The Complete Bu
Process Handbook
Body of Knowledge from Process Modeling to BPM

Volume I

The Complete Business Process Handbook

Body of Knowledge from Process Modeling to BPM

Volume I

Mark von Rosing
Chairman of the Global University Alliance

August-Wilhelm Scheer
Founder of the Institute for Information Systems (IWi)

Henrik von Scheel
CEO of LEADing Practice

AMSTERDAM • BOSTON • HEIDELBERG • LONDON
NEW YORK • OXFORD • PARIS • SAN DIEGO
SAN FRANCISCO • SINGAPORE • SYDNEY • TOKYO

Morgan Kaufmann Publishers is an Imprint of Elsevier

Acquiring Editor: Steve Elliot
Editorial Project Manager: Kaitlin Herbert
Project Manager: Priya Kumaraguruparan
Cover Designer: Greg Harris

Morgan Kaufmann is an imprint of Elsevier
225 Wyman Street, Waltham, MA 02451, USA

ISBN: 978-0-12-799959-3

British Library Cataloguing in Publication Data
A catalogue record for this book is available from the British Library

Library of Congress Cataloging-in-Publication Data
A catalog record for this book is available from the Library of Congress

For information on all MK publications visit
our website at www.mkp.com

16 17 18 19 20   10 9 8 7 6 5 4 3 2

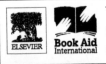

Working together
to grow libraries in
developing countries

www.elsevier.com • www.bookaid.org

Contents

Author Biographies...xxv
Foreword xciii
Abbreviations xcix
Introduction to the Book..ciii

Phase 1 1

Henrik von Scheel, Mark von Rosing, Marianne Fonseca, Maria Hove, Ulrik Foldager
Introduction 1
Process Concept Evolution 1.0 2
    Sun Tzu 2
    Adam Smith 4
    Taylorism..5
    Henry Ford..7
End Notes 8

Phase 2: Process Concept Evolution 2.0..11

Henrik von Scheel, Mark von Rosing, Maria Hove, Marianne Fonseca, Ulrik Foldager
Introduction 11
Gantt Chart 13
Frank B. Gilbreth 14
Allan H. Mogensen 16
Boeing B17 17
Benjamin S. Graham 18
ASME: American Society of Mechanical Engineers 18
Functional Flow Block Diagram of PERT 20
    Functional Flow Block Diagrams 20
    PERT: Program Evaluation Review Technique................................21
Data Flow Diagrams and IDEF 22
    Data Flow Diagram 22
    Integrated Definition 23
    IDEF0 Overview: Function Modeling Method 23
    IDEF1 Overview: Information Modeling Method 24
    IDEF1X Overview: Data Modeling Method 24
    IDEF3 Overview: Process Description Capture Method 25
    IDEF4 Overview: Object-Oriented Design Method 25
    IDEF5 Overview: Ontology Description Capture Method 25
Zero Defects 25
Toyota Production System 27

Jidoka: Highlighting/Visualization of Problems 28
Just-In-Time: Productivity Improvement 28
The 14 Principles of TPS 30
End Notes 34

Phase 3: Process Concept Evolution 3.0 37

Mark von Rosing, August-Wilhelm Scheer, John A. Zachman, Daniel T. Jones, James P. Womack, Henrik von Scheel

Introduction 37
Prof. Dr. Dr. H.c. Mult. August-Wilhelm Scheer 39
Introduction 39
A New Way of Thinking: Linking Process and Information Concepts 40
Architecture of Integrated Information Systems (ARIS) 41
Additional Important Aspects 42
Conclusion 42
John A. Zachman—the Arrival of Enterprise Architecture 42
Introduction 42
The Zachman Framework for Enterprise Architecture 43
Perspectives of the Framework 44
Conclusion 46
Lean Thinking, Lean Practice and Lean Consumption 46
The evolution of Toyota's practices 46
The evolving understanding of Lean 47
The spread of Lean and Lean Consumption 48
Conclusion 49
Business Process Reengineering 50
Dr Michael Hammer 50
Introducing Business Process Reengineering 50
Width before Depth 51
The Three Levels of Management 52
The Three Important Ingredients 52
The Business Process Reengineering Cycle 53
Methods and Approaches to Business Process Reengineering 54
Business Process Reengineering Project and Success Criteria 55
The Pros of Business Process Reengineering 56
The Cons of Business Process Reengineering 57
Conclusion 57
Total Quality Management 58
Introduction 58
Implementing Total Quality Management in the Organization 59
Key Elements for Change 59
The Use of Total Quality Management in Process Work 61

Tools for TQM 63
   House of Quality or Quality Function Deployment 63
   Taguchi Techniques 64
   Pareto Diagrams 64
   Process Diagrams 65
   Cause & Effect Analysis Diagrams 66
   Statistical Process Control 66
   The PDCA Cycle 66
   Business Excellence and EFQM 69
   Conclusion 69
Six Sigma 70
   Introduction 70
   What Six Sigma Means 70
   The Purpose of Six Sigma 70
   DMAIC 71
   DMADV 72
   Conclusion 72
End Notes 73

Phase 4: What Is Business Process Management? 79
Keith Swenson, Mark von Rosing
Introduction 79
Definition and Research 79
Insights Gained 83
   BPM Is Not About Automation of Processes 83
   BPM Is Done by People Concerned Primarily with Improvement
   of the Process 84
   Misrepresentations of BPM 84
   BPM Is Not a Product 84
   BPM Is Not a Market Segment 84
   An Application Does Not Do BPM 84
   BPM As a Service Is Not Application Hosting 85
   Entire Organizational Units Do Not Do BPM 85
   BPM Is Not Merely Anything that Improves Business 85
   BPM Is Not All Activities Supported by a BPMS 85
   Just Because You Can Do Something with a BPMS Does Not Mean It Is BPM 85
   Participating in a Process Is Not Doing BPM 86
   Implementation (Coding) of the Process Application Is Not BPM 86
   Making a Suggestion for Process Improvement Is Not BPM 86
   Improving a Single Step of a Process Is Not BPM 86
Conclusion: One Common Definition 87
End Notes 88

The BPM Way of Thinking 89

Mark von Rosing, Henrik von Scheel, August-Wilhelm Scheer
Introduction 89

The Value of Ontology 91

Mark von Rosing, Wim Laurier, Simon Polovina
Introduction 91
What Is Ontology? 91
Ontology Classification Based on Context Dependency 92
Ontology Maturity and the Maturing Process 92
State of the Art 93
Conclusions and Directions for Future Research 95
End Notes 96

The BPM Ontology 101

Mark von Rosing, Wim Laurier, Simon Polovina
Introduction 101
The BPM Ontology as a Folksonomy: Sharing Fundamental Process Concepts 101
The BPM Ontology as a Thesaurus: Structuring Process Knowledge
by Defining Relations 106
The BPM Ontology as a Frame: The Ontological Structure of the
Leading Practice Process Meta Model 114
Discussion of the BPM Ontology 119
Summary 120
End Notes 121

Process Tagging—A Process Classification and Categorization
Concept 123

Mark von Rosing, Neil Kemp, Maria Hove, Jeanne W. Ross
Introduction 123
Logical Clustering: Learning from other Areas 123
Conceptual and Logical Process Classification and Categorization 125
Classification of Process by Method of Execution 128
The Nature of Process Decomposition 130
Describing Work 133
Process Area 136
    What Is a Process Area? 136
    How to Identify Process Areas 137
    How Is a Process Area Documented? 137
Process Group 139
    What Is a Process Group? 139
    Why Separate Process Group and Business Service as Unique Concepts? 140

How to Identify Process Groups 140
How Are Process Groups Documented? 142
The Nature of Process Groups 143
Process 143
What Is a Process? 143
How to Identify Processes 144
How Are Processes Documented? 144
The Nature of Processes 147
Process Lifecycle Verb Taxonomy 147
Process Step 147
What Is a Process Step? 147
How to Identify Process Steps 147
How Are Process Steps Documented? 150
The Nature of Process Steps 157
Activity 157
What Is an Activity? 157
How to Identify Activities 157
How Are Activities Documented? 157
The Nature of Activity 158
The Work System 158
What Is the Work System? 158
How to Determine the Work System 159
How Is the Work System Documented? 159
Procedure 159
What Is a Procedure? 159
How to Identify Procedures 160
How Are Procedures Documented? 160
Connecting the Work Spaces 160
Process Scenarios 161
Process Type 162
Process Tier 165
Process Nature 165
Miscategorization and Misclassification 169
Conclusions 169
End Notes 170

Why Work with Process Templates 173

Mark von Rosing, Maria Hove, Henrik von Scheel, Ulrik Foldager

Introduction 173
The Relationship Between Business Process Management Ontology
and Process Templates 173
What Are Process Templates? 175

Process Maps 175
Process Matrix 177
Process Model 178
The Most Common Process Templates 181
Benefits of Process Templates 181
Conclusion 183
End Notes 184

The BPM Way of Working 185

Henrik von Scheel, Mark von Rosing, August-Wilhelm Scheer
Introduction 185

Business Process Trends 187

Mark von Rosing, August-Wilhelm Scheer, Henrik von Scheel, Adam D.M. Svendsen, Alex Kokkonen, Andrew M. Ross, Anette Falk Bøgebjerg, Anni Olsen, Antony Dicks, Asif Qumer Gill, Bas Bach, Bob J. Storms, Callie Smit, Cay Clemmensen, Christopher K. Swierczynski, Clemens Utschig-Utschig, Dan Moorcroft, Daniel T. Jones, David Coloma, Deb Boykin, Dickson Hunja Muhita, Duarte Gonçalves, Fabrizio aria Maggi, Fan Zhao, Fatima Senghore, Fatma Dandashi, Fred Cummins, Freek Stoffel, Gabriel von Scheel, Gabriella von Rosing, Gary Doucet, Gert Meiling, Gert O. Jansson, Hans Scheruhn, Hendrik Bohn, Henk de Man, Henk Kuil, Henrik Naundrup Vester, Jacob Gammelgaard, James P. Womack, Jeanne W. Ross, Jeff Greer, Jens Theodor Nielsen, John A. Zachman, John Bertram, John Golden, John M. Rogers, Jonnro Erasmus, Joshua von Scheel, Joshua Waters, Justin Tomlinson, Karin Gräslund, Katia Bartels, Keith D. Swenson, Kenneth Dean Teske, Kevin Govender, Klaus Vitt, Krzysztof Skurzak, LeAnne Spurrell, Lloyd Dugan, Lotte Tange, Mads Clausager, Maria Hove, Maria Rybrink, Marianne Fonseca, Mark Stanford, Marlon Dumas, Mathias Kirchmer, Maxim Arzumanyan, Michael D. Tisdel, Michel van den Hoven, Mikael Munck, Mike A. Marin, Mona von Rosing, Nathaniel Palmer, Neil Kemp, Nils Faltin, Partha Chakravartti, Patricia Kemp, Peter Franz, Philippe Lebacq, Rich Hilliard, Richard L. Fallon, Richard N. Conzo, Rod Peacock, Ronald N. Batdorf, Sarel J. Snyman, Scott Davis, Simon M. Polovina, Stephen White, Steve Durbin, Steve Willoughby, Thomas Boosz, Thomas Christian Olsen, Tim Hoebeek, Tom Preston, Ulrik Foldager, Victor Abele, Vincent Snels, Volker Rebhan, Wim Laurier, Yr Gunnarsdottir, Yury Orlov, Zakaria Maamar, Ekambareswaran Balasubramanian, Mai Phuong, Régis Dumond

Introduction 187
The Importance of Trends 187
Maturity of the Subject 188
Mega Trends 189
Emerging Trends 190
Process Trends 191
Early Adoption 191
Early Adopter of Process Trends 193

Industry Adoption 204
    Industry Adoption of Process Trends 205
Standard Adoption 211
Standards Adoption of Process Trends 211
Conclusion 216
End Notes 216

BPM Center of Excellence 217

Mark von Rosing, Maria Hove, Henrik von Scheel

Introduction 217
The Challenge BPM CoE Faces 217
What Happens Without a BPM CoE? 220
Cause and Effect Matrix 222
Lessons Learned Regarding BPM CoE 222
    Work of a BPM CoE 224
    Typical BPM CoE Roles 226
    BPM CoE Process Life Cycle 227
    BPM CoE Portfolio Process Management 227
    A Clear Understanding and Approach to BPM Governance 229
    A BPM Maturity Holistic View in BPM CoE 232
    BPM Performance Management Is Executed Within the BPM CoE 233
    BPM Alignment to Value So That the Strategic Intent
    Is Woven Into the BPM CoE 234
    Alignment of BPM CoE to Existing Enterprise Standards,
    Enterprise Architecture, Enterprise Modeling, and Other
    IT Disciplines 235
    Continuous Improvement and BPM CoE Change Management 236
Conclusion 238
End Notes 238

Understanding Business Process Management Roles 241

Mark von Rosing, Neil Kemp, Maxim Arzumanyan

Introduction 241
Motivation for Defining Your BPM Roles 241
Relevance Context 242
What Is a Role? 242
Standards that Link to Role Concepts 246
Current Methods 247
Role Context 248
Abilities to Act 250
    Rights versus Hierarchical Power 250
Role Profile 251
    Categories of Working Roles 251

Common Roles Involved with Role Modeling 252
Roles within BPM 253
Typical BPM CoE Roles 254
   BPM CoE Stakeholders 254
   Process Owner 255
   BPM CoE Manager 256
   Business Process Portfolio Manager 256
   Process Project Manager 257
   Process Expert 257
   Business Process Analyst 257
   Process Engineer 258
   Process Architect 258
   Enterprise Architect 259
   Process Support Desk 259
   Methods and Tools Specialist 259
   Business Process Management Tool Administrator 259
   Training Specialist 259
Additional Roles 260
Role Profile within BPM CoE 261
Role Profile within BPM Projects 262
Conclusion 263
End Notes 263

**Working with the Business Process Management
(BPM) Life Cycle** 265
*Ulrik Foldager, Mark von Rosing, Maria Hove, Joshua von Scheel, Anette
Falk Bøgebjerg*
Introduction 265
Phase 1: Analyze—Project Preparation and Blueprint 266
   Step 1: Identify Critical Business Factors 270
   Step 2: Describe Process Goals 270
   Step 3: Choose Building 271
   Step 4: Check for Process Reference Content 273
   Step 4a: Process Reference Content Available 273
   Step 4b: Define High-Level Process Landscape Based on Process Reference
   Content 275
   Step 4c: Analyze Match of Process Reference Content 276
   Step 4d: Processes That Do Not Match Process Reference Content 276
   Step 4e: Understand As-Is High-Level Process Landscape 277
   Step 5: No Process Reference Content Available 278

Phase 2: Design—Project Realization and Design 278
  Step 6: Process Planning and Design 280
  Step 7: Define Process Map 282
  Step 8: Design Solution 283
  Step 9: Case-Based Process Concept 283
  Step 10: Value-Based Process Concept 284
  Step 11: Standardize and Integrate 285
  Step 12: Process Requirement Management 286
  Step 13: Processes Cannot Be Adapted 287
Phase 3: Build—Final Project Preparation 287
  Step 14: As-Is Analysis 291
  Step 15: To-Be Value-Driven Process Design 291
  Step 16: Harmonize Variants Based on Value-Driven Process Design 292
  Step 17: To-Be Documentation and To-Be Organizational Structure 293
  Step 18: Match Processes to Process Reference Content 294
  Step 19: Processes with Variants 294
  Step 20: Directly Adaptable Processes 295
Phase 4: Deploy/Implement—Go Live 295
  Step 21: Decide on Process Implementation (Based on Requirements) 299
  Step 22: Process Rollout 299
  Step 23: Add Process Rewards 300
  Step 24: Enable Process Performance Measurements 301
  Step 25: Define Performance Indicators Based on Value Drivers 302
  Step 26: Harmonize Terms 303
  Step 27: Establish Process Ownership 303
Phase 5: Run/Maintain—Run Processes and Govern Performance 306
  Step 28: Process Measurements, Monitoring, Reporting, and Audits 307
  Step 29: Perform Scoping of Gaps 310
  Step 30: Choose Building Blocks 310
  Step 31: Evaluate Potential Solutions 312
  Step 32: Analyze Variances 312
  Step 33: Estimate Impact 314
Phase 6: Continuous Improvement—Continuously Optimize and
Develop Processes 316
  Continuous Improvement: Performance and Value Drivers 318
  Step 34: Prioritize Improvement Areas 320
  Step 35: Manage Process Update 324
  Step 36: Performance Change Management 324
  Step 37: Business Innovation and Transformation Enablement 325
  Step 37a: Value Model 327

Step 37b: Revenue Model 329
Step 37c: Cost Model 330
Step 37d: Service Model 331
Step 37e: Operating Model 333
Step 37f: Performance Model 336
Conclusion 336
End Notes 340

The Chief Process Officer: An Emerging Top Leadership Role 343

Mathias Kirchmer, Peter Franz, Mark von Rosing
Introduction 343
The Emerging Role of the CPO 343
Key Tasks of the CPO 345
Positioning of the CPO in the Organization 346
Conclusion 347
End Notes 347

iBPM—Intelligent Business Process Management 349

Nathaniel Palmer
The Evolution of Intelligent BPM 350
From Automation to Orchestration: The Realignment of BPM Around
Service-Oriented Architectures 351
Apply SOA Strategies to Integrating Unstructured Information 352
    Leveraging Content As a Service 353
Realizing Adaptability: Shifting from Event-Driven to Goal-Driven 353
    Goal-Driven Scenarios 354
Phase Three: Intelligent BPM 354
    Adaptability Begins with Reading Signals 355
Intelligent BPM Leverages Big Data 356
    Faster Adaptation Is Not Necessarily Faster Decisions 358
The Value of Social Media to Intelligent BPM 359
    The Ability to Mobilize 360
Conclusion 360
End Notes 361

Evidence-Based Business Process Management 363

Marlon Dumas, Fabrizio Maria Maggi
Introduction 363
Evidence-Based BPM: What for? 363
The Answer: Process Mining 364
Descriptive Approaches 365
Process Performance Analytics 366

Automated Process Discovery 366
Model Enhancement 367
Deviance Mining 368
Process Variant and Outlier Identification 369
Predictive Approaches 369
Case Studies and Lessons in Evidence-Based BPM 370
Case Studies in Automated Process and Variant Discovery 370
Case Studies in Deviance Mining 371
Case Studies in Predictive Monitoring 373
Conclusion 373
End Notes 374

Social Media and Business Process Management 377

Zakaria Maamar, Henrik von Scheel, Mona von Rosing

Introduction 377
The Digital Mind-set Is Changing 377
Social Media Are Reshaping Business 379
Enabling Customer-Centricity 383
Lessons Learned Around Social-Oriented Process Modeling 384
Target Marketing Campaigns with Social Media 385
Improving the Prospect Qualification Process 386
Customer Profile Data for Process (Simplification) 386
Customer Notifications for Process (Visibility) 387
Alternative Channels for Sales 387
Selection of the Right Offering/Solution 387
Social Media and BPM for Customer Servicing 387
Customer Relationship Management 388
Social Media Process Flow 392
Conclusion 392
End Notes 394

BPM and Maturity Models 395

Gabriella von Rosing, Krzysztof Skurzak, Henrik von Scheel, Maria Hove

Introduction 395
Historic Development of Maturity Models 396
The Different Stages of Maturity Models 399
The Missing Parts of the Maturity Models 401
BPM Maturity Model 403
Maturity Levels 403
    Business Process Maturity: Level 1 403
    Business Process Maturity: Level 2 404

Business Process Maturity: Level 3 404
Business Process Maturity: Level 4 404
Business Process Maturity: Level 5 405
From Maturity Level Assessment to Maturity Benchmark 421
Conclusion 424
End Notes 424

The BPM Way of Modeling

The BPM Way of Modeling 427

Mark von Rosing, Henrik von Scheel, August-Wilhelm Scheer

Introduction 427

Business Process Model and Notation—BPMN

Business Process Model and Notation—BPMN 429

Mark von Rosing, Steve White, Fred Cummins, Henk de Man

Introduction 429
What Is BPMN? 429
The Historic Development of BPMN 430
The BPMN Notations/Shapes 431
BPMN Diagrams 439
To Point (1) Private (Internal) Business Processes 439
Public Processes 440
Collaborations 441
To Point (2) Choreography 441
To Point (3) Conversations 442
BPMN Usage 443
Diagram Point of View 444
Understanding the Behavior of Diagrams 444
BPMN Example 444
BPMN Caveats 447
The Future of BPMN 447
Fulfilling the BPMN Vision 448
Implementation Level Modeling 449
Case Management Modeling 451
Conclusions 452
End Notes 452

Variation in Business Processes

Variation in Business Processes 455

Mark von Rosing, Jonnro Erasmus

Introduction 455
Business Process Variance: What Is It? 455
Complications and Challenges 457
Solution Description 459

When Should Variation Be Allowed and How Much Is Enough? 459
Defining and Justifying Business Process Variance 462
Modeling of Business Process Variance 464
Managing Business Process Variances 468
Cost Calculation of Process Variances 470
Lessons Learned 471
Conclusion and Summary 472
End Notes 472

Focusing Business Processes on Superior Value Creation: Value-oriented Process Modeling 475

Mark von Rosing, Mathias Kirchmer

Introduction 475
Value Is a Different Kind of Concept for Process Teams 475
Targeting Value 476
Segmentation of Business Processes 477
Value-oriented Design 481
Value-oriented Process Modeling 483
Value-oriented Implementation 484
Value-oriented Process Governance to Sustain Value 489
Conclusion 491
End Notes 491

Sustainability Oriented Process Modeling 493

Gabriella von Rosing, David Coloma, Henrik von Scheel

Introduction 493
Situation, Complications, and the Main Questions 493
Conditions, Circumstances, and Complexity 494
The Main Questions Covered 495
The Answer 496
The Way of Thinking Around Sustainability Oriented Process Modeling 496
Sustainability Oriented Process Modeling: The Way of Working 497
Understanding Your Organization's Sustainability Personality 499
Building and Transforming the BPM CoE and Organization's
Culture Toward Sustainability 499
Developing the Organization's Business Model 499
Developing the Sustainability's Life Cycle 500
Building the Organization's Sustainability Maturity Model 501
Developing the Sustainability Value Model 502
Developing the Sustainability Revenue Model 504

Sustainability Oriented Process Modeling: Way of Modeling 505
Sustainability Oriented Process Modeling: Way of Implementing 507
Sustainability Oriented Process Modeling: Way of Governing 508
Benefits of Combining BPM and Sustainability Oriented Process Modeling 508
Conclusions 509
End Notes 509

Information Modeling and Process Modeling 511

Hans-Jürgen Scheruhn, Mark von Rosing, Richard L. Fallon

Introduction 511
Intended Audience 511
Process Life Cycle 512
    Analyze (and Discover) 513
    Design 514
    Build 515
    Deploy/Implement 516
    Run/Maintain (Monitoring) 516
    Continuous Improvement 516
Process Attributes 516
    Process Flow and Process Resources 516
    Data Flow 517
    Process Automation (Application) 517
Why the Subject Is Important and the Problems and Challenges
It Will Solve 517
Information Models Within As-Is and To-Be Models 518
    As-Is Modeling 521
    Determining the Hierarchy Level 521
    Meta Information Objects Within Information and Process Modeling 524
Example As-Is Model (Sales and Distribution) 529
    Business Process Model and Notation Model 529
    Event-driven Process Chain Model 531
    Entity–Relationship (ER) Model 534
    To-Be Modeling 536
Example of To-Be (BPMN) Model (Materials Management) 536
    Unified Modeling Language Model 538
    Star Scheme 538
    Information Engineering 538
    Balanced Scorecard Cause-and-Effect Chain 543
Lesson Learned 544
What Worked 544
What Did Not Work 546

Conclusions 547
  Findings and Summary 547
End Notes 548

The BPM Way of Implementation and Governance 551
Mark von Rosing, Henrik von Scheel, August-Wilhelm Scheer
Introduction 551
End Notes 551

Applying Agile Principles to BPM 553
Mark von Rosing, Joshua von Scheel, Asif Qumer Gill
Introduction 553
What Is Agile? 553
Agile Characteristics 555
Agile Values 556
Agile Principles 556
Agile Practices 557
Agile versus Traditional Ways of Working 557
Agile BPM 559
  The Benefits and Limitations of Agile and How to Apply It to BPM 560
  An Agile BPM Method 562
  Agile Terminology 570
  Building Agile Capabilities in the BPM CoE 573
Agility Adoption and Improvement Model 574
Conclusion 575
End Notes 576

BPM Change Management 579
*Maria Hove, Marianne Fonseca, Mona von Rosing, Joshua von Scheel,
Dickson Muhita*
Introduction 579
Lessons Learned Around BPM Change Management 579
Lessons Learned of the Outperformers and Underperformers 581
Lessons Learned Around Benefit and Value Realization 582
Leading Practice Suggestions on What Really Works Well 582
  BPM Change Management in the Analyze Phase 585
  BPM Change Management in the Design Phase 588
  BPM Change Management in the Build Phase 589
  BPM Change Management in the Deploy/Implement Phase 589
  BPM Change Management in the Run/Maintain Phase 592
  BPM Change Management in the Continuous Improvement Phase 593
  Perform Managerial Governance Activities Across all Phases 596

Conclusion 596
End Notes 597

Business Process Management Governance 599

Maria Hove, Gabriella von Rosing, Bob Storms
Introduction 599
Why Is BPM Governance Important? 599
What Is BPM Governance? 600
BPM Center of Excellence and Governance 601
How Does BPM Governance Work? 604
BPM Governance and Incident Management 606
BPM Portfolio Management and Governance 607
Lessons Learned 609
Benefits and Value of BPM Governance 610
Conclusions 611
End Notes 611

Business Process Portfolio Management 613

Mark von Rosing, Hendrik Bohn, Gabriel von Scheel, Richard Conzo, Maria Hove
From Business Process Management to Business Process Portfolio
Management 613
Common Pitfalls When Implementing BPPM 614
  Not All Process Portfolios are Equal 614
  Changes to a Process Portfolio Can be Implemented Over Several
  Years, Yet Budgets are Allocated Yearly 615
  Organization Has a Silo Mentality 615
  Lack of Information on Processes 615
  Getting Reliable and Accurate Information on Processes 615
  Inadequate Portfolio Management Skills 615
  Additional Time Constraint on Busy Executives 616
Establishing BPPM 616
Comparison of PPM, BPPM, and BPM 617
Creating a BPPM Competency 618
  Guiding Principles 618
  Analysis Phase 619
  Design Phase 619
  Build Phase 619
  Deploy/Implement Phase 619
  Run/Maintain Phase 620
  Continuous Improvement Phase 620

Alignment Considerations When Implementing BPPM 620
Strategic Alignment 621
Social Alignment 621
Processual Alignment 621
Technical Alignment 621
BPPM Life Cycle 621
Business Process Portfolio Planning and Alignment Phase 622
Opportunity Management Phase 622
Variation/Change Management Phase 622
Approval Phase 624
Opportunity Realization Phase 624
Feedback Loop Communication 626
Feedback Loop 626
Continuous Improvement Phase 627
Business Process Hierarchy 627
Business Process Area 628
Business Process Group 628
Business Process 628
BPPM Information, Measurements, and Reporting 628
BPPM Information for Measurement and Reporting 629
BPPM Measurements and Reporting 630
Summary of Establishing BPPM 630
Lessons Learned From Implementing BPPM 630
Right Time to Implement BPPM 630
Effect of Limited or No Implemented BPPM in the Long Run 631
Conclusions 631
End Notes 633

Real-Time Learning: Business Process Guidance at the Point of Need ...635

Nils Faltin, Mark von Rosing, August-Wilhelm Scheer

Introduction 635
Real-Time Learning to Close the Knowledge Gap 637
Bite-Sized Learning Units 637
Electronic Performance Support: Delivering Knowledge at the
Point of Need 638
Business Process Guidance 638
Components of a BPG System 639
BPG in Practical Use 639
Supporting Entry of Correct Data 639
Supporting Multiple Applications 640

Enhancing Communication with the Support Desk 640
Introducing BPG in an Organization 641
    Creating a Repository of Microlearning Content 641
Major Steps to Create the Repository 642
Conclusions and Outlook 642
End Notes 643

Business Process Management Alignment 645

Mona von Rosing, Henrik von Scheel, Justin Tomlinson, Victor Abele, Kenneth D. Teske, Michael D. Tisdel

Introduction 645
Background to a New Way of Looking at Alignment for BPM 645
Alignment of BPM 647
Establishing Alignment to BPM 647
Business Scenarios That Would Require Business Process Alignment 652
    Stakeholder Alignment 652
    Alignment Portfolio, Program, and Project Management Challenges 652
    Merger and Acquisition 654
    Align BPM with Business Intelligence to Achieve Business
    Process Excellence 654
    Align BPM with Master Data Management for Master Data
    Governance, Stewardship, and Enterprise Processes 654
    Align BPM with SOA for a Business-Driven, Service-Oriented
    Enterprise 654
    Align BPM with Cloud for Business Process as a Service 655
Benefits of BPM Alignment 655
Conclusions 656
End Notes 656

Business Process Outsourcing 657

Mark von Rosing, Gary Doucet, Gert O. Jansson, Gabriel von Scheel, Freek Stoffel, Bas Bach, Henk Kuil, Joshua Waters

Introduction 657
Business Process Outsourcing: What Is It? 657
Business Process Outsourcing Value Case 658
The BPO Market 660
Business Process Outsourcing: Possible Pitfalls 661
Business Process Outsourcing: How to Go About It 662
    Step 1: Fully Understand the Expenditure Category 665
    Step 2: Supplier Market Assessment 665

Step 3: Prepare a Supplier Survey 666
Step 4: Building the Strategy 666
Step 5: RFx Request for ... .667
Step 6: Selection 667
Step 7: Communicate with Your New Suppliers 668
Conclusions 668
End Notes 669

The Business Process Management Way of Training and Coaching 671

Mark von Rosing, Henrik von Scheel, August-Wilhelm Scheer

Introduction 671

The Need for a Standardized and Common Way of Process Training 673

Mark von Rosing, Marianne Fonseca, Ulrik Foldager, Joshua von Scheel

Introduction 673
Skills Requirements 673
Learning Versus Forgetting Curve 674
Standardized Way of Training for Process Professionals 675
End Notes 676

Process Expert Training 677

Content of the Program 678
Process Expert Learning Model 679
What the Practitioner Gets 679

Process Architect Training 681

Content of the Program 682
Process Architect Learning Model 682
What You Get 683

Process Engineer Training 685

Content of the Program 686
Process Engineer Learning Model 687
What You Get 687
Conclusions 687

Process Owner Training 689

Program Type 689
Content of the Program 690

Process Owner Learning Model 691
   Needed Skill for Abstraction Level for a Process Owner 691
What the Practitioner Gets 692

Conclusion 693

Author Index 695
Subject Index 697

Author Biographies

Mark von Rosing

Prof. Mark von Rosing is in every way an innovator impacting developments, standards, frameworks, methods, and approaches around the world. He founded, in 2004, the Global University Alliance (GUA), the largest nonvendor academic platform for academic collaboration. As a part of the GUA work he has been involved in developing 96 Enterprise Standards and 51 Industry Standards. He is a leader in the industry in developing standards. He has not only founded the largest Enterprise Standard community "LEADing Practice" used by practitioners and organizations around the world, but also has a main role in developing standards in the following standard bodies:

- **World Wide Web Consortium (W3C):** Prof. Mark von Rosing is leading development member of the World Wide Web Consortium (W3C). The W3C purpose is to lead the World Wide Web to its full potential by developing protocols and guidelines that ensure the long-term growth of the Web/Internet. Prof. Mark von Rosing is thereby part of developing the internet principles and standards that will help radically improve the way people around the world develop new technologies and innovate for humanity. See the link under LEADing Practice that is a strategic liaison partner of W3C www.w3.org/2001/11/StdLiaison#L.
- **ISO:** As a leader and development member of "The International Organization for Standardization (French: Organisation internationale de standardization)"; known as ISO, Prof. Mark von Rosing coordinates the development of international standards among various national standards organizations. Prof. von Rosing is thereby a leading mind in promoting worldwide proprietary, industrial, and commercial standards. The standards focused on at the moment are ISO 42010, the Systems and software engineering Architecture description, as well as ISO 279 the Innovation standard.
- **Energetics:** As a core development of the energy standard body Energetics, Prof. Mark von Rosing develops the energy standards used by countries and companies around the world. This also includes the standards used by the upstream oil and gas organizations around the world, improving their business model, performance concepts, process models, and data models.

- **Object Management Group (OMG):** Prof. Mark von Rosing is cochair and leading development member of the software standards in OMG. This development includes:
  - Value Delivery Modeling Language (VDML)
  - Business Planning and Motivation Modeling (BMM)
  - Business Process Modeling Notations (BPMN)
  - Semantics of Business Vocabulary and Rules (SBVR)
  - Decision Model and Notation (DMN)
  - Risk and Threat Modeling.
- **The Information Security Forum (ISF):** Prof. Mark von Rosing is a core team development member of the Information Security Forum. Investigating, clarifying and resolving key issues in information security, and developing best practice methodologies, processes, and solutions that meet the business and IT needs around security.

Additional standard developments that are worthwhile mentioning:
  - Research collaboration and developer with IEEE standards.
  - Codeveloper of the Global TOGAF Business Architecture Methods & Certification Development Group.
  - Development member of the NATO standards, including EA, BPM, Capabilities and joint mission execution.
  - Built the BPM and EA curriculum for the SAP University Alliance (+900 universities).
  - SAP AG Method developer e.g., ASAP, SAP Agile, BPM, Enterprise Architecture (EAF).

Author of multiple publications among them in the last 3 years:
  - SAP Press bestseller: "Applying real-world BPM in an SAP environment"
  - IEEE publication "defining the profession of the Business Architect" as well as the publication "How to integrate Enterprise Architecture and BPM"
  - Springer: Conceptual Structures in LEADing and Best Enterprise Practices as well as The Impact of Culture Differences on Cloud Computing Adoption
  - Future Strategies Inc. and the Workflow Management Coalition (WfmC) "Passports to Success in BPM."

Henrik von Scheel

International recognized thought leader and the driving force behind the Enterprise Modelling revolution and a pioneer in linking strategy with operational execution. For most Fortune 500 and public organizations, Henrik von Scheel is synonym for a visionary, game changer, and a challenger striving to defy outmoded business models.

Recognized as a strategy and business process management thought leader, advisor, mentor, and coauthor of SAP Press bestseller book: Applying real-world BPM in a SAP environment. He has made a significant contribution to the enterprise modeling discipline—whether by driving standards, expanding the technology, or pushing process improvement in a new direction.

Together with Global University Alliance, he has evolved mainstream process thinking, approaches, and styles through his efforts in standards bodies, books, academic publications, and published reference content, such as extended BPMN, Object Modelling (Business, Service, Process, Information & Data), BPM enabled Innovation & Transformation, BPM Centre of Excellence, BPM Alignment, Social BPM, BPM & Enterprise Architecture, BPM Change Management, BPM Lifecycle, BPM Maturity, Value BPM, Goal-Oriented Process, and BPM Industry Accelerators, etc.

Henrik is the CEO of LEADing Practice—#1 Enterprise Standard provider, setting the agenda for 56 industries. He serves as ADVISORY BOARD MEMBER at Google EMEA, Gazprom, Global University Alliance, and Chairman of Capital Investment Partners. Awarded "The NEXT 100 Top Influencers of the European Digital Industry in 2012" among the most important Europeans shaping our digital future.

Advising executives how to tackle THE BLIND SPOTS or "change gap"— discover the WHY, define the WHAT, and deliver the HOW. Enabling executives to transform and innovate existing business models and their service model to design tomorrow's enterprises. His trademark is the unique ability to help organizations master the rare discipline of developing their core competitive and differentiated aspects. Translating the "Big Picture" into operational execution using layered architectural rigor and applying leading practice, industry and best practice with the IT team.

August-Wilhelm Scheer

Professor Dr Dr h.c. mult. Scheer is founder of the Institute for Information Systems (IWi) at Saarland University and was its director for 30 years. His publications in the field of business information systems are today considered standard references and are very well known across the global market.

The Y-CIM production model, created by Prof. Scheer, serves as an overall framework for integrating operative information systems in the manufacturing industries.

Prof. Scheer was honored with the Lifetime Achievement Award in 2013 by the Global University Alliance on behalf of +300 universities, in recognition of his long-term impact and contribution to evolve the academic world and organization's structural thinking of how to apply enterprise modeling today.

Leaving his mark on this generation and generations to come, pushing the bar with his research and focus on information and business process management, Prof. Scheer has, among others, brought to us:

- Link between processes and information.
- His contribution to the academic world: in 1975, Scheer took over one of the first chairs for information systems and founded the Institute for Information Systems (IWI) at the Saarland University, which he led until 2005.
- His contribution to the Software world: In 1984, he founded IDS Scheer, a Business Process Management (BPM) software company, which is still today the market leader.
- His contribution to Enterprise Modeling: The ARIS House which is one of the first Enterprise Modeling concepts that combines and organizes information of an organization in five interrelated views: data, function, organization, output, and control.

His contribution to the Process Modeling community: He developed among others two main concepts for Business Process Modeling:

- Business content in Value-added Chain Diagrams (VCD).
- Process content in Event-driven Process Chains (EPC).

He is widely regarded as the founder of the BPM industry.

In 1984, he founded the international software and consulting company IDS Scheer AG. Until 2009, he expanded the business to become one of the leading IT companies in Germany. In 1997, he founded the imc AG located in Saarbrücken and in 2000, the Scheer Group GmbH, which participates in innovative high-tech companies, such as the Scheer Management Consulting & Solutions GmbH. He is forerunner and companion of the future project "Industry 4.0" initiated by the German federal government. The network of IT companies within the Scheer Group is actively participating in the implementation of projects along with well-known industry and research partners.

Adam D.M. Svendsen

Adam D.M. Svendsen, PhD (Warwick, UK), is an intelligence and defense strategist, educator and researcher, and a Consultant at the Copenhagen Institute for Futures Studies (CIFS), Denmark. His research work has been pursued internationally, including in the US, Canada, and across Scandinavia.

He has been a Visiting Scholar at the Center for Peace and Security Studies (CPASS), Georgetown University, has held a postdoctoral fellowship based in the Centre for Military Studies (CMS), Department of Political Science, University of Copenhagen, Denmark, and he has worked at Chatham House on the International Security Programme and at IISS, London.

He has also worked as a Strategic Intelligence consultant, trained at European defense and emergency planning colleges, lectured at senior/advanced level at the Royal Danish Defence College (FAK), taught at the University of Nottingham, has participated in several conferences, workshops, and in a Track II UK-US Strategic Dialogue.

Together with work cited in testimony to the UK Parliament, he has multisector award-winning media and communication experience, including authoring several peer-reviewed publications, such as the three books: Intelligence Cooperation and the War on Terror: Anglo-American Security Relations after 9/11 (London: Routledge/Studies in Intelligence Series, 2010); Understanding the Globalization of Intelligence and The Professionalization of Intelligence Cooperation: Fashioning Method out of Mayhem, both (Basingstoke: Palgrave Macmillan, 2012).

Alex Kokkonen

Alex Kokkonen, PhD, FCMA is an accomplished executive with extensive international and multi-industry experience established over a 25 year career. Alex has genuine global experience gained across Europe, Asia, and North America in seven industries, including the Healthcare, Defense, Consulting, FMOCG, IT, Telecommunications, Airline and Finance industries working for major multinational blue chip companies such as Johnson & Johnson, Unilever, Serco Defence, Nokia, IBM, and Deutsche Bank. Alex has extensive team leadership and project delivery experience in multicultural environments across several business functions. She has successfully held a variety of multidisciplinary leadership positions in Strategy development,  Commercial management, Financial control, IT strategy, IT management, HR systems implementations, Process and system standardization, outsourcing, and several ERP implementations, delivering successfully in a variety of diverse cultural settings.

Alex completed her PhD in Information Systems; Business Process Management focused on the characterization of expertise in the context of BPM from the Queensland University of Technology in Brisbane, Australia. Alex also holds an MBA from Deakin University, Melbourne, a Master in Education (Educational Leadership and Management) from the Royal Melbourne Institute of Technology, and a Master in Applied Social Science (Counseling) from the Australian College of Applied Psychology. Alex is a Fellow of the Chartered Institute of Management Accountants (FCMA), a Fellow of the Australian Institute of Management (FAIM), and a Chartered Practicing Project Director (CPPD). She is currently finalizing a Doctorate in Business Administration (DBA) with Deakin University focused on organizational consciousness.

Publications include: Challenges for BPM Education: The Importance Relevance of Business Process Expertise (Kokkonen, 2007), Business Process Intelligence (Genrich et al., 2008), Expertise in the Context of Business Process Management (Kokkonen and Bandara, 2010), and Expertise in the Context of Business Process Management (Kokkonen and Bandara, 2014).

Genrich, M., Kokkonen, A., Moormann, J., zur Muehlen, M., Tregear, R., Mendling, J. & Weber, B. 2008, 'Challenges for business process intelligence: discussion at the BPI Workshop 2007', in Business Process Management Workshops Lecture Notes in Computer Science Volume, Brisbane, Australia, vol. 4928, pp. 5–10

Kokkonen, A. 2007, 'BPM education: the importance relevance of business process expertise', in 5th International Business Process Management Conference, Brisbane, Australia.

Kokkonen, A. & Bandara, W. 2010, 'Expertise in the illustrative context of Business Process Management', in M. Rosemann & J. von Brocke (eds), Business Process Management Springer, vol. 2.

Kokkonen, A. & Bandara, W. 2014, 'Expertise in the Illustrative Context of Business Process Management', in M. Rosemann & J. von Brocke (eds), Business Process Management Springer, vol. 2.

Andrew Ross

Andrew Ross has a significant background in corporate transformation activities spanning three decades and multiple industries. Using a hands-on approach to applying process, systems, and operational excellence thinking over this time has enabled a number of multinationals to embed and sustain what Ross likes to term "organic continuous improvement" cultures. These approaches empower and build capability within existing workforces to drive sustained change over long periods of time.

Ross received an MBA from RMIT (Royal Melbourne Institute of Technology), focused on International business in 2012 and is extending his personal perspectives through his ongoing executive development at MIT Sloan (USA) currently.

Core to each of these transformation programs led by Ross is a common method, approach, and application of process, systems, and operational excellence across the enterprise. This has enabled large complex organizations like the Mayne Group, National Australia Group and now the Westpac Group to establish a common way of thinking, working, and modeling process architecture whilst equipping their large disparate workforces to embrace, own, and build on these methods, enabling them to become a part of their everyday operational rhythm and way of improving business outcomes.

Ross currently is leading a team that is redesigning the relationship between business, application, information, and technology reference models across the Westpac Group to enable the rapid change that is required in banking services to become truly responsive to the digitized customer needs.

Westpac Group is Australia's First Bank and its oldest company, celebrating 200 years in 2017. This year the Group was voted as the world's most sustainable bank according to the 2014 Dow Jones Sustainability Indices (DJSI) Review.

Anette Falk Bøgebjerg

She is the Director of Business Process Management (BPM) at LEGO Group's, overall responsible for the project management of the creation of business process documentation throughout the LEGO Group and responsible for the daily management of a central team to build, expand, and maintain the entire framework for business process documentation and BPM.

Anette has been with LEGO Group for 18 years and a renowned public speaker on process and innovation.

She received, in 2013, for the LEGO case story, the prestigious 2013 BPM Gartner Group award for adopting Leading Practice and advance process modeling to create a platform for knowledge, collaboration, and optimization. She emphasized the importance of engaging with and educating business users about the use of BPM to overcome natural resistance to change. The focus on BPM, managed internally by a core BPM team and BPM ambassadors, has improved organizational agility and flexibility, created coherence across business processes, and established a strong foundation for continuous improvement.

Gartner Group evaluation: "The LEGO Group: Best BPM Organization. The LEGO Group, famous for its LEGO bricks, strives to develop children's creativity through play and learning. It recognized that BPM was important to create a platform for knowledge, collaboration and optimization. It also understood the importance of engaging with and educating business users about the use of BPM to overcome natural resistance to change. Its focus on BPM, managed internally by a core BPM team and BPM ambassadors, has improved its organizational agility and flexibility, created coherence across business processes, and established a strong foundation for continuous improvement."

Anette is LEAD Process Architect certified.

Anni Olsen

Anni Olsen has been with Carlsberg since 1976, mainly within process improvement programs and system implementations. Anni is a graduate in economics and business administration from Copenhagen Business School and has many years of experience with the more practical aspects of process improvement and change management.

During the last few years Anni has been part of Carlsberg's large scale standardization program, BSP1, where she has been part of defining the Carlsberg Business Process Model including its end-to-end processes, level definitions, and coverage. Anni has been leading the selection of ARIS as the Business Process Analysis tool, as well as the implementation; this included defining both the process mapping standards and establishing the process governance. During the extensive work with mapping all the processes in Carlsberg for the first time, she facilitated process integration between different functions and was the link between different aspects such as processes, roles, master data, etc. Currently, Anni is overall responsible for the process integration and oversees that processing standards are being followed.

Anni has been a key player in implementing Business Process Management in Carlsberg due to her strong capability of bridging systems and processes and ensuring adoption in the local business units. Anni trains the local organizations in understanding and using the Business Process Model where she is also often involved in both issue identification and solution support.

Antony Dicks

Antony is a business architect at Nedbank in South Africa. He is an enterprise architect practitioner, specializing in guiding innovation and transformation across IT and business.

He has developed business investment road maps in the retail and financial industries. This included the successful modernization of EDCON's retail chain's store system and coordination of a major technology transformation at Nedbank.

Having studied psychology and practiced as an enterprise architect, he has worked on refining practices around road maps to accommodate technical, business, and people aspects. Anthony is a certified LEAD Enterprise Architect.

Dr Asif Q. Gill

Dr Asif Q Gill is a result-oriented experienced author, coach, consultant, educator, researcher, speaker, trainer, and thought leader. He has a PhD Computing Science, MSc Computing Science and Master of Business. When completing his PhD at University of Technology in Sydney, he was awarded the Australian Postgraduate Award for Industry (APAI).

Asif has extensive experience in both agile and non-agile software development environments, displaying a deep appreciation of their different perspectives in a number of IT-enabled business process improvement and transformation industry projects of varying sizes. The focus of his work is to help teams and organizations to improve and transform their human and IT capabilities by leveraging lean agile practices and emerging technologies. He enjoys communicating and managing challenging and conflicting tasks.

Asif is the regional representation for Global University Alliance Regions, providing a local and international platform where universities and thought leaders can interact to conduct research, comparison, and explore leading practices, best practices as well as to develop missing practices.

Asif has authored 2 books and 35+ articles. He is often invited and involved as a professional speaker, conference chair, organizer, and reviewer for a number of quality academic and industry conferences. Certified in ITIL, Lean Six Sigma, TOGAF, and Project Management.

Johan S. Bach

Johan S. Bach has already been involved in large projects with a major focus on Service-Oriented Architecture. This has resulted in more efficient development and operational costs reduction with a maximum strong coupling to business innovation. This strong focus led him to the SAP Quality Award for Large Enterprises in 2010. In order to stay connected with peer organizations he is chair at the SAP Process Integration community since 2009.

Having a strong technical background, electronics and later technical computer science, he participated in projects like ATM (ABN-AMRO's automated teller machine), Dutch Railways switch from paper to electronic travel products for the consumer market. Now he is involved in reorganizing the back office for administering all public transport transactions.

Bach has been active in the Lead Enterprise Architecture method since the early days. He has been part of the Lead exam committee and has seen a lot of practitioners, material. This resulted in a more profound knowledge and wider view on Enterprise Architecture.

Repositioning and rethinking middleware is giving the companies, he worked for, the flexibility to be maneuvrable as the market is dictating.

He is a certified LEAD Process eXpert, LEAD Value eXpert as well as LEAD Enterprise Architect. Johan is furthermore LEADing Practice community founder and member of LEADing Practice Board of Directors, and was cochairman of that board.

Robert J Storms

Worked for over 25 years as a Canadian government civil servant, in leadership roles encompassing the domains of Finance, Human Resources, and Information Technology including extensive business transformation experience. Last position Manager of Business Architecture for Human Resources Development Canada.

He has been part of creating business models, defining the operating model, process mapping entire departments as well as SAP and Oracle blueprinting and implementation.

Robert is certified LEAD Business Architect and LEAD Process-, Value-, Service-, and Innovation & Transformation eXpert certified. In the LEADing Practice Community is he responsible for creating and maintaining the Process Maps and its reference content.

Callie Smit

Callie Smit is the Chief Enterprise Architect at South African Reserve Bank. The South African Reserve Bank is the central bank of South Africa.

Its functions include the formulating and implementing of South Africa's monetary policy, ensuring the efficiency of South Africa's financial system and educating South Africa's citizens about the monetary and economic situation of the country. Unlike the reserve banks of most commonwealth nations, the South African Reserve Bank has always been privately owned.

Callie is certified as a LEAD Enterprise Architect.

Cay Clemmensen

Veteran in the area of business modeling, service model renewal, and value modeling. Started working with financial institutions three decades ago to help them streamline their business models and align business and IT. As specialist in enterprise engineering, enterprise modeling, and enterprise architecture he has worked with international organizations, optimizing and transforming the way of working.

Cay was responsible for the Global IBM SAP partnership. In 2004, he joined the LEADing Practice community as a core founding member.

He has personally developed the Enterprise Standards around Value Modeling, Value Engineering, and Value Architecture. After this he has applied value-based process design or value-based service design.

Cay is a certified Value eXpert and Value Architect.

Christopher K. Swierczynski

Chris Swierczynski's career spans lecturing, R&D, Functional and Project Management, LEAD Enterprise Architecture and Business Lean Six Sigma. For the last 14 years he has been focusing on Process Architecture and Business Process Management improving and optimizing business processes at such companies as Plessey, Telefunken, NYNEX/Verizon, Global Tele-Systems, VeriSign, Cendant, and Electrolux.

Throughout his career within telecom, security, finance, leisure, and consumer goods industries he has been demonstrating creativity, talent, and passion for enterprise improvement and innovation.

In 1983, Chris was one of the four start-up founders and a dynamic leader of a team who invented revolutionary voice data telecom system, with packet switching at the desktop and throughout network, long before comparable technology was introduced—a decade before Internet became a meaningful part of daily life.

Between 1991 and 1998, he established, managed, and optimized operations at NYNEX/Verizon Communications in Europe and SE Asia.

Since 2008, Chris has been the driving force behind the introduction of BPM for a global business transformation at AB Electrolux.

Clemens Utschig-Utschig

Clemens works for Boehringer Ingelheim, one of the top 10 researching pharmaceutical companies in the world. In his current role, he heads the architecture practice for marketing and sales—focusing on enabling the digital revolution.

Before joining BI he worked at the Oracle Headquarters in the United States as platform architect, working with the Fusion Applications development as advisor and supported customers all around the world on their journey toward implementing enterprise-wide SOA.

During his platform engineering years, Clemens was responsible for cross-product integration, strategic standards, as well as a member to the Oracle's SOA platform steering committee, and served on the OASIS TC for Service Component Architecture. In 2006, Clemens cofounded the "Masons-of-SOA", an intercompany network founded by architects of Oracle Germany, Opitz, SOPEra (Eclipse Project Swordfish founders), and EDS, with the mission of spreading knowledge, fostering discussion, and supporting SOA programs across companies and borders. After 14 articles on advanced SOA topics in the German Java Magazin, three patterns in Thomas Erl's SOA Design Patterns catalog, they are currently working on "Next Generation SOA"—slated to release as part of the Service Oriented Computing Series of Prentice Hall for late 2010. Clemens is also a coauthor of the SOA Manifesto.

Dan Moorcroft

Dan is CEO and Founder at QMR Consulting & Professional Staffing; Chairman, Dean's Advisory Board (Telfer School of Management) at University of Ottawa, and Advisory Committee Member—Professional Services Acquisition Advisory Committee at Public Works and Government Services Canada.

A C-Level Executive in Professional Services, Government, and Information Management and Information Technology with proven leadership ability of both small and large teams in both the private and public sectors.

Change leader with keen attention to detail and who builds effective teams empowered with accountability and focused on service delivery, with a record of dramatic improvements in policy and process, cost savings, and P&L.

Innovative business development pioneer with outstanding record of project success. Analytical visionary adept at developing new strategies and aligning technology to grow the business. Executive team player and strong communicator who thrives on responsibility and accountability. Dan has a Master of Business Administration (MBA) Degree and undergraduate law degree. Functionally bilingual French and English.

Daniel T. Jones

Professors Daniel Jones and James P. Womack are the fathers of the "Lean Thinking today". Founder and Chairman of the Lean Enterprise Academy in the UK, Prof. Daniel T. Jones is a senior advisor to the Lean Enterprise Institute, management thought leader, and mentor on applying lean process thinking to every type of business.

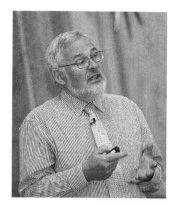

He is the author of the influential and popular management books that describe the principles and practice of lean thinking in production:

- The Machine that Changed the World
- Lean Thinking: Banish Waste and Create Wealth in Your Organization
- Seeing the Whole Value Stream
- How Companies and Customers Can Create Value
- Breaking Through to Flow, Creating Lean Dealers, and Making Hospitals Work

A sought-after keynoter, Jones also has organized Lean Summit conferences in Europe, including the Frontiers of Lean Summit, the First Global Lean Healthcare Summit, and the Lean Transformation Summit.

Prof. Jones advises organizations in different sectors on their lean transformations, helped to establish the first company university in the UK at Unipart, wrote the UK Government's Rethinking Construction report and Lean Thinking for the NHS.

Prof. Jones holds a bachelor's degree in economics from the University of Sussex.

David Coloma-Guerrero

CEO of Cynertia, a business and IT consulting firm in Barcelona, where he leads its business consulting practice, specialized in advising on strategy and innovation to companies with aggressive growth intents.

Prof. Coloma-Guerrero is Director of the Scientific Secretariat of Next World Congress, an international futures congress, and is also a special advisor to the vice president of the autonomous government of Catalonia on foresight and analysis.

Board Member of the Global University Alliance, he lectures at the graduate school of the Universitat Politècnica de Catalunya on service

management and engineering as well as in lean start-up creation, in which he shares his experience as a technology venture capital investor.

Previously, David has been planning manager in the Department of Interior of the autonomous government of Catalonia, responsible for designing strategies, organization, and processes for the deployment of its police services, as well as for its budget planning and controlling.

Deb Boykin

Director BPM/Global Business Architect at Pfizer Pharmaceuticals

Deb has over 30 years of experience specializing in the areas of process methodology and is now the Business Process Management Accountable for managing the activities necessary to develop and sustain Pfizer's enterprise Business Architecture program.

Responsibilities include managing the activities necessary for the development of a robust yet agile Business Architecture repository, ensuring; alignment between SAP Solution Manager and ARIS process objects, alignment of Business Processes with Business Intelligence metrics, linkage with SAP training curricula, integration with Lean/Six Sigma

initiatives. Additionally responsible for providing thought leadership on BPM direction and trends within the industry, keeping abreast of emerging BPM tool suites, and developing courseware in support of the Business Architecture program.

Deb was a contributing author to the book Business Process Management: The SAP Roadmap published in November 2008. Deb has received awards for the Best Practice Partner for Process Measures and Analytics: The Right Data for the Right Decisions by APQC in 2008, Emerging BPM Best Practice by APQC in 2005,

Business Process Excellence Verve Award at Process World in 2007, and the Pfizer PGS Mission Award, November 2012.

Dickson Hunja Muhita

Chartered IT professional and entrepreneur experienced in significantly bettering operations through Information and communications technology (ICT), enterprise architecture, business process management and mentoring.

Professionally certified in LEAD Enterprise Architecture, Business Process Management, and CPA and a member of the Association of Enterprise Architects, British & Australian Computer Society, and Information Systems Audit Control Association (ISACA).

Experience at strategic and operational levels in strategy & architecture, business change, solution development & implementation. This is in large complex organizations with geographically dispersed ICT environments and during initiation of major organization change projects. Organizations include the Australian Bureau of Statistics, Finance & Services NSW govt., Ipswich City Council, RACV, Brightstar Corporation, Xstrata Copper, Monash University, and the European Union Business Assistance Scheme.

Proprietor and Principal Consultant at DHM Consulting Pty and occasional guest lecture at Monash University and LEADing Practice Regional Advisory Board member for Australia and New Zealand.

Dickson is certified as LEAD Enterprise Architecture, OMG-Certified Expert in BPM, Business Process Management (BPTrends Associate & Enterprise), Modeling (BMM, BPMN, EPCs, ARIS house, ArchiMate), Accounting Systems & ERPs; Tools (ARIS, Sparx Enterprise Architect, IBM Rational).

Duarte Gonçalves

Duarte Gonçalves is a registered professional engineer with a BEng in Electronics Engineering, an MEng in Computer Engineering and a PhD in Engineering Development and Management. He is currently employed by the CSIR as a Principal Systems Engineer.

Dr Gonçalves has been involved in engineering surveillance systems for the South African National Defence Force (SANDF) and has consulted to the Karoo Array Telescope and led a renewable energy project as a systems engineer. As part of effort to develop systems engineering skills at the CSIR and nationally, he has developed a practice-based systems engineering program, which is being presented at Wits University. More recently, he has been involved in Force Planning and Design for the SANDF. He currently leads a Whole-of-Society approach to strategy development at the CSIR with border security and rhino poaching as the first applications of the approach.

Dr Gonçalves has a strong interest in *trans*disciplinary problems that span engineering, social sciences, and strategy.

Ekambareswaran Balasubramanian (EK)

Has rich experience in leading and developing strategies, products, solutions and consulting services based on information technology for many industries since 1996. Primary industries include Automotive, Supply Chain, Manufacturing, Healthcare, Banking and Financial Services.

EK has a global work experience covering USA, Europe and Asia.

Some of his major focus areas were Business and Solution Architectures, Product Development, Research and Development, Technology and Architecture Assessment, Product and Process Certifications, Business Process and Business Rules Management.

EK has strong technology and process background. He has architected and developed products and solutions using various technologies covering Telematics, Cloud, Mobile, Web and Enterprise applications. He has architecture and technology certifications to his credit. From the process perspective, he has supported and implemented OMG, CMM, ISO and AGILE based processes. Very early in his career, by 2001, he has worked with KPMG to receive CMM Certification for a company while serving as Software Engineering Process Group lead.

To keep up with the market, business and technology trends, EK has collaborated with many leading research organizations including Gartner, Forrester, SBD, IHS and Strategy Analytics.

During his career, EK has collaborated with many innovative companies for strategic decisions, standards and solutions, including Salesforce.com, Microsoft, IBM, Akamai, Teradata, Oracle and SAP, to name a few.

EK received his master's degree in Computer Applications from Anna University, India, in 1996, his bachelor's degree in Computer Science from University of Madras, India, in 1993.

He currently resides in USA with his family.

Fabrizio Maria Maggi

Fabrizio Maria Maggi received his PhD degree in Computer Science in 2010. He then joined the Architecture of Information Systems research group, Eindhoven University of Technology, before moving to University of Tartu, where he currently holds a senior researcher position.

Fabrizio's areas of research span process modeling and process analysis. He has coauthored more than 50 articles on process mining, automated revision of business process models, declarative business process modeling, monitoring of business constraints at runtime, service-oriented architectures, service choreographies, and service composition.

He serves as Program Committee Member of several international conferences and workshops in the business process management field.

Fan Zhao

Faculty member of Computer Information Systems and Decision Sciences in Florida Gulf Coast University. PhD in Management Information Systems, University of Nebraska-Lincoln (2006).

Dr Zhao is a member of the Decision Science Institute, Association for Information Systems, and IEEE. Research interests in enterprise resource planning, data mining, human–computer interaction, e-commerce, and customer relationship management.

Fatima Senghore, PMP

Fatima Senghore is a certified Project Management Professional with 12 years of professional experience in federal and commercial consultancy providing program and project management support. Currently, Fatima is employed with Valador Inc. and is the Data Manager and IT Lead for NASA's Office of Education Infrastructure Division; her responsibilities include supporting the evolution and maintenance of the agency's education applications, performance reporting, and portfolio management. In addition she serves as adjunct faculty within the Industrial Engineering Department at Morgan State University. Fatima has experience increasing efficiencies, solving problems and providing innovative solutions. In addition to her PMP certification Fatima is a certified ScrumMaster.

Fatima is currently pursuing her doctorate in the Department of Engineering Management and Systems Engineering at George Washington University. She received her Masters of Science in Industrial Engineering from Florida A&M University and her Bachelors of Science in Industrial Engineering from Morgan State University, where she was a NASA fellow. Recent publications include "Using Social Network Analysis to Investigate the Potential of Innovation Networks: Lessons Learned from NASA's International Space Apps Challenge."

Fatma Dandashi

Dr Dandashi works at the MITRE Corporation which is a not-for-profit company that operates multiple federally funded research and development centers where she applies knowledge and expertise in systems engineering, information technology, operational concepts, and enterprise modernization to address various sponsors' critical needs. In this role, Dr Dandashi supports DoD on standards development for Model-Based Systems Engineering (MBSE) and architecture-based analysis modeling languages (UML, SysML, BPMN) and frameworks (Unified Profile for DoDAF/MODAF (UPDM)). Dr Dandashi is a co-chair of the Analysis and Design Task Force at the Object Management Group.

Dr Dandashi is an International Council on Systems Engineering (INCOSE) Certified Systems Engineering Professional. She holds a PhD in Information Technology from GMU, a master of science degree in computer science from the University of Louisiana (Lafayette), and a bachelor of arts degree in computers/business administration from the Lebanese American University.

Dr Dandashi has presented at conferences and published numerous papers at INCOSE, SISO, ACM, and IEEE affiliated publications/conferences.

Fred A. Cummins

Fred A. Cummins is an independent consultant doing business as Agile Enterprise Design, LLC. He is a former HP and EDS Fellow. He has developed solutions or functioned as an analysis and design consultant across multiple industries including manufacturing and distribution, financial services, transportation, insurance, health care, and government.

Fred has been cochair of the Business Modeling and Integration (BMI) task force at OMG (Object Management Group) for 14 years. He has been an active participant in the development of a number of OMG specifications, and most recently was a leader in the development of the Case Management Model and Notation (CMMN) specification and the Value Delivery Modeling Language (VDML) specification. CMMN supports the design of event-driven, adaptive processes to improve planning, coordination, and collaboration of knowledge workers. VDML provides a business design abstraction appropriate for business leaders that brings together multiple dimensions of business design including organization, capabilities, processes, resources, performance measurements and the creation and delivery of customer value. The BMI task force is also responsible for a number of other business-focused specifications including BPMN (Business Process Model and Notation), BMM (Business Motivation Model), SBVR (Semantics of Business Vocabulary and Rules), and DMN (Decision Model and Notation).

Fred has presented at conferences, authored numerous papers, and published three books, most recently Building the Agile Enterprise with SOA, BPM, and MBM (Elsevier, 2009).

Gabriel von Scheel

Gabriel is a big scale thinker who loves the details just as much. Recognized for his business logic and design thinking that simplifies complexity and problem solving though visual thinking.

He helps businesses to solve complex problems through his visual thinking in workshops and hands-on projects. Gabriel has helped teams learn to solve complex problems by relearning how to see.

Through his mix of unique visual, analytical skills, and attention to details he has been a significant contributor to the process improvements, mapping, diagrams, performance and value indicators, maturity, lifecycles, and modeling of this book.

He is a rising star in the making and ONE TO WATCH.

Gabriella von Rosing

She has specialized as a Business Architect and the Sustainability Development of the Enterprise. She is thereby in business modeling and strategic execution for the development and improvement of an organizations revenue, service and value model as well as cost, performance and operating model. She applies the mentioned principles to organizations Business Architecture in defining the organizations business relevant meta object and mapping a Business Model, Strategy Map. Value Drivers, Performance Drivers, Scorecards and Process Architecture work, e.g., process optimization/innovation, performance and value creation. In the past years, she has supported, coached and consulted dozens of organizations around the world. Her cross-cultural background as well as her cross-disciplinary background of business, economics, change and sustainability theory and practice enables her to work with managers and employees from different companies and of different nationalities and professions.

Gabriella led the development of the LEADing Practice change management standard, with attached change management reference content. This development included the coordination and leadership of 3900 practitioners, +400 universities, professors, lecturers and researchers (from the Global University Alliance), that among others included:

- Research and analyze what works around change management (best practice), and what are unique practices for changes applied by leading organizations (leading practices).
- Identify common and repeatable change patterns which provide the basis for the LEADing Practice Change Management Enterprise Standards.
- Develop "Change Management Reference Content" that increases the level of re-usability and replication within the field of enterprise modeling, enterprise engineering and enterprise architecture.
- Extended with change management accelerators that adopt and reproduce the identified change management best practices and leading practices.

Gabriella is a certified Change eXpert & LEAD Business Architect Certified.

Gary Doucet

An experienced Enterprise Solution Architect and Information Management and Information Technology Executive with over 30 years of experience, including 7 years as the Government of Canada's Chief Architect.

Gary has deep experience in enterprise architecture, program management, product development, systems integration, business transformation, and various technologies.

Gary is the lead author/editor of "Coherency Management—Architecting the Enterprise for Alignment, Agility and Assurance" and contributor/editor to several other publications and professional journals. He has, by invitation, presented to venues around the globe as a keynote speaker for his thought leadership in architecture, e-business, business transformation, and systems engineering.

After completing a large business blueprint exercise for a large back office transformation based on LEADing Practice and involving ERP solutions for HR and Finance he was invited to work in the central agency of the Government of Canada on an effort to do the same thing enterprise wide.

His passion is coherency and he is an avid practitioner of "Just Enough" strategies, value-based engineering and he is a proud LEAD© Certified Architect.

Gert Meiling

Gert Meiling, MBA, is a practitioner of business architecture and since 1997, working in the Fashion and Sporting Goods industry predominantly in the areas of management accounting and performance management. Currently, he is working for Tommy Hilfiger and Calvin Klein and works on the management reporting, including measurements, business monitoring, performance management, and business intelligence. Thereby, working both with business and IT to seamlessly merge these worlds into solutions that support the achievement of organizational objectives.

He received a bachelor degree in business studies from the Windesheim University of Applied Sciences in Zwolle in 1996 and a masters degree after completing the International Action Learning MBA Program at Business School Netherlands in 2011.

Gert O. Jansson

Gert has an extensive and broad background from the private sector. His main experience originates from Eastman Kodak Company. He has held several positions within the company in different regions. He has been working for the Scandinavian region, the UK region, and also the US and Canadian region.

His background is mainly within Supply Chain, Business Controlling and Project Management. He has been involved in pilot projects, scale, and scope projects.

Gert has seen a huge giant such as Kodak trying to adjust and adapt to a never-ending changing environment. The Rise and Fall of a Blue Chip Giant. Since he left Eastman Kodak, he has been working as a consultant within other industrial sectors.

Gert is the Vice President of Enterprise Standards at LEADing Practice for North European Region.

He has a University degree in Business and Administration, Diploma in Engineering and is certified as an LEAD Enterprise Architect.

Prof. Hans-Jürgen Scheruhn

Dr Hans-Jürgen Scheruhn, Professor at the Hochschule Harz University in Wernigerode, Germany, Department of Automization and Computer Science, since 1994. Dr Scheruhn teaches Business Process Management with Enterprise Resource Planning Systems (ERP) and related subjects.

He obtained his PhD in Engineering from Hanover University, Germany, in 1988. Starting as a System Analyst the same year, Product Manager, and later as head of the Product Marketing department, Dr Scheruhn was responsible for SAP R/3 at Siemens, Hanover, Germany. He jointly offers certified courses with Atos/Siemens IT Solutions and Services GmbH.

Dr Scheruhn's research focuses on Information Model-Based Implementation of Business Information Systems and Workflow Management. He has published about 50 international articles and several books, one of them in cooperation with KPMG Consulting.

He also has got experience from numerous ERP projects with companies like Salzgitter Stahl AG. Together with the SAP University Competence Center (UCC) in Magdeburg he has investigated its ITIL Compliance and has implemented the entire UCC Online Course Management based on SAP ERP. He also works as a Consultant for the implementation of SAP ERP at the Bundesagentur für Arbeit in Nürnberg, Germany.

Dr Scheruhn has been teaching ERP graduate courses in several international Universities of Australia, New Zealand, the United States, Cuba, and Spain. He is a Professor of Management at Krannert School of Management, Purdue University, and GISMA Business School in Hanover, Germany, Courtesy Faculty at Florida Gulf Coast University (FGCU), a Former Lecturer of Enterprise-Systems Teaching Team at the University of Technology Sydney (UTS) and he obtained a "Profesorado" at the Universidad de Alicante (UA).

Dr Scheruhn is a Board Member and Head of Information Management Research & Development at the Global University Alliance. Providing an international platform where universities and thought leaders can interact to conduct research, comparison, and explore leading practices, best practices, as well as to develop missing practices. He is a certified LEAD Enterprise Architect.

Henk de Man

Henk de Man is an architect with over 20 years of experience in IT and Business concepts. He has a successful track record of commercializing research insights to launch world-class Enterprise Application Software products, in the areas of ERP, Lean Enterprise, and BPM, that today serve a global customer base to integrate and smoothly run their business operations while serving as platforms for business transformation.

In his current position as cofounder of VDM-bee, he focuses on supporting business managers, analysts, and architects with Business Model Innovation, Transformation and Management technology on mobile platforms.

Over the years, Henk served as active developer and implementer of OMG specifications in related areas, in particular Value Delivery Modeling Language (VDML), Structured Metrics Metamodel (SMM), and Case Management Model and Notation (CMMN).

Henk also participated in European Research and authored and coauthored various articles and papers in these areas.

Henk Kuil

Henk Kuil, Bachelor ICT, specialization Software Engineering in 1987. During his study his fascination has been initiated for meta programming and meta languages. He started work at the Medical Informatics in Rotterdam as a coresearcher in a PhD dissertation on self-descriptive data models for user-level integration. Equipped with the academic background, Henk moved to a small business startup, specialized in knowledge-based systems, where he worked on one of the first commercial data mining systems, CAPTAINS, used by KLM to assist cockpit career planners at KLM Royal Dutch Airlines.

Currently Henk works as a LEAD enterprise architect at the MRO business of Air France/KLM, where he is involved in redesign of the application landscape. Moving from nonstandard processes and custom applications to standard processes based on three COTS application suites.

He is a certified LEAD Process eXpert, LEAD Value eXpert as well as LEAD Enterprise Architect. Henk is furthermore LEADing Practice community founder and member of LEADing Practice Board of Directors, and was cochairman of that board from 2012 to 2014.

Dr Hendrik Bohn

Dr Hendrik Bohn is a LEAD Business Architect at Nedbank in South Africa. Since 2009, he has worked at several financial institutions advising on Enterprise Architecture practices, strategy, and portfolio planning. Before moving to South Africa, he had comanaged two award-winning European R&D IT integration projects and facilitated the formulation of R&D projects between industry and academia. He also worked as external expert evaluator for funded European R&D projects for the European Commission. In 2009, he received his PhD in Engineering from the University of Rostock, Germany, for his research on Web Services process management for embedded devices. He has coauthored over 20 publications around research and position papers.

Henrik N. Vester

Henrik N. Vester is the Co-Chair of the Global Business Process User Group at LEADing Practice. Pioneering and helping Fortune 500 organizations on how to apply business process best practices, industry practices, and leading practices. Standing at the frontline how to get business value by linking business process to strategy with operational execution.

He started his journey toward becoming a recognized Business Process Management (BPM) trendsetter and trusted advisor, for a number of global organizations. In the Royal Danish Navy, in the early 1980s, he was one of the first pioneer's educated, to support the organization transform from a mainframe base service model, to the world of Personal Computers.

Henrik has since then been working on a number of Enterprise scale Business Transformation Projects, mainly in highly regulated industries like food manufactures and pharmaceuticals. Always in the role as the person who connects business, people, processes, methodologies, regulations, and technology. He also translates extremely complex theories and relationships, between regulations and enterprise architectures, into practical models and tools for all levels of the business.

Henrik is currently managing and advising a number of technology startups and consulting companies in the BPM space. His main focus remains how to add value to the clients, by leveraging his waste experience and knowledge. Working directly with the transformation teams, helping keep the business core differentiators and value drivers in focus for the projects.

Over the past 20 years, Henrik has been a presenter and keynote speaker at international conferences. Henrik is a certified LEAD Enterprise Architecture.

Jacob L. Gammelgaard

Jacob L. Gammelgaard has a background from finance and holds a master of science degree in E-business.

He has 11 years of experience with large strategic business and IT projects in international environments from companies like Coloplast A/S and FLSmidth A/S.

Jacob has been responsible for several standardization programs and has as a result vast practical experience in working with standardizing business processes and systems and linking company strategy to the operational level. In Coloplast A/S Jacob was responsible for designing a corporate ERP-template for Sales, Distribution, Manufacturing, and Finance and succeeded in implementing the solution to 25 sites in 2.5 years.

Following his time in Coloplast Jacob took a position in FLSmidth in connection with the Helios Program. In FLSmidth, Jacob has been responsible for setting up the Global Business Process Management organization and governance. Jacob is heading the department responsible for designing the +450 global business processes needed in FLSmidth to run the daily business. He has furthermore been involved in the ongoing implementation of the ERP and PDM solution in co-operation with the deployment department and Solution- and Enterprise Architects.

To ensure the important strong governance of the finished solution Jacob has also been involved in creating a governance organization. The foundation for the governance set up is the involvement of a group of area specific Executive Business Process Owners. The Executive Business Process Owners are members of a Change Advisory Board, which is responsible for approving/rejecting and prioritizing the incoming business initiatives and change requests.

James P. Womack

Management expert James P. Womack, PhD, is the founder and senior advisor to the Lean Enterprise Institute, Inc., a nonprofit training, publishing, conference, and management research company chartered in August 1997 to advance a set of ideas known as lean production and lean thinking, based initially on Toyota's business system and now being extended to an entire lean management system.

The intellectual basis for Cambridge, MA-based Institute is described in a series of books and articles coauthored by Womack and Daniel Jones over the past 20 years. The most widely known books are: *The Machine That Changed the World* (Macmillan/Rawson Associates, 1990), *Lean Thinking* (Simon & Schuster, 1996), *Lean Solutions* (Simon & Schuster, 2005), and *Seeing The Whole Value Stream* (Lean Enterprise Institute, 2011).

Articles include: "From Lean Production to the Lean Enterprise" (Harvard Business Review, March–April, 1994), "Beyond Toyota: How to Root Out Waste and Pursue Perfection" (Harvard Business Review, September–October, 1996), "Lean Consumption" (Harvard Business Review, March–April, 2005).

Womack received a BA in political science from the University of Chicago in 1970, a master's degree in transportation systems from Harvard in 1975, and a PhD in political science from MIT in 1982 (for a dissertation on comparative industrial policy in the US., Germany, and Japan).

During the period 1975–1991, he was a full-time research scientist at MIT directing a series of comparative studies of world manufacturing practices. As research director of MIT's International Motor Vehicle Program, Womack led the research team that coined the term "lean production" to describe Toyota's business system.

Womack served as the Institute's chairman and CEO from 1997 until 2010.

Jeanne W. Ross

Jeanne W. Ross is the founder and pioneer of our operating model thinking today. She is an organizational theorist and Principal Research Scientist at MIT Sloan School of Management for Information Systems Research.

Jeanne W. Ross directs and conducts academic research that targets the challenges of senior level executives at Center for Information Systems Research's more than 80 global sponsor companies.

She studies how firms develop competitive advantage through the implementation and reuse of digitized platforms. Her work has appeared in major practitioner and academic journals, including *MIT Sloan Management Review, Harvard Business Review, The Wall Street Journal, MISQ Executive, MIS Quarterly*, the *Journal of Management Information Systems, IBM Systems Journal*, and *CIO Magazine*.

She is coauthor of three books: *IT Savvy: What Top Executives Must Know to Go from Pain to Gain* (2009), *Enterprise Architecture as Strategy: Creating a Foundation for Business Execution* (2006) through Harvard Business School Press, and *IT Governance: How Top Performers Manage IT Decision Rights for Superior Results* (2004). She has served on the faculty of customized courses for a number of major corporations, including PepsiCo, McKinsey, General Electric, TRW, Pfizer, News Corporation,

Commonwealth Bank of Australia, IBM, and Credit Suisse. She regularly appears as a speaker at major conferences for IT executives.

Jeanne earned a BA at the University of Illinois, an MBA from The Wharton School at the University of Pennsylvania, and a PhD in management information systems from the University of Wisconsin–Milwaukee. She is a founding senior editor and former editor in chief of *MIS Quarterly Executive*.

Jeff Greer

Jeff Greer is the Vice President of IT Strategy and Business Architecture at Cardinal Health, a US Fortune 21 Company. In his role, Jeff is responsible for spearheading the creation, implementation, and advancement of Cardinal Health's overall enterprise IT strategy and business architecture framework—including responsibility and oversight for IT strategies and processes for all mergers, acquisitions, and divestitures.

Over the last 4 years, Jeff has been the visionary, leader, and champion of business architecture and business process management at Cardinal Health—working to develop the tools, methods, and approaches linking strategy, execution, and operations. He has presented and published about his business architecture experiences at Cardinal Health, including:

"Using Business Architecture to Manage Complexity and Drive Change," Gartner, 2014. "Leading Companies Leverage Business Architecture to Integrate Business and IT Execution," Gartner Research, 2013. "Bridging the Architecture Talent Gap—Cardinal Health," Corporate Executive Board, 2012.

Prior to joining Cardinal Health, Jeff was a consultant with A.T. Kearney within their Strategic IT Practice. Jeff received a B.A. in philosophy from Vanderbilt University and a Master of Business Administration from Vanderbilt's Owen Graduate School of Management.

Jens Theodor Nielsen

Jens Theodor Nielsen, Chief Adviser at the Danish Defense Command, has worked with strategic business development within the Danish Defense since 2006. Over the years, he has contributed to several development initiatives with his strong focus on business optimization and IT alignment. At the Defense Command he holds special responsibility for developing strategic process management initiatives and for promoting the Business Process Management perspective.

Since the year 2000, Jens Theodor Nielsen has also worked with ERP planning. He was a project participant for 4 years in the SAP implementation project at the Danish Defense Command and worked 1 year as SAP Consultant for a the consulting company NNIT. Since 2006 he has been a Danish representative in the SAP Defense Interest Group (DEIG).

In 2006 Jens Theodor Nielsen introduced the methodology Managing Successful Programmes (MSP) as a tool for strategic alignment of business and IT at the Danish Defense Command. When the first program was launched in 2008 he had the lead on developing the program blueprint and describing an envisaged to-be process architecture. He has since then been a keen ambassador for combining the use of Program Management with Enterprise Architecture and Business Process Management.

Together with retired Commander Senior Grade Torben Claus Dahl from the Royal Danish Navy, Jens Theodor Nielsen has developed The Value Driver Model©, which outlines the interrelationship between strategic Corporate Governance, Core Business, BPM and Management of IT, as well as other Capacities. A first version of this model was presented in the publication "Real-World BPM in an SAP Environment" published by SAP Press in 2010. The Value Driver Model© is a private consultancy product and not in use within the Danish Defense.

Jens Theodor Nielsen is a Certified LEADing Enterprise Architect and within networks contributes to the development of BPM and EA thinking. He has lectured on BPM at the IT University in Copenhagen, and he has been invited as speaker at a number of conferences in Europe.

John Arthur Zachman

Father of Enterprise Architecture concepts. Author of the Framework for Enterprise Architecture, the Enterprise Ontology.

Founder and Chairman of Zachman International, an Enterprise Architecture research and education company.

Executive Director of FEAC Institute (Federated Enterprise Architecture Certification Institute) awarding certifications in DoDAF (Department of Defense Architecture Framework), FEAF (Federal Enterprise Architecture Framework), and Zachman (Zachman Ontology).

Author of numerous articles including seminal articles on Enterprise Architecture and teacher and apologist for the Ontological approach versus Methodological approaches for Enterprise Architecture.

John E. Bertram

John E. Bertram is a certified LEAD Business Architect. He is recognized for his trademark and unique ability to transform and innovate existing business and service models; translating the "Big Picture" into operational execution by applying leading practice, industry- and best practice with the IT teams.

John is acknowledged for his ability to identify, plan, and create value by aligning business strategies with information technologies. Drilling Business Objectives "big-picture" down to Critical Success Factor and Key Performance Indicators at strategically, tactical, and operational level on business, technology, and applications.

John has been instrumental in developing the Call/contact Enterprise Standards with LEADing Practice that interconnects business model, value management/architecture, measurements, analytics, service orientation, testing, process modeling/architecture, as well as information modeling/architecture. Supporting complex organization call/contact center works effectively, that is, transform organization to optimize costs and drive out value, draw more direct and explicit links to strategic targets, understand the value potential of call/contact centers by integrating them directly into their core and supporting processes, and finally linking cost to performance—answering client demands in a manner that makes business sense and aligns with acceptable service standards.

John has a passion to discover the Why, define the What, and deliver the How. With a wide range of private and public section experience, John currently works for the Canadian Government and is responsible for aligning Project & Portfolio initiatives in a complex environment.

John E. Golden

John Golden has an extensive background reflecting a 30-plus year consulting career delivering process improvement, automation requirements, and architecture services and solutions spanning automotive, manufacturing, healthcare, energy, financial, consumer goods, and temporary staffing industries. John holds a bachelors degree in business leadership and administration and an associates in computer science.

Since the 1980s, John has been both a practitioner and manager of business solution teams delivering leading edge consulting services to Fortune 1000 companies. During this time, John filled a principal role in the development of a proven, repeatable, and commercially available full lifecycle project execution methodology, along with supporting service offerings, and training materials. This methodology is currently in practice at dozens of federal, state, and public organizations.

John has served many clients as a business transformation consultant and engagement manager. Using proven and repeatable approaches and John's attention to customer needs and details, he has facilitated dozens of process change, organizational change, and (model-based) automation requirements analysis/design projects to a successful conclusion.

John Martin Rogers

John Rogers is a practicing Enterprise Architect and Business Architect with over 30 years consulting experience in Government, Utilities, and the Mining Industries, full system development lifecycle experience, including 15 years with SAP rollout and support projects. His burning passion is to help organizations find holistic ways to innovate and better deliver on their mission.

Jonnro Erasmus

Jonnro Erasmus is a forerunner in the use of requirements analysis and functional models for enterprise and industry systems. He is a senior researcher at the Council for Scientific and Industrial Research and a registered professional engineer with the Engineering Council of South Africa. He has developed solutions and consulted clients across multiple industries, including manufacturing, energy, transportation, and government.

Jonnro specializes in analysis and design of large, complex systems, to identify risks, dependencies, and opportunities. He spent several years developing and implementing business processes at a major electricity utility, where he pioneered the development of process building blocks and how they are combined to deliver different products and services. He has also had the responsibility of managing interdependent risks between major construction projects of both public and private enterprises. Jonnro is currently the research coordinator for the Product Lifecycle Management research group of the Global University Alliance and is pursuing research into supply chain integration for his PhD.

Jonnro has presented at conferences, authored several papers and is an active participant in the International Council on Systems Engineering and the Association of Enterprise Architects. He is also a certified LEADing Practice EA eXpert and a certified TOGAF9 practitioner.

Joshua von Scheel

Joshua has been the main force in the outperformers versus underperformer's study, researching, and evolving mainstream key management models, tools, and practices.

His effort to interconnected key models, tools, and practices across Business (business competencies, services, processes and value) Application (application and data) with Technology (platform and infrastructure) have been published in standards bodies and reference content.

Acknowledged for his Value and Performance contribution to this book, such as:

Value: Value expectations and requirements (e.g., service, process, data, etc.), value drivers (external and internal), value bottlenecks/value clusters, value measurements, value maps, matrices, and models, revenue model, value-based costing, value-based modeling as well as value management.

Performance: Performance expectations and requirements (e.g., service, process, data, etc.), performance drivers (external and internal), performance bottlenecks, performance measurements, business performance indicators (BPIs), and key performance drivers in performance maps, matrices.

Recognized as a practitioner with an extraordinary business understanding and abilities in his field. Discovering relationships of objects not seen before. He has the potential to break the sound barrier of conventional thinking.

Certified LEAD Value eXpert and Process eXpert. A true Jedi Knight and proficient in his field of expertise.

Joshua Waters

In his work he is specialist as a LEAD Business Architect and with his unique background in business and change management, he is specialized in business innovation and transformation. With the mentioned business knowledge, he mixes his business approach with a blend of business oriented and people change aspects. He applies the mentioned principles to organizations Business Architecture in defining the organizations business relevant meta object and mapping their Competencies, Business Model, Strategy Map, Value Drivers, Performance Drivers, Scorecards, and Process Architecture work, e.g., process optimization/innovation, performance, and value creation.

In LEADing Practice, Joshua is responsible for the business measurements and performance indicator standards and the relevant reference content. This responsibility included the coordination and leadership of the LEADing Practice +3900 practitioners, as well as the coordination with the +400 universities, professors, lecturers, and researchers from the Global University Alliance.

Joshua is a certified Business Architect as well as LEAD Enterprise Architect.

Justin Tomlinson

Founder of ValueAdd group AG, an international group of entrepreneurs, thought leaders, business leaders, and senior advisors using proven frameworks, methods, approaches, and tools to identify, plan, create, and realize value throughout organizations.

Justin's professional passion is helping organizations eliminate "fake work" by aligning stakeholder expectations with operational performance. Author of "The People Quadrant," "Leading the People-Side of Change," and "Tapping Human Potential through Social Organization Design and Workplace 3.0."

Justin is a certified LEAD Transformation Architect.

Karin Gräslund

While's serving as research assistant at a university, Prof. Dr Karin Gräslund, together with her professor and three PhD colleagues, established a medium-sized company for state-of-the-art, innovative IT consulting when their projects changed from scientific exploration to repetitive and proven consulting methods. She has also worked in the non-academic sector, developing expertise in business intelligence projects and business case modeling for IT projects while working for SAP, among other companies. Today, she teaches informatics and Information Management in the Bachelor of Business Administration program and Finance Information & Enterprise Performance Management in the Master of Controlling & Finance program of the Wiesbaden Business School. She has also taught in several other universities around the world for over 10 years.

Her current interests include enterprise performance, evidence-based management, sustainability and user-experience management.

In 2006, she cofounded two roundtables in the SAP University Alliance (SAP UA Business Intelligence and Business Process Management) and is member of the non-vendor academic platform for academic collaboration. As part of her SAP University Alliance work, she has been involved in developing enterprise and industry standards, with OMG, LEADing Practice, and more. She has also contributed to the Global TOGAF Business Architecture Methods & Certification Development

Group and the BPM and EA curriculum for the SAP University Alliance (+900 universities).

Publications during the last 3 years:

- Contributed to the IEEE publication "Defining the Profession of the Business Architect" as well as the publication "How to integrate Enterprise Architecture and BPM"
- Karin Gräslund, Jana Nizold: IntegRisk – Risikointegrierendes und –adjustierendes Performancemanagement - Literaturüberblick zur Integration von Risikomanagement in einen Closed-Loop Ansatz zur nachhaltigen Unternehmenssteuerung -, in Heiß; Pepper; Schlingloff; Schneider (Hrsg.) Proceeding Informatik 2011, GI-Lecture Notes in Informatics 2011, p. 84 and 020,134.pdf
- Karin Gräslund "Einführung Business Intelligence", in Uwe Haneke, Stephan Trahasch, Tobias Hagen, Tobias Lauer (Herausgeber): "Open Source Business Intelligence (OSBI): Möglichkeiten, Chancen und Risiken quelloffener BI-Lösungen", autumn 2010. Published in TWDI
- Karin Gräslund "Strategieberatung vs. künstliche Intelligenz - Permanente Überprüfung der Lösung" Tagesspiegel/Handelsblatt Beilage FORUM (50 Jahre Top-ManagementBeratung) Page 7 from 5 May 2014.

Katia Bartels

Graduated in International Business and Languages with specialization in Marketing. Katia started her career combining two areas of interest: Customer Relationship Management and Technology Information. During her IT years she specialized and focused on Sales/eCommerce, Marketing and Service processes and how these areas could be supported by better IT solutions.

Throughout her career she's been able to do different assignments in her roles as Application & Solution Architect, Project Management, Trainer & Coach, but also deployment of strategy & methodologies across companies.

From 2010 till 2012 she worked as Global Architect for Professional Services and Consumer Care for Philips. Katia currently works as European Enterprise IT Architect at Office Depot, where she is closely involved in back end consolidation and integration as well in the innovation of the eCommerce platforms.

Worked together with SAP in an innovation partnership for Social Media Engagement and with different suppliers as SAP, Microsoft and Salesforce.com developing Customer Value Prototyping initiatives.

Katia is certified Togaf 9 and LEADing Practice Enterprise Architecture Expert with 13 years' experience with IT solutions, mainly SAP, as Consultant and Architect with international experience.

Keith D. Swenson

Keith Swenson is Vice President of Research and Development at Fujitsu North America. As a speaker, author, and contributor to many workflow and BPM standards, he is known for having been a pioneer in collaboration software and Web services.

He is currently the Chairman of the Workflow Management Coalition and has led agile software development teams at MS2, Netscape, Ashton Tate and Fujitsu. In 2004, he was awarded the Marvin L. Manheim Award for outstanding contributions in the field of workflow.

Coauthor on more than 10 books. In 2010, his book "Mastering the Unpredictable" introduced and defined the field of adaptive case management and established him as a top influencer in the field of case management.

Kenneth D. Teske

A results-driven joint command and control professional with more than 30 years of demonstrated leadership and management success in military, academia, and defense contracting organizations from tactical though strategic levels.

Ken has a wide-ranging experience analyzing, determining, articulating, and advocating war-fighters' command and control requirements improving organizational productivity.

Recognized with the prestigious "FRONTIER RUNNER of the year" (2014) as codeveloper of the "Unity of Effort" Framework. Responsible as the Lead Operational Architect of process flows of the "Unity of Effort" Framework.

Ken is a Senior Multi-Discipline Integration Analyst at Cydecor detailed to US Special Operations Command, DOD Joint Staff J6, and the Naval Research Laboratory.

Author of numerous articles and professional papers. Retired as a United States Army Sergeant Major from the Department of Defense.

Certified LEAD Enterprise Architecture and Practitioner.

Kevin Govender

Strategy and Enterprise Architecture

Profile: As the Group Chief Enterprise Architect, Mr Kevin Govender is responsible for the IT strategy, enterprise architecture, research, and innovation. Mr Govender's responsibilities include providing leadership and direction as well as developing, maintaining, and leveraging the strategy and enterprise architecture across organization to support the company strategy and focus on business outcomes.

Achievements: During his 20 years of work experience, Mr Govender's expertise is attributed to the various roles he has played in other organizations prior to joining Transnet, namely Ernst & Young, Discovery, Accenture, Nedcor, and Unilever. He has worked in many diverse industries and consulted to various organizations. He has extensive experience in strategy, business intelligence, business advisory, management consulting, portfolio and program management, SAP assurance and implementation, and implementing turnaround, transformational and improvement programs.

Academic Qualifications: Mr Govender received a Bachelor of Technology in industrial engineering from the Durban University of Technology in 1998, an executive leadership program from the University of Cape Town Business School in 2008, and a postgraduate diploma (honor's degree) in management practices in business leadership from the University of Cape Town Business School in 2014.

Areas of Interest: Mr Govender's key interest includes business strategy, innovation, research, and new technologies.

Klaus Vitt

Klaus Vitt (Dipl.-Ing. FH; Dipl.-Math. Univ.) served as the Chief Executive Officer of the German Federal Employment Agency (Bundesagentur für Arbeit) from 2006 to June 2014.

Currently serving as the Chief Information Officer of German Federal Employment Agency, responsible for strategy, planning, and governance, security, and process management of information technology.

Mr Klaus Vitt has served as the Chief Information Officer and Member of Board of Management at T-Com since 2001. Mr Vitt was responsible for information and process management at T-Com.

He began his career in 1979 at Sperry Univac. Since 1980, he served as a System Engineer at the Applied Data Research software house. He moved to Bertelsmann in 1982 as an international IT coordinator and took increasingly responsible positions in various areas, served as head of the computing.

Mr Klaus Vitt was recognized for his leadership with the "LEADing Practice Transformation" project of 2013 out of 120 compelling transformation projects. He has transformed the largest service provider of the German labor market into a modern service provider and an efficiency-oriented service agency, meanwhile fulfilling important legal mandates. Bundesagentur für Arbeit currently has approximately 100,000 employees and during the course of the year 7.77 million people newly registered as unemployed while at the same time 7.72 million people found a new job.

The transformation initiative is a major undertaking with all odds against it: a structural approach and with surgical precision mapping all tasks, activities, functions, roles, and processes across departments and organizations and interlinking the data with the information flow and services of 13.82 billion euros in unemployment benefits in 2012.

Krzysztof Skurzak

Krzysztof is an Enterprise Architect at NATO Allied Command Transformation (ACT) at the headquarters at Norfolk, Virginia. His role in NATO ACT includes:

- To further develop the NATO enterprise architecture framework
- To develop the capability framework for the conduct of future combined joint operations
- To develop the NATO process reference content
- To enable joint collaboration between the NATO partners

Krzysztof is a certified LEAD Enterprise Architect and is the contact point between LEADing Practice and NATO and the strategic partnership they have. Joint developments with the NATO Framework for Collaborative Interaction, include:

- To further develop the NATO semantic tools
- To tailor and develop the NATO Enterprise Architecture Framework
- To help NATO apply and tailor Enterprise Standards

LeAnne Spurrell

Founder Logica Consulting Inc., an Ottawa-based SAP consulting firm formed in 1998 to provide SAP consulting services to Canadian federal government clients. Strategic Partner, QMR Consulting, created their SAP/ERP practice.

LeAnne's SAP Public Sector expertise has made her a trusted strategic advisor for many Canadian government executives. She has crafted a niche practice in SAP business process reengineering and SAP workflow automation projects.

As a visionary in her field, she has designed a custom project management methodology to accelerate SAP automation initiatives, the WF-SWAT Accelerated Automation™ approach.

LeAnne has gathered a dream team of SAP consultants to work with her on automation projects, known as the SAP Workflow SWAT team (WF-SWAT™). The WF-SWAT™ team is an elite team of senior SAP consultants specializing in automation project delivery.

LeAnne and her team guide an organization through the process of business process reengineering, change management, and technical automation resulting in streamlined processes, cost savings, and new efficiencies.

Lloyd Dugan

Lloyd Dugan is the Chief Architect for Business Process Management, Inc. (BPMI), providing BPM, BPMN, EA, and SOA modeling, system design, and architectural advisory services.

He is a widely recognized thought leader in the development and use of leading modeling languages, methodologies, platforms, and tools in these areas. He is also an Independent Consultant that designs executable BPMN processes that leverage Service Component Architecture (SCA) patterns (aka BPMN4SCA), principally on the Oracle BPMN/SOA platform. He has provided IT advisory services to major public sector clients, most recently for the Deputy Chief Management Office (DCMO) of the U.S. Department of Defense (DoD) and the Department of Veterans Affairs (VA), Office of Information Technology (OIT)/Architecture & Strategies Division (ASD), and to private and hybrid sector clients for over 28 years, including work in housing, mortgage insurance/banking.

His experience ranges from Business Process Reengineering (BPR) to System Development Life Cycle (SDLC) phases, including sizing, modeling, simulation, design, development, testing, implementation, and operation of effective integrated business systems. He developed and delivered BPMN training to the Department of Defense (DoD), presented on it at national and international conferences, and coauthored the seminal BPMN 2.0 Handbook, chapter on "Making a BPMN 2.0 Model Executable" sponsored by the Workflow Management Coalition.

He is an OMG-Certified Expert in BPM (OCEB)—Fundamental. He is also a member of standards organizations, such as the OMG's BPMN Model Interchange Working Group (MIWG) that is charged with resolving model interchange issues. He is also a member of the WfmC, including the Business Process Simulation Working Group (BPSWG) that developed a specification for simulation of process models done in the standard modeling language of BPMN.

He has an MBA from Duke University's Fuqua School of Business.

Lotte Tange

Lotte Tange is VP Business Process & Information Management at Carlsberg. She is a former auditor and has been part of numerous BPM & IT implementation and optimization initiatives, developing business solutions across different industries; however, lately mainly within the FM0CG Beverage segment.

Lotte has been with Carlsberg for 13 years, where she has been heading the development and establishment of Business Process Management, Information Management, and Master Data Management as part of the consolidation of acquisitions within the Carlsberg Group. Lotte has been a key driver of the mobilization and implementation of Carlsberg's Standardization Program (BSP1), where she has been responsible for the business process, master data, and BI solution design of Carlsberg's new operating model in Western Europe, covering all main functional areas such as Sales, Logistics, Planning, Procurement, Production, and Finance. One of the key deliverables has been the development and continuous improvement of the standard Carlsberg Business Process Model, where all business processes are mapped, (re)-designed, documented and interlinked from an End-to-End perspective. The transformational implementation in the business units, shared service centers, and central functions has been a pivotal part of Lotte's achievements, where the new business process model has been instrumental in standardizing new ways of working.

Lotte has throughout her career had a central role in bridging business and IT, succeeding in optimizing business processes, increasing efficiencies, and leveraging scale globally.

Mads Clausager

Mads Clausager has a background in process optimization, business consulting, and software development. He has extensive knowledge and experience with BPM and its enabling technologies from engaging with customers in transformation initiatives within Banking, Transportation, and IT industries, as well as being the Nordic BPM Leader in IBM.

Mads is currently Senior IT Manager in Maersk Line, one of the world's leading container shipping companies, where he is driving multiple large-scale process-driven transformation projects within the customer service area, and with specific focus on the order handling processes.

Mads has been a speaker at Gartner's BPM Summit about "Delivering Results with Agile BPM using Lean, Kanban and Cost of Delay", as well as at several customer events arranged by various vendors.

Mads holds a Master in IT-ledelse og Strategi at IT University of Copenhagen.

Mai Phuong

Mai Phuong is the Systems Engineer at Northrop Grumman Electronic Systems. Northrop Grumman is a leading global security company providing innovative systems, products and solutions in unmanned systems, cyber, C4ISR, and logistics and modernization to government and commercial customers worldwide.

We hold ourselves to a higher standard, both in the products we deliver and in the way we conduct ourselves throughout the entire customer experience. Because, after all, we are in the business of securing a great deal more than just our place in the market. Our mission is to be at the forefront of technology and innovation, delivering superior capability in tandem with maximized cost efficiencies. The security solutions we provide help secure freedoms for our nation as well as those of our allies. Squarely meeting our obligations, fiscally and technologically, isn't just a business goal, but a moral imperative. To that end, as we evolve as a company, the responsibility we feel for our country and the citizens and troops we help support grows with us.

Mai Phuong received the Northrop Grumman Technology All-Star awards in 2014.

Maria Hove

International recognized researcher and thought leader in the field of business model, performance modeling, and value modeling. She has worked for many fortune 500 organizations and for governments around the world.

Maria leads multiple researches in the Global University Alliance (GUA), the largest nonvendor academic platform for academic collaboration.

As a part of the GUA work, has she been involved in developing multiple Enterprise Standards as well as Industry Standards. Within the context of BPM her speciality is

- Align business processes to business goals
- Process Innovation & Transformation Enablement (PITE)
- BPM & Operating Model
- BPM Change Management
- BPM Governance
- BPM Portfolio Management
- Continuous Process Improvement Author of multiple publications among them the IEEE publication "How to Integrate Enterprise Architecture and BPM," as well as for Future Strategies Inc. and the Workflow Management Coalition (WfmC) "Passports to Success in BPM." Maria is a certified Process eXpert & LEAD Process Architect as well as Business Architect Certified.

Maria Rybrink

Maria Rybrink is the Head of Business Process & Information Management at TeliaSonera and she is leading a core team of highly skilled process and information experts with the focus to drive and further develop TS Centers of Excellence for Business Processes and Enterprise Information Management.

The BPM and EIM Centers of Excellence at TeliaSonera have the accountability to globally establish harmonized and standardized BPM and EIM Frameworks. The Frameworks include the governance, architecture, methodologies, methods, guidelines, organization, tools, and skills necessary to ensure that the TeliaSonera Process and Information/Data Transformation is successfully implemented, sustained, and improved in TeliaSonera functions.

TeliaSonera provides network access and telecommunication services that help people and companies communicate in an easy, efficient, and environmentally friendly way and offer services in the Nordic and Baltic countries, the emerging markets of Eurasia, including Russia and Turkey, and in Spain.

Marianne Fonseca

Marianne is specialized in analyzing and designing organizations by assessing the business model, competencies, services, processes, and data. She has been the driving force in the outperformers versus underperformer's study and Global BPM trend study in collaboration with the Global University Alliance.

Marianne helps organizations to succeed in business transformation and innovation by improving the decision making and drive business outcomes. She specializes in

- Align business processes to operational goals
- Process innovation based on operational objectives
- Link activities to Business Model transformation
- Identify process requirements
- Focus on pain points, bottlenecks, and benchmarking
- Develop process standardization
- Ensure process integration
- Continuous process improvement

Marianne leverages her previous experience in paralegal, project management, and research to advise organizations how to apply best practices, industry practices, and leading practices in the real world. She is certified LEAD Process eXpert.

Mark Stanford

Mark Stanford is the Senior Director of Program Management at iGrafx. Mark is the resident product and solutions expert, staying abreast of all product strategy and evolution initiatives to ensure new process management solutions are in alignment and best serving the needs of iGrafx customers.

Mark cowrote and delivered a four-part executive webinar series with Professor Mark von Rosing covering business innovation and transformation, cost reduction, the operating model, and performance management. Mark is also a member of the LEADing Practice Community and is "Process eXpert" certified.

Mark coauthored the Winter Simulation Conference paper titled "Are business managers and non-technical consultants ready for low-cost discrete-event simulation? A survey of users".

Stanford holds a bachelor of science in computer science from Oregon State University and a master of science in Management from the Graduate School of Business, Stanford University where he is a Sloan Fellow.

Marlon Dumas

Marlon Dumas is Professor of Software Engineering at University of Tartu, Estonia where he leads a research group of around 20 members focused on evidence-based approaches to business process and software process management. The group specializes on the use of data mining methods to identify and analyze process improvement opportunities.

Prof. Dumas is also Strategic Area Leader at STACC: a collaborative research center that gathers 10 IT organizations with the aim of conducting industry-driven research in service engineering and data mining. In this context, Prof. Dumas leads a cooperative research project with Microsoft's Skype Division aimed at developing scalable methods to analyze Skype's social graph for predictive purposes.

From 2000 to 2007, Prof. Dumas worked in the Business Process Management (BPM) research group at Queensland University of Technology in Australia where he worked in several research projects in the field of BPM and Service-Oriented

Computing with SAP's Brisbane Research Centre. These cooperative research projects led to half a dozen patents.

Professor Dumas has been recipient of best paper awards at the ETAPS'2006, BPM'2010, and BPM'2013 conferences and recipient of the 10-year most influential paper award at MODELS'2011 conference. He is coauthor of the textbook "Fundamentals of Business Process Management" (Springer).

Prof. Dumas is regional represener at the Global University Alliance. Providing an international platform where universities and thought leaders can interact to conduct research, comparison, and explore leading practices, best practices, as well as to develop missing practices.

Mathias Kirchmer

As innovative top executive Dr Kirchmer has worked for over 20 years in an international environment, serving clients across different industries and sizes. Dr Kirchmer is a visionary leader, thought leader, and innovator in the field of Business Process Management.

Dr Kirchmer has combined his broad practical business experience with his extensive academic research. This systematic integration has led to pioneering management approaches that have proven to be both sustainable and provide immediate benefits.

Most recently, Dr Kirchmer has founded BPM-D, a company focused on enabling the next generation enterprise by leveraging the discipline of BPM. He is now Managing Director and Co-CEO of this organization.

Before Dr Kirchmer has been Accenture's Managing Director & Global Lead for BPM. He developed inventive BPM services resulting in significant revenue growth. Dr Kirchmer's major process initiatives transformed business for his clients and created significant assets internally at Accenture. He became the face of Accenture's BPM Practice.

Prior to joining Accenture, Dr Kirchmer was the CEO of the Americas and Japan and The Chief Innovation & Marketing Officer for IDS Scheer, a leading provider of software and consulting solutions for BPM, best known for its ARIS software.

Dr Kirchmer is an affiliated faculty member at the University of Pennsylvania, Widener University, Philadelphia University, and the Universidad of Chile. In 1984, he received a research fellowship from the Japan Society for the Promotion of Science. Dr Kirchmer published six books and numerous articles making him a much sought after speaker and expert.

Dr Kirchmer holds a PhD in Information Systems (Saarbrucken University), a Master in Business Informatics (Karlsruhe Technical University), as well as a Master in Economics (Paris-IX-Dauphine).

Maxim Arzumanyan

Maxim Arzumanyan is a researcher and a lecturer at Saint-Petersburg State University of Telecommunications developing and running new academic courses on Enterprise Architecture and Business Process Management.

Cofounder and curator of an open free ad hoc educational and research program on Enterprise Architecture "GameChangers Enterprise Architecture Track" in Russia.

Maxim has taken part in such projects as business transformation and engineering, EA methodology development, IT architecture development, IT-strategy development, and BPM implementation in different roles including project manager and project architect.

Author of more than 30 publications in the field of EA, BPM, IT, and education.

In 2014, Maxim has become a LEAD Enterprise Architect and Board member at Global University Alliance.

Michael D. Tisdel

Mike Tisdel is a Senior Multi-Discipline Integration Analyst and Operational Architect detailed to the Department of Defense, Joint Staff J6, and United States Special Operations Command. In this role he conducts analysis and assessments and evaluates war-fighter needs, plans, requirements, programs, and strategies providing Special Operations and Joint Force impacts and potential solutions in support of the guidance from Chairman of the Joint Chiefs of Staff.

Mr Tisdel has over 30 years of experience both uniformed and as a contractor in leading people, conducting planning & analysis, and managing capabilities in the Department of Defense. His planning and operational experience ranges from the tactical through strategic levels in the United States Air Force, Joint, and Special Operations Forces.

Previously, he served as team member of the Building Partnerships—Planning Synchronization Framework project as an architect of the process, Solution Developer of the "Unity of Effort Framework" and coauthor of the Solution Guide.

Recognized with the prestigious "FRONTIER RUNNER of the year" (2014) as codeveloper of the "Unity of Effort" Framework.

He received several military awards for meritorious service and has been published in the International Command and Control Research and Technology Program periodicals.

Mr Tisdel is an operational architect at Cydecor. He holds a Bachelors of Science in Flight Technology from Central Washington University and is a graduate from multiple Professional Military Education schools in the US Air Force.

Certified LEAD Enterprise Architecture and Practitioner.

Mikael Munck

Mikael Munck was named CIO of the year by Danish "Computerworld" in 2012 and is widely recognized for this frontier thinking in adopting leading practice. Mikael was promoted to Global Head of Technology and Operations at Saxo Bank in January 2014.

At Saxo Bank, the leading online trading and investment platform, Mikael has pushed the frontier boundaries of superior client service and competitive pricing; challenging the tradition of working with software development and testing. The idea to adopt best- and industry practices and developing leading practice in order to better interlink project management, software development, and testing with value creation (based on the strategy).

Mikael Munck joined Saxo Bank in November 2009 following the Bank's acquisition of Initto, a privately held IT services provider for which Mikael served as CEO, having cofounded the company in 2003.

Mikael Munck brings considerable experience from the IT and financial sectors, having worked as Portfolio Manager within banking, and as General Manager for SunGard and as CEO of Aloc Bonnier, both software and IT services companies for the financial market, prior to founding Initto.

Mikael is member of the Board of Directors at LEADing Practice and holds a MSc in finance from the Copenhagen Business School.

Mike A. Marin

Mike Marin is an IBM Distinguished Engineer and the chief architect for the IBM Case Manager product. Marin is also a Distinguished Engineer and life member of the Association for Computing Machinery (ACM). He is currently the chair of the OMG's Case Management Modeling and Notation (CMMN) revision task force.

Mike has more than 20 years of experience designing and developing system software, including several commercial workflow, Business Process Management (BPM), and case management products.

Mike has been an active participant in standard organizations including OMG, OASIS, and WfmC, where he has contributed on several workflow, BPM, and case management standards. Mike is a Fellow of the Workflow Management Coalition (WfmC) and has received the Excellence Award for his technical contributions to the WfmC standardization efforts.

Mona von Rosing

In her work she is a specialist in LEAD Business Innovation & Transformation Architect and with her unique background of business psychology and business economics, she is specialized in business transformation, change, and strategic execution for the development and improvement of an organization's revenue, service, and value model as well as cost, performance, and operating model. With her business knowledge she mixes her business approach with psychological change topics and approaches within her specialty of Change and Alignment. She has participated in the global research in Enterprise Philosophy. The

research focused on how Enterprise Philosophy considers the prismatic fundamental principles that underlie the formation and operation of a business enterprise. Thereby the nature and purpose of a business, for example, is it primarily property or a social institution; its role in society or the accrued function concerning collective consciousness?

Mona has furthermore led the development of the LEADing Practice Alignment-Unity Framework. The Alignment-Unity Framework was developed together with US Department of Defense, the Department of Homeland Security, Department of Justice, and Department of State, Joint Staff (J6 and J7), US Northern

Command, US Southern Command, National Guard Bureau. Mona was the business analyst from LEADing Practice who developed the standard with the following external people:

- The Project lead, Ms. Angela Winter, Joint Staff J7, US Government
- The developers, Mr. Mike Tisdel and Ken Teske, Joint Staff J6, US Government
- Mr. Martin Westphal, Vice Director, Joint Staff J6, US Government
- Mr. Stuart Whitehead, Deputy Director C5I, Joint Staff J6, US Government
- General Jon Thomas, Deputy Director, Future Joint Force Development, US Government

    The Alignment-Unity Framework aims to:

- Unify common stakeholders, objectives and size the common mission critical aspects across complex missions and multidimensional warfare such as cyber war, combating of weapons of mass destruction, combating translation organization crime and security corporations.
- Achieving information sharing the unity of effort to meet national security US Department of Defense with the Department of Homeland Security, Department of Justice, and Department of State.
- Alignment and Unity Stakeholder Map
    - Alignment and Unity QuickScan
    - Alignment and Unity Maturity TCO-ROI evaluation
    - Alignment and Unity Maturity Benchmark
    - Alignment and Unity Development Path
- Alignment-Unity Framework Stages: Align, Compare and Unify.

    Mona is a certified Change eXpert & LEAD Transformation Architect as well as Business Architect Certified.

Nathaniel Palmer

A best-selling author, practitioner, and rated as the #1 Most Influential Thought Leader in Business Process Management (BPM) by independent research, Nathaniel has been the Chief Architect for large-scale and complex projects involving investments of $200 million or more.

Nathaniel has coauthored a dozen books on technology and business transformation including "Intelligent BPM" (2013), "How Knowledge Workers Get Things Done" (2012), "Social BPM" (Future Strategies), "Excellence in Practice" (2007), as well as the "Encyclopedia of Database Systems" (2007), and "The X-Economy" (2001) and "Mastering the Unpredictable," which reached #2 on the Amazon.com Bestsellers List in 2008.

Nathaniel was the first individual named as Laureate in Workflow. He has been featured in media ranging from Fortune to The New York Times, and has authored several articles in publications such as Intelligent Enterprise, KMWorld, CIO, and InformationWeek, as well as a featured expert on National Public Radio, World Business Review, and The Emerald Planet in conjunction with Internet pioneer Vint Cerf.

He is a regular speaker at leading industry forums including those by AGA, AIIM, Forrester, Gartner, FSO Knowledge Xchange, and SOA Symposium, as well as featured in national media such as CIO, Fortune, NPR, and The New York Times. He also serves as Executive Director of Workflow Management Coalition, the industry's longest-standing BPM adoption group.

Neil Kemp

Neil Kemp is the Director, Value Team (North America). With more than 30 years' experience, Neil has extensive experience in model-driven computing, business analysis, and architecture.

In his consulting career he has worked for multiple departments within the Federal Government of Canada and for a number of municipalities, provinces, and also with private sector clients.

Mr Kemp holds an MBA from Queens University at Kingston, and is certified LEAD Enterprise Architect, TOGAF, and Project Management Professional in good standing with the Project Management Institute.

Author of numerous articles and professional papers and recognized as Modeler of the year (2013).

Nils Faltin

Dr Nils Faltin is leading the research department at IMC, a company providing solutions for technology-enhanced learning. He has managed and contributed to several large European research projects in business process aware competency management, adaptive learning solutions, performance support, project-based learning, and reflective learning.

Before joining IMC he worked at research institutes developing new forms of interactive online learning for engineering and computer science students. PhD in computer science education at the University of Oldenburg, Germany.

Partha Chakravartti

Partha Chakravartti is an accomplished senior enterprise architect with over 20 years of progressive experience across Automotive, Aerospace, Hi-Tech, Pharmaceuticals, Information Technology Services, and Government. He has successfully architected complex business solutions through cross-organizational and global teaming, for private and public sectors.

Partha is the Global Director of Enterprise Architecture at Astra Zeneca in charge of Application/Platform strategy and Road maps. In the past, he has led business-driven technology innovation at the Bureau of Census and drove transparency of investments in FAA, aligning to the Open Government initiative.

In his 10 years' tenure with IBM, Partha has led multiple Global IT solutions at General Motors, Ford, Toyota, Boeing, Land Rover, Honeywell, and founded a supply chain solutions practice for IBM.

Partha has multiple publications, professional memberships, certifications, recognitions and awards, and one patent. He is on the board of Tier 1 automotive supplier. He has chaired multiple profit and nonprofit organizations.

Partha holds a Bachelor's degree in Electrical Engineering from IIT and a Masters in Computer Science from Wayne State University.

Peter Franz

Peter Franz is one of the two cofounders of BPM-D. He has been working at the forefront of Business Process Management for many years as part of a 30-year career with Accenture. Since setting up the innovative new company he has assisted a number of companies in establishing a BPM discipline and has developed a number of innovative approaches to pragmatically solve implementation issues. These have been encapsulated in the (Patent Pending) BPM-D™ framework.

He is a results-driven executive with a pragmatic ability to create the spark in a business strategy through a clearly articulated execution strategy; and then drive toward this goal. He has led very substantial change programs across a number of industries including: Energy, Financial Services, Logistics, Travel Services, Utilities, and Consumer Goods.

Mr Franz has authored a book on this subject and has developed related executive level courses that can be adapted to various audiences.

Mr Franz holds a Masters degree in Information Systems and a Bachelors degree in Computer Science from the University of Witwatersrand in South Africa and is a certified BPM professional (CBPMP).

Philippe Lebacq

Philippe Lebacq is a lead architect for the Development of Process & Methodology and Expert Tester for Testing Tools Administration at Toyota Motor Europe.

Toyota first began selling cars in Europe under an official distributor agreement in 1963. Since then, the company has matured into the leading Japanese car manufacturer in this highly competitive market. Toyota directly and indirectly employs around 94,000 people in Europe and has invested over EUR 8 billion since 1990.

Toyota's operations in Europe are supported by a network of 30 National Marketing and Sales Companies across 56 countries, a total of around 3,000 sales outlets, and nine manufacturing plants.

Régis Dumond

Régis Dumond, CSEP, is responsible for the implementation of system engineering methods and tools in "Direction Générale de l'Armement (DGA)," the defence procurement agency of the French ministry of defense.

He is also the French Representative of Architecture Capability Team NATO in charge of enterprise architecture aspects, in particular the definition of the NATO Architecture Framework (NAF), and the panel of the Information System and Technology NATO Science and Technology Organization (STO).

He is a member of the French Association for Standardization (AFNOR) on the subject of the engineering system and contributor to the future ISO 42020 Systems and software engineering—Architecture Processes and Work Products.

He was the Resilient Affiliate at the Software Engineering Institute (SEI) in the product line team.

Regis is certified TOGAF and IREB, and member of the INCOSE.

Rich Hilliard

Rich Hilliard is a consulting software systems architect to public and private sector clients. He is project editor of ISO/IEC/IEEE 42,010, *Systems and software engineering—Architecture description*, the internationalization of IEEE Standard 1471:2000. Software systems architecture services including stakeholder and concern analyses, architectural viewpoint definition, architectural view modeling, modeling and analysis to address extra-functional concerns (e.g., quality of service, performance, safety, and security), and best practices on architecture description using ISO/IEC/IEEE 42010 (IEEE Std 1471).

Rich is vice-chair of IFIP Working Group 2.10 on Software Architecture; invited expert for The Open Group Architecture Framework next version; and member of the IEEE Computer Society and the Free Software Foundation.

Author of +40 publications, articles, and professional papers.

Richard N. Conzo

Richard Conzo is a Senior Consultant of Lean Six Sigma Project & Program Management at Verizon. His Process/Project Management leadership impacts a national base of 6000 engineering and operations representatives performing operational readiness functions that include Technology Testing, Service Order and Billing updates, and Regulatory review.

He is one of Verizon leading performers championing for "Out Of The Box" process solutions that support new product deployment and business transformation. He is a certified Lean Six Sigma Black Belt, Project Management Professional (PMP) with 25 years of Telecommunications and IT experience. He is also a certified adjunct professor for Boston College School of Project Management.

Rod Peacock

Rod Peacock is a Chief Architect at European Patent Office at the second-largest European organization, employing 7 000 staff from over 30 countries.

European Patent Office support innovation, competitiveness and economic growth across Europe through our commitment to high quality and efficient services delivered under the European Patent Convention.

Rod serves on the Board of Directors at LEADing Practice and is certified as a LEAD Enterprise Architect.

Richard Fallon

Richard Fallon works as an independent consultant on SAP developments and BPM/BPR projects. He completed his Bachelor of Engineering Degree in Digital Systems Engineering at Sunderland Polytechnic in 1987.

Richard has worked on the development of hardware and software solutions over a variety of industry sectors, including R&D/nuclear industry (Rolls-Royce IRD), IT (UNISYS), credit card processing (First Data), telecommunications (A1), and pharmaceutical (Novartis) on assignment in France, USA, UK, Australia, Japan, Taiwan, Austria, and Switzerland.

In 2012, he completed a Master of Science in Technology Consulting at Sheffield Hallam University, which included completing his master thesis "Evaluating the extent to which REA can enhance ERP systems, using SAP as an exemplar."

He is currently in the process of completing his PhD into Transaction Orientated Architecture (TOA) in Enterprise Systems where he sees the opportunity to convert the industrial experience and insights he has gained over the last 27 years into new theories and solutions for enterprise systems.

Ronald N. Batdorf

Ron Batdorf is currently a sought out Government Civilian leader with expertise in Engineering, System Architecture, Enterprise Architecture, Cloud Computing Dynamics, and Human Interaction Analysis for US Department of Defense at US Joint Staff.

He provides engineering solutions and thought leadership to the DoD and the Federal Government. Ron has worked as a leader in the defense industry for the US Navy, USACOM, USJFCOM, and Joint Staff as well as several years in leadership roles within industry in industrial engineering, business development, and overall profit/loss management.

In his previous position, he worked on cloud and IT strategies for US Joint Forces Command. He recently moved on to Joint Staff J6 to work on a defense-oriented application lifecycle management platform dynamics. Ron has a keen understanding of multiple engineering disciplines and how system of system engineering is intertwined with human factors. As a leader in the industry he actively engages with Joint Staff, National Labs, other Combatant Commands, Services, and Agencies.

Ron has written a White Paper on "New Vision for Command & Control," as well as other thought pieces including: "Enterprise Architecture Life Cycle," "Process-Oriented Architecture", "Net-Centric Pyramid" and "Flash Jobs" and others topics related to managing change.

Certified LEAD Enterprise Architect.

Sarel J. Snyman

Sarel J. Snyman is a SAP consultant with extensive practical specialist knowledge and practice in cross-modular solution design and integration management for ERP solutions.

He has extensive full lifecycle project experience from several large multicompany implementation projects. These international projects included rollouts in FICO, FICO-JVA, AA, MM, SD, PP, CRM, and Fund and Grant management, as well as CS and precious metal accounting solution with integration to BW, BPC, and other logistic modules.

In the projects Sarel has worked on, he has held positions of Integration Manager and Consultant,

Project Development Manager, Solution Design Manager, Project Manager, and Principle FICO Consultant.

Sarel has substantial business experience working as a financial and logistic manager in the mining, steel, and chemical industries.

Scott Davis

Scott Davis is a Director for Costing Policy and Training, Costing Center of Expertise at Treasury Board of Canada Secretariat.

Scott Davis is currently a Director with the Office of the Comptroller General (OCG) at the Treasury Board of Canada Secretariat, where he is responsible for government-wide policy related to financial management, costing, and charging (Costing Policy and Training, Costing Center of Expertise).

Prior to joining the Office of the Comptroller General, he was the Director of Program Office, Integrated Financial and Materiel System at Public Works and Government Services Canada.

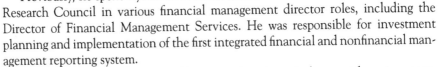

Previously, he spent 5 years with the National Research Council in various financial management director roles, including the Director of Financial Management Services. He was responsible for investment planning and implementation of the first integrated financial and nonfinancial management reporting system.

Mr Davis spent the first part of his career in private industry with various companies across the United States and Canada, focused on accounting and reporting.

Mr Davis obtained his BBA in accounting from Bishop's University and is a Certified Professional Accountant.

Simon M. Polovina

Prof. Dr Simon Polovina engages in roles that draw upon his expertise in Enterprise Architecture and Conceptual Structures (CS), which harmonizes the human conceptual approach to problem solving with the formal structures that computer applications need to bring their productivity to bear.

Prof. Dr Polovina is a reader in Business Computing within the Department of Computing at Sheffield Hallam University, UK. He was a

Principal Investigator for the recently completed European Commission 7th Framework Programme project CUBIST ("Combining and Unifying Business Intelligence with Semantic Technologies"), where he applied CS and comanaged the project. CUBIST centered on applying smart technologies (namely CS and the Semantic Web) to Business Intelligence. It was a €4m project funded under topic 4.3: Intelligent Information Management. Simon is the Enterprise Architect for CENTRIC (Centre of excellence in terrorism, resilience, intelligence & organised crime research).

Prof. Dr Polovina is Cochairman of the Global University Alliance that partners with the LEADing Practice (Leading Enterprise Architecture Development) practitioner community. Simon has many years of industrial experience in accounting and information and communication technologies (ICT), and has published widely with over 90 learned publications to date.

His interests include the use of Smart Applications and how they can detect novel or unusual transactions that would otherwise remain as lost business opportunities or represent illicit business or criminal activity. He is editor-in-chief of the International Journal of Conceptual Structures and Smart Applications (IJCSSA). He has expertise in Enterprise Architecture, Service-Oriented Architecture, Business Process Management, SAP technologies, Web technologies, Java, Object-oriented Analysis and Design, Conceptual Modeling of organizations as Multiagent Systems, and in Interaction Design.

Stephen A. White

Stephen A. White, PhD, has over 25 years of process modeling experience, ranging from modeling pilot workload to commercial business processes, and has been involved in most aspects of business process modeling software, from product management, design, consulting, training, and technical writing.

During the 2000s decade, he was active in the development of business modeling standards. For the BPMI organization, he was the chair of Notation Working Group and on the board of directors. He was the primary author/editor of the BPMN 1.0 and BPMN 2.0 specifications.

As an IBM representative for BPM standards, he continued work on BPMN as chair of the OMG Finalization Task Force for BPMN 1.1 (Spec Editor) and chair of OMG Revision Task Force for BPMN 1.2 (Spec Editor). He followed this work by being the coauthor/editor of BPMN 2.0 Technical Specification.

During that time, he published many white papers and book chapters on BPMN as well as being coauthored "BPMN modeling and reference guide" book. He is currently a design researcher for IBM's BPM Software and continues to Blog and give conference presentations on BPMN.

Steve Durbin

Steve Durbin is Managing Director of the Information Security Forum (ISF). His main areas of focus include the emerging security threat landscape, Cyber security, BYOD, Big data, Cloud security, and Social media across both the corporate and personal environments.

Steve is a regular speaker and chair at global events and is often quoted in publications such as the *Financial Times*, *Wall Street Journal*, *Forbes*, *Deutsche Presse*, *Süddeutsche Zeitung*, *CIO Forum*, *ZD Net*, and *Information Week* on topics directly affecting board effectiveness and the challenges of operating multinational businesses in a cyber enabled world.

Formerly at Ernst & Young, Steve was responsible for the growth of the firm's entrepreneurial markets business in Europe, Middle East, India, and Africa. He has been involved with mergers and acquisitions of fast-growth companies across Europe and the USA, and has also advised a number of NASDAQ and NYSE listed global technology companies.

Steve has considerable experience working in the technology and telecoms markets and was previously senior vice president at Gartner. As global head of Gartner's consultancy business, he developed a range of strategic marketing, business, and IT solutions for international investment and entrepreneurial markets. He has served as an executive on the boards of public companies in the UK and Asia in both the technology consultancy services and software applications development sectors.

Steve has also served as a Digital 50 advisory committee member in the United States, a body established to improve the talent pool for Fortune 500 boards around information governance and he was recently ranked as one of the top 10 individuals shaping the way that organizations and leaders approach information security careers in 2014. He is currently chairman of the Digiworld Institute senior executive forum in the UK, a think tank comprised of Telecoms, Media, and IT leaders and regulators. Steve is a Chartered Fellow of the Chartered Institute of Marketing.

Contact details.
Steve Durbin, Managing Director.
US Tel: +1 (347) 767 6772.
UK Tel: +44 (0)20 3289 5884.
UK Mobile: +44 (0)7785 953 800.
Email: steve.durbin@securityforum.org.
Web: www.securityforum.org.
Twitter: @stevedurbin
LinkedIn: http://uk.linkedin.com/in/stevedurbin.

Stephen William Willoughby

Steve Willoughby's BPM experience spans more than 10 years. Since 2003, Steve has been focusing on process improvement, business analysis, and Enterprise Architecture Initiatives. He holds a bachelor's of science degree in business management from the University of Findlay, and a masters of business in operational excellence from The Ohio State University.

Beginning his career as a Process Engineer, he helped develop a Repository of Process Knowledge and create a Process Improvement Methodology that resulted in millions in savings for an innovative telecommunications company. He then migrated to working on a major CRM application implementation where he was creating processes, requirements, and design documentation.

From there he moved into consulting and has had the opportunity to work on SAP implementations, Six Sigma Initiatives, Enterprise Architecture Programs, Business Architecture and Capability Modeling, Lean Initiatives, and Implementation of Process Modeling Methodologies.

He has also contributed to the development of Operational Excellence Strategies and Programs. Looking at ways to instill Operational Excellence thinking into the entire organization from the top down. Implementing strategies and tools at every level of the organization to tie into the Strategic Plan and ensure that all areas and levels are working together to achieve the common goals set forth.

Mr Willoughby has leveraged his practical experience with BPM tools and techniques to support successful project implementation with a variety of clients, including some Fortune 500 companies, in retail, finance, automotive, government, and telecommunication industries.

Dr F.P. Stoffel RA RC

Mr Freek Stoffel is LEAD Enterprise Architect. He has been working for more than 20 years on financial business transformations, and on the development of the correlated best practices in Finance and IT.

In 1993, he cofounded a consulting company with a focus on project, process, and change management, a visionary position at the time. This consulting practice grew into a global organization of 250 employees the moment it was sold to an

investor. As per 2000, Freek focused on the use of Business Intelligence systems and their interaction with ERP transaction systems at international companies. In 2012 he completed this with Enterprise Architecture as a third and overarching competence.

Freek has successfully managed complex business/IT change programs in many different organizations such as the Government of Canada, Tommy Hilfiger/PVH, BHP Billiton, BAM Group, DSM, and Philips. He has also been contributor to the Enterprise Architecture body of knowledge of LEADing Practice since 2012.

Thomas Boosz

Thomas Boosz is the Chief Business Architect at the Federal Employment Agency of Germany (Bundesagentur für Arbeit).

Mr Thomas Boosz was recognized for his leadership with the LEADing Practice Transformation project of 2013 out of 120 compelling transformation projects. He has transformed the largest service provider of the German labor market into a modern service provider and an efficiency-oriented service agency, meanwhile fulfilling important legal mandates.

Bundesagentur für Arbeit currently has approximately 100,000 employees and during the course of the year 7.77 million people newly registered as unemployed while at the same time 7.72 million people found a new job.

The transformation initiative is a major undertaking with all odds against it. Meanwhile, with a structural approach and with surgical precision mapping all tasks, activities, functions, roles and processes across departments and organizations and interlinking the data with the information flow and services of 13.82 billion euros unemployment benefits in 2012.

Thomas Chr. Olsen

Thomas Chr. Olsen is member of the Global Supply Chain Management group within Novozymes—the world's leading company within bio innovation and industrial enzyme manufacturing.

Thomas has a 16-year career track at Novozymes spanning various functional disciplines within the company. His specialty is Strategy Design and Strategic Management. Over the years Thomas has worked on several major efficiency transformation and most recently Lean projects in the Supply Operations. He has

management experiences from manufacturing and later within the Development & Optimization discipline. Thomas has been focusing on designing organizational and people processes to support business development; this includes talent and leadership development, performance leadership, and the design of optimal organizational structures to ensure and enhance optimal business performance.

In addition to working with internal management processes Thomas is much in demand as a consultant and facilitator for especially innovation and ideation sessions with various major companies. He is part of the LEADing Practice community.

Tim Hoebeek

Tim Hoebeek is a LEAD Enterprise Architect and Principal Consultant at SAP, helping customers with different challenges across different architectural domains. He is primus inter pares for Enterprise Architecture within the SAP EMEA Architect Community.

Before joining SAP, Tim worked as a lecturer at Erasmushogeschool Brussel. He taught both industrial engineering students and prospective bachelors in computer science and covered different topics, ranging from microelectronics and programming to ERP systems and economics.

Between 2001 and 2005, he worked as a researcher at the Vrije Universiteit Brussel, first on a research project on digital media, mainly new technologies for digital television, and after that on a project on innovation in education, focusing on content and knowledge management and applying these concepts to the integrated education of civil engineer–architect students.

He received his degree in industrial engineering in 2000, building a distributed home automation system as thesis project. In 2001 he received a degree in Management, a Master in Business Administration in 2002 and a degree in Applied Computer Science in 2006.

Tim holds numerous SAP certifications, technology certifications, is TOGAF 9 and LEAD Enterprise Architect certified.

Tom W. Preston

Tom Preston, CPA, CMA, CIA, CISA, CSCP, and PMP is a Principal at a large international consulting firm and leads their ERP Advisory Services capabilities. Mr Preston directly oversees technology teams supporting multiple US Department of Defense (DoD), ERP optimization projects as well as managing big data supply chain analytics projects for a large US DoD client. Mr Preston is a certified SAP Integration and Business Process Expert and has over 22 years leading large scale financial systems and business analytics projects across the DoD, Civilian, and Intelligence Agencies and commercial clients. In this role, he provides executive level financial management consulting and ERP related functional and technical expertise for clients seeking to implement or optimize their financial management, supply chain, and business intelligence systems. Mr Preston is also the executive sponsor and graduate of the Booz Allen/Indiana University Kelley School of Business (Top 15 B-School) ERP and Business Analytics graduate certificate programs.

Articles include: "Business Analytics in the Federal Government" (Indiana University Institute for Business Analytics, Spring 2012), "Leveraging Data in the Public Sector" (Indiana University Institute for Business Analytics, Fall 2012) and blog interview "An Executive Curriculum, Handpicked by Your Employer" (Bloomberg Businessweek August 2013, interview by Francesca Di Meglio).

Mr Preston received a BS in accounting from the University of Tennessee in 1988, an MS in finance and information systems from Carnegie Mellon University in 1990, and an MBA from the Indiana University Kelley School of Business in 2014.

Ulrik Foldager

Ulrik Foldager is a concept developer within all major architecture disciplines, such as Process Architecture, Value Architecture, Service Architecture, Business Architecture, and Layered Enterprise Architecture.

His innovative and unconventional way of thinking has often led him to being accused of "thinking out of the box." This is due to his expertise and area of specialization and unique way of communicating complex scenarios of information into simple models and visualizations that are easy to grasp and comprehend—a powerful tool that enables him

to convey complex information to management and stakeholders on all levels across organizational boundaries.

In this book, he has contributed to the authoring of the History of Process Development, Business Process Outsourcing (BPO), Value-Oriented Process Modeling, BPM & Maturity Models, as well as around BPM Change Management.

Ulrik Foldager is Head of the Process Architecture at LEADing Practice and responsible for Process Reference Content.

Certified LEAD Process Architect, Value Architect, and Enterprise Architect.

Victor Abele

Victor Abele is Senior Director General in the Government of Canada.

Recognized Business Transformation leader, senior project executive, and enterprise service delivery specialist.

Acknowledged for his leadership to develop Business Strategy and implement transformation and change management that deliver tactical and operational performance.

Victor is the Chairman of Board of Directors at LEADing Practice. Certified LEAD Enterprise Architect and Transformation Architect.

Father and grandfather, cuisine, and travel enthusiast.

Vincent J. Snels

Vincent J. Snels is Information Architect at Nationale Nederlanden at the NonLife Business Unit. He's had almost 20 years' experience in the IT Architectural competency in this company and has participated both in business as well as IT transformation and innovation projects. Optimizing and improving process flow as well as the information and the service flow, he has experience of the Non-Life domain as well as domains in Marketing & Sales and Management Information.

He is a certified LEAD Process eXpert, LEAD Value eXpert as well as LEAD Enterprise Architect.

Volker Rebhan

Dr Volker Rebhan is the responsible Product Manager for the Virtual Jobmarket at the Federal Employment Agency of Germany (Bundesagentur für Arbeit).

Mr Dr Volker Rebhan was recognized for his leadership with the "LEADing Practice Transformation project of 2013" out of 120 compelling transformation projects, for his ability to transform the largest service provider of the German labor market into a modern service provider and an efficiency-oriented service agency, meanwhile fulfilling important legal mandates.

Bundesagentur für Arbeit currently has approximately 100,000 employees and during the course of the year 7.77 million people newly registered as unemployed while at the same time 7.72 million people found a new job.

The transformation initiative is a major undertaking with all odds against it. Meanwhile, with a structural approach and with surgical precision mapping all tasks, activities, functions, roles, and processes across departments and organizations and interlinking the data with the information flow and services of 13.82 billion Euros unemployment benefits in 2012.

Wim P.R. Laurier

Wim Laurier is an associate professor in management information systems at Université Saint-Louis in Brussels (Belgium), and a voluntary postdoc researcher at Ghent University (Belgium).

In 2010–2011, he worked as Instructor at the Department of Accounting and MIS of the Alfred Lerner College of Business and Economics, University of Delaware (USA), and at the Eli Broad College of Business, Michigan State University (USA). Wim holds a Bachelor (2004), Master (2006), and PhD degree (2010) in Applied Economic Sciences from Ghent University (Belgium). He is working on enterprise modeling using different methodologies at SMASH (Séminaire en Mathématiques Appliquées aux Sciences Humaines), which is also led by him.

Prof. Laurier is a Board Member and Head of Enterprise Ontology Research & Development at the Global University Alliance. Providing an international platform where universities and thought leaders can interact to conduct research, comparison, and explore leading practices, best practices, as well as to develop missing practices.

His research interests include business and enterprise ontologies, conceptual modeling, enterprise information systems, and business processes simulation models. Wim's research has been presented at workshops and conferences such as OTM, ICEIS, EOMAS, ISAmI, VMBO, EIS and published in Decision Support Systems (DSS), Journal of Database Management (JDM), Information Systems Management

(ISM), Lecture Notes in Computer Science (LNCS), Lecture Notes in Business Information Processing (LNBIP), and Advances in Soft Computing (AISC). In 2011, he was a workshop chair at the 5th International Workshop on Value Modeling and Business Ontology (VMBO).

Ýr Gunnarsdóttir – OE/CI Process Leadership at Shell International

Ýr has over a decade's experience of leading business strategy and process and performance management initiatives. She has been on the front line in developing Continuous Improvement and Operational Excellence approach within multiple Fortune 500 companies. Enabling them to enhance and align strategy, business planning, and KPIs with the reality of daily operations and behavioral challenges in the spirit of Continuous Improvement and Operational performance.

Fundamental to delivering above in her experience with some of the larger more complex matrix organizations is establishing a culture of Continuous Improvement. One of the ways this can be achieved is by understanding what the key business priorities are and aligning them with the desired outcomes. There is no silver bullet for this but by bringing cross-functional teams together, and facilitating understanding of the specific goals, drivers, key cultural elements, and the customer perspective delivers end-to-end efficiency in a credible and sustainable manner.

Yury Orlov

Experienced business and IT leader with impressive charisma and outstanding skills gained in various projects in areas like Business Transformation; Enterprise Modeling; Enterprise architecture design, implementation, and governance; Business Process Architecture development.

Having worked throughout his career in big international companies like IBM and Ernst & Young, Yury has successfully been uniting worldwide leading EA and BPM practices together with knowledge of Russian specifics.

In 2011 Yury decided to focus on EA and Enterprise Modeling areas and he founded Smart

Architects, now being the leading "pure" EA consulting company in Russia. Yury is a certified LEAD Enterprise Architect.

In 2014, Yury was honored to become Advisory Board Member for Russia in LEADing Practice community.

Zakaria Maamar

Dr Zakaria Maamar is a professor and assistant dean in the College of Technological Innovation at Zayed University (ZU) in Dubai, United Arab Emirates.

Prior to joining ZU in 2000, he held a Defense Scientist position with Defense R&D Canada—Valcartier. In conjunction with this position, he was appointed as Adjunct Professor and Associate Researcher with the Computer Sciences and Software Engineering Department and the Research Center on Geomatics both at Laval University in Quebec City. His research interests are primarily related to service sciences theories and methods, context-aware computing, and social computing.

Prof. Dr Maamar has published over 100 peer-reviewed papers in journals and conferences, is the founder of the International Symposium on Web Services, and regularly serves on the program and organizing committees of several international conferences and workshops.

Prof. Dr Maamar graduated for his MSc and PhD in Computer Sciences from Laval University in 1995 and 1998, respectively.

Michel van den Hoven

Philips, Order to Cash Business Architect & BPM.

Already as a young child Michel always was exploring the optimal way of doing things, and with preference in an automated way. This later on resulted in a professional career with a strong passion for processes and the supporting information technology, building upon the fields of Electrical Engineering and Business Administration.

Today Michel's specialties are among others: Business Architecture, Business Process Management, Project Management, Manufacturing Operations Management, Supply Chain Management, Information Technology. As the role of Business Architect in Philips, he is supporting the Business Transformation of Philips in the Order to Cash area to ensure that the strategic intent of the business is effectively executed by guiding the organizations through the business, process, and technology changes necessary to execute the Philips Accelerate! Strategy.

With the global Business Process Owners and Enterprise Architecture team he uniquely translates the enterprise vision and strategy in building blocks defined in a reliable, repeatable and manageable structure, enabling agility within the organization to improve business value and improve customer experience. Furthermore he is part of developing structures, methods and approaches in the several stages of the business transformation and in the several areas of enterprise modeling, enterprise engineering, enterprise modeling and enterprise architecture.

Foreword

This book has been put together to help you explore Business Process concepts and to understand what BPM really is all about.

We wrote this book for YOU—the individual. You may be a business executive, manager, practitioner, subject matter expert, student, or researcher. Or maybe an ambitious career individual who wants to know more about business process concepts and/or BPM, what it is all about and how to apply it.

This, The Complete Business Process Handbook, provides a comprehensive body of knowledge written as a practical guide for you—by the authorities that have shaped the way we think and work with processes today. You hold the first of three books in the series in your hand.

- The first volume endows the reader with a deep insight into the nature of business process concepts and how to work with them. From BPM Ontology, semantics, and BPM Portfolio management, to the BPM Life Cycle, it provides a unique foundation within this body of knowledge.
- The second volume bridges theory and application of BPM in an advanced modeling context by addressing the subject of extended BPM.
- The third volume explores a comprehensive collection of real-world BPM lessons learned, best practices, and leading practices examples from award-winning industry leaders and innovators.

We wish you well on your Business Process journey and that is why we also have invested years putting this Handbook series together. To share the knowledge, templates, concepts, best and leading practices. To ensure high quality and standards, we have worked and coordinated with standard development organizations like International Organization for Standardization (ISO), Object Management Group (OMG), Institute of Electrical and Electronics Engineers (IEEE), North Atlantic Treaty Organization (NATO), Council for Scientific and Industrial Research (CSIR), MITRE—a Federally Funded Research and Development Center, European Committee for Standardization (CEN), The Security Forum, World Wide Web Consortium (W3C), and LEADing Practice.

We have also identified and worked with leading organizations and with their process experts/architects, and have described their practices. Among them are LEGO, Maersk Shipping, Carlsberg, FLSmidth, the US Government, Airfrance, KLM, German Government, SaxoBank, Novozymes, the Canadian Government, US Department of Defense, Danish Defense, Johnson & Johnson, Dutch Railway, Australian Government, and many more. Last but not least the Global University Alliance consisting of over 400 universities, lecturers, and researchers have analyzed and examined what works, again and again (best practice), and what are the unique practices applied by these leading organizations (leading practices). They then identified common and repeatable patterns, which provide the basis for the BPM Ontology, BPM Semantics, the BPM standards, and the process templates found in this book.

We have worked years on this book, and as you just read, you will find contributions from standard bodies, governments, defense organizations, enterprises, universities, research institutes and individual thought leaders. We put these chapters and their subjects carefully together and hope you enjoy reading it—as much as we did writing, reviewing and putting it together.

Name	Organization
Mark von Rosing	Global University Alliance
August-Wilhelm Scheer	Scheer Group GmBH
Henrik von Scheel	LEADing Practices, Google Board
Adam D.M. Svendsen	Institute of Future Studies
Alex Kokkonen	Johnson & Johnson
Andrew M Ross	Westpac
Anette Falk Bøgebjerg	LEGO Group
Anni Olsen	Carlsberg Group
Antony Dicks	NedBank
Asif Gill	Global University Alliance
Bas Bach	NS Rail
Bob J Storms	LEADing Practices
Callie Smit	Reserve Bank
Cay Clemmensen	LEADing Practices
Christopher K. Swierczynski	Electrolux
Clemens Utschig-Utschig	Boehringer Ingelheim Pharma
Dan Moorcroft	QMR
Daniel T. Jones	Lean UK
David Coloma	Universitat Politècnica de Catalunya, Spain
Deb Boykin	Pfizer Pharmaceuticals
Dickson Hunja Muhita	LEADing Practices
Duarte Gonçalves	CSIR—Council for Scientific and Industrial Research
Ekambareswaran Balasubramanian	General Motors
Fabrizio Maria Maggi	University of Estonia
Fan Zhao	Florida Gulf Coast University
Fatima Senghore	NASA
Fatma Dandashi	MITRE

Name	Organization
Freek Stoffel	LEADing Practices
Fred Cummins	OMG
Gabriel von Scheel	LEADing Practices
Gabriella von Rosing	LEADing Practices
Gary Doucet	Government of Canada
Gert Meiling	Tommy Hilfiger
Gert O Jansson	LEADing Practices
Hans Scheruhn	University of Harz, Gemany
Hendrik Bohn	Nedbank
Henk de Man	OMG, VeeBee
Henk Kuil	KLM, Air France
Henrik Naundrup Vester	iGrafx
Jacob Gammelgaard	FLSchmidt
James P. Womack	Cambridge University-Massachusetts Institute of Technology (MIT)
Jeanne W. Ross	Cambridge University-Massachusetts Institute of Technology (MIT)
Jeff Greer	Cardinal Health
Jens Theodor Nielsen	Danish Defense
John A. Zachman	Zachman International
John Bertram	Government of Canada
John Golden	iGrafx
John M. Rogers	Government of Australia
Jonnro Erasmus	CSIR—Council for Scientific and Industrial Research
Joshua von Scheel	LEADing Practices
Joshua Waters	LEADing Practices
Justin Tomlinson	LEADing Practices
Karin Gräslund	RheinMain University-Wiesbaden Business School
Katia Bartels	Office Depot
Keith Swenson	Fujitsu
Kenneth Dean Teske	US Government
Kevin Govender	Transnet Rail
Klaus Vitt	German Federal Employment Agency
Krzysztof Skurzak	NATO ACT
LeAnne Spurrell	QMR

Name	Organization
Lloyd Dugan	BPM.com
Lotte Tange	Carlsberg Group
Mads Clausager	Maersk Group
Mai Phuong	Northrop Grumman Electronic Systems
Maria Hove	LEADing Practices
Maria Rybrink	TeliaSonera
Marianne Fonseca	LEADing Practices
Mark Stanford	iGrafx
Marlon Dumas	University of Tartu
Mathias Kirchmer	BPM-d
Maxim Arzumanyan	St. Petersburg University
Michael Tisdel	US Government, DoD
Michel van den Hoven	Philips
Mikael Munck	SaxoBank
Mike A. Marin	IBM Corporation
Mona von Rosing	LEADing Practices
Nathaniel Palmer	BPM.com, Workflow Management Coalition (WfMC)
Neil Kemp	LEADing Practices
Nils Faltin	Scheer Group GmBH
Partha Chakravartti	AstraZeneca
Patricia Kemp	LEADing Practices
Peter Franz	BPM-d
Philippe Lebacq	Toyota
Régis Dumond	French Ministry of Defense, NATO, ISO
Rich Hilliard	IEEE, ISO
Richard L. Fallon	Sheffield Hallam University
Richard N. Conzo	Verizon
Rod Peacock	European Patent Office
Ronald N. Batdorf	US Government, DoD, Joint Staff
Sarel J. Snyman	SAP Solution Design
Scott Davis	Government of Canada
Simon Polovina	Sheffield Hallam University
Stephen White	IBM Corporation
Steve Durbin	Information Security Forum

Name	Organization
Steve Willoughby	iGrafx
Thomas Boosz	German Government
Thomas Christian Olsen	NovoZymes
Tim Hoebeek	SAP
Tom Preston	Booz Allen Hamilton
Ulrik Foldager	LEADing Practices
Victor Abele	Government of Canada
Vincent Snels	Nationale Nederlanden
Volker Rebhan	German Federal Employment Agency
Wim Laurier	Université Saint-Louism Bruxelles
Ýr Gunnarsdottir	Shell
Yury Orlov	Smart Architects
Zakaria Maamar	Zayed University, United Arab Emirates

Abbreviations

A2A	Application to application
AAIM	Agility adoption and improvement model
ACM	Adaptive case management
ADDI	Architect design deploy improve
API	Application programming interface
APQC	American productivity and quality center
B2B	Business to business
BAM	Business activity monitoring
BCM	Business continuity management
BEP	Break even point
BI	Business intelligence
BITE	Business innovation and transformation enablement
BOM	Business object management
BPA	Business process analysis
BPaaS	Business process as a service
BPCC	Business process competency center
BPD	Business process diagram
BPE	Business process engineering
BPEL	Business process execution language
BPEL4WS	Business process execution language for web services
BPG	Business process guidance
BPI	Business process improvement
BPM	Business process management
BPM CM	Business process management change management
BPM CoE	Business process management center of excellence
BPM LC	Business process management life cycle
BPM PM	Business process management portfolio management
BPMaaS	BPM as a service
BPMI	Business process management institute
BPMN	Business process model and notation
BPMS	Business process management system
BPO	Business process outsourcing
BPPM	Business process portfolio management
BPR	Business process reengineering
BRE	Business rule engine
BRM	Business rules management
CDM	Common data model
CE-BPM	Cloud-enabled BPM
CEAP	Cloud-enabled application platform
CEN	European committee for standardization
CEP	Complex event processing
CM	Configuration management
CMS	Content management system
COBIT	Control objectives for information and related technology

CPO	Chief process officer
CRM	Customer relationship management
CSF	Critical success factor
CSIR	Council for Scientific and Industrial Research
CxO	Chief x officer
DB	Database
DBMS	Database management system
DMS	Document management system
DNEAF	Domain neutral enterprise architecture framework
DSDM	Dynamic systems development method
EAI	Enterprise application integration
EITE	Enterprise innovation & transformation enablement
EMR	Enterprise-wide metadata repositories
EPC	Event-driven process chain
EPSS	Electronic performance support system
ERM	Entity relationship modeling
ERP	Enterprise resource planning
ESB	Enterprise service bus
FEAF	Federal enterprise architecture framework
FI	Financial
iBPM	Intelligent business process management
IDE	Integrated development environment
IE	Information engineering
IEEE	Institute of electrical and electronics engineers
ISO	International Organization for Standardization
ITIL	Information technology infrastructure library
KPI	Key performance indicator
L&D	Learning and development
LEAD	Layered Enterprise Architecture Development and/or LEADing Practice
MDM	Master data management
NATO	North Atlantic Treaty Organisation
NIST	National Institute of Standards and Technology
OCM	Organizational change management
OLAP	Online analytic processing
OLTP	Online transaction processing
OMG	Object management group
PDC	Process data collection
PIM	Process instance management
PM	Portfolio management
PM	Project management
PMBOK	Project management body of knowledge
PMO	Project management offices
POA	Process oriented architecture
PPI	Process performance indicator
PPM	Project portfolios management
PPPM	Portfolio, program and project management
PRINCE	PRojects IN Controlled Environments
QM	Quality management

ROI	Return on investment
SBO	Strategic business objective
SCM	Supply chain management
SCOR	Supply chain operations reference model
SD	Sales and distribution
SNA	Social network analysis
SOA	Service oriented architecture
SPI	Service performance indicator
SRM	Supply relationship management
SW	Software
TCO	Total cost of ownership
TOGAF	The open group architecture framework
TQM	Total quality management
UI	User interface
ULM	Unified modeling language
USGAP	United States general accounting principles
VDML	Value delivery modeling language
VNA	Value network analysis
W3C	World Wide Web consortium
xBPMN	eXtended business process model and notation
XLM	Extensible markup language
XMI	Metadata interchange
XSD	XML schema definition

Introduction to the Book

Prof. Mark von Rosing, Henrik von Scheel, Prof. August-Wilhelm Scheer

It is not a new phenomenon that the markets are changing, however, the business environment in which firms operate lies outside of themselves and their control. So, while it is their external environment, which is always changing, most changes on the outside affect the need for innovation and transformation on the inside of the organization. The ability to change the business and to manage their processes is symbiotic, which is, among others, one of the reasons for such a high Business Process Management (BPM) adoption rate in the market. It is, however, important to note that unlike some analysts might claim, the size of the market and its adoption is in no way an indicator of maturity. As a matter of fact, the maturity of many of the BPM concepts can be low, even though the adoption is widespread. So while the high demand for BPM as a management method and a software solution, and the maturing BPM capabilities develop and unfold, the challenge quickly develops to provide concise and widely accepted BPM definitions, taxonomies, standardized, and integrated process templates, as well as overall frameworks, methods, and approaches.

Written as the practical guide for you—by the authorities that have shaped the way we think and work with process today. This handbook series stands out as a masterpiece, representing the most comprehensive body of knowledge published on business process. The first volume endows the reader with a deep insight into the nature of business process, and a complete body of knowledge from process modeling to BPM, thereby covering what executives, managers, practitioners, students, and researchers need to know about:

- Future BPM trends that will affect business
- A clear and precise definition of what BPM is
- Historical evolution of process concepts
- Exploring a BPM Ontology
- In-depth look at the Process Semantics
- Comprehensive Frameworks, Methods, and Approaches
- Process analysis, process design, process deployment, process monitoring, and Continuous Improvement
- Practical usable process templates
- How to link Strategy to Operation with value driven BPM
- How to build BPM competencies and establish a Center of Excellence
- Discover how to apply Social Media and BPM
- Sustainable Oriented process Modeling
- Evidence-based BPM
- Learn how Value and Performance Measurement and Management is executed
- Explore how to enable Process Owners

- BPM Roles and Knowledge Workers
- Discover how to develop information models within the process models
- Uncovering Process Life cycle
- BPM Maturity
- BPM Portfolio Management and BPM Alignment
- BPM Change Management and BPM Governance
- Learning a structured way of Thinking, Working, Modeling, and Implementing processes.

This book is organized into various chapters that have been thoughtfully put together to communicate many times a complex topic into a replicable and manageable structure—that you as a reader can apply. Furthermore, the book is structured into six parts with the intention to guide you in turning business processes into real assets.

In Part I, we introduce a comprehensive "history of process concepts" from Sun Tzu's, to Taylorism, to Business Process Reengineering to Lean and BPMN, providing the reader with an in-depth understanding of the evolution of process thinking, approaches, and methods: a fundamental insight to what has shaped and what is shaping process thinking.

In Part II, we introduce the "Way of Thinking" around Business Process with focus on the value of Ontology, and a comprehensive BPM Ontology—the essential starting point that creates the guiding principles.

In Part III, we establish a "Way of Working" with Business Processes—the critical discipline of translating both strategic planning and effective execution. Exploring the current and future process trends that you need to be aware of with a detailed practical guide on how to apply them in areas such as BPM Life cycle, BPM Roles, process templates, evidence-based BPM, and many more.

In Part IV, provides essential guidance to help you in a "Way of Modeling" in traditional Process Modeling concepts to BPMN and Value-Oriented Process Modeling, how to work with and model Business Processes variations, as well as how to interlink information models and process models.

In Part V, we focus on the "Way of Implementation" and "Way of Governance"—the approach the practitioner follows in order to apply and steer what exists, spanning issues ranging from BPM change management, agile BPM, business process outsourcing, and holistic governance to project, program, and portfolio alignment.

In Part VI, we focus on the "Way of Training and Coaching"—to provide insight into ideal process expert, process engineer and process architecture training, from online to class-based learning and coaching.

While this book certainly can be read cover to cover, depending on where you are in your Business Process journey, you may wish to choose a different path. If you are new to Business Process concepts, you might start at the beginning, with part I. If you are beginning a BPM project, or it has already begun its journey, or you are looking for inspiration, we recommend using the book as a reference tool to access it by the topic of interest.

But no matter how you plan on building your knowledge, the book has been designed and architected to be a guide and a handbook able to create the right way of thinking, working, modeling implementation, and governance.

Phase 1: Process Concept Evolution

Henrik von Scheel, Mark von Rosing, Marianne Fonseca, Maria Hove, Ulrik Foldager

INTRODUCTION

The term *process* comes from the Latin word *processus* or *processioat*, which translates as a performed action of something that is done, and the way it is done. A process is, therefore, a collection of interrelated tasks and activities that are initiated in response to an event which aims to achieve a specific result for the consumer of the process. Processes constantly occur and happen all around us, in all that we do throughout the course of the day. They are the basis of all actions that involve concepts such as time, space, and motion, and they shape and bend to the very reality in which we exist.

Imagine yourself reading this chapter. You glance briefly to the side of your table only to realize that your coffee cup is now empty. A process is then sparked and initialized, and you (1) get up from your chair, (2) lift your cup from the table, (3) walk into the kitchen, (4) pour yourself another cup of coffee, (5) you then return to your chair, and (6) sit down and continue reading. That, in itself, is a process by nature. This is just one example of a very simple and descriptive process so as to better illustrate its elusive concept.

A *business process*, however, is the same as a process, but with one major difference, namely with the emphasis on the word *business*. A business process is a collection of tasks and activities (business operations and actions) consisting of employees, materials, machines, systems, and methods that are being structured in such a way as to design, create, and deliver a product or a service to the consumer.

As such, a *business process* can be understood in the following way:

- It is a placeholder for the action (process area).
- An action is taking place (process group).
- A business task is taking place (business process).
- The location of the business task in the sequence (process step).
- The way the business task is carried out (process activity).

Business processes consist of nucleus tasks and activities that are connected with each other, and are categorized and grouped. High-level business processes occur in a far more abstract context, as they are, usually, utilized to illustrate how a business carries out many different sets of operations. The entire marketing department of a large corporation, for example, can be described as a process group, although it depends entirely on the process structure of each individual organization. A business process can also consist of minor activities within the business process itself, and in such a case, these minor activities are called subprocesses. One ought to view the processes in the big picture first (captured in the process map) since a business process can trigger many tasks and subprocesses but also initiate other processes. In that way, you often see a connection between the different processes (both the value-adding processes and the non-value-adding processes) that are involved in the servicing of a client. Business processes are usually illustrated by different readable business process diagrams—for example through the use of Business Process Modeling Notation[1] diagrams. Business Process Modeling Notation (BPMN) is a standardized, visual (graphical) modeling representation used to illustrate business process flows. It provides an easy to use, flow-charting notation that is independent of the implementation environment. Business processes are used to illustrate, document, and shape the way an organization carries out its business operations across all organizational levels, i.e., both the strategic, tactical, and operational business levels.

There are four major phases in the historical development of business processes. The first phase is launched with the introduction of Sun Tzu's *Art of War* in the era of Ancient China. In the *Art of War*, Sun Tzu describes military strategies and tactics where he would assign specific tasks to certain people and calculate the resources needed for the execution of these tasks. Thousands of years later, we share with you Adam Smith's observations of work processes, which eventually inspired Taylor's "Scientific Management." The main problem in the implementation of Scientific Management is that it does not integrate the person behind the machine, and this leads us to the second phase, in which Allan H. Mogensen, Frank Gilbreth, and Ben Graham involved the worker in optimizing the processes. Finally, the visualization and digitalization of processes leads to the third and fourth (present) phase, in which the processes are being implemented and, to some extent, executed through the use of information systems and technology (Figure 1).

PROCESS CONCEPT EVOLUTION
Sun Tzu

Sun Tzu (also rendered as Sun Zi) was a Chinese military general, strategist, and philosopher and is assumed to have lived his life from around 544–496 BC in ancient China. He is traditionally credited as the author of *The Art of War*[2]—an extremely influential ancient Chinese book on military strategy. Traditional accounts state that the general's descendant Sun Bin also wrote a treatise on military tactics, also titled *The Art of War*.

Sun Tzu's work has been praised and employed throughout East Asia since its composition. During the twentieth century, *The Art of War* grew in popularity and saw practical use in Western society as well. *The Art of War* is composed of 13 chapters, each of which is devoted to one aspect of warfare. It is commonly known to be the definitive work on military strategy and tactics of its time and has had an influence on Eastern and Western military thinking, business tactics, legal strategy, and beyond. In his work, Sun Tzu describes a subtle yet abstract use of process activities to fulfill specific goals, precisely as business processes today are used to fulfill the goals of a company. He describes carrying out specific sets of tasks and activities and then assigning resources to the execution of these tasks and their related activities in order to complete certain objectives, and thereby, fulfilling the strategies of warfare.

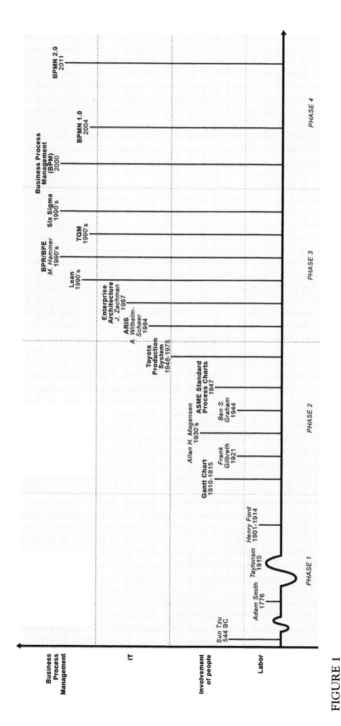

FIGURE 1

The historical evolution of processes over the course of time.[3]

It should also be noted, however, that in 604 AD, Shotoku Taishi (573–621), the Prince of Holy Virtue, was a Japanese regent, statesman, and scholar who established a set of guidelines that served as the constitution of Japan at the time. In these documents, after studying the Chinese administration, he described the relations between Buddhism and what we would call public administration. These observations were later worked over and expanded and used as the foundation for the Japanese administration. Shotoku Taishi specified how tasks and responsibility best could be placed in the different branches of the administration. This is one of the earliest abstract views of the relation between organizational format and goals that the authors of this chapter have been able to identify.

Adam Smith

Adam Smith (1723–1790) was a Scottish moral philosopher and a pioneer of political economy. One of the key figures of the Scottish Enlightenment,[4] Smith is best known for two classic works: *The Theory of Moral Sentiments*[5] (1759), and *An Inquiry into the Nature and Causes of the Wealth of Nations*[6] (1776). While his exact date of birth is not known, Adam Smith's baptism was recorded on June 5, 1723, in Kirkcaldy, Scotland. He attended the Burgh School, where he studied Latin, mathematics, history, and writing. Smith entered the University of Glasgow when he was 14 years old and in 1740 he went to Oxford.[7]

In 1748, Adam Smith began giving a series of public lectures at the University of Edinburgh. Through these lectures in 1750, he met and became lifelong friends with Scottish philosopher and economist David Hume. This relationship led to Smith's appointment to the Glasgow University faculty in 1751.

In 1759, Smith published *The Theory of Moral Sentiments*, a book whose main contention is that human morality depends on sympathy between the individual and other members of society. On the heels of the book, he became the tutor of the future Duke of Buccleuch (1763–1766) and traveled with him to France, where Smith met with other prominent thinkers of his day, such as Benjamin Franklin[8] and French economist Anne-Robert-Jacques Turgot.[9]

After toiling for nine years, and with his work from 1776, *An Inquiry into the Nature and Causes of the Wealth of Nations* (usually shortened to *The Wealth of Nations*), Adam Smith changed the traditional way of viewing the production process. Smith's work is best known for his invisible-hand analogy of market pricing and self-regulation by the individual actors acting out of their own best interests. In this work, Smith uses the well-known example of the production of pins in which a specialized line of production can increase the production capability.[10] Furthermore, he is one of the first to do movement and time studies, and he suggests that the work processes can be split up in many parts. Smith's work is not only considered the first modern work of economics and the "father of modern economics"[11] but is also one of the main sources of inspiration for Taylorism.[12]

Smith's ideas are a reflection on economics in light of the beginning of the Industrial Revolution, and he states that free-market economies (i.e., markets based on capitalism) are the most productive and beneficial to their societies. He goes on to argue for an economic system based on individual self-interest led by an "invisible hand," which would achieve the greatest good for all. In time, *The Wealth of Nations* won Smith a far-reaching reputation, and the work, considered a foundational work of classical economics, is one of the most influential books ever written.

In 1787, Smith was named rector of the University of Glasgow, and he died just three years later at the age of 67.

Taylorism[13]

Frederick Winslow Taylor (1856–1915), efficiency engineer and inventor, was born in Germantown, Philadelphia, Pa., the youngest child of Franklin and Emily Annette (Winslow) Taylor. He was a descendant of Samuel Taylor, who settled in Burlington, N. J., in 1677.[14]

His father was a lawyer, more interested, however, in literature than law; his mother was an ardent abolitionist and a coworker with Lucretia Mott [q.v.] in this cause. Taylor received his early education from his mother. In 1872, after two years of schooling in France and Germany, followed by 18 months of travel in Europe, he entered Phillips Exeter Academy at Exeter, N. H., to prepare for the Harvard Law School. Though he graduated with his class two years later, his eyesight had in the meantime become so impaired that he had to abandon further study. Between 1874 and 1878, he worked in the shops of the Enterprise Hydraulic Works, a pump-manufacturing company in Philadelphia, where he would learn the trades as a pattern-maker and machinist.

In the latter year, he joined the Midvale Steel Company, Philadelphia, as a common laborer. In the succeeding 12 years, he not only rose to be chief engineer (1884), but in 1883, by studying at night, obtained the degree of M.E. from Stevens Institute of Technology, Hoboken, N. J. In 1884, he married Louise M. Spooner of Philadelphia. His inventions during these years that affected improvements in machinery and manufacturing methods were many, the outstanding one being the design and construction of the largest successful steam hammer ever built in the United States (patent No. 424,939, Apr. 1, 1890). After three years (1890–93) as a general manager of the Manufacturing Investment Company, Philadelphia, operating large paper mills in Maine and Wisconsin, he began a consulting practice in Philadelphia—his business card read "Systematizing Shop Management and Manufacturing Costs a Specialty"—which led to the development of a new profession.

Behind this lay Taylor's years of observation and study of manufacturing conditions and methods. From these he had evolved a theory that, by scientific study of every minute step and operation in a manufacturing plant, data could be obtained as to the fair and reasonable production capacities of both man and machine, and that the application of such data would, in turn, abolish the antagonism between employer and employee and bring about increased efficiencies in all directions. He had, in addition, worked out a comprehensive system of analysis, classification, and symbolization to be used in the study of every type of manufacturing organization.

For five years, he successfully applied his theory in a variety of establishments, administrative and sales departments, as well as shops. In 1898, he was retained exclusively for that purpose by the Bethlehem Steel Company in Bethlehem, Pa. In the course of his work there, he undertook with J. Maunsel White a study of the treatment of tool steel, which led to the discovery of the Taylor–White process of heat treatment of tool steel, yielding increased cutting capacities of 200–300 percent. This process and the tools treated by it are now used in practically every machine shop of the world. While he was at Bethlehem, too, Taylor's ideas regarding scientific management took more concrete form. Being convinced of the results that would be attained if these principles should be generally adopted throughout the industrial world, he resigned from the Bethlehem Steel Company in 1901, returned to Philadelphia, and devoted the remainder of his life to expounding these principles, giving his services free to anybody who was sincerely desirous of carrying out his methods. While he met with many unbelievers among both employers and employees, he lived to see his system widely applied. In 1911, the Society to Promote the Science of Management (after his death renamed the Taylor Society) was established by enthusiastic engineers and industrialists throughout the world to carry on his work and legacy.

Among Taylor's contributions to the technical journals were "A Piece-Rate System"[15] (Transactions of the American Society of Mechanical Engineers, vol. XVI, 1895), an exposition of the principles on which his system of management was subsequently based, and "Shop Management," which was translated and published in almost every country of Europe. As an active member of the American Society of Mechanical Engineers, he served as vice-president in 1904–05 and as president in 1906, when he delivered as his presidential address an exhaustive monograph *On the Art of Cutting Metals*.

In 1911, Frederick Winslow Taylor published his work *Principles of Scientific Management*.[16] The purpose of this method, which is also known as Taylorism, is to identify the optimum method to achieve a certain goal. By categorizing people as a machine that can be manipulated, the factory processes could be streamlined and optimized. Taylor was among those who did the most to systematize the production technique and make it more scientific. Before the turn of the century, work processes and organization were based on experience, tradition, and, as seen from a production point of view, sheer chance. Taylorism meant a development of time and method studies and job analysis. The jumping-off point was the way the best and fastest workers performed a certain job. Taylor put a lot of emphasis on the standardization and specialization of the work—for both workers, foremen, and planners—and on the importance of increased quality control. Along with the practician Henry Ford, the car manufacturer, Taylor was among those who contributed the most to the development of the capitalist large-scale industry.[17]

Scientific Management is based on objective data, like measuring the time required for a certain job, which helped you set expected quotas for the workers. At the same time, the system was supposed to show the value of the work, and thus ensures the worker a reasonable salary for a job well done. Taylor was convinced that all interests were considered, which has not always been the case in practice. Taylorism was also the jumping-off point for Henry Ford, who created his own very successful production machinery. Taylor based his theory on the assumption that industrial growth required a large-scale influx of workers from the primary trades to the industry. These were workers with no industrial experience. This made it expedient to ensure a strong specialization and strict control, which would leave nothing to chance. But Taylor also claimed that most workers are lazy and stupid and solely interested in their salary; therefore, they will be better off with no responsibility and only simple jobs.

Taylorism has a bad reputation these days since it contributed to creating a self-fulfilling prophecy. Based on the assumption that workers are lazy and stupid, they created boring jobs that left no room for growth. Naturally, the workers reacted with apathy in a situation like that. This cemented the employer's belief that workers simply lacked skills, and that increased the strict control. The kind of work that these guidelines created has contributed to the alienation within the industry.

Frederick Winslow Taylor died in Philadelphia of pneumonia, survived by his widow and three adopted children.

Henry Ford[18]

Famed automobile manufacturer Henry Ford was born on July 30, 1863, on his family's farm in Wayne County, near Dearborn, Michigan. When Ford was 13 years old, his father gifted him a pocket watch, which the young boy promptly took apart and reassembled. Friends and neighbors were impressed and requested that he fixed their timepieces too. Unsatisfied with farm work, Ford left home the following year, at the age of 16, to take an apprenticeship as a machinist in Detroit. In the years that followed, he would learn to skillfully operate and service steam engines and would also study bookkeeping.

In 1888, Ford married Clara Ala Bryant and briefly returned to farming to support his wife and son, Edsel. But three years later, he was hired as an engineer for the Edison Illuminating Company. In 1893, his natural talents earned him a promotion to chief engineer. All the while, Ford developed his plans for a horseless carriage, and in 1896, he constructed his first model, the Ford Quadricycle. Within the same year, he attended a meeting with Edison executives and found himself presenting his automobile plans to Thomas Edison. The lighting genius encouraged Ford to build a second, better model.

After a few trials building cars and companies, in 1903, Henry Ford established the Ford Motor Company. Ford introduced the Model T in October of 1908, and for several years, the company posted 100 percent gains. However, more than for his profits, Ford became renowned for his revolutionary vision: the manufacture of an inexpensive automobile made by skilled workers who earn steady wages. Inspired by Taylorism, Ford started his mass production[17] and revolutionized the production process. In 1914, his plant in Highland Park, Michigan, could produce a complete frame every 93 min thanks to innovative production techniques. This was a remarkable improvement in comparison with the former production time of 728 min.

Through the use of a conveyer belt, the breaking down of work processes and careful coordination and operations, Ford gained serious profits in productivity.

In 1914, Ford started paying his employees five dollars a day, which was almost double the salary paid by other manufacturers. He cut the working hours from nine to eight hours for a three-shift working day at the factory. Ford's mass production techniques would finally make it possible to build a Model T every 24 s. Ford's affordable Model T and the way it was produced has changed American society for good. As more Americans became car owners, the patterns of city life changed. As the United States saw a traffic increase in the suburbs, a highway system was established, and the population could transport itself anywhere it wanted to. From a social perspective, Henry Ford was marked by seemingly contradictory viewpoints. In business, Ford offered profit sharing to select employees who stayed with the company for six months and, most importantly, who conducted their lives in a respectable manner.

The company's "Social Department" looked into an employee's drinking, gambling, and otherwise uncouth habits to determine eligibility for participation. Ford was also an ardent pacifist and opposed World War I, and even funded a peace ship to Europe. Later, in 1936, Ford and his family established the Ford Foundation to provide ongoing grants for research, education, and development. But despite these philanthropic leanings, Ford was also a committed anti-semite, going as far as to support a weekly newspaper, The Dearborn Independent, which furthered such views.

Henry Ford died of a cerebral hemorrhage on April 7, 1947, at the age of 83, near his Dearborn estate, Fair Lane. Ford, considered one of America's leading businessmen, is credited today for helping to build America's economy during the nation's vulnerable early years. His legacy will live on for decades to come.[19]

End Notes

1. BPMN: The business process modeling notation, Patrice Briol, s. l. s. n. 2008.
2. The Art of War, Sun Tzu (author), B. H. Liddell Hart (Foreword), Samuel B. Griffith (Translator), Oxford University Press, 1971.
3. Process Evolution Timeline Model, LEADing Practice Business Process Reference Content #LEAD-ES20005BP.
4. Great Thinkers of the Scottish Enlightenment, BBC, from http://www.bbc.co.uk/history /scottishhistory/enlightenment/features_enlightenment_enlightenment.shtml.
5. The Theory of Moral Sentiments, Adam Smith, 1759 from http://www.earlymoderntexts. com/pdfs/smith1759.pdf.
6. An Inquiry into the Nature and Causes of the Wealth of Nations, Adam Smith, 1776 from http://www.gutenberg.org/files/3300/3300-h/3300-h.htm#link2HCH0028.
7. Smith A., The Biography.com website, (2014), Retrieved 11:52, August 11, 2014, from http://www.biography.com/people/adam-smith-9486480.
8. Benjamin Franklin from http://www.biography.com/people/benjamin-franklin-9301234.
9. Anne-Robert-Jacques Turgot from http://www.econlib.org/library/Enc/bios/Turgot.html.
10. The History of Management Thought, Daniel A. Wren, Wiley, 2005.
11. Davis William L., Figgins B., Hedengren D., and Klein D.B., "Economic Professors' Favorite Economic Thinkers, Journals, and Blogs," Econ Journal Watch 8, no. 2 (May 2011): 126–146.

12. The History of Management Thought, Daniel A. Wren, Wiley, 2005.
13. American genesis: A century of invention and technological enthusiasm, 1870–1970, Thomas Parke Hughes, University of Chicago Press, 2004.
14. *Dictionary of American Biography Base Set*, Frederick Winslow Taylor, American Council of Learned Societies, 1928–1936.
15. The visible hand: The managerial revolution in American business, Alfred Dupont Chandler, Belknap Press, 2002.
16. The Principles of Scientific Management, Frederick Winslow Taylor, Courier Dover Publications, 1998.
17. Henry Ford, mass production, modernism and design, Ray Batchelor, Manchester University Press, 1994.
18. The People's Tycoon: Henry Ford and the American Century, Steven Watts, Vintage Books, 2006.
19. Ford H., The Biography.com website, (2014), Retrieved 11:34, August 11, 2014, from http://www.biography.com/people/henry-ford-9298747.

Phase 2: Process Concept Evolution

Henrik von Scheel, Mark von Rosing, Maria Hove, Marianne Fonseca, Ulrik Foldager

INTRODUCTION

Throughout the first phase of the historical development of processes, we elaborated on some of the key figures who are widely regarded as pioneers—both in academia as well as in business—and laid the foundation for the upcoming—as well as today's—process studies and the use of them in organizations across the world. The second phase of the historical evolution of process flows incorporates a far more extensive use of human involvement, however, and tells the story of human interaction around processes, process flows, tasks, and activities, as well as the necessary application and consumption of resources that are associated with carrying out each of these tasks and activities.

Upon entering the second phase, we are introduced to Henry Laurence Gantt, an American engineer who is best known for his planning methodology.[1] This methodology helped him realize major infrastructure projects including the construction of the Hoover Dam in the United States. His manager, Frederick W. Taylor, involved Gantt in a number of large infrastructure projects. Together with Taylor, Henry Gantt applied different scientific management principles in order to implement these projects successfully.

While closing in on the twentieth century, Frank B. Gilbreth introduces us to much more efficient bricklaying techniques, as he studies the sequence and number of physical movements associated with laying down each brick upon the construction of a building. By studying and documenting the movements associated with physical labor, he found that one would be able to reduce the number of movements required in order to carry out a specific task. This enabled him to effectively reduce the number of physical movements associated with that particular task, and thus, improve the flow of the process by shortening the time consumption while increasing productivity. He would also be the first person ever to document the flow of a process through the use of a so-called Process Chart, as he coined it.

Later on in the early 1930s, Allan H. Mogensen evolved upon this methodology through the study of motion pictures, which enabled him to further improve upon the sequence of activities that was involved with each task. He created process diagrams—a more detailed and elaborate version of Frank Gilbreth's process charts—to document each task that enabled him to understand and visualize the activities that were involved with that task. This would allow him to reduce the number of motions required to carry out a particular task, and reducing the time needed to complete it. These techniques were used in hospitals at the time and would thereby be used to increase the likelihood of survival of patients during surgery by reducing the need for unnecessary movements and activities.

At the end of the 1930s, William E. Boeing would then take these practices, and the knowledge thereof, and learn how to effectively break down a process into smaller bits, thereby enabling him to simplify and improve processes that were involved with the building of both civilian as well as military aircraft. Through the use of these enhanced process techniques, Boeing would become able to supply the American Air Force with the B-17 Flying Fortresses and B-29 Superfortresses during the Second World War that were able to carry heavy military equipment, such as nuclear bombs and other material. It would become one of the first very good examples of process documentation for process flows and breakdown.

In the 1940s, Ben S. Graham would then take these process practices that he had acquired from Allan H. Mogensen and Lillian Gilbreth (the wife of Frank B. Gilbreth) into office work in order to simplify paperwork and work more efficiently with information at an office desk. He used his own techniques to map out the processes of the employees that worked with paperwork—nonphysical and non-manufacturing labor—which would later be used across the world today. It is also known as Business Process Improvement, although the term was not coined as such at that time.

In 1947, the American Society of Mechanical Engineers—or ASME—would become the first organization to develop and establish an international standard of process symbols, and document how to use them in process charts and process diagrams. Shortly thereafter, namely in the 1950s, Functional Flow Block Diagrams began to surface that would commonly be used to describe processes in development and production system environments.

In 1957, the PERT methodology was introduced and is utilized to illustrate and analyze program-related tasks. This was particularly helpful, as it would give employees and managers involved with programs the ability to set up timelines, estimated durations, and the following efficiency evaluation—with a focus on time consumption—in each program.

With the introduction of the Data Flow Diagram, engineers would have a tool to produce a graphical illustration (process diagrams) that would place information blocks into the flow of a process, giving them the ability to see how and where data would be stored in the process, as well as which kind of input would be delivered to what and the consequential output of this behavior. Around nearly the same time, we see the arrival of IDEF (Integrated Definition), which was developed by Knowledge Based Systems, Inc. (KBSI). IDEF would introduce methods of function modeling, information modeling, data modeling, and object-oriented design, as well as a methods for capturing process and ontology descriptions.

In the 1960s, the theory of Zero Defects was established and expressed the idea that *a product that meets the requirements of the consumer is the right product.* In 1979, Philip Crosby penned *Quality Is Free: The Art of Making Quality Certain,*[2] which would introduce a 14-step quality improvement program designed to not only improve quality but also reduce an unnecessary waste of resources in production facilities.

At the end of the second phase, Taichi Ohno and Shigeo Shingo developed the Toyota Production System (TPS) between 1948 and 1975. In 1988, Taichi Ohno explained the philosophies and concepts behind TPS through the publication of *Just-in-Time for Today and Tomorrow*.[3] TPS focuses mainly around two different concepts: (1) *Jidoka*, which means that when a problem occurs, the equipment stops immediately, preventing defective products from being produced, and (2) *Just-in-Time*, in which each process produces only what is needed by the next process within the continuous flow of production processes.

GANTT CHART

Henry Laurence Gantt, AB, ME, (1861–1919) was an American engineer and famous management consultant who is best known for his planning methodology. This methodology helped him realize major infrastructure projects, including the construction of the Hoover Dam in the United States. Henry Gantt graduated with a bachelor's degree (AB) from McDonogh School (United States) in 1878. Then he went on to the Stevens Institute of Technology (New Jersey, United States) to obtain his master's degree in engineering (ME). After obtaining this degree, Gantt worked as a teacher until 1887. From 1887, Henry Gantt chose a new challenge and joined Midvale Steel Company in Philadelphia, United States. His manager, Frederick W. Taylor, involved Gantt in a number of large infrastructure projects. Together with Taylor, Henry Gantt applied different scientific management principles in order to implement these projects successfully.

Henry Gantt worked for Midvale Steel Company until 1893. He continued his career as a management consultant and developed his famous planning methodology. Henry Gantt also developed a task and bonus system of wage payment and measurement instruments to provide an insight into worker efficiency and productivity. In 1916, inspired by Thorsten Veblen, Gantt set up a trade association that was aimed at the development of industrial efficiency within political processes. In addition, he called into question the industrial system under control of managers and Polakov's analysis[4] of inefficiency within the industrial sector.

While Ford implemented Taylorism in practice, Henry Gantt chose to illustrate the process work behind it all. This way of keeping track of all processes is utilized all over the world today. The Gantt chart that we know today was created from 1910 to 1915, and it was later published in the entire western world.[5] A Gantt chart is a type of bar chart that illustrates a project schedule. Gantt charts illustrate the start and finish dates of the terminal elements and summary elements of a project. Terminal elements and summary elements comprise the work breakdown structure of the project. Modern Gantt charts also show the dependency (i.e., precedence network) relationships between activities. Gantt charts can be used to show current schedule status using percent-complete shadings and a vertical "TODAY" (the "TODAY" indicator describes what happens on that particular day or at this particular time) line as shown in (Figure 1).

Gantt charts (see Figure 1) have become the common method to present the phases and activities in a project's work breakdown structure thus making it comprehensible to a wide audience. Although now regarded as a common charting technique, Gantt

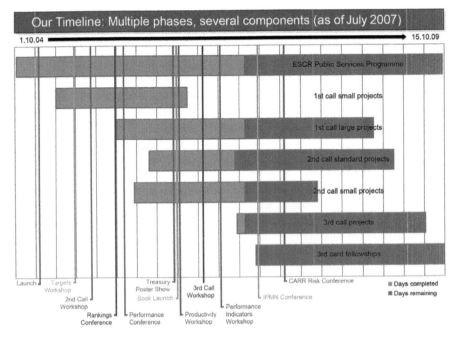

FIGURE 1

Seen as a whole, a Gantt chart is a useful tool to get a general idea of the process work and to be able to control it, but it does have its short comings that you need to take into consideration.[6]

charts were considered extremely revolutionary when first introduced. This chart is also used in information technology to represent data that have been collected.

Even though a Gantt diagram is useful and valuable to smaller projects, which fits nicely on a single sheet or on the screen, they tend to become a bit too overwhelming for projects that include a lot of activities. Larger Gantt charts are unsuitable for most computer screens, and they do not give the intended easy overview. Gantt charts are also criticized for not having more than a little information in each area of the screen. Projects are often more complicated than can be illustrated effectively in a Gantt chart. Since the horizontal bars in a Gantt chart have a fixed height, they cannot be representative of the work-load in the time phase (resource requirements) of a project. In the model below, all activities have the same size, but in reality the work-load itself can be much different. Another criticism states that activities in a Gantt chart show a planned work-load as a constant.

FRANK B. GILBRETH

Born in Fairfield, ME, on July 7, 1868, Gilbreth broke into the construction industry as a bricklayer shortly after his high school graduation. In the course of his work, Gilbreth observed that each bricklayer approached his job differently, some seemingly more efficient than others. He then began analyzing their motions to determine which approach to bricklaying was the best. Hence, his pioneering work in motion analysis and how it was applied to the workforce was under way. Over the years, he developed many improvements in bricklaying. He invented a scaffold that was easily adjusted to allow the worker to be at the most advantageous level at all times. He created a system whereby bricks were stacked on the scaffold in such a manner that the worker could easily pick up a brick in one hand and mortar in the other. By using some of the previously established best practices that he had observed, and some that he made up himself, he improved his performance by 190%. This led Gilbreth to improve his theories on how to find the best practices.[7,8] He used different methods to gain a better understanding of the movements that people performed while doing a certain job—first he filmed them, and later, he divided the hand movements into 17 minor standard movements. To monitor the processes and these movements in a work situation, he developed the "process chart" and the "flow diagram." The flow diagram is a diagram that shows the separate parts of a process.[9]

Gilbreth learned every trade in the construction business and advanced to superintendent without the typical three years of apprentice work. At the age of 27, Gilbreth started his own contracting firm, where he patented many inventions, including a concrete mixer and concrete conveyor system. He adopted the slogan "Speed Work" for his company and expressed his goals as the elimination of waste, the conservation of ability, and the reduction of cost. He was lauded for the application of these principles in the rapid construction of the Augustus Lowell Laboratory of Electrical Engineering for the Massachusetts Institute of Technology. His company was involved in a variety of construction projects, including dams, canals, houses, factory buildings, and an industrial facility. He eventually expanded his business to England.[10]

Gilbreth had the good fortune to meet Lillian Evelyn Moller, and they married in 1904. In addition to raising 12 children and being the subject of the Hollywood movie *Cheaper by the Dozen*, they became one of the great husband–wife teams of science and engineering. Together, they collaborated on the development of a micromotion study as an engineering and management technique and introduced the application of psychology to industrial management. They saw the need to improve worker satisfaction, which would in turn improve overall job performance and worker efficiency. Gilbreth designed systems to ease worker fatigue and increase productivity by studying each movement a worker made, and in doing so, document the best way to perform the task. They also considered the physical comfort of the worker and their innovations in office furniture led to the study of ergonomics.

In 1907, Gilbreth met engineer and inventor Frederick Winslow Taylor and became a proponent of the Taylor System of Time Study.[11] Frank and Lillian were instrumental in creating the Taylor Society. In 1912, the Gilbreths left the construction industry to focus their efforts on scientific management consulting. They broke with Taylor in 1914 and formed their own scientific management company with the intent to focus on the human element of management, as well as the technical.

They felt Taylor's "stop-watch" approach was primarily concerned with reducing process times, whereas the Gilbreths focused on making processes more efficient by reducing the motions involved. The Gilbreths continued their micromotion studies in other fields, pioneering the use of motion pictures for studying various aspects of work and workers.

In the early months of World War I, Gilbreth studied industrial processes and machinery in Germany. As wounded soldiers began returning home, Gilbreth applied his principles to improving surgical procedures and was the first to use the motion-picture camera in the operating room for educational purposes. He was also the first to propose that a surgical nurse serve as a "caddy" to the surgeon by handing surgical instruments to the surgeon during a procedure. He also helped rehabilitate injured soldiers by developing ways to help them manage their daily activities.

In 1920, ASME instituted its Management Division, which Gilbreth had helped to establish. He became one of the most widely known engineers in the US and Europe and reaped financial rewards and many professional honors. At an ASME conference in 1921, Gilbreth became the first to present a structured method to document process flow. He called his presentation "Process Charts—First Steps in Finding the One Best Way."[12] Seen as a whole, the purpose of Gilbreth's work was to develop the worker's full potential through effective training, new work methods, improved working environment and tools, and a healthy psychological outlook on life.[13]

Frank B. Gilbreth suggested the inaugural international management congress that was held in Prague in 1924. He was stricken with a heart attack shortly after the conference and died on June 14, 1924, while traveling from his home in Montclair, NJ, to New York City.

ALLAN H. MOGENSEN

Allan H. Mogensen, also known as Mogy, (Pennsylvania, May 1901–March 1989), was an American industrial engineer and authority in the field of work simplification and office management. He is noted for popularizing flow charts in the 1930s and is remembered as the "father of work simplification."

In the 1920s, Mogensen received his BA in Industrial Engineering at Cornell University, where he had studied the methods of Frank Gilbreth. Afterward, he started as an industrial engineering consultant, among other places at Eastman Kodak. During his consultancy practice, he experienced that improvements made by employees on the work floor were the most successful. Mogensen's career started at a time when there was a dramatic increase in productivity. This was due to Scientific Management, which Frank Gilbreth had further improved on by increasing the efficiency of the analysis and the adding of techniques, which made it possible for people to make an increased output with a slightly improved effort. Even so, some of the workers saw this as a new way of taking advantage of them,[14] and at times it led to such an intense opposition as to destroy the entire process.

In the 1930s, Mogensen further experimented with time and motion studies using motion pictures. In 1932, Allan H. Mogensen invented the "Work Simplification", which is defined as the organized utilization of common sense.[15] Mogensen made use of process diagrams to organize and study the work, and he tapped into the common sense of the one performing the work in order to develop ideas for improvement.[16] One of Allan H. Mogensen's main points was that the one performing the task was the one best suited to improve it. What sets his method apart from earlier methods is the fact the he sees the people performing the work as the most vital resource when it comes to an ongoing improvement of the work processes.[17] By involving each individual worker in the process, he achieves two things: (1) he reduces the opposition to the implementation of the scientific management methods and (2) he gets input to improvement of the processes. In 1937, he had organized the process enough to be able to start arranging his conferences.

During the early 1940s, Mogensen was noted for making movies of operations in hospitals, where he discovered that surgeons could work faster by avoiding lost motions, and in doing so reduce the mortality rate. At Lake Placid, Mogensen kept organizing the Work Simplification Conferences for almost 50 years.

BOEING B17

Boeing is an American plane manufacturer producing planes for both civilian and military use. The company was founded in Seattle in the United States by William E. Boeing and George Conrad Westervelt on July 15, 1916, and was named B&W after their initials. Later, the name was changed to Pacific Aero Products, and in 1917, it became Boeing Airplane Company. William E. Boeing had been educated at Yale University, and originally he had earned a lot of money in the forest industry. He acquired a certain knowledge of a breakdown of work processes, simplification, and improvement in dealing with the work that was being done, and thus, the work-flow and the context of processes. He put this knowledge to use in the design and production of airplanes.

Toward the end of the 1930s, Boeing constructed the world's largest passenger plane, the Boeing 314 Clipper, which could hold 90 passengers during daytime flights and 40 passengers during night flights. The plane was designed in cooperation with Pan American World Airways and was used for long-distance international flights. It was a seaplane that could take off and land on the water.

During the Second World War, the company manufactured aircraft for the military and is known for its bombers. The production rate went up dramatically, and they produced about 350 planes each month. These planes were primarily B-17 Flying Fortresses and B-29 Superfortresses. It was planes of the latter type that carried the nuclear bombs to Hiroshima and Nagasaki in Japan, thus contributing to ending the Second World War through the pacification of Japan.

It was a great technological triumph, but the greatest innovation was the handling of the complexity of the job. They started working with checklists. Checklists are not just useful for making sure that every detail is carried out, but also in controlling the context in which it is done.[18] Nowadays, checklists are used in many places, and not just in aviation, but also for precision tasks such as surgery and laser carving. It is one of the first good examples of process documentation for complicated workflows and the breakdown of processes.

BENJAMIN S. GRAHAM

Benjamin S. Graham, Sr. (1900–1960) was a pioneer in the development and use of scientific management and industrial improvement techniques for office work. He is to this day recognized as the founder of "paperwork simplification." He saw a growing need for improvement in dealing with information back in the 1940s when leaders and office staff still constituted a minority of the workforce.[19] Benjamin S. Graham's work sprang from Mogensen's, and focused on the simplification of the work processes.

He was trained in "Work Simplification" by Allan Mogensen and Lillian Gilbreth, later, and adapted Gilbreth's flow process diagrams which had been used to improve the rather complex business processes in factory work. He worked at the Standard Register Company of Dayton, Ohio, and his job was to work out processes so that the employees could study them and streamline them. Graham was invited to participate in Mogensen's conferences to teach simplification of paperwork. His technique for the mapping of processes is used all over the world for business process improvement. While Mogensen's work focused on factory work, Graham adapted the process to integrate the indirect workforce, which he called "Paperwork." He defines this in the light of two terms: "The desired purpose or end result" and "paperwork includes absorption, transmission, analysis, communication, and storing of information/facts".[20]

Graham finds the above information very important, since it will be used as management tools for the employees. He said, "Earlier the purpose was to help the leadership in their decision-making, but it seemed that the message was not being conveyed to the employees. Therefore, the employees constantly tried to "increase production, improve quality, and reduce costs, but in vain, since they had not been given any guidelines." Graham felt that the employees should be involved in the accumulated knowledge.

ASME: AMERICAN SOCIETY OF MECHANICAL ENGINEERS

The American Society of Mechanical Engineers—also known as ASME[21]—is a not-for-profit membership organization that enables collaboration, knowledge sharing, career enrichment, and skills development across all engineering disciplines towards the goal of helping the global engineering community develop solutions to benefit lives and livelihoods. Founded in 1880 by a small group of leading industrialists, ASME has grown through the decades to include more than 130,000 members in 158 countries. Circa thirty-thousand of these members are students.

From college students and early-career engineers to project managers, corporate executives, researchers, and academic leaders, ASME's members are as diverse as the engineering community itself. ASME serves this wide-ranging technical community through quality programs in continuing education, training and professional development, codes and standards, research, conferences and publications, government relations, and other forms of outreach.

A process chart is one of the simplest forms of mapping procedures. Process charts are a common "language" between different groups of people and across several branches of an organizational environment. A set of different process diagrams are designed to meet the needs at a certain level or step in the analysis, and they can be used at a very detailed level (for the monitoring of the activities at a certain place of work) but also in a much larger system, process, or procedure level. The different forms of process diagrams share a common set of symbols, but some have other symbols for specific and specialized steps within the process. The most common and well-known process symbols (of which there are only five) were first announced by the American Society of Mechanical Engineers and are known as the ASME symbols[22] (see Figure 2).

Operation: The Operation symbol represents the handling of goods, preparing and putting away, loading and unloading, and all sorts of activities that do not include the exchange of information. This includes physical "paper carrying" and "electronic paper carrying" activities (i.e., the typing of electronic documents and the use of software applications), and usually there are more of these symbols than any other on the chart.

Checking: The Checking symbol represents the checking of an object to see if it is "all right." The Checking symbol is not used when dealing with normal checking routines within a given work. The purpose of this symbol is to check if a certain job has been done correctly. The Checking symbol is often followed by correction routines.

Transport: The Transport symbol represents a movement from one area of work to another. It is not used for minor movements within a given area of work. The purpose of this symbol is to illustrate the movements that separate the employees from one another and, thus, requires time and resources when the employees have to cooperate across the organizations. These movements are often time-consuming and expensive.

Storage: The Storage symbol represents a period where nothing happens at the step being monitored. We should show the occurrence of storage, when it involves a period of neglect of an existing project, and thus is of importance for the subsequent processes.

Delay: The Delay symbol represents a period which is extended. How short or how long this period is depends on the situation. We should show the occurrence of delays when they involve the consumption of time and when they are of importance to the subsequent processes.

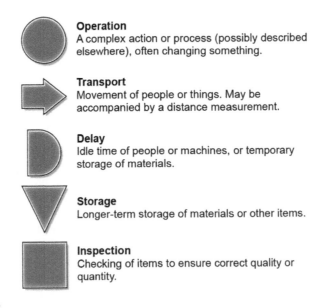

Operation
A complex action or process (possibly described elsewhere), often changing something.

Transport
Movement of people or things. May be accompanied by a distance measurement.

Delay
Idle time of people or machines, or temporary storage of materials.

Storage
Longer-term storage of materials or other items.

Inspection
Checking of items to ensure correct quality or quantity.

FIGURE 2

ASME symbols (Ref. 23).

FUNCTIONAL FLOW BLOCK DIAGRAM OF PERT
Functional Flow Block Diagrams

Functional Flow Block Diagrams (FFBD) surfaced in the 1950s. They are a way of illustrating and describing the processes in a development and production system environment and are a multitiered, time-sequenced, step-by-step flow diagram of a system's functional flow. The FFBD notation (see Figure 3) is widely used in classical systems engineering and is one of the classic business process modeling methodologies, along with flow charts, data flow diagrams, control flow diagrams, Gantt charts, PERT diagrams, and IDEF.[24] FFBDs are also referred to as Functional Flow Diagrams, functional block diagrams, and functional flows.[25]

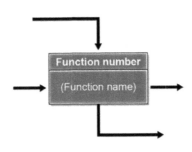

FIGURE 3

FFBD Functional block (Ref. 26).

The purpose of this method is to show the sequential relations between all the functions in a given system. FFBD illustrates the chronological sequence of functional occurrences. The amount of time spent on each function or the time period between two functions are not indicated. FFBD has its focus on functions and shows only which function is to be carried out, but not how this is to be done.

The first structured method for documenting process flow was introduced by Frank B. Gilbreth to members of the American Society of Mechanical Engineers (ASME) in 1921 in his presentation "Process Charts—First Steps in Finding the One Best Way." Gilbreth's tools quickly found their way into industrial engineering curricula. In the early 1930s, Allan H. Mogensen began training business people in the use of some of the tools of industrial engineering at his Work Simplification Conferences at Lake Placid, New York.

A 1944 graduate of Mogensen's class, Art Spinanger, took the tools back to Procter and Gamble where he developed their Deliberate Methods Change Program.[27] Another 1944 graduate, Benjamin S. Graham, Director of Formcraft Engineering at Standard Register Industrial, adapted the flow process chart to information processing with his development of the multiflow process chart to display multiple documents and their relationships. In 1947, ASME adopted a symbol set as the ASME Standard for Operation and Flow Process Charts, derived from Gilbreth's original work. The modern FFBD was developed by TRW Incorporated, a defense-related business, in the 1950s. In the 1960s, it was exploited by NASA to visualize the time sequence of events in space systems and flight missions. FFBDs became widely used in classical systems engineering to show the order of execution of system functions.

PERT: Program Evaluation Review Technique[28]

PERT is a method to analyze the tasks involved in completing a given program, especially the time needed to complete each task, and to identify the minimum time needed to complete the entire program. PERT was developed primarily to simplify the planning and scheduling of large and complex programs and was developed for the United States Navy Special Projects Office in 1957 to support the United States Navy's Polaris nuclear submarine program.[29] It was able to incorporate uncertainty by making it possible to schedule a program while not knowing precisely the details and durations of all the activities. It is more of an event-oriented technique rather than being start- and completion-oriented, and it is mostly used in projects where time is the major factor rather than the cost. It is often applied to large-scale, one-time, complex, nonroutine infrastructure and research and development programs.

An example of this was for the 1968 Winter Olympics in Grenoble, which applied PERT from 1965 until the opening of the 1968 Games. This program model was the first of its kind, a revival for scientific management, founded by Frederick Winslow Taylor (Taylorism) and later refined by Henry Ford (Fordism).

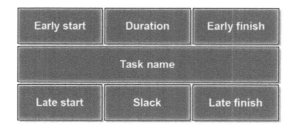

FIGURE 4

The PERT diagram (Ref. 30).

Figure 4 shows one way to describe a PERT diagram. Early start (ES) is the earliest possible starting point. Early finish (EF) is the earliest possible finishing point. EF–ES = duration of the task. The latest starting point (LS) and the latest finishing point (LF) is stated as well.

PERT uses terms like Slack or Float, Lead Time, Lag Time, Critical Way, Fast Tracking, and Crashing. Slack (or Float) states the amount of time that a given task can be delayed without resulting in a delay of the total program. Slack = LF–EF. Lead Time describes when a subsequent task can start before the previous task has been completed. In contrast to this is Lag Time, which describes the waiting time between two tasks (drying time). The Critical Way is the way through the project where you do not experience any Slack. If a task on the Critical Way is delayed, this will result in a total delay if you are using either Fast Tracking or Crashing. Fast Tracking means that you re-plan (if at all possible) and perform several tasks simultaneously on the Critical Way. The advantage of Fast Tracking, as opposed to Crashing, is that there is no increased consumption of resources as a result of the re-planning. Crashing is an attempt to catch up or accelerate activities on the Critical Way by speeding them up. This almost always results in an increased use of resources.

DATA FLOW DIAGRAMS AND IDEF

Data Flow Diagram

A Data Flow Diagram (DFD) is a graphical representation of the "flow" of data through an information system (as shown on the DFD flow chart in Figure 5), modeling its process aspects. Often it is a preliminary step used to create an overview of the system that can later be elaborated. DFDs can also be used for the visualization of data processing (structured design) and show what kind of information will be input to and output from the system, where the data will come from and go to, and where the data will be stored. It does not show information about the timing of processes or information about whether processes will operate in sequence or in parallel.

FIGURE 5

An example of a Data Flow Diagram (Ref. 31).

It is common practice to draw the context-level data flow diagram first, which shows the interaction between the system and external agents that act as data sources and data sinks. This helps to create an accurate drawing in the context diagram. The system's interactions with the outside world are modeled purely in terms of data flows across the system boundary. The context diagram shows the entire system as a single process and gives no clues as to its internal organization.

This context-level DFD is next "exploded" to produce a Level 1 DFD that shows some of the detail of the system being modeled. The Level 1 DFD shows how the system is divided into subsystems (processes), each of which deals with one or more of the data flows to or from an external agent, and which together provide all of the functionality of the system as a whole. It also identifies internal data stores that must be present in order for the system to do its job and shows the flow of data between the various parts of the system.

Integrated Definition

IDEF is an abbreviation of Integrated Definition. It is a modulation method that is used in system and software design. It is a broad-spectrum model, and it covers a lot of applications within data modulation, simulation, object-oriented analysis/design, and gathering of information (Figure 6).

IDEF contains a lot of different variables, of which the most commonly used is IDEF0, which is the only model described here. IDEF0 is focused on describing decisions, actions, and activities in an organization or a system. Just like DFD, IDEF0 shows the data flow between various functions.

IDEF0[32] Overview: Function Modeling Method

IDEF0 is a method designed to model the decisions, actions, and activities of an organization or system. IDEF0 was derived from a well-established graphical language, the Structured Analysis and Design Technique (SADT). The United States Air Force commissioned the developers of SADT to develop a function modeling method for analyzing and communicating the functional perspective of a system. Effective IDEF0 models help to organize the analysis of a system and to promote good communication between the analyst and the customer. IDEF0 is useful in establishing the scope of an analysis, especially for a functional analysis.

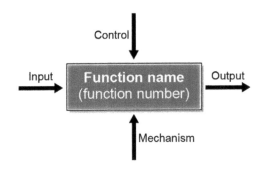

FIGURE 6

IDEF0 basis format (Ref. 33).

IDEF1[34] Overview: Information Modeling Method

IDEF1 was designed as a method for both analysis and communication in the establishment of requirements. IDEF1 is generally used to (1) identify what information is currently managed in the organization, (2) determine which of the problems identified during the needs analysis are caused by lack of management of appropriate information, and (3) specify what information will be managed in the TO-BE implementation.

IDEF1 captures the information that exists about objects within the scope of an enterprise. The IDEF1 perspective of an information system includes not only the automated system components, but also non-automated objects such as people, filing cabinets, telephones, etc. IDEF1 was designed as a method for organizations to analyze and clearly state their information resource management needs and requirements. Rather than a database design method, IDEF1 is an analysis method used to identify the following:

• Information collected, stored, and managed by the enterprise.
• Rules governing the management of information.
• Logical relationships within the enterprise reflected in the information.
• Problems resulting from the lack of good information management.

IDEF1X[35] Overview: Data Modeling Method

IDEF1X is a method for designing relational databases with a syntax designed to support the semantic constructs necessary in developing a conceptual schema. A conceptual schema is a single integrated definition of the enterprise data that is unbiased toward any single application and independent of its access and physical storage. Because it is a design method, IDEF1X is not particularly suited to serve as an AS-IS analysis tool, although it is often used in that capacity as an alternative to IDEF1. IDEF1X is most useful for logical database design after the information requirements are known and the decision to implement a relational database has been made. Hence, the IDEF1X system perspective is focused on the actual data elements in a relational database. If the target system is not a relational system, for example, an object-oriented system, IDEF1X is not the best method.

IDEF3[36] Overview: Process Description Capture Method

The IDEF3 Process Description Capture Method provides a mechanism for collecting and documenting processes. IDEF3 captures precedence and causality relations between situations and events in a form natural to domain experts by providing a structured method for expressing knowledge about how a system, process, or organization works. IDEF3 descriptions can do the following:

- Record the raw data resulting from fact-finding interviews in systems analysis activities.
- Determine the impact of an organization's information resource on the major operation scenarios of an enterprise.
- Document the decision procedures affecting the states and life-cycle of critical shared data, particularly manufacturing, engineering, and maintenance product definition data.
- Manage data configuration and change control policy definition.
- Make system design and design trade-off analysis.
- Provide simulation model generation.

IDEF4[37] Overview: Object-Oriented Design Method

The intuitive nature of object-oriented programming makes it easier to produce code. Unfortunately, the ease with which software is produced also makes it easier to create software of poor design, resulting in systems lacking re-usability, modularity, and maintainability. The IDEF4 method is designed to assist in the correct application of this technology.

IDEF5[38] Overview: Ontology Description Capture Method

The IDEF5 method provides a theoretically and empirically well-grounded method specifically designed to assist in creating, modifying, and maintaining ontologies. Standardized procedures, the ability to represent ontology information in an intuitive and natural form, and higher quality results enabled through IDEF5 application also serve to reduce the cost of these activities.

ZERO DEFECTS

The theory of Zero Defects was first brought into use in the space and defense industry in the United States in 1960. The term Zero Defects expresses the idea that a product which meets the requirements of the consumer is the right product. If the product can do more or less than needed, it is a waste of resources.

Thus, a cheap product can be just as good as an expensive one if it meets the expectations of the client.

In 1979, quality expert Philip Crosby penned *Quality Is Free: The Art of Making Quality Certain*, which preserved the idea of Zero Defects in a 14-step quality improvement program and the concept of the "Absolutes of Quality Management." Zero Defects seeks to directly reverse the attitude that the amount of mistakes a worker makes does not matter since inspectors will catch them before they reach the customer. This stands in contrast to activities that affect the worker directly, such as receiving a paycheck in the correct amount. Zero Defects involves reconditioning the worker to "take a personal interest in everything he does by convincing him that his job is just as important as the task of the doctor or the dentist."

According to Crosby, there are four Absolutes:

1. **Quality is conformance to requirements**

   Every product or service has a requirement: a description of what the customer needs. When a particular product meets that requirement, it has achieved quality, provided that the requirement accurately describes what the enterprise and the customer actually need. This technical sense should not be confused with more common usages that indicate weight or goodness or precious materials or some absolute idealized standard. In common parlance, an inexpensive disposable pen is a lower-quality item than a gold-plated fountain pen. In the technical sense of Zero Defects, the inexpensive disposable pen is a quality product if it meets requirements: it writes, does not skip or clog under normal use, and lasts the time specified.

2. **Defect prevention is preferable to quality inspection and correction**

   The second principle is based on the observation that it is nearly always less troublesome, more certain, and less expensive to prevent defects than to discover and correct them. It saves a lot of human power and cost of inspection and correction. For example, if a person changes the poor condition brake shoes of his bike before next riding, then it will save a lot of the rider's energy and reduce the risk of accident on the road, not to mention the generation of new defects in the bike due to poorly conditioned brake shoes, which when observed later will have a higher cost of repair.

3. **Zero Defects is the quality standard**

   The third is based on the normative nature of requirements: if a requirement expresses what is genuinely needed, then any unit that does not meet requirements will not satisfy the need and is no good. If units that do not meet requirements actually do satisfy the need, then the requirement should be changed to reflect reality. Furthermore, the idea that mistakes are inevitable is rejected out of hand. Just as the CEO wouldn't accept "mistakenly" not getting paid occasionally, his/her chauffeur "mistakenly" driving them to the wrong business, or their spouse "mistakenly" sleeping with someone else, so the company should not take the attitude that they'll "inevitably" fail to deliver what was promised from time to time. Aiming at an "acceptable" defect level encourages and causes defects.

4. **Quality is measured in monetary terms—the Price of Nonconformance (PONC)**

The fourth principle is key to the methodology. Phil Crosby believes that every defect represents a cost, which is often hidden. These costs include inspection time, rework, wasted material and labor, lost revenue, and the cost of customer dissatisfaction. When properly identified and accounted for, the magnitude of these costs can be made apparent, which has three advantages. First, it provides a cost justification for steps to improve quality. The title of the book *Quality is Free* expresses the belief that improvements in quality will return savings more than equal to the costs. Second, it provides a way to measure progress, which is essential to maintaining management commitment and to rewarding employees. Third, by making the goal measurable, actions can be made concrete, and decisions can be made on the basis of relative return.

Another principle that Crosby stresses is that it is much cheaper and more efficient to prevent errors than to check and remedy errors later. Crosby formulated the idea that Zero Defects was what was expected, and one defect or error means that the product does not meet the expectations. In cases where the product meets the needs but not the expectations, the expectations will have to be adapted to the need.

Crosby thought that every error or defect represented an expense, which is often camouflaged. Whether it is control, lost materials, reparations, or extra labor, this expense has to be made visible. By mapping these factors, you would gain three advantages:

1. An expense that can justify the quality improvement effort.
2. A valuable measuring tool that allows you to monitor the progress and motivate or reward the employees.
3. A valuable foundation for decisions on where to put in an extra effort.

Crosby's principles had their renaissance in the 1990s when the battered American car industry needed to make cuts in the budget. By increasing the requirements to the suppliers, they could downsize several quality control functions and, thus, save a lot of money.

TOYOTA PRODUCTION SYSTEM

Toyota's production system (TPS) was developed between 1948 and 1975 by Taichi Ohno, Shigeo Shingo and the grandchild of the founder of Toyota, Eiji Toyoda. One of the most popular books written by the founders themselves is *Just-In-Time for Today and Tomorrow* (Ohno et al., 1988), which accounts for the philosophy behind TPS. TPS is based on a scientific production method.[39] When Eiji Toyoda returned from a trip to the United States to learn about mass production from Ford, the factory manager at Toyota, Taiichi Ohno, was given the task of improving the production processes at Toyota to achieve the same level of productivity as Ford. Toyota had only limited funds and, therefore, had to find a way to increase flexibility and efficiency.

This lead to the Toyota Production System (TPS). The TPS concept focuses on a set of main ideas. The first is the elimination of all waste. Waste is to be understood as anything superfluous that does not add any value (i.e., defect components, unnecessary processes, downtime, etc.). The other two main ideas are a constant improvement of processes as well as people (we respect others) and teamwork (stimulate personal and professional growth).

The Toyota Production System (TPS) was established based on two concepts: The first is called "jidoka" (which can be loosely translated as "automation with a human touch"), which means that when a problem occurs, the equipment stops immediately, preventing defective products from being produced; The second is the concept of "Just-in-Time," in which each process produces only what is needed by the next process in a continuous flow.

Jidoka: Highlighting/Visualization of Problems

Quality must be built in during the manufacturing process!

If equipment malfunction or a defective part is discovered, the affected machine automatically stops, and operators cease production and correct the problem. For the Just-in-Time system to function, all of the parts that are made and supplied must meet predetermined quality standards. This is achieved through jidoka.

1. Jidoka means that a machine safely stops when the normal processing is completed. It also means that, should a quality/equipment problem arise, the machine detects the problem on its own and stops, preventing defective products from being produced. As a result, only products satisfying quality standards will be passed on to the following processes on the production line.
2. Since a machine automatically stops when processing is completed or when a problem arises and is communicated via the "andon" (problem display board), operators can confidently continue performing work at another machine, as well as easily identify the problem's cause to prevent its recurrence. This means that each operator can be in charge of many machines, resulting in higher productivity, while continuous improvements lead to greater processing capacity.

Just-In-Time: Productivity Improvement

Making only "what is needed, when it is needed, and in the amount needed!"

Just-in-Time means producing quality products efficiently through the complete elimination of waste, inconsistencies, and unreasonable requirements on the production line. In order to deliver a vehicle ordered by a customer as quickly as possible, the vehicle is efficiently built within the shortest possible period of time by adhering to the following:

1. When a vehicle order is received, a production instruction must be issued to the beginning of the vehicle production line as soon as possible.
2. The assembly line must be stocked with the required number of all needed parts so that any type of ordered vehicle can be assembled.
3. The assembly line must replace the parts used by retrieving the same number of parts from the parts-producing process (the preceding process).
4. The preceding process must be stocked with small numbers of all types of parts and produce only the numbers of parts that were retrieved by an operator from the next process.

Based on the basic philosophies of jidoka and Just-in-Time, the TPS can efficiently and quickly produce vehicles of sound quality, one at a time, that fully satisfy customer requirements.

The entire Toyota "house" is shown in Figure 7. The roof can only be held up by Just-In-Time (JIT) and Jidoka, which is achieved through people's efforts and the reduction of waste. The idea of minimizing waste led to the Lean principle, which states that any activity that does not add value must be cut off.

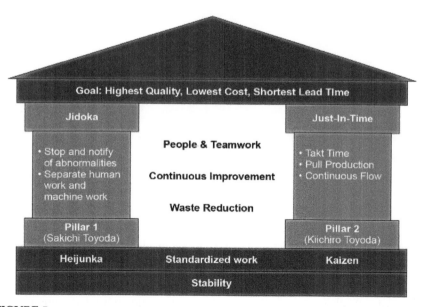

FIGURE 7

The TPS house (Ref. 40).

Toyota identified seven kinds of waste that had to be eliminated: overproduction, waiting time, unnecessary transport, over processing or misprocessing, superfluous storage, unnecessary movement, defects, and unutilized employee creativity. The entire Toyota concept states that only by combining JIT and Jidoka can you achieve the goal of the best quality, lowest costs, shortest lead time, the greatest safety, and high morale.

The 14 Principles of TPS

All in all, there are 14 principles in TPS, which are divided into four main areas[41] that we will describe in the following sections. These four sections are illustrated as a pyramid in Figure 8.

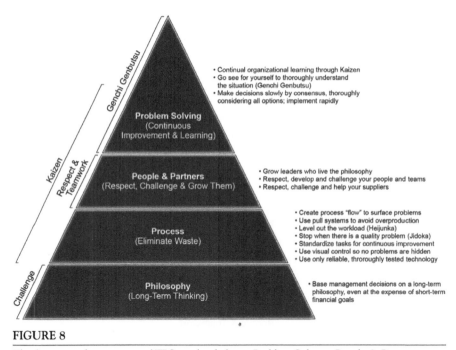

FIGURE 8

The four overriding sections of TPS are divided into Problem Solving, People & Partners, Process, and Philosophy.

Long-Term Philosophy

Principle 1: Base your management decisions on a long-term philosophy, even at the expense of short-term financial goals.

• Have a philosophical sense of purpose that supersedes any short-term decision making. Work, grow, and align the whole organization toward a common purpose that is bigger than making money. Understand your place in the history of the company and work to bring the company to the next level. Your philosophical mission is the foundation for the other principles.

- Generate a value of the customer, society, and the economy—it is your starting point. Evaluate every function in the company in terms of the ability to achieve this.
- Be responsible. Strive to decide your own fate. Act with self-reliance and trust in your own abilities. Accept responsibility for your own conduct and maintain to improve the skills that enable you to produce added value.

The Right Process Will Produce the Right Results

Principle 2: Create continuous process flow to bring problems to the surface.

- Redesign work processes to achieve high-value-added, continuous flow. Strive to cut back to zero the amount of the time that any work project is sitting idle or waiting for someone to work on it.
- Create flow to move material and information fast, as well as to link processes and people together so that problems surface right way.
- Make flow evident throughout your organizational culture. It is the key to a true continuous improvement process and to developing people.

Principle 3: Use "Pull" system to avoid overproduction.

- Provide your downline customers in the production process with what they want, when they want it, and in the amount they want it. Material replenishment is initiated by consumption in the basic principle of just-in-time.
- Minimize your work in process and warehousing of inventory by stocking small amounts of each product and frequently restocking based on what the customer actually takes away.
- Be responsive to the day-by-day shifts in customer demand rather than relying on computer schedules and systems to track wasteful inventory.

Principle 4: Level out the workload (heijunka).

- Eliminating waste is just one-third of the equation for making Lean successful. Eliminating overburden to people and equipment and eliminating unevenness in the production schedule is just as important—yet, generally not understood at companies attempting to implement Lean principles.
- Work to level out the workload of all manufacturing and service processes as an alternative to the start/stop approach of working on projects in batches that is typical at most companies.

Principle 5: Build a culture of "stopping to fix problems to get quality right the first time".

- Quality of the customer drives your value proposition.
- Use all the modern quality assurance methods available.
- Build into your equipment the capability of detecting problems and stopping itself. Develop a visual system to alert team or project leaders that a machine or process needs assistance. Jidoka (machines with human intelligence) is the foundation for "building in" quality.

- Build into your organization support systems to quickly solve the problems and put in place countermeasures.
- Build into your culture the philosophy of stopping or slowing down to get quality right the first time to enhance productivity in the long run.

Principle 6: Standardized tasks are the foundation for continuous improvements and employee empowerment.

- Use stable, repeatable methods everywhere to maintain the predictability, regular timing, and regular output of your processes. It is the foundation for the flow and pull.
- Capture the accumulated learning about a process up to a point in time by standardizing today's best practices. Allow creative and individual expression to improve upon the standard; then incorporate it into the new standard so that when a person moves on, you can hand off the learning to the next person.

Principle 7: Use Visual Control so no problems are hidden.

- Use simple visual indicators to help people determine immediately whether they are in standard condition or deviating from it.
- Avoid using a computer screen when it moves the worker's focus away from the workplace.
- Design a simple visual system at the workplace where the work is done to support flow and pull.
- Reduce your reports to one piece of paper whenever possible, even for your most important financial decisions.

Principle 8: Use only reliable, thoroughly tested technology that serves your people and process.

- Use technology to support people, not to replace people. Often it is best to work out the process manually before adding technology to support the people.
- New technology is often unreliable and difficult to standardize and, therefore, endangers "flow." A proven process that works generally takes precedence over new and untested technology.
- Conduct actual tests before adopting new technology in business processes, manufacturing systems, or products.
- Reject or modify technologies that conflict with your culture or that might disrupt stability, reliability, and predictability.
- Nevertheless, encourage your people to consider new technologies when looking into new approaches to work. Quickly implement a thoroughly considered technology if it has been proven in trials and if it can improve the flow in your processes.

Add Value to Your Organization by Developing Your People and Partners

Principle 9: Grow leaders who thoroughly understand the work, live philosophy, and teach it to others.

- Grow leaders within, rather than buying them from outside the organization.
- Do not view the leader's job as simply accomplishing tasks and having good people skills. Leaders must be role models for the company's philosophy and the way of doing business.
- A leader must understand the daily work in great detail so that he or she can be the best teacher of your company's philosophy.

Principle 10: Develop exceptional people and teams who follow your company's philosophy.

- Create a strong, stable culture, in which company values and beliefs are widely shared and lived out over a period of many years.
- Train exceptional individuals and teams to work within the corporate philosophy to achieve exceptional results. Work hard to reinforce the culture continually.
- Use cross-functional teams to improve quality and productivity and enhance flow by solving difficult technical problems. Empowerment occurs only when people use the company's tools to improve the company.
- Make an ongoing effort to teach individuals how to work together as teams toward common goals. Teamwork is something that has to be learned.

Principle 11: Respect your extended network of partners and suppliers by challenging them and helping them to improve.

- Have respect for your partners and suppliers and treat them as an extension of your business.
- Challenge your outside business partners to grow and develop. It shows that you value them. Set challenging targets and assist your partners in achieving them.

Continuously Solving Root Problems Drives Organizational Learnings
Principle 12: Go and see for yourself to thoroughly understand the situation (genchi genbutsu).

- Solve problems and improve processes by going to the source and personally observing and verifying data, rather than theorizing on the basis of what other people or the computer screen tell you.
- Think and speak based on personally verified data.
- Even high-level managers and executives should go and see things for themselves, so they will have more than a superficial understanding of the situation.

Principle 13: Make a decision slowly by consensus, thoroughly considering all options; implement decisions rapidly.

- Do not pick a single direction and go down that one path until you have thoroughly considered alternatives.
- Nemawashi is the process of discussing problems and potential solutions with all of those affected, to collect their ideas and get agreement on a path forward. This consensus process, though time-consuming, helps broaden the

search for solutions, and once a decision is made, the stage is set for rapid implementation.

Principle 14: Become a learning organization through relentless reflection (hansei) and continuous improvements (kaizen).

- Once you have established a stable process, use continuous improvement tools to determine the root cause of inefficiencies and apply effective countermeasures.
- Design processes that require almost no inventory. This will make wasted time and resources visible for all to see. Once waste is exposed, have employees use a continuous improvement process (kaizen) to eliminate it.
- Protect the organizational knowledge base by developing stable personnel, slow promotion, and very careful succession systems.

End Notes

1. ToolsHero.com: Henry L. Gantt from http://www.toolshero.com/henry-gantt.
2. Philip B. Crosby *Quality Is Free: The Art of Making Quality Certain: How to Manage Quality–So That It Becomes A Source of Profit for Your Business*, (1979).
3. Taiichi Ohno and Setsuo Mito., *Just-In-Time for Today and Tomorrow*, (1988).
4. *Mastering Power Production: The Industrial, Economic and Social Problems Involved and Their Solution*, (Walter Nicholas Polakov, 1923).
5. Gantt H.L. et al., published by The Engineering Magazine, New York, 1910; republished as Work, Wages and Profits, Easton, Pennsylvania, Hive Publishing Company, 1974.
6. Gantt Chart from http://www.gantt.com/.
7. *The One Best Way, Frederick Winslow Taylor and the Enigma of Efficiency*.
8. The Ben Graham Corporation, "Business Process Improvement Methodology for Graham Process Charting Software", 57–58.
9. http://pascal.computer.org/sev_display/search.action;jsessionid=C022AFA5E46051D302 D9E138E7A90DAF. D. 30. October 2009 –kl. 20.00 (Software and System Engineering Vocabulary).
10. Frank Bunker Gilbreth, Tom Ricci, http://www.ASME.org, 2012.
11. F. W. Taylor: Critical Evaluations in Business and Management, Volume 2, John Cunningham Wood, Michael C. Wood, Taylor & Francis, 2002.
12. Dr. Ben S. Graham. Jr, *Flowchart*.
13. George C.S., *The history of management thought*, 100–101.
14. Dr. Ben S. Graham Jr., Allan Mogensen and his Legacy, p. 5.
15. Mogensen A.H., *Common sense applied to motion and time study*, (McGraw-Hill, 1932).
16. Ben G, Rediscover Work Simplification, 1–2.
17. Allan H. Mogensen, Carry Out a Methods Improvement Program, 1949 at http://www.nickols.us/Mogensen.pdf.
18. Schamel J., *How the Pilot's Checklist Came About*. (FAA Flight Service Training, Retrieved 12 January 2007). "The idea of a pilot's checklist spread to other crew members, other Air Corps aircraft types, and eventually throughout the aviation world".
19. http://en.wikipedia.org/wiki/Benjamin_S._Graham 30.09.2009 21:34.
20. Ben S., Graham Sr., *Paperwork Simplification*.
21. https://www.asme.org/.

22. A.S.M.E. *standard operation and flow process charts, developed by the A.S.M.E. Special committee on standardization of therbligs, process charts, and their symbols,* (1947).

23. Henzold G., *Geometrical Dimensioning and Tolerancing for Design, Manufacturing and Inspection.* 2nd ed., (Oxford, UK: Elsevier, 2006).

24. Thomas Dufresne and James Martin, *Methods for Information Systems Engineering: Knowledge Management and E-Business* (2003).

25. *Task Analysis Tools Used Throughout Development* (FAA, 2008).

26. Graham B. B., *Detail Process Charting: Speaking the Language of Process* (2004).

27. Motivating People to Work: The Key to Improving Productivity, Warren C. Hauck, Industrial Engineering and Management Press, 1984.

28. Tim Weilkiens., *Systems Engineering with SysML/UML: Modeling, Analysis, Design,* 287.

29. Malcolm D.G., et al., *Application of a Technique for Research and Development Program Evaluation Operations Research* vol. 7, no. 5, (September–October 1959), 646–669.

30. Tim Weilkiens., *Systems Engineering with SysML/UML: Modeling, Analysis, Design* (2008), 287.

31. John Azzolini., *Introduction to Systems Engineering Practices.* (July 2000).

32. http://www.idef.com/IDEF0.htm.

33. *ICAM Architecture Part II, Volume V–Information Modeling Manual (IDEF1), AFWAL-TR-81–4023, Materials Laboratory, Air Force Wright Aeronautical Laboratories, Air Force Systems Command,* (Wright-Patterson Air Force Base, Ohio 45433, June 1981).

34. http://www.idef.com/IDEF1.htm.

35. http://www.idef.com/IDEF1x.htm.

36. http://www.idef.com/IDEF3.htm.

37. http://www.idef.com/IDEF4.htm.

38. http://www.idef.com/IDEF5.htm.

39. Ohno T., *Toyota Production System: Beyond Large-scale Production* (Productivity Press Inc, 1995).

40. Liker J.K., Chapter 3 "The TPS House Diagram" *The Toyota Way: 14 Management Principles from the World's Greatest Manufacturer* (McGraw Hill, 2004).

41. Jeffrey Liker, *The Toyota Way: 14 Management Principles from the World's Greatest Manufacturer,* First edition, McGraw-Hill (2003).

Phase 3: Process Concept Evolution

Mark von Rosing, August-Wilhelm Scheer, John A. Zachman, Daniel T. Jones, James P. Womack, Henrik von Scheel

INTRODUCTION

In this book, we have until now covered key figures like Adam Smith, Frederick Winslow Taylor, Henry Ford, and many others who have dramatically impacted the way of thinking of, working with, and how we model processes. This chapter of the book will elaborate on the move from process-centric work around labor and people to the coupling of information technology (IT) aspects with process modeling aspects. We witness a much wider and more profound involvement of IT with the incorporation of processes in business and organizations across geographical borders and cultural differences.

With the entry of Phase 3 at the beginning of the 1980s, Professor August-Wilhelm Scheer founded his company, IDS Scheer, in Germany. IDS Scheer is a consulting and development firm focusing on business process management (BPM)[1] and is widely regarded as a frontrunner and pioneer of today's BPM industry. Professor August-Wilhelm Scheer would later launch the Architecture of Integrated Information Systems (ARIS) concept in 1991—a system concept that would allow company data to be associated with information flows, function, and control while simultaneously be supervised by different management viewpoints for the sake of business clarity and a better control of circumstances and process execution within the organization.

In 1987, John Zachman (born December 16, 1934), an American business and IT consultant and early pioneer of Enterprise Architecture[2], published his initial framework named "A Framework for Information Systems Architecture"[3] in an article in the IBM Systems Journal. This would lead to the ongoing development of what is now known as the Zachman Framework for Enterprise Architecture—a conceptual development of a framework that intends to establish principles for and to document how an enterprise is constructed and designed through the use of accountabilities, responsibilities, interrogatives, functions, control, information and process flows, infrastructure and technology, etc. This framework would be the very first concept to relate an entire enterprise with information systems and business processes and—although not discussed in this chapter—would then spark the development of many more frameworks in the future.

After World War II, Taiichi Ohno and Shingeo Shingo created the "Just In Time," "Waste Reduction," and "Pull System" concepts for Toyota, which, together with other flow management techniques, resulted in the Toyota Production System (TPS).[4] Ever since its initial conception during the early 1970s, the TPS has undergone industrial evolution and matured dramatically while being constantly improved upon by industry professionals as well as throughout the academic world. In 1990, James Womack summarized the TPS concepts to create Lean Manufacturing[5] at a time when Japanese expertise was spreading to the West, and the success achieved by companies applying these principles and techniques became undeniable. Then, in 2005, James P. Womack and Daniel T. Jones published an article in the Harvard Business Review describing a new theory called "Lean Consumption."[6] While "Lean Manufacturing" set out ways to streamline manufacturing processes, Lean Consumption *minimizes customers' time and effort by delivering exactly what they want, when, and where they want it.*

Perhaps one of the biggest ideas in the 1990s was conceived by Dr Michael Hammer, an American engineer, management author, and a former professor of computer science at the Massachusetts Institute of Technology (MIT), as he introduced the business world to a concept he called business process reengineering (BPR).[7] BPR involves the redesign of core business processes to achieve improvements in productivity, cycle times, and quality. In BPR, companies start with a blank sheet of paper and rethink existing processes to deliver more value to the customer. The terms *process improvement, process excellence,* and *process innovation* were all coined by Dr Michael Hammer.

In the 1980s to the 1990s, a new phase of quality control and management began. This became known as total quality management (TQM).[8] Having observed Japan's success of employing quality management, western companies started to introduce their own quality initiatives.[9] TQM developed as a catchall phrase for the broad spectrum of quality-focused strategies, programs, and techniques during this period, and became the center of focus for the western quality movement.[10]

A typical definition[11] of TQM includes phrases such as the following:

- Customer focus
- The involvement of all employees
- Continuous improvement
- The integration of quality management throughout the entire organization

Although the definitions were all similar, there was confusion. It was not clear what sort of practices, policies, and activities needed to be implemented to fit the TQM definition. Some of the tools involved with the implementation of the TQM concept in organizations were such as:

- House of Quality or Quality Function Deployment (QFD)[12]
- Taguchi techniques[13]
- Pareto diagrams[14]
- Process diagrams
- Cause and effect analysis diagrams—also known as root cause analysis
- Statistical process control (SPC)[15]
- The Plan, Do, Check, Act (PDCA) Cycle[16]
- The EFQM Excellence Model[17] or simply "business excellence"

In the early and mid-1980s, with Chairman Bob Galvin at the front, Motorola engineers decided that the traditional quality levels—measuring defects in thousands of instances—did not provide enough granularity. Instead, they wanted to measure the defects per million instances. Six Sigma[18] was then theorized by Bill Smith in 1986, upon formulating the strategic concepts of Motorola.[19] Motorola developed this new standard and created the methodology and the needed cultural change associated with it. Since then, hundreds of companies around the world have adopted Six Sigma as a way of doing business. This is a direct result of many of America's leaders openly praising the benefits of Six Sigma, leaders such as Larry Bossidy of Allied Signal (now Honeywell) and Jack Welch of General Electric.

PROF. DR. DR. H.C. MULT. AUGUST-WILHELM SCHEER

Introduction

One of the key figures in leading the new ways of thinking, working and modeling with business processes was the German Professor and Entrepreneur August-Wilhelm Scheer. He developed the concept of using the business process as the anchor for his "architecture of integrated information systems" (ARIS)[20] covering design, implementation, execution and control of business processes. His approach is considered innovative and groundbreaking. Scheer founded his first company, IDS Scheer AG, based on his ARIS approach. IDS Scheer is an international software and consulting company that develops, markets, and supports Business Process Management (BPM) solutions around the world. The software tool "ARIS Toolset"[21] became the global market leader for process modeling and repository tools. Amongst many other things, the following can be mentioned that Prof. Scheer has developed or left his mark upon by pushing the bar with his research, entrepreneurship as well as his focus on integrating business and IT:

- The link between process management and information technology. The ability to link processes and IT changed everything around process concepts, including the way of thinking, working, modeling and automating processes.
- His contribution to the academic world includes: In 1975 Scheer took over one of the first chairs for information systems and founded the Institute for Information Systems (IWI) at the Saarland University, which he led until 2005.
- His contribution to the Software world includes: In 1984 he founded IDS Scheer—a Business Process Management (BPM) software and consulting company. Its flagship product, the ARIS Toolset, is still today the market leader.
- His contribution to the Process Modeling[22] community includes: He developed among others the 2 main methods for Business Process Modeling:
  1) Value-added Chain Diagrams (VCD).
  2) Event-driven Process Chains (EPC).
- His contribution to Enterprise Modelling and Architecture includes: The ARIS House which is one of the first Enterprise Architecture and Modeling frameworks that combines and organizes information of an organization in five interrelated views: data, function, organization, output, and control (Figure 1).

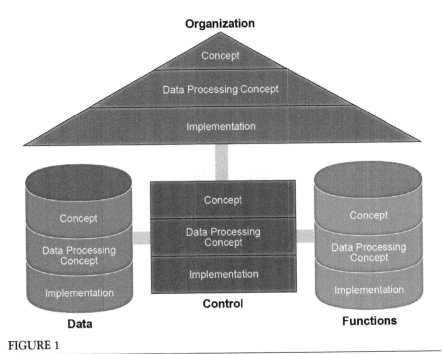

FIGURE 1

The Architecture of Integrated Information Systems (ARIS) model.

Prof. Scheer is widely regarded as the founder of the BPM industry. In this chapter we briefly explain why.

A New Way of Thinking: Linking Process and Information Concepts

It was in 1984 when two important events took place; Scheer's thinking about "IT oriented Business Administration"[23] was published, and in the same year he founded IDS Scheer which can be regarded as the frontrunner and foundation of the BPM industry. The notion of "business process" had been front and center of IDS Scheer from the beginning. Other important book publications followed, for example "Business Engineering"[24], "CIM—The Factory of the Future"[25] and, of course, the two books on ARIS. IDS Scheer quickly became a sought after advisor for large companies like Bosch and Daimler. The major business processes of the "CIM Organization" has been represented in the popular "Y Model"—a symbol that is a distinguishing feature of IDS Scheer's company logo.

Parallel to the set-up of his company IDS Scheer, Prof. Scheer researched methods of business user-oriented description of information systems[26] and the underlying technologies. Contrary to previous traditional thinking, the business process was now being treated as the critical link between people and IT. The ability to link process and information technology changed everything around process management approaches because Scheer's approach met the demand for simplicity for the business user and—at the same time—delivers the methodological stringency for the transfer of process design into information technology-based execution. This approach is also represented in the ARIS Framework and was already being rolled out globally in 1991.

Architecture of Integrated Information Systems (ARIS)

Architecture of Integrated Information Systems (ARIS) is an approach to enterprise modeling and enterprise architecture. It offers methods for managing the entire life cycle of processes while taking a holistic view of the organization, data, functions, deliverables, and last but not least, the control flows (Figure 1). Based on the ARIS Framework[27], the ARIS software tool was developed—the ARIS Software tool is a modelling and repository software system.

The ARIS Framework facilitates the use of all available modeling methods, including the mentioned previously Event-driven Process Chains (EPC) and the Business Process Modeling Notation (BPMN). The ARIS Toolset supports over 250 modeling methods. These modeling methods address the different views on a business process as it is illustrated in ARIS (see Figure 2).

- Organizational view
- Data view
- Control view
- Functional view

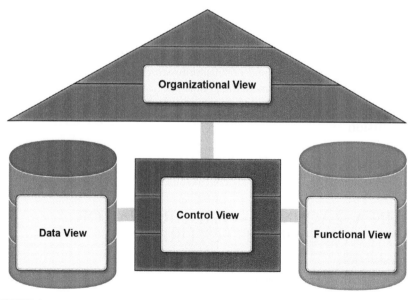

FIGURE 2

The Architecture of Integrated Information Systems (ARIS) view model.

Each view of ARIS can be described in different levels of abstraction, starting with a pure business layer, ending in an implementation-oriented IT description layer. This allows the systematic link of business approaches to the underlying enabling IT.

Additional Important Aspects

In 1997, Scheer also founded a company focused on innovative learning and education technologies and approaches, called IMC AG. This company addresses the people-side of a process implementation. Other company start ups quickly followed—all of them focusing on topics around the integration of business processes and IT.

In 2003, Scheer was awarded the Philip Morris Research Prize and the Ernst & Young Entrepreneur of the Year Award. In December 2005, he received the Erich Gutenberg price and in the same month the Federal Cross of Merit first class of Germany was awarded to him. In 2005 he was elected a fellow of the "Gesellschaft für Informatik", a renowned German research organization. Since 2006, Scheer has been a member of the council for innovation and growth of the Federal Government of Germany. In 2007, he was honored as a "HPI-Fellow" by the Hasso-Plattner Institut (HPI) für Softwaresystemtechnik" and was elected President of the German Association for Information Technology, Telecommunications and New Media.

In 2010, Scheer was awarded the Design Science Lifetime Achievement Award at the University of St. Gallen. He received the award as a recognition of his contribution to design science research.

In 2014, the Global University Alliance (a collaborative, academic alliance consisting of more than 300 universities) and the LEADing Practice Community (a professional community consisting of more than 3200 certified practitioners) decided to honor August-Wilhelm Scheer with the LEADing Practice Lifetime Achievement Award in recognition of his long-term impact and contribution to evolve both the business and academic world and organizations structural way of thinking and way of working around enterprise modelling concepts.

Conclusion

Scheer has revolutionized the way we manage processes and link business to information technology. Frameworks like ARIS and the Y-CIM model have fundamentally transformed academia and practice regarding business process management.

JOHN A. ZACHMAN—THE ARRIVAL OF ENTERPRISE ARCHITECTURE

Introduction

John A. Zachman is the originator of the first "Concept of the Framework for Enterprise Architecture," which is widely regarded as the birth of enterprise architecture. With the arrival of the first enterprise architecture descriptions, concepts and frameworks, there was a clear link being established and built between the already established—although young and immature—business process landscape that had evolved prior to the introduction of enterprise architecture. This link, in particular, was mostly focusing on establishing a connection between ownerships (who is accountable), interrogatives (why are we doing this, and how should we do it), information systems[28] (connecting data to functionality and information flows), and the need for detailed representation of all of these functions and activities.

Zachman is not only known for his work on enterprise architecture, but is also known for his early contributions to IBM's Information Strategy methodology (Business Systems Planning)[29] as well as to their executive team planning techniques (Intensive Planning). Mr. Zachman retired from IBM in 1990, having served them for 26 years. He is the founder and chairman of Zachman International, an enterprise architecture research and education company. He is also the Executive Director of FEAC Inc, the Federated Enterprise Architecture Certification Institute, that issues certifications for DoDAF (the Department of Defense Architecture Framework), FEAF (the Federal Enterprise Architecture Framework), and Zachman (the Zachman Ontological Framework).[30]

Mr. Zachman serves on the Executive Council for Information Management and Technology (ECIMT) of the United States Government Accountability Office (GAO) and on the Advisory Board of the Data Administration Management Association International (DAMA-I) from whom he was awarded the 2002 Lifetime Achievement Award. In November 2013, he was acknowledged for Achievement and Excellence for Distinguished Innovative Academic Contribution by the IEEE Systems, Man and Cybernetics Society Technical Committees on Enterprise Information Systems and on Enterprise Architecture and Engineering. In August 2011, he was awarded the General Colin Powell Public Sector Image Award by the Armed Services Alliance Program. He was awarded the 2009 Enterprise Architecture Professional Lifetime Achievement Award from the Center for Advancement of the Enterprise Architecture Profession as well as the 2004 Oakland University Applied Technology in Business (ATIB) Award for IS Excellence and Innovation.

Mr. Zachman has been focusing on enterprise architecture since the 1980s and has written extensively on the subject, and he is also the author of the book *The Zachman Framework for Enterprise Architecture™: A Primer on Enterprise Engineering and Manufacturing.*[31]

The Zachman Framework for Enterprise Architecture

"A framework as it applies to enterprises is simply a logical structure for classifying and organizing the descriptive representations of an enterprise that are significant to the management of the enterprise as well as to the development of the enterprise's system (with the aim of) rationalizing the various concepts and specifications in order to provide for clarity of professional communication, to allow for improving and integrating development methodologies and tools, and to establish credibility and confidence in the investment of systems and resources."

John Zachman, 2003

The Zachman Framework for Enterprise Architecture[32] is a two-dimensional classification scheme for descriptive representations of an enterprise. It was derived through observation of descriptive representations (design artifacts) of various physical objects like airplanes, buildings, ships, computers, etc., in which it was empirically observed that the design artifacts (the descriptive representations, the product descriptions, the engineering documentation) of complex products can be classified by the audience for which the artifact was constructed (the Perspective) as well as classified by the content or subject focus of the artifact (the Abstraction) (Figure 3).

Perspectives of the Framework

Different perspectives are being represented over the process of engineering and manufacturing complex products. The descriptive representations of the product that are prepared over this process are designed to express concepts and constraints relevant to the various perspectives. That is, not only do the design artifacts depict the necessary engineering information, but they depict it in such a fashion that it is intelligible to the perspective (audience) for which they were created.

The principal perspectives are easily identifiable including:

1. **The Owner's Perspective (Row 2)**[33]—the recipient (customer, user) of the end product (e.g., airplane, house, enterprise, etc.). These descriptive representations reflect the usage characteristics of the end product, what the owner(s) are going to do with the end product, or how they will use it once they get it in their possession. This is the conceptual view of the end product, whatever the owner can think about relative to its use.
2. **The Designer's Perspective (Row 3)**—the engineer, the architect, the intermediary between what is desirable (Row 2) and what is physically and technically possible (Row 4). These descriptive representations reflect the laws of nature, the system, or logical constraints for the design of the product. This is the logical view of the end product. For enterprises, this is the logical representation of the enterprise which forms the basis for the white collar system, the record-keeping system of the enterprise as well as the basis for the design of the blue-collar system, the material manipulation system for manipulating the tangible aspects of the enterprise.
3. **The Builder's Perspective (Row 4)**—the manufacturing engineer, the general contractor, the employer of some technical capacity for producing the end product. These descriptive representations reflect the physical constraints of applying the technology in the construction of the product.

Empirically, there are two identifiable additional perspectives which include:

1. **A Scope Perspective (Row 1)**[34]—the context that establishes the universe of discourse, the inner and outer limits, the list of relevant constituents that must be accounted for in the descriptive representations (models) for the remaining perspectives.

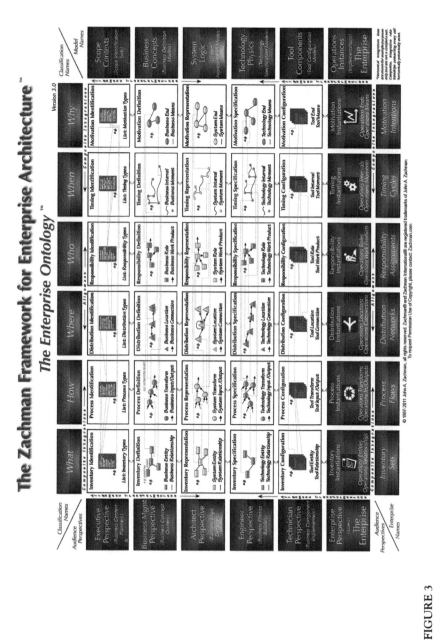

FIGURE 3

The most up-to-date (in 2014) version of the Zachman Framework for Enterprise Architecture.

2. **An Out-of-Context Perspective (Row 5)**—a detailed description that disassociates the parts or pieces of the complex object for manufacturing purposes. These out-of-context representations play a part in the transformation from the media of the design of the product to the media of the end product itself. For example, in physical products, like airplanes, the medium of the design is typically paper and ink (or more recently, electronic). Whereas, the media of the end product itself is aluminum, titanium, composites, etc. The out-of-context artifacts are employed in this media transformation between the media of the design and the media of the end product. For enterprises, these are the product specifications relating the technology constraints of row 4 to the vendor products in which the technology constraints are materialized.

Conclusion

As a part of the historic development of process concepts, we have covered the influential and key people and concepts impacting the way of thinking, working, and modeling of processes. In this context, we have focused in this section on what John A. Zachman, Sr. has developed and published and how it changed enterprise modeling and enterprise architecture around the world. His concept of adding different views as the anchor for answering relevant questions of what, how, where, who, when, and why was innovative and groundbreaking in every way. His contribution to enterprise modeling, enterprise engineering, and enterprise architecture[35] has left its mark on this generation and generations to come.

LEAN THINKING, LEAN PRACTICE AND LEAN CONSUMPTION
The evolution of Toyota's practices

Lean thinking and Lean practices are generic versions of the Toyota Production System (TPS) and the Toyota Way of Management system.[36] Lean did not derive from theory, but through observing practices at Toyota that were delivering superior performance in terms of product quality, efficiency (hours per car) and time-to-market for new products, leading Toyota to eventually become the largest car maker in the world.

The problem the founder of TPS, Taiichi Ohno, was trying to solve in the 1950s was how to build several different products on the limited equipment that Toyota could afford at that time. Instead of resorting to producing in batches, he carried out many pioneering experiments to build an integrated production system that was able to make a variety of products in single-piece flow in line with demand. This challenged the assumptions that there is a trade-off between quality and productivity, and that bigger batches lead to economies of scale and lower costs. His experiments also led to the development of many new tools, such as Kanban pull systems and SMED quick changeovers.[37] Ohno also built on Toyota's Jidoka system for making abnormalities visible immediately, and was invented in the 1930s.

However, the distinguishing feature of Ohno's approach was to challenge and teach front line and support staff how to design their own work, using the Training Within Industry system pioneered during WWII in the USA.[38] This enabled the front line to establish a standard way of doing their work as a baseline for improvement, which in turn enabled them to see and respond to any deviations from this standard immediately. In analyzing the root causes of the many issues that interrupted their work, he also taught them how to use the scientific approach to solving problems, using Deming's PDCA method.

Indeed it is the repeated daily practice of PDCA that develops the capabilities of individuals and teams to continually improve their work and improve the performance of the system as a whole. Toyota is often quoted as saying it "makes people in order to make cars". These enhanced problem solving capabilities enabled Ohno to link activities together, remove all kinds of buffers and delays and with much shorter lead times, and to use simpler planning systems driven by demand rather than by forecasts. This accelerating continuous improvement system is called Kaizen.[39]

Similar logic was used to develop very different approaches in other areas of the business including managing product development projects, production engineering of right-sized tooling, supplier coordination and sales and marketing. Eiji Toyoda, the long-time Chairman of Toyota, also used these principles to build a management system to support Kaizen and to focus and align activities towards key corporate objectives, called the Toyota Way.[40] Again the key to doing so is building common capabilities at every level of management to plan and solve business problems using another version of PDCA called A3 thinking.[41]

The evolving understanding of Lean

TPS was developed in the 1950s and was taught to its suppliers in the 1970s and brought together as a management system in the Toyota Way in 2001. It continues to evolve as Toyota faces new challenges today. Likewise, our understanding of Lean has deepened over time. We initially bench marked their superior performance and coined the term Lean to describe this system in *The Machine that Changed the World*.[42] This caused quite a stir across the global auto industry and beyond.

But it quickly became apparent that simply collecting and training all the lean tools was not enough for others to follow Toyota's example. The authors (James P. Womack and Daniel T. Jones) set out to observe Toyota's leading practices in more detail and those of other pioneering leading practice organizations who had learnt directly from Toyota's practices. From this, they were able to distil a set of five principles behind a Lean system and a common action path to realize them in *Lean Thinking*.[43]

One of the insights from this research is that no one can see or is responsible for the horizontal sequence of activities that creates the value customers pay for, from concept to launch, from raw material to finished product and from purchase to disposal. Vertically organized departments instead focus solely on optimizing their activities and assets to make their numbers.

To help teams to see the end-to-end processes or value streams they are involved in we used another Toyota tool, which we called Value Stream Mapping.[44] As teams map their value streams they realize the problem is not the people, but a broken process, and having stabilized their own work they now see new opportunities for collaboration to improve the flow of work and align it with the pull from real customer demand.

In industry after industry, they saw value streams that used to take many months from beginning to end now take a matter of days, with far fewer defects and more reliable delivery. This is only possible because front line staff know how to react quickly and tackle the root causes of problems that will *arise* in any tightly synchronized and interdependent system. It is also much easier to adapt to changing circumstances. Over time, these emergent capabilities achieve superior performance than systems designed and supported solely by experts. This is the main difference between Value Stream Analysis and Business Process Reengineering.

The other insight is that the traditional approach to managing by the numbers and through functional politics at HQ wastes a lot of management time, fails to align activities with corporate objectives, hides problems and takes management away from front line value creating activities. Relying on expensive enterprise systems to force compliance with the command and control instructions from the top has in many cases made things worse and much harder to adapt to changing circumstances.

Toyota use a very different strategy formulation process, called Hoshin Kanri, to define the overall direction of the organization and to conduct a dialogue up and down the organization on proposed actions to achieve it, again based on PDCA.[45] As a result, resources and energies are prioritized and aligned through a visual process that reaches right down to the front line. This also lays the basis for collaboration across functional silos. Management in turn spends a lot more time at the front line, understanding their issues, eliminating obstacles and coaching problem solving. In this way management learns by helping colleagues to learn and does this by asking questions rather than telling them what to do. This builds very different behaviors and an environment where employees are challenged to fulfil their potential.[46]

The spread of Lean and Lean Consumption

Lean thinking and Lean practice has spread across almost every sector of activity, from retailing and distribution, discrete and process manufacturing, service and repair, financial services and administration, construction, software development and IT, healthcare and service delivery in governments. It has even created a framework for improving the viability of digital startups.[47] While the focus on value creation, value streams and learning is common, the sequence of improvement steps varies for different types of activity. However, Lean practices seem to work equally well in different cultures.

The full potential of Lean is realized when it is embraced by the whole supply chain. Toyota's aftermarket parts distribution system is still the global benchmark supply chain, delivering near perfect availability of the basket of parts at the point of use with only a tenth of the lead time and inventory in the pipeline from the point of production.[48] Not surprisingly this inspired retailers like Tesco and Amazon to develop their own rapid response distribution systems that are essential for convenience retailing and home shopping. Manufacturers like GKN have also moved away from concentrating activities in focused factories in distant low cost locations to creating rapid response supply chains to serve customers in each region.[49] GE is also using Lean to design a new product range and production system for household appliances in North America, bringing this activity back from China.

While most of the attention has been focused on the upstream supply chain, Lean actually begins with the customer's use of the product or service. In Lean Solutions, James Womack and Daniel Jones developed a framework for using Lean to define value from the user's perspective.[50] Consumption is in fact a series of processes that interact with the provider's processes. Mapping both processes reveals where they are broken and cause mutual frustration and unnecessary cost. This reveals opportunities for improving user experience at lower cost and even new business models. In the digital age it is now possible to track the customer's use of the product or service and enter into a two way dialogue with them. In a very real sense, customers and users are becoming an important part of the supply chain delivering today's products and services and co-developing tomorrow's solutions.

Conclusion

From the above it should be clear that Lean is not just another improvement methodology, but a very different set of behaviors and management system. It is not just a set of tools for production operations in the auto industry, but a much broader framework for creating more productive value creation systems in all kinds of sectors and activities. Readers should be aware of the confusion that is caused by partial descriptions of Lean that often miss the key elements that make it work as a system.

Lean shares the same scientific approach to the analysis of work as many other improvement methodologies, like BPR, Six Sigma and TQM. But it differs from them in how it is used. Rather than experts using scientific methods to design better systems, Lean builds superior performance by developing the problem solving capabilities of the front line, supported by a hands-on management system.

Lean is therefore a path or journey of both individual and organizational learning, and leads to more challenging and fulfilling work for those involved. It is learnt by doing through repeated practice rather than by studying books or in the classroom. While it is driven by practice, and not theory, Lean raises many interesting new hypotheses about learning and collaborative working for different academic disciplines to think about and research.

BUSINESS PROCESS REENGINEERING

Dr Michael Hammer

Michael Hammer[51] (1948–2008) was an American engineer, management author, and a former professor of computer science at the MIT, and is most commonly known as the founder of the management theory of BPR. BPR was widely perceived as one of the biggest business ideas of the 1990s—which Hammer defined as "the fundamental rethinking and radical redesign of business processes to achieve dramatic improvements in critical measures of performance." The terms *process improvement*, *process excellence* and *process innovation* all came from him.

The idea, first propounded in an article in Harvard Business Review[52], was later expanded into a book that Hammer wrote with James Champy, the founder of CSC Index, a consulting firm. The book[53] sold several million copies. So popular was reengineering that one survey in the 1990s showed it to have been adopted by almost 80% of Fortune 500 companies. It was often blamed for the widespread layoffs that became part of almost every company's radical redesign at that time.

As an engineer by training, Hammer was the proponent of a process-oriented view of business management. He earned BS and MS degrees and a Ph.D. in EECS from the MIT in 1968, 1970, and 1973, respectively. He was a professor at the MIT in the department of computer science and lecturer in the MIT Sloan School of Management. Articles written by Hammer were published in business periodicals, such as the Harvard Business Review and The Economist. TIME named him as one of America's 25 most influential individuals[54] in its first such list. *Reengineering the Corporation*[55] was ranked among the "three most important business books of the past 20 years" by Forbes magazine.

Introducing Business Process Reengineering

Business Process Reengineering focuses exclusively on redesigning the core business processes of an organizational unit—or the enterprise as a whole. The aim is to increase productivity, improve process cycle times and the resulting quality thereof. The basic idea of BPR is to completely rethink an organization's core processes from scratch by turning to focus on processes that deliver the most value to the consumer (whether external or internal). This approach often leads to the adoption of a brand new value delivery system with a dramatically increased attention and focus upon the needs of the customer. The overall goal is to simply—and entirely—eliminate non-productive activities in two key areas; first, it includes the redesign of functional organizations into cross-functional teams to increase productivity and efficiency across organizational boundaries; second, the usage of technology to achieve a much higher degree of data dissemination in order to greatly improve decision making.

Many times before, companies simply haven't received the expected performance boost from the use of usual methods such as process rationalization and process automation. Heavy investments in information technology, in particular, has shown to deliver increasingly disappointing results because many companies tend to use technology to mechanize and automate old or, in some ways, redundant ways of doing business. As Albert Einstein once said: "Insanity: doing the same thing over and over again and expecting different results." It is important to note that technology is but a tool that acts on behalf of its user, so if you do not rethink and redesign how your processes should perform as well as educate employees on the process changes, you'll almost always end up with disappointing results when it comes to meeting the performance and value expectations from the original goals of business process redesign. The result is that technology is used only to speed up process execution while leaving existing processes intact.

Using technology to speed up process execution—in exchange of focusing on process redesign—simply will not adhere to the importance of addressing fundamental performance deficiencies. Job designs, business work flows, information flows, control, monitoring and governance mechanisms as well as organizational structures often come of age continuously across different competitive environments throughout history. Most of these areas tend to be geared towards effectiveness, efficiency and control, however, but in today's global business ecosystem, the terms to really look out for and pay attention to are around *process innovation, process speed* and *process quality.*

Width before Depth

Hammer realized early on that the processes really proved useful when you worked together across organizational borders—it may even be something as simple as cooperation among departments. Compare this with the fact that most process initiatives take place within one's own sphere of power. Of course, it is quite okay to find your sea legs in-house at first, but you meet the real possibilities and problems when you venture out of your own sphere of power. It is so much easier to get the internal areas to behave, both because of your direct authority, but also because the individual subprocesses are well known. You have to work in a more factual manner if you are to cooperate with/persuade an external partner, whom you have no authority over.

The reason being that the real potential for savings lies in the cooperation between two organizations, since you need a customer need to fulfill in order to make such a cooperation viable. And there must be a need for interorganizational contact in order to fulfill this customer need. The relevant optimizations at this level will have a lot of potential since we are optimization on a larger scale.

This touched on yet another point; *processes need width before depth,* which means that we identify and establish the overriding processes end-to-end, *before we go deeper into them.* We do this when the coherence and the external requirements have been established. This point of view matches the concepts of Mura—a Japanese term meaning "unevenness; irregularity; lack of uniformity; nonuniformity; inequality." Mura is a key concept in the TPS as one of the three types of waste (muda, mura, muri).[56]

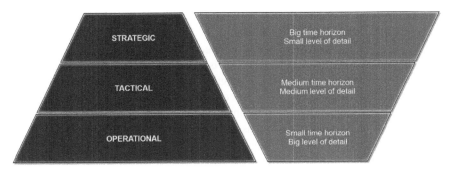

FIGURE 4

The three levels of management.

The Three Levels of Management

As employees become more and more specialized and as leadership no longer knows the most about the various disciplines (see phases 1 and 2), a need arises for making projects across the board in companies, and thus the project culture, emerged. Most organizations today are process-driven and have a flat structure. Decisions are still being made on a strategic (planning), tactical (management), or operational (executional) level, and depending on the leadership level, the decisions have a longer or shorter time horizon, and a greater or lesser level of detail. The process flow and the tasks that this solves will only benefit the company, however, if they are connected to the company's overriding goals.[57]

Figure 4 illustrates the three levels of management combined with the time horizon and level of detail. The levels of management are interconnected via information streams. From the leadership, who are the ones to decide the strategic part, and downward in the hierarchy, the level of agency is limited more and more the further you go down.

This is done through plans and budgets. From the lower level, control information, i.e., reports, are sent upward and become more and more detailed the higher you get in the hierarchy. The authors behind BPR were Michael Hammer and James A. Champy. The concept looks at the organization's business processes from a "clean slate" point of view and then decides how to best redesign and reconstruct these processes so as to improve the way they run the company.[58] In spite of the fact that BPR is considered a concept from the early 1990s, you could argue that there is nothing new in reengineering.[59]

The components of BPR existed before 1990, when the first articles about BPR were written. But it was not until the 1990s that these components were brought together to form a coherent management concept.

The Three Important Ingredients

Business Process Reengineering (BPR) is all about creating change by identifying and focusing on business processes and then make them more efficient by simplifying

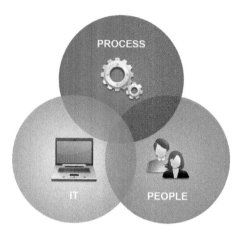

FIGURE 5

Illustration of the vital integration of process, information technology, and people.

them with the use of modern technology and the involvement of the entire organization. This means that you are not just looking at parts of the organization of individual technologies. When BPR is launched, the business process, technology, and the organization have to be developed simultaneously (Figure 5).

In BPR, the three circles should not slide away from one another. Even though these three parts of BPR cannot and must not be separated, IT is considered the key element in BPR (Hammer, 1990).

The Business Process Reengineering Cycle

A Business Process Reengineering (BPR) cycle[60] can be illustrated in the following way (Figure 6).

First you identify the process, and then an analysis of the existing process is carried out. Then, you design the new process, which is ultimately implemented. A clarification of the cycle follows below. Before launching a BPR project, the company should typically start with a BPR pre-analysis to identify the state of the present business process and establish the level of interaction between the organization, the technology, and the processes. Ambeck and Beyer[61] claim that the changes brought on by BPR happen when the development of processes, technology, and organization take place simultaneously and in accordance with the company's strategy and vision. Furthermore, they write that this exact approach is very different from the traditional methods where technological, organizational, and strategic issues are kept separate, which can result in a loss of overview and synergy effects.

A company's BPR project portfolio can span from the minor here-and-now processes of a shorter duration to longer lasting, complex processes, which require greater improvements and typically lasts from 1 to 6 months. Last, but not least, there can be long, continual process improvements, which can last from a few months to several years.

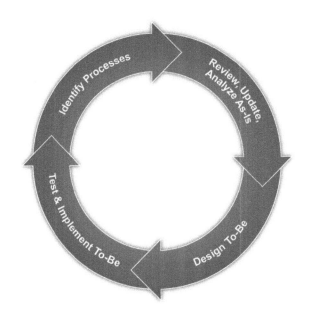

FIGURE 6

The Business Process Reengineering cycle.[62]

Methods and Approaches to Business Process Reengineering

In the literature written about BPR, several methodical approaches are mentioned. A BPR method can, in many ways, be compared to a road map, which helps the driver get his bearings before, during, and after the road trip. The same goes for BPR. You need to know where you are and where you are going and at the same time find the right way. Then you can start the process (the road trip), and then you can continuously check how far you have come. In the following, we will look at three different methods, where one thing is in common, the fact that their approach to the BPR project is divided into steps.

One such approach to BPR is process reengineering life cycle (PRLC).[63] The method was developed by Dr Subashish Guha. PRLC is based on analysis of different BPR methods in use today. Guha (et al.) has studied the different BPR methods, and even though the studies did not result in a standard BPR method, they showed that all the different BPR methods follow the same principle—the aforementioned *step* principle, which can be divided into three overriding phases (Figure 7).

By identifying the company's visions and goals, you can decide where to concentrate your efforts. Then, by identifying which processes to work with, you can ensure that those processes support the company's visions and goals. In that way, you can be sure that the effort is worthwhile. If you have not identified visions and goals, you risk spending time and resources on a process that should have been cut off.

You have to understand the existing processes—what they do for the company and how they fit together. This is important if you are to create an optimum

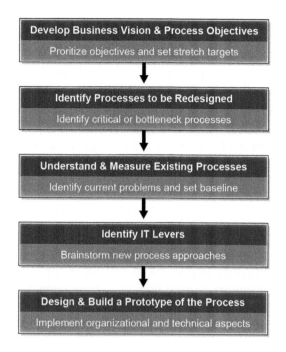

FIGURE 7

The five steps of process redesign.[64]

redesign. Otherwise, you risk ending up with a design that does not deliver the desired result. If you are aware of the IT level in your company, it can provide you with ideas for new approaches to processes. Where are we, and where are we going? When all of this is in place, you can test the new process. The process must be implemented, and you have to take organizational changes and technical aspects into consideration.

Hammer and Champy postulate that the article "Business Process Reengineering: Analysis and Recommendations" is not very detailed concerning the BPR techniques,[65] which has probably resulted in the wide range of methods.

Business Process Reengineering Project and Success Criteria

In his account of BPR, Nicolaisen reaches the criteria, stated below, that need to be realized in order to say that BPR has been a success since the criticism in the report from 1994, "State of re-engineering rapport" states that two-thirds of the initiatives had either unsatisfactory or mediocre results. This is in line with the estimate made by several of the BPR founders that between 50 and 70% of all BPR project results are unsatisfactory:

- Whether or not the project fulfilled the requirements set up for it, for instance, if you have utilized the right innovative technology or if you were able to reach an agreement on the necessary changes.

- Whether or not the project created competitive advantages for the company, like have you increased customer satisfaction or have you boosted morale and productivity among the employees.
- Whether or not the project has improved the results on the bottom line, like if you have increased your market shares, increased your profits, or improved ROI.

Even though the company follows the PRLC principles or some other method and/or uses the five steps, in process change, this does not imply that BPR has been successful. The company has to be ready for change. Smith divides change up in two, a nonradical change, which is low risk and, therefore, has a greater chance of success, and it does not require a lot of resources.[66]

Apart from this, the leadership needs to have enough clout and the ability to communicate the radical changes, so as to minimize opposition to change among the employees. You need to employ a process "owner," who is responsible for keeping the reengineering team together and ensure progress. The reengineering team often consists of 5 to 10 individuals who will examine the existing processes and then redesign and implement the processes. Aside from the 5 to 10 individuals, the team should have consultants or coworkers from other departments.[67]

There are a lot of project criteria for a successful BPR; it is, therefore, important that the company has the right approach and an understanding of how demanding the process can be.

The Pros of Business Process Reengineering

When companies work with BPR, they should be able to identify company processes and analyze and redesign if need be. Kaplan and Murdock feel that this way of working provides the company with certain advantages when it comes to their core processes,[68] and at the same time, the company is encouraged to focus on the results of the entire company and not just the results of a single department.

The advantages of working with business process reengineering can be summed up as follows[69]:

- Optimizing business processes
- Improving efficiency and higher quality
- Reducing costs
- Better working environment and understanding among employees
- Increasing flexibility and the ability to handle change
- Creating a foundation for growth
- Increasing cooperation between departments

To get a BPR project to succeed, it is important, aside from having the full support of the leadership, to have the right people aboard. Senior management needs to be represented in management committees, and there is a need for project managers and BPR consultants.

Davenport states that even though BPR is demanding, it is a process that the company should consider as it ultimately creates a bonus for the company both financially and competitively. Through the process work, the company might eventually expose processes that need to be eliminated or redesigned.[70]

The Cons of Business Process Reengineering

We do not feel that there are any disadvantages of a successful BPR, and we have not been able to find any documentation that indicates this. But there are some issues that the company needs to take into consideration when planning to implement BPR. These issues have to do with the company's resources to meet the project criteria. The leadership could feel that the organization is not ready for change, and then they should gradually make changes in the culture of the organization before implementing BPR.

Another issue could be whether or not the organization can allocate the needed resources to provide the leadership with the necessary clout.

And finally, it can be difficult to implement a BPR if the organization is not International Organization for Standardization (ISO) certified, i.e., all processes have been documented. If you attempt to implement BPR in an organization in which all the processes have not been documented or established, it can require a lot of resources. This could mean that a BPR in itself will not create financial profit, but combined with an ISO certification and cheaper insurances, the overall financial benefit of the BPR can be increased. An added bonus of BPR could be that all procedures are identified and written down. This could then be used for an implementation of activity-based costing (ABC) or time-driven activity-based costing (TDABC), in which the project group normally requires a lot of resources to identify processes, speak to employees, and maybe even measure resource consumption themselves. To implement an ABC or TDABC under this condition would require fewer resources and can create an added profit.

Conclusion

Setting up a business process re-engineering initiative and designing the many different projects involved in the execution of such an initiative is a daunting task for any organization. Not only does the process redesign itself pose a number of technical challenges, but one of the most prominent issues comes from the requirement of organizational change management. LEGO[71] has portrayed this issue in detail when they set out to document all of their business processes across their organizational boundaries. As redesigning the core business processes of any organization requires a different point of view and take on both performance and value delivery, there will be a fundamental need for the employees involved with such projects to change not only their way of thinking and their way of working, but also their way of modeling with processes. It is therefore vital for any leadership to incite and govern employee adaptation and education so that the organization has acquired the correct skills to carry out such projects successfully, and also to enable them to govern and monitor the processes and their performance. This will ultimately enable the organization as a whole to continuously improve and adapt processes to a constantly changing business environment.

TOTAL QUALITY MANAGEMENT

Introduction

Total Quality Management (TQM) as defined by the International Organization for Standardization (ISO) as:

> *"...a management model for an organization, centered on quality, based on the participation of all its members, and achieves long-term success through client satisfaction, and creates advantages for all members of the organization, and the society as a whole."*
> **source: ISO 8402:1994.**

In Japan, TQM consists of four process steps:

1. *Kaizen*: Focuses on "constant process improvement", on making the processes visible, measurable and repeatable.
2. *Kansei*: An examination of the way the consumer uses the product, which leads to improvement of the product itself.
3. *Atarimae Hinshitsu*: The idea and the way that "things function as they are supposed to."
4. *Miryokuteki Hinshitsu*: The idea that "things need an aesthetic quality"

TQM is therefore not a new concept, even though that in the shape and form we know it now, it is said to have been formed and influenced by W. Edwards Deming, Philip B. Crosby, J. M. Juran, and Kaoru Ishikawa. Deming was a consultant for Toyota, and TQM and Toyota Production System have many common traits. There are other related concepts and techniques like Six Sigma and Lean that are very closely related to TQM and its concepts of "constant process improvement," customer feedback loops, on making the processes visible, measurable and repeatable. Six Sigma was created by Motorola, which also uses TQM. Some of the companies that have implemented TQM include Ford Motor Company, Motorola, NXP Semiconductors (formerly Philips Semiconductor, Inc), SGL Carbon and Toyota Motor Company.[72]

Throughout the 1980s, American companies adopted TQM concepts and standardized their processes with Baldrige standards and Six Sigma since 1990. Companies today need to be flexible and innovative to be competitive. This requires the companies to have the methods and the software to distance themselves from their competitors. Future generations of companies are based on best practice with an integrated, holistic perspective on process leadership. A renowned expert in this field, W. Edwards Deming, stated 14 steps to the recognized implementation of TQM[38]:

1. Create a common purpose and goal.
2. The leadership decides on transformation and it is they that should promote change.
3. Integrate quality into the product; do not depend on inspection to expose problems.
4. Establish long-term relations based on performance rather than price.

5. Constant improvement of product, quality, and service.
6. Start training people.
7. Focus on leadership.
8. Dispel fear
9. Tear down barriers and silos between departments.
10. Abstain from preaching to the employees.
11. Support, help, and create improvements.
12. Remove barriers for pride, arrogance in a job well done.
13. Implement an energetic program for learning and self-improvement.
14. Have everyone in the organization work on the transformation.

These 14 steps best describe what the concept of TQM encompasses. The concept can also be summed up in five simple main points:

1. Continuous improvement
2. Employee empowerment
3. Analysis, comparing and benchmarking
4. Just-In-Time (JIT) principles
5. Knowledge of the TQM tools

This main point provides an opportunity to explain the use of TQM in process work, see "The Use of TQM in Process Work".

Implementing Total Quality Management in the Organization

According to Hashmi,[73] the first task is to consider if the organization is ready for the change that the implementation of TQM will bring. The right prerequisites for the implementation of TQM deal with the company history, its present needs, the implementation of initiatives leading to TQM, and the quality of the existing staff. An organization with a culture of flexibility will be better prepared to implement TQM. If this flexibility does not exist, it is important that the leadership makes changes so that they can become culture bearers in the implementation of ¡TQM in order to perform the required change management. In other words, a holistic approach to change is needed.

The next task previous to the implementation of a new system like TQM is identification of the tasks to be solved, establishing the necessary leadership structures, preparation of strategies for support of involvement, design of communication tools in accordance with the change, and the allocation of resources for the implementation.[74]

Key Elements for Change

When implementing TQM, one attempts to establish a company culture in the entire organization, where focus is on constant improvement of quality. Dr S. Kumar[75] describes eight key elements that an organization should focus on to ensure a successful implementation of TQM.[75]

The key elements are *Ethics, Integrity, Trust, Training, Cooperation, Leadership, Recognition,* and *Communication.* These can be illustrated in the following way (Figure 8)[76]:

The foundation consists of ethics and integrity: The basis for ethics is an ethical code in the organization. This organization must include all persons, and it serves as a guideline for their performance in their jobs. Integrity includes traits like honesty, morals, values etc., which the customers would expect of the organization. Trust in connection with the customers is essential to all persons in the organization since customer satisfaction is of the essence.

The bricks are made up of training, cooperation, and leadership: Training is extremely important in connection with productivity. For the leadership, the task is to ensure the skills of the employees, teamwork, problem-solving, decision-making etc. Cooperation ensures a faster and probably better solution to a problem. At the same time, there is a constant improvement in the processes and the work, and the employees feel safe in solving problems amongst themselves. Leadership is seen as the most important element in TQM. The visions, strategies, values, etc., that form the basis for the culture of the organization must come from the leadership. It is essential to have a leadership that is dedicated to leading, and so effectively. This goes for the low-level leader as well as for senior management. The leadership must support the entire process and have an extensive knowledge of the process and be personally involved in the initiation of methods, systems, and measurement to be able to realize the company goals.

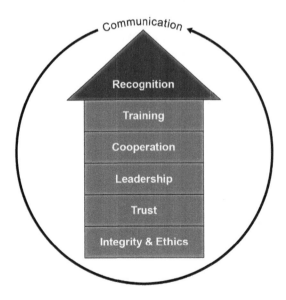

FIGURE 8

Components and key elements in connection with the implementation of Total Quality Management.[77]

The mortar is communication and that is what binds the entire organization together: The communication must ensure a common and frequent frame of reference and must ensure a common way of understanding of the concepts and ideas that are being spread among the individuals in the organization. This also involves contractors and customers. The leadership needs to maintain an open communication with the employees, and the common frame of reference ensures that both the receiver and the sender understand the information that is communicated.

The roof is recognition: Recognition is a very important element in the system, and it should be granted immediately after the completion of a task. A task can be both suggestions for improvements and actual improvements based on suggestions. Recognition can lead to increased self-worth, higher productivity, better quality, and a faster performance of the task. You could argue that there is a relatively close connection between Deming's 14 steps and Kumar's eight key elements as focus areas.

It is obvious that leadership is important to a successful implementation of TQM since the management needs to be in the front on several levels, and in many ways drive the process, or at the very least, support the employees in the process. The implementation of TQM is of importance to management itself, too. Lakhe and Mohanty (1994) argued that not only did the implementation of TQM mean a radical change in the culture of the organization, but it also meant that the leadership actually had to start leading the employees, and at the same time, there needs to be a constant process for quality improvement.

This puts a lot of pressure on the individual manager's flexibility and his or her role as a culture bearer and motive power. You cannot help reaching the conclusion that the implementation of TQM will not be a success until everyone in the organization has come to an understanding of these eight key elements and acts accordingly.

The Use of Total Quality Management in Process Work

Why work on quality—why is it important? According to Figure 9,[78] quality provides market shares and reduces costs.

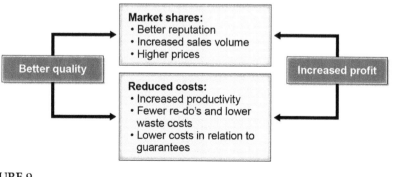

FIGURE 9

Total Quality Management's figure for quality.

Besides, quality has an influence on the company's reputation and legal responsibilities. The involvement of TQM in process work can best be communicated with a basis in the aforementioned five main points for TQM.

1. **Constant improvement:** In Japan, they use the term "Kaizen," and in the United States and Europe, "Six Sigma" is used to describe efforts in this field. The point is to set higher goals all the time and constantly improve all processes.
2. **Empowerment of employees:** The idea is that the people who work with the process, like the ones running the machines in a production plant, are also

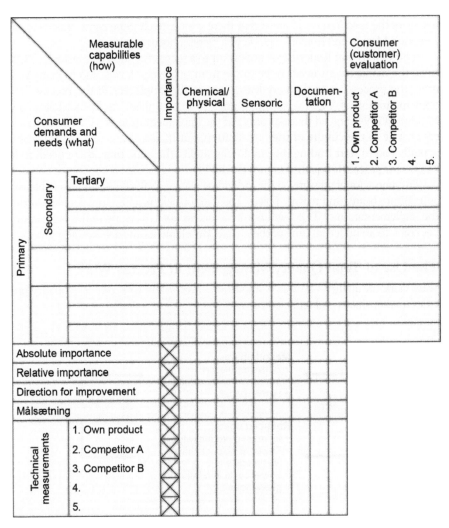

FIGURE 10

House of Quality.[79]

those who know the process best, and thus, are best equipped to improve upon it. We speak of a "quality circle", which consists of a group of employees who meet and discuss work-related problems. These quality circles have proven to provide results in the form of improved productivity and quality.

3. **Benchmarking**: Benchmarking involves best practice in the process work, so that a demonstrated standard of performance represents the highest possible goal for the company within a certain type of process. You make a serious effort to reach that goal. You benchmark within every field and across all departments. TQM requires a measurable benchmarking.

4. **Just-in-Time (JIT)**: The philosophy from JIT stands for constant improvement and proactive problem solving. On a more tangible level, it means minimizing storage via control measures.

5. **A knowledge of the TQM tools**: The management should continually train all employees in the use of TQM, and for this purpose, you utilize tools from Quality Function Deployment (QFD) and "House of Quality" (Figure 10), Taguchi-techniques, Pareto diagrams, process diagrams, cause and effect diagrams, and Statistical Process Control (SPC). The tools are described in greater detail in the upcoming section of this chapter.

TOOLS FOR TQM

House of Quality or Quality Function Deployment

Breyfogle (1999) has listed the following 10 items for the "translation" of the input coming from the organization in the house of quality, which will then be used as useful information for the entire organization:[80]

1. Make a list of the characteristics of your customers. This list can be made through interviews with customers and/or research and studies.
2. Identify the importance of each of these characteristics. This information can be gleaned from the customer studies.
3. Get the customer's input on the existing design and the competitors' designs.
4. Designers need to make up a list of the technical features to meet the customer's characteristics.
5. Relations should be identified in relation to the matrix and assigned a qualitative value (weak, medium, strong).
6. Technical tests must be done on existing designs and competitors' designs to measure objective differences.
7. The importance of all technical features should be calculated as either absolute values or sorted by their relative importance.
8. The difficulties of maneuvering each technical feature must be evaluated.
9. Correlation matrices are to be worked out.
10. Goal values for each technical feature should be established. This could be based on the customers' evaluation in step 3. Based on the calculations of the technical importance under step 7 and the evaluation of the technical difficulties under step 8, choose which technical features to focus on.

QFD is used early in the production process to determine where to launch a special effort in the quality work. Basically, you need to translate customer needs into specific features, which can be designed and produced. The House of Quality is a graphical tool that can provide a visual picture of how well the company meets the (prioritized) customer needs.

Taguchi Techniques

Taking the fact that most problems originate from product or process design, there are three concepts, of which we will mention two:

1. **Sturdiness of quality**: The product must be produced in uniform quality, regardless of changing, external factors. The variation in input materials must not influence the quality.
2. **Quality loss function**: This function is a simple mathematical function that describes how costs increase the more the product deviates from the targeted customer needs. This function can help you set the limits for acceptable and unacceptable product output, which could be utilized in the company's financial management (Figure 11).

Pareto Diagrams

In 1906, the economist Vilfredo Pareto illustrated in his research a stunting discovery: 80% of the land in Italy was owned by just 20% of the people. This principle is today known as the Pareto principle—or 80–20 rule—and has been widely adopted

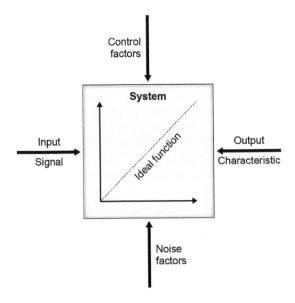

FIGURE 11

An example Taguchi diagram.

and used across all aspects of business, economics, mathematics, and processes—just to name a few.[81] The Pareto analysis is applied in a straightforward technique to prioritize the root-cause and/or problem solving, subsequently that the first part resolves the greatest number of problems.[82] It is based on the idea that 80 percent of problems may be caused by as few as 20 percent of causes.

Identify a list of problems, followed by scoring and mapping each of the problems by root-cause and subsequently summarizing the scores of each group. At this point, the effort of finding the source of the problem should be clear, and work is then focused on finding an answer or a solution to the root-cause of the problems for the highest scoring group. The Pareto analysis thereby not only identifies the most important problem to solve, it also provides the use of a rating system as to how difficult the problem will be to solve Figure 12.[83]

Process Diagrams

Process diagrams describe the sequence of events in a process, for instance, around the manufacture or sales of a product or a service to a customer. You can glean vital information from these diagrams, such as data accumulation,

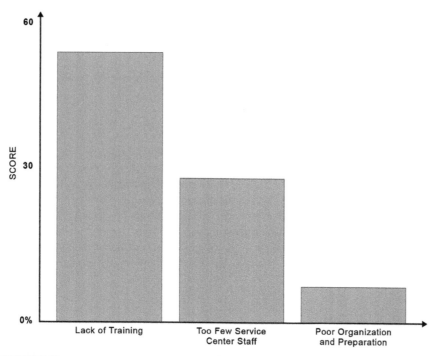

FIGURE 12

An example of a Pareto analysis chart showing that 51 complaints are due to employee lack of training, 27 complaints are due to too few service center staff, and seven complaints are about poor organization and preparation.

FIGURE 13

An example of a simple sales process diagram.[84]

isolation, accumulation of problem areas, ideal areas for audits, opportunities for reduction of transport distances, etc. In the process diagram of Figure 13, we see an illustration of a very simple and generic sales process—from customer engagement to closing the deal.

Cause & Effect Analysis Diagrams

In 1960, Professor Dr. Kaoru Ishikawa established the cause and effect analysis discipline. Often referred to as a fishbone diagram as the technique maps the possible causes of a problem in a diagram that looks a lot like an entire fishbone stripped of meat. This method visualizes the challenges and problems in a situation in relation to possible causes and complications. The four steps to use the cause and effect analysis are:[85]

1. Identify the challenge and problem (situation).
2. Identify the complication and main factors involved
3. Identify potential root causes.
4. Analyze and examine your diagram.

These diagrams are used for identification of possible quality problems and for locating appropriate areas for inspection (Figure 14).

Statistical Process Control

Statistical Process Control (SPC) is a technique of quality control which uses statistical methods. SPC is applied in order to monitor and control a process. Monitoring and controlling the process ensures that it operates at its full potential. At its full potential, the process can make as much conforming product as possible with a minimum (if not an elimination) of waste (rework or scrap). SPC can be applied to any process where the "conforming product" (product meeting specifications) output can be measured. Key tools used in SPC include control charts, a focus on continuous improvement, and the design of experiments. An example of a process where SPC is applied is manufacturing lines[86] (Figure 15).

The PDCA Cycle

Deming developed a model for use for constant improvement.[87] The model is known as the PDCA Cycle (Figure 16). Throughout this cycle you look at the following:

1. **Plan**—you have to establish the goals, and then the necessary processes to meet the goals of the organization.

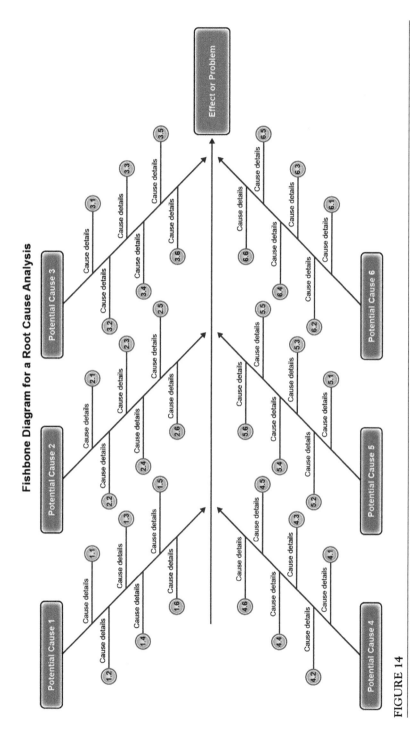

FIGURE 14

A root cause analysis (cause and effect) fishbone diagram.

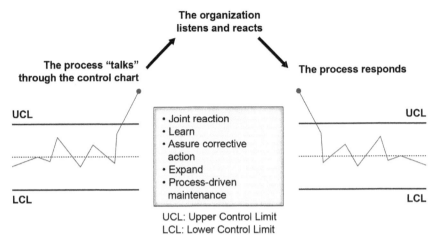

FIGURE 15

A statistical process control chart.

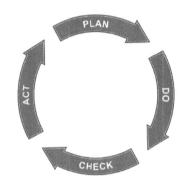

FIGURE 16

The Plan-Do-Check-Act (PDCA) cycle.

2. **Implement** the processes.
3. **Monitor and evaluate** the processes and the results in relation to the goals and report the results.
4. **Act and make decisions** on possible areas of improvement. Evaluate the entire PDCA process and, if necessary, modify it before the next implementation phase.

The model presupposes that the organization is flexible or that the right culture and the support of the management is a given. It is interesting to note that Deming in the PDCA cycle argues for a monitoring of results and for prompt action on this monitoring. In his 14 steps to the implementation of TQM, he argues that the improvement of quality should not be a consequence of inspection and measuring, but should rather be integrated with the product. To improve on the quality of a certain product or service, the starting point must be a frame of reference to measure the improvement against.

Business Excellence and EFQM

The principles and tools from total quality management (TQM) are also known as "business excellence" when they are applied to management and general improvements of the company. The stakeholder value, customer focus, and process management are the parameters the company needs to improve on through a systematic approach.[88] (Figure 17).

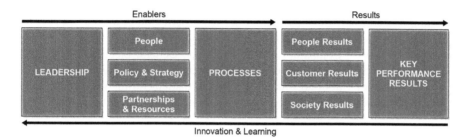

FIGURE 17

A systematic approach to business excellence.

Conclusion

Quality management as a foundational discipline has been around for many years now, and it has gained a significant focus and attention of, in particular, the manufacturing industry. Total Quality Management (TQM) has since its early development phases in the 1940s laid the groundwork for an organizational management discipline that focuses on quality across organizational boundaries and disciplines. The involvement of people in this discipline is all-encompassing, and as such, implementing TQM in any organization requires a heavy investment of both time and resources. Training is also required for the personnel, but for many companies, it is generally considered—if implemented right and adequately—to be worth the effort.

Some of the many benefits that TQM has to offer are:
- The ability to produce high quality products for the end consumer
- Elimination of waste, and reduction of the resources needed to produce goods
- Continuous process improvement and product optimization
- Achieve labor savings due to the streamlining of processes
- Increased product quality awareness across the company

SIX SIGMA

Introduction

Six Sigma, or 6σ as it is also written, is a collection of methods, techniques and tools for process improvement. The basic thinking of Six Sigma can be traced back to Carl Friedrich Gauss (1777–1855) as a measurement standard by introducing the concept of the normal curve. In the 1920s, Walter Shewhart demonstrated that sigma imply where a process requires improvement. In 1986, Bill Smith and Mikel Harry, two engineers at Motorola were accredited to having developed "Six Sigma", and in 1995, Jack Welch made it the central business strategy of General Electric.

Today, the principles are widely adopted across industry sectors, and in recent years the Six Sigma ideas have merged with the Lean manufacturing methodology, naming it Lean Six Sigma. The Lean Six Sigma methodology aims to support the business and operational excellence by focusing on variation, design, waste issues and process flows.[89] Companies such as Motorola, General Electric, Verizon, and IBM uses Lean Six Sigma as a growth strategy to rethink and transform themselves through efficiency—from organizational setup to manufacturing, software development to sales and distribution, and finally for service delivery functions.

What Six Sigma Means

Sigma is used in statistics to indicate a deviation from the standard of 99,99999980268%.[90] This means that almost no errors are produced. In reality a process that is designed to be in accordance with Six Sigma may not continue to do so. It has been empirically proven that, in time, it decreases from 6 to 4.5 sigma. It is debated whether or not the 1.5 is universal, but nobody doubts that there is a decrease.[91]

The Purpose of Six Sigma

The purpose of Six Sigma is to improve the quality of process outputs by identifying and removing the causes of defects (errors) and minimizing variability in manufacturing and business processes. It uses a set of quality management methods, including statistical methods, and creates a special team of people within the organization (Champions, Black Belts, Green Belts, Yellow Belts, etc.) who are experts in these methods. Each Six Sigma project carried out within an organization follows a defined sequence of steps and has quantified value targets, for example:[92]

- Reduce process cycle time.
- Reduce pollution.
- Reduce costs.
- Increase customer satisfaction.
- Increase profits.

Six Sigma makes a distinction between improving existing processes and designing new ones. For this purpose, Deming's Plan-Do-Check–Act cycle has been developed into the following two methodologies (DMAIC of DMADV).

DMAIC

DMAIC (define, measure, analyze, improve, and control) is used for projects aimed at improving an existing business process. The DMAIC project methodology has five phases (Figure 18):

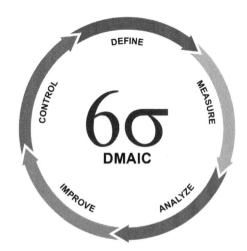

FIGURE 18

The Six Sigma DMAIC (define, measure, analyze, improve, and control) model.

1. **Define** the system, the voice of the customer and their requirements, and the project goals, specifically.
2. **Measure** key aspects of the current process and collect relevant data.
3. **Analyze** the data to investigate and verify cause-and-effect relationships. Determine what the relationships are, and attempt to ensure that all factors have been considered. Seek out the root cause of the defect under investigation.
4. **Improve** or optimize the current process based upon data analysis using techniques such as design of experiments, poka yoke or mistake proofing, and standard work to create a new, future-state process. Set up pilot runs to establish process capability.
5. **Control** the future-state process to ensure that any deviations from the target are corrected before they result in defects. Implement control systems such as SPC, production boards, visual workplaces, and continuously monitor the process.

Some organizations add a "recognize" step at the beginning, which is to recognize the right problem to work on, thus yielding an RDMAIC methodology.[93]

DMADV

DMADV (define, measure, analyze, design, and verify) is used for projects aimed at creating new product or process designs. The DMADV project methodology, also known as DFSS (Design for Six Sigma[94]), also features five phases (Figure 19):

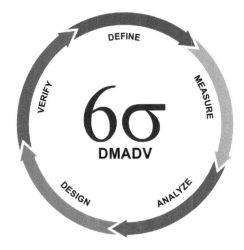

FIGURE 19

The Six Sigma DMADV (define, measure, analyze, design, and verify) model.

1. **Define** design goals that are consistent with customer demands and the enterprise strategy.
2. **Measure** and identify CTQs (characteristics that are Critical To Quality), product capabilities, production process capability, and risks.
3. **Analyze** to develop and design alternatives.
4. **Design** an improved alternative, best suited per analysis in the previous step.
5. **Verify** the design, set up pilot runs, implement the production process, and hand it over to the process owner(s).

First you define the goal in accordance with the demand and the strategy. Then, you measure and identify the quality criteria for the product and process and the risks involved in both. The analysis will result in several designs, which are compared and analyzed to find the very best design. Then, you verify if the chosen design meets the goal, and then you launch it.

Conclusion

We have in the above section elaborated on what Six Sigma is and the way of thinking and working around the concept. One of the things to consider is why to choose Six Sigma in the first place? You could, of course, consider other process methodologies that require a higher (Zero Defect) or lower level of accuracy. In the end, it's a question of cost-benefit in every situation. Both improvement methodologies

(Six Sigma and Zero Defect) are based on the analysis of data. It is therefore important to know that Six Sigma requires very precise data to yield any benefit. If the performance and measuring tools are not accurate enough, you cannot calculate the process improvements accurately. The accuracy of the measuring is proportional with the cost of measuring, and this can be a hindrance that will ultimately make you choose other optimization or improvement techniques, such as BPR or Lean, rather than Six Sigma.

Regardless, Six Sigma offers a substantial range of adequate benefits and rewards once it has been successfully implemented in an organization. Some of the most sought for benefits are for instance:

- The goal is to improve the process quality to a level of less than 3.4 errors per one million possibilities.
- Six Sigma distinguishes between designing a new process and improving an existing one.
- Six Sigma is as a concept aware of the roles and qualifications of the involved parties in the process management.
- Six Sigma is designed to correct an existing process, but is not suited to create new products or technologies.
- It provides a clear focus for achieving measurable and quantifiable financial advantages.
- It increases focus on strong leadership and support.

It provides a clear duty to make decisions based on verifiable data instead of merely guessing.

End Notes

1. Business Process Management: Profiting From Process, Roger Burlton, Sams Publishing, 2001.
2. An Introduction To Enterprise Architecture: Third Edition, Scott A. Bernard, AuthorHouse, 2012.
3. A framework for information systems architecture, John A. Zachman, IBM Systems Journal, Vol 26. No 3, 1987.
4. Toyota Production System: Beyond large-scale production, Taiichi Ohno, Productivity Press, 1988.
5. Ibid.
6. Lean Consumption, J.P. Womack and D.T. Jones, *Harvard Business Review*, 2005.
7. Reengineering Work: Don't Automate, Obliterate, Michael Hammer, *Harvard Business Review*, 1990.
8. Total Quality Management: Origins and evolution of the term, Martínez Lorente, Ángel Rafael, Emerald Group. Publishing Limited, 1998.
9. Quality Management: Strategies, Methods, Techniques, Tilo Pfeifer, Hanser, 2002.
10. A History of Managing for Quality: The Evolution, Trends, and Future Directions of Managing for Quality, Joseph M. Juran, ASQC Quality Press, 1995.
11. What is total quality control? The Japanese way, Kaoru Ishikawa, Prentice Hall, 1985.
12. The House of Quality, John R. Hauser, Don Clausing, Harvard Business Review, 1988.

13. Application of Taguchi Method for Optimizing Turning Process by the effects of Machining Parameters, Krishankant, Jatin Taneja, Mohit Bector, Rajesh Kumar, International Journal of Engineering and Advanced. Technology, 2012.

14. Quantitative methods for quality improvement, Hart, K. M., & Hart, R. F., ASQC Quality Press, 1989.

15. Foundations of statistical quality control, Barlow, Richard E.; Irony, Telba Z., Institute of Mathematical Statistics, Hayward, CA, 1992.

16. Statistical Method from the Viewpoint of Quality Control, Walter A. Shewhart, W. Edwards Deming, Dover. Books on Mathematics, 2011.

17. EFQM Excellence Model, AKYAY UYGUR, SEVGI SÜMERLI, International Review of Management and Business Research, 2013.

18. The Six Sigma Handbook, Fourth Edition, Thomas Pyzdek, Paul Keller, McGraw-Hill Education, 2014.

19. *The Six Sigma Way: How GE, Motorola, and Other Top Companies are Honing Their Performance*, Pande, P. S., Robert P, Neuman and Roland R., Cavanagh, McGraw-Hill Professional, 2001.

20. Architecture of Integrated Information Systems: Foundations of Enterprise Modelling, August-Wilhelm Scheer, Springer, 1992.

21. Start-ups are easy, but..., August-Wilhelm Scheer, Springer, 2001.

22. ARIS—business process modeling, August-Wilhelm Scheer, Springer, 1999.

23. Computer: A Challenge for Business Administration, August-Wilhelm Scheer, Springer, 1985.

24. Business Process Engineering: Aris-Navigator for Reference Models for Industrial Engineers/Book, August-Wilhelm Scheer, Springer, 1995.

25. CIM Towards the Factory of the Future, August-Wilhelm Scheer, Springer, 1994.

26. Principles of efficient information management, August-Wilhelm Scheer, Springer, 1991.

27. ARIS – Business Process Frameworks, August-Wilhelm Scheer, Springer, 1998.

28. A framework for information systems architecture, John A. Zachman, IBM Systems Journal, 1987.

29. Business systems planning and business Information control study: a comparison, John A. Zachman, IBM Systems Journal, 1982.

30. John Zachman's Concise Definition of The Zachman Framework™, John A. Zachman, Zachman International, Inc., 2008.

31. *The Zachman Framework for Enterprise Architecture™: A Primer For Enterprise Engineering and Manufacturing*, John Zachman, Zachman International, 2003.

32. The Zachman Framework For Enterprise Architecture: Primer for Enterprise Engineering and Manufacturing, John A. Zachman, Zachman International, Inc., 2003.

33. Conceptual, Logical, Physical: It Is Simple, John A. Zachman, Zachman International, Inc., 2000–2011.

34. Architecture, John A. Zachman, Zachman International, Inc., 2007–2011.

35. Cloud Computing and Enterprise Architecture, John A. Zachman, Zachman International, Inc., 2011.

36. The original texts are Taiichi Ohno, The Toyota Production System, Productivity Press, Oregon, 1988 and The Toyota Way, Toyota Motor Corporation, Tokyo, 2001.

37. The Lean Lexicon, Lean Enterprise Institute (LEI), Cambridge, 2003, The use of these tools is described in a series of workbooks published by LEI, including Creating Continuous Flow, 2001, Making Materials Flow, 2003 and Creating Level Pull, 2009.

38. For a description of TWI see Donald A. Dinero, *Training Within Industry*, Productivity Press, New York, 2005.
39. Masaki Imai, Kaizen, McGraw Hill, New York, 1991.
40. Jeff Liker, The Toyota Way, McGraw Hill, New York, 2004.
41. John Shook, Managing to Learn, Lean Enterprise Institute, Cambridge, 2009.
42. James P Womack, Daniel T Jones & Daniel Roos, The Machine that Changed the World, Rawson Macmillan, New York, 1991.
43. James P Womack & Daniel T Jones, Lean Thinking, Simon & Schuster, New York, 1996 and 2003.
44. John Shook and Mike Rother, Learning to See, Lean Enterprise Institute, Cambridge, 1998.
45. Pascal Dennis, Getting the Right Things Done, Lean Enterprise Institute, Cambridge, 2009.
46. This management system is described in Jeff Liker and Gary Convis, The Toyota Way to Lean Leadership, McGraw Hill, New York, 2012, Mike Rother, Toyota Kata, McGraw Hill, New York, 2010 and Michael and Freddy Balle, Lead with Respect, Lean Enterprise Institute, Cambridge, 2014.
47. Eric Ries, The Lean Startup, Penguin, New York, 2013.
48. Described in detail in Chapter 4 of Lean Thinking, ibid.
49. The Tesco and GKN examples are outlined in Daniel Jones and James Womack, Seeing the Whole Value Stream, Lean Enterprise Institute, Cambridge, 2011.
50. James Womack and Daniel Jones, Lean Solutions, Simon & Schuster, New York, 2005.
51. The Economist Guide to Management Ideas and Gurus, Tim Hindle, 2012.
52. Reengineering Work: Don't Automate, Obliterate, Michael Hammer, Harvard Business Review, 1990.
53. Reengineering the Corporation: A Manifesto for Business Revolution (Collins Business Essentials), Michael Hammer, James Champy, Harper Business Essentials, 2006.
54. Time 25: They Range In Age From 31 To 67, Time Magazine, 1996.
55. Michael Hammer and James Champy. *Reengineering the Corporation: A Manifesto for Business Revolution*, (Harper Business, 1993).
56. Identifying and Eliminating The Seven Wastes or Muda, Rene T. Domingo, Asian Institute of Management.
57. von Rosing, M., Hagemann Snabe, J. Rosenberg, A. Møller, C. Scavillo, M. *Business Process Management – the SAP® Roadmap*, 2009.
58. Hammer, M., "Reengineering Work: Don't Automate, Obliterate", *Harvard Business Review*, July/August,1990, 104–112.
59. The New Industrial Engineering: Information Technology and Business Process Redesign, Davenport, Thomas &. Short, J., Sloan Management Review, 1990.
60. A Practical Guide to Business Process Re-engineering, Mike Robson, Philip Ullah, Gower Publishing, Ltd., 1996.
61. Kristian D. Ambeck and Peter Beyer, *The Road to Renewal* (Danish publication).
62. Hammer, Michael and Champy, James, Reengineering the Corporation: A Manifesto for Business Revolution, (Harper Business, 1993), Chapter 1 excerpt.
63. Business Process Reengineering: Building a Comprehensive Methodology, Subashish Guha, William J. Kettinger & James T.C. Teng, Taylor & Francis Group, 1993.
64. Davenport, Thomas, *Process Innovation: Reengineering work through information technology*, (Harvard Business School Press, Boston, 1993).
65. Maureen Weicher, William W. Chu, Wan Ching Lin, Van Le and Dominic Yu, *Business Process Reengineering: Analysis and Recommendations*.

66. Smith, K.K., "Philosophical Problems in Thinking about Organisational Change", in Change in Organisations, (Jossey-Bass, Oxford, 1982).
67. Michael Hammer; James Champy, *Reengineering the Corporation*.
68. Kaplan, R.B. and Murdock, L., "Rethinking the Corporation: Core Process Redesign", *The McKinsey Quarterly*, No. 2, 1991.
69. There's no Better Time to Do Business Process Improvement than the Bad Time, Hutex™ Management Consulting.
70. Thomas H. Davenport, Laurence Prusak and H. James Wilson "Article from Computerworld: Reengineering revisited: What went wrong with the business-process reengineering fad. And will it come back?"
71. LEADing BPM Practice Case Story, Mark von Rosing, Henrik von Scheel, Anette Falk Bøgebjerg, LEADing Practice, 2013.
72. T. Priyavrat, (2007),'Teams, Traits And Tasks [QT3] For Total Quality', Quality World, Vol V, April 2007.
73. Hashmi, K. "Introduction and Implementation of Total Quality management (TQM)".
74. Beckhard, R., Pritchard W. *Changing the Essence* (San Francisco: Jossey-Bass, 1992).
75. Kumar, Dr. S., 2006 *Total Quality Management*, 13–17. ISBN-10: 8131805689.
76. Nayantara Padhi. Total Quality Management of Distance Education. The Eight Elements of TQM. ISBN-10: 0415961602.
77. Thareja, P., "Each One is Capable (Part 16 of A Total Quality Organisation Thru' People). FOUNDRY", *Journal For Progressive Metal Casters*, Vol. 20, No. 4, July/Aug, 2008.
78. Thareja, P., Each One is Capable (Part 16 of A Total Quality Organisation Thru' People). Journal: Foundry, July/August 2008, Vol. 20, No. 4, P61-69. ISBN20083325.
79. Breyfogle, F.W., *Implementing Six Sigma: Smarter Solutions Using Statistical Methods*, (John Wiley & Sons Inc., New York, NY, 1999).
80. Breyfogle, F.W. 1999, Implementing Six Sigma: Smarter Solutions Using Statistical Methods, John Wiley & Sons Inc., New York, NY. ISBN-10: 0471265721.
81. Mandelbrot, Benoit; Richard L Hudson (2004). The (mis)behavior of markets: A fractal view of risk, ruin, and reward. New York: Basic Books. p. 153.
82. Vijay K. Mathur, "How Well Do We Know Pareto Optimality?" Journal of Economic Education 22#2 (1991) p. 172–78.
83. The Economics of Vilfredo Pareto, Renato Cirillo, Routledge, 1978.
84. Sales Process Diagram, LEADing Practice Business Process Reference Content #LEAD-ES20005BP.
85. Ishikawa, Kaoru (1985) [First published in Japanese 1981]. What is Total Quality Control? The Japanese Way. Prentice Hall. ISBN 0-13-952433-9.
86. Barlow, R. E. & Irony, T. Z. (1992) "Foundations of statistical quality control" in Ghosh, M. & Pathak, P.K. (eds.) Current Issues in Statistical Inference: Essays in Honor of D. Basu, Hayward, CA: Institute of Mathematical Statistics, p. 99-112.
87. Deming, W.E., "Out of The Crises" MIT Center for Advanced Engineering Study, 1986. ISBN-10: 8176710377.
88. Priyavrat, Thareja. GEMI (Global Environmental Management Aman Mohamed Initiative: Total Quality Environmental Management. The Primer. Washington D.C.: GEMI, 1993.
89. Pande, P. S.; Neuman, Robert P.; Cavanagh, Roland R. (2001). The Six Sigma Way: How GE, Motorola, and Other Top Companies are Honing Their Performance. New York: McGraw-Hill Professional.

90. Adams, C.W., Gupta, Praveen, *Six Sigma Deployment*. Butterworth-Heinemann, Burlington, MA, 2003.
91. Stamatis, D.H., *Six Sigma Fundamentals: A Complete Guide to the System, Methods, and Tools*, (Productivity Press, New York, 2004) p. 1.
92. Mikel J. Harry, The Vision of Six Sigma: Tools and Methods for Breakthrough, Volume II, Fifth Edition, January1, 1997. ASIN: B003X67OX4.
93. Webber, L., Wallace, M. *Quality Control for Dummies*, December 15, 2006.
94. De Feo, J.A., Barnard, W. Juran, *Institute's Six Sigma Breakthrough and Beyond – Quality Performance Breakthrough Method*, (Tata McGraw-Hill Publishing Company Limited, 2005).

Phase 4: What Is Business Process Management?

Keith D. Swenson, Mark von Rosing

INTRODUCTION

As explored in an earlier chapter, the term *business process modeling* was coined in the field of systems engineering by S. Williams in his 1967 article entitled, "Business Process Modeling Improves Administrative Control."[1] However, it was not until the 1990s that the term became popular[2] and the term *process* became a new productivity paradigm.[3] Companies were encouraged to think in terms of processes instead of functions and procedures. Today, there are multiple books, white papers, articles, blogs, and even entire conferences on the subject of business process management (BPM). However, many people still struggle to find a precise definition of BPM. As we will show, viewpoints vary wildly, making people unclear whether BPM is a process, technology, or management discipline. The answer depends upon whom you ask. If the question is asked of a technology company, most likely the definition of BPM will be centered more on technology than business. Going into this analysis, we believed that there was a strong bias toward technology within the industry, as indicated by the way that software companies refer to BPM in the context of the capabilities of their particular technology, such as SAP to describe the BPM Netweaver engine or Oracle to describe their BPM collaboration platform. We are greatly concerned by the way that the BPM acronym is used loosely, with its meaning depending upon the context. The lack of a widely accepted definition has arguably had the single most harmful effect on the industry.

DEFINITION AND RESEARCH

During a concerted review and assessment of approximately 100 articles, we found dozens of differing definitions of BPM; what was offered as authoritative meanings varied significantly by publication, which creates a significant problem. Without a common understanding of BPM, one cannot make a conclusive statement about what BPM does or how one might or might not use it. The goal of this research effort is to find the definition that most closely represents the concept that people (expert and otherwise) generally have for the term BPM. To this end, we want to uncover a definition that will resonate with most people in a meaningful and useful way when we say "BPM." With the goal to find a common definition, we will cite well-known definitions of BPM, then provide our analysis of the usefulness in terms of various contexts, such as business, technology, length, etc.

Cambridge Dictionary Online: "(BPM is) the development and control of processes used in a company, department, project, etc. to make sure they are effective."

This definition does not say anything about process efficiency or quality and ignores the idea of process improvement, all of which are necessary parts of BPM. With the focus on development and control, the definition might lead the reader to take on a very technology-centric view that suggests a focus on the automation aspects of processes, and it is the automation that is the focus and goal of BPM. The larger view is that processes exist outside of development, and they are subject to examination and improvement with or without technology.

Rummler and Brache, Improving Performance: How to Manage the White Space in the Organization Chart: "(BPM is the) management of the series of steps that a business executes to produce a product or service."

Management of the work steps is clearly an aspect of process. This definition potentially conflates the automation of the tasks (i.e., the process) with the continual improvement of the process over time. The reader could easily confuse the term "management" as used here with the idea of automation, but BPM is not necessarily or even particularly about automation.

Smith and Fingar, BPM: The Third Wave: "(BPM is) management of the complete and dynamically coordinated set of collaborative and transactional activities that deliver value to customers."

The idea of coordination imparts a sense that control and stewardship are aspects of the management of business process, but it does not talk about improvement. Management of the activities is different from the management of the process. This definition focuses on transactional work, ignoring the idea that work may be transformational or tacit within a process that delivers value. This definition lacks the specificity that would clearly show that process and process management can exist without automation.

Martyn Ould, BPM: A Rigorous Approach: "(BPM is the) management of a coherent set of activities carried out by a collaborating group to achieve a goal."

The management of activities of one instance of a process is different than the management of the flow of activities in a set of processes over time. The goal of BPM is not to successfully complete one process, but to control, steward, and continually improve all processes over time. This facet is not clear in this definition. Again we fear that management, in this setting, could be interpreted as automation.

Marlon Dumas, et al., Fundamentals of BPM: "BPM is the art and science of overseeing how work is performed in an organization to ensure consistent outcomes and to take advantage of improvement opportunities."

This is a very good definition. It is important that a definition of BPM clarify that it takes a process-oriented approach as opposed to a function-oriented approach. That being said, this definition, because it talks only of work and outcomes, could also be seen to apply to improvements aimed at a single step (unit of work) of a process in isolation of the entire process.

Wikipedia article on BPM, captured around November 28, 2013 (*for clarity, the text not directly related to defining BPM has been removed*): "BPM has been referred to as a 'holistic management' approach to aligning an organization's business processes with the wants and needs of clients. BPM uses a systematic approach in an attempt to continuously improve business effectiveness and efficiency while striving for innovation, flexibility, and integration with technology. It can therefore be described as a 'process optimization process.' ... As a managerial approach, BPM sees processes as strategic assets of an organization that must be understood, managed, and improved to deliver value-added products and services to clients."

This is poorly written and clearly far too long to be a definition. The gratuitous use of "holistic" does not help in understanding, nor do the many uses of vague, conditional phrases (e.g., "has been," "could be," "attempt"). More to the point, there is no requirement for a reference to technology in the definition and an overemphasis on other areas.

IBM: "BPM is a discipline that leverages software and services to provide total visibility into an organization. Discover, document, automate, and continuously improve business processes to increase efficiency and reduce costs."

This narrowly defines BPM as software and services, conveniently matching the sort of thing that IBM can supply. There is wide agreement in the field that BPM is a management discipline, which could be done on paper and pencil if necessary; software is not a necessary ingredient.

Association for Information and Image Management: "BPM is a way of looking at and then controlling the processes that are present in an organization. It is an effective methodology to use in times of crisis to make certain that the processes are efficient and effective, as this will result in a better and more cost efficient organization."

This is a fairly reasonable definition, but positioning BPM as something to be used in a crisis is not consistent with what most people see as being an essential aspect.

BPM Institute, "What is BPM Anyway? BPM Explained": "(BPM is a) process of managing your business processes; a management discipline; a technology or set of technologies; a rapid application development framework. First and foremost, BPM is a process and a management discipline."

Here, BPM is defined as just about anything you want. Again, there is confusion with the technology perspective. BPM is certainly not a rapid application framework. This definition simply does not help people understand what BPM is.

Paul Harmon, 2005: "(BPM is) a management discipline focused on improving corporate performance by managing a company's business processes."

This is very good for a short definition. However, it is not clear about whether BPM is the management of the tasks within a single process (e.g., automation) or the means of how processes are repeatable, modified, and improved over time. It is important to say a few more words to make it clear that BPM is the latter and to emphasize the need to care for processes as part of the going concern of the enterprise.

Gartner: "BPM is the discipline of managing processes (rather than tasks) as the means for improving business performance outcomes and operational agility. Processes span organizational boundaries, linking together people, information flows, systems and other assets to create and deliver value to customers and constituents."

This definition is not bad, although a little bit wordy. It does not fully capture the idea of stewardship or control of the process in the steady state.

Hammer, cited by Tim Weilkiens in Object Management Group's Certified Expert in BPM: "(BPM is a) structured approach to performance improvement that centers on the disciplined design and careful execution of company end to end processes."

This definition is exclusively about design and execution can easily be confused with automation of processes.

CIO Magazine: "BPM is a systematic approach to improving a company's business processes."

This definition needs to mention a process-oriented approach as opposed to a functional-oriented approach. It speaks solely to improvement, thus ignoring the idea of controlling and making decisions about the operating processes.

BusinessDictionary.com: "(BPM is an) activity undertaken by businesses to identify, evaluate, and improve business processes. With the advancement of technology, BPM can now be effectively managed with software that is customized based on the metrics and policies specified by a company. This type of action is essential to businesses seeking to improve process performance related issues so that they can better serve their clients."

This definition is not bad, although a bit wordy. The focus on technology is somewhat misplaced.

Techopedia: "BPM is a concept that focuses on aligning all organizational elements to improve operational performance. The BPM strategy is categorized with holistic management approaches which are used to develop better business efficiency, while channeling organizations toward more creative, flexible and technologically-integrated systems."

It is unclear what is meant by "aligning all organizational elements," "channeling organizations," or "holistic management." This is missing the aspect that BPM by nature is process oriented, and that performance must be measured across the entire process, as opposed to only a single step of the process. There is a problem using the term management as a way to describe what happens within the nature of BPM, so it would be helpful if this point of clarification was made.

Popkin Software, BPMN and BPM: "BPM is concerned with managing change to improve business processes."

Although this definition is nice and short, the use of business process within the definition makes it circular. The definition needs more explanation about how this is accomplished. It ignores the idea of controlling the process on an ongoing basis.

IBM Redbook, BPM Enabled by SOA: "BPM is most often associated with the life cycle of a business process. The process life cycle spans identifying and improving processes that deliver business capability to deploy and manage the process when it is operational. What is often forgotten is managing process performance after a process is operational."

The mention of "deploying a process" might be construed as a technological view centered on process automation, as might be the phrase "process is operational." There is no idea of control, or oversight, care for processes as an asset of value.

PC Magazine: "(BPM is a) structured approach that models an enterprise's human and machine tasks and the interactions between them as processes."

This is a very technological view, particularly the mention of "machine tasks". BPM might or might not use modeling, but this definition implies that BPM is the modeling of the process, and not the work that people do to steward or improve a process.

Business Analysis Body of Knowledge: "BPM covers a set of approaches that focus on how the organization performs work to deliver value across multiple functional areas to a customer. BPM aims for a view of value delivery that spans the entire organization and views the organization through a process-centric lens."

Although this definition avoids the technology bias, there is nothing that speaks to the nature of "management." It looks to be an analytic method rather than a management discipline.

INSIGHTS GAINED

We have discussed at length what many authorities see as representing BPM and observed what we believe to be the key shortfall of each case. In this section, we elaborate on what was learned about the nature of process to synthesize the best features of what we observed and to address the limitations we noted. The specific desire is to understand what works in terms of good patterns and to reflect on what does not work, thereby exposing useful antipatterns.

BPM Is Not About Automation of Processes

The implication is that BPM is not about automating business processes (in the "paving the cowpaths" meaning) but about improving them. It presumes that you view business as a set of processes, and BPM is the act of improving those processes. It is important to note that "skill" is different from "skill improvement." This can be confusing. For example, in competitive situations the two ideas are often intertwined: What is the act of playing tennis, if not also the act of trying to improve the way you play tennis? However, in other contexts, it is easier to distinguish: The activity of driving is different than taking a driving course to improve the way you drive. In the same way, reengineering a process is not simply about automating what is currently there. Some will say that automation by itself is an improvement over a manual process. BPM is the activity of discovering and designing the automated process, and it is done when the finished application is deployed to the organization. The running of the processes is not part of BPM. However, monitoring the process to find areas of improvement would still be an important part of BPM.

BPM Is Done by People Concerned Primarily with Improvement of the Process

A business process will involve many people, but how many of them are concerned with improving it? Some will insist that improvement is everyone's job. That is, the receptionist should be thinking about how to improve the operations if possible. This interpretation is too broad to be useful. The in-house cook adding a new spice to a menu item—making it taste better, motivating more employees to eat in the building, cutting down on wasted time driving to an outside restaurant, and improving the amount of information interactions between workers, thus resulting in better performance—is not BPM by any account. Everybody in a business is working to do their best job, and every good job helps the business, but all of this is not BPM. BPM must be narrowly defined as the activity done by people who actively and primarily look specifically at the business processes and try to improve them. Clearly, those people must solicit input from as many others as possible, but those others are not doing BPM.

Misrepresentations of BPM

In this section, we suggest a variety of different ways that people abuse the BPM term and offer our thoughts on why the point is problematic.

BPM Is Not a Product

There is a product category called BPMS, which is a BPM suite or BPM system. Gartner has introduced a new product category called "intelligent BPMS." What is included depends very much on the vendor. Analysts have attempted to list features and capabilities that are necessary, but those features change from year to year. For example, in 2007, the suggestion was that BPM suites must have a Business Process Execution Language (BPEL) execution capability, but today this is entirely ignored or forgotten.

BPM Is Not a Market Segment

Again, there might be a market segment around products that support BPM or BPMS products, but BPM itself is a practice. Vendors may be labeled as a "BPMS vendor", which simply means they have some products that can support the activity of BPM, among other things.

An Application Does Not Do BPM

The application might be the result of BPM activity. Once finished, it either controls the business process or supports people engaged in doing the business process. It may, as a byproduct, capture metrics that help further improvement of the process.

In this sense, an application supports BPM in the same way that a receptionist may support BPM by coming up with good ideas; that is not enough to say that the application, or the receptionist, is "doing" BPM.

BPM As a Service Is Not Application Hosting

We use the term business process as a service to mean applications hosted outside the company that supports more than one function of a business process. Like the application above, it does the process, but it does not do BPM.

Entire Organizational Units Do Not Do BPM

To say that a company is doing BPM is simply a way of saying that there are some people in the company who are doing BPM. This kind of abstraction is normal. It should be obvious that when a company or division claims to be doing BPM, the majority of the people there are not actually doing BPM.

BPM Is Not Merely Anything that Improves Business

Some argue that every activity is part of a process, because a process is just a set of activities. Then, any action taken to improve any activity is BPM. We have argued against this interpretation because such a broad interpretation would make BPM meaningless: It would mean anything. There is broad acceptance that BPM is a practice of methodically improving a process that supports business, and that improvements in part of the process must be done only after the consideration of the entire end-to-end process.

BPM Is Not All Activities Supported by a BPMS

As mentioned earlier, a BPMS supports many things (e.g., application development) that are not BPM. A BPMS that only supported the exact activity of BPM would not be as useful as one that brought a lot of capabilities together. It is, however, a common mistake for people to say that because a BPMS supports something, it is then an aspect of BPM. While it is true that someone who does BPM needs to document a process, it is not true that anyone who documents a process is doing BPM. Also, while it is true that many BPMS support designing a screen form, it is not true that designing a screen form is BPM. The activity of BPM is fairly well defined, but a BPMS supports a much wider set of activities.

Just Because You Can Do Something with a BPMS Does Not Mean It Is BPM

A BPMS is designed to support the activity of BPM. However, there are many things a BPMS can do that are not BPM.

Participating in a Process Is Not Doing BPM

A manager approving a purchase order is not doing BPM, even though that approval is an activity in a process. A bank manager rejecting a loan application is not doing BPM, even though this activity is a step in a business process. These people are doing jobs that are part of a process, but they are not doing BPM.

Implementation (Coding) of the Process Application Is Not BPM

An application developer designing a form for data entry as a step in a process is not doing BPM at that moment. Once the "to-be" process has been adequately spelled out, the actual implementation of the application that supports it is no longer actively engaged in improving the process. A small caution should be noted here: Applications are often developed incrementally—show the customer, get feedback, improve, and iterate—and the process may be improved incrementally as well. Those incremental improvements should be included as the activity of BPM, but the activity of implementation of the application is not BPM. The criteria are clear: If you are actively and primarily engaged in improvement of the process, then it is BPM; otherwise, it is engineering.

Making a Suggestion for Process Improvement Is Not BPM

There is a distinction between many people who make suggestions and those who then actually do the BPM. When a process analyst is involved in BPM, it is expected that they will solicit lots of information about what is and is not working, as well as suggestions on how it might work. Those people who give the feedback are helping the BPM work but are not themselves doing BPM.

Improving a Single Step of a Process Is Not BPM

Some people have the mistaken idea that any possible action that improves a process is BPM, no matter how small. A person doing BPM needs to have some kind of big-picture view of the process; it has been described as an "end-to-end" view of the process. Optimizing one step in a process, without knowledge of the entire process, is exactly what Hammer and Champy were warning about: To understand the correct optimizations, we need to consider those optimizations within the context of a complete business process. A workman smoothing gravel on a road is improving all of the process that involves driving on that road, but it is not BPM because he does not have visibility of the whole process. The engineer finding a way to double the bandwidth of a fiber-optic cable is improving all the processes that require communications, but this is not BPM either. An office worker who finds that OpenOffice 4 helps to create documents faster than some other word processor is improving all the processes that involve writing documents; this is not BPM either. To have a discussion about BPM, we can consider only those activities by people who have a view to, and consider the effect on, the entire end-to-end process.

CONCLUSION: ONE COMMON DEFINITION

From the above analysis and comparison of definitions, as well as a long research discussion led by Keith Swenson, among others, on the LinkedIn BPM Guru group, bpm.com forum, Association of Business Process Management Professionals forum, and other places, brings us to propose this definition:

> Business process management (BPM) is a discipline involving any combination of modeling, automation, execution, control, measurement, and optimization of business activity flows in applicable combination to support enterprise goals, spanning organizational and system boundaries, and involving employees, customers, and partners within and beyond the enterprise boundaries.

This definition is designed to be short enough to use regularly in both business and technology context without gratuitous words. However, there is a trade-off: a longer definition might be clearer, perhaps at the cost of being more cumbersome. Here is clarification of what we mean by these words:

- BPM is a discipline: It is a practice; it is something you do. Predominant in the definitions is the idea that BPM is something you do, not a thing you own or buy. It is described in many definitions as a practice. There was wide agreement on this: Well over 90% of the participants expressed this view.
- Business stems from the state of being busy, and it implies commercially viable and profitable work. A business exists to provide value to customers in exchange for something else of value.
- Process means a flow of business activities and seeing those activities as connected toward the achievement of some business transaction. Flow is meant loosely here: The order may or may not be strictly defined.
- A person doing BPM must consider a process at the scope of interrelated business activities that holistically cooperate to fulfill a business objective. This is the key difference from a functional view of business, where the production of the different classes of output might be optimized independent of the other functions. In a complex system, such as a modern business, it is well known that local optimization of part of the system will rarely lead to good overall results. A BPM practitioner must consider the metrics of the entire system when evaluating a specific process.
- Modeling means that they would identify, define, and make a representation of the complete process to support communication about the process for the purpose of creating a shared understanding and to provide the tools to exercise control. There is no single standard way to model, but the model must encompass the process.
- Automation refers to the work that is done in advance to assure the smooth execution of the process instances. In many cases, this means writing software, but it might include building machinery or even creating signage to direct participants in the process.
- Execution means that instances of a process are performed or enacted, which may include automated aspects. Conceptually, the process instance executes

itself, following the BPM practitioner's model, but unfolding independent of the BPM practitioner.

- Control means that there is some aspect of making sure that the process follows the designed course. This can be strict control and enforcement, or it might be loose control in the form of guidelines, training, and manual practices.
- Measurement means that effort is taken to quantitatively determine how well the process is working in terms of serving the needs of customers.
- Optimization means that the discipline of BPM is an ongoing activity, which builds over time to steadily improve the measures of the process. Improvement is relative to the goals of the organization and ultimately in terms of meeting the needs of customers.
- Enterprise is used here simply to mean a business organization or organizations where people are working together to meet common goals; it does not need to be exceptionally large, and it does not need to be for profit.
- The mention of enterprise goals is included here to emphasize that BPM should be done in the context of the goals of the enterprise, and not some small part of it. This might seem a bit redundant in one sense: Any improvement of a process must be an improvement in terms of the enterprise goals; anything else would not be called an improvement.
- Within and beyond the enterprise boundaries recognizes that the enterprise is part of a larger system. Customers are part of the business process. Their interaction, along with those of employees, should be considered as part of the end-to-end interaction.

Our goal was to find a common definition. Our request is that you endorse this definition of BPM, so that there exists a common definition that we can use as a basis of creating shared understanding and advancing the discipline. We believe that a single common definition is of critical value to the entire marketplace; this wish started our research and analysis and led to the definition. In the aim and objective to isolate the single prominent definition, we did not wish to single out definitions. However, we realize that with such a publication, there will probably be people who will say, "I would prefer if the definition had X, or didn't have Y."

Everyone has an opinion. The question we asked ourselves—and we think that you should ask yourself—is this: Does this common definition cover the concepts that are inherent in the idea of BPM? To that end, our work is built on research and analysis, and single opinions were avoided to unite and build a common understanding of the subject.

End Notes

1. Williams S., "Business Process Modeling Improves Administrative Control," in *Automation* (December 1967), 44–50.
2. Michael Hammer, "Reengineering Work: Don't Automate, Obliterate," *Hardvard Business Review* (July 1990).
3. Asbjørn Rolstadås, "Business Process Modeling and Reengineering," in *Performance Management: A Business Process Benchmarking Approach* (1995), 148–150.

The BPM Way of Thinking

Mark von Rosing, Henrik von Scheel, August-Wilhelm Scheer

INTRODUCTION

In this part, we introduce the "way of thinking" around business process concepts. We focus on the value of an ontology and the business process management (BPM) ontology, which is the essential starting point that creates the guiding principles. We also provide structural concepts around strategic definitions, such as wants, needs, direction, issues, and problems.

Here, we explore how BPM ontology can be applied within the areas of process modelling, process engineering, and process architecture. It provides the fundamental process concepts that can be used to document corporate knowledge and structure process knowledge by defining relation process concepts (e.g., the order of process steps).

We feel this way of thinking enables the right abstraction level and allows an understanding of the underlying thoughts, views, visions, and perspectives.

Today, many BPM and/or process frameworks, methods and/or approaches, such as LEAN, Six Sigma, BPR, TQM, Zero Defect, BPMN, and BPMS, have their own vocabularies. Each of these vocabularies has its own definition of terms, such as business process, process step, process activity, events, process role, process owner, process measure, and process rule.

Ontology is an essential discipline that can support understanding and structuring of BPM knowledge, create and define the fundamental concepts, and provide semantic relations and correlations between these concepts. Such definitions are not incorporated in contemporary BPM practice in an integrated and standardized way. Therefore, we present an ontology for BPM. Our focus will be on the value of an ontology and the BPM ontology itself.

This discussion builds the foundation for the rest of the book, as the BPM ontology includes our shared vocabulary (i.e., folksonomy) that structures knowledge in two ways. First, it allows practitioners to structure their business knowledge by adding meaningful relationships between the vocabulary terms. Second, it organizes concepts in hierarchic "is-a" relationships, which allow for a polymorphic inheritance of properties.

The Value of Ontology

Mark von Rosing, Wim Laurier, Simon M. Polovina

INTRODUCTION

It is generally accepted that the creation of added value requires collaboration inside and between organizations.[1] Collaboration requires sharing knowledge (e.g., a shared understanding of business processes) between trading partners and between colleagues. It is on the (unique) knowledge that is shared between and created by colleagues that organizations build their competitive advantage.[2] To take full advantage of this knowledge, it should be disseminated as widely as possible within an organization. Nonaka distinguished *tacit* knowledge, which is personal, context specific, and not so easy to communicate (e.g., intuitions, unarticulated mental models, embodied technological skills), from *explicit* knowledge, which is meaningful information articulated in clear language, including numbers and diagrams.[3]

Tacit knowledge can be disseminated through *socialization* (e.g., face-to-face communication, sharing experiences), which implies a reduced dissemination speed, or can be *externalized*, which is the conversion of tacit into explicit knowledge. Although explicit knowledge can take many forms (e.g., business (process) models, manuals), this chapter focuses on ontologies, which are versatile knowledge artifacts created through externalization, with the power to fuel Nonaka's knowledge spiral. Nonaka's knowledge spiral visualizes how a body of unique corporate knowledge, and hence a competitive advantage, is developed through a collaborative and iterative knowledge creation process that involves iterative cycles of externalization, combination,[4] and internalization.[5] When corporate knowledge is documented with ontology, a knowledge spiral leads to ontology evolution.[6]

The next section of this chapter defines ontologies, discussing their level of context dependency and maturing process. The third section of this chapter discusses the state of the art in a business context, while the fourth section introduces directions for future research and development. A summary is presented in the last section.

WHAT IS ONTOLOGY?

The term *ontology* can refer to a philosophical discipline that deals with the nature and the organization of reality.[7] Ontology, as a philosophical discipline, is usually contrasted with epistemology, which is a branch of philosophy that deals with the nature and sources of our knowledge. However, an *ontology* is an artifact—more precisely, an intentional semantic structure that encodes the set of objects and terms that are presumed to exist in some area of interest (i.e., the universe of discourse or semantic domain), the relationships that hold among them, and the implicit rules constraining the structure of this (piece of) reality.[8,9] In this definition, *intentional* refers to a structure describing various possible states of affairs, as opposed to exten-sional, which would refer to a structure describing a particular state of affairs. The word *semantic* indicates that the structure has meaning, which is defined as the rela-tionship between (a structure of) symbols and a mental model of the intentional structure in the mind of the observer. This mental model is often called a *concep-tualization*.[10] Semantics are an aspect of semiotics, like syntax, which distinguishes valid from invalid symbol structures, and like pragmatics, which relates symbols to their meaning within a context (e.g., the community in which they are shared).[11]

ONTOLOGY CLASSIFICATION BASED ON CONTEXT DEPENDENCY

Ontologies can be classified according to their level of context dependency.[12] *Top-level* or *foundational ontologies* are context independent because they describe very general concepts, such as space, time, and matter, which ought to be found in any context. *Task* and *domain ontologies* all relate to the context of a specific domain (e.g., banking, industry) or task (e.g., accounting, sales). Domain and task ontology terms are specializations of top-level ontology terms or terms used in a domain or task ontology with a wider scope (e.g., business-to-business (B2B) sales is a subcontext of sales), which means that they are directly or indirectly founded on top-level ontology terms. Finally, *application ontologies* relate to a very specific context (e.g., accounting in the banking industry, B2B sales in a single sales department). Their terms can be defined as specializations of domain and task ontology terms.

ONTOLOGY MATURITY AND THE MATURING PROCESS

Ontologies can also be classified according to their level of maturity. At the low-est level of maturity, we find *emerging ontologies*, which are rather ad-hoc, not well-defined, individually used, and informally communicated natural-language artifacts.[13] Within the ontology spectrum, which ranges from highly informal to formal ontolo-gies, controlled vocabularies, glossaries, and thesauri, are suitable ontology formats for such informal ontologies. A *controlled vocabulary*, which is a finite list of terms with a unique identifier, is the most rudimentary ontology. A *glossary*, which is a controlled vocabulary in which each term's meaning is given using natural language statements, is a slightly richer ontology.[14] Both controlled vocabularies and glos-saries provide a list of unrelated or implicitly related terms. Some of these emerging ontologies mature to become *folksonomies* or common vocabularies, which are shared within and collaboratively improved by a community. Like most emerging ontolo-gies, folksonomies use an extensional notion of conceptualization, which means that the terms are defined through examples rather than through descriptions.[15]

Folksonomies can mature to become *formal ontologies* through the organization of their terms using relationships. These relationships can be ad hoc, as in thesauri, or hierarchical, as in classification schemes.[16] A *thesaurus* increases ontology expressiveness by adding relations (e.g., synonyms) between terms in a controlled vocabulary. However, thesauri do not necessarily provide an explicit term hierarchy (e.g., specialization-generalization), which is a feature of classification schemes. A *classification scheme* contains informatory "is-a" relations, a *class hierarchy* strict specialization–generalization relation. Strict specialization–generalization relations create a treelike hierarchy, with a generic term as the root and more specific terms, which inherit meaning from the more generic concepts (e.g., the root) they are related to, as branches and leafs. The formality level of a class hierarchy can be increased by adding instantiation as a relation. Instantiation distinguishes between a meaningful term, which is often called a class (e.g., a car), and the terms that are examples of this class, which are often called instances (e.g., my car, your car). Inference rules can be derived from classification schemes and class hierarchies. For example, if a car is a kind of vehicle, then my car is also a vehicle. This implies that everything that can be said about vehicles can be said about my car. At a higher level of thesaurus expressiveness, *frames* include information about potential properties and relationships of classes and their instances (e.g., a car might have a price).[17]

The final phase in the maturing process is called the axiomatization.[18] An *axiom* is a statement for which there is no counter-example or exception.[19] *Value restrictions*, which increase the expressiveness of a frame by discriminating valid from invalid relationships between properties of classes and their instances,[20] are examples of axioms. Other examples of axioms include mathematical equations that relate properties, or logical restrictions on classes and their instances (e.g., disjointness constraint). Some ontologies also provide heuristic value restrictions (e.g., most cars consume fuel, most cars have one owner).

When an ontology was not formalized earlier, the axiomatization phase is often combined with the articulation in a formal language. This formality is a critical aspect of a well-known ontology definition, which dictates that an ontology needs to be a "formal specification of a shared conceptualization."[21] In this definition, the word *specification* requires that an ontology is an appropriate representation of its universe of discourse, which is typically referred to as but not limited to a (semantic) domain. The word *shared* refers to the need for social agreement about and shared understanding of the terms in the ontology. *Formal* refers to the fact that ontologies are frequently written in a formal (and often also machine-readable) language, which is a set of finite symbol structures taken from a finite alphabet of symbols[22] and defined by syntax.

STATE OF THE ART

Building and maturing an ontology is a collaborative and iterative process that requires thought and effort. The process also produces several valuable byproducts, including a better understanding of the organization.[23] Through documentation, structuring, and analysis of business process information, ontology development has been found to support business process detection,[24] continuous process refinement,[25] and defining process performance indicators.[26] Ontology engineering also requires discussion, which may yield valuable feedback, to reach consensus and obtain a conceptualization that is shared by all stakeholders. LEGO refers to this shared conceptualization as "One truth for all."[27] Several domain ontologies for business have been developed. Their main purposes are knowledge exchange[28] and knowledge management covering and bridging[29] several subdomains of business (e.g., business plans and other strategies,[30-36] operations,[37,38] finance,[39] accounting[40,41]), and auxiliary disciplines (e.g., information management,[42,43] requirements engineering,[44,45] information systems design,[46] and the development of the semantic web[47]).

Corporate knowledge is often visualized using conceptual modeling grammars (e.g., business process modeling notation (BPMN)). It has been demonstrated that an ontological assessment of such a modeling grammar (through semantic mapping) increases the perceived usefulness and ease of use.[48] An ontological assessment uses the knowledge embedded in ontologies to assess the expressiveness of modeling grammars by mapping grammar constructs to concepts of a relevant ontology.[49] The resulting mapping is called a semantic mapping and is proof of a modeling grammar's ontological commitment. The grammar constructs can be textual, iconic, or diagrammatic and are often referred to as symbols.[50] A semantic mapping can reveal grammar incompleteness, construct redundancy, excess, and overload.[51] *Construct deficit* occurs when one or more ontology concepts lack an equivalent grammar construct, which signals that the grammar is incomplete. *Construct redundancy* occurs when an ontology concept corresponds with two or more grammar constructs. *Construct excess* can be observed when one or more grammar constructs lack an equivalent ontology concept. *Construct overload* occurs when a grammar construct matches with two or more ontology concepts.

Next to symbols that can be mapped to ontological concepts, *modeling grammars* provide rules that prescribe how symbols, which refer to ontology concepts, can be combined to model real-world phenomena.[52] In formal languages, these rules are embedded in a proof theory, which consists of a set of inference rules.[53] These inference rules prescribe how new combinations of symbols can be derived from existing combinations of symbols. Consequently, a proof theory, together with the syntax and semantic mapping, permits a mathematical evaluation of a grammar's correspondence with the semantic domain.[54,55] In the ideal scenario, the set of all valid models generated from a modeling grammar's symbols and its (inference) rules covers the entire domain and nothing but the domain (i.e., every real-world phenomenon from the semantic domain can be modeled, and it is impossible to create a model that does not belong to the set of intended models).

Semantic mappings can also be applied to validate and integrate ontologies. When two or more ontologies that cover the same semantic domain share the same concept, the concept is more likely to belong to the semantic domain. When a concept occurs in only one of several ontologies that share the same domain, the concept is more likely to be redundant. The LEADing Practice community has applied semantic mappings to validate its ontology and integrate it with the ontologies of other frameworks and methods (e.g., The Open Group Architecture Framework (TOGAF), Control

Objectives for Information and Related Technology (COBIT), Information Technology Infrastructure Library (ITIL), Layered Enterprise Architecture Development (LEAD)).[56] However, most semantic mappings are applied in data management for the purpose of enterprise application integration[57] or database integration,[58] or to build a semantic[59,60] or pragmatic web.[61] Additionally, the semantic mappings allow for an automated translation of a concept from one ontology (e.g., applied in database A) to another equivalent ontology (e.g., applied in database B).

A lot of corporate knowledge is documented using diagrammatic languages (e.g., BPMN). An ontological evaluation of such languages through a semantic mapping of their symbols has been observed to improve their expressiveness and clarity. Consequently, semantic mappings between domain ontologies and domain-specific modeling languages[62,63] would allow organizations to improve these languages for the purpose of interorganizational communication. Semantic mapping might also allow organizations to develop unique intraorganizational languages based on an organization's application ontology for strategic information. Such an intraorganizational language might be defined as an extension of BPMN (e.g., extended business process modeling notation (X-BPMN)[64]) or as a completely independent language, which might need to respect the "physics of notation."[65]

Markup languages such as the Ontology Web Language (OWL), Resource Description Framework (RDF) and Knowledge Interchange Format (KIF) allow ontologies to be processed and distributed by computers, which allows for an automated combination and evaluation of (inter)organizational ontological knowledge.[66-68] Although some efforts have been made to formalize enterprise ontologies (e.g., REA (economic Resources, economic Events, and economic Agents)[69]) or best practices,[70] most applications of ontology in an organizational context are currently limited to building less formal ontologies (e.g., folksonomies). Therefore, organizations should invest in formalizing shared knowledge (e.g., big data).

CONCLUSIONS AND DIRECTIONS FOR FUTURE RESEARCH

This chapter defined ontology engineering as a discipline that can support corporate knowledge creation through the definition of fundamental concepts, as well as semantic relations and correlations between these concepts. Such definitions are not incorporated in contemporary BPM practice in an integrated and standardized way. Therefore, it would be advisable to develop an ontology for BPM.

A BPM ontology could include, among others, the following:

- It should state the primary concepts,[71] such as the entities/objects involved in BPM.
- It should define each of these primary involved concepts.
- It should define the relationships between these concepts.
  - It should preferably describe these relationships using class hierarchies.
  - These class hierarchies should preferably be based on existing classifications.
- It should describe the properties of the concepts and relationships above.

- It should define a set of value restrictions, such as how and where can the process objects be related (and where not).
- It should be supported by as large a user community as possible.
- It should be vendor neutral and agnostic, therefore allowing it to be used with most existing frameworks, methods, and/or approaches that have some of its mentioned meta-objects.
- It should be practical.
- It should have fully integrated and standardized relationship attributes.

Within the context of a BPM ontology, what are the properties of process (meta) objects and how do they relate to other (meta) objects?

- It should define how to organize and structure viewpoints and concept associations.
- It should structure process knowledge.
- It should establish guiding principles for creating, interpreting, analyzing, and using process knowledge within a particular (sub) domain of business and/or layers of an enterprise or an organization.

End Notes

1. Brandenburger A. and Nalebuff B., *Co-opetition* 1st ed., xiv (New York: Doubleday, 1996), 290.
2. Nonaka I., Umemoto K., and Senoo D., "From Information Processing to Knowledge Creation: A Paradigm Shift in Business Management," *Technology in Society* 18, no. 2 (1996): 203–218.
3. Practice L., *Hands-on Modelling Templates* (2014); Available from: http://www.leadingprac tice.com/tools/hands-on-modelling/.
4. Combination aggregates explicit knowledge to create new explicit knowledge (e.g., analysis, reporting).
5. Internalization transforms shared explicit knowledge into personal tacit knowledge (e.g., learning, studying).
6. Liu J. and Gruen D. M., "Between Ontology and Folksonomy: A Study of Collaborative and Implicit Ontology Evolution," in *Proceedings of the 13th International Conference on Intelligent User Interfaces* (Gran Canaria, Spain: ACM, 2008), 361–364.
7. Guarino N. and Giaretta P., "Ontologies and Knowledge bases: Towards a terminological clarification," in *Towards Very Large Knowledge Bases: Knowledge Building and Knowledge Sharing*, ed. N. Mars (IOS Press, 1995), 314.
8. Ibid.
9. Genesereth M. and Nilsson N., *Logical Foundations of Artificial Intelligence* (Los Altos, CA: Morgan Kaufmann, 1987).
10. Gruber T. R., "A Translation Approach to Portable Ontology Specifications," *Knowledge Acquisition* 5, no. 2 (1993): 199–220.
11. Cordeiro J. and Filipe J., "The Semiotic Pentagram Framework – A Perspective on the Use of Semiotics within Organisational Semiotics." in *7th International Workshop on Organisational Semiotics* (Setúbal, Portugal, 2007).
12. Guarino N., "Semantic Matching: Formal Ontological Distinctions for Information Organization, Extraction, and Integration," in *SCIE* (1997), 139–170.

13. Braun S., et al., "The Ontology Maturing Approach for Collaborative and Work Integrated Ontology Development: Evaluation Results and Future Directions," in *International Workshop on Emergent Semantics and Ontology Evolution ESOE, ISWC 2007* (Busan, Korea, 2007).

14. Lassila O. and McGuinness D. L., "The Role of Frame-based Representation on the Semantic Web," *Nokia Research Center* (2001).

15. See note 13 above.

16. See note 14 above.

17. See note 14 above.

18. See note 13 above.

19. Bahrami A., *Object Oriented Systems Development* (Boston, Mass, London: Irwin/McGraw-Hill, 1999), 411.

20. See note 14 above.

21. Borst W. N., "Construction of Engineering Ontologies for Knowledge Sharing and Reuse," in *Center for Telematics and Information Technology* (Enschede: Universiteit Twente, 1997), 227.

22. Gold E. M., "Language Identification in the Limit," *Information and Control* 10 (1967): 447–474.

23. Lamsweerde A. V., "Formal Specification: A Roadmap," in *Proceedings of the Conference on the Future of Software Engineering* (Limerick, Ireland: ACM, 2000), 147–159.

24. Damme C., Coenen T., and Vandijck E., "Turning a Corporate Folksonomy into a Lightweight Corporate Ontology," in *Business Information Systems*, ed. W. Abramowicz and D. Fensel (Springer Berlin Heidelberg, 2008), 36–47.

25. Prater J., Mueller R., and Beaugard B., *An Ontological Approach to Oracle BPM* (Oracle, 2011).

26. del-Río-Ortega, Resinas A. M., and Ruiz-Cortés A., "Defining Process Performance Indicators: An Ontological Approach," in *On the Move to Meaningful Internet Systems: OTM 2010*, ed. R. Meersman, T. Dillon, and P. Herrero (Springer Berlin Heidelberg, 2010), 555–572.

27. von Rosing M., von Scheel H., and Falk Bøgebjerg A., *LEADing BPM Practice – Case Story* (2013).

28. ISO/IEC, "Information Technology – Business Operational View Part 4: Business Transaction Scenario – Accounting and Economic Ontology," in *ISO/IEC FDIS 15944-4: 2007(E)* (2007).

29. Antunes G., et al., "Using Ontologies to Integrate Multiple Enterprise Architecture Domains," in *Business Information Systems Workshops*, ed. W. Abramowicz (Springer Berlin Heidelberg, 2013), 61–72.

30. Yu E.S-K., *Modelling Strategic Relationships for Process Reengineering* (University of Toronto, 1995), 181.

31. Osterwalder A. and Pigneur Y., *Business Model Generation: A Handbook for Visionaries, Game Changers, and Challengers* (Hoboken, NJ: Wiley, 2010).

32. Osterwalder A., Pigneur Y., and Tucci C. L., "Clarifying Business Models: Origins, Present and Future of the Concept," *Communications of AIS* 2005, no. 16 (2005): 1–25.

33. Hulstijn J. and Gordijn J. "Risk Analysis for Inter-organizational Controls," in *12th International Conference on Enterprise Information Systems (ICEIS 2010)* (Funchal, Madeira, Portugal, 2010).

34. Kort C. and Gordijn J., "Modeling Strategic Partnerships Using the E3value Ontology – A Field Study in the Banking Industry," in *Handbook of Ontologies for Business Interaction*, ed. P. Rittgen (Hershey, PA: Information Science Reference, 2007).

35. Gordijn J., Yu E., and van der Raadt B., "E-service Design Using i* and e/sup 3/value Modeling," *Software, IEEE* 23, no. 3 (2006): 26–33.

36. Gordijn J. and Akkermans H., "Designing and Evaluating E-Business Models," *IEEE Intelligent Systems* 16, no. 4 (2001): 11–17.

37. Geerts G. L. and O'Leary D., "RFID, Highly Visible Supply Chains, and the EAGLET Ontology," in *Working Paper* (Newark, DE: University of Delaware, 2008).

38. Haugen R. and McCarthy W. E., "REA, a Semantic Model for Internet Supply Chain Collaboration," in *Business Object Component Workshop VI: Enterprise Application Integration (OOPSLA 2000)* (2000).

39. Council E, *Financial Industry Business Ontology* (2014); Available from: http://www.edmcouncil.org/financialbusiness.

40. Geerts G. L. and McCarthy W. E., "An ontological Analysis of the Economic Primitives of the Extended-REA Enterprise Information Architecture," *International Journal of Accounting Information Systems* 3, no. 1 (2002): 1–16.

41. Geerts G. L. and McCarthy W. E., "Augmented Intensional Reasoning in Knowledge-Based Accounting Systems," *Journal of Information Systems* 14, no. 2 (2000): 127.

42. Fensel D., "Ontology-based Knowledge Management," *Computer* 35, no. 11 (2002): 56–59.

43. Benjamins V. R., Fensel D., and Perez A. G., "Knowledge Management Through Ontologies," *PAKM 98. Practical Aspects of Knowledge Management. Proceedings of the Second International Conference* (1998), 5/1–12.

44. Gordijn J., "Value-based requirements engineering: Exploring Innovative E-commerce Ideas," in *Exact Sciences* (Amsterdam: Free University of Amsterdam, 2002), 292.

45. Gordijn J., Akkermans H., and Van Vliet H., "Value Based Requirements Creation for Electronic Commerce Applications," in *Proceedings of the 33rd Hawaii International Conference on System Sciences* (IEEE Computer Society, 2000).

46. Hruby P., *Model-driven Design Using Business Patterns* xvi (Berlin: Springer, 2006), 368.

47. Obrst L., et al., "The Evaluation of Ontologies, Towards Improved Semantic Interoperability," in *Semantic Web: Revolutionizing Knowledge Discovery in the Life Sciences*, ed. C. Baker and K-H. Cheung (New York: Springer Verlag, 2006), 139–158.

48. Rosemann M., et al., "Do Ontological Deficiencies in Modeling Grammars Matter?" *MIS Quarterly* 35, no. 1 (2011): 57–A9.

49. Shanks G., Tansley E., and Weber R., "Using Ontology to Validate Conceptual Models," *Communications of the ACM* 46, no. 10 (2003): 5–89.

50. Harel D. and Rumpe B., "Meaningful Modeling: What's the Semantics of 'Semantics'?" *Computer* 37, no. 10 (2004): 64–72.

51. Wand Y. and Weber R., "Research Commentary: Information Systems and Conceptual Modeling–A Research Agenda," *Information Systems Research* 13, no. 14 (2002): 363–376.

52. Ibid.

53. See note 23 above.

54. See note 12 above.

55. See note 23 above.

56. Practice L., *Interconnects with Existing Frameworks* (2014); Available from: http://www.leadingpractice.com/about-us/interconnects-with-main-existing-frameworks/.

57. Uschold M. and Gruninger M., "Ontologies and Semantics for Seamless Connectivity," *Sigmod Record* 33, no. 4 (2004): 58–64.

58. Liu Q., et al., "An Ontology-Based Approach for Semantic Conflict Resolution in Database Integration," *Journal of Computer Science and Technology* 22, no. 2 (2007): 218–227.

59. Berners-Lee T., Hendler J., and Lassila O., "The Semantic Web – A New Form of Web Content That is Meaningful to Computers will Unleash a Revolution of New Possibilities," *Scientific American* 284, no. 5 (2001): 34.

60. Shadbolt N., Hall W., and Berners-Lee T., "The Semantic Web Revisited," *IEEE Intelligent Systems* 21, no. 3 (2006): 96–101.

61. Schoop M., De Moor A., and Dietz J. L. G, "The Pragmatic Web: A Manifesto," *Communications of the ACM* 49, no. 5 (2006): 75–76.

62. Walter T., Parreiras F. S., and Staab S., "OntoDSL: An Ontology-Based Framework for Domain-Specific Languages," in *Proceedings of the 12th International Conference on Model Driven Engineering Languages and Systems* (Denver, CO: Springer-Verlag, 2009).

63. Guizzardi G. and Wagner G., *Towards Ontological Foundations for Agent Modelling Concepts Using the Unified Fundational Ontology (UFO), in Agent-Oriented Information Systems II* (Springer, 2005), 110–124.

64. Practice L., *The LEADing Practice – EXtended BPMN Standard* (2013).

65. Moody D., "The Physics of Notations: Toward a Scientific Basis for Constructing Visual Notations in Software Engineering," *Software Engineering, IEEE Transactions on* 35, no. 6 (2009): 756–779.

66. Kalfoglou Y. and Schorlemmer M., "Ontology Mapping: The state of the Art," *Knowledge Engineering Review* 18, no. 1 (2003): 1–31.

67. See note 47 above.

68. Rijgersberg H., Wigham M., and Top J. L., "How Semantics can Improve Engineering Processes: A Case of Units of Measure and Quantities," *Advanced Engineering Informatics* 25, no. 2 (2011): 276–287.

69. Gailly F., Laurier W., and Poels G., "Positioning and Formalizing the REA Enterprise Ontology," *Journal of Information Systems* 22, no. 2 (2008): 219–248.

70. Polovina S., Von Rosing M., and Laurier W., "Conceptual Structures in LEADing and Best Enterprise Practices," in *21st International Conference on Conceptual Structures (ICCS 2014)* (Iasi, Romania, 2014).

71. Within the context of BPM, these concepts are also called entities or objects.

The BPM Ontology

Mark von Rosing, Wim Laurier, Simon M. Polovina

INTRODUCTION

Many business process management (BPM) and/or process frameworks, methods, or approaches (e.g., Lean, Six Sigma, Business Process Reengineering (BPR), Total Quality Management (TQM), Zero Defect, Business Process Modeling Notation (BPMN), Business Process Execution Language (BPEL)) have their own vocabulary. Each of these vocabularies has its own definition of terms, such as business process, process step, process activity, events, process role, process owner, process measure, and process rule. This chapter introduces a BPM ontology that can be applied within the area of process modeling, process engineering, and process architecture. It provides fundamental process concepts that can be used to document corporate knowledge and structure process knowledge by defining relation process concepts (e.g., the order of process steps). The BPM ontology is presented as a shared vocabulary (i.e., folksonomy) that structures knowledge in two ways. First, it allows practitioners to structure their business knowledge by adding meaningful relationships between the vocabulary terms. Second, it organizes concepts in hierarchic "is-a" relationships that allow a polymorphic inheritance of properties.

The BPM ontology presented in this chapter should help to remedy the inconsistent use of these terms by providing benchmark terms and definitions and mapping those terms and definitions to the terms in the vocabularies of other existing frameworks. As these mappings demonstrate the shared use of terms in the BPM ontology and several business standards and reference frameworks, we could argue that the BPM ontology documents (i.e., externalizes) a tacit business folksonomy that was mainly shared through socialization before.[1] Part of the BPM ontology presented here is an explicit business folksonomy that is supported by a wide community of practitioners and academics.[2]

This explicit business folksonomy is presented in the next section of this chapter. The BPM Ontology as a Thesaurus: Structuring Process Knowledge by Defining Relations then presents the BPM ontology as a thesaurus, focusing on the meaningful relationships that exist between the concepts of this business folksonomy. The BPM Ontology as a Frame: The Ontological Structure of the LEADing Practice Process Meta Model demonstrates how this thesaurus can be formalized as a frame, using conceptual graphs (CGs). The BPM ontology is discussed in Discussion of the BPM Ontology, and its advantages are summarized in the final section.

THE BPM ONTOLOGY AS A FOLKSONOMY: SHARING FUNDAMENTAL PROCESS CONCEPTS

All ontologies have a controlled vocabulary as a foundation. Because the BPM ontology is an extensive ontology that has the ambition to cover all aspects of business (as opposed to academic ontologies), its terms are organized in a top-level domain and multiple intersecting subdomains. The top-level ontology is kept relatively simple, consisting of four main terms: object, meta-object, object group, and object meta-model. *Objects* refer to something that is within the grasp of the senses and that which a subject relates to. They represent a piece of reality in a model or a document. *Meta-objects* create, describe, or equip objects. A meta-object defines an object's type, relation attributes, functions, control structures, etc. *Object groups* serve to group objects with a common purpose, goal, aim, target, objective, and sets. In the BPM ontology, object groups collect meta-objects related to a subdomain. *Object meta-models* are precise definitions of meta-objects, the semantics[3] of the relationships they are involved in, and the rules that apply to them.[4]

BPM ontology terms are assembled into two groups: composition and decomposition (meta-objects). The decomposition meta-objects are presented in Table 7.1 and allow modelers to structure processes. Categorizations assemble

Table 7.1 *Decomposed Process Meta-Objects*

Process Object	Description
Process area (categorization)	The highest level of an abstract categorization of processes.
Process group (categorization)	A categorization and collection of processes into common groups.
Business process	A set of structured activities or tasks with logical behaviors that produce a specific service or product.
Process step	A conceptual set of behaviors bound by the scope of a process that, each time it is executed, leads to a single change of inputs (form or state) into a single specified output. Each process step is a unit of work normally performed within the constraints of a set of rules by one or more actors in a role, which are engaged in changing the state of one or more resources or enterprise objects to create a single desired output.
Process activity	A part of the actual physical work system that specifies how to complete the change in the form or state of an input, oversee, or even achieve the completion of an interaction with other actors and which results in the making of a complex decision based on knowledge, judgment, experience, and instinct.
Event	A state change that recognizes the triggering or termination of processing.
Gateway	Determines the forking and merging of paths, depending on the conditions expressed.
Process rule	A statement that defines or constrains some aspect of work and always resolves to either true or false.
Process measurement (process performance indicator)	The basis by which the enterprise evaluates or estimates the nature, quality, ability, and extent as to whether a process or activity is performing as desired.

Table 7.1 Decomposed Process Meta-Objects—cont'd	
Process Object	Description
Process owner	A role performed by an actor with the fitting rights, competencies, and capabilities to take decisions to ensure work is performed.
Process flow (including input/output)	A stream, sequence, course, succession, series, or progression, all based on the process input/output states, where each process input/output defines the process flow that together executes a behavior.
Process role	A specific and prescribed set of expected behavior and rights (authority to act) that is meant to enable its holder to successfully carry out his or her responsibilities in the performance of work. Each role represents a set of allowable actions within the organization in terms of the rights that are required for the enterprise to operate.

heterogeneous groups, whereas classifications assemble objects into order (e.g., through the use of strict part-whole or sequencing semantics). For example, a process area can cluster otherwise independent processes; process steps need to follow each other.

The decomposed process meta-objects listed in Table 7.1 can be used in process architecture and process engineering, as they allow for process decomposition. These fundamental concepts can be combined with auxiliary concepts to produce the semantic richness needed by practitioners. These auxiliary concepts are called process composition meta-objects and represent various process aspects such as strategy, goals, critical success factors, performance indicators, reporting, services, applications, and/or data. Together, process composition and decomposition meta-objects provide a structuring mechanism that facilitates the developments of corporate ontologies (e.g., combining the decomposition meta-object process step with the decomposition meta-object risk invites practitioners to think about the risks of each process step they identify). The composition meta-objects, which are shown in Table 7.2, intersect with several subdomains of business (e.g., process, strategy). Consequently, they can be reused for the elicitation of risks, costs, and other aspects of business in several subdomains of business next to processes.

In addition to the decomposed process meta-objects, other meta-objects relate to the concept of process modeling. The related meta-objects are called composed process meta-objects and are considered an essential part for any practitioner working with and around innovation and transformation across various relevant subjects (vs siloed process modeling, engineering and architecture view). The additional related meta-objects fundamental to the various process concepts are shown in Table 7.2.

Table 7.2 *Process Composition Meta-Objects*

	Composed Process Meta-Object Descriptions
Goal (e.g., business, application, technology)	A desired result considered a part of the organizational direction, aims, targets, and aspirations.
Objective (critical success factor)	Time-bounded milestones to measure and gauge the progress towards a strategy or goal.
Value indicator (critical success factor)	Any of a series of metrics used by an enterprise, to indicate its overall ability to achieve its mission.
Performance indicator	Any of a series of metrics used by an enterprise, to indicate its overall success or the success of a particular area in which it is engaged.
Performance expectation	The manner in which, or the efficiency with which, something reacts or fulfills its intended purpose as anticipated by a specific stakeholder.
Performance driver	Those variables that are critical to develop the means and overall performance of an enterprise.
Quality	A state of excellence or worth, specifying the essential and distinguishing individual nature and the attributes based on the intended use.
Risk	The combined impact of any condition or events, including those cause by uncertainty, change, hazards, or other factors that can affect the potential for achieving these objectives.
Security	The objects or tools that secure, make safe, and protect through measures that prevent exposure to danger or risk.
Business measure	Any type of measurement used to gauge some quantifiable component of an enterprise's performance.
Report	The exposure, description, and portrayal of information, about the status, direction, or execution of work within the functions, services, processes, and resources of the enterprise.
Timing	A plan, schedule, or arrangement when something should happen or be done or take place.
Business area	The highest level meaningful grouping of the activities of the enterprise.
Business group	An aggregation within an enterprise, which is within an enterprise area.
Business competency	An integrated and holistic set of related knowledge, skills, and abilities, related to a specific set of resources (including persons and organizations) that combined enable the enterprise to act in a particular situation.
Business resource/actor	A specific person, system, or organization that initiates or interacts with the defined functions and activities. Actors may be internal or external to an organization.
Business role	A part that someone or something has in a particular defined function, activity, or situation. A resource/actor may have a number of roles.
Business function	A cluster of tasks creating a specific class of jobs.

Table 7.2 Process Composition Meta-Objects—cont'd

	Composed Process Meta-Object Descriptions
Business owner	A role performed by an actor with the rights, rules, competencies, and capabilities to take decisions for the part of enterprise for which stewardship responsibilities have been assigned.
Cost	An amount that has to be paid or given up to obtain the use or access to something.
Revenue	The realized income of an enterprise or part thereof.
Object (business and information)	A real-world thing of use by or which exists within the enterprise and information objects reveal only their interface, which consists of a set of clearly defined relations. In the context of the business competency, the relevant objects are only those which relate to the enterprise's means to act.
Product	A result and output generated by the enterprise. It has a combination of tangible and intangible attributes (features, functions, usage).
Contract	An agreement between two or more parties that establishes conditions for interaction.
Business rule	A statement that defines or constrains some aspect of behavior within the enterprise and always resolves to either true or false.
Business compliance	The process or tools for verifying adherence to rules and decisions.
Location	A facility, place, or geographic position.
Business channel	A means of access or otherwise interacting within an enterprise or between an enterprise and its external partners (customers, vendors, suppliers, etc.).
Business workflow	A stream, sequence, course, succession, series, and progression as well as order for the movement of information or material from one enterprise function, enterprise service, or enterprise activity (worksite) to another.
Business service	The externally visible ("logical") deed or effort performed to satisfy a need or to fulfill a demand, meaningful to the environment.
Service flow (including output/input)	A set of one or more service input output states, where each service state defines a step in the service flow that, when entered, executes a behavior.
Service measurement (Service Performance Indicator (SPI) and Service Level Agreement (SLA))	The basis by which the enterprise evaluates or estimates the nature, quality, ability, or extent of the services. The commitments of a business service are assessed.
Logical application component	An encapsulation of application functionality that is independent of a particular implementation.
Physical application component	A deployable part of a software product, providing identifiable functions and existing within a specific version of the product.
Application function	The specification of a significant aspect of the internal behavior of the application, which acts as a broader description of a set of application features.
Application task	The automated behavior of a process activity performed by an application.

Continued

Table 7.2 *Process Composition Meta-Objects—cont'd*	
Composed Process Meta-Object Descriptions	
Application service	An externally visible unit of functionality, provided by one or more components, exposed through well-defined interfaces, and meaningful to the environment.
Application/system flow	The specification of the sequence in which two application task processes (or an application task and an application event or gateway) are executed, one of which provides an output, which is an input to the other.
System measurement	Measures that are defined and implementable within an application.
Application/system report	Reports that are defined and implementable or implemented within or by an application.
Application roles	A role performed by an actor with the rights, competencies, and capabilities to take decisions about an application, its behavior, and properties.
Application rule	A business rule implemented within and able to be executed by an application.
Data object	A logical cluster of all sets of related data representing an object view of a business object.
Data table	A physical specification of the means of arranging data in rows and columns while being stored in physically persistence structures.
Data flow	The specification of the sequence in which data moves from one state to another.
Data owner	A role performed by an actor with the rights, competencies, and capabilities to take decisions about the aspects of data for which stewardship responsibilities have been assigned.
Data rule	Criteria used in the process of determining or verifying values of data or generalizing certain features of data.
Platform device	A set of platform components configured to act as a modular part of a platform.

THE BPM ONTOLOGY AS A THESAURUS: STRUCTURING PROCESS KNOWLEDGE BY DEFINING RELATIONS

The process objects that have been defined through a search for process composition and decomposition meta-object instances in an organization require additional structure.

Structuring the process knowledge includes identifying the existing classes and groups of process objects and the relations between them and the characteristics that unite or differentiate them. The following criteria facilitate grouping:

- *Identity*: allows users to distinguish an object from any other object and distinguishes objects from meta-objects, which have no identity.
- *State*: is the aggregate of an object's properties, including its relations with other objects, meta-objects, classes, etc.
- *Behavior*: distinguishes between legal and illegal state changes.

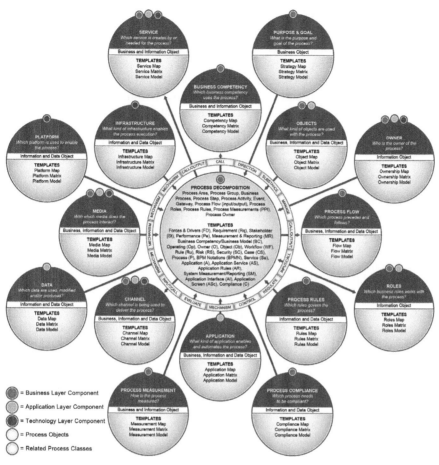

FIGURE 7.1

The 16 basic process classes and groups.[5]

Although relations are mainly defined at the level of meta-objects (e.g., in corporate ontologies), the BPM ontology contains a set of archetypal relations that have been observed to apply to almost any process. These relations have been defined at the level of meta-object groups, which means that they apply to object groups in corporate ontologies, elicited using these meta-objects. Sixteen meta-object groups can be identified. Although these groups contain meta-objects, they are not meta-objects. Their relations with the process meta-object group are summarized in Figure 7.1, which is an overview of these 16 classes and how they relate to the process objects. These 16 groups assemble composition meta-objects, which can be observed in several areas of business other than processes. Consequently, this template can be reused to represent the relations between these 16 groups and other aspects of business.[6]

Next to the meta-object relations visualized in Figure 7.1, process composition meta-objects do not only have relationships to the central concept of a business process, but also with multiple other areas. These relations provide an important tool to assess the details of a corporate business ontology, as each object that belongs to one of these 16 meta-object groups is expected to be related to any business process object in order to obtain a complete business process specification. Consequently, a process specification that is missing one or more of these essential objects in its relationships will be considered to be malformed and incomplete. This approach is expected to provide a powerful tool to assist in the identification and capture of all relevant process aspects.

The following process meta-objects and relations are expected to exist within most organizations:

1. The *business competency meta-object group* relates to the following meta-objects: organizational construct, business capability, business resource/actor, business function, product, location, report, timing, revenue, and cost. They intersect with the process meta-object groups as a business calls upon its *business competencies*, or organizational skills and knowledge, which are part of its business model and thereby the organizational structure, to create value within the organization and for its customers via its processes, events, and decisions, or gateways, which are decomposed process meta-objects.

    The relations between business competency and process meta-objects include descriptions of relations between cost and the process objects, of which some examples are given below:

    a. Cost occurs when executing a task within a business process, cost can therefore be related to a business process.
    b. Cost accrued at an event can be associated and tracked.
    c. Cost measures can be specialized within a process measurement (process performance indicator).
    d. Cost control is, among others, the responsibility of a process owner.
    e. Cost compliance can be ensured through process rules.
    f. Cost flow can be found in various process flows.

2. The *purpose and goal meta-object group* contains the following meta-objects: driver (value/performance), strategy, goal, objective, value indicator, value expectation, value proposition, performance indicator, performance expectation, quality, risk, and security. They intersect with the meta-objects of the purpose and goal meta-object groups as business strategies will dictate the *purpose and goals (value)* that provide directions for the process objects. This includes business process objectives, performance expectations, and performance indicators, which can be measured and linked back to the strategy through process performance indicators (PPIs).

    Below is an example of the semantic relations between performance drivers, which belong to the purpose and goal meta-object group and the process objects:

    a. Performance driver influences choices of process owner.
    b. The categorization of process areas and groups can be influenced by performance drivers.
    c. Performance drivers influence the design of business processes.

    d. Events realize the various performance drivers.

    e. Performance driver sets criteria for the direction of the gateways.

    f. Performance driver sets criteria for the execution of the process flow (including input/output).

    g. Performance drivers set presentation criteria for the process role.

    h. Process rules are set based on various performance drivers.

    i. Process measurements (PPI) can be tracked and reported against the performance drivers.

3. The *object meta-object group* has the following members: business objects, information objects, and data objects. They need to be considered because (parts of) business, information, and data objects give *substance* to business process tasks and services. A business process uses, modifies, and/or produces business information and data objects on several hierarchical levels; data objects with data components, business processes with information objects, and business process tasks with data services.

    Below is an example of the semantic relations between the information objects and the process objects:

    a. Business process areas and groups consume and develop information objects relevant for decision making.

    b. Business processes use, produce, and store information objects.

    c. Information objects change the state of an event.

    d. Gateways produce and consume information objects.

    e. Information objects are produced and consumed by process roles.

    f. Process rules regulate the compliance of specific information objects.

    g. Information objects are a part of any process measurement (PPI).

    h. Process owners have the responsibility for the information objects involved in the process.

4. The *owner meta-object group* contains the following: Business owner, process owner, service owner, application owner, data owner, platform owner, and infrastructure owner. They are important because multiple owners can have the authority to steward or *manage* business processes. All owners have specific responsibilities that result in different desires, demands, and various performance and value expectations. In the context of business processes, the business process owners have the responsibilities connected to business tasks, process flow, service, creating value, achieving performance goals set by the strategy adhere to security, and maintaining compliance standards within the "work system."

    Below is an example of the semantic relations between the business owner and the process objects:

    a. Business owners define through the business goals the direction of the business process.

    b. Business owners set performance criteria for the business process.

    c. Business owners create and specify the performance indicators within the process measurements (PPI).

    d. Process owners work with business owners.

    e. Business owners govern the process flow.

    f. Business owners are involved in the verification and conformance of the process rules.

5. The *flow meta-object group* consists of the following: business workflow, process flow, service flow, information flow, data flow, and application/system flow. They should be considered because business processes *call and provide output* to the business process flow, which interacts with several different flows within the business. These flows include the business workflow, information flow, data flow, etc., all interacting with the process flow.

    Below is an example of the semantic relations between the information objects and the process objects:

    a. Business processes are found within the information flow.

    b. Events sequence the information flow.

    c. Information flows have gateways.

    d. Information flow crosses the process flow (including input/output).

    e. Process measurements (PPI) are a part of the information flow.

    f. Process owners are involved with the creation of certain information flows.

    g. Information flows and their rules can be derived from process rules.

6. The *roles meta-object group* has the following members: business role, process role, service role, and application role. It is important to consider them because the enacted business process roles *input and call* the processes through the process steps and activities so as to be supported by the roles of the respective business functions and tasks.

    Below is an example of the semantic relations between the business roles and the process objects:

    a. The process group categorizes business roles into its groups.

    b. Business roles execute the tasks in the business process and activities.

    c. The process role is a form of the business role.

    d. Process owners interact with various business roles.

    e. Business roles participate within the process flow.

    f. Business roles abide by the process rules.

7. The *rules meta-object group* contains the following: business rule, process rule, service rule, application rule, data rule, platform rule, and infrastructure rule. Business process rules *regulate* the processes, which are then instantiated in services and implemented within applications that enable these processes, data that they consume or produce, and security behavior. This must also both be adhered to and embedded within the different parts of the planning, creation, realization, and governance processes of the business processes.

    Below is an example of the semantic relations between the business rules and the process objects:

    a. Business rules regulate business process tasks.

    b. Business rules ensure the correctness of process flow (including input/output).

    c. Business rules apply to gateways.

    d. Business rules relate to process roles.

    e. Business rules are contained within process rules.

    f. Business rules are measured by process performance indicators (PPIs).

    g. Business rules are also a part of the responsibility of process owners.

8. The *compliance meta-object group* contains the following: business compliance, application compliance, data compliance, platform compliance, and infrastructure compliance. When designing, building, implementing, updating, working with, or terminating business process tasks, events, and services, it is essential to demonstrate the level of *control* necessary to demonstrate process compliance with respect to applicable policies, guidelines, standards, and regulations through the use of governance controls, risk management, audits, evaluation, security, and monitoring.

    Below is an example of the semantic relations between business compliance and the process objects:

    a. Business compliance verifies execution of business processes.

    b. Business compliance verifies execution of the gateway.

    c. Process flow (including input/output) conforms to business compliance.

    d. Business compliance assesses the performance process role.

    e. Business compliance verifies conformance to the design of the process rule.

    f. Business compliance evaluates process measurements (PPIs).

    g. Business compliance assesses the performance of process owners.

9. The *application meta-object group* contains the following: logical application component, physical application component, application module, application feature, application function, application task, application/system report, and application/system. An *application* is a *mechanism* used to automate a business process, and/or its steps, activities, events, and flows. Applications are also used to automate process reporting through the use of system measurements and system reporting.

    Below is an example of the semantic relations between the application tasks and the process objects:

    a. The application task partially or fully automates the business process and process activities.

    b. Gateways are automated by application tasks.

    c. The application task partially or fully automates process flow (including input/output).

    d. Process rules are partially or fully automated by application tasks.

    e. Process owners desire application task automation.

10. The *measurement meta-object group* contains the following: business measure, service measure, process measure, and system measure. The measurement indicators are the basis by which we *evaluate* the business processes; their outputs and results can all be measured. Process measurements or their automated equivalent, the system measurements, are linked to business reporting (at the strategic, tactical, and operational levels) through scorecards, dashboards, and cockpits, which aid in this assessment.

Below is an example of the semantic relations between the business measurements and the process objects:

a. Business process performance is tracked by business measures.
b. Events can be tracked against business measures.
c. Business measures are found within the process flow (including input/output).
d. Process roles are evaluated against business measures.
e. Process rules are tracked and reported by business measures.
f. Process owners report part of the business measures.

11. The *channel meta-object group* contains the following: business channel, service channel, application channel, data channel, platform channel, and infrastructure channel. The value delivery to those that benefit from the output of a process occurs through business and technology *channels*. The business channel stages can range from marketing, sales, distribution, business service, and so on.

Below is an example of the semantic relations between the business channel and the process objects:

a. Business channels require execution of business processes and process activities.
b. Business channels require execution of gateways.
c. Business channels involved within the process are the responsibility of process owners.
d. Business process flow participates in the business channel.
e. Process rules regulate the business channel.

12. The *data meta-object group* contains the following: data component, data entity, data objects, and data table. Process execution is the mechanism by which *data* are created, used, or consumed.

Below is an example of the semantic relations between the data objects and the process objects:

a. Data objects are related to business processes and activities.
b. Data objects change state at an event.
c. Data objects abide by process rules.
d. Data objects are within process measurements (PPIs).

13. The *media meta-object group* contains the following: business media, application media, data media, platform media, and infrastructure media. *Media* is the mechanism that is part of any process by which inputs or outputs of a process are held. There are many kinds of media involved within a process, such as paper, visual, or auditory for manual processes; screens, memory, or disks may act as media for automated processes.

Below is an example of the semantic relations between the business media and the process objects:

a. Business media are supplied or consumed by business processes and process activities.
b. Gateways use business media.
c. Business media are produced at events.
d. Process owners have the responsibility for the business media.

14. The *platform meta-object group* consists of the following: physical platform component, and platform device. A *platform* is a mechanism used to enable process automation; for example, a platform component enables an application component, and a platform service enables an application service and thereby a business service. Platforms such as laptops, smart phones, or tablets are used to access processes.

     Below is an example of the semantic relations between the platform devices and the process objects:

     a. Platform devices generate and participate in a business process.
     b. Platform devices are used by process roles.
     c. Platform devices participate within the process flow.
     d. Platform devices change the state of events.

15. The *infrastructure meta-object group* contains the following: physical infrastructure component and infrastructure device. From a process architecture perspective, processes are automated with dedicated technology, which use a mechanism to draw on *infrastructure* for their ability to execute. For example, a process rule engine resides on infrastructure components, and infrastructure services support the platform services.

     Below is an example of the semantic relations between the infrastructure and the process objects:

     a. Automated business processes reside on physical infrastructure components.
     b. Physical infrastructure components host business process engines (rules, measures, etc.).

16. The *service meta-object group* contains the following: business service, application service, data service, platform services, and infrastructure services. Business services are what actually deliver value within the organization and to its customers. They do this when they call upon and provide output to the processes necessary to instantiate them. This is because value creation is subject to the relationships between business processes and their resources, tasks, events, and the services they deliver. Although there is a distinction between manual and automated services, the division is captured within the process notations, which relate the automated service to the relevant web services, application services, data services, platform services, and infrastructure services and the business services to their manual counterparts.

     Below is an example of the semantic relations between the business compliance and the process objects:

     a. Business services are realized by business processes.
     b. Business services resolve events.
     c. Business services are provided to process roles.
     d. Business services are regulated by process rules.
     e. Business services are measured by process measures.
     f. Business services are governed by process owners.

THE BPM ONTOLOGY AS A FRAME: THE ONTOLOGICAL STRUCTURE OF THE LEADING PRACTICE PROCESS META MODEL

The business process ontology that is embedded in the LEADing Practice narratives, models, tables, and diagrams can be explicated and interrelated by bringing them together in a universal conceptual structure, such as conceptual graphs (CGs).[7–9] CGs provide a graphical interface for first-order logic that enables the visualized objects and relations in the ontology to be articulated as a (class) hierarchy and, by linking (meta)objects to each other through their object relations, the direct and indirect interrelationships in business processes can be discovered. It is the vehicle by which LEADing Practice's ontology and semantics foundation can be applied to enterprises wishing to understand and improve their own processes.[10]

Figures 7.2 and 7.3 show an extract from the meta-object ontology of the business layer and application layer, respectively, taken from LEADing Practice's *Process Architecture Reference Content*.[11] The objects are shown as a CG type hierarchy, linking subtypes (subobjects) to their supertypes (superobjects). Thus, in Figure 7.2

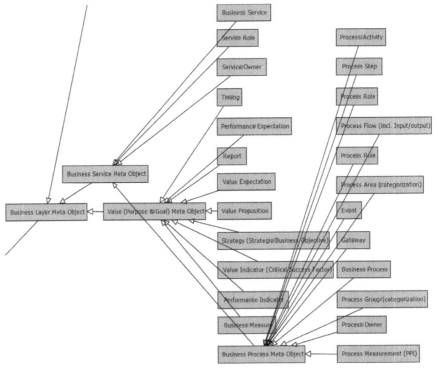

FIGURE 7.2

Extract from the business layer meta-object ontology.

for example, the subtype to supertype path is Process Owner < Business Process Meta-Object < Business Service Meta-Object < Business Layer Meta-Object < Top (not shown). Another is Product < Business Competency Meta-Object < Business Layer Meta-Object < Top. In Figure 7.3, an example is Data Service < Data Meta-Object < Application Layer Meta-Object < Top. Another is Application Module < Application Meta-Object < Application Layer Meta-Object < Top. The "<" symbol can be read as "is a"; for example, product is a business competency meta-object. It is also transitive; thus, for example, process owner < (is a) business layer meta-object. Furthermore, it is polymorphic; properties affecting a superobject will cascade to *all* of its subobjects. Thus, if we make an assertion about the business layer meta-object, for example, then that assertion will also apply to all its subobjects; in this case, all the objects shown in Figure 7.2. Note that it does not apply the other way; thus, for example, an assertation made about the product will only affect that object. Otherwise, it would wrongly affect everything that comes under Business

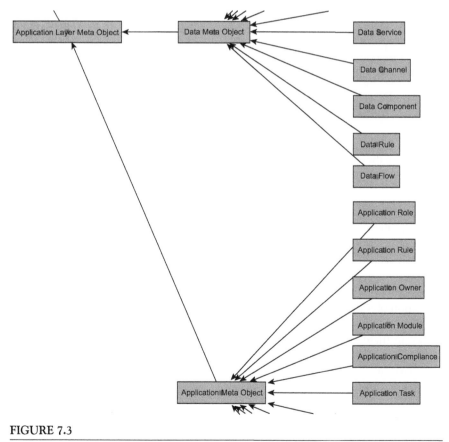

FIGURE 7.3

Extract from the application layer meta-object ontology.

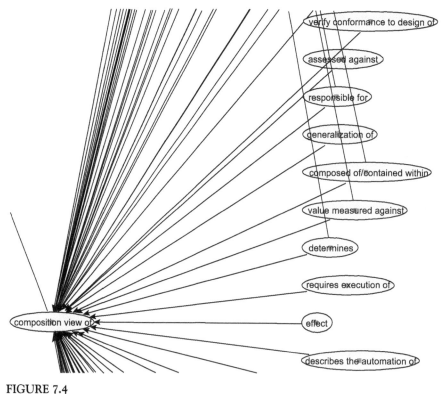

FIGURE 7.4

Extract from the composition relation ontology.

Competency Meta-Object < Business Layer Meta-Object < Top. Consequently, we have the ability to apply reasoning at multiple levels of the ontology.

Figures 7.4 and 7.5 similarly describe extracts of the object relations of the ontology as a CG relation hierarchy. The relations are structured to capture the composition-decomposition views in LEADing Practice's process architecture reference content.[12] The "<" (is a) rules also apply to object relations, such as requires execution of < decomposition view < link (not shown), in Figure 7.4. An example from Figure 7.5 would be participates in < decomposition view < link. Although not shown in these figures, some of the relations are subrelations of both the composition view and decomposition view. These are indicated by relations in the figures that have two lines going from them, one of which goes off the figure to the other view as its superrelation. One such example in Figure 7.4 is "participates in." That relation also has composition view as its superrelation. The "based on" relation in Figure 7.4 only has the decomposition view as its superrelation. Examples of both sorts of relations also appear in Figure 7.3.

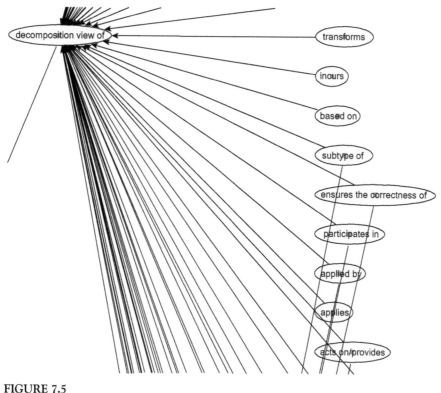

FIGURE 7.5

Extract from the decomposition relation ontology.

Figures 7.6 and 7.7 show extracts of the objects linked by their relations for the business process composition and decomposition attribute taxonomy, respectively, based on the object and relation ontology of the earlier figures. Semantics is thereby added to these taxonomies, as each object is described by its relation to other objects through the ontological structure defined in the CGs of Figures 7.2–7.5. Accordingly, for example, business process is delivered by business service. Business Service < Business Service Meta-Object; thus, properties (assertions) applied to this meta-object would cascade to business service (but not vice versa as explained earlier). Business process is not on this hierarchical path, so it would be unaffected. Of course, any properties applied to the business layer meta-object would affect them both. The same pattern applies to the object relations. Overall, we can see how this multilevel behavior affects the context of each object in relation to its others. Properties applied to the superobject and relations are thereby reused at their sublevels. Such relationship models also act as the test that properties are not applied at too high a level, as that would highlight oversimplification through overgeneralization. Conversely, when common properties are discovered at a common sublevel, they can be generalized and reused over those objects. This generalization and specialization can be updated in

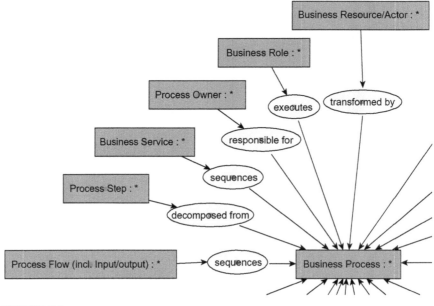

FIGURE 7.6

Extract from the business process composition attribute taxonomy.

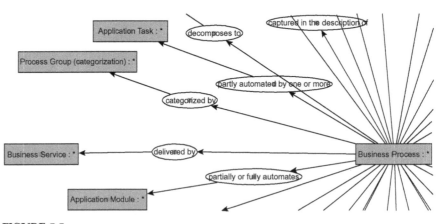

FIGURE 7.7

Extract from the business process decomposition attribute taxonomy.

the light of new best practices; notably, those best practices are being applied through CG logic rather than loosely on less formal foundations. Understanding is assisted by how objects are linked to other objects (directly and indirectly) through their relations, thus adding context to how the generalizations may be applied.

The CGs shown in each figure were drawn in the CoGui[13] software. As well as a CG editor, CoGui enables the first-order logic reasoning of CGs, as was outlined

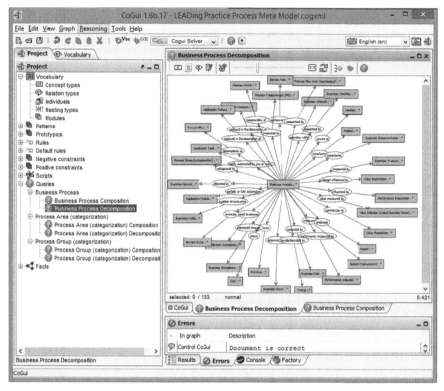

FIGURE 7.8

Example of querying the process meta-model.

earlier. Consequently, as Figure 7.8 indicates, the business process decomposition (and composition) meta-model can be used to query the models of a given enterprise. This enables the enterprise to test the conformity of their business models against the rich body of knowledge underpinned by LEADing Practice's ontology and semantics, identifying where the enterprise's own business processes might require further maturity.

DISCUSSION OF THE BPM ONTOLOGY

The BPM ontology is an empiric ontology, meaning that its roots lie in practice, as it was developed by practitioners documenting their practical knowledge of the field rather than having originated from theory and academics specialized in a restricted area of business. Consequently, it is one of the few ontologies that has the ambition to cover all aspects of business. To attain the desired level of completeness, the ontology is complemented with elicitation support, such as the guiding principles for creating, interpreting, analyzing, and using process objects within a particular domain and/or layers of an enterprise or an organization. The BPM ontology also offers a set of principles, views, artefacts, and templates that have detailed meta-object relations and rules that apply to them, such as how and where can the process objects be related (and where not). Because the BPM ontology has the ambition to support a large community, it is open-source within the community and vendor neutral or agnostic, so it can be used with most existing frameworks, methods and/or approaches that have any of the meta-objects mentioned in this document. The mapping can be found online.[14]

By sharing knowledge within the community, practitioners have found and documented repeatable patterns[15] for process-related objects, structures, and artefacts. This has led to the identification of 16 cross-domain meta-object groups that provide additional structure to the ontology, and it may lead to the development of 16 orthogonal task ontologies (e.g., describing costs or risks) that intersect with domain ontologies (e.g., business processes). However, further research is needed to determine whether or not such a decomposition is feasible and desirable.

The ontology is also complemented by a framework that helps practitioners transform their (ontological) knowledge of a process into process models and (new) working methods. To be able to cope with the complexity of the real world, the framework allows practitioners to (temporarily) simplify their (mental) models by taking partial views on their knowledge. These viewpoints are especially useful in the context of process engineering, process modeling, and process architecture.

SUMMARY

The BPM ontology's primary purpose is to provide a shared vocabulary for practitioners and academics in the business domain. This purpose was achieved by selecting terms from other business process ontologies embedded in existing frameworks, standards, and approaches and mapping them to their equivalent, which is often the exact same term, in the BPM ontology. Because practitioners need more than just a glossary to describe the aspects of business, this folksonomy is enriched with relationships between meta-objects to build a business thesaurus. This frame has been complemented with rules and a framework that should help practitioners to transform their process knowledge in competitive advantage. This will help practitioners to achieve the following:

- Identify the relevant process objects
- Decompose the process objects into the smallest parts that can, should, and need to be modeled, and then compose the process objects entities before building them (through mapping, simulation, and scenarios)
- Visualize and clarify process object relationships with the process artefacts by using maps, matrices, and models (alternative representation of information)
- Reduce and/or enhance the complexity of process modeling, process engineering, and process architecture principles by applying the process decomposition and composition standard (see decomposition and composition reference content)[16]
- Model the relevant process objects through the architectural layers
- Adding process requirements (see requirement reference content)

- Provide a structured process blueprinting and implementation (see blueprint and implementation reference content).

This chapter also demonstrated how parts of this thesaurus (i.e., the BPM ontology) have been determined and how the entire thesaurus will be formalized as a frame, which allows for polymorphic property inheritance.

In the next chapters, the BPM ontology's meta-objects, groups, categorizations, strict specialization–generalization relations, and rules will be elaborated in detail, with examples. For further information on semantic process relations, process decomposition and composition, layered modeling, process engineering, and process architecture or how the BPM Ontology content can be used, we refer the reader to the *Business Process Reference Content*.[17]

End Notes

1. Practice L., (2014b). Interconnects with Existing Frameworks, from: http://www.leadingp ractice.com/about-us/interconnects-with-main-existing-frameworks/.
2. Practice L., (2014a). Community Open Source, from: http://www.leadingpractice.com/ab out-us/community-open-source/.
3. A Process Ontology & Process Semantic Description, Views, Stakeholders and Concerns.
4. Rosing M. v. (Producer), *Objects and Object Relations around Business Modelling and Business Architecture* (2014). Retrieved from: http://www.leadingpractice.com/wp-content/ uploads/presentations/LEADing%20Practice%20&%20OMG%20Business%20Architec ture%20and%20Business%20Modelling.pdf.
5. Practice L., (2014c). The Leading Practice Process Reference Content #LEAD-ES20012BC.
6. LEADing Practice Business Process Reference Content #LEAD-ES20005BP.
7. Chein M. and Mugnier M-L., *Graph-based Knowledge Representation: Computational Foundations of Conceptual Graphs, Advanced Information and Knowledge Processing* (Springer, 2008).
8. Polovina S., *An Introduction to Conceptual Graphs Conceptual Structures: Knowledge Architectures for Smart Applications* (Springer, 1997), 1–15.
9. Sowa J., *Conceptual Structures: Information Processing in Mind and Machine* (Addison-Wesley, 1984).
10. PDF of Diagram on www.leadingpractice.com Homepage, (2014). LEADing Practice. Retrieved from: http://www.leadingpractice.com/wp-content/uploads/2014/02/LEAD-Frameworks-Enterprise-Engineering-Enterprise-Modelling-Enterprise-Architecture.pdf.
11. Process Architecture Reference Content, (2014). Retrieved from: http://www.leadingpra ctice.com/enterprise-standards/enterprise-architecture/process-architecture/.
12. See note 11 above.
13. CoGui: A Conceptual Graph Editor, (2014). LIRMM. Retrieved from: http://www.lirmm.fr/cogui/.
14. See note 1 above.
15. The definition of a pattern used here is the description of the repeatable and mostly used/ generic specifications and relations of a topic, not all theoretically possible specifications or relations.
16. LEADing Practice decomposition and composition reference content, LEADing Practice, 2012 content.
17. See note 6 above.

Process Tagging—A Process Classification and Categorization Concept

Mark von Rosing, Neil Kemp, Maria Hove, Jeanne W. Ross

INTRODUCTION

Categorization and classification have been around for a long time. Classical categorization first appeared in the context of Western philosophy in the work of Plato[1] who, in his Statesman dialogue, introduced the approach of grouping objects based on their similar properties.[2] This approach was further explored and systematized by Aristotle in his Categories treatise, where he analyzed the differences between classes and objects.[3] Aristotle also intensively applied the classical categorization scheme in his approach to the classification of living beings (which used the technique of applying successive narrowing questions such as "Is it an animal or vegetable?" "How many feet does it have?" "Does it have fur or feathers?" and "Can it fly?"), establishing the basis for the formulation of natural taxonomy. Classification is an important tool in science. It reduces the complexity of a body of work easily as it exposes patterns and structures to provide a clearer picture of the area of interest, serving to assist in understanding the relationships and acting as a baseline for subsequent work.

LOGICAL CLUSTERING: LEARNING FROM OTHER AREAS

Within many parts of enterprise modeling, enterprise engineering, and enterprise architecture there is clarity in the classification and categorization of the objects involved. For example, data practitioners distinguish between:

- Data types, in terms of master data, metadata, tacit data and transactional data.
- Data levels, where the decomposed and composed relationship of data components, data objects, data entities, data services and data tables is established in terms of their relationship and how they assemble by order.
- Data nature, where data are grouped into either structured or unstructured data. For the most part, structured data refers to information with a high degree of organization, such that inclusion in a relational database is seamless and readily searchable by simple, straightforward search engine algorithms or other search operations; unstructured data are essentially the opposite.

Figure 1 illustrates the data classification and categorization forms.

This data example shows logical clustering in terms of data categorization and classification. In each case, these data tags provide the data expert with important information about the properties and features of the data, and tools that give insight into how to organize the data to maximize their utility, protect them, and so on.

Data Classification / Categorization	Data Class / Category
Level *(decomposition)	Data Component
	Data Object
	Data Entity
	Data Service
	Data Table
Nature**	Structured
	Unstructured
Type**	Master
	Meta
	Transaction
*Classify = to assemble by order **Categorize = to divide into groups	

FIGURE 1

Data classification and categorization.

The reason such a tagging is beneficial is that the properties and features of data should be understood in terms of their relationship to the larger, overarching system or structure. Logical data clustering in this case works to uncover the data nature, data type, and data levels, and thereby the aspects of their structure. These relations constitute a combined structure, and behind the properties and features in the surface phenomena there are laws of context that are a part of the complex structure. This is exactly what the logical clustering of classification and categorization tries to identify. The concept of identifying properties and features in terms of type, nature, tiers, and levels has been applied in a diverse range of fields, including anthropology, sociology, psychology, engineering, economics, positivism, functionalism, conflict theories, mathematics, to name but a few. Therefore, while concepts of logical clustering exist in nearly all the mentioned areas and also nearly all areas of information technology (IT), from application modeling, to measurements, reporting, business intelligence, etc. this maturity does not exist to this degree within the process/business process modeling (BPM) world. Although some concepts exist regarding how to tag a process according to management, or a main or supporting process, there are almost no existing concepts for process nature or process decomposition, or at least, none that put it all together for an integrated and standardized process-tagging concept.

We believe this adds to process modeling, process engineering, and process architecture difficulties and the high cost of process work. The purpose of this chapter is thus to set out a process-tagging scheme for process categorization, and process classification, which will provide insight to the nature of process from multiple dimensions.

CONCEPTUAL AND LOGICAL PROCESS CLASSIFICATION AND CATEGORIZATION

The classical Aristotelian worldview claims that categories are discrete entities characterized by a set of properties that are shared by their members. In analytic philosophy, these properties are assumed to establish the conditions that are both necessary and sufficient to capture meaning. According to the classical view, categories should be clearly defined, mutually exclusive, and collectively exhaustive. This way, any entity of the given classification universe belongs unequivocally to one and only one of the proposed categories. However, both within enterprise engineering and within enterprise architecture there is a more modern variation of the classical approach that derives from attempts to explain how knowledge is represented. In this approach, classes (clusters or object entities) are generated by first formulating their conceptual descriptions and then classifying the object entities according to the descriptions and possibly relations. Figure 2 illustrates an example from the view of the enterprise layers, e.g., Business, application, and technology, and the conceptual representation, of how the categories with their object entities relate to each other.

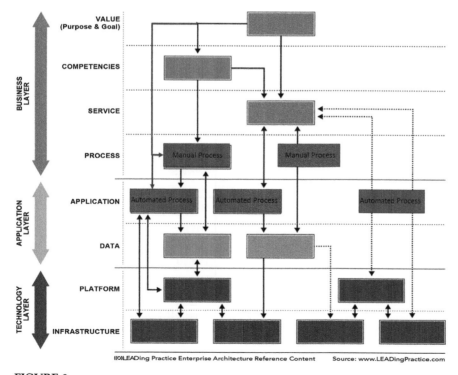

(((O))LEADing Practice Enterprise Architecture Reference Content   Source: www.LEADingPractice.com

FIGURE 2

Example of layered architecture categories and their relations to each other.

The layers within Figure 2 are in fact one classification of the parts of an enterprise that illuminates a relationship between the layered objects and the various subjects and provides the basis for the conceptual and logical clustering of the identified objects.

Conceptual and logical object clustering is the technique in which objects are identified, understood, and differentiated into their specific categories. Such concepts are also applied and presented in the BPM ontology categories (groups).

We realize that conceptual and logical object clustering is a paradigm shift toward traditional grouping, categorization, or even ordinary data clustering by generating a concept description for each generated categorization or classification potential, providing clustering of the labels for certain objects and enabling integrated and standardized classification and categorization within and across the layers allows accurate prediction of class labels as well as future-proofing areas that will be added, including the specification of object attribute relations, semantic rules, and sub-layer category labels. The task of clustering involves recognizing the inherent structure in a set of objects together by similarity into classes based on:

- Attribute relations
- Semantic rules
- Specific sub-layer categories and how the clustered objects can relate to other objects.

By using the classifications and categories such as presented in Figure 3 a logical cluster of the processes may be formed. On the other hand, clustering areas with no standardized classification and categorization labels are referred to as unsupervised classification, learning, or clustering.

Classification / Categorization	Class / Category
Level *(decomposition)	Process Area
	Process Group
	Process
	Steps
	Activities
Type*	Management
	Main
	Supporting
Tiers*	Strategic
	Tactical
	Operational
Nature*	Simple/Static
	Generic/Hybrid
	Complex/Dynamic

*Classify = to assemble by order
**Categorize = to divide into groups

FIGURE 3

Process classification and categorization.

Below is an overview of the classification and categorization of the business processes:

- Process decomposition captures the manner by which the process objects are broken down into simpler forms of objects. The business process area can be decomposed into one or more business Process Group(s), while a Business Process Group is made up of multiple business processes. The business process, in turn, can be broken down into process steps and then further into process activities.
- A process type categorizes the process based on the role of the process, differentiating between processes that focus on planning and control (management), those that are the main processes for the production of output, and those that are necessary for the main processes to execute (support).
- The process nature is categorized by the nature of the processes based on their complexity.
- Process tiers classify processes into one of three tiers, distinguishing between processes that are strategic, tactical, or operational.

In the BPM Ontology chapter, we learned about the importance of understanding the nature of a process object, its description, and its relations. The purpose of this chapter is to explore the nature of processes, the hierarchical semantic relations for identifying how the description of work can best be organized and used by process modelers, process engineers, and process architects. The intent is that resulting descriptions can be done independently of the particulars of implementation, but they can be used as the basis for relating both logical and physical descriptions, the dynamic aspect of business operations, and that both the descriptions and their specification be described as a set of persistent classes and relationships.

This approach attempts to set out a repeatable pattern leading to a means to capture and represent work at levels that are typically the subject of business process analysis in BPMs and system models.

The expectation is that by making a method to describe business process behavior that is highly structured, the quality of models will improve, the result will be more accessible to stakeholders, the level of rework and process variances will reduce, and the results will be more predictable and testable. Process modeling will move from a condition where the result depends less on the ability of the specific worker and will become a more repeatable capability in the BPM team and or the BPM center of excellence (CoE).

The key difficulty that comes from traditional techniques for representing process work is that too many decisions are left in the hands of the business analyst. Specifically, when modeling work without a proper context, the start and stop points for any subject to be explored and represented can be arbitrary, resulting in depictions of work that cannot be compared with each other. Similarly, in these same circumstances, the level at which work is modeled can vary widely, and standards, if they exist, whether from Business Process Modeling Notation (BPMN), Unified Modeling Language (UML), or the Consortium for Advanced Management–International (CAM-I), are not particularly helpful. Although the modeler may strive to describe work at a specific level of abstraction, it is almost impossible to do and the resulting work will end up at different levels of detail. Fundamentally and finally, when one examines process at different levels of abstraction, one finds that processes at each of the levels have both different relationships and their own unique set of attributes, meaning nontrivial functional dependency of the item of interest fully depends on the name of each instance.

The result does not diminish existing work on structured methods of documenting and representing work, but it provides a framework that allows work on process design to be more accurately positioned in terms of the problems addressed and the value of the particular model used. It also provides a means both to keep the components of a specific process model at a common level of exposition and to permit models to be placed into a context to allow for a greater understanding of the context of the work.

CLASSIFICATION OF PROCESS BY METHOD OF EXECUTION

In the ground-breaking book, "Enterprise Architecture as Strategy", Ross et al.[4] identify that the way processes are executed can be classified two ways. They observe that processes may be classified based on the extent to which parts of the organization perform the same process the same way and the extent to which these same processes share data.

- Process Integration – the extent to which processes within the same organization share data
- Process Standardization – the extent to which parts of the organization perform the same process the same way

Each category can be measured as being "high", or "low".

These classifications work together to create a set of extremely powerful second order categories that will inform the way the processes are implemented and how the technology to enable these processes can best be deployed. These secondary categories describe four possible operating strategies (Figure 4).

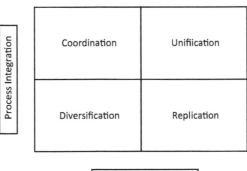

FIGURE 4

Application of process standardization and process integration to create an operating model.[4,5,6]

What is ironic is that these classifications were developed to differentiate essential aspects of process but have rarely been applied in that context, but are frequently applied in many other contexts.

- Coordination – low process standardization (interactions or processes are local, based on local requirements) but high process integration (data are shared across the enterprise).
- Unification – both high standardization and integration (data and processes are universally similar across the business). In this situation data and processes can be centrally managed to achieve economies of scale, and reduce cost and risk within the infrastructure.
- Diversification – businesses requiring low standardization (few data standards need exist) and low integration (operations are unique within the separate business units). Business units are largely autonomous.
- Replication – high standardization (transactions have limited variations and are designed centrally) but low integration (few customers are shared so data are locally owned). These conditions are seen in franchises, or retail chain stores.

These strategies are explicit, conscience design choices that lead to investment and operating decisions. The decision as to how a company wants to operate with regard to standardizing and integrating processes across various organizational domains (e.g. business units, geographies, product lines, franchises). It doesn't speak to the implications of those decisions so much as it facilitates discussions as to how a company wants to pursue its business model. By examining how the data and process **should be used** the enterprise creates a "foundation for execution". By selecting the strategy, understanding the implications on the method of execution and therefore on the classification of process standardization and process integration enterprises can achieve higher profitability, faster time to market, and lower IT costs.[4]

THE NATURE OF PROCESS DECOMPOSITION

One of the fundamental difficulties with modern process practices for understanding and representing business with structured (graphical) process models revolves around the analysis and representation of work, the representation of actions involving mental or physical effort done to achieve a purpose or result. The core of the difficulty with describing work is that there is little clarity and less agreement about what is meant by work or with respect to how to organize its descriptions in ways that are meaningful, repeatable, and reusable. Methodologies, most of which are focused on software implementation of behavior, talk about using a variety of methods to analyze and design workflows and processes within an organization, using such terms as "process," "sub-process," "activity," "task," "procedure," "transaction," or "step" to describe the way work is executed but without distinguishing the nature of one from another. Indeed, most attempts at clarification simply classify process into levels of detail. By failing to offer definitions whose perspective and context are clear, they unfortunately fail before they start.

It may be that a factor with existing approaches to describing work is that they are based on the old assembly line thinking invented by automotive manufacturing, and that this approach does not directly scale to address their application in a different context.

When capturing the details of work on an assembly line, the place where the flow starts and stops is clear. Owing to the tangible nature of the work involved, where modeling a workstation on the entire line, both the nature of the work and the scope are clear. Anyone can point out and relate to where the work starts and where it ends. Work starts at the factory door or at the start of the line and ends with a completed product. In addition, whether building subassemblies out of individual components or doing final assembly of a vehicle, the items being manipulated are clear. This clarity does not easily transfer from the physical world of transformational work to the more conceptual world that is aimed at processing information.

We have already covered this in the chapter entitled "What Is BPM," but we already see the first signs of this problem when we examine the literature, which is full of definitions for process. Although a small selection of the more commonly used definitions show a certain level of consistency, none of them provides the clarity needed to provide testable criteria, to ensure an analyst is able to be clear regarding where the work being documented is to start, where it is to end, or what level of representation is applicable to address the business problem at hand.

The core idea of a process is that any piece of definable work will always produce a specific product (or economic service); i.e., the reason for the existence of the process is the output of the product or service that it produces. In our context, an attribute or feature of a process is the output it is designed to create; each time the process is executed it will create a new instance of its product or service, and the thing that it is designed to produce remains consistent each time the process is performed.

Consider the following:

1. "A process is a group of related activities that together creates a result of value for clients."[7] This tells us that there is some sort of relationship between "process" and "activity" without giving any illumination as to what either is, or providing tests that we can use to any great effect.
2. "A business process is a series of steps designed to produce a product or service."[8] This definition tells us that there is a relationship between "process" and "steps" but leaves us no wiser.
3. "A business process is a series of logically connected business events and the logical connection is to a bigger scenario such as 'source to pay.'"[9] This view of the subject says that a process and an event are the same thing, while indicating that a series of processes is part of some larger idea.
4. "A process describes a sequence or flow of activities in an organization with the objective of carrying out work. Processes can be defined at any level from enterprise-wide processes to processes performed by a single person. Low-level processes can be grouped together to achieve a common business goal."[10] This

is just another way of saying that a process can be anything you want; it does not help if one is trying to create a testable, repeatable specification.

In the end, all of these definitions offer a view of process that is akin to a *matryoshka* or Russian nesting doll of decreasing size placed one inside the other with no way to distinguish where the dolls are in the hierarchy without having other dolls in the set to provide a basis for comparison.

Figure 5 shows a set of five nested *matryoshka* dolls and a set of five undifferentiated processes that are similarly nested. In the case of either the dolls or any of the processes, it is not possible to distinguish members of the set without additional information. This lack of information creates a challenge for making the documentation and representation of work a repeatable process, where the start and stop of the description is meaningful and results in a complete specification, and where the level of description is suited to the problem being addressed and the result desired.

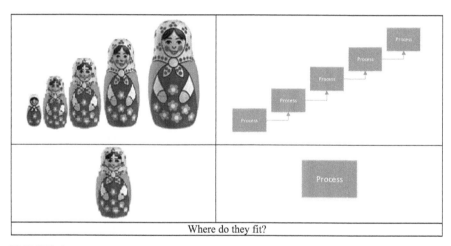

FIGURE 5

Nested dolls and nested processes.

At its simplest level, APQC's Process Classification Framework (PCF) is a list that organizations use to define work processes comprehensively and without redundancies. The goal of the PCF is to create an inventory of the processes practiced by most organizations, categorize them, and align them according to a standard system.

Processes are organized into levels. Level 1 processes are a simple categorization of service. Level 2 processes capture more detail within the same process, and so on.

In counterpoint to this, the SAP ASAP (Accelerated SAP) process hierarchy makes a partially useful attempt to distinguish among levels of complexity in processes. The SAP process hierarchy arguably offers the most advanced thinking on the classification of processes within a hierarchy, and therefore offers an excellent starting point. Key members of this hierarchy are as follows:

1. Level 1 Process Areas: A high level aggregation of deliverable processes.
2. Level 2 Process Groups: "A bundle of processes that belong to the same area of responsibility dealing with similar tasks and activities for functional or other reasons".[11] This suggests that processes can be bundled based into arbitrary classification, i.e., "for functional or other reasons," a definition that might have been useful except that the bundling can be for any arbitrary reason.
3. Level 3 business processes: "The business process is the level that aggregates business-oriented functions or steps into a unit that is meaningful and comprehensive in the sense that the steps or functions incorporated are essential to fulfill a business mission-related task; i.e., a business process is defined by steps that transform an input into an enriched output."[12] Without knowing what a "business mission-related task" is and without clarity on how "steps or functions" are organized this definition does not directly advance our understanding.
4. Level 4 process steps: "An activity performed by a user or a piece of software together with other process steps forming a business process."
   The SAP process hierarchy specification offers specific guidance about the creations of process steps, specifying that:
   a. A process step is an activity related to exactly one object (e.g., a human, a sheet of paper, a purchase order (system), etc.).
   b. A process step is typically executed by one person and documented using an appropriate representation of the object (paper, data in an IT system, etc.).
   c. From a user interaction point of view, a process step is a single work task in a causal workflow without role change. A process step is typically identified by the fact that the task owner has all necessary responsibilities to execute the task. A process step can be performed by a single human being or by interaction between human/system and system/system."
   Although it should be evident that work can be performed by things other than "users" or "software," such as by machines, not only is the intent of this definition with its supporting tests exactly the type of guidance we are looking for, it appears to be extremely useful with regard to understanding the nature of process. We will also choose not to be confused by the use of the term "activity" in this definition and assume what is meant is "work."
5. Level 5 activities: "Activities are the lowest granularity for business process modeling and reflect the single actions a user or a system performs to fulfill the process step; i.e., filling in the fields of a special mask consists of activities as each field has to be filled to end the step." Again, other than being transactional work-centric and focused on "modeling," this definition provides clear guidance about the nature of work at this level of granularity.

The challenge, then, in part is that these definitions need to be expanded to embrace all forms of work—transformational, transactional, and tacit—and to provide greater clarity at all levels of this hierarchy so as to create an integrated set of testable, definitions with supporting criteria that can be used to produce consistent, repeatable results that can be applied to obtain similar results by two or more analysts working to understand, document, and represent the decomposition of work. Table 1 summarizes the key classification schemes for classifying process detail/decomposition.

Table 1 *Overview of Different Views of Process Levels*

		APQC PCF	LEAD Process Levels	SAP Process Levels	SAP Solution Manager	SCOR
Levels	1	Category	Process area	Business area		
	2	Process Group	Process Group	Process Group		
	3	Process	Business process	Business process	Scenario	Level 1
						Level 2
	4	Activity	Process step	Business process variant	Process	Level 3
	5		Process activity	Process step	Process step	Level 4
	6			Process activity		

DESCRIBING WORK

An important tool in setting out the components of any set of ideas is a diagram in the form of a structured model that shows the constituent parts of the idea and how they relate; i.e., in UML, a class model is organized within a larger framework that ensures clear boundaries are applied. Whereas class models are typically used in business analysis and software engineering to describe the structure of the information within the domain of interest, they can also be used to set out the structure of the ideas that make up the standard for describing how to express these ideas. This type of structural model is, or at least it should be, an important tool in specifying any notation-centric standard, or in any situation where the exchange of ideas or insight has a significant role.

> The challenge in attempting to bring clarification to subjects such as this is one of semantics. It is important to distinguish between the label put on ideas and the idea. The fact that "activity" as a label within BPMN or used within the LEAD process hierarchy or the SAP process hierarchy has a particular meaning in the case and the way in which "activity" is used in this document should not be taken to mean they are the same thing just because the labels are coincidently the same.

The class model for describing work that this chapter applies is set out in Figure 6 – Simplified Class Model for Describing Work. Note that "activity" is the "coal face" where work is first truly exposed; when information, for example, is created, updated, and consumed; where a transaction is finalized or where inputs complete their transformation into a final output; and where decisions are made. The remaining aspects, process area, Process Group, process, and process step, are logical and conceptual components that provide an organizing context to the level, manage the way we

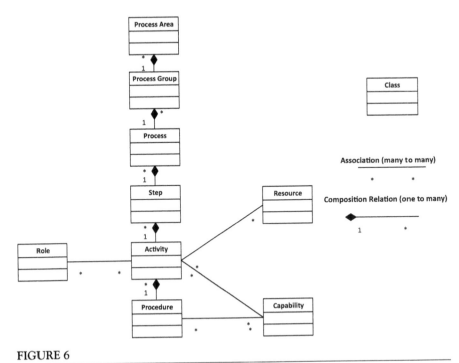

FIGURE 6

Simplified class model for describing work.

describe and understand how value or products are being achieved, and are part of the means by which we connect work at the level of process activity to strategy, which is where its value is actually exposed.

The most general classification of a process is a process area, the highest possible level of aggregation of processes. A process area may be broken down into Process Groups, logical sets of work necessary and sufficient to produce an output that is in a form that has value to the enterprise. Process Groups represent a categorization and collection of processes into a set that covers the full set of work needed to plan, provision, deliver, and decommission the resources over which they operate so as to create the desired valued output. Note that the reason for a Process Group is for its ability to create something of value. While this falls within the possible reasons set out within the SAP hierarchy, this is much more specific and has significant implications that will be discussed later.

Each instance of a process within a Process Group transforms a set of inputs into a specific instance of an output that is complete and useful in that it leads specifically to the value that shapes the scope of its Process Group. At its core, a process is a set of structured actions with logical behavior that produce a specific economic service or product. Processes have a specific typing that identifies the steps needed for its completion in a controlled manner. A process step represents a conceptual set of behaviors bound by the scope of a process which, each time it is executed (exceptions aside), leads to a single change of inputs (form or state) into a single specified output. Each process step is a unit of work normally performed within the constraints of a set of rules by one or more actors in roles that are engaged in changing the state of one or more resources or business objects to create a single desired output.

A process step is in turn composed of activities. An activity is a part of the actual physical work system that specifies how to complete the change in the form or state of an input, oversee, or even achieve the completion of an interaction with other actors, and which results in the making of a complex decision based on knowledge, judgment, experience, and instinct. Each activity is a single repeated, complete, and discernible action required to complete the process based on the process type and on the policies that specify the requirements for its completion. The completion of an activity can be tested for conformance to some standard and will always lead to the completion of a specific output. Through the completion of an activity an actor in a role may change or record the state of a resource.

At an additional level of detail, the actions required to complete an activity may be captured in procedure as a set of contiguous actions, i.e., in a common "swim lane"[13] with no intervening activities performed by another role, which are part of the set of actions required to complete the process. Procedures are based on or shaped by individual or organizational capability, or by leverage-specific capabilities. That is, the features of the resources that act to enable the work will shape how that work is executed, leading to a different script.

A final layer exists; this layer is not the subject of "Architecture", but of analysis. This layer is not included in Figure 6 because this is the realm of "Procedure". This level of skilled work, where human and other capabilities connect to the work. Figure 7 shows how treating the components of a vehicle as being different classes of things

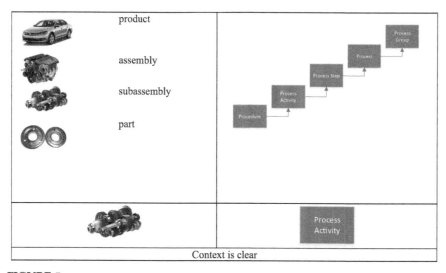

FIGURE 7

Components and processes existing in differing contexts.

and similarly viewing the types of processes, not as the same things, but as discrete and separate things makes the context of each clear.

A significant result of this framework is that no process will appear in more than one progress group (but will appear in the Process Group in which it adds to the ability to create value). Similarly, a step will appear in exactly one process, an activity will be within exactly one step, and a procedure will provide detail for exactly one activity. Economies of scale and reuse of resources are possible, but how these opportunities are found or expressed is not shown in this model.

It would seem clear from the above that each layer of process is actually in a different conceptual space in which each view of what constitutes process is different from the others, with different relationships, properties, and indeed purpose. In other words, breaking down a process is not about more detail, but about identifying the sub-assemblies from which the parent is constructed. In this view, the parent component is an assembly of components with features that are different and distinct from them; they are not a *matryoshka*, but are in a container–piece relationship.

Not focusing on apparently shared labels used to name these things, but paying attention to the essential features, attributes, and relationships of each level, we see that process is not a single thing but a set of things that must be viewed as different objects. The result of this thinking is that we move away from the idea that processes exist in a hierarchy where differentiation is about levels of granularity, but that they are actually different things with unique features, relationships, and behavior.

By recognizing the separate context of the various elements, it is possible to exploit the similarities within each layer of decomposition to identify better, more repeatable methods of capturing and representing the different aspects in a standard form.

PROCESS AREA
What Is a Process Area?

A process area is a high-level, abstract aggregation of a set of Process Groups that frames or positions the context of the Process Group as to its nature. A business competency may be described by the process areas needed for that competency to perform as expected.

How to Identify Process Areas

A process area is categorized according to either:

- Enterprise business areas, business units, or divisions
- End-to-end flow of process areas

How Is a Process Area Documented?

The documentation of a process area is produced in a Process Map, illustrated in Figure 8; (more on this is in the following chapter on process templates). There are various ways to graphically illustrate process areas; however, there are no standards of how to present

Process Area
Defense Navy Administration
Naval Force Planning
Force Generation
Navy Force Employment

FIGURE 8

Illustration of defense Navy process area example of a Process Map (list).

them. In this context, it is vital to know that BPM notations do not show Process Areas in their notations. The first example of this documentation presented will be value chain diagrams from ARIS (Architecture of Integrated Information Systems) (see section on Prof. Scheer); then in other variations of that we see organizations use to illustrate their process areas or the flow of process areas and groups.

In the following, we present various ways that we see organizations represent their process areas:

- Representation of process areas in a Process Map, with a defense Navy process area example
- Value-added chain diagram: Figure 9 – Illustration of a Value added Chain Diagram-example ITIL V3 Process Areas, shows the IT service centric process areas and the supporting Process Groups.

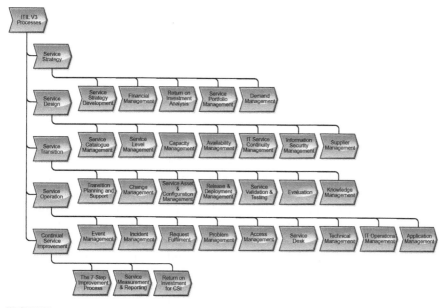

FIGURE 9

Illustration of a value-added chain diagram: example of ITIL V3 process areas.

- A Process Area could be illustrated by the organizational entities and their relationship to each other. This can be seen in the example of defense organizational entities and the command, reporting, and information relationship (Figure 10). While we also do not say in the example that this is a good way of illustrating process areas, nevertheless we also see such illustrations graphically showing the process areas and how they in their command, reporting, and information relationship work together

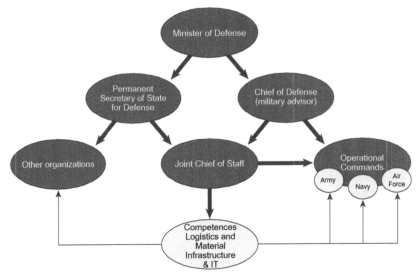

FIGURE 10

Process area based on enterprise/business high-level relations.

PROCESS GROUP

What Is a Process Group?

A Process Group is a bundle of processes that acts as a container to combine a coherent and complete set of processes, which together produce a final output that provides a specific benefit or value to a specific set of stakeholders. These stakeholders may be either internal or external to the enterprise. A well-formed Process Group will consist of a complete set of processes that describes the activity required to carry out the full set of work required for the business to deliver both the valued output that the Process Group is intended to produce and all the business objects within its operational cycle. The requirement to establish a Process Group is determined by exploring options to achieve economies of scale within the work of the enterprise and by exploring the chain of value necessary for the enterprise to achieve its purpose and address the needs and requirements of its marketplace.

Within a Process Group, there is exactly one process (and, as we will see, one process step and one process activity) that delivers the output for which the Process Group is valued. All other processes that are within the group and as part of the larger package are there to ensure that the main process has everything it needs to ensure the value desired from this work is delivered.

Generally, a Process Group provides a specific capability to the enterprise to operate a delegated center of operation within an enterprise, or to operate the infrastructure of the enterprise itself. Examples of what is achieved by the processes within a Process Group include any well-bounded set of processes that provide the enterprise with the ability to produce a cohesive output, for internal or external consumption, that solve a specific business problem.

A key feature of a Process Group is that it contains the set of work supported by relevant capabilities necessary to deliver the entire set of work required to deliver the desired value over all phases of value creation for the output it exists to produce. In formulating the way work can be performed in an enterprise, the opportunity to achieve an economy of scale through the sharing of resource that encapsulates this value is critical. Although it is not obvious, this relation is in fact significant. By scoping a Process Group not based on functional or other reasons, but solely to the type of value produced, two results are achieved: First, a repeatable basis for identifying the purpose of and processes within a Process Group is established, and secondly, a Process Group becomes the means by which a Business Service is provided the resources it needs to fulfill its intended purpose.

When it is determined that a product produced by a process within a Process Group can be organized so the enterprise can benefit from the result in a sharable fashion, two things happen: First, the product ceases to be viewed for what it is, but is judged for its value, thus being separated from the other members of its current Process Group to become the final valued output of a new Process Group. Second, this simultaneously necessitates its being supported by its own unique set of capabilities, including the full set of processes necessary to ensure it is able to deliver the value expected of it within its own value chain.

Why Separate Process Group and Business Service as Unique Concepts?

The idea of a service in this sense (which should not be confused with the idea of an economic service, which is a class of intangible commodities and has no meaningful part in these concepts, except tangentially) is that the complexity of resources used to produce an output can be hidden from the consumer and can then be reused for different purposes, together with the policies that should control usage. Once the complexity is hidden, the consumer of the service, whether data, application, infrastructure, platform, or business, is able to access the output of a service with no understanding or knowledge of anything that happens behind the interface. The whole point of a service is that the consumer of the service does not need to know any of the magic needed to provide the value they are looking for. As a consumer of a Business Service, I am simply looking for something to be achieved; the details of who, what, where, when, how, etc. are not of interest to me, and actually none of my business. To put it another way, I am interested in the value accrued from the relationship and leave the details to the service provider.

A Business Service in this context is "The externally visible ('logical') deed, or effort performed to satisfy a need or to fulfill a demand, meaningful to the environment." To be instantiated, a Business Service requires a full set of capabilities, processes, information, major systems, people, organizational structures, etc. Thus, the concept of service allows for both simplification of the relationship between provider and consumer and separation of value and effort. It does not actually do away with the need to account for, describe and ensure the enterprise has access to the capabilities while exploring how to design the enterprise so as to deliver value.

To be clear, as the customer of a process I am in the process and therefore am aware of what is happening, whereas when I am a customer of the service, I simply make requests of the service and receive that which I seek and therefore acquire the value I am seeking without gaining significant insight into who is doing the work, how the work is done, how exceptions are handled by the service provider, where the work is performed, and so on (or at least, should not be made aware of these if the service is designed and operating properly).

How to Identify Process Groups

A Process Group must meet all the following conditions:

1. Every Process Group will have a single output identified that it is accountable to produce.
2. The output of the Process Group must be in a final valued form (recognized through the fact that the output is recognized as value imparted from within the enterprise through a Business Service, which is held as accountable for value through a contract, service level agreement, or similar vehicle).
3. The Process Group output must address the recognized needs of an identified group and be received by at least two categories of recipients.
4. A single, unique owner is accountable for the output.
5. The Process Group must be represented by a Business Service created to encapsulate the set of resources and business processes needed to produce the output.
6. The output Business Service must be either consumed by two or more other Business Services, two or more recipients of the Business Service, or some combination.
7. A Process Group must be independent of all other Process Groups such that if any other Process Group or groups for some reason cease to exist the Process Group in question continues to exist and remains unchanged in terms of its output. (Though it will be required to perform additional processes to address the shortfall.)

Further, a Process Group will consist of multiple processes that are each of one of five types; all five types must be represented in the processes of a Process Group:

1. Planning processes that describe the work of determining how the Business Service will respond to demands. Planning processes operate on a planning cycle, or in response to a contingency.
2. Provisioning processes that describe the work of preparing the Business Service to respond to demands in accordance with plans. Provisioning processes operate in response to a routine drawdown of resources, or in response to a contingency or required protective or stewardship activity.
3. Delivery processes that operate repeatedly when each request for a Business Service output is received.
4. Deregister/decommission processes that recognize the lifecycles of resources, suppliers, Business Service outputs, or Business Service recipients and operate according to the lifecycle stages of these elements
5. Oversight processes monitor, provide feedback, and thus control the performance of the other processes within the Process Group.

In the simplest organization there will only be three Process Groups: those needed to manage the organization itself; those needed to operate the organization; and those needed to plan, provision, deliver, and terminate the creation of the single thing that represents the value proposition central to its purpose by meeting the needs of the target community that it services. That being said, even the smallest organization will draw on services beyond its doors to give itself the wherewithal to achieve its purpose and carry out the production of its valued output, no matter what it is. As the organization grows in size, it will seek to differentiate itself within its environment and to optimize cost and value. This leads to the need and ability to hollow out aspects of the initial process set so as to specialize, standardize, achieve economies of scale, or use specialized resources capable of addressing high-complexity/low-value Business Services, in the process perhaps changing the mix of services it provides for itself and those it draws from the market. Every time this occurs, the affected process will disappear from the set of processes that existed before to be replaced by a Business Service that delivers not the product, but the value of that product, while simultaneously adding a new and complete Process Group to instantiate for the Business Service the necessary planning, provision, delivery, and deregistration processes, while addressing the need to ensure oversight of this new feature.

How Are Process Groups Documented?

Documentation of Process Group is done in a Process Map, illustrated in Figures 11 and 13 also (more on this is in the following chapter on process templates). A Process Group is named based on the valued output it is accountable for producing, prefixed with a verb that imparts the finality of what is accomplished. Verbs such as "provide" (provide funding, provide food), "furnish" (furnish car, furnish payment), "address" (address question, address complaint), and "steward" (steward funds, steward buildings) are appropriate, as are others in Figure 11.

Defense Navy Process Map	
Process Area	**Process Group**
Defense Navy Administration	Exercise Controls and Analysis
	Execute Navy Budget
	Grants Management—Grantee
	Manage Employee Resources
	Manage Position Plan
	Formulate Budget
	Locality Management
	Manage Vehicle Fleet
	Provide Medical and Health Service
	Conduct Analytics
	Manage Financials
	Manage Human Capital
	Deliver Corporate Services
	Provide Operations Support
Naval Force Planning	Develop Strategic Plan
	Develop Naval Force Requirement
	Develop Naval Force Goal
	Develop Naval Force Plan
Force Generation	Create Navy Master Data
	Create Basic Navy Organization
	Manage Navy Personnel
	Manage Navy Equipment
	Develop Organization
	Conduct Individual Training
Navy Force Employment	Deploy Navy
	Manage Navy IT Landscape
	Organizational Flexibility
	Deliver Mobile Personnel and Organizational Management
	Provide Collective Naval Training

FIGURE 11

Illustration of defense Navy Process Map with Process Groups structured based on the process areas.

As no sequence constraints are implied by Process Groups, they cannot be captured in anything more than a Process Map (a process list) and no structured model will represent relationships between or among a set of Process Groups (as it is defined by the structure of the process areas).

The Nature of Process Groups

Process Groups may be tagged and categorized based on the nature of the valued output of each Process Group. They can also be tagged in terms of their financial impact and their value contribution, as well as whether they are strategic, tactical, or operating in nature or in terms of their lifecycle in the delivery of value: provision, planning, delivery, and decommissioning of their ability to create value.

PROCESS

What Is a Process?

Although we say that a set of processes is decomposed from a Process Group, this does not mean that a process is simply more detail about the actions needed to complete the goal of a Process Group.

A process, like a progress group, is conceptual; it contains no choices, but will be a member, along with other processes, of the chain of dependent work within the complete Process Life Cycle presented in Figure 12, which is necessary and sufficient for the output of the Process Group to be realized. Each Process Group will consist of the set of processes required to plan, prepare, and deliver its valued output.

In each case, a process will produce a single, usable, and complete business object: a product, a control object, or information object, any of which can then be consumed as a single thing, which makes it essential to fulfill the requirements to complete something that is needed by the enterprise as a means to act. Within transactional work, this will include the set of work required to complete any business object directly related to the purpose of the progress group, and within

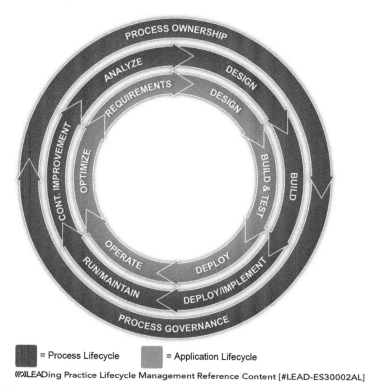

= Process Lifecycle   = Application Lifecycle

((O)LEADing Practice Lifecycle Management Reference Content [#LEAD-ES30002AL]

FIGURE 12

Process Life Cycle.

transformational work, anything that leads to the creations of the product or economic service that is central to its purpose or mandate. Although the output of a Process Group, the thing of value, and the output of one of the processes in a Process Group may appear to be identical, the purpose of the Process Group is to produce the thing of value, and the purpose of all other work and their associated business objects is to be the means by which that value is produced in a controlled, effective, and efficient method.

The process lifecycle is actually another classification scheme for categorizing processes, distinguishing among those that are part of specifying the conception, planning, and arrangement of processes, the processes that are required to take what was designed and bring it to operation, when it is then monitored, and finally those processes necessary to analyze or assess the performance of one or more processes. (See more on process lifecycle in the BPM Process Life Cycle chapter.)

How to Identify Processes

Each process will produce a single, complete, and meaningful result that contributes to the completion of the valued output necessary for the conclusion of the work of a Process Group. This output may be a transformation of a business object (through transformational work), the result of a complete set of transactions that produce a control object (achieved by transactional work), or the creation of new knowledge or insight (tacit work).

When creating a process, the name given the process will be derived from its goal. The process goal is an atomic statement describing the result of the successful completion of the process based on the process type and output produced.

The output of the process is the resource whose goal it is for the process to change the state of. In better English, we could say that it is the goal of a process to change one or more inputs into a specific output each time it is executed.

Processes are named by referring to the business object that is completed by the process, suffixed with a verb that gives a sense of completion. Verbs such as "determine," "complete," and "answer" provide this sense of completion, whereas "draft," "develop," and "propose" lack the finality needed to convey the needed completeness and will result in candidate processes that will not stand up to further decomposition.

How Are Processes Documented?

Documentation of business processes is captured in a Process Map. An example of such a Defense Process Map is illustrated in Figure 13.

Because processes are a logical view of work and at a level of abstraction where they simply identify what the result of the expended effort is, there is no means to identify the impact of the process not succeeding. That being said, processes have preconditions that must be met or dependencies that must be satisfied. Therefore, whereas a model map may be used to show the inventory of processes, a process model will show the dependency chain required.

Defense Navy Process Map		
Process Area	**Process Group**	**Defense Navy Business Process**
Force Generation	Create Navy Master Data	Create Reference Force Elements
		Create Jobs
		Maintain Material Planning Objects
		Create Material Container
		Maintain Equipment Package
	Create Basic Navy Organization	Create Unit
		Define Stock Elements
		Define Provision Elements
		Maintain Support Relationship
		Maintain Authorized Personnel
		Maintain Real Estate Requirements
		Activate Unit
		Connect to Functional Area Services
		Measure Handling
		Close Unit
	Manage Navy Personnel	Post Personnel
		Move Personnel
	Manage Navy Equipment	Compare Authorized and Actual Material
		Request Equipment
		Finalize Request of Equipment
		Convert Request to Order
		Loan Equipment
		Issue Equipment to a Person
		Return Personal Equipment
	Develop Organization	Create Working Organizations
		Transfer Technical Objects
		Loan Equipment
		Change Supply Relationships
		Change Maintenance Relationship
		Delimit Structures
		Reassign Structures
	Conduct Individual Training	Provide Academic Services
		Grade
		Audit Degree
		Advise Information

FIGURE 13

Illustration of a Defense Navy Process Map with business processes structured by Process Groups and process areas.

Any set of these processes may, at any time, be of interest for any reason. These may be assembled into a scenario that is captured in a Process Map. Figure 14–Example Process Map presents an example of process relationship for the processes to provide repaired cars in response to requests provided by customers.

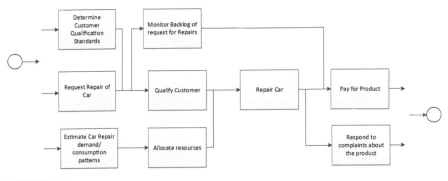

FIGURE 14

Example of a Process Map.

The graphic shows the sequencing relationships between each of the processes of interest for an example set of processes organized to show the sequence of dependency for the completion of each process.

The narrative for this fragment of a larger Process Map would be "… once the request for repair of car" has been received, the customer is qualified based on the customer qualification standards. At the same time, using the estimates of car repair demand/consumption patterns, resources are allocated and available to carry out repairs to cars. Once the request for repairs has been accepted, until the car is repaired the backlog of work will be monitored. When a car has been repaired, it must be paid for and there may

> This example only shows the processes and their flows for the set of processes included in the list in Figure 14. A well-formed Process Map will always include the necessary oversight, planning, provision, delivery, and deregistration processes.

be a requirement to respond to complaints about some aspect of the work.

Processes are named by combining the noun phrase that identifies the name of the completed output, the thing that is the result or purpose of the work with a verb that expresses the idea that the work to create in output results in something that is in its final, complete, and finished form. The product of a process is a complete, well-formed business object. The business object may a thing; a car or a person; a control object (used to record or track the progress to complete the valued output of a Process Group) such as a budget or plan; or an information object employed within the Process Group.

A Process Map will only contain the processes within a Process Group. The Process Map will show the chain of dependency for the completion of the processes necessary to plan, provide, and deliver the valued output as well as the processes necessary to monitor or oversee the work and to dispose of or deregister resources upon the decision to terminate execution of the Process Group.

THE NATURE OF PROCESSES

When tagging and categorizing processes they may be characterized as Main, Management, or Supporting, or as being Strategic, tactical, or operational in nature.

PROCESS LIFECYCLE VERB TAXONOMY

Because we see a lot of inconsistency in Process Maps and in existing process reference content such as the Supply Chain Operations Reference model (SCOR) or American Productivity & Quality Center (APQC), we created a process verb taxonomy to help you describe and classify processes throughout the entire process lifecycle. As illustrated in Figure 15, this enables the process expert, engineer, or architect to describe and classify

Process Lifecycle Verb Taxonomy

ANALYZE	DESIGN	BUILD	DEPLOY/IMPLEMENT	RUN/MAINTAIN	CONT. IMPROVEMENT
Analyze	Aim	Accept	Accomplish	Administer	Adjust
Appraise	Align	Adapt	Achieve	Assign	Alter
Approximate	Arrange	Assemble	Activate	Audit	Amend
Ascertain	Begin	Assure	Apply	Calculate	Boost
Assess	Blueprint	Build	Assimilate	Chronicle	Change
Capture	Categorize	Chart	Carry out	Communicate	Condense
Clarify	Characterize	Check	Cause	Conserve	Convert
Collate	Classify	Codify	Close	Control	Coordinate
Collect	Cluster	Combine	Complete	Engage	Correct
Consider	Commence	Compile	Conclude	Exchange	Decrease
Count	Compare	Compose	Conduct	Fix	Diminish
Demand	Convene	Configure	Conform	Govern	Eliminate
Detain	Describe	Confirm	Deliver	Handle	Enhance
Detect	Design	Constitute	Deploy	Keep	Escalate
Diagnose	Determine	Construct	Do	Maintain	Improve
Discover	Devise	Craft	Educate	Manage	Incorporate
Estimate	Display	Create	Employ	Measure	Moderate
Evaluate	Draft	Customize	Evolve	Monitor	Modernize
Examine	Draw	Define	Execute	Operate	Modify
Explore	Drive	Develop	Finish	Oversee	Optimize
Find out	Enter	Enact	Generate	Preserve	Realign
Forecast	Enumerate	Enlarge	Get done	Process	Reassess
Formulate	Establish	Erect	Implement	Oversee	Reconsider
Gage	Form	Expand	Include	Promote	Redevelop
Gather	Format	Extend	Initiate	Protect	Redirect
Gauge	Found	Fabricate	Instigate	Reconcile	Redraft
Identify	Idea	Increase	Integrate	Record	Reduce
Inspect	List	Itemize	Interlink	Recover	Reevaluate
Investigate	Negotiate	Make	Launch	Register	Reexamine
Judge	Obtain	Manufacture	Migrate	Reintroduce	Reform
Learn	Organize	Match	Perform	Report	Refresh
Observe	Outline	Pilot	Present	Respond	Regulate
Recognize	Plan	Procure	Progression	Retain	Renew
Reflect on	Plot	Provide	Put into action	Retire	Renovate
Research	Prepare	Purchase	Put into operation	Run	Reorganize
Review	Prioritize	Raise	Put into service	Save	Reprioritize
Revise	Propose	Rank	Realize	Service	Restore
Search	Quantify	Scan	Reallocate	Set up	Restructure
See	Recommend	Secure	Set off	Supervise	Revert
Seek out	Select	Shape	Shift	Support	Revolutionize
Study	Sketch	Systemize	Teach	Turn on	Rework
Survey	Start	Test	Train	Update	Standardize
Think about	Suggest	Translate	Transfer	Uphold	Transfigure
Understand	Verify	Unify	Transition	Withdraw	Transform

©LEADing Practice Business Process Reference Content [#LEAD-ES20005BP]

FIGURE 15

Process verb taxonomy to help describe and classify processes.

processes in the areas of process analysis, process design, process building, process implementation, process maintenance/monitoring, and continuous process improvement.

PROCESS STEP
What Is a Process Step?

A process step exists as an essential part of what is required to control a process. In each case of a process step, one of the two roles involved initiates the sequence by performing one or more aspects of the work and a second role is involved in completing other parts of the process before the output needed to complete the process is achieved.

A process step is part of the journey to completion of a business object that is produced by a particular process. Each process step, as with a process, will contain the name of the business object that is at the center of the work. Each step will also contain a verb or verb phase taken from the steps derived from the pattern of process steps based on the nature of the process. At this level, although the work is specific, there is nothing to indicate or specify how each action will be accomplished.

How to Identify Process Steps

A process step is a unit of work that is related to exactly one object (e.g., human, sheet of paper, purchase order (system)) and that is executed by one role.

The specifics of the steps involved in a process are based on two factors. The first is the nature of the process, which then permits the core steps to be defined. There are five process types:

1. Respond to request (prepare request, submit request, receive request, act on request, provide response, accept response)
2. Provide or publish an output (prepare output, provide output, receive output)
3. Provide or publish an output and confirm receipt (prepare output, provide output, receive output, verify conformance of output to requirement, confirm receipt of output, receive confirmation of receipt of output)
4. Collaborate to produce a shared output (collaborate on output)
5. Monitor and respond (observe conditions, assess conditions, determine action required, provide direction/assessment, receive direction/assessment)

Superficially, these may look like work that already exists within a process, but this is not the case.

Consider that the sequence of work within the example process includes "request repair for car," "qualify customer," and "repair car." Although this appears to be redundant, it pays to keep in mind the motivation or purpose of each level of work. When we consider these processes, it is important to remember that they are each about the creation of value, whereas at the level of steps the concern has to do with control. Therefore, whereas "request repair for car" is within the continuum of the production of a product (in this case, a repaired car), when we explore how that value is created and controlled, we find a number of viable choices. Two actors can collaborate to determine what the request for the repair of the car should look like to provide to a third party, or one actor can request assistance from another in describing the requirement, or one role can provide the specification of the requirements to a second, who must then act. This decision is central to the idea of achieving control.

The second factor contributing to describing a complete process is driven by seven process-oriented policies.[14] These independent policies will dictate the steps required to flesh out or be added to a process to complement and complete the set core process. The relevant process policies (with the options for each identified) are:

1. When are payments for the output made? (n/a, before, now, later)
2. When is value provided relative to the request? (now, later)
3. Is a profile of the service partner (customer or supplier) maintained? (yes, no)
4. How is price for the output established? (n/a, negotiate, standard pricing)
5. Are the rights to the output transferred? (yes, no)
6. Is the output tracked after the transaction? (yes, no)
7. Is the output prefabricated or made to order? (inventoried, built to order)

Collectively, the answers to these questions and steps identified through the process type complete the list of steps necessary to capture the specification of work at this level. For example if the answer to Question 4, "How is price for the output established?" where that the price is determined by standard pricing, the process step "look up product price on price list" would have to be added. If the answer to this question indicated that prices are determined via negotiation, the process step "negotiate product price" would be needed.

From these patterns, we can see that a process step might legitimately be named in the following manner:

- For a process intended to "respond to (a) request," such as the process to answer a request for an appointment:
  - Provide request for appointment
  - Receive request for appointment
  - Determine appointment
  - Provide response to request for appointment
  - Receive response to request for appointment
  - Examine response to request for appointment
- For a process intended to "provide or publish an output," such as the process to:
  - Provide invoice
  - Receive invoice
  - Accept invoice

Both of these example sets of process steps may be incomplete owing to the influence of the process policies in place for each process, but the additional process steps "create request for appointment" must be added in the first example and "produce invoice" in the second because in either case the particular business object is available except by being "made to order" (Policy 7).

Similarly, in both cases the process owner has the discretion to decide whether a profile of the service partner (customer or supplier) is maintained (Policy 3). In cases where the profile exists, another process step, "obtain address for appointment/invoice," is required, and in cases where it is not there would be no additional step. A similar set of decisions is required for each of the process policies in an additive process in which the only point at which the set of process steps making up a particular process will be known is once all the questions have been addressed.

How Are Process Steps Documented?

Process steps may be documented in a structured model that identifies the events (things outside the work that initiate, and terminate the actions described in the model) and the steps required to move the business object to completion.

This modeling approach requires no sub-process, no transaction activity, and no call activity, and only the most basic form of work.

It should be noted that the analysis of activities can only be carried out after either the physical roles are determined from the organization design, from policy, or through practice associated with project- or team-based roles.

In Figure 16 – Example Process Step Model, we see the set of process steps based on the "provide or publish an output" pattern, with no requirement for a payment or other policy-driven steps, except for "develop customer qualification standards," or "built to order," which is added for clarity.

When the decision is made for the product to be delivered not by obtaining it from inventory but by a "build to order" mechanism, a decision must be made as to how the product is to be built. A standard set of choices, where each requires a different set of process steps, is available (not all are required in all cases). Options for building the product are:

- In a product[15,16] manufacturing context: project,[17] jobbing,[18] batch,[19] assembly,[20] or continuous.[21]
- In an economic service[22] context: project, jobbing, batch, or assembly

It is at the level of the process step we see business objects being connected to work. Resources are consumed and output products are produced. In information-centric work the control objects that are consumed and created can be identified and linked to the work that uses or produces them.

While the information flow associated with the control object can be represented separately, in an information flow model, the Process Step Model in Figure 16 shows the sequence of work and where the information structures fit into and connect with the behavior part of the larger equation, which is the complete design and specification of the business to show how control of the work will be maintained and tracked. Figure 17 provides a clearer picture of the work, identifying not just the sequence of work, but the business objects involved in the work and their respective flows.

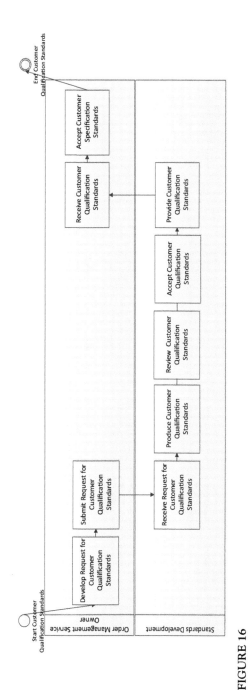

FIGURE 16

Example of a process step model.

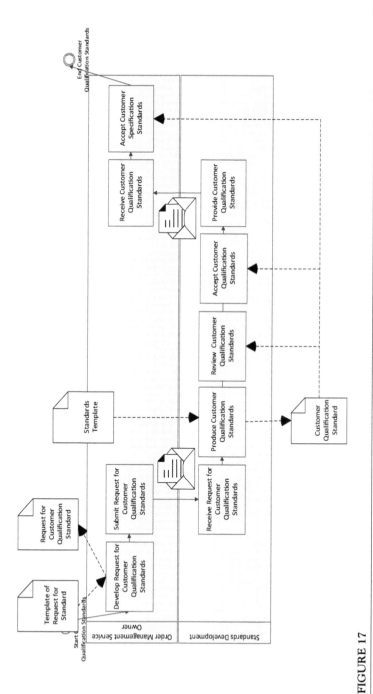

FIGURE 17

Example of a Process Step model with information flows.

The above example Process Step model shows that in the top lane the actor in the initiating role (Order Management Service Owner) would "develop request for customer qualification standard" and then "submit the request for customer qualification standard" to the actor in the receiving role (Standards Writer), represented by the lower lane, who would then first "receive request for customer qualification standard" and then "produce/review/approve customer qualification standard" before "providing the customer qualification standard" back to the requestor, who will first "receive customer qualification standard" and then "accept the customer specification standard," thus complete all steps for the process "produce customer specification standard." Again, this model could be modified to include additional process steps for any one or more of the remaining process policy decisions or to more specifically expose the actual details of the means used to produce or develop the standards, likely project, or jobbing type work.

In this model, the Process Steps are augmented within information flows that show that four business objects are involved in the process: the template for requesting a standard, the request for customer qualification standard, a standards template, and the customer qualification standard itself.

Notice that in these models we are dealing only with the sequence of actions required for the successful, normal behavior to perform the work and therefore complete the process. These steps do not expose the results of decisions, only the activity needed to obtain a decision, and at this level the sequence of work does not change. On the other hand, every one of the steps making up a process may be affected by a set of policies that will affect the sequence of work. Exception conditions, which may result in the work product moving in some manner other than the ideal path seen at the level of the step, are exposed at this level. These exception conditions may occur because of one or more of the following failure types:

1. Execution failure
2. Deadline expiration
3. Resource unavailability
4. External triggers
5. Constraint violation

Each and any of these failure types may occur during any step. Although the complete specification of the rules for handling each failure may be required, care should be taken in performing, documenting, or executing actions in conditions where these failure modes exist, because the result can be a significant explosion in the options of how this work may flow. Of course, this complexity makes process models using existing, standard techniques complex to model and virtually impossible to verify. By separating the failure modes that are applied to a set, from the choices that are about the application of rules within the step, accidental complexity is reduced.

The nature of each of these failure modes is as follows:

1. **Execution failure:** Execution failures during the execution of a step will typically mean the work item is unable to progress and no further steps are possible within the normal flow. This may result in escalation of the execution of work to a different role or that handling of the work by other roles is required.

2. **Deadline expiration:** Commonly there is a requirement for a step to be completed in or by a particular time constraint. If this cannot happen, exception handling involving other roles different from the above case may be required.
3. **Resource unavailability:** Often the execution of work requires access to one or more resources during its execution, and fails due to either no resource is found to do the work, or the resource becoming unavailable during the course of the work. If these are not available to the work item at initiation, it is usually not possible for the work item to proceed. This may require some combination of other activities actions to:
   a. Obtain the necessary resources
   b. Reallocate resources
   c. Abandon the execution of work
   d. Re-specify the execution of work
   Examples of this type of failure include having inadequate information or the incorrect information necessary to perform a transaction.
4. **External trigger:** Events external to an activity may affect the ability to act on the execution of work and may therefore require some alternative form of handling. Events may occur in activities that are not directly linked to the work in question being executed. They may occur anywhere within the process model or even in other process models. Addressing the impact of these external triggers will typically mean that current execution of work needs to be halted or possibly undone and some alternative action taken. Examples of an external trigger include the requestor who initiates a process cancelling the request, a systematic breakdown of the process, such as a failure of enabling automation.
5. **Constraint violation (including inadequate authority to approve):** Constraints in the context of an activity are typically found within the information integrity requirements needed and operational consistency of the business. On-going monitoring is generally required to ensure that they are enforced. Implementation of routines to identify and handle constraint violations detected within the context of a step is similar to the issue of dealing with external triggers. Typically, the constraint will detect and need to deal with the violation, although there is no reason why the constraint could not be specified and handled at a block or process level.
6. To address its failure condition, each exception case should be modeled separately as a separate overlay to the activities in the activity baseline. These conditions can lead to the creation of multiple paths, any number of which can result in failure of the activity, and therefore the affected parent process, to complete. Then it is at the level of the steps where work occurs and the possibility of failure exists.

Each instance of a failure mode can be seen in Figure 18 as triggering an event that moves the workflow from the current, planned, sequence to a new, exception flow. Each exception condition is terminated by an intermediate event, which can

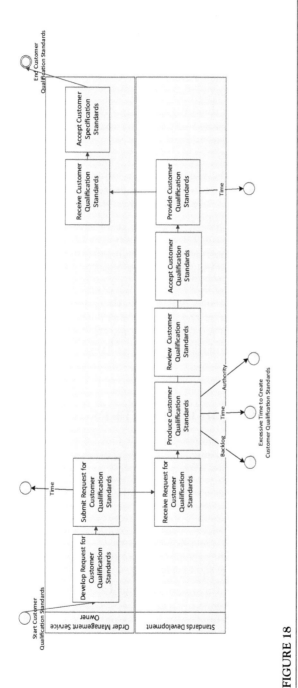

FIGURE 18

Example of a Process Step with Exceptions.

then in turn be recognized as the triggering event for the appropriate workflow; i.e., if the Standards Developer takes too long to "Develop the Customer Qualification Standard," this will trigger the workflow that transfers the work from the current workflow to a new workflow that is not on this model and therefore can be addressed as a single bundle of behavior, capturing each escalation path and its rules and behavior as a discrete package. Because each exception condition and its associated work is now both well-bounded and focused on a single aspect of the work, the ability to develop and validate the specification is now standardized and repeatable.

The decision to establish and enforce any exception condition is wholly within the discretion of any actor engaged in the process. In the example, the time from the "request for customer qualification standards" and their actual receipt is monitored and if the intervening process to "submit the request for customer qualification standards" takes too long, the process may be interrupted and completed through a separate exception process. Similarly, the step to "provide customer qualification standards" may also be escalated or subject to exception handling based on time criteria. Finally, the process to "develop the customer qualification standards" themselves may be escalated if it remains in the backlog too long, the standards development resource has an issue with the authority available to do the work, or they take too long with this work. In each case, the exception condition flows to an event that is then mirrored by an equivalent event that indicates the start of the applicable process designed to address the implied work. Of course, the potential exists for the control policies for every process step to have the potential to experience failure for any combination of the failure conditions.

THE NATURE OF PROCESS STEPS

When tagging or categorizing process steps, they may be identified as simple/static, generic/hybrid, or complex/dynamic.

ACTIVITY

What Is an Activity?

The activities of a process are classified within each of the process steps. Activities describe work. Each activity specifies one of the inputs consumed within the activity and exposes it as work separate from the work needed to transform it, or is the transaction that produces the output identified as being the result of completing the step.

Process activities provide the details of the complete set of actions required to produce an output from a process step. The flow between activities exposes the impact of failure of the work to complete successfully, i.e., the content of a data field is not available where it is required or does not conform to the specification, or a part is not of acceptable quality, and so on.

An activity is the part of the actual physical work system that specifies how to complete the change in the form or state of the inputs, oversee, or even achieve the completion of an interaction with other actors and seeing the decisions that must be made, who makes them, and under what circumstances.

At this level, we are capable of exposing and capturing the individual atomic questions that a worker must ask and answer to complete the step.

How to Identify Activities

At this level, we are capable of exposing and capturing the interaction with the individual atomic objects that a worker in a role can view, access, and/or manipulate within the work.

Activities will be of one of two types:

1. There will be one activity that will always recognize the work to convert some set of inputs into an output (transformational work), complete a transaction within rule-based work, or, in situations of high ambiguity, reach a judgment or conclusion (tacit work)
2. The remaining activities are each associated with one of the inputs consumed in creating the output

How Are Activities Documented?

Process activities are documented in a structured model that identifies the events (things outside the process that initiate, terminate, or happen during the course of the action described in the model), and the set of activities required within the scope of the business step.

In the example shown in Figure 19 the work becomes much more concrete. The context of the activity is well-bounded by the process step within which it is classified. The events that show the start and end of the process activity model are the

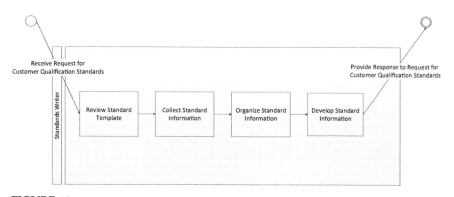

FIGURE 19

Example of a process activity model.

names of the proceeding and following steps and the process activities themselves are individual, discrete actions that are complete to address a specific problem, or challenge on the way to completing the step. The focus of each item of work is on accomplishing or completing a different thing. Whereas all activity is carried out by a single role in most cases, including this example, this is not always the situation. In collaborative work, multiple roles may again appear at this level, but the purpose of each activity can be described by a single verb.

THE NATURE OF ACTIVITY

Process activities may be tagged or categorized as simple/static, generic/hybrid, or complex/dynamic and may be of the type: create, maintain, transmit, receive, track, find, store, pay, observe, assess, or destroy.

THE WORK SYSTEM
What Is the Work System?

The work system is composed of the combination of human work performing an activity aided by one or more resources that provide capability in performing this work; i.e., each resource acts as a package of capabilities to enable the work or act as a multiplier on what the human could reasonably accomplish without the aid of the resource.

Work system design seeks to optimize the contribution of a range of capabilities in the performance of a set of work to appropriately deliver the desired value and cost combination. Conception and execution of the work system will of necessity require that the designers address the problem through the interplay of the components to create a holistic understanding of the parts in relation to the whole such that all the parts of a work system relate (directly or indirectly) to the creation of a single specific result.

The nature of the activities will depend on the features of the capabilities available to enable the work. While it seems complicated, this is a simple concept. Let us illustrate this simplistic example, where the work system for digging a hole with a shovel (which draws on the capability of a small tool, a shovel), is different from digging a hole with a back end loader (which will draw on the different capabilities in this package of equipment). Similarly, the activity for entering process, resources, work tasks, and data into SAP will, for example, be different from executing the equivalent work in PeopleSoft.

How to Determine the Work System

Only one business role (which may or may not be fulfilled by multiple actors performing that role and which is supported by a resource providing particular capabilities) will be involved in the activities needed to complete an activity. Each activity may be enabled through any number of capabilities.

One challenge of developing the work system is that it requires a mode of thinking at odds with much current practice, which focuses on disciplines that are analysis-centric. Analysis, by definition, is about the decomposition of a problem into its parts to formulate an understanding of the constituent parts of the problem so as to study the parts and their relationships, and to reach a conclusion. Rather than taking the reductionist approach of traditional design of work, the work system design involves understanding how things influence each other within a whole. Although thinking about each part is critical to understanding, thinking about the whole is critical to creating a work environment that cost-effectively optimizes the tradeoffs between human and machine capabilities to create a result that supports the larger enterprise strategy and cost.

How Is the Work System Documented?

The work of the human is in one "swim lane" and the work of each capability is each captured in a separate one.

One example of the method for documenting work might be to capture transactional work enabled by a software system. Such a specification requires a clear understanding of the work involved, as set by the step that provides the context to the work, the nature of the work (transformational, transactional, or tacit), as well as that of the enabling capabilities to create a work system that finds the optimal balance between the manual and automated parts.

PROCEDURE

What Is a Procedure?

Whereas Process Groups, processes, and process steps are conceptual and process activities describe tangible work, procedure actually specifies how the work is done and will typically represent common agreed-upon practice controlled at a supervising (human or machine) level. Using the specification of the design of software or other capabilities is the means to capture the behavior and information aspects of systems or machines at the lowest externally observable level. Procedures are captured within the design of the product and within the manuals of operations and are an essential part of the product behavior.

A clear understanding of the context of the work is required to document a work system. Every domain of human endeavor and the standards for describing work in each domain has its own requirements as to what is needed. Within those domains enabled by software-based systems, different tools to describe activity are often also necessary, with distinctions based on the solution architecture being employed so as to both cleanly separate process or business logic from software implementation and provide a complete specification of application behavior and therefore a specification of the application interface, or the features of other capabilities and the work to be performed by each role when using the system, providing input to training aides, application manuals, and other products.

How to Identify Procedures

Each procedure will reference a single object that the role can view, access, or manipulate in a transactional application with a graphical user interface. The objects might include menu items, buttons, fields, scroll bars, a specific tool such as a steering wheel or a particular switch on the steering column, and so on.

How Are Procedures Documented?

The language of specification of procedures will vary based on the specifics of the capabilities and combinations of capabilities being used. For example, even with software design, the specification for each of a report, interface, conversion, enhancement, or form may be different.

CONNECTING THE WORK SPACES

To understand how these views of work connect, it is useful to view them in an integrated manner. This is shown in Figure 20.

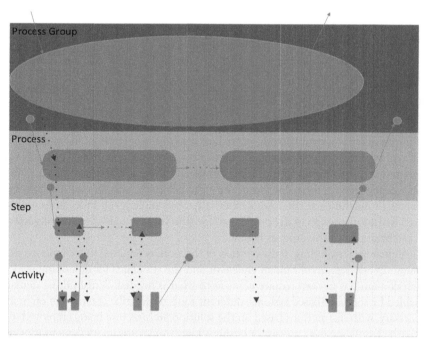

FIGURE 20

Integrated view for process hierarchy.

The view of work in which value is delivered occurs within the Process Group and at this level appears to be seamless. To expose the work needed to provide the product that delivers this value I must look into the processes, and then if I want to understand how the delivery of the processes is controlled I will look into the relevant process steps, and from there, if I want to actually understand the work involved I need to examine the process activities. What this means is that, as one enters a process, the work goes through a series of steps that start with the desire to create value and end with the work required to provide the control. In the course of this, the product needed to obtain the value is produced. In the case of software enabled transactional work, this occurs when the operator, working within an activity, presses the "Enter" key to complete the final activity needed to complete the final piece of work. This triggers the event that ends the activity flow, which provides the final piece of control needed to complete the product, necessary to obtain the value, all completing instantaneously.

PROCESS SCENARIOS

Process scenarios express the user story of how work is performed to achieve a particular result, using reusable design objects at the appropriate level to express the concern through the exploration of the process hierarchy. Although the hierarchy captures work as level, well-bounded components with a purpose in terms of the creation of value, production of useable products, maintenance of control, or the actual execution of work, it does not actually expose how the business uses or consumes these processes in the pursuit of a specific business purpose; process scenarios do this extremely well.

To develop a meaningful scenario, three questions must be asked and answered.

1. What is the purpose of the scenario; i.e., is it intended to show production of products or how control will be maintained, or is it to show the actual execution of work.
2. What is the defined objective of the work?
3. Where is the birth of the process relative to the scope of the analysis?

A Process Map may be used to capture the processes within a single Process Group, or be within a scenario drawn on the processes of multiple Process Groups to show a more complex set of linkages. For example, a Process Groups scenario map may call on processes within the process management Process Group, budgeting Process Group, procurement process, and payment groups to show the processes that cross a wide swath of an enterprise to fully execute an integrated procurement cycle, not only including the processes directly implicated in such a body of work, but showing all necessary oversight, planning, provision, delivery, and deregistration processes.

PROCESS TYPE

Tagging processes according to their type categorizes the processes based on their role within the enterprise in terms of whether they are essential management, process supporting processes, or represent a primary process within the enterprise. This is identified and correctly used in competency modeling, business model design, as part of the value chain, accountability, or operating model view.

Management processes will appear in the accountability view and may be subject to decisions about how activities are designed and implemented. Management processes are engaged in planning, budgeting, control, oversight, and monitoring of main or supporting processes.

Main processes are processes within a process that deliver the output.

Supporting processes are processes that are necessary to ensure the main process is given everything it needs to meet the purpose for which it was designed, deployed and is operated.

As you can see in Figure 21, management processes control the organization. Main processes produce the products/services for customers. Support processes provide resources for main processes. Together, they constitute the hierarchy or process architecture of an organization.

While most organizations are familiar with categorizing process types in their organizations, we feel compelled to point out the mistakes regarding tagging process types. The most common mistake in tagging process types is not understanding the difference between *categorizing process types and competency types*. The tagging of process types into main processes, also called core processes, does not recognize the difference between the nature of processes and the role of competency; where the latter concept is generally used in literature and by most

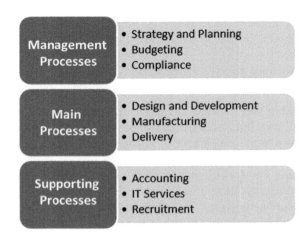

FIGURE 21

Example of process types.

executives to identify the organization's ability to be responsive to its external environment.[23] Strategic competitiveness and differentiation have been defined in the literature as an organization's ability to identify major changes in the external environment to quickly commit one's competencies to new courses of action, and to act promptly when it is time to halt or reverse them.[24] Organizations in every industry face competitive forces and develop strategies to define their direction. With the ability to classify competencies into core-differentiated competencies, core competitive competencies, or non-core competencies, it enables sorting of the role played by each competency in the execution of the strategy, the creation of value, and the link to the relevant business model discipline. Through renewal of the core competitive and core-differentiated competencies, one enables renewal in terms of business model innovation and transformation.[25] However, this requires understanding one's competencies according to the value they provide and where and how they provide it to the enterprise.

When decomposing process type classification to recognize management processes, main (core) processes, or supporting processes, it is possible for a process of any of these types to be within any one of core differentiating, core competitive or the non-core competencies. This means a non-core competency will have management processes, main (core) processes or supporting processes, so will core differentiating competency as well as a core competitive competency. Therefore, while they are two very different tagging mechanisms, one is applied within process modeling and another within competency/business modeling. Except that both are tagging mechanisms, they have nothing to do with each other and we actually understand how the mix-up came about. As shown in Figure 22, a main process will go across non-value creating as well as value creating aspects. So will a management process and a supporting process; they are all part of various service flows to the outcome, e.g., customer value creation.

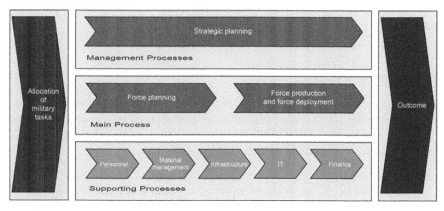

FIGURE 22

Process types in a defense example.

Therefore, while process also can be viewed as a "value chain" in which each process, step, and activity contributes to the result, some management, main, and supporting activities directly contribute value, while others may not. However, we all know that all processes have and consume enterprise resources independent of the value creation and realization. The challenge for managers is to eliminate steps that do not add value and to improve the efficiency of those that do. Within the main processes, there will be aspects that are non-value creating, also aspects that do.

A more detailed version of the Process Map defense example is found in Figure 23.

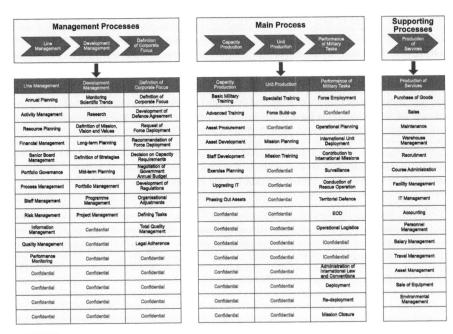

FIGURE 23

Process types in a more detailed Process Map defense example.

PROCESS TIER

In addition to process tagging in terms of process classification and process categorization, processes can be tagged according to their strategy, tactics, and operational tiers. The reason this applies to all processes is that all processes exist within the strategic, tactical, or operational aspects of the organization.

- **Strategic aspects:** This tier affects the entire direction of the firm. An example may be the mission, vision, strategic business objectives, and specific business performance indicators and business plans. The strategic tier has long-term, complex decisions made by executives and senior management, and the measurement reporting view used is for the most scorecards.

- **Tactical aspects:** The aspects at this tier are more medium-term, subjects of less complex decisions and primarily performed by middle managers. They follow from strategic decisions and aim to meet the critical success factors. The way to do this is for governance, evaluation, reports, control, and monitoring, and the measurement reporting view used is, for the most dashboards.
- **Operational aspects:** At this tier, decisions are made day-to-day by operational managers. They are simple and routine, and the measurement reporting view used is, for the most cockpits.

Figure 24 illustrates an example of the "Enterprise Tiers" and relevant process context.[26]

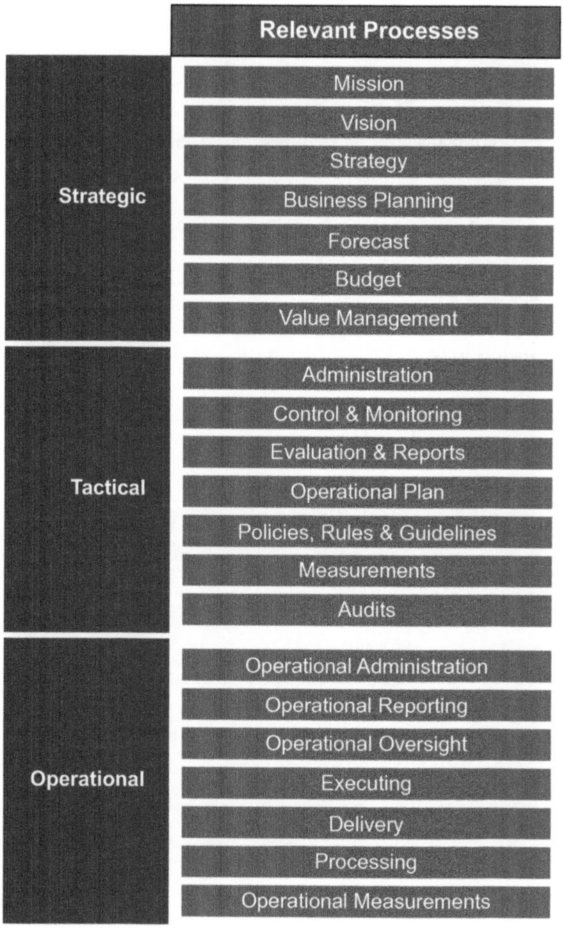

Relevant Processes
Strategic · Mission · Vision · Strategy · Business Planning · Forecast · Budget · Value Management
Tactical · Administration · Control & Monitoring · Evaluation & Reports · Operational Plan · Policies, Rules & Guidelines · Measurements · Audits
Operational · Operational Administration · Operational Reporting · Operational Oversight · Executing · Delivery · Processing · Operational Measurements

FIGURE 24

Example of "Enterprise Tiers" and relevant process context.

As demonstrated in Figure 24, the enterprise tiers represent tagging possibilities that link the processes, the goal and objective view, decision making, and the system measurement and reporting view. Beside the ability to classify processes according to strategic, tactical, and operational processes, and relate the processes to the right accountability level, ideal for process ownership, process governance, process analytics, and reporting, tier tagging enables information or the service flow between the enterprise tiers, making the tier process tagging a powerful tool (Figure 25).

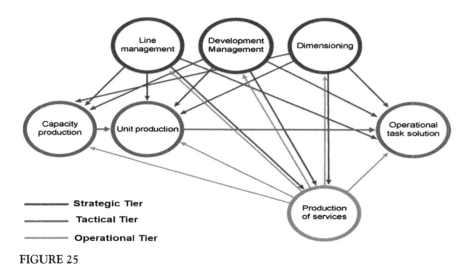

FIGURE 25

Example of enterprise tiers and the relations across tiers.

Tiers	Business Process	Process Step	Business Process Activity	Solution Area	WorkFlow
1. Strategic	Develop and manage strategies	Develop HR strategy	Identify strategic HR needs	Portal	End-to-end Process Integration
2. Tactical	Manage treasury operations	Manage treasury policies and procedures	Develop and confirm internal controls for treasury	ERP	Human capital management
2. Tactical	Manage IT knowledge	Develop IT knowledge management strategy	Plan IT knowledge management actions and priorities	ERP	Corporate services
2. Tactical	Dispose of assets	Dispose of product/service assets	Perform sale or trade	Portal	User Product/service/ivity Enablement
2. Tactical	Develop product and services	Design, build, and evaluate product and services	Build prototypes	ERP	Corporate services
2. Tactical	Develop and maintain information technology solutions	Develop the IT development strategy	Establish sourcing strategy for IT development	ERP	Corporate services
3. Operational	Develop and maintain information technology solutions	Develop the IT development strategy	Define development processes, methodologies, and tools standards	ERP	Corporate services
3. Operational	Manage taxes	Develop tax strategy and plan	Develop foreign, national, state, and local tax strategy	ERP	Corporate services

FIGURE 26

Detailed example of sorting processes according to enterprise tiers.

In Figure 26 is a more detailed example of how the tagging of the processes according to strategic, tactical, and operational views is an ideal way to go across end-to-end processes and see connections in the different tiers.

PROCESS NATURE

Not all processes are created equal. Some processes are simple and highly repeatable, and involve the same transactional and transformation work that can be done over and over; others are more complex or dynamic, involved in cases where the rules either are not clear, or are chaotic or subject to dynamic change. Understanding the nature and importance of processes is therefore central to effective process management and the basis for developing a successful business process management basis. Characteristics of the tagging process are as follows:

1. Simple and static processes are well understood, highly repeatable and are carried out multiple times in exactly the same way.
2. Generic and hybrid processes have mixed components and objects-like resources, tasks, measures, or rules, but similar properties.
3. Characteristics of complex and dynamic processes are that they are difficult and challenging, the way they are carried out changes over time, and the rules, practices, and procedures of this class of process are subject to ongoing evolution.

The ability to tag processes and categorize them according to their simple, hybrid, and complex nature enables the link to process drivers, reporting, process automation, and even risk, the operating model, as well as cost and value.

- **Process drivers and process nature:** Understanding the factors that lead to the drivers, e.g., performance and value drivers of a particular process, provides a means not only of understanding what to consider when evaluating the operations of a process, but also of developing the approach to improving it. When we consider the factors that influence process design, we see that many organizations are looking at performance drivers when modeling processes. However, we do know that the focus cannot only be about performance; by the nature of many of the process drivers, we must be concerned with value creation and realization.
- **Cost and process nature:** When we consider the factors that influence process design, we see that many organizations are looking at processes with a cost-centric view. Although it should not be this way, for some organizations BPM is all about cost. This is where the identification of cost factors in the processes is an ideal tool. In the simple and hybrid processes, cost cutting

through standardization is a huge potential, whereas human-based cost cutting, which is generally achieved by training or other means that improve human performance, must occur for processes that are more complex. More straightforward standard cost cutting is normally applied for the less complex processes.

- **Value aspects and process nature:** Once the enterprise truly understands which processes are of value, it is appropriate to invest in optimization of performance to include all factors of the nature of the process and thereby the simple, hybrid, and complex processes that are a part of value creation and realization.

- **Process reporting and process nature:** Reports are periodic accounts of the activities of the enterprise, whereas the other reporting tools are real-time or near real-time communications tools for providing information in such a way as to connect the activities to their strategic and tactical tiers. Where scorecards are a summary record of events of the execution, dashboards provide at-a-glance views of key performance indicators relevant to a particular objective, and cockpits provide real-time/actual measurement of dynamic and especially complex processes. In this case, because the concerns are just about control, all that is required here is the application of sound standards and guidelines.

- **Process automation and process nature:** Human replacement by machine or automation achieves a lower cost of operations. First, aspects of human labor were replaced with simple process automation. Today, both simple and complex processes are automated across the enterprise. For processes that tend to be either more complex or more valuable, it makes sense to seek improvements through exploring and developing methods and practices to achieve greater value before automating them. Generally, transaction volumes aside, investment in automation or other capabilities should receive low priority when the process is cost focused and simple; the business case will not be there unless the transaction volumes are significantly larger than elsewhere in the process landscape. Understanding the dimensions of a particular process nature is necessary to its automation design.

- **Risk aspects and process nature:** When considering the effects of uncertainty on process design and operations, risk increases as complexity increases. Whereas the probability and impact of variation in the performance of a process are consistent within processes of the same nature, when considering other than simple and static processes the reason for the risk varies. Variations within simple processes are generally not material to their performance and therefore not of concern to the extent that explicit risk management-centric oversight is required. On the other hand, when considering bottlenecks in processes, a phenomenon in which a single or limited number of components, aspects, or resources affect or otherwise limit the capacity, affecting performance and value, the same bottleneck would have a different impact on a high-value process than it would on a lesser-value process. Therefore, considering the process nature, one distinguishes between pain points, weakness cluster, and value clusters.

- **Operating model and process nature:** An operating model is an abstract representation of how an organization operates, or could operate, across process, organization, and technology domains to achieve its purpose and execute its strategy. The operational model is orthogonal to the previous models. Whereas all other models examine strategic importance and process complexity within a particular context, the operating model considers the implications of relative process standardization and integration irrespective of its value or relative complexity.

MISCATEGORIZATION AND MISCLASSIFICATION

It is important to mention that, while the logical clustering of categorization and classification is important and brings many benefits, there are also some common mistakes that are made. For the most part these errors occur due to a logical fallacy in which diverse and dissimilar objects, concepts, entities, etc. are grouped (categorization) or sorted by order, based upon illogical common denominators, or common denominators and relations based on over generalization of perceived underlying patterns are made. It is therefore relevant as illustrated in this document, to have the right decomposed levels and relationship in place as well as the right tier, type and the nature identified.

CONCLUSIONS

While this chapter should be seen and used as a description of what process tagging is and how it can be applied, it does not show all aspects of where the concepts can be useful. It attempted to build a basis of a structured way of thinking, working, modeling, and implementation of process classification and categorization. It endeavored to provide a standardized terminology, build common understanding, and make available the standardized and integrated classification and categorization tags to processes, enabling process practitioners to use the process tagging reference content to:

- Identify the relevant process tags
- Identify the process nature and enable understanding
- Specify process complexity
- Decompose the relevant process levels into the smallest parts that can, should, and need to be modeled, and then compose the entities to the right content through mapping, simulation, and scenarios

- Model the relevant process meta objects through the architectural layers (process architecture relevant)
- Visualize and clarify the process tags with the process templates by using maps, matrices, and models (alternative representation of information)
- Reduce and/or enhance complexity of process modeling, engineering, and architecture principles applying a common logical clustering
- Provide a structured process content that can be used for blueprinting and implementation

The beauty and power of this approach is that it enables understanding of the nature of a process, its levels, the relationships, enabling that the requirements for analysis are explicit, the starting and ending points are abundantly clear, and the level of analysis is set in each case by the context of the view of perspective of the containing description of work.

End Notes

1. Cohen H. and Lefebvre C., eds., *Handbook of Categorization in Cognitive Science* (Elsevier, 2005).
2. http://oll.libertyfund.org/index.php?option=com_staticxt&staticfile=show.php%3Ftitle=166&Itemid=99999999.
3. Cohen H. and Lefebvre C., eds., Ibid.
4. Ross, Jeanne; Weill, Peter; Robertson, David C. Enterprise Architecture As Strategy: Creating a Foundation for Business Execution. Harvard Business Review Press (2006).
5. Ibid.
6. Ibid.
7. Dr M. Hammer, *Business Process Re-engineering*.
8. H. Smith and P. Fingar, *Business Process Management*.
9. BPMN.
10. http://www.modelio.org/documentation/metamodel/Metamodel_HTML/90.html.
11. http://wiki.scn.sap.com/wiki/display/ModHandbook/Process+Hierarchy.
12. Ibid.
13. Within a single role. A swim lane is a graphical tool for showing a collection of steps, or activities for which a specific role is responsible.
14. Business information analysis and integration technique (BIAIT): the new horizon, Walter M. Carlson IBM, ACM SIGMIS, Volume 10 Issue 4, Spring 1979.
15. Products are tangible and discernible items.
16. Process choice is demand driven. Three primary questions bear on the selection of the production process step:
   a. How much variety in products or services must be provided?
   b. What degree of equipment flexibility will be needed?
   c. What is the expected volume of output?
17. Initiate, plan, execute, close out.
18. Specify, design, obtain materials, set up, create components, assemble, finish, test, accept, take down.
19. Set up, create components, assemble, finish, test, accept, take down.

20. Produce, test, accept.
21. Ibid.
22. An economic service is the production of an essentially intangible benefit, either in its own right or as a significant element of a tangible product, which through some form of exchange satisfies an identified need.
23. Hamel and Prahalad, 1994; Sull, 2009.
24. Shimizu and Hitt, (2004).
25. Burgelman, 1983.
26. LEADing Practice-Categorization & Classificaion Body of Knowledge, 2014.

Why Work with Process Templates

Mark von Rosing, Maria Hove, Henrik von Scheel, Ulrik Foldager

INTRODUCTION

In the Business Process Management (BPM) Ontology and Semantics chapter, we provided you with a detailed and extensive description of the concept of ontology and semantics: what they are, what their purpose is, and perhaps most importantly of all, how to use them effectively in the BPM way of thinking, the BPM way of working, and the BPM way of modeling.

Although we see an immense amount of literature on the adoption and implementation of BPM in a rapidly growing market, what surprises us is the low level of maturity of standards in terms of consistent and integrated templates to describe process. Because we see this as one of the main reasons for high-cost and low-value creation around process analysis, process mapping, process documentation, and process governance, we have chosen to focus in this chapter on process templates.

The chapter will specify what process templates are, the relationship between BPM ontology and semantics and how it links directly to the concept of templates, why they are needed, where they can be applied, and the benefits of applying them.

We believe that the principles of process templates are relevant to any organization, independent of industry, business model, or operating model.

THE RELATIONSHIP BETWEEN BUSINESS PROCESS MANAGEMENT ONTOLOGY AND PROCESS TEMPLATES

When an organization decides to make use of ontology and semantics to lay the foundation of what we call "process things," it is done for a vast variety of purposes (we will be naming a few of them throughout this chapter), but the most important one is that once you have established a specific and clear definition for a meta object, for example, this definition will be available to all relevant employees across organizational boundaries of the enterprise after it has been documented and published for use. This means that a common understanding and consensus has been reached within the organization for what name a particular meta object has for whenever you are referring to that particular meta object. Of course, this makes it a lot more practical for organizations to handle objects in the bigger picture: not just for documenting, but also for using them when modeling, engineering, and architecting process concepts and solutions, regardless of the business unit and/or business requirement. In the sense of semantics, then, it allows you to accurately describe how a particular object relates to another particular object (regardless of object type or hierarchical location). This has to be defined as well, of course, but just like the ontology definitions, an organization must also reach a common understanding and consensus in semantic relationships regarding how exactly each object relates to another. This is meticulous work and takes time and effort, but it is nevertheless extremely important to avoid common pitfalls.

Thus, we know what to call a particular object. In our case, we choose to use the driver meta object (through the creation of our ontology), and we know how the driver meta object relates to a business process meta object (because we have also defined a set of semantics that accurately describe how they influence and relate to each other). If we would then create a process template in which the relationship to a value driver is relevant, we would be able to use the business process meta object and place it in the process template, for both information and documentation purposes, as well as the ability to relate it to other aspects further on. We would most likely be identifying and listing (for example, in columns in an Excel spreadsheet) values such as the name of each business process meta object, where it is located, what resources it uses, etc. Maps are always used within the concept of the BPM way of thinking, which is the starting point, and where the conceptual aspects are covered. With this planner's view we generate and describe business concepts, document important and essential information regarding the business, and create a general overview of more or less anything of importance.

Continuing from this path, we would next create a process matrix for the purpose of relating the value driver meta object (in a row next to the columns in the Excel spreadsheet) to the relevant business process meta object. Matrices are almost always created within the concept of the BPM way of working, because here we begin to actually take action and relate objects to each other. Keep in mind that whenever you are creating a matrix, you are actively using the information provided to you through the previous creation of a process map. The map provides you with the information you need to create an efficient process matrix. By creating a process matrix, we then allow ourselves to identify directly and accurately which kind of value driver (whether internal or external) has an impact on the business process (regardless of impact type, although it has to carry some importance because we expect to note down information that affects the business somehow, and bearing that in mind that it is therefore worth documenting) on the business processes of the organization (regardless of business unit). Not only do we describe which value driver affects which business process, we can also identify exactly how the value driver affects the business process, where the impact occurs, what the consequences are, and who is responsible (role object) and who is accountable (owner object) for acting upon this knowledge.

Last but not least, we could—if deemed necessary and/or beneficial—create a process model to build a visual representation of how these value drivers would affect the business processes of the organization. Process models, as the name implies, are mostly used within the concept of the BPM way of modeling. Here we visually illustrate behaviors, relationships, connectivity, location, function, and purpose. Keep in mind, however, that a model always makes use of both the process map and the process matrix. The map and the matrix are your source of information; the model is how you would visualize this information.

As you can see, this is why the BPM ontology and semantics have real business value, because you have put down definitions of *what* (ontology) the objects are and *how* (semantics) they relate to other objects. As you can imagine, this is an essential piece of information for any process expert (process modeler), process engineer, and/or process architect in daily work. This is also the foundation and the reason why our process templates are 100% standardized and integrated with each other, enabling the ability to share process objects across various process templates.

WHAT ARE PROCESS TEMPLATES?

A process template is a documentation product such as a process map, process matrix, or process model. Process templates are created to describe some aspect of a process, a process landscape, process flow, process solution, or state. In enterprise architecture, these would be called artifacts. Templates enable the capture and relation of objects within the same template or across multiple templates, each of which promotes its own view. Process templates enable the capture and relation of process-centric objects within the same template or across multiple templates, each of which promotes its own view of a process.

The purpose of having process templates that address the various process concepts is to set out or describe how to organize and structure the viewpoints and process objects associated with the various disciplines and bring them together to create a common understanding. Standard process templates are important because they establish the elements of the artifacts, i.e., the relevant process objects to be addressed when the template is used.

Within the set of templates presented in this chapter, each template is part of an overarching ontological and semantically based specification that ensures that all of the objects are appropriately related. Reuse of the content of one process template or view for another is therefore ensured. Without this standardization and integration, the process templates create more work and cost, and are actually of little value. What many practitioners and organizations do not realize is the importance of having such integration and standardization across the landscape of this work, and therefore the value of the result.

Years of research in the Global University Alliance[1] have identified the semantic relations of the various process objects and how they can be applied within different contexts. These relationships are built into the process templates, e.g., process maps, process matrices, and/or process models.

PROCESS MAPS

A process map is intended to be an accurate list and representation of a set of decomposed and/or composed process objects. The purpose of this map is to inventory and create a list of all processes in the enterprise.

The content of a process map is based on which objects/elements can be related so the columns of the map conform to the semantic rules within the context in which they are being used.

This list helps us to understand the breadth of functionality provided by each of the processes. It will also provide a centralized and official overview and record of the key processes in the enterprise, each situated within the specific process area and process group in which it participates as well as linking in the channel, stakeholder, owner, and role/resource (including the manager) involved. Table 1 is an example of such a process map.

Members of the BPM team carry out the tasks necessary to complete the process map in the manner described in Table 2.

Mapping a process enables the following, among others:

- Identify relevant processes, including the name of the process
- Specify a unique process identifying number or ID
- Specify the level of process detail (see process levels in process tagging chapter)
- Link the involved business units and stakeholders to the relevant process
- Detail the process owners, in terms of which process is owned by whom
- Other process roles involved this can include:
  - Process roles

Table 1 *Example of a Process Map*

	What Specification:					Who Specification:			
Process#	Business Process area	Process Groups	Business Process	Process Steps	Process Activities	Stakeholder Involved	Process Owner	Managers Involved	Roles/ Resources Involved
#									

Table 2 *Example of How a Process Map is Based on Semantic Rules and Tasks*

The "what" specification: Identify, select, and categorize the business processes.	
Rules	Process relates directly to business construct, i.e., when collecting the inventory of processes within a sliver or slice of the enterprise
Tasks	• Identify and categorize the process areas related to the business areas or the end-to-end flow areas. • Specify and categorize the process groups based on the related business groups or the end-to-end flow groups. • Select, label, and categorize the business processes according to the groups. • Spot the process steps related to the business process. • Identify the process activities related to the process steps and business processes.
The "who" specification: Identify the relevant stakeholder, owners, and managers involved.	
Rules	Process relates directly to role and to resource (stakeholder) and owners, i.e., when collecting the inventory of processes related to a community within the enterprise
Tasks	• Identify and categorize the stakeholders linked to the business processes. • Specify the business process owners and categorize them according to their business process ownership. • Spot and categorize the business process-related managers. • Recognize, classify, and label the roles/resources of the business processes.

- Process approver, in terms of who approves the process and/or the work
- Process checker, in terms of who checks the work

As we have already mentioned, the above reasons determine the design and content of what is within such a process map and therefore how such a process map looks.

PROCESS MATRIX

Process matrices show the relationship between two specific sets of decomposed (broken down) objects in a process-centric context. The core idea of the process matrices is that they each consist of a set of process objects that semantically have primary and therefore direct natural relations to each other. The result is that these are always in the form of two lists (a row and a column) in which the process objects with which they share a relationship are each rated according to them within the body of the matrix. Within the process matrix, this allows one to relate the unfamiliar to the familiar, thus connecting process objects in the different layers (composition).

Table 3 is a process matrix illustrating the columns of the process map combined with performance indicators. Using this template would result in the content of every column having a minimum of one process indicator.

The process-performance indicator matrix's capture should be based on enterprise modeling and architecture rules outlined in Table 2. In addition to those rules and tasks, the rules and tasks outlined in Table 4 are applied when completing Table 3.

Reasons for creating process matrices can include:

1. Link processes to business goals and strategy
2. Create value-oriented process relations
3. Relate business competencies and processes
4. Understand the end-to-end process flow
5. Identify process problems and pain points—fixing a defective or inefficient process
6. Specify which business objects, information objects, and/or data objects are involved

Table 3 *Example of a Process Matrix Showing How Processes Relates to Performance Indicators*

	Indicators Process Number	What Specification:			Who/Whose Specification:			
		Business Process	Process Steps	Process Activities	Stakeholder Involved	Process Owner	Managers Involved	Roles/ Resource Involved
Performance Indicator 1	#							
Performance Indicator 2	#							
Performance Indicator N	#							

Table 4 *Relationship of Process Objects to Performance Indicators and Tasks Associated With It*	
Performance Indicator: A metric used by an enterprise to indicate its overall success or the success of a particular area in which it is engaged.	
Rules	(D) Process relates to performance (performance indicator).
Tasks	• Associate and tie the performance indicator(s) to the business processes. • Associate and tie the performance indicator(s) to the process steps of the business process. • Associate and tie the performance indicator(s) to the process activities of the business process. • Associate and tie the performance indicator(s) to the stakeholders involved in the business process. • Associate and tie the performance indicator(s) to the process owners of the business process. • Associate and tie the performance indicator(s) to the managers involved in the business process. • Associate and tie the performance indicator(s) to the roles/resources involved in the business process.

7. Connect performance indictors to processes
8. Improve the operating model
9. Reduce process cost
10. Associate relevant rules to the processes
11. Identify and relate compliance aspects
12. Process automation
13. Process measurements and reporting as part of the organizational analytics and decision making
14. Service model improvement

As we have mentioned, these reasons determine the design and content of what is within such a process matrix and therefore how such a process matrix should look. For example, reporting would require process matrices with the following relations: other relations' performance indicators (measures), business goals, and who would receive what report.

PROCESS MODEL

Once information has been collected and organized in the process maps and/or process matrices, a process model may be crafted to enable the complex set of resulting information to be used in different disciplines, and within this to be communicated more easily to stakeholders, management, and leadership. The fully integrated and standardized process templates enable the practitioner to work and model with the process objects throughout all aspects of the enterprise (business, application, and technology) with more confidence in the completeness and alignment of their information. Their semantic relations and connection are governed not only by the

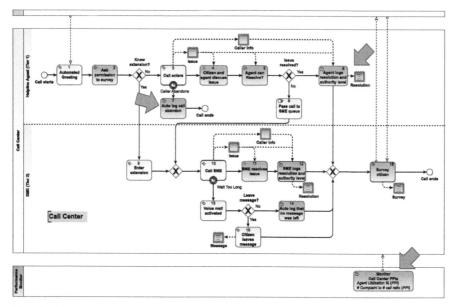

FIGURE 1

Example of process model, with measurements and reports specified within notations (Example modeled in iGrafx®).

objects, but also by the process modeling rules and tasks, which ensure how and where the process templates interlink and share common process objects.

An example of such a process model is illustrated in Figure 1, which demonstrates processes, roles involved, interactions, data aspects, and measurements and reporting aspects.

In this example, through a process such as described in Table 1, the stakeholders, managers, and owners identified in the process map are related to the performance indicators through the process matrix (Table 3). If such a vertical alignment of measurements across levels is ignored, it is possible that activities or processes will be measured in ways that do not contribute to the overall success of the organization. The danger to an organization might even be that the performance indicators could lead to conflicts in strategy or value creation. Together, the process map in Table 1 and process matrix in Table 3 and the process model in Figure 1 provide a good example of how it is possible to relate the relevant process information.

The process maps, process matrices, and process models that specify the semantic relations in this illustration are just examples. As such, they do not show all possible relations that exist. Other views of other information are possible. We could, for example, choose to organize this same information by processes, measurements, or the data involved. An example of an alternative view is found in Figure 2, in which the sales call center from Figure 1 shows a sales analysis and a cost of goods sold analysis by process.

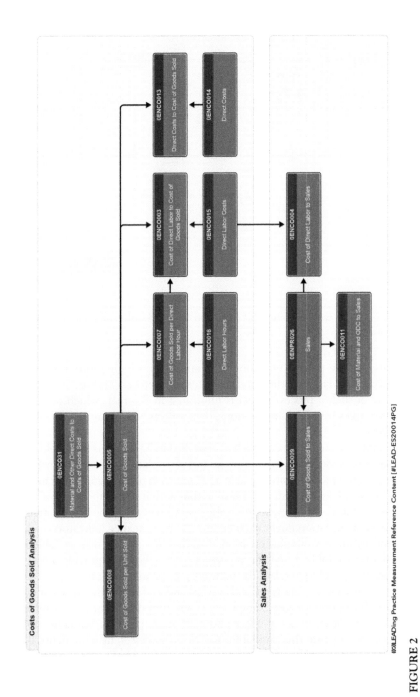

(©)LEADing Practice Measurement Reference Content [#LEAD-ES20014PG]

FIGURE 2

Example of automated process measure, e.g., SAP system measurement with the relevant processes, data object queries, transaction codes, and process flow relations. [2]

THE MOST COMMON PROCESS TEMPLATES

As we have just explained, the process templates consist of process maps, matrices, and models that capture the relevant process elements (meta objects). Each of these process templates is based on a specific view with particular stakeholder concerns, to enable process identification, creation, and realization in achieving the outlined needs and wants. For this, the process templates identify the relevant stakeholders, their requirements and concerns, the process descriptions and their semantic rationale, and the corresponding tasks to the specific views and viewpoints. Each of these process templates is thereby built to support a particular need and want.

Figure 3 illustrates an overview of the most common process templates. All of the process templates listed are fully integrated and standardized, enabling full reusability of shared aspects between process templates, where 1 in Figure 3 shows the objects in the process maps, 2 shows the objects in the process matrices, and 3 shows those of the process models. The specific process templates therefore not only show which objects are within what template, specifying whether it is a map, matrix, or model, it furthermore shows where the object of one template can be reused in another: where the objects have and should be integrated and standardized, because they are the same. That most organizations do not have such integrated and standardized process templates is the single source of the high costs of modeling, engineering, and architecture and the low maturity of output.

BENEFITS OF PROCESS TEMPLATES

One of the strangest things we have heard is that "real process experts do not use templates," or "templates are a substitute for a real subject matter experts." However, we have learned through hard experience that there are times when using one is not only the most appropriate choice, but frequently the sole choice that addresses the problem. Some benefits to using process templates are that:

- They ensure consistency with project artifacts
- All subject matter experts work in a standardized way
- They ensure cross-integration of templates
- They save time with templates
- They are reusable
- They enable better governance
- They are less expensive
- They are faster to populate across various teams
- They develop routine
- They maintain consistency among various team members and artifacts
- They immediately lift the artifacts to maturity level 3 and 4
- They develop a standard in your BPM Center of Excellence (CoE)
- If you are a non-designer, use templates to give a more professional edge to your own marketing materials.
- They get things done faster

Process Objects \ Templates	FD	VMG	Rq	ST	S	BSC	Pe	MR	BC	Rev	Co	Op	I	Ro	O	OC	Ob	WF	Ru	RS	SC	CS	P	BPMN	Se	A	AS	AR	AM	AI	Asc	C	D	PL
Process Area (categorization)	1,2	2	1,2	1,2,3	1,2,3		2,3	2,3	2			1		2,3	2,3	2,3		2,3					1,2,3	2										
Process Group (categorization)	1,2	2	1,2	1,2,3	1,2,3		2,3	2,3	2			1		2,3	2,3	2,3		2,3					1,2,3	2										
Business Process	2	2	1,2	1,2,3								1										2,3	1,2,3	2,3	2	2								
Process Step			2,3							2	2							2,3	2,3	2	2		1,2,3	3	2	2								
Process Activity			2,3							2	2							2,3	2,3	2	2		1,2,3	3	2	2								
Events			2,3							2	2							2,3	2,3			2	2,3	3	2		2,3							
Gateways			2,3																2,3				2,3	3	2		2,3							
Object (Business & Information & Data)			2,3										1,2,3				1,2	1,2,3	2,3				2,3	2,3	2,3									
Process Flow (incl. Input/output)			2,3						1,2,3	3	3						2	1,2,3					3	3	2,3	3	2			3	2,3		1	1
Process Roles			2,3											1,2			2,3						2,3	2,3	1,2		2							
Process Rules			2,3																1,2,3				2,3	2,3				2,3				1,2		
Process Measurement (PPI)						2,3	1,2,3	1,2,3	1,2,3	2,3	2,3												2	2,3					1,2					
Process Owner	2	2	1,2,3	1,2,3	2,3	2,3	2,3	2,3	1,2,3	1,2	1,2	2,3			1,2								1,2,3	2,3	2,3									

1 = Map   2 = Matrix   3 = Model

FIGURE 3

The most common process templates.[3]

- They maintain artifact consistency
- They simplify updates and changes
- Process templates can be used by the various people who work with processes, i.e., process experts, process engineers, and process architects. As a matter of fact, aspects of the templates can be reused across the various process roles.
- There are many ways to personalize them without sacrificing the benefits and consistency of the process templates. If your team has unusual needs, you can customize a process template and then create the BPM project.

Remember that the process templates we have illustrated are designed based on a complete view of the enterprise semantics and are therefore fully integrated and standardized with each other. This means that we know which aspects of one process template can be reused in another template. A further advantage is that the process templates are designed to meet the needs of most process experts/teams in many different settings and to be fully integrated into the BPM lifecycle, BPM roles, BPM governance, and BPM change management. Working with the various process templates we present in this book is a smart idea and will lift your maturity and save significant amounts of time and money.

CONCLUSION

In this chapter, we have focused on process templates and why they are important within organizations working with their processes. The subject is therefore relevant for BPM CoE, BPM teams, process experts, and other subject matter experts working with processes.

We covered what process templates are, how they can be used, and where they can or should be applied to draw on the ontology and semantic-based process relations standardized to ensure reusability and replication of success in outlining the correct connection points based on a common relationship pattern of the process objects.

We furthermore detailed the differences between process templates in terms of process maps, process matrices, and process models, and ended with the benefits and value of process templates.

We showed that by using process templates to manage the different kinds of highly connected information and relations the process creation is ensured and that:

- The process map (which lists the various related objects to capture the decomposed unrelated objects) is a critical design tool
- The process matrix (which is composed in terms of relating specific objects together) provides the continuity for and interconnection between a process map (a representation of decomposed and/or composed objects)
- A process model (a representation of interconnected and related objects) is critical to integrating and standardizing the process templates and tools of the practitioner.

Furthermore, it is an essential part of supporting, integrating, and standardizing the practitioner's way of thinking, working, and modeling.

As already shown, the illustrated process map, process matrices, and process models and the specification of semantic relations are just examples. Because they were examples, not all possible relations were specified. However, all of the possible relationships for the various process templates will be illustrated with detailed examples in the various chapters across Volumes 1 and 2 of *The Complete Business Process Handbook.*

End Notes

1. http://www.globaluniversityalliance.net/.
2. Enterprise Cost Model, LEADing Practice Measurement Reference Content [#LEAD-ES20014PG].
3. Common Process Templates Overview, LEADing Practice Business Process Reference Content [#LEAD-ES20005BP].

The BPM Way of Working

Henrik von Scheel, Mark von Rosing, August-Wilhelm Scheer

INTRODUCTION

In this part, we establish a way of working with business processes—the critical discipline of translating strategic planning into effective process execution. We explore both the current and future business process trends that we advise you to be fully aware of in order to be best prepared for many of the coming business process changes on the global scale. We also provide a perspective regarding what is hype and what is real to allow you to make critical decisions about what to possibly adopt, transform, and innovate within your organization.

The way of working around business processes is structured to provide you with a practical guide for how to organize, classify, align, arrange, and quantify business process management (BPM) concepts and to select and use process objects and/or process templates/artifacts in the systemized and categorized way that they need to be applied and used within your process initiatives. This is described around important topics such as:

- What are the current and future business process trends?
- Building BPM competencies: the BPM Center of Excellence
- How to use process templates
- The various BPM roles
- Working with the BPM lifecycle
- Uncovering a detailed guide for how to work with process analysis, process design, process deployment, process monitoring, process maintenance, and continuous process improvement
- Determining the potential of working with BPM maturity models
- Discovering how BPM alignment management enables identification of duplicated business processes, tasks, roles, measures, and reports; unleashes reusability and unifies initiatives
- Realizing the impact and opportunities in intelligent business process management (iBPMN): From automation to orchestration—the realignment of BPM around service-oriented architecture (SOA)
- How evidence-based BPM seeks to instill a data-driven approach
- Understanding how social media and BPM fit together

Business Process Trends

Mark von Rosing, August-Wilhelm Scheer, Henrik von Scheel, Adam D.M. Svendsen, Alex Kokkonen, Andrew M. Ross, Anette Falk Bøgebjerg, Anni Olsen, Antony Dicks, Asif Qumer Gill, Bas Bach, Bob J. Storms, Callie Smit, Cay Clemmensen, Christopher K. Swierczynski, Clemens Utschig-Utschig, Dan Moorcroft, Daniel T. Jones, David Coloma, Deb Boykin, Dickson Hunja Muhita, Duarte Gonçalves, Fabrizio Maria Maggi, Fan Zhao, Fatima Senghore, Fatma Dandashi, Fred Cummins, Freek Stoffel, Gabriel von Scheel, Gabriella von Rosing, Gary Doucet, Gert Meiling, Gert O. Jansson, Hans Scheruhn, Hendrik Bohn, Henk de Man, Henk Kuil, Henrik Naundrup Vester, Jacob Gammelgaard, James P. Womack, Jeanne W. Ross, Jeff Greer, Jens Theodor Nielsen, John A. Zachman, John Bertram, John Golden, John M. Rogers, Jonnro Erasmus, Joshua von Scheel, Joshua Waters, Justin Tomlinson, Karin Gräslund, Katia Bartels, Keith D. Swenson, Kenneth Dean Teske, Kevin Govender, Klaus Vitt, Krzysztof Skurzak, LeAnne Spurrell, Lloyd Dugan, Lotte Tange, Mads Clausager, Maria Hove, Maria Rybrink, Marianne Fonseca, Mark Stanford, Marlon Dumas, Mathias Kirchmer, Maxim Arzumanyan, Michael D. Tisdel, Michel van den Hoven, Mikael Munck, Mike A. Marin, Mona von Rosing, Nathaniel Palmer, Neil Kemp, Nils Faltin, Partha Chakravartti, Patricia Kemp, Peter Franz, Philippe Lebacq, Rich Hilliard, Richard L. Fallon, Richard N. Conzo, Rod Peacock, Ronald N. Batdorf, Sarel J. Snyman, Scott Davis, Simon M. Polovina, Stephen White, Steve Durbin, Steve Willoughby, Thomas Boosz, Thomas Christian Olsen, Tim Hoebeek, Tom Preston, Ulrik Foldager, Victor Abele, Vincent Snels, Volker Rebhan, Wim Laurier, Yr Gunnarsdottir, Yury Orlov, Zakaria Maamar, Ekambareswaran Balasubramanian, Mai Phuong, Régis Dumond

INTRODUCTION

Business process and business process management (BPM) concepts have matured over the years and new technology, concepts, standards and solutions appear. In this chapter we will therefore focus on the current and future process trends. We will elaborate on the importance of trends, the maturity of the subject, giving a perspective on what emerging trends, industry trends, mega trends are, what is hyped at the moment, and what has reached a market adoption where it has started to become the de facto standard in terms of mega trends that has achieved a dominant position by public acceptance.

THE IMPORTANCE OF TRENDS

A trend is defined as a general direction in which something is developing or changing.[1] Trends involve looking at the statistical analysis of historical data over a selected time frame and charting the progression. If the data suggest consistent increases, decreases, or even constancy or flatness, a trend exists. Businesses of all sizes use these kinds of data to help predict the future or shape strategic decisions.

So why are trends important? Because trends help you prepare for the future! From a business perspective, there are three main types of trend: emerging, industry, and mega trends. If organizations ignore any of them, the business drivers or trends may eventually evolve to become a direct threat to their existing business model. If embraced, they hold the key for the next opportunity for growth.

For example, business process has matured over a decade into a management discipline that treats processes as assets that directly contribute to enterprise performance by driving operational excellence and business process agility. Today, business process has become an essential source of performance that supports business success, some of which are:

- Optimizing the performance of end-to-end business processes that span functions as well as processes that might extend beyond the enterprise to include partners, suppliers, and customers (the value chain).
- Making the business processes visible (and thus explicit) to business and information technology (IT) constituents through business process modeling, monitoring, and optimization/simulation.
- Keeping the business process model in sync with process execution and empowering business users and analysts to use the model to improve process performance and outcomes.
- Enabling the effective integration of process activities, business measurements, rule management, content integration, and greater collaboration to set the base for continuous improvement.
- Enabling rapid iterations of processes and underlying systems for continuous process improvement and optimization.
- Delivering measurable improvement to enterprise performance that directly contributes to organizational success and competitive advantage.
- BPM is just one approach to the larger challenge known as business process improvement (BPI). Other approaches to BPI include business process re-engineering (BPR) and business process automation.

Hence, both executives and practitioners are focusing on process trends to gain a competitive advantage by being the early adopter. Our focus is on process mega trends and emerging trends as the driving force that will change how organizations work with and apply these trends successfully to their process landscape in order to gain a competitive advantage in the future.

MATURITY OF THE SUBJECT

The adoption of trends is tightly connected to the maturity. The rise of business process engineering and re-engineering results from a paradigm shift[2] that has already occurred by moving away from the previous function-oriented management practices. The new focus is now more towards practices that focus on customer value. The result of this shift also necessitated consideration of the enterprise strategy, structure, and culture that are required to support the new infrastructure.

According to a survey done by PriceWaterhouseCoopers AG,[3] organizations are critically aware of the importance of BPM to the future success of their business. To remain competitive, senior executives have identified the importance of the continuous optimization of business processes in terms of quality and efficiency for their administrative and production business processes[4] while retaining the differentiation among core competitive, core differentiating, and non-core processes. The survey found that many of these executives believed that their business would no longer exist in as little as 10 years if efforts to continuously improve and optimize their business processes were not pursued. In a similar tone, many of these executives saw that another key factor to the success of an organization is the collection and analysis of appropriate key process performance indicators.

Often when a trend emerges and the maturity is low, early adoption investors take advantage of the opportunity and develop unique leading solutions. Such practices from the leaders are called leading practices. Leading practices define and strengthen competitive advantage, innovation, and efficiency in the core differentiating competencies with a focus on the revenue model and value model. They are called the out-performers and are the first to take advantage of the new emerging trends and thereby outperform the market.

When a trend is in its early hype stages and becomes more mature, industry leaders adopt, invest, and develop industry practices to out-compete their peers. This is called industry adoption. Industry practices improve competitive parity and standardize core competitive competencies with a focus on performance models and service models. They are called industry leaders because they have the advantage of emerging trends and outperform the majority of the competition in their respective markets.

Finally, as the trend matures with wide adoption and years of experience it has becomes a standard or a best practice. The adoption becomes a best practice when organizations begin to improve and standardize their non-core competencies that focus on the cost model and the operating model. Such organizations are considered followers who take advantage of best practices that are non-core to their business, while gaining the full advantage of trends with low risk and cost.

MEGA TRENDS

Mega trends are changes that are slow to form a tendency, but are likely to affect the future in all areas in the next 10–15 years, such as globalization, technology, economy, the workforce, demographics, politics, and the environment (Figure 1). Once in place, mega trends influence a wide range of activities, processes, and perceptions in businesses, governments, and societies, possibly for decades to come. They are the underlying forces that drive trends (i.e., aging population).

Process mega trends are already shaping the future. No one should dwell in neither the past nor the present, and there some trends that will definitely have a significant impact on how organizations apply and take advantage of processes in the next 10 years.

Both current and future process mega trends have enormous potential and will definitely change, improve, and revolutionize the future. Business process management

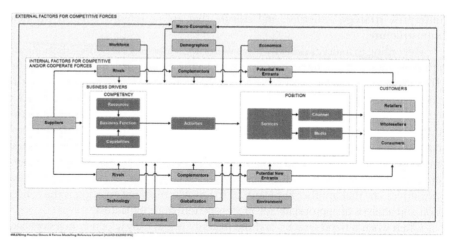

FIGURE 1

Megatrends as the driver of competitive forces.[5]

provides the context and best mechanism to achieve the full potential of technology trends for the next decade. BPM is at the inflection of underlying technologies and human participants, providing the perfect place to leverage technology trends while providing a business context.

EMERGING TRENDS

Emerging trends are maturing tendencies driven by mega trends that influence industry trends at different levels, such as process-driven case management, a technology mega trend and a trend in the insurance industry.

Emerging trends can be illustrated in many ways, e.g., hyper cycles (Gartner), radar systems (Forrester), mind-map footprints (Frost & Sullivan), usage curves and product lifecycles (Boston Consulting Group), and underground station lines. Common to all of them is an emphasis on a specific view that misleads the reader; the most popular one is the annually published Gartner Hyper-Cycle.

For those unfamiliar with these charts, the basic structure starts with a technology trigger near the origin of time and is visibly followed by a quick rise to the "peak of inflated expectations" that is often driven by a combination of unrealistic claims by proponents and the hopes of users desperate to believe those claims. The exaggerated peak of hype is inevitably followed by a crash of popularity into the so-called "trough of disillusionment." Many ideas just die here and drop off the curve, but for others a more realistic set of expectations develops as believers and early adopters begin to experience measurable benefits. It serves to push the idea (sometimes with changes) up the "slope of enlightenment."[6] This gradual advance passes an important point of inflection on the performance S curve known as the attitude confirmation. The next landmark is crossing a social chasm at another critical inflection point called the attitude plateau.[7] Once an idea successfully

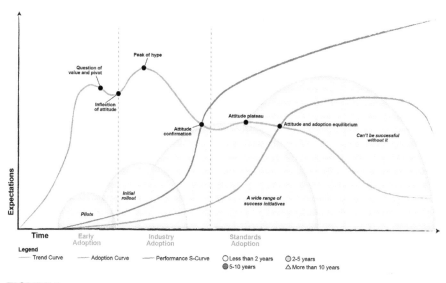

FIGURE 2

Process trends, which incorporates trends, actual adoption, performance, and the maturity life cycle.[8]

crosses the chasm, it plateaus as a generally recognized productivity concept for that industry. Some ideas fly quickly along these curves, passing older ideas that seem to just plod along at a much slower pace.

Hence, we have chosen to illustrate the emerging process trends in a hype trend model to give an independent and agnostic view of process trends, which incorporates trends, actual adoption, performance, and the maturity life cycle (Figure 2).

PROCESS TRENDS

Based on agnostic and vendor neutral research with the Global University Alliance and in consensus with their key authorities and leaders, we agreed on the following emerging process trends (Figure 3) that will influence the future of how organizations will adapt to, work with and apply processes.

EARLY ADOPTION

Trend phase: Pilots to initial rollout	Market penetration: Low	Maturity: Emerging
Benefit rating: Very high	Investment required: High	Risk: Very high

Characteristic: A potential trend breakthrough kicks things off. Early proof-of-concept stories and media interest trigger significant publicity. Often no usable

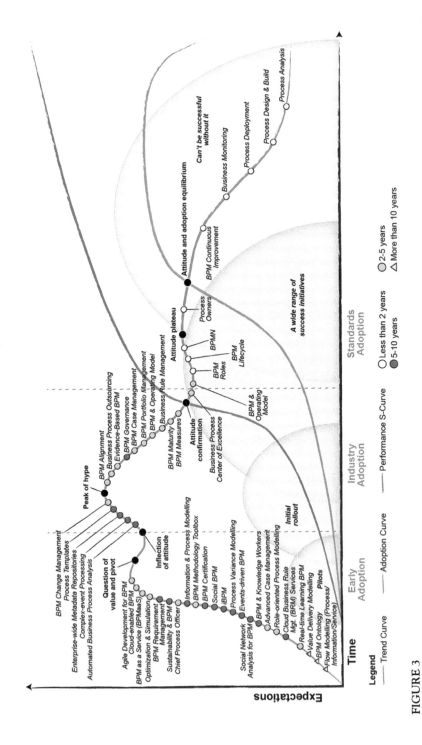

FIGURE 3

Business process trends.[9]

products exist and commercial viability is unproven. Early publicity produces a number of success stories—often accompanied by scores of failures. Few organizations take action; many do not.

Trends are less than 5–10 years from mainstream adoption. It requires a high level of investment and high risk with the potential to deliver core differentiating aspects.

Business Performance Impact: Early adoption invests to take advantage of the opportunity and develop LEADing Practices. The LEADing Practices define and strengthen competitive advantage, innovation, and efficiency in the core differentiating competencies with focus on the revenue model and value model. They are called the outperformers and are the first to take advantage of the new emerging trends, and thereby outperform the market.

EARLY ADOPTER OF PROCESS TRENDS

1. **Extended Flow Modeling (a part of X-BPMN).** The next generation of BPM will benefit from the evolution of modeling approaches currently being advanced in architecture and engineering, enhancing a structured way of thinking, working, and modeling. Learning from other principles enables reuse of models as well as standardization of various concepts. What is especially relevant is the interlink between process flow, information flow, and service flow. Organizations realize the need to model the various flows both separately and together. We already see the first technology enabling such modeling; see example from iGrafx: www.igrafx.com/solutions/business-challenges/process-modeling

2. **BPM Ontology.** Many BPM and/or process frameworks, methods, and approaches such as Lean, Six Sigma, BPR (Business Process Reengineering), TQM (Total Quality Management), Zero Defect, BPMN (Business Process Modeling Notation), BPMS (Business Process Management Suite) have their own vocabulary. Each of these vocabularies has its own definition of terms such as business process, process step, process activity, events, process role, process owner, process measurement, and process rule. This variety of definitions might hamper communication. On one hand, the same word might have different meanings in different frameworks, methods, and approaches (i.e., homonymy). On the other hand, different words might have the same meaning in various frameworks, methods, and approaches (i.e., synonymy). When communicating, people are often unaware of homonymy and synonymy and expect the same words to have the same meaning and different words to have a different meaning, which might lead to miscommunication among people with different backgrounds (i.e., with training in a different framework, method, or approach). What is needed is a shared vocabulary (e.g., a folksonomy) that ensures a consistent use of terms. In a weak interpretation, such a folksonomy could be used as a central ontology to which all framework, method, and approach vocabularies are mapped to determine which words have the same and which have a different meaning in different frameworks, methods, and approaches. In a strong interpretation, such a central ontology

that defines fundamental process concepts and the relations between them (e.g., the ability to define a sequence of process steps) could be used as the reference vocabulary to describe, document, and structure process knowledge. Both interpretations would profit from a validated reference ontology. Hence, the need for a BPM ontology that can be applied within the areas of process modeling, process engineering, and process architecture is clear.

3. **Value-Oriented Process Modeling.** Often referred to as value-oriented process design or value delivery modeling (VDML), emerged in an era focused on the automation and optimization of business processes in the context of established business organizations. As such, they tended to focus on process flow within and between organizations, typically within individual lines of business. As the scope of automation expanded, processes were linked electronically but tended to preserve existing organizations and relationships, optimizing processes within lines of business, optimizing processes at an operating level. Value planning, value identification, value creation, and value realization are not really methods and approaches used by process teams today. However, advances in technology, global competition, and continuous business change have increased the need for business agility with a focus on the creation of customer value and optimization of business processes across the enterprise. This requires the ability of top management to analyze and guide the design of the business focusing on customer value, consolidating sharable capabilities, and linking business strategy to business transformation through a shared understanding of the desired business design and key objectives. In this area, we also see technology move in this direction, where VDML has been adopted as an object management group (OMG) modeling standard and is expected to be available in 2015.

4. **Real-time Learning BPM.** Organizations around the world struggle to crack the code for improving the effectiveness of managers, salespeople, scientists, and others whose jobs consist primarily of interactions with other employees, customers, and suppliers, and complex decision making based on knowledge and good judgment. As process and BPM adoption rise in organizations, enabling processes and continuous improvement around the knowledge workers and similar employees working in complex processes is a new challenge. Business processes are the heart of an organization and the support of the business processes by application systems is central to each organization. Introducing new applications requires employees to become trained and educated for them, often by multi-day presence trainings in advance.

When the software is rolled out organization-wide, it is expected that the cost and time savings will materialize in short time. However, user errors slow down the efficiency of the new software and with it the execution of the connected business processes. Although they have been trained, employees are not able to use the new technology efficiently. Even though knowledge workers are often the core of many organizations, enablement of these employees with specific guidance at their point of need in a manner consistent with kaizen principles of quality and continuous improvement is frequently poor. In the following section, we show how real-time learning based on business process guidance (BPG) can help employees to get along better with new processes. It is expected that real-time learning through BPG will grow in importance in the future.

a. More changes: Processes and applications will change even more frequently in the future, triggering a need for training and support among the employees using them.

b. More collections of applications: Instead of one large system installed and configured on premise, we will often see a collection of applications provided as a service out of the cloud. This asks for process guidance that works across applications and that can be configured and equipped with content by the user organization.

c. Social networks will be used more at work: We will also see more knowledge sharing and peer support using social network technologies at the workplace. Social BPG will provide users with access to social network communication channels and will help filter and display only messages that are relevant based on the process and application context of the user.

d. Users will influence provision of content: Statistics from software usage and user feedback will become an important source for content authors to provide additional content and improve the existing support content in the BPG system.

e. BPG will extend beyond the office: Mobile devices will bring process guidance to new areas such as repair and maintenance of machines. First prototypes are built in research projects where information and work instructions will be displayed with augmented reality techniques on top of live pictures taken through the built-in camera. Users can call experts that support them directly, seeing the machine in real time through the camera.

f. BPG is already a good concept supporting the introduction of new processes and applications and its potential will grow in the future as it enables the organization.

5. **Cloud Business Rule Management (BRM) Services.** Business rules are actionable elements of business policy; they are implicit and explicit business directives that define and describe guidance for taking a business action. Externalizing policies and rules create a need to manage them as an important business resource, and BRM has emerged as a structured discipline guiding business rule definition, categorization, governance, deployment, and use throughout the business life cycle. BRM is supported and enabled in this need to manage rules as an important business resource by two technology types: the business rule engine (BRE) and BRM system (BRMS). A BRE is core software that executes business rules that have been segregated from the rest of the application logic, matching a collection of rules (the rule set) against a set of given conditions to determine which rules apply. A BRMS is a comprehensive suite built around a BRE that facilitates the creation, registration, classification, verification, deployment, and execution of business rules. BRMS products constitute a modern incarnation of BRE products. A critical

distinction between a traditional BRE and a BRMS is that a BRMS incorporates support for seven capabilities: the execution engine (the BRE), repository, integrated development environment rule model simulation, monitoring and analysis management and administration rule templates. When BRMS or BRE functionality is provided as a core capability hosted in a cloud, it is called cloud BRM services. Cloud BRM services are a type of platform as a service (PaaS). Cloud BRM services can be obtained either as a separate offering or as a feature of a BPM PaaS. The primary business impact of cloud BRM services will derive from the business impact of BRM proper; cloud BRM services are just an alternative delivery vehicle for a concept BRM that can increase quality decision making when properly understood. Although BRM concepts have been prevalent in certain industries (for example, financial services) and in well-documented processes (for example, underwriting), there is no inherent limit to BRM's industry and process reach. Therefore, cloud BRM services have a similar potential reach, with an emphasis on "potential."

6. **Role-Oriented Process Modeling.** Traditional BPM and requirement concepts are insufficient for today's EA, business model, and value-driven approach to organization operational execution and strategic management, whereas requirements must support, link, and be decomposed from top objectives down to technology requirements. Consequently, business processes are architected and designed as a system of activities reflecting and supporting achievement of an organization's goals, strategies, and objectives. All of these can be classified as high-level business requirements. A role-oriented (people oriented) process modeling approach and discipline is required to create process-centric organizations as high level requirements must be decomposed, layered, and used to identify, model, architect, design, implement, and operate cross-functional process scenarios, each with a defined purpose, value-driven activity, and measurable outcomes (performance indicators) that relates directly to the desired business objectives (high-level requirements). All of these are functional capabilities, which are also requirements.

7. **Advanced Case Management.** This is at the nexus of BPM and enterprise content management (ECM) usage scenarios, and involves a mix of collaborative, unstructured, and structured processes. We see in multiple organizations requirements beyond traditional process modeling; among others, it is about empowering participants in a process by removing context tunneling and providing better support for exception handling, the ability to control flow and cross-flow information visibility. Organizations around the world have therefore started to invest in case management. The information model includes both data and documents, so changes in values, metadata, and life cycle state can all be used to model the case.

8. **BPM Knowledge Worker.** Introducing new applications requires employees to become trained and educated for them, often by multi-day presence trainings in advance. When the software is rolled out organization-wide, it is expected that the cost and time savings will materialize in short time.

However, user errors slow down the efficiency of the new software and with it the execution of the connected business processes. Although they have been trained, employees are not able to use the new technology efficiently. Organizations are looking for better ways to provide the needed knowledge to their employees at the time of need. A new approach is real-time learning, in which information about the business process is presented to users automatically together with support on using software applications. It is gaining stronger acceptance in the market as a supplement or replacement to traditional software rollout training.

9. **Social Network Analysis for BPM.** Social network analysis (SNA) tools analyze patterns of relationships among people in groups. They are useful for examining the social structure and interdependencies (or work patterns) of individuals and organizations. SNA involves collecting data from multiple sources (such as surveys, e-mails, blogs, and other electronic artifacts), analyzing the data to identify relationships, and mining it for new information (such as the quality or effectiveness of a relationship). Organizational network analysis is a form of SNA that examines the information flow among individuals, and it depicts the informal social network, typically of groups working in the same enterprise. Value network analysis examines the deliverables exchanged among roles, typically groups of people from multiple organizations who need to work together. SNA scans social media to identify influential people, associations, or trends in the collective.

10. **Evidence-Based BPM.** As organizations gain awareness of the latent business value locked in their back-end systems' data stores, evidence-based BPM will become a day-to-day management tool rather than the subject of ad hoc initiatives triggered by punctual process performance issues. This shift will lead to the emergence of evidence-based process governance frameworks, allowing managers to effectively set up and steer long-term evidence-based BPM programs that deliver measurable value via continuous process improvement. In turn, increased evidence-based BPM maturity will spawn the deployment of real-time and predictive evidence-based BPM methods that will allow process stakeholders to respond to fine-grained process performance issues as they arise or even before they arise. In other words, evidence-based BPM methods will push the boundaries of contemporary business process monitoring practices by extending them with real-time predictive analytics. Evidence-based BPM will also enable continuous process auditing, whereby compliance violations are detected on a day-to-day basis, in contrast to contemporary postmortem process auditing approaches. Combined, these developments will bring BPM to the level of modern data-driven marketing approaches. Ultimately, every business process redesign decision will be made with data, backed by data, and continuously put into question based on data.

11. **Process Variance Modeling.** Business process variance should be seen as a viable way of allowing small differences in the way the core business functions are performed. It is advisable to introduce variation only in those business

processes that represent the core-differentiating competencies of the organization. This will allow an enterprise to develop its own practice and deliver unique value to clients and other stakeholders. For non-core and core-competitive competencies, best practice and industry best practice should suffice. Business process variance can be modeled in three different ways, depending on what is expected. If the aim is only to capture slight differences in the inputs, outputs, controls, and mechanisms of processes, it will be adequate to create only variances at the process activity or task levels. However, if the actual steps of the variant processes are different, true process variances can be used by presenting all the variances together in a single model or document, or a separate distinct process may even be developed. The modeling approach taken has a major impact on the management of the business processes and variances. When certain commonality between the master process and its variants is important, additional BPM techniques are necessary to maintain this traceability. This will require a great deal of attention to be given to establishing and maintaining the traceability links between the variants. Separate and distinctive processes introduce more process content, but standard BPM is applied because traceability to the master process is unnecessary. When introducing process variance, caution should be taken and the amount of variation should be minimized. If the development and modeling are not sufficiently controlled, the amount of additional and unnecessary content will quickly become unmanageable. However, if it is done well, it is an excellent way for organizations to acknowledge and embrace unique value enablers without losing out on the many benefits of business process modeling and management.

12. **Intelligent BPM (iBPM).** Recent evolution towards iBPM strategies and technology is the inclusion of more sophisticated reporting capabilities within the BPM environment itself. This is both enabled and in many ways necessitated by the greater flexibility of the architectures introduced with the BPM suites that provide BPM Phase 2 capabilities. With these environments, the ability to support non-sequential, goal-driven models is greatly increased, requiring more feedback (reporting) to enable successful execution of this type of less deterministic process models. With few exceptions, reporting on process events and business performance was previously done only after a process had executed, or otherwise within a separate environment disjointed from the process. This obviously prevented any opportunity to affect the direction of a process, but was based on a limitation of the management process as well as system and software architectures. Specifically with regard to BPM, process models were most commonly defined as proprietary structures, and in many cases compiled into software. Thus, changes either required bringing down and recompiling an application or were otherwise limited to discrete points in the process (such as exceptions and yes/no decision points).

13. **Social BPM.** This is a concept that describes collaboratively designed and iterated processes. These processes mirror the way work is performed from a doer's

perspective and experienced from a receiver's perspective. Social BPM is a concept that describes collaboratively designed and iterated processes. These processes mirror the way that work is performed from a doer's perspective and experienced from a receiver's perspective to harness the power of continuous learning. Social BPM resides at the intersection of process and collaborative activity. It is supported by BPM and social software that makes process design more visible and holistic. This includes the ability to support all process activities, such as collaboration, social networking, collective activities, and communications, that are a natural part of work to create a holistic process design that is open to influence and change from a variety of perspectives (for example, from customers, partners, suppliers, and employees). The value of social BPM is that it connects structured and unstructured knowledge-centric tasks by understanding the needs of each user (internal and external) and combines social technologies to achieve the process outcome. As such, social BPM moves BPM closer to design by doing. In practice, there are two distinct implementations of social BPM: one for process design and the other for process iteration. Social BPM design enables a group to collaboratively work on the design of a process. Social BPM iteration is the act of harnessing knowledge about how the process is experienced while it is being performed, and acting on this to change the process to better reflect preferences and shifts in the user experience. The business practice director will be the driving force to integrate social BPM techniques into process analysis and design.

14. **BPM Certification.** The need for skilled and experienced personnel to lead and participate in BPM activities is clear. The BPM profession requires a vendor neutral and agnostic Process eXpert and Process Architect certification with cross-disciplines, e.g., Business Process Principles (BPR, Six Sigma, TQM, Lean, etc.), BPMN 2.0, eXtended BPMN, Process Monitoring, Value-Based Process Modeling, Continuous Improvement Approach, and Architectural Layer Modeling (Business, Application, and Technology). The eclectic nature of that skill and, by definition, the individuals who possess it, is also clear. Given the diversity of skills and experiences needed, would recruiters be better off looking for someone who is already certified in BPM? Certification in BPM, as discussed here, refers not only to certification in methodologies used in BPM (such as Six Sigma or IT Infrastructure Library) or a vendor-specific tool or methodology. Instead, we are referring to more generic, broadly scoped training in BPM as a discipline. There is growing interest in this type of certification, and a number of organizations have established their own distinct approaches to curricula, exams, assessments, and certifications for BPM.

15. **BPM Methodology or BPM Methodology Toolbox.** These serve as solution accelerators and often feature commonly accepted practices for selected business processes. Process templates are becoming alternatives to traditional applications in certain process domains and industries, particularly when these process templates are based on an ICE, such as a BPMS. Today,

there is no unified BPM methodology. Instead, there are discrete methodologies that can be applied depending on the change or improvement being sought. The BPM methodologies apply across BPI (such as Six Sigma, Lean thinking, kaizen, Rummler-Brache, and business process re-engineering), application development (such as scrum, feature-driven development, and extreme programming), project management as well as implementation (PRINCE2, PMBOK, etc.), and change/transformation management. A growing number of BPM vendors provide methodologies that range from project implementation to broader BPI approaches. Consulting and system integration vendors are also incorporating BPM methods into their service delivery methodologies. However, choosing the right agnostic and vendor-neutral overachieving approach to methodologies that interconnect with all of them is required. Business process management methodologies initially operate with performing and driving business process intelligence (BPI) projects and rely on expert knowledge from seasoned BPI practitioners to be effectively used.

16. **Information and Process Modeling.** Also called anti-pattern information modeling, is the need to support information models with a more flexible process execution by avoiding well-known restrictions present in conventional BPM and workflow technology. The trend for information modeling in the market is about the challenge regarding process and information modeling and how one can produce adequate as-is and to-be process models that incorporate information models. Anti-pattern information modeling is often incorrectly understood to be concerned only with data modeling. The answer to this is not easy and is discussed in the X-BPMN chapter. One of the biggest challenges is the mistake that most BPM and BPMN concepts do not consider the process in its full context. A process always has a context; not considering its context in the purpose and goals perspective of the business is devastating. It keeps away the context that so many are looking for: the value perspective. Not considering the context to the business competencies can have the effect that nobody knows which processes are a part of the core differentiating competencies and which support the core competitive competencies of the organization. It does not matter how much we analyze the process itself; it cannot reveal this information. The same goes for services; whereas we all know that activities (processes) are needed to create services, most organizations do not know which processes create what kind of service. Therefore, their process models do not consider the most vital aspects of the various value offerings to the consumers of the processes (e.g. employees and/or customers). Modeling the process without considering its relevant context results in process models that the executives and many others from the business or even architecture teams cannot use. We see too many BPM programs/projects within organizations that limit their as-is and to-be process models in this way. To structure the X-BPMN process groups, we categorize the relevant process context into layers.

17. **Chief Process Officer.** We increasingly see in organizations a new top management position emerging, which we call the chief process officer (CPO). The CPO oversees the BPM-discipline of an organization, which creates significant value by moving business strategy systematically into people and IT-based execution at a pace and with certainty. The CPO works as a value scout across organizational boundaries, building an agility network for the organization. The need for this development is driven through digitalization in many companies. The CPO makes sure that IT is used in a way that produces the best business value. In a time when most technology moves to the cloud, business processes become a critical asset of an organization. The CPO manages these process assets using an outcome-driven process management discipline.

18. **Sustainability and BPM.** The management of organizations has experienced some interesting trends. The first one is a stronger focus on delivering value with a more comprehensive definition of it, encompassing not only financial aspects but also other stakeholder interests that put pressure on building more sustainable societies. Secondly, process management is a way of improving an organization's performance. And the third is the pervasiveness of IT as both a resource and an enabler. The need for organizations to become more sustainable from an economic, ecological, and social point of view through the management of processes and with a strong IT bend is clear. Therefore, a growing trend is to codify and guide through specific practices that, by linking strategy to operations, drive joint improvements in shareholder returns, the ecological footprint, and social impact, ideally from a life cycle point of view.

19. **BPM Requirements Management.** Whether for business innovation, transformation, or technology development, requirements management is the most widely used concept influencing design of anything in any industry. Consequently, it also influences design of business processes, both functional and end-to-end scenarios ("Our enterprise is our processes"). As a result, it impacts how well the organization operates.

    Today, BPM requirements management has become critical for any organization, heavily influencing the quality of its business designs and corporate results. The significance of the requirement concept to any organization lies in the fact that it is a key information carrier, interpreter, bridge to, and translator of desired enterprise goals with process and technology realization designs and performances using decomposition and mapping of high-level requirements into a network of more granular requirements. It applies throughout all pertinent types of enterprise layers (business, process, application, data, technology, organization, governance, etc.). In essence, requirements exist everywhere in any organization within each layer of its architecture and drives everything an organization does. Requirements are not stand-alone entities. They relate, decompose, or compose into other types of more granular requirements. Requirements are dynamic. They change, are impacted by changes to other requirements, or are added as new by business or technology. Requirements must therefore be continuously managed.

BPM requirements management requires a standardized terminology, builds common understanding, and makes available the standardized and integrated BPM requirement templates, enabling users of the BPM requirements managements body of knowledge to:

a. Identify the relevant objects to which the requirements have a relationship.

b. Decompose the business, application, and technology objects into the smallest parts that can, should, and need to be modeled, and then compose the detailed requirements to the objects' entities before building them (through mapping, simulation, and scenarios).

c. Visualize requirement relations to the specific object with the requirements templates/artifacts by using the requirements maps, matrices, and models.

d. Reduce and/or enhance complexity of requirements modeling, requirements engineering, and the use of requirements within architecture when applying the decomposition and composition standards.

e. Model the relevant requirements through the objects within the enterprise layers.

f. Add value perspective to requirements management.

g. Provide structured blueprinting and implementation that has specific phases for incorporating high-level and detailed business, application and technology requirements.

20. **Optimization and Simulation**—This enables organizations to experiment with a process, quickly determine process alternatives, and identify which alternatives are likely to produce the best outcomes under certain conditions. Optimization and simulation tools are useful technologies to, in essence, support process experimentation. These tools use a more scientific approach to process design and implementation. Optimization and simulation tools for BPM use an explicit process model (that is, an imitation of a business process) and enable the user (that is, the experimenter) to experiment with the process over time. Optimization and simulation allow the experimenter, perhaps a business process analyst, to see how the process holds up over time or in response to specific events. Does it bog down? Does the process break? What might we predict based on past behavior in production? Are there enough resources to handle all the calls, loans, claims, and other demands? Should you shift resources, and are they available? In other words, optimization and simulation allow you to run the process as if it were running in the real world. However, unlike processes running in the real world, if the optimized and simulated process breaks, no one gets hurt. It's all a simulation and it can be re-optimized and rerun. Using simulation and optimization tools, the assumptions, constraints, and scenarios of a process context can be verified with more certainty before the process model is actually deployed in the real world. Clearly, a prerequisite for performing business process optimization and simulation is that you must have an explicit business process model: the "imitation" mentioned in the definition. Business process modeling is a technique to graphically express how business processes and associated strategies are interrelated. Process modeling is used to better

understand and diagnose the business process, as well as the behavior of all
the participating constituents within the process. Whereas process modeling is
generally a static representation of the business process under study, simulation
adds a dynamic component to this model. This technology profile specifically
reflects the use of optimization and simulation tools when applied to designing and improving business processes by using explicit process models. It does
not cover constraint-based optimization and simulation tools that are used for
digital control systems, factory scheduling, transportation route scheduling, and
other operations research and decision management applications that are not
centered on process models.

21. **Business Process Modeling as a Service (BaaS).** BaaS gives you the opportunity to outsource your complete BPM so you can concentrate on your core
business. The BPM as a service model (BaaS) is a service-oriented solution.
Explained simply, BaaS is the outer shell of infrastructure as a service, BaaS,
and software as a service: for example, combining all BPM services, from
process analysis to real-time enterprise management, to integrated on-demand
services: (1) automation of business processes, (2) process analysis and
modeling with different specifications and scenarios, (3) process automation
and process simulation using IBM BPM standard, (4) BPM and real-time
enterprise management using new intelligence methods based on the BPM
suite and BPM standard, (5) integration of technologies, e.g., RFID, and (6)
integration of mobile devices (e.g., smartphones).

22. **Cloud-Enabled BPM (CE-BPM).** BPM technologies help manage the work
of a single organization or multiple organizations. Business processes are the
actual work of a single organization or multiple organizations. Business processes
include formally defined activities as well as informal work practices. In addition, business processes may involve human and application activities, and they
may be structured or unstructured. A CE-BPM platform is a platform for managing business processes in a private or public cloud. CE-BPM is often confused
with BPMaa-S and BPMPaaS, which refers to the delivery of BPM technology
functionality as a service by a cloud service provider, whereas CE-BPM refers
to a cloud-enabled BPM technology product. CE-BPMs are typically purchased
by enterprises to run shared business process service centers in a private cloud.
A vendor may use the same technology in its BPMPaaS and its CE-BPM. The
only difference is in the delivery model. BPMPaaS is delivered as a service;
CE-BPM is delivered as a product and then is used to provide a public or private
cloud service by an ESP or an internal IT organization. ESPs use CE-BPM as
the underlying application infrastructure to deliver SaaS and business process
utilities in the public cloud, as well as cloud-enabled outsourcing in community
clouds. Providers of BPMPaaS may use their own or a third-party CE-BPM
platform. A CE-BPM exhibits cloud-enabled application platform capabilities
(see Gartner Reference Architecture for Cloud-Enabled Application Platforms).
A CE-BPM must include at least one of the following BPM run-time capabilities:
flow management, rule management, optimization and simulation, or BAM. It may

optionally include a variety of design-time BPM capabilities, such as business process modeling and automated business process discovery.

23. **Agile Development for BPM**. This represents a development methodology that is a highly accelerated, incremental approach aimed at delivering high-priority, demonstrable business value. Agile development for BPM combines management disciplines as well as agile software development methods. The nature of agile BPM means process improvement or physical process implementation starts before the models are fully complete, avoiding the big design up-front problem, which delays benefits realization. Agile development for BPM methods is defined in terms of values, principles, and best practices rather than overly prescriptive plan-driven processes. Lean and agile practices of collaboration, customer focus, short cycles, and value delivery are applied to BPM suites (BPMSs) and BPM technologies, as well as the BPM (the process of process improvement) cycle. Agile BPM builds on the growing trends of social BPM and business process analysis (BPA) for the masses, both of which increase user involvement in process discovery, modeling, and implementation. Agile BPM methods attempt to establish a high level of collaboration among business process owners, architects, and the IT organization. They also attempt to flatten the project and organizational structure, often through self-organizing teams. Agile BPM methods are based on empirical process control, which accepts requirements changes and validates project direction with short, business-focused delivery cycles. Use of agile BPM is most necessary in situations requiring frequent process change, and is particularly important for continuous process improvement use scenarios.

INDUSTRY ADOPTION

Trend phase: "Initial roll out" to "a wide range of successful initiatives"	
Market penetration: Medium–Low	*Maturity*: Medium
Benefit rating: High	*Investment required*: Medium–High

Characteristic: Early publicity produces a number of success stories, often accompanied by scores of failures. Some companies take action; many do not. More instances of how the technology can benefit the enterprise start to crystallize and become more widely understood. Second- and third-generation products appear from technology providers. More enterprises fund pilots; conservative companies remain cautious.

Trends are less than 5 years from mainstream adoption. They require a medium level of investment and medium risk with the potential to deliver industry competitive advantage.

Performance impact: Industry leaders adopt, invest, and develop industry practices to outcompete their peers. Industry practices improve their competitive parity and standardize core competitive competencies with a focus on the performance model and service model.

They are called the industry leaders because they outperform their peers with their advantage of emerging trends.

Industry Adoption of Process Trends

1. **Automated Business Process Analysis (BPA).** (BPA for the masses.) This provides a simpler modeling approach tailored to business roles rather than technical roles, enabling BPA tools to become popular among businesspeople. The resulting benefits will include faster realization of the desired business performance improvements and better ability to meet time and budget targets, owing to better process understanding as well as extra insight into process impacts to avoid unpleasant surprises. Business process analysis for the masses is a developing trend toward a simpler modeling approach tailored to business roles, rather than a technical or BPA expert. It is simpler in that it uses familiar business terms, with attention to business goals and outcomes, and less inclusion of technical terms to support implementations. Because this trend will enable BPA tools to become popular among business people, Gartner referred to it as "BPA for the masses." The traditional BPA tool category has focused on the need of business architects and analysts to collaborate with others, requiring more robust methods and tooling than many business process modelers care to deal with. However, BPA for the masses will be targeted directly at business staff regardless of position or role, to provide them with easy-to-grasp insights into their own business processes. The goal is to capture the informal shadow process, concepts, and information often missing in more formal in-process modeling and user requirements definitions. BPA for the masses tooling allows for collaboration around communities of interest to develop peer interactions, knowledge exchanges, and consensus building. Harvesting information from common formats such as Microsoft's Excel, Word, PowerPoint (EVP) and Visio is a key requirement, as is the ability to communicate either with BPA traditional models or with common business formats. We expect BPA for the masses to be increasingly delivered via thin clients on-premise or the cloud through SaaS, because this will allow for communities to grow unimpeded. We see increased use of mobile technology for capturing at the source process-related information, which allows for BPA where needed.

2. **Complex-Event Processing (CEP).** CEP is the basis for many pattern-based strategies, particularly those that require continuous intelligence. When combined with BPM, CEP not only helps detect patterns, it allows an organization to quickly act on those patterns through executable business processes. CEP is a style of computing that is implemented by event-driven, continuous intelligence systems. CEP differs from other kinds of computing in that insight is

derived by combining information from multiple data points (event objects). A CEP system uses algorithms and rules to process streams of event data that it receives from one or more sources. It generates new summary-level facts (called complex events) and puts them in context to identify threat and opportunity situations. This information is then used to guide the response in sense-and-respond business activities. CEP is event-driven because the computation is triggered by the receipt of event data. CEP systems run continuously, so they are available to act as soon as the data arrive. Data is processed immediately upon arrival. In contrast, time-driven and request-driven IT systems store the data when it arrives, and processing is triggered later by a clock (in a time-driven system) or by a request from a person or computer program (in a request-driven system). One can produce complex events in a scheduled computation (time-driven processing) or in response to an ad hoc user query or method call (request-driven processing). However, the term "CEP" is generally only applied to event-driven processing.

Here, we focus on general-purpose, reusable event-processing software platforms that are customized at development time to implement CEP applications. The core of these platforms is a software engine that runs the CEP algorithms and rules. Commercial event-processing platform products typically include development and administrative tools; other tools to implement graphical business dashboards and alert end users; and adapters for various input event data sources and output devices.

3. **Enterprise-wide Metadata Repositories**. Metadata is defined as "information that describes various facets of an information asset to improve its usability throughout its life cycle". Generally speaking, the more valuable the information asset, the more critical managing the metadata about it becomes because the contextual definition of metadata provides the understanding that unlocks the value of the data. Examples of metadata are abstracted levels of information about the characteristics of an information asset, such as its name, location, perceived importance, quality, or value to the organization, as well as its relationship to other information assets. Metadata can be stored as artifacts in metadata repositories in the form of digital data about information assets that the enterprise wants to manage. Metadata repositories are used to document and manage metadata (in terms of governance, compliance, security, and collaborative sharing) and to perform analysis (such as change impact analysis and gap analysis) using the metadata. Metadata repositories can also be used to publish reusable assets (such as application and data services) and browse metadata during life cycle activities (design, testing, release management, and so on) in the common sources of metadata, should meet enterprise-wide metadata management needs. These include several categories of metadata repositories, such as those used in support of tool suites (tool suite repositories), project-level initiatives and programs (community-based repositories), and those used to federate and consolidate metadata from multiple sources (enterprise repositories)

to manage metadata in a more enterprise-wide fashion. Here, we focus on the state of the repository markets—because there are now many sub-markets—in terms of this need to federate and consolidate metadata in an enterprise-wide manner. We are seeing more and more organizations, even those that already own enterprise repositories, acquiring several other best-of-breed repositories, each focused on different communities of users in projects and programs involving data warehousing, master data management, business process modeling and analysis, service-oriented architecture (SOA), and data integration—just to name a few—types of communities. In each case, these community-focused repositories have shown benefits in improved quality and productivity through an improved understanding of the artifacts, the impact queries, and the reuse of assets, such as data and process artifacts, services, and components. This has resulted in the subsetting of what once was the enterprise repository market into smaller communities of interest, using solutions that are less expensive and easier to manage. However, attempting to federate metadata across multiple repositories to provide an enterprise-wide view of metadata is no simple task, but rather a cornerstone of advanced process modeling.

4. **Process Templates.** "Process templates" is an overarching term that describes pre-built business process design, execution, and management artifacts that accelerate time to solution. They are also known by various names such as "solution frameworks," "solution templates," "solution kits," "starter kits," "process accelerators," and "process pods." Process templates should be agnostic and vendor neutral. Typically, process templates are graphical and are based on process flows, rules or SOA. The contents vary dramatically among vendors or providers. Some offer simple visual process models that are useful in jump-starting discussions about target processes for improvement. Others provide pre-built detailed process models, technical reference models, candidate service definitions, technical service libraries, rule sets, user interface templates, simulation scenarios, recommended governance policies, delivery and deployment guides, and process improvement methodologies. Some vendors sell process templates as products, whereas others treat them as software assets primarily intended for use in professional service engagements. Process templates are not intended to deliver 100% of a solution. Instead, they are meant to be changed by an implementer. A process template can be extended (that is, the implementer can add capability beyond what was provided by the original assets). It can also be adjusted or configured to accommodate the unique requirements of a process. In many cases, process templates are designed to allow business stakeholders to extend the solution, not just IT personnel.

Process templates use models to manipulate one or more aspects of the process. Some templates are broad (including activities, rules, work flows and user interfaces) and some are narrow, such as a rule set only. Nevertheless, in the BPM market, model-driven pre-built solution content is typically referred to as process templates.

With process templates, the resulting application is driven by the metadata reflected in the process model. This means that the application's behavior is determined by direct manipulation of the explicit process model, rather than through the setting of parameters or by writing code. Instead of parameters, which restrict application behavior to predetermined options only, a process orchestration engine reads the explicit business process model and directly executes it.

5. **BPM Change Management.** The implementation of a BPM change management program demands a whole new way of working in an organization, and also implies looking differently at your organization. This is something that many organizations underestimate. Old, existing ways of working and managing/directing people must be changed. This fact alone begs for a clear change at the management level, but it also requires change at lower organization levels. This new way of working should be accepted before working in a process-oriented manner can become successful. When organizations decide to implement process improvements and/or BPM, they must not only pay attention to the new possibilities and the factors that stimulate successful implementation; they must also be aware of the restrictions. These restrictions or barriers are often bound to the organization culture, to the comfort one obtains from holding a certain position, and to power and status. Management must deal with these barriers and actively deal with the factors that stimulate implementation as well. Clear and accurate communication is important for successful change management. This implies a need to build integrity and trust, which will have implications for the specific tactics that will be adopted in implementing the changes required. There are many tactics that can be selected from the tool kit for each area, and the actual tactics adopted will need to match the particular business, but if you have a framework from which to select, the likely success of your BPM change management project is increased.

6. **BPM Alignment.** BPM alignment focused on reusability and accelerated automation needs an understanding of what alignment is, how to develop an alignment competency, and what considerations should be made by organizations to ensure alignment is adequately adopted. Alignment of BPM provides for the policy or strategy of the organization to drive the alignment of BPM portfolios, programs, and projects that require the relevant stakeholders (business process owners) to the develop a common understanding of their business process so that there is a transformation of business process from as-is through to-be. The to-be business processes that have been aligned can then be used in enterprise transformation and innovation to enable improved financial measures of performance and replication of the same success across project, portfolio, and programs. The BPM alignment objective is combined with BI MDM, SOA, and/or the cloud; the strategic value and the effect on the organizational performance are significant.

7. **Business Process Outsourcing (BPO).** This is likely to yield high benefits to BPO providers as well as buyers. To gain maximum benefit, a BPO program should go through a formal close-down. There is no point in arguing lost causes once irrevocable decisions have been taken. Staff and companies alike need to accept the new situation and move forward. However, there will be a lot of information generated during the life of the program, and this will have been stored with varying degrees of formality by the team members. This information needs to be formally filed away for future reference. In this light, there are no simple criteria to conduct an outsourcing versus in-house analysis. The benefits associated with outsourcing are numerous, and one should consider each project on its individual merits. Ongoing operational costs that may be avoided by outsourcing are also a consideration. In a nutshell, outsourcing allows organizations to be more efficient, flexible, and effective, while often reducing costs.

8. **Evidence-Based BPM.** As organizations gain awareness of the latent business value locked in their back-end systems' data stores, evidence-based BPM will become a day-to-day management tool rather than the subject of ad hoc initiatives triggered by punctual process performance issues. This shift will lead to the emergence of evidence-based process governance frameworks, allowing managers to effectively set up and steer long-term evidence-based BPM programs that deliver measurable value via continuous process improvement. In turn, increased evidence-based BPM maturity will spawn the deployment of real-time and predictive evidence-based BPM methods that will allow process stakeholders to respond to fine-grained process performance issues as they arise or even before they arise. In other words, evidence-based BPM methods will push the boundaries of contemporary business process monitoring practices by extending them with real-time predictive analytics. Evidence-based BPM will also enable continuous process auditing, whereby compliance violations are detected on a day-to-day basis, in contrast to contemporary postmortem process auditing approaches. Combined, these developments will bring BPM to the level of modern data-driven marketing approaches. Ultimately, every business process redesign decision will be made with data, backed by data, and continuously put into question based on data.

9. **BPM Governance.** Governance in organizations is not a new trend; as a matter of fact, few industries are not demanded to prove compliance in multiple areas. Governance in terms of monitoring, evaluation, and audits are part of all organizations, daily tasks. The trend we have seen for years and now with the advanced abilities of process intelligence, evidence-based process mining, rules modeling and performance management. BPM governance become a part most organizations apply. By tackling compliance as well as continuous improvement via BPM governance, the organizations have an agile way to more easily respond to regulatory change, enable faster decision making, and link it to the continuous improvement loop.

10. **BPM and Enterprise Architecture.** BPM and enterprise architecture (EA) should be an integrated part of the enterprise modeling, engineering, and architecture concepts. There are multiple benefits and different ways to combine the disciplines to create the needed business transformation and innovation, that could achieve the quality and longevity for enterprises. The key distinction for BPM as a discipline is added focus on flexible and dynamic process design and process orchestration and automation through enabling architecture. In addition to reduced costs through continued improvement and automation, BPM provides the foundation for converged and agile business and IT responsiveness and is the key to applying the principles. The success of interlinking BPM with EA derives from the proper coordination between planning and execution of the overlapping principles in the approaches. This, in turn, requires a company's understanding of EA and the process life cycles of the enterprise and the establishment of appropriate collaboration between EA and BPM governance approaches to ensure interlinking of the described approaches.

Whereas value management, BPM, and EA each have value on their own, we have described how they are naturally synergetic and work best when used together for better business performance and value outcomes and strategic alignment of business and IT. When these approaches are used together, performance drivers and operational excellence and thereby possible improvement areas are provided by the BPM context that outlines where to change the input–output model and provides an understanding of where to create the value and how and where to measure performance. Business architecture provides the design principles for solution transformation, and the rest of EA provides the discipline for translating business vision and strategy into architectural change. Although governance principles can apply the needed standards and rules, all are required for sustainable continuous improvement, optimization, and innovation. It is important to realize the value of direct collaboration across the described boundaries. Only when supported by appropriate collaboration and governance processes can BPM and EA roles work effectively together toward the common goals of the enterprise. The key to business–IT alignment and what glues it all together is the processes and activities. The notion of having business process optimization and integration of approaches has been around for a long time. Yet, around the same time that EA and governance became a mainstream topic in the context of business and IT alignment, the focus in many process optimization communities shifted subtly to BPM to go beyond an optimization approach.

11. **BPM Case Management.** In the past few years, the ECM and BPM markets have converged into a common use case called case handling, case management, or adaptive case management. The goal of case management is to make knowledge workers more productive by empowering them with control over the process outcome; providing them with full visibility and ability to manipulate all process data; and allowing them to collaborate to manage and evolve to completion each process instance. This trend is an evolution of the document-centric BPM that is motivating vendors to provide a deeper integration

between ECM and BPM technology. Vendors are incorporating collaboration technology for knowledge workers to manage the data and outcome of each process instance. The result is that BPM products are becoming more flexible, are better integrated with ECM technology, and provide better collaboration environments for knowledge workers.

STANDARD ADOPTION

Trend phase: "A wide range of successful initiatives" to "Cannot be successful without"	
Market penetration: High	*Maturity*: High
Benefit rating: Low–Medium	*Investment required*: Low

Characteristic: Mainstream adoption starts to take off. Criteria for assessing provider viability are more clearly defined and become a standard of whom to apply it to. The technology's broad market applicability and relevance are clearly paying off.

Trends are widely mainstream adopted and deliver out-of-the-box functionality.

Performance Impact: Wide adoption and years of experience have become standard or best practice. Organizations adopt to best practices to improve and standardize the non-core competencies with focus on the cost model and operating model. Organizations such as these are referred to as followers, and take advantage of best practices that are non-core to their business while gaining full advantage of trends with low risk and cost.

STANDARDS ADOPTION OF PROCESS TRENDS

1. **BPM and Operating Model.** Is an abstract representation of how an organization operates across resource, process, organization, and technology domains to accomplish its functions. This includes decision as to how a company wants to operate with regard to standardizing and integrating processes across various organizational domains (e.g. business units, geographies, product lines, franchises). It facilitates discussions as to how a company wants to pursue its business model. The purpose of an operating model is to categorize the organization into groups of how it operates, to increase understanding and suggest opportunities for improvement. In the context of BPM, an operating model can be used in various ways:

    a. A BPM operating model refers to both the level of integration and standardization of the BPM concepts, the BPM team, a shared facility, and how it operates in enabling process innovation and transformation for the organization.

    b. The BPM Center of Excellence (COE) acts both as the initiation point and the organization's custodian to the point of accountability of its processes, tasked with ensuring sustainability, maturity, governance, alignment, as well as the measurements and reporting that makes BPM successful.

    c. BPM portfolio management also needs to consider the organizational operating model as well as the level of process standardization and integration across the BPM portfolio.

    d. For BPM alignment management, it is essential to define the level of process standardization and integration for any alignment initiative.

    e. The BPM teams develop process templates that need to be integrated and standardized across various operating components.

2. **Business Rule Management (BRM).** BRM guides business rule definitions, categorizations, governance, deployments, and use throughout the business life cycle. When combined with other BPMTs, BRMs simplify process change and accelerate process agility. Two level-setting definitions are required before discussing BRMs: (1) Business rules: implicit and explicit business directives that define and describe guidance for taking a business action (a decision, constraint, option, or mandate—for example, if an applicant wants more than $1 million in insurance coverage and he has high blood pressure, he will be charged at a higher rate). (2) BRM: a structured discipline guiding business rule definition, categorization, governance, deployment, and use throughout the business life cycle. BRM is defined as a comprehensive business rule offering that facilitates the creation, registration, classification, verification, deployment, and execution of business rules in the support of BRM. A BRM is the next-generation evolution of the more-mature technological foundation known as a business rule engine (BRE). A critical distinction between a traditional BRE (execution engine only) and a BRM is that the latter is much more than an execution engine and development environment. A BRM goes well beyond a BRE and broadens the historical technology ecosystem to incorporate rich support for seven key component areas: execution engine, repository, integrated development environment rule model simulation, monitoring and analysis management and administration, and rule template.

3. **BPM Center of Excellence (BPM CoE).** A BPM CoE represents an internal consultancy and promoter of BPM, including training and awareness, and offers a "one-stop shop" that provides services to multiple BPM projects, programs, and initiatives. The BPM CoE implements, chooses, and supports the guidelines, standards, and tools, and offers services that enable the enterprise to progress with and adopt BPM. A well-planned process improvement strategy includes a BPM CoE model that best fits an organization's needs as it starts up or grows its BPM program. A BPM CoE is essential for BPM to become institutionalized within an organization. The BPM CoE acts as an internal consultancy and promoter for BPM, including training and awareness, and offers a "one-stop shop" that provides services to multiple BPM projects, programs, and initiatives. The BPM CoE implements, chooses, and supports the guidelines, standards, and tools, and offers services that enable the enterprise to progress with and adopt BPM. A well-planned process improvement strategy includes a BPM CoE model that best fits an organization's needs as it starts up or grows its BPM program. A BPM CoE guides process improvement projects by applying

standards and proven techniques to ensure that they deliver business value and can be leveraged for future efforts supporting business agility. It delivers a standard methodology (or methodology toolbox where multiple approaches are required), repository, and best practices for engaging in process redesign and transformation activities. These may cover the disciplines of modeling, real-time measurement, and content management rules. The center offers multi-disciplined senior process improvement staff who support work ranging from consulting on small projects to turnkey program management for large and complex transformation efforts.

The implementation models for a BPM CoE will vary. The BPM CoE can be centralized or federated, and may report into the business, IT, or a blended relationship. Business process directors who understand the necessary capabilities to guide the enterprise's BPM efforts and what capabilities already exist in the organization may choose to incorporate the needed components into existing competency centers or governance groups to achieve the same outcomes. The BPM CoE is not just for large enterprises; midsized and small organizations can have a fully functional BPM CoE. The requirement is not staffing, but functionality. One person can manage this function and establish a BPM program. Some organizations use alternative naming for the BPM CoE: for example, "business process CoC" or "process and service improvement group."

4. **BPM Roles.** To succeed with any business process initiative today, it is crucial to understand the BPM roles, features of a role, motivation, measurements, and challenges faced in identifying and using business process-centric roles today. Clarity shed regarding the BPM roles will provide accountability. The concept of "role" is separate and distinct from the persons or things that access the rights of and perform its responsibilities. Given the rights granted in a business context and supported by the skills and knowledge needed to exercise those rights, a role can be treated and managed as a conceptual thing of significance in the design of enterprises and organizations. Therefore, a standard way of thinking, working, modeling, and governing is applied to exploration of the nature of roles to create a standardized and repeatable method for identifying, characterizing, and documenting roles and then this approach is applied to finding and describing the roles needed within the BPM COE.

5. **BPM Life Cycle.** The organizational requirements of implementing a usable and effective BPM life cycle in any organization is a demanding task in itself; even more difficult is the need to structure the life cycle in a way that fully and in a detailed and explicit manner revolves around accomplishing not only process-related goals, but more importantly, business objectives, goals, and strategy. In a nutshell, processes are essentially a sequenced flow of steps and activities that have been specifically designed to achieve a defined business objective and eventually allow for the fulfillment of a strategy on behalf of the organization. Thus, processes act as a chain reaction of actions that are indirectly responsible

for fulfilling the strategy of an organization; and ultimately, that is the goal. Most BPM and process life cycles focus almost exclusively on process-oriented solutions and goals and more or less circle around technical problems and other non-business related challenges. That is where many organizations go about it the wrong way. As mentioned earlier, processes are but a tool to fulfill the goals of the business. With that in mind, it is important to maintain a strong focus on business objectives and goals when designing the structure and the steps involved with the BPM life cycle. Process goals have to serve the needs of the business, and designing a tight collaboration between process objectives and goals and business objectives and goals is of the utmost importance.

6. **Business Process Model and Notation** (BPMN). BPMN is a standard for business process modeling that provides a graphical notation for specifying business processes in a Business Process Diagram, based on a flowcharting technique similar to activity diagrams from a unified modeling language. The objective of BPMN is to support BPM for both technical users and business users by providing a notation that is intuitive to business users, yet able to represent complex process semantics. The BPMN specification also provides mapping between the graphics of the notation and the underlying constructs of execution languages, particularly business process execution language. The primary goal of BPMN is to provide a standard notation readily understandable by all business stakeholders. These include the business analysts who create and refine the processes, the technical developers responsible for implementing them, and the business managers who monitor and manage them. Consequently, BPMN serves as a common language bridging the communication gap that frequently occurs between business process design and implementation. Currently there are several competing standards for business process modeling languages used by modeling tools and processes. Widespread adoption of the BPMN will help unify the expression of basic business process concepts (e.g., public and private processes, choreographies), as well as advanced process concepts (e.g., exception handling, transaction compensation). BPM initiative developed BPMN, which has been maintained by the OMG.

7. **BPM Continuous Improvement.** Organizations continue to invest massive amounts of money and time in improving their business processes. Why? Because of the imperative to optimize their business operations for their markets, even as their markets shift with changing customer expectations and the accelerating drumbeat of competition. The pull away from structured processes to more ad hoc and exception management, with a higher degree of process flexibility, as well as the need to support mobile solutions, are the core drivers of the current BPM landscape[10]. BPM is charging toward a market opportunity of 6.6 billion USD and will be the basis of the next generation of packaged apps. This BPM landscape report lays out the path to the future state and describes the impact of this shifting landscape on business, customers, and partners.

8. **Business Monitoring or Business Activity Monitoring (BAM)**—This describes the processes and technologies that provide real-time situation awareness, as well as access to and analysis of critical business performance indicators, based on event-driven sources of data. BAM is used to improve the speed and effectiveness of business operations by keeping track of what is happening now and raising awareness of issues as soon as they can be detected. BAM describes the processes and technologies that provide real-time situation awareness, as well as access to and analysis of critical business performance indicators, based on event-driven sources of data. BAM is used to improve the speed and effectiveness of business operations by keeping track of what is happening now and raising awareness of issues as soon as they can be detected. BAM applications may emit alerts about a business opportunity or problem, drive a dashboard with metrics or status, make use of predictive and historical information, display an event log, and offer drill-down features. Events from a BAM system may trigger another application or service, communicated via a messaging system. The processing logic of a BAM system may use query, simple-stream or CEP.

9. **Process Development.** Process deployment is where the organization launches, implements, executes, deploys, activates, completes, concludes and transitions the processes to execution (go live). The process release and deployment management in the BPM life cycle aims to plan, schedule, and control the movement of releases to test in live environments. The primary goal of release management and deployment management is to ensure that the integrity of the live environment is protected and that the correct components are released on time and without errors.

10. **Process Design and Build.** Business process design is the concept by which an organization understands and defines and design the business activities that enable it to function. Process design is concerned with designing the processes of a business to ensure that they are optimized and effective, meet customer requirements and demands, and support and sustain organizational development and growth. A well-designed process will improve efficiency, deliver greater productivity, and create more business value. The most common initiatives behind business process design projects are:
    a. Customer and supply chain management
    b. Operational performance improvement
    c. Business process integration, standardization, and automation
    d. Cost reduction
    e. Creating new business opportunities

Business process design typically occurs as an early, critical phase in BPM projects rather than as an end in itself.

11. **Process Analysis.** Process analysis is a standard practice in the market that helps managers improve the performance of their business activities. The ultimate goal when organizations model business processes is to describe what

the business does in a hierarchy of detail from a high level down to the level where processes of the business become visible. In this content process analysis is a step-by-step breakdown of all the relevant process aspects, including the inputs, outputs, and the BPM COE operations that take place during the phase. It can be a milestone in continuous improvement. The process analysis approach consists of the following steps: (1) definition of the scope and the objectives of the study, (2) documentation of the status quo and definition of performance measures, (3) assessment and performance evaluation, and (4) development of recommendations.

CONCLUSION

In this chapter we have focused on the current and developing process trends. We have given a perspective on emerging trends, industry trends, and mega trends and have detailed and explained the trends for organizations to be able to learn from others to see what new trends are emerging and what others do successfully. Our recommendation is clear: Executives and process practitioners should make adoption decisions based on the ability to learn from others. Our experience has shown that it has a much higher benefit–risk ratio and performance curve.

End Notes

1. *The Oxford English Dictionary* (published by the Oxford University Press, 2014).
2. van Rensburg A., "A framework for business process management," *Computers & Industrial Engineering* 35, (1998): 217–220.
3. Müller T. Zukunftsthema geschäftsprozessmanagement. 'Zukunftsthema Geschäftsprozessmanagement.'pwc-PricewaterhouseCoopers. February 2011. PricewaterhouseCoopers AG (2012).
4. Business Process Intelligence, Daniela Grigori et al., Computers in Industry Vol. 53, Elsevier B.V., 2004.
5. LEADing Practice Driver & Forces Modelling Reference Content #LEAD-ES20001PG.
6. Everett M, *Diffusion of Innovations: Technology & Engineering* (Rogers: Press of Glencoe, 1962).
7. Geoffrey A. Moore, *Crossing the Chasm* (Publisher Capstone, 2000).
8. LEADing Practice Business Process Reference Content #LEAD-ES20005BP.
9. Ibid.
10. Prepare For 2013's Shifting BPM Landscape, Craig Le Clair, Alex Cullen, Julian Keenan, Forester Media, INC., 2013.

BPM Center of Excellence

Mark von Rosing, Maria Hove, Henrik von Scheel

INTRODUCTION

To achieve the organizational objectives of business process management (BPM), the implementation of a BPM office or center of excellence (CoE) is a key component of success in the management of business processes. BPM is not a discipline that can be done on one day and then disregarded the next; it must be considered as a consistent business stream that flows through an organization, preventing the organization and its processes from slipping back, making ongoing improvements to organizational processes, and providing the means to execute the strategic objectives of the various stakeholders. This business stream—the stewardship or management of business processes—BPM, is similar to other business disciplines that require an initiation point and a means to ensure ongoing sustainability as the organization builds its maturity. The BPM CoE acts as both the initiation point and the organization's custodian and point of accountability of its processes, tasked with ensuring sustainability, maturity, governance, alignment, as well as the measurements, reporting, templates, and artifacts that makes BPM successful.

THE CHALLENGE BPM CoE FACES

For most organizations, a number of pain points[1] exist with respect to implementing and sustaining a successful BPM CoE. As they do this, they need to be aware of what happens when a BPM CoE is not in place to guide and govern the overall BPM. For the executive, the reasons as well as the consequences of not implementing a successful and ongoing BPM within the organization are important.

- **Not managing the processes across all areas:** Within the organization, only some of the parts have completed detailed process mapping, orchestration, and optimization. This leaves process integration across the entire enterprise structure disjointed and unmanaged. A process will simply stop at the end of a department, line of business, or other business unit's logical boundary. The result is the hampering of service and information flows and duplication of roles, resulting in inefficiency.
- **No mandate to make the necessary changes, i.e., no business process charter:** The business process charter defines the mandate for initiating improvement targets.[2] It gives process owners direction and approval for their initial focus on BPM improvements.[3] These targets should tell the process owner the areas in which executives want to see improvements, e.g.,
  - Standardize the budget process, i.e., "Reduce the 15 different budget processes we currently have to one."

- Increase the accuracy of the data entry inputs from 65% to 95%.
- Reduce the total cycle time from ordering to delivery from 18 h to 2 h.
- **No vision for the future**: BPM should never be content with always delivering the as-is processes. BPM that does not have a future vision of the ever-changing business will forever lag behind the business changes and hence deliver a much lower value than what is expected. At executive forums, the Return on Investment (ROI) will always be questioned.
- **Lack of BPM budget**: As a resulting lack of budget in the BPM CoE, only a percentage of the processes are converted from as-is to to-be. Because only processes in the to-be state are a true representation of the business, the organization is left in a state of permanent under-delivery and underperformance. The old way of doing things creeps back in and the result is a step forward but two steps backward. Confusion is created and the results for an organization are self-limiting.
- **Lack of clear rules for participation in BPM within the organization**: A clear lack of defined roles and responsibilities[4] of who should work with BPM creates divisions, and a lack of accountability and responsibility pervades the organization. This results in missed improvement targets and an organization whose business processes stagnate, adding little value even in cases where much potential exists.
- **Not enough skilled resources in the BPM CoE to fulfill the mandate**: A lack of skilled resources such as business analysts available for each project results in a distinct lack of quality and causes major delays in projects such as Enterprise Resource Planning (ERP) implementations that are reliant on business processes. This adds to project costs and untimely delays.
- **Lack of benchmarking and best practice**: No standard or point of reference guidelines have been set for business process modeling, orchestration, or optimization. This leads to significant variations in BPM quality and often results in having the record of the business processes in separate BPM repositories and tools that do not communicate with one another. This leads to a disjointed set of business processes across the entire organization.
- **BPM governance**: The cost and complexity of adhering to compliance requirements are a drain on resources and a significant pain point. In many cases, particularly where the compliance relates to maintaining BPM (e.g., in keeping process changes and the record of these changes updated), BPM CoE support is needed to satisfy these requirements effectively. The requirements are the same across the enterprises, yet each line of business or department addresses them individually, and this is expensive. Furthermore, enterprises devote resources to compliance unnecessarily. Because the requirements are so complex and their resources are limited, enterprises may not meet the requirements to the extent that they would wish.
- **BPM alignment**: Although the information technology (IT) marketplace may convey the impression that BPM is easy and simple, the reality is that BPM is not easy. The complexities of a BPM implementation have their roots in the

architectural challenges (alignment across the layers of business, application, and technology) in building composite applications. These include orchestration of user interfaces, integration with systems of record, managing nonfunctional aspects such as transactional requirements, availability, governance, performance, and scalability, and so on.[5] BPM development is certainly not easy and therefore the alignment of its construct into an enterprise can be seen as a major pain point. In addition, the visibility of BPM solutions to end users makes this architectural alignment focus even more important.

- **Performance management**: Performance management of business processes enables executives to be informed as significant events and trends occur in their businesses. It assists managers in aligning performance goals and identifies areas of opportunity and concern related to BPM investment and results. Current approaches to BPM performance management are cumbersome and inflexible and solve only part of the problem. They do not extend from the organizational objectives down to the level of the individual manager or employee and they do not provide a link between business consulting and the systems required to monitor and manage BPM performance. As a result, employees do not work at optimal productivity, which negatively influences performance and employee satisfaction and reduces customer retention.[6]

- **Value management**: BPM value management is the pursuit and stewardship of the anticipated benefits of processes that are of worth, importance, and significance to a specific stakeholder or group of stakeholders. In many organizations no relationship between BPM and value exists. Because of this, the nature of BPM and its contribution to stakeholder value is not anticipated in the organizational strategy. This means that BPM investments that can otherwise improve the worth of the organization are isolated and have little or no influence on providing the means to achieve strategic ends. The final result is an organization that has little consideration for the way in which its information, service, and data flows operate and which people are involved in these aspects, leading to duplications of task, ineffectual data services, and poor information within reporting and measurements.

- **BPM maturity**: BPM maturity relates to the degree of formality and optimization of process management. Many organizations only adopt a single view of BPM maturity; they consider only one of the following three possible maturities:
  - Maturity in developing BPM solutions
  - Maturity in adopting BPM solutions
  - Maturity of governance through BPM solutions

  For organizations that take one of these narrow views, they are left at a disadvantage in their global competitiveness. Maturity cannot be considered in only one realm; it needs to have a holistic approach, and hence the maturity against which BPM performance is measured needs the same perspective.

- **Lack of an adequate change management approach within the BPM CoE**: Managing change is tough, but part of the problem is that there is little agreement regarding what factors most influence transformation and innovation initiatives. Ask five executives to name the one factor critical to the success of these portfolios and you are likely to get five different answers.[7] What is missing, we believe, is a focus on the hard factors. These factors bear three distinct characteristics:

- Organizations are able to measure the change in direct or indirect ways
- Organizations can easily communicate their importance, both within and outside organizations
- Businesses are capable of influencing those elements quickly

Some of the hard factors that affect a transformation and innovation initiatives are:

- The time necessary to complete the initiative
- The number of people required to execute it
- The financial results that intended actions are expected to achieve

WHAT HAPPENS WITHOUT A BPM CoE?

What happens if an organization does not have a sound BPM CoE in place? Some of the symptoms attributed to organizations not properly analyzing, selecting, and managing its BPM improvements are related to the process as described in Figure 1 below.

In Figure 1, we see business events, business processes, and business decisions each as separate. Connecting them, through BPM, to a common view that is maintained and managed via BPM allows insight into the business events to be applied, through business decisions, to affect the business processes, and vice versa.

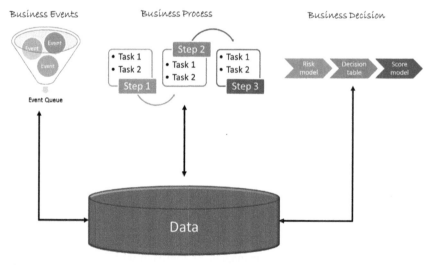

FIGURE 1

Business events driving business decisions through business process management.

- **Lack of business agility to react to business events**: Events range from those that take place in the course of normal operation or that may occur as planned or unplanned occurrences that drive responses and processes internal to a business and result in a business decision: for example, the introduction of mobile technology as a service. BPM applies designs to improve the detection, identification, and response to associated business events with efficiency and effectiveness.

Why it is important: The increasing speed of commerce is introducing more events per day, per minute, and per second for many businesses, increasing the backlog of challenges in the event queue. Hence, efficient detection and response to just a fraction of these events can result in millions of dollars gained or saved per year. It makes sense that businesses are focusing on improving their performance in identifying events or event patterns, as well as generating the right response, at the right time, and for the right reason.[8]

- **Inability to implement BPM technology**: BPM technologies have become cornerstone products for enterprise software vendors. BPM is solidly rooted as a core element of their product stack and continues to drive complementary software development, including B2B integration, content management, and decision making.[9] Lack of a BPM CoE that helps select the correct BPM technology suited to the organization and works to ensure that its implementation as part of the wider ERP implementation is effective leads to:
  - Ineffective use of organization resources
  - Inability to adjust with agility and flexibility to meet changing business requirements and customer expectations
  - Inefficient response time to internal and external events
  - Limited the speed at which an organization can bring new products or services to market
  - Reduction of customer satisfaction
  - Reduction of competitive advantage and positioning

Why it is important: Consider a manufacturing organization that loses millions of dollars because of an underperforming logistics operation. When orders are unable to be shipped, the root cause may be lack of consistent and efficient processes that create challenges to compensate and adjust priorities, resources, and tasks.

High-performing organizations invest in BPM approaches and technologies to better address business challenges that cause inefficiencies, lost revenue, and lower customer satisfaction. Improving the way business processes are managed is a critical component for improving operational performance.

- **Inability to assist decision making**: Decision management helps organizations extract strategic decision-making logic from traditional programmed solutions into a central repository maintainable by business experts. It improves operational performance by facilitating faster time to market for decision-making changes and enabling organizations to react better to market opportunities.

Why it is important: Staying competitive in a fast-moving market requires agility, flexibility, and precision. Decision making has created value for organizations across many industries with diverse business challenges, and creates a decision-making platform allowing organizations to align business policies to market challenges and opportunities.

- **Cross-functional, resource, and cause and effect challenges:** This point highlights several areas in which a poor or nonexistent BPM CoE leads to business challenges in which the following symptoms exist:
  - Project and functional managers often clash over scarce BPM resources
  - Priorities of BPM initiatives frequently change, with resources constantly reassigned
  - BPM initiatives begin as soon as approved by senior managers, irrespective of the resources availability
  - Even if the strategic BPM initiative is implemented, the organization frequently does not achieve the desired improvement, because it is not measured against a benchmark or baseline.
  - There is no comprehensive document (BPM charter) that links all of the organization's BPM undertakings to the strategic plan
  - The list of BPM initiatives is not properly prioritized. Therefore, it is presumed that all ideas should be implemented simultaneously.

CAUSE AND EFFECT MATRIX

The symptoms associated with a lack of the abilities described in the previous section and not fulfilled through a BPM CoE unfortunately represent only half of the story. The additional consequences are portrayed in Figure 2. These effects include a reluctance to eliminate or align BPM initiatives and the need to engage in the maintenance of an ever-widening tunnel, rather than support a decreasing funnel of BPM pipeline portfolio process projects, which then lead to a chronic lack of resources, poor quality, missed deadlines, and inconsistent process mapping, orchestration, and optimization, and eventually to shortfalls within strategic objectives.

A logical outcome of such an approach is the apparent lack of real to-be processes that capture the essence of an organization's way of working, standard operating procedures or policies are misunderstood between departments, and alignment between other disciplines is missing.[10]

The answer to the pain points and the symptoms highlighted above is the development of a BPM CoE. The BPM CoE is discussed in some detail in the next section with reference to a portfolio management approach.

LESSONS LEARNED REGARDING BPM CoE

In the following section, our aim is to communicate some of the knowledge or understanding gained about what a BPM CoE could and should look like in the form of the specific construct, participating roles, the work, the perspective it brings to the portfolio of work, and the services delivered.

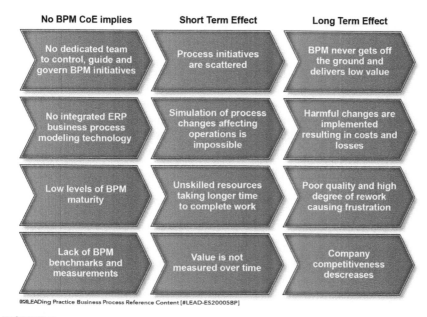

No BPM CoE implies	Short Term Effect	Long Term Effect
No dedicated team to control, guide and govern BPM initiatives	Process initiatives are scattered	BPM never gets off the ground and delivers low value
No integrated ERP business process modeling technology	Simulation of process changes affecting operations is impossible	Harmful changes are implemented resulting in costs and losses
Low levels of BPM maturity	Unskilled resources taking longer time to complete work	Poor quality and high degree of rework causing frustration
Lack of BPM benchmarks and measurements	Value is not measured over time	Company competitiveness descreases

(©)LEADing Practice Business Process Reference Content [#LEAD-ES200058P]

FIGURE 2

Short- and long-term effects of limited to no business process management (BPM) center of excellence (CoE).[11]

One of our biggest lessons learned is the importance of viewing the BPM CoE from a portfolio approach and thereby interlinking BPM alignment, BPM governance, and BPM change management: the many programs and projects the BPM CoE needs to govern and align. Such considerations will shape the specifics of the BPM CoE approach[12] and the services offered to the larger organization. On the other side, this defines what kind of roles need to be involved in the BPM CoE as well as how they will work together with multiple other teams, e.g., business architects, transformation experts, change managers, application architects. After all, the work that the BPM CoE will do or support will involve parts or full aspects of the process life cycle[13] and all its roles, tasks, and deliverables in such a manner that the lines of governance are clear and that portfolio, program, and project management team should have a clear line of alignment and integration. The clear suggestion is therefore that your BPM CoE construct include:

1. The definition of which work needs to be done and how (the work of the BPM CoE)
2. The roles needed in the BPM CoE
3. Portfolio process management
4. All execution is done through and managed within the process life cycle
5. A clear understanding and approach to BPM governance

6. A BPM maturity holistic view in the BPM CoE
7. BPM performance management described for BPM executed within the BPM CoE
8. BPM alignment to value so that the strategic intent is woven into the BPM CoE
9. Alignment of the BPM CoE to existing enterprise standards, enterprise architecture, and enterprise modeling and other IT disciplines
10. Enabled business decisions through evidence-based BPM
11. Continuous improvement in terms of change management in the BPM CoE

We will cover points 1 and 2 in this chapter; the rest of the points are covered in other chapters.

Work of a BPM CoE

A BPM CoE refers to a team, a shared facility, and an entity that provides leadership, evangelization, best practices, research, support, and/or training for the management of business processes. A BPM CoE is a tool that can be used to revitalize stalled BPM initiatives.[14] Its mandate is to govern, steward, and control a process life cycle across a set of roles, tasks, and activities. The BPM CoE integrates its function into the specific strategic, tactical, and operational layers within the enterprise. Furthermore, a BPM CoE will work closely with portfolios, programs, and projects, especially those that are involved with the implementation of applications and technology, and where they involve complex ERP solutions.

To position the BPM CoE services accurately, it must have the authority to oversee and consider the link between the process initiatives within its mandate of execution and all the enterprise layers, e.g., business, application, and technology. Furthermore, the scope of any initiative must be done within a portfolio approach.[15] For a portfolio approach to work and to result in the alignment of multiple initiatives necessitates an understanding of the existing and targeted process architecture. This is depicted in Figure 3.[16] For most process practitioners, introducing a portfolio approach requires an understanding of where program and project levels fit in against the process scope. It further requires they understand how the process portfolio, program, and project levels interact across the enterprise layers and against aspects of time and detail.

As with any other CoE, the BPM CoE does not simply develop on its own; it is not self-creating and it needs to be initiated, integrated, and aligned to the greater enterprise structure. This is the main failing in the current development approach taken with many BPM CoEs. In most instances, organizations attempt to take a shortcut and develop their BPM CoE by leveraging its creation on the back of the services it is to deliver, instead of initiating and sustaining it with consideration of an enterprise portfolio perspective. Taking an enterprise portfolio approach aids strategic alignment, collaboration between process and

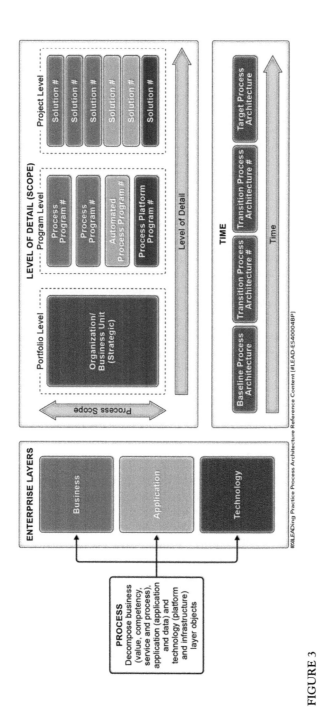

lf@LEADing Practice Process Architecture Reference Content (#LEAD-ES40004BP)

FIGURE 3

Business process management center of excellence management of the enterprise layers process decomposition and composition.[17]

architectural work, and the creation of a direct relationship between BPM initiatives and business innovation. Where business innovation is one of the driving forces for change and therefore identifying and creating value, the BPM CoE created in this manner offers a vastly improved way of implementing changes and sustaining results.

The enterprise portfolio approach deals with the various levels within the enterprise structure (Figure 3). The enterprise layers (business, application, and technology) have processes that require decomposition and composition. The BPM CoE is the responsible party that should take control of the process decomposition and composition.

The highest level, the portfolio, deals with the high-level scope initiatives and is able to differentiate the process into strategic aspects as well as define the process automation requirements. The program levels deal with the tactical scope initiatives of the business, application, and technology as the level of scope detail increases; furthermore, it develops the process automation within the tactical level. The third level is the project level, which deals with the operational scope initiatives and detailed process automation across the operation level. At this level, the business, application, and technology business process requirements are considered in detail.

The BPM CoE development should consider the technology landscape, which it simply has not done in the past. As is represented in Figure 3, technology process development is described over time to ensure adequate integration and alignment within the enterprise portfolio approach. The technology process architecture similarly develops over time from a baseline toward a target (to-be) process architecture through transitional phases of process architecture. This ensures that the technology process architecture can meet the application and business demands and requirements enabling business innovation.

Typical BPM CoE Roles

One of the primary areas of responsibility for the delivery element of a BPM CoE is to provide the staffing, expertise, and experience required to execute the pipeline of programs and projects within the portfolio. This requires a staffing model and a resource pool, aligned with roles in the BPM CoE.

Any staffing model for BPM projects should take into account a need for scalability to keep pace with BPM adoption across the enterprise. This scalability can be enabled by understanding the specialization of various roles involved in successfully implementing a BPM project, and the recommended level of involvement by these roles in each project. These resources are likely to start being used for multiple projects as resource demands grow for the BPM CoE.[18]

The BPM CoE roles are highlighted in Figure 4.[19,20]

Such roles within the BPM CoE ensure that there is an accountability framework for creating decisions and determining the services, architecture, standards, and policies for continuous management of business processes. Over all, they ensure

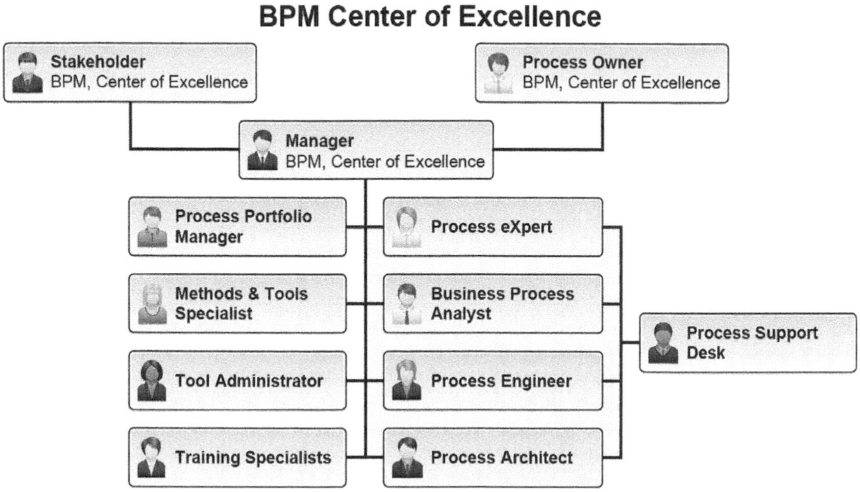

BPM Center of Excellence

FIGURE 4

Typical business process management center of excellence roles.

the sustainability, maturity, governance, and alignment, of processes both horizontally from end to end across the enterprise, but in a manner that ensures their connection and contribution to strategy.

BPM CoE Process Life Cycle

The BPM CoE roles work in various programs and projects where the specific tasks always relate to a specific phase of the process life cycle; therefore, the roles, tasks, and deliverable part of the portfolio, program, and project can be managed within the process life cycle. This is done through managing the deliverables/artifacts assigned to the specific roles and their tasks within the process life cycle[21] (Figure 5). Because the process management life cycle has already been aligned to the project management life cycle, the key touch points can be highlighted for specific focus on governance and value delivery.

The process life cycle is controlled, directed, and governed by the BPM CoE across all areas of the business. The BPM CoE requires a specific team of skilled individuals to accomplish this.

BPM CoE Portfolio Process Management

Another key feature of the BPM CoE is the alignment of the portfolio inputs processes to outputs flow. It describes how a BPM CoE would integrate a portfolio working model into its current state of working. It helps define how the daily

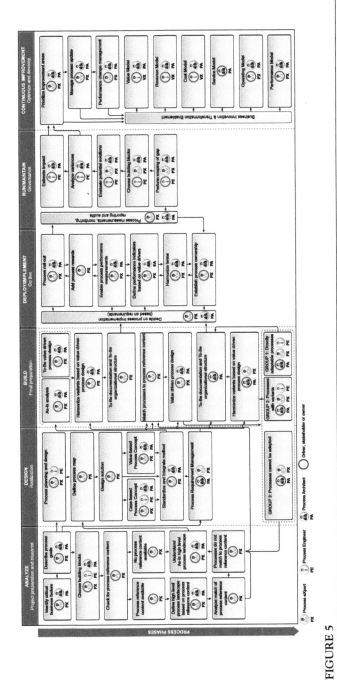

FIGURE 5

Process management life cycle.[22]

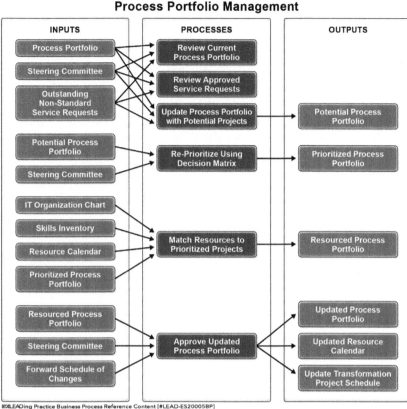

FIGURE 6

Business process management center of excellence operational portfolio management expected inputs processes–outputs/deliverables.

operation of a BPM CoE would function based on input criteria, which would result in the initiation of a defined set of processes and respective expected outputs from these processes. This is shown in Figure 6.[23,24]

The outputs of the processes are in essence the deliverables that a BPM CoE should consider enabling through its ongoing operation.

A Clear Understanding and Approach to BPM Governance

Governance must deal with two aspects: governed guidelines, and governing guidelines. The Open Group's SOA Governance Framework[25] calls these aspects governed and governing, respectively. Any of the first type prescribes activities to be done within the core discipline (in this case, the core discipline is BPM), whereas the second type makes sure that all that needs to be done is actually completed.

Research suggests that BPM governance, by providing guidance on models, metrics, and management accountability, is the way to reduce chances for failing large-scale BPM initiatives.[26] To achieve this the BPM CoE needs to define the approach to governance. Part of this work is to ensure that there is a good understanding across all layers of the organization of what BPM governance is. This means that the executives, managers, and individual contributors each understand their role in adhering to the BPM governance laid out by the BPM CoE.

A strong governance framework for BPM needs to be used to help guide the BPM approach. For more information, see the BPM governance chapter. A high-level overview of relevant topics is presented in Figure 7.

The alignment category (guidelines ensuring strategic and tactical alignment of BPM with enterprise business objectives, investment policies, other initiatives, and stakeholders) includes the following guidelines:

- BPM guiding principles
- High-level business process architecture
- Business process portfolio management (prioritizing BP for redesign/automation)
- BPM investment policies
  - Project planning, approval, and funding
  - BPM budget access and transparency policies

FIGURE 7

Business process management (BPM) center of excellence governance guidelines.

- Business process metrics, Key Performance Indicators (KPIs) and business activity monitoring
- Business process end user and stakeholders policies
- BPM standards

The methods category (guidelines prescribing methodologies, best practices, and standards for modeling, implementing, and commissioning business processes) includes the following guidelines:

- Business process life cycle methodology
- Business process analysis and modeling
- Business process design and testing
- Business process integration with information, services, and rules

The operations category (guidelines prescribing operational procedures and best practices for BPM, BPMS, and underlying infrastructure) includes the following guidelines:

- Business process platform sharing
- BPMS infrastructure operations
- BPMS infrastructure support
- Business process end user support
- Business process monitoring and control
- Business process measurements and reporting

The people category (guidelines for sponsorship, roles, and organizations, resources management and training, knowledge management, and communication) includes the following guidelines:

- Executive sponsorship policies
- BPM roles, responsibilities, and accountability
- Skills, expertise, labor division, and assignment
- BPM Knowledge Management
- BPM education and training
- Collaboration and communication

The chart in Figure 7, breaks BPM governing guidelines into two categories.

The processes category (guidelines prescribing the steps for governing processes) includes the following guidelines:

- Compliance verification
- Dispensation
- Monitoring and reporting
- Business control

The knowledge category (guidelines for managing and communicating content, resources, and facilities involved in the planning, execution, measurement, and analysis of the governing processes) includes the following guidelines:

- Governance roles, responsibilities, and accountability
- Governance education and training

- Information management and communication
- Policy management and take-on
- Environment management

A BPM Maturity Holistic View in BPM CoE

As discussed in the BPM maturity chapter, the term "maturity" relates to the degree of formality and ripeness of practices within a specific field, from ad hoc practices to formally defined steps, managed result metrics, active optimization, and improvement of the processes. Maturity models have the aim to improve existing practices from and can be viewed as a set of structured levels that describe how well the behaviors and practices of an organization can reliably and sustainably produce required outcomes. A maturity model can be described as a structured collection of elements that describe certain aspects of maturity in an organization. A maturity model in the context of a BPM CoE may, for example:

- Provide a quick scan of the status quo
- Identify where there is low maturity and therefore a place to start
- Provide a way to define what improvement the BPM CoE will focus on
- Provide an approach for prioritizing actions
- Provide the benefit of a community's prior experiences
- Provide a common language and a shared vision

A maturity model can be used as a benchmark for comparison and as an aid to understanding. In the BPM maturity chapter, we elaborated on the need to view the maturity of the process in its context of:

- The purpose and goal of the process, including aspects such as link to strategic business objectives, goals, critical success factors, value drivers, performance indicators, requirements, etc.
- The relationship to the organizational aspects such as business areas and groups, business competencies, business capabilities, etc.
- Which business, information and/or data objects are involved in terms of input, output, storage, etc.
- Its flows and interlink to services flow, information flow, and even value flow.
- The owners involved, which can be the process owners, but also business area owners, services owners, or data owners
- The various roles involved, which span from traditional process roles to application roles and service roles
- The various rules and compliance aspects involved, e.g., business rules, process rules, service rules, and security and data rules that influence and direct the various aspects of the process
- Automation in terms of application modules involved, and application tasks as well as application services
- Of the various measurements in terms of KPIs, Process Performance Indicators (PPIs), and Service Performance Indicators (SPIs) that are part of reporting and real-time decision making

- Data aspects involved, including the data components, data entities, data objects, and possibly the data services and data tables
- Which media and channels are involved
- Technological aspects from platforms aspects such as platform services and platform devices (mobile devices) to infrastructure aspects
- Services that are created within the process as well as the service flow that goes across the various processes

In a BPM CoE context, however, the challenge with existing BPM maturity models is that the BPM CoE maturity is not really considered through the multiple perspectives in which it needs to be considered. A BPM CoE maturity model needs to covers at least the following perspectives:

1. The maturity of developing the BPM standards
2. The BPM services offered
3. The BPM governance set in place
4. Instituting BPM security
5. Organizing change management around BPM initiatives
6. Ensuring latest BPM development are aligned
7. Executing BPM transformation
8. Adopting BPM solutions

An overview of the additional BPM CoE maturity aspects is illustrated in Figure 8.

BPM Performance Management Is Executed Within the BPM CoE

For BPM adoption, governance, and related value aspects to be successfully implemented, ongoing BPM performance management must be included in the overall concept to be managed by the BPM CoE for performance management to provide a complete solution designed to assist the business in identifying the appropriate metrics to maximize value for the business, translate them into objectives for managers and employees throughout the organization, and to provide employees at all levels of the organization the capabilities and feedback they need to optimize their performance.

Implementing such a BPM performance management methodology can provide significant bottom line business benefits, and provide growth in annual savings. Benefits include:

- Increasing employee productivity
- Increasing customer satisfaction and retention
- Increasing revenue
- Reducing employee attrition and costs associated with it
- Reducing performance management workload
- Reducing hiring and training costs
- Reducing learning curve for new hires
- Reducing IT workload

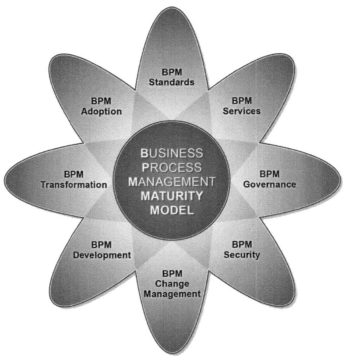

(IC)LEADing Practice Maturity Reference Content (#LEAD-ES60003AL)

FIGURE 8

Considering the additional business process management (BPM) center of excellence maturity aspects.[27]

Furthermore, such a performance management system can be used within the BPM CoE to measure and optimize any business process, including the performance management process itself. This can result in a self-perpetuating virtual cycle of continued performance optimization, leading to exponential improvement over time.

BPM Alignment to Value So That the Strategic Intent Is Woven Into the BPM CoE

As already discussed in the value-driven process design chapter, one of the most challenging aspects in business is to get the agreement of value aspects from a group of people (employees, managers, and executives) who have come from different backgrounds and cultures and have different competing forces and drivers. Added to this mix is the requirement to align the BPM to the defined value within the organization so that the strategic intent of the business operations is captured as a common thread which a BPM CoE can integrate. The capturing of value aspects is seen as vital as it sets the direction for the various BPM CoE projects and the process execution. Contrary to ordinary BPM approaches, BPM alignment understands that an organization can simultaneously pursue multiple strategies and goals and needs to align the underlying execution. For example, an organization can pursue both high growth and profits by defining unique critical success factors that break the conventional value–cost tradeoff by simultaneously pursuing both differentiation in the market and low cost in its operations. Although these would be two different projects, they can have lots of common steps, tasks, and maybe even artifacts. This is where BPM alignment to value is relevant; it captures value elements and aligns them and the underlying BPM initiatives.

Alignment of BPM CoE to Existing Enterprise Standards, Enterprise Architecture, Enterprise Modeling, and Other IT Disciplines

A BPM CoE cannot and should not exist in isolation within any organization; this principle drives the alignment of BPM to enterprise standards, enterprise architecture, enterprise modeling, and other disciplines. Furthermore, process is one of the four key pillars of enterprise management and is therefore a fundamental integration stream indicated in Figure 9.

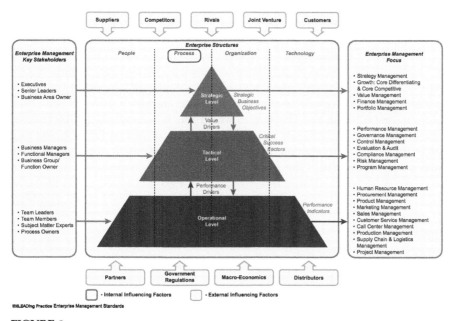

FIGURE 9

Business process management integration across the enterprise through process.[28]

The BPM CoE should thus have an influence across all major levels in the organization. The CoE should be an integral part of an alignment management framework that the business sets up, ensuring that participation in daily operational activities as well as in the portfolio, program, and project management delivery is attained, sustained, and optimized.

Continuous Improvement and BPM CoE Change Management

A challenge faced by both newly formed and well-matured BPM CoEs is the continuous expectations to make ongoing improvement in response to changing needs, wants, performance, and/or value concerns/expectations.[29] Change is not something that could or might happen to the modern enterprise; it is happening. It is a fact of any BPM initiative or BPM portfolio, and thus any BPM CoE. The issue of change therefore requires considerable consideration.

Change management is a process and the use of tools and techniques to manage the people side of change processes to achieve the required outcomes, and to realize the change effectively within the individual change agent, the inner team, and the wider system[30]: in this case, the BPM CoE and the complete enterprise organization. Change scope encompasses the addition, modification, and removal of anything that could have an effect on the BPM portfolio, BPM programs, BPM projects, BPM services, or specific processes within the various organizational flows. Consequently, for any BPM CoE, BPM change management is a critical and core competency that must be the center around which the changes will be happening. In the modern BPM CoE organization, we believe that they will realize that this competency becomes a core differentiator and a link to stakeholder value and performance expectations.

BPM change management has linkages to many other key BPM services such as changes to the process itself, process architectures, procedures, systems, process measurements, performance metrics, process monitoring, process reporting, process compliance, and process documentation, as well as changes to BPM services, BPM projects, and other items. The way in which this is accomplished is by building change interventions at regular intervals throughout the process life cycle and then using these change interventions to ensure communication/feedback to relevant stakeholders (Figure 10). The feedback loop occurs only during the run/maintain

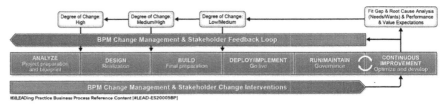

FIGURE 10

Process life cycle with business process management (BPM) change management interventions and change feedback loop.[31]

and continuous improvement phases. It cannot occur during the previous phases because they have been closed as part of the project/portfolio.

- Degree of change—low: changes that can be achieved with low work amounts are referred to by different names in the various BPM CoEs: fast changes, quick changes, or even standard changes. All have one thing in common: they have a low degree of change and are for the most part preauthorized because they have low risk, are relatively common, and follow a known procedure or work flow.
- Degree of change—medium: Changes that can be achieved with medium work amount are for the most referred to as normal change requests.
- Degree of change—high: Changes that include a high degree of change can also have different names. Some of the names are big change, strategic change, major incident change, and emergency change. All not only have a high degree of change in common, they also have a certain relationship to performance and value creation, and therefore must be implemented as soon as possible.

Change interventions do not just occur in the process life cycle; they have to be planned into specific points in the process phases. The degree of change determines the amount of change intervention required. This is detailed in Figure 11, which defines what tools should be used against what degree of change and the degree of active involvement required by the stakeholders in adopting the change.

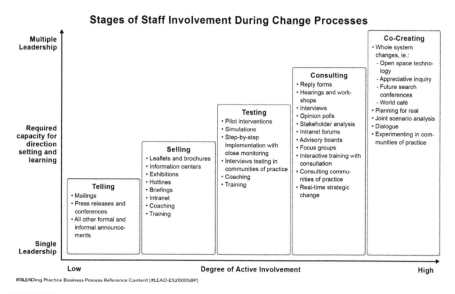

FIGURE 11

Stages of stakeholder involvement.[32]

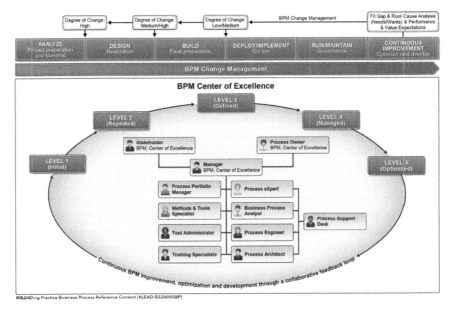

FIGURE 12

Consolidated business process management (BPM) center of excellence model.[33]

CONCLUSION

The key to successful BPM is a BPM CoE.[34] The BPM CoE helps establish and improve BPM maturity and ensures a consistent and cost-effective way of offering BPM services. This chapter elaborated on the need to manage BPM initiatives with allocated roles and responsibilities through a BPM CoE, managing the portfolio, programs, and projects through their specific process life cycle and the changes accruing. In this chapter we therefore illustrated the key aspects of a BPM CoE, as shown in Figure 12: the life cycles, roles, and process portfolio, program, projects, and changes that occur as a part of continuous improvement of the organization. This is combined with a maturity view on BPM through five levels, all of which need to be balanced together to enable value identification, creation, and realization.

End Notes

1. Pain points are areas that organizations can make improvements to.
2. Sandy Kemsley, *Business Process Discovery* (2011), www.tibco.com.
3. Gabriel Kemeny and Micheal Reame, *Creating a Charter for Your Process Improvement Project* (2010), http://www.processgps.com/.
4. Dan Morris, *7 Key Roles You Need in Your BPM Center of Excellence* (2013), http://www.processexcellencenetwork.com/.
5. S. Simmons and D. Wakeman, "BPM Voices: Don't forget the basics of software design when architecting BPM solutions." *IBM Business Process Management Journal* (2014).

6. K. Forbes, *Driving Business Value Through Performance Management* (2002) http://www. crmxchange.com/whitepapers/pdf/bluepumpkin-WP_PerformanceManagement.pdf.

7. Harold L. Sirkin, P. Keenan, and A. Jackson, "The hard side of change management." *Harvard Business Review* (2005).

8. Dyer L. and Ericksen J, "Complexity-based agile enterprises: putting self-organizing emergence to work", in *The Sage Handbook of Human Resource Management*, ed. A. Wilkinson et al (London, 2009).

9. Unlocking the Potential of Business Process Management", *iGrafx* (2013), www.igrafx.com.

10. LEADing Practice Business Process Reference Content #LEAD-ES20005BP.

11. Portfolio Management Reference Content LEAD-ES10019AL.

12. Portfolio Management Reference Content LEAD-ES10019AL.

13. Business Process Reference Content LEAD-ES20005BP.

14. M.O. George, *The lean six sigma guide to doing more with less* (John Wiley and Sons, 2010):261, ISBN: 9780470539576.

15. Taken from the Portfolio Management Reference Content LEAD-ES10019AL.

16. LEADing Practice Process Architecture Reference Content LEAD-ES40004BP.

17. LEADing Practice Layered Enterprise Architecture Reference Content #LEAD-ES40001AL.

18. L. Dyer, Andrew Forget, Fahad Osmani, Jonas Zahn, *Creating a BPM Center of Excellence (CoE) IBM Redbooks* (2013), www.ibm/redbooks.

19. LEADing Practice Business Process Reference Content LEAD-ES20005BP.

20. LEADing Practice Process Architecture Reference Content LEAD-ES40004BP.

21. LEADing Practice Business Process Reference Content LEAD-ES20005BP.

22. LEADing Practice Business Process Reference Content #LEAD-ES20005BP.

23. LEADing Practice Business Process Reference Content #LEAD-ES20005BP.

24. LEADing Practice Portfolio Management Reference Content #LEAD-ES10019AL.

25. S.O.A. Governance Framework The Open Group (2009), http://www.opengroup.org/pubs/catalog/c093.htm.

26. A. Spanyi, BPM Governance. BPMInstitute.org (2008), http://www.bpminstitute.org.

27. LEADing Practice Maturity Reference Content #LEAD-ES60003AL.

28. LEADing Practice Enterprise Management Reference Content [#LEAD-ES10EMAS].

29. A part of the Change Management Reference Content (LEAD-ES60002AL).

30. H. Nauheimer, *The Change management tool book. Creative Commons Attribution-Share-Alike 3.0 Unported License.*

31. LEADing Practice Business Process Reference Content #LEAD-ES20005BP.

32. LEADing Practice Business Process Reference Content #LEAD-ES20005BP.

33. Asim Akram, *BPM Center of Excellence* (2013) www.bpminstitute.org.

34. LEADing Practice Business Process Reference Content #LEAD-ES20005BP.

Understanding Business Process Management Roles

Mark von Rosing, Neil Kemp, Maxim Arzumanyan

INTRODUCTION

In this chapter we will explore what a role is, discuss the features of a role, and seek to understand the motivation and challenges we face in identifying and using business process-centric roles today. This chapter also provides a summary of the profile of the factors or features needed to flesh out or give specific form to the roles in a business process management (BPM) center of excellence.

MOTIVATION FOR DEFINING YOUR BPM ROLES

Role modeling, role engineering, and various terms such as "rights," "privileges," and "permissions"[1] may be used to communicate the idea of a part in which someone or something engages or does in a particular defined function, activity, or situation.

Successful BPM requires a structured and repeatable method of exploring, finding, specifying, and/organizing roles in both the organizational structure and its programs and projects. It also requires use of a complete set of roles that have stewardship, including, for example, the roles within a BPM center of excellence (CoE) (see chapter on BPM CoE).

Business processes and therefore BPM are concerned with three general types of things: process objects, consisting of the processes, gates, and events that are performed in a sequence; business objects that are consumed, transformed, and created by the process objects; and rules about participation in the work and ensuring that the work is done in accordance with its requirements (see chapter on BPM requirements management). Of the three, the controls on participation lead to the need to explore roles and is perhaps the least understood. It presents a great challenge to BPM today.

Within existing business process thought, there is a certain amount of confusion as to the nature of roles. Interestingly, for example, although the business process modeling notation (BPMN) standard, the reference standard for describing processes, refers to the term "role," it offers no specification or description as to what it means. It therefore is useful to examine the idea of "role" and its related concepts closely to tease apart the ideas and exploit the value and insight we can gain as a result. As we do this, it is important to keep some points in mind.

1. A repeatable process is needed, such that two analysts given the same problem are likely to come up with similar results: i.e., when determining the roles required to execute a particular design, they will be able to find a set of roles with similar properties or characteristics. This is a part of alignment and standardization.

2. We want to provide a method to separate the logical intent of the work being described from the constraints and realities of execution. Treating roles as logical constructs and position and actors as being purely physical in nature allows the subject matter expert to gather business requirements about the rules and constraints of behavior and therefore focus on the needs of the business, not the issues related to what the business has in terms of capabilities. This separation between logical and physical is critical because it gives us the means to create forward-looking (to-be, should-be, and might-be) designs without being constrained by current restrictions, thinking, or organizational structure. Such structured thinking is part of role engineering and we believe that role modeling could greatly benefit from the insights gained through such an approach.

3. It is important to simplify the problems related to understanding work through the elimination of concerns about organizational aspects of where the work is done. This allows the analyst to concentrate on the nature of the work being explored without being distracted by whatever tradeoffs are part of the current organization design.

4. In the early stages of analysis, we do not want to spend time on capacity issues, i.e., the number or deployment of the actual resources that will be required to perform the work, when the specific nature of the work itself is unclear. Our requirement is to first address "what" and then address "how."

For these reasons, it is essential to develop a strong understanding of roles that reflects the value being sought by the strategy, which can in turn be communicated within an enterprise to address the above points.

RELEVANCE CONTEXT

Today's frequent practice for identifying the roles required to develop new processes designs or to otherwise transform or innovate the business into some future way of operations is to use the current roles, or worse, the current positions, or worse yet, the current people within the projected new processes. The result of designing new processes with incomplete insight into the logic of the work needed to perform the process really means that the results are literally compromised from the start.

In a Forrester Research survey of over 100 business process and application professionals, 86% of participants said that poor support for cross-functional processes is a significant or very significant problem. In addition, almost 70% reported that the lack of insight into process results is a significant or very significant problem for enterprise applications. The resolution of the methods to identify and allocate roles is one key to resolving this challenge.

WHAT IS A ROLE?

Roles and role relationships are the building blocks of any enterprise. The idea of a role is a business concept that can exist entirely without reference to technology, although it can be captured and enabled through automation.

The methods used to identify, define, and deploy these business components is of interest for executives or managers concerned with creating an organization capable of operating in the manner they desire. In particular, they are used to assigning process owners to each process across the enterprise and within the business process hierarchy.

Roles are often thought of as "assigned positions in the organization, each with specific accountabilities and authorities,"[2] or the set of activities that someone may perform to complete a process.[3]

Instead of treating the ideas of role, position (job title), and actor as equivalent or synonymous, we must, as The Open Group Architecture Framework (TOGAF) suggests, consider them to exist as distinct though related things,[4] or similarly, as LEAD states, consider that a role is "a part that someone or something has in a particular defined function, activity, or situation. A resource/actor may have a number of roles."[5]

We already know that good design practice tells us to separate the logical intent of a design from its physical description, whether designing software, a building, or an organization.[6] Because of this, these latter definitions are more appealing. Making a distinction between the concept of "role" versus that of "resource" or "actor" is therefore appealing. It meets our requirements and is therefore of more use to us than cases in which the differences are not as explicit.

If we limit the idea of a role to being **a set of rights granted in a business context and supported by the skill and knowledge needed to exercise those rights**, then within the design process we do not need to worry about anything more than what are the rights, skills, and knowledge. Later, in a separate and distinct design process, we can work out how to transition from the current or as-is rights to the target or to-be rights, which is an important aspect of business transformation. Alternatively, if the required skills and knowledge do not exist, gaps between what is required for the roles to be performed and what is required of available actors may be solved by training, or recruiting the resources, or through acquiring a going concern that has what is necessary.

A further problem and limitation in current thinking about roles is that many organizations do not appreciate that, as illustrated in Figure 1, business processes and their end-to-end flows cross multiple organizational business units, and therefore likely necessitate the involvement of multiple roles. These processes and the roles that interact with them must therefore be connected such that the various control types, properties, tasks, and objects in which a role is involved are each engaged in a sound manner.

Business processes not only run across multiple business units; when examined end-to-end, we see that as they flow they interact with multiple roles within the organization. For these reasons, the roles and how they are assembled in the organization to deliver the strategic intent change across each flow and are influenced by this context. Any exploration of role context must therefore include developing an understanding of the business units in which a role exists, but also the:

- Business areas: The highest-level meaningful grouping of the activities of the enterprise
- Business groups: An aggregation within an enterprise that is within a business area

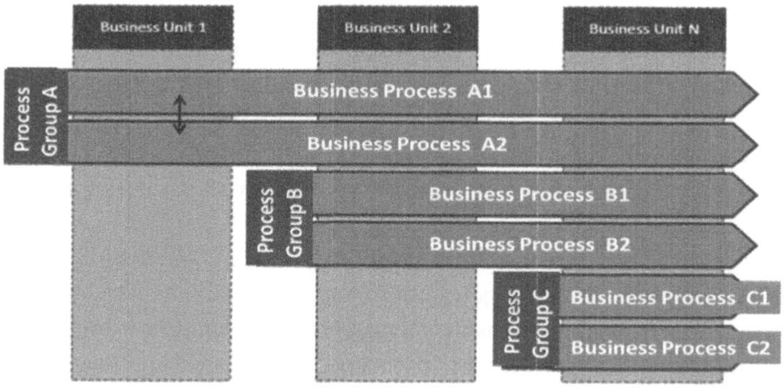

FIGURE 1

How business processes and end-to-end flows cross multiple organizational business units.

- Business functions: A cluster of tasks creating a specific class of jobs
- Service areas: A high-level, conceptual aggregation of provided services
- Service groups: An aggregation of services based on a common factor or domain that exist within a common service area.
- Business services: The externally visible ("logical") deed or effort performed to satisfy a need or to fulfill a demand, meaningful to the environment

The need to quantify the business process with all its role types and the related properties, tasks, etc., requires application of the principle of the separation of duties (separation by sharing of more than one individual in one single task is an internal control intended to prevent fraud and error). This must be done without regard to the design or form of the organizational construct or the specific areas and groups in which the process activities take place. The result is that the analyst is better able to identify duplication of duties, business functions, tasks, services, and their associated resources and actors, and for employees, the actors in the enterprise that actually do the work, better see themselves in the creation of value. This is a significant point because when workers cannot see themselves in the work or do not understand how they add value, all sorts of problems may arise:

- If they are unable to see how their work directly contributes to a specific outcome that the customer values, they may be poorly motivated
- They do not have enough authority to do a good job
- A confusing process with multiple handoffs, many approvals, and rework caused by people not having complete and accurate information from an earlier step can lead to limited cooperation
- Limited cooperation can come from attitude again, or functional silos that are vying with one another

On the other hand, if they see a strong connection between the employee, and their work, the role they perform in carrying out this work makes sense to them.

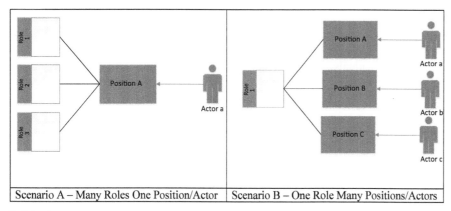

FIGURE 2

Scenarios relating roles to other components of the organization.

Similarly, during transformative change, it is always important that the employees be able to see themselves in the future plans of the enterprise; by providing strong links to the work, this is made easier.

As we see in Figure 2, many roles can be assigned to a single position or actor; similarly, one role can actually be performed, if it is deemed necessary, by many resources, who would then be granted all the same rights and have the personal competency to perform and engage in the same work. By separating the resource loading and work distribution questions that are inherently distinct from the role implementation and capacity issues, these can be ignored until the later stages of design as we focus on the parts that are played within the business process. In addition, hidden in this representation is resolution of conflict–separation of function and control: cashier versus daily depositor versus bookkeeper versus supervisor.

This should be consistent with personal experience; a person can act in many roles at the same time or at different times. We know in our personal lives that a person can, for example, be a daughter, mother, soccer coach, lawyer, and wife within the same person. Similarly, it would be reasonable for a large organization to have many accounts receivable clerks, many programmers, etc.

In the formal sense, a role is a set of rights and privileges (authorizations and accountabilities) together with human capability (skills, knowledge, and present and future decision-making ability) involved in the execution of a set of tasks:

1. The role of teacher involves specific instructional skills used to impart knowledge of a particular kind (e.g., mathematics, history, English literature) within an institutional framework (i.e., the authorizations).
2. The role of application security analyst involves the use of specific analysis skills that apply security principles (i.e., the knowledge) to the evaluation of computer programs (i.e., the accountability) for ensuring the protection of data and processes within an automated software product.[7]

The context for the definition of role is applicable only within an organization, whether public, private, or not for profit. Although individuals acting on their own behalf have roles, they are not subject to the same methods of classification. For example, individuals acting on their own behalf in transformational or transactional work may be assigned the role of customer and act in this role throughout all views of the work.

STANDARDS THAT LINK TO ROLE CONCEPTS

Standard development bodies have categorized and classified how to think, work, and/or model roles within the context of their framework, method, and approaches. The standards developing organizations, standards bodies, or standards setting organization (such as governments) are, among others:

- The Object Management Group (OMG), a technology standards consortium. The OMG Task Forces develop enterprise integration standards for a wide range of technologies and an even wider range of industries. The OMG's modeling standards have specific aspects of roles including:
  - Model-driven architecture
  - BPMN
  - Business motivation model
  - Value Delivery Modeling Language
- Control Objectives for Information Technology (COBIT)—COBIT is an IT Governance Framework created by Information Systems Audit and Control Association (ISACA) as a centralized source of information and guidance in the field of auditing controls for computer systems. IT's Control Objective PO4.6—Establishment of Roles and Responsibilities—is contained within Process. Define the IT Processes, Organization, and Relationships.

- ITIL (formally known as Information Technology Infrastructure Library) is concerned with IT service management. The ITIL roles are employed to define responsibilities. In particular, they are used to assign process and service roles to the various ITIL processes and to illustrate responsibilities for the single activities within the detailed process descriptions used in all ITIL phases and steps
- The Open Group is a global consortium that enables the achievement of business objectives through IT standards. With more than 400 member organizations, it has a diverse membership that spans various sectors of the IT community. The Open Group, among others, has developed the framework and methods around TOGAF and TOGAF 9.X; although it has no artifacts to classify and/or categorize roles, it has the following meta objects and relationships related to a role:
  - Role is performed by an actor
  - Role accesses a function
  - Role decomposes role
- Although much of the body of work produced by these groups (OMG, COBIT, ITIL, TOGAF) is useful for understanding and applying roles in their specific context, it must generally be used with caution in another context: The

charters of most of the organizations and therefore their respective body of knowledge are focused almost exclusively on a specific way of thinking, working and modeling and are often very technology-centric based. The execution and enabling of roles and their function in the stewardship of technology is interesting in the context of this chapter, but so are the much larger questions about their nature, purpose, discovery, and use across all aspects of the business, not just with respect to the management of technology.

- The International Organization for Standardization is an international standard-setting body composed of representatives from various national standards organizations. The role modeling in ISO standards are not managed across the standards but rather within the specific standard.
- The Institute of Electrical and Electronics Engineers (IEEE) is a professional association dedicated to advancing technological innovation and excellence. The IEEE's constitution defines the purposes of the organization as "scientific and educational." In pursuing these goals, the IEEE serves as a major publisher of scientific journals and organizer of conferences, workshops, and symposia (many of which have associated published proceedings). The role modeling in IEEE standards are not managed across their standards but rather within the specific standards.
- The LEADing Practice, with over 100 Enterprise Standards and its open source community, is one of the largest development organizations in the world. Its Enterprise Standards are the result of years of international industry research, mostly carried out by the Global University Alliance, which consist of over 400 universities that bring together professors, lecturers, and/or researchers from all over the world to improve enterprise architecture practices. Its Enterprise Standards are therefore de facto standards, capturing what has been shown to work well and expert consensus on repeatable patterns that can be reused and replicated. The various LEAD enterprise standards are packaged as reference content and are both tool agnostic and vendor neutral. The material is designed to be tailored and implemented by any organization, large or small, regardless of its various frameworks, methods, products/services, or activities. In terms of role modeling, LEADing practice has Role Modeling Reference Content LEAD ID ES20012BC; however roles are modeled in the following additional enterprise standards:
  - Competency Modeling Reference Content LEAD ID ES20013BC
  - Business Process Reference Content LEAD ID ES20005BP
  - Measurement Reference Content LEAD ID ES20014PG
  - Value Model Reference Content LEAD ID ES20007BCPG
  - Service Model Reference Content LEAD ID ES20008BCBS
  - Performance Modeling Reference Content LEAD ID ES20009BCPG
  - Operating Model Reference Content LEAD ID# ES20010BC

CURRENT METHODS

There is implied recognition in current techniques that one actor may actually have different roles, but there are no generally used techniques to tease the roles apart, understanding whether the roles are complete or appropriate.

Traditional methods for identifying roles generally rely on interviews, observation, or questionnaires aimed at the current resources, performing the current processes, within the current organization to identify what the actor does.

The assumptions embedded in the current method are numerous:

1. That the existing organization is correct, complete, and reflective of the work to be done
2. That all processes exist and are at most subject to incremental change or other methods to find the current set of roles that exist in an organization
3. That the processes in which the subject is engaged are the correct processes, or that any variances can be addressed through minor adjustments
4. That the processes are positioned correctly with respect to their value proposition, i.e., that they exist inside a competency that reflects the business strategy and that the strategy has not and will not change, that the alignment of the organizational competency to the strategy is appropriate (core or non-core) and that both the process design and role profile are complete, leveled, and well-bounded (have consistent start and end points)

Even if these assumptions were false, those in the process cannot pinpoint problems with its current design and usually do not envision the best solutions.

As a further concern, the current practice has two fundamental limitations:

1. It provides no baseline with which to benchmark the completeness, veracity, or applicability of the role, its positioning, the work involved, its rights, or anything else
2. There is no way to determine from the list of roles created by this method whether the list itself is complete and/or whether the roles are well set

The net result is that suggestions or insights about changes are generally evolutionary and look at the problem only at its edges. That is to say, because the existing participants really only have experience with their existing work and their existing way of working, it is difficult for them to step out of this world and imagine a situation where the rules are different. Only someone who is outside the work in question has the context and tools, and may provide the insight to create truly innovative new processes, flows, and roles by challenging the assumptions embedded in these methods.

ROLE CONTEXT

When we think about anything, it is always good to place it in its proper context. The context of roles is critical to our understanding of what they are and to shape our thinking about how to use them.

Every role captures four essential lenses through which the world views the role and the role connects with the world. Generically, these are:

1. The way of thinking, which is the world view of the enterprise taken from the perspective of the purpose the role seeks to achieve and the goals it sets for itself.

2. The way of working, which is the critical discipline applied to translate the identified drivers, expectations, and requirements into a form that guides the effort to expose the roles. It structures the arrangement of effort and work by translating the way of thinking into a structural approach for action.
3. The way of modeling, or the approach followed by the analyst so as to make an objective assessment of what is necessary and sufficient to complete the work. The way of modeling is the conceptual framework, language, and relationships.
4. The way of governing, which relates to decisions and guidance that define expectations and goals, grant power, or verify and ensure value identification and creation in the life cycle(s) of interest.

Figure 3 shows a role in the context of its way of thinking, way of working, way of modeling, and way of governing and how through the entire context the objects the role interacts with, artifacts (templates), and life cycle steps are consistent. The figure further distinguishes between the properties of a role that are both inherent in the role and unchanging or static, and those that are dynamic and unique.

For every role described, there will be a set of properties or a profile that speak to each of these factors.

What many organizations do not realize is that there is something in common between the areas where roles need to be applied. The common things are the role objects. Global University Alliance research identifies the semantic relations of the

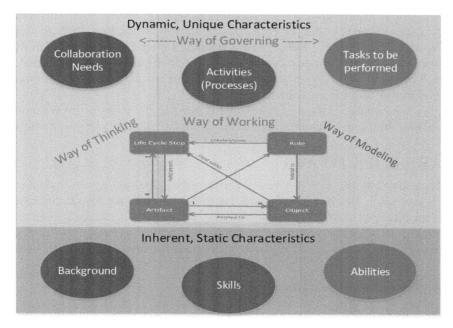

FIGURE 3

Context of role.

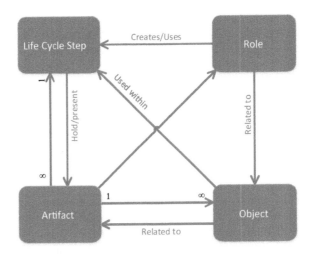

FIGURE 4

Key role relationships.

various role objects and how they can be applied within different disciplines.[8] The relations of the role objects are built into its role templates and artifacts, e.g., role maps, role matrices, and/or role models.

These properties influence the ability of the role to interact with other components, or objects within the enterprise. Figure 4 shows the logical relationships between the objects that have the most significant interaction with roles. In this figure, we see that a role captures or uses a life cycle step that has an object that is used within it and that holds or presents one or more artifact. We also see that roles interact with artifacts and with objects.

The importance of these relationships and therefore this model is that it exposes and links the role in its complete context so that all of its parts may be fully understood.

ABILITIES TO ACT

There are many ways in which we describe the rights, privileges, powers, and immunities of which roles may be composed. Fundamentally, roles are described in terms of the permitted actions that can be performed on resources (including information objects). However, for the purpose of clarity it is useful to distinguish between those that are involved with business processes and those that are situational dependent.

Rights versus Hierarchical Power

There is little agreement on what is meant by the rights to which a role has access. Although it is easy to say that rights are about how the role participates in the activity, it is not necessarily clear what we mean by this.

If we distinguish between the working relationships of roles and the relationship of a role with the work itself, we can see that two different sets of patterns emerge.

1. Role authority about either horizontal or vertical relationships between roles
2. Roles that are engaged in and have a direct relationship to work

In *Requisite Organization*, Elliot Jaques identified "task assignment role relation-ships" as "vertical" interactions and "task initiating role relationships" as "horizontal" in nature. Both these are made in the context of the organization structure or design and are relevant only in subordinate–superior relationship structures and are not core to BPM in a direct sense. What is important is the distinction between the nature of role relationships, which are about authority, and the work-centric roles, which are about responsibility. The difference between responsibility and authority is clear; responsibility is associated with execution, whereas accountability is about results and ultimate ownership. Actors possessing roles in a management hierarchy engage in task delegation, whereas within BPM, they exercise their rights and perform work. Whereas hierarchical structures and/organizational design work with roles, the rights associated with roles in this context are not directly part of BPM, which is the focus of this chapter.

ROLE PROFILE

To understand the specific set of rights granted to a role, its business context and the supported skill and knowledge needed to exercise those rights require an understanding of each of the areas identified in Table 1. These properties provide a profile of the role.

Categories of Working Roles

With business processes, the most common categorized role groups found in most organizations are business, process, service, and application. Table 2 gives an over-view of the typical role categories within an organization.

The purpose of having such a role categorization is to define how to organize and structure the viewpoints and role objects associated with the various disciplines, e.g., business role, process role, service role, and/or application role applying the concepts. This has proven to help companies with some of the most common and complex advanced role principles, dilemmas, and challenges that enterprises must confront today. This includes, but is not limited to:

- The role definitions used in the enterprise and their content; most large orga-nizations have duplications and other redundancies in their roles and thereby their processes, leading to major inefficiencies and ineffectiveness
- The way specific roles link to the business model, and whether they are value creating is often unclear when viewing them just from the process perspective
- The link between roles and the competency type within which they work, e.g., core differentiating, core competitive, non-core. This is not possible to identify from process modeling alone; therefore, the link between roles and competency types is seen as vital
- The relationship of various roles with measurement and reporting for advanced decision making

Table 1 *Role Profile*	
Feature	**Description**
Organizational roles	The name of the role or roles included in the profile (multiple roles may be included to address different levels of experience)
Background and experience	Specialized accumulated knowledge or skill acquired by experience over a period of time and which is inherent in the work
Focus area	The class of output or functional area in which the role is involved
Relation to strategy	How the role connects to strategy and brings value to the enterprise
Business services	The business services in which the role participates and the nature of the participation
Task	Work that the role performs
Abstraction level	Identifies whether the context of the roles is strategic, tactical, and/or operational
Needed skill for abstraction level	Identifies the conceptual level of thinking of the role: concrete (thoughts and deeds tied to physical things), symbolic (descriptions connect to symbols that represent things which are treated as real or concrete), or conceptual (concepts that pull ideas together)
Products	The outputs of the work
Decisions	The choices the role is called upon to make
Scope	The boundary of decision making for the role
Way of governance	Objects of which the role participates in the life cycle
Life cycle phase	States within the life cycle of an object that are of concern to the role
Cross-competencies (roles)	Areas of similar background that overlap or work in conjunction with these roles

COMMON ROLES INVOLVED WITH ROLE MODELING

Now that the overall pattern or structure of a role has been given form, we can apply this knowledge to give general shape and direction to the roles needed. What is needed within BPM is the set of rights granted in a business context and supported by the skill and knowledge needed to exercise those rights, necessary to manage the business process life cycle.

Table 2 *Typical Role Categories within Enterprise Engineering, Enterprise Modeling, and Enterprise Architecture*	
Business role	A part that someone or something has in a particular function, activity, or situation
Owner role	A set of **responsibilities** assigned with the rights, competencies, and capabilities to take decisions about an object, its behavior, and properties Examples include the: • Process group owner, who is responsible for the production of value • Business process owner, who is responsible for the creation of a useable product • Process step owner, who is responsible for ensuring the process is in control • Process activity owner, who is responsible for creating value through the work • Application owner, who is responsible for decisions about an application
Process role	A prescribed set of expected **behavior** and rights (authority to act) that is meant to enable its holder to successfully carry out his or her work. Each role represents a set of allowable actions within the enterprise in terms of the rights that are required for the business to operate
Service role	A prescribed set of expected behavior and rights that is meant to enable its holder to successfully carry out his or her **accountability** in the delivery of value. Each role represents a set of allowable actions within the enterprise in terms of the rights that are required for the business to operate Examples include the: • Service owner, who is accountable for the realization of value • Client service owner, who is accountable for obtaining value
Application role	A set of rights identified as part of the allowable behavior of a software application

ROLES WITHIN BPM

The transition to an enterprise that is permanently equipped to adopt change requires the ability to manage the targeted business processes. This necessitates an increased process orientation, leading to modifications in the organizational and operational structure of the modern enterprise.[9] To capture all the roles within BPM needed to achieve this objective would necessitate a complete specification of the strategic design of the enterprise in question. It would require identification of the situation or environmental variables relevant to the enterprise and strategic response to this situation in the form of the competency group as well as the subordinate variables, strategies, and responses that generate the business competencies. Once the context for the activity of the business has been established, it would be necessary to explore the process groups and the business services necessary to address these conditions to obtain the desired economies of scale, or to address the need for robustness and other variables affecting the strategic organizational design. Only then does the context exist to expose the full set of roles necessary to realize the process design and roles required.

This design would have to integrate a number of areas of concern that an enterprise may factor into, or connect with, its capacity to steward its business processes and therefore be part of its BPM strategy. The list of the knowledge areas might include:

- Strategic planning
- Business design
- Enterprise architect
- Change management
- Configuration management
- Process management
- Project management
- Value management
- Architecture alignment
- Performance measurement

Organizationally, these roles and their involvement may vary depending on the organizational style, strategy, and other factors; however the following section provides an overview of the typical roles in a BPM (CoE).

TYPICAL BPM CoE ROLES

One of the primary areas of responsibility for the delivery element of a BPM CoE is to provide the staffing, expertise, and experience required to execute the pipeline of programs and projects within the portfolio. This requires a staffing model and a resource pool, aligned with roles in the BPM CoE.

Any staffing model for BPM projects should take into account a need for scalability to keep pace with BPM adoption across the enterprise. This scalability can be enabled by understanding the specialization of various roles involved in successfully implementing a BPM project, and the recommended level of involvement by these roles in each project. These resources are likely to start being used for multiple projects as resource demands grow for the BPM CoE.[10]

Multiple additional roles can be found in a BPM CoE. This depends on many factors such as industry, BPM CoE size, the specific mission, and the focus of the portfolio, program, and/or project. The most common BPM roles are highlighted in Figure 5.[11,12]

BPM CoE Stakeholders

The BPM stakeholders could have many roles in the organization; however, by definition of being a stakeholder, they represent someone that has an interest in the

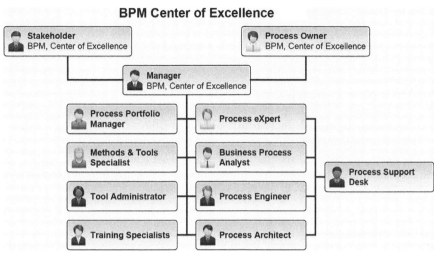

FIGURE 5

Typical business process management (BPM) CoE roles.[13]

BPM CoE. This could be for an entire portfolio or a specific program or project. No matter the position, this role is accountable for the successful initiation, implementation, and sustainability of the BPM CoE. Their responsibility is to:

- Deliver the necessary strategic guidance
- Provide direction
- Arrange alignment
- Enable funding for to the BPM CoE

Other stakeholders can, as mentioned, have an interest in a specific BPM portfolio, program, and/or project and therefore similarly advocate for these narrower areas of concern.

Process Owner

The process owner is responsible for the governance of process performance and process change and defines the process mission, vision, tactics, goals, and objectives, and selects the key performance indicators (KPIs) and measures that align with the organization's strategies. Process owners monitor and report process performance against these KPIs and on the health of execution versus plans. Furthermore, they are involved in synchronizing process improvement plans with other process owners within the value chain and other interfacing processes. Their process aim is to continuously increase the maturity of the process and sustain each level of maturity. The business process owner typically has the following role-specific responsibilities:

- Is number one cheerleader for team
- Coordinates with the business on purpose of the processes
- Has authority and accountability for current and newly developed processes
- Has end-to-end focus and responsibility
- Creates and charters team based on organization's business goals
- Appoints process team leader
- In conjunction with the process portfolio manager sets schedule for team
- Provides guidance, information, and support to team
- Meets periodically with BPM project manager for team status
- Informs other parts of organization about the BPM team's work
- Stays informed of activities happening elsewhere that may impact team's activities and coordinates between team and those activities

BPM CoE Manager

The BPM CoE manager supervises and manages all process management activities at a group or business unit level, and manages a team of business process experts that report into the BPM CoE and whose mandate is organization-wide. The BPM CoE manager should have experience with BPM methods and should be comfortable with a leadership role. The BPM CoE manager typically has the following role-specific responsibilities:

- Develop the BPM CoE strategy
- Set the BPM CoE objectives
- Business process management CoE representation to the business
- Brings BPM awareness to the business
- Work with the chief process officer
- Ensure BPM CoE funding
- Work with stakeholders to define BPM needs and wants
- Work with the BPM portfolio managers
- Provides BPM governance coordination between the process owner
- Coaches BPM CoE portfolio and project managers

Business Process Portfolio Manager

The business portfolio manager coordinates the organization-wide portfolio of projects, along with the associated alignment to organization strategy, the development of the BPM pipeline of projects, and their approval and subsequent execution in a program or project. The business process portfolio manager typically has the following role-specific responsibilities:

- Cross-functional representation
- Provides portfolio objectives
- Work with stakeholders to define BPM portfolio
- Provides consultation on process portfolio to process owner

- Provides process alignment methodology to program and project team
- Coordinates training for team
- Coaches portfolio team leader on process agenda and strategic direction
- Provides link to portfolio stakeholders
- Assists BPM team in portfolio methodology execution so that portfolio goals and milestones are met
- Brings portfolio awareness of group dynamics uses to BPM team

Process Project Manager

This role is typically a senior project manager who has experience with large projects, establishing methods, and providing governance, and quality control across multiple projects. Typically, this role is a full-time commitment. Responsibilities of the process project manager include:

- Estimates, plans, and manages the overall BPM project
- Creates, manages, and drives the BPM project methodology within the BPM CoE
- Enables the delivery team with project methods and a business value focus
- Leads the BPM Program sub-team and is a member of this sub-team
- Work with project stakeholders
- Cross-functional project representation
- Brings project awareness to BPM team

Process Expert

The process expert combines business analysis and various process subject matter expertise with enhanced process modeling skills. The role is to interpret the business requirements, and based on specific process knowledge and expert modeling skills, to develop the process models with both business and application context. The process expert typically has the following role-specific responsibilities:

- Be a subject matter expert in process-related project
- Develop input to business case for BPM project
- Analyze processes, including process landscape
- Capture process requirements
- Design processes, including process transformation and process innovation
- Build process models, e.g., BPMN
- Process deployment and rollout
- Process monitoring
- Continuous process improvement

Business Process Analyst

Business process experts work as internal process management consultants on projects and are in charge of executing BPM excellence and in rolling out BPM knowledge into all projects. They have the required expertise and skills in BPM as well as good understanding of project management. The business process analyst typically has the following role-specific responsibilities:

- Be a subject matter expert in business-related matters
- Work with the business stakeholders
- Develop the business case for BPM projects
- Participate in process analysis
- Capture business requirements
- Agree and work on process transformation and process innovation
- Work with process owners
- Business process management alignment
- Process deployment and rollout
- Continuous process improvement

Process Engineer

Process engineers focus on the design, operation, control, and optimization of business, application, and technology processes. They use specific engineering principles to enable better enterprise related processes. Process engineers typically have the following role-specific responsibilities:

- Construct and maintain the endeavor-specific process from the process landscape
- Evaluate process tools for consistency with the organizational process landscape and process life cycle and/or endeavor-specific
- Ensures that the endeavour-specific process is constructed based on endeavour-specific needs prior to process tool selection, rather than being driven by the early selection of a potentially inappropriate process tool
- Provide input to the environment team regarding required process tool support
- Provide local guidance and mentoring in the proper adoption and use of the endeavor process.
- Identify, document the enterprise's own leading practices, disseminate, and evangelize industry best practices and common best
- Work to support strategic process initiatives including recommending improvements to the organizational process framework
- Support multiple endeavors within a local region
- Staff regional process help desks
- Present local training on process-related topics
- Research advances in process engineering (e.g., new software development methods) practices

Process Architect

The process architect works with senior business stakeholders as a process linkage, structure, and change agent in shaping and fostering continuous improvement, business transformation, and business innovation initiatives related to processes. Process architects build an effective description of the structural design of the general process system for the BPM team/project that makes up the business process programs or the change programs. Process architects typically have the following role-specific responsibilities:

- Provide advice on the structure of the link between business models and process models
- Link between strategy, objectives, and process purpose and goals
- Relationship between process measurements, business reporting, and analytical decision making
- Association between business rules and process rules
- Increase the level of process automation
- Link between process flow, information flow, and service flow

Enterprise Architect

An enterprise architect is a person responsible for the organization, administration of conceptual, logical, and physical relationships and connectivity of specific objects and artifacts within and across the enterprise to each other (and the environment) to understand to enable transformation, performance, or value.

Process Support Desk

The task of the process support desk is to assist in maintaining and supporting ongoing BPM initiatives as a first line of contact to resolve BPM issues and risks that are raised against BPM operational and project-related queries. The process support desk can also be responsible for BPM issue management support, BPM governance support, and even BPM change management support.

Methods and Tools Specialist

Methods and tools specialists' role is to ensure that the correct BPM tool set is being used consistently across all projects. They share knowledge about BPM tool usage with project teams and BPM CoE members, and research and look for improvements in the current BPM tool sets and set out methods for their adoption.

Business Process Management Tool Administrator

The BPM tool administrator controls and administers management of the BPM tool set. This includes managing the authorization profiles and ensuring that business process owners maintain governance over their area of processes through the available BPM tool set.

Training Specialist

The BPM training specialists are individuals who evangelize the business with BPM understanding and knowledge transfer. They maintain the BPM training curricula and ensure that project teams have the latest information and/or updates on the BPM tools and methods.

ADDITIONAL ROLES

In the context of the enterprise, ancillary roles are not secondary roles although the actors involved may well have roles that require them to be involved in processes owing to the nature of those roles.

Overseeing the process centric roles will be the competency group owner, who is accountable for ensuring the enterprise maintains and exercises the where-withal to respond to external forces, drivers, or situations that are within the purview of the competency group. The competency group owner is answerable for achieving strategic business objectives set by the enterprise owner. As such, the competency group owner is a source of oversight on the collective process groups within the competency group, but also an escalation and exception point to ensure exception conditions for these processes are addressed in a manner con-sistent with the strategy. Similarly, the competency owner has the same account-ability and process involvement as the competency group owner, but only for their competency.

These roles become involved in process management either directly through their oversight and stewardship functions or within escalation and exception man-agement. As with the process-centric roles, these roles each may be supported by a role that administers the flow of information.

At the apex of the accountability chain is the role with the greatest scope. This, of course, is the enterprise owner, who is ultimately answerable for the strategy and alignment of the processes, for investment in their capabilities, and as the final esca-lation and oversight point.

Each of these roles will be supported by an administrative role whose purpose is to exercise the duties needed to support the affairs of the principal. It should be remembered that this generic set of roles does not imply a specific number of actors, nor does it imply anything about the organizational hierarchy; a design decision is a function of the size of the organization, its strategy, and other factors.

Such roles within the BPM CoE ensure that there is an accountability frame-work for creating decisions and determining the services, architecture, standards, and policies for continuous management of business processes. Over all, they ensure the sustainability, maturity, governance, and alignment of processes horizontally from end-to-end across the enterprise, but in a manner that ensures their connec-tion and contribution to strategy.

Specific roles actually work with the definition, categorization, and classification of roles in an organization. The role that creates and defines other roles is often found in the form of the human resource officer, whereas the roles that categorize and classify other roles in the organization are also found in the disciplines of enterprise modeling, engineering, and architecture. Table 3 gives an overview of the typical roles involved with the categorization and classification of roles in an organization.

Table 3 *Typical Roles Involved with the Definition, Categorization, and Classification of Roles in an Organization*

Enterprise Modelers	Enterprise Engineers	Enterprise Architects
Business analyst	System engineer	Business architect
Process expert	Process engineer	Process architect
Information expert	Value engineer	Service-oriented architect
Service expert	Quality engineer	Information architect
Change/transformation expert	Software engineer	Solution architect
	Technology engineer	Data architect
		Technology architect
		Enterprise architect

ROLE PROFILE WITHIN BPM CoE

Table 4 applies the role profile to record sets of rights granted the roles within the BPM CoE, the business context, and the supported skill and knowledge needed to exercise those rights required to perform the work in each of the areas.

Table 4 *Role Profile for Process Management Roles*

Feature	Description
Organizational roles	• Senior process expert and consultant • Senior process method specialist • Process engineer • Quality/production/manufacturing engineer • Junior and senior process architect
Background and experience	• Business management and business engineering
Focus area	• Identify architectural process requirements • Focus on architectural pain points and bottlenecks • Define the process architecture standards • Ensure cross-flows to process and information • Continuous architectural process optimization
Relation to strategy	• Align business processes to architectural goals • Architectural alignment based on process objectives • Link process architecture to business model transformation
Task and services	• Work with process owner • Identify cross process requirements • Categorize processes • Benchmark process architecture maturity • Define process architecture standardization and integration • Align process measures and monitoring to information

Continued

Table 4 *Role Profile for Process Management Roles—cont'd*	
Feature	**Description**
Abstraction level	• Tactical • Operational (solution specific processes)
Needed skill for abstraction level	• Concrete • Descriptive • Design
Map, matrix, and models	• Stakeholder matrix • Process owner matrix • Process requirement map and business case • Process map/matrix, and models (BPMN) • Objects matrix • Performance map, matrix, and model • Reporting matrix and model • Process roles matrix • Process rules matrix • Operating model • Business process modeling notation model • Process media and channel • Process maturity model • Process innovation and transformation matrix and model
Decisions	• Architectural requirement decisions; process, task, event, and gateways • Architecture scenario decisions; rules, flow, and measurements
Scope	• Enterprise, area, • Project • Process flow
Way of governance	• Process life cycle • Value life cycle (performance) • Transformation life cycle (optimization)
Life cycle phase	• Process analysis • Process design • Process implementation • Continuous process improvement
Cross-competencies (roles)	• Value expert • Service expert • Process architect

ROLE PROFILE WITHIN BPM PROJECTS

In BPM projects, these role profiles can be applied in various forms depending on their business context in terms of title, roles, and responsibility. Thus, in addition to the role categorizations and classifications specified in Table 4, we suggest specifying the various forms the BPM roles could have in the various projects. This includes, as illustrated in Table 5, specification of the project title, roles and responsibility in the project.

Table 5 *Example of Project Role Specification*		
Project Title	**Project Role**	**Project Responsibilities**
<Title>	<Role>	• <Responsibility>
<Title>	<Role>	• <Responsibility>
<Title>	<Role>	• <Responsibility>
<Title>	<Role>	• <Responsibility>
<Title>	<Role>	• <Responsibility>

CONCLUSION

We have shown that the concept of "role" is separate and distinct from the persons or things that access the rights and perform its responsibilities. We have shown that as a set of rights granted in a business context and supported by the skill and knowledge needed to exercise those rights, a role can be treated and managed as a conceptual thing of significance in the design of enterprises and organizations.

We have applied a standard way of thinking, working, modeling, and governing to the exploration of the nature of roles to create a standard and repeatable method for identifying, characterizing, and documenting roles, and then applied this approach to finding and describing the roles needed within the BPM CoE.

End Notes

1. Newman J., Rhona Newman, "Role, Right and Rationality in the Business Process," in *ElnfUhrung yon CSCW-Systemen in Organlsationen*, ed. Ulrich Hasenkamp (Braunschweig/Wiesbaden: © Friedr. Vieweg & Sohn Verlagsgesellschaft mbH, 1994).
2. Jaques E., Requisite Organization.
3. Body of Knowledge (BABOK)™.
4. Version 9.1 "Enterprise Edition".
5. LEAD Object Definitions.
6. John A. Zachman, *Conceptual, Logical, Physical: It Is Simple*.
7. http://www.modernanalyst.com/Careers/InterviewQuestions/tabid/128/ID/1197/How-do-you-define-a-role.aspx.
8. http://www.globaluniversityalliance.net/research-areas/industry-standards/.
9. Stefan Eicker, Jessica Kochbeck and Peter M. Schuler, Employee Competencies for Business Process Management (University of Duisburg-Essen).
10. Lisa Dyer, Andrew Forget, Fahad Osmani, Jonas Zahn, *Creating a BPM Center of Excellence (CoE) IBM Redbooks* (2013), www.ibm/redbooks.
11. Taken from the Business Process Reference Content LEAD-ES20005BP.
12. Taken from the Process Architecture Reference Content LEAD-ES40004BP.
13. LEADing Practice Business Process Reference Content #LEAD-ES20005BP.

Working with the Business Process Management (BPM) Life Cycle

Mark von Rosing, Ulrik Foldager, Maria Hove, Joshua von Scheel,
Anette Falk Bøgebjerg

INTRODUCTION

Business processes are collections of one or more linked activities that realize a business objective or policy goal, such as fulfilling a business contract and/or satisfying a specific customer need. The life cycle of a business process involves everything from setting up process goals and requirements, capturing the process in a computerized representation, as well as automating the process. This typically includes specific steps for measuring, evaluating, and improving the process. Currently, commercially available workflow management systems (WFMSs) and business process modeling tools (BPMTs) provide for complementary aspects of business process life-cycle management.

Furthermore, new concepts and interoperating tools in these categories are emerging to provide comprehensive support for managing the entire business process life cycle. In this chapter, we provide an overview and an evaluation of the Process Life Cycle phases, as well as details around process modeling, analysis, automation, and coordination capabilities. The life cycle represents the course of developmental changes through which the process evolves in terms of transformation and/or innovation as it passes through six different phases during its lifetime. From process analysis, design, construction, deployment, implementation, as well as governance and continuous improvement. The life cycle helps guide the practitioner to complete categorizations of process areas and groups, mapping of processes, their steps, activities, operations, improvements, and planned changes for the future by using change management as the driving force in the project.

The Process Life Cycle consists of a set of steps and phases in which each step and phase uses the results of the previous one. It provides a highly useful sequence of actions that any Business Analyst, Process Expert, Process Engineer, Process Architect, Business Architect, and/or Enterprise Architect can follow during any process-oriented projects. This can be used in combination of various process methods and approaches such as Business Process Reengineering (BPR), Business Process Management (BPM), Lean, and Six Sigma exist today, but no end-to-end BPM Life-cycle models have been developed in the market thus far. However, parts of the BPM Life Cycle can be found within Control Objectives for Information and related Technology (COBIT) and Information Technology Infrastructure Library (ITIL) v2 and v3, which are both Application and Service Life-cycle concepts, but they concentrate only very little on process maturity and the architectural aspects of processes.

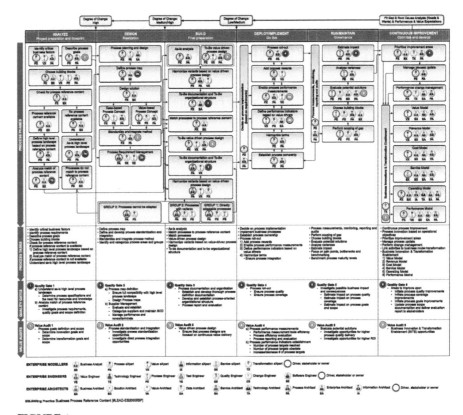

FIGURE 1

The BPM Life Cycle at a glance.

Ref. 1.

The proposed BPM Life Cycle concept interlinks with, and can be integrated with, the previously mentioned life cycles and helps practitioners place focus on all process-relevant aspects from business and application requirements to process modeling, engineering and architecture (see Figure 1).

PHASE 1: ANALYZE—PROJECT PREPARATION AND BLUEPRINT

The ultimate goal when we model business processes is to describe what the business does in a hierarchy of detail from the top level down to the level at which documents and other types of specific information components become visible. When we analyze processes, the information we discover will come from many sources and at many levels of abstraction and granularity. This information helps ensure consistency and completeness if we try to answer the same questions for each process that we encounter throughout the process landscape. In this context,

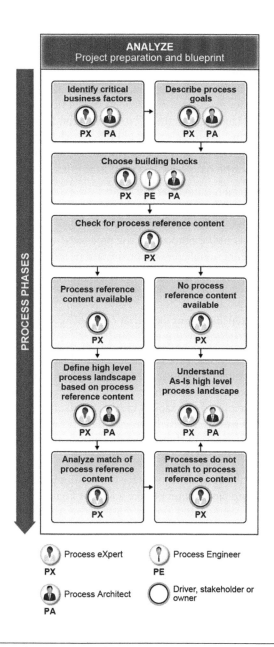

FIGURE 2

The Analyze phase of the BPM Life Cycle.

Ref. 2.

process analysis is a step-by-step breakdown of all the relevant aspects, including inputs, outputs, and the BPM Center of Excellence (CoE) operations that take place during the phase.

As an example, if our goals are strategic, we would be taking a top-down approach and interviewing senior executives or managers with a holistic and big picture view of an organization to identify the critical business factors and the process goals. Process recognition on this level tends to yield processes that are very abstract or very generic, partitioning activity into large, goal-oriented chunks. Among the questions, the answers for which describe processes at this level, are:

- What are the critical business factors?
- Which processes exist?
- What are the names of the processes?
- What are the goals and/or purposes of the processes?
- What industries, functional areas, or organizations are involved with the processes?
- Who are the stakeholders, owners, and/or participants in the processes?
- What is the process landscape?
- Does process reference content exist that could be used?
- Do the current processes present problems?

The process analysis phase can, therefore, be used to improve understanding of how the process operates, determine potential targets for process alignment with business goals, and identify increasing efficiency. Asking questions and recording their answers in a disciplined way rapidly creates a web of related information about interconnected processes from which we can develop models. The various BPM roles will get more information that is useful if they both ask questions and record the answers, using;

1. a standard vocabulary and definitions for the various process concepts described (see the BPM Ontology chapter or take a look at Figure 3).
2. process reference content that already exists within the domain in which the organization is working [3].

In this chapter, we will show the kinds of reference content that already exist. The 1st phase, the Process Analysis Phase (see Figure 2), is the phase in which the organization's processes are analyzed, captured, and defined based on the business goals and specific process requirements (e.g., business needs and wants), as well as on any interlinked business and process demands. Process goals and detailed process requirements are defined, choices are clarified through blueprinting, and the initial process maps are populated with the identified processes. Traditional output of the analyze phase would be problem analysis, As-Is analysis, measurement analysis, as well as establishment of business goals. This phase includes a link to change management and the continuous improvement loop through change management of the BPM Life Cycle. The degree of changes made during this phase is considered high.

Process Lifecycle Verb Taxonomy

ANALYZE	DESIGN	BUILD	DEPLOY/IMPLEMENT	RUN/MAINTAIN	CONT. IMPROVEMENT
Analyze	Aim	Accept	Accomplish	Administer	Adjust
Appraise	Align	Adapt	Achieve	Assign	Alter
Approximate	Arrange	Assemble	Activate	Audit	Amend
Ascertain	Begin	Assure	Apply	Calculate	Boost
Assess	Blueprint	Build	Assimilate	Chronicle	Change
Capture	Categorize	Chart	Carry out	Communicate	Condense
Clarify	Characterize	Check	Cause	Conserve	Convert
Collate	Classify	Codify	Close	Control	Coordinate
Collect	Cluster	Combine	Complete	Engage	Correct
Consider	Commence	Compile	Conclude	Exchange	Decrease
Count	Compare	Compose	Conduct	Fix	Diminish
Demand	Convene	Configure	Conform	Govern	Eliminate
Detain	Describe	Confirm	Deliver	Handle	Enhance
Detect	Design	Constitute	Deploy	Keep	Escalate
Diagnose	Determine	Construct	Do	Maintain	Improve
Discover	Devise	Craft	Educate	Manage	Incorporate
Estimate	Display	Create	Employ	Measure	Moderate
Evaluate	Draft	Customize	Evolve	Monitor	Modernize
Examine	Draw	Define	Execute	Operate	Modify
Explore	Drive	Develop	Finish	Oversee	Optimize
Find out	Enter	Enact	Generate	Preserve	Realign
Forecast	Enumerate	Enlarge	Get done	Process	Reassess
Formulate	Establish	Erect	Implement	Oversee	Reconsider
Gage	Form	Expand	Include	Promote	Redevelop
Gather	Format	Extend	Initiate	Protect	Redirect
Gauge	Found	Fabricate	Instigate	Reconcile	Redraft
Identify	Idea	Increase	Integrate	Record	Reduce
Inspect	List	Itemize	Interlink	Recover	Reevaluate
Investigate	Negotiate	Make	Launch	Register	Reexamine
Judge	Obtain	Manufacture	Migrate	Reintroduce	Reform
Learn	Organize	Match	Perform	Report	Refresh
Observe	Outline	Pilot	Present	Respond	Regulate
Recognize	Plan	Procure	Progression	Retain	Renew
Reflect on	Plot	Provide	Put into action	Retire	Renovate
Research	Prepare	Purchase	Put into operation	Run	Reorganize
Review	Prioritize	Raise	Put into service	Save	Reprioritize
Revise	Propose	Rank	Realize	Service	Restore
Search	Quantify	Scan	Reallocate	Set up	Restructure
See	Recommend	Secure	Set off	Supervise	Revert
Seek out	Select	Shape	Shift	Support	Revolutionize
Study	Sketch	Systemize	Teach	Turn on	Rework
Survey	Start	Test	Train	Update	Standardize
Think about	Suggest	Translate	Transfer	Uphold	Transfigure
Understand	Verify	Unify	Transition	Withdraw	Transform

FIGURE 3

The process life-cycle verb taxonomy model can be used to help identify the terminology associated with the organization's BPM life cycle around analyzing, designing, building, implementing, running, and improving business processes.

Ref. 4.

Step 1: Identify Critical Business Factors

To identify and define process goals effectively, an organization must first and foremost identify the existence and possible impact of any internal and external value and performance drivers and how they relate to the critical business factors. This is primarily done to identify the drivers for change, plan for the requirements, identify the resources needed, and relate to the process landscape the most critical business factors that are expected to impact the organization. For the most part, this step typically involves identifying both the internal and external value and performance drivers that may impact the design and creation of new business processes and/or to create an effective and reliable environment in which to support an eventual reengineering of existing processes. The output of step 1 is consumed by step 2.

Typical tasks that are done within this step:

- Identify which critical value and performance drivers are impacting and/or influencing the process landscape
- Prioritize value and performance drivers based on level of impact, severity, and/or urgency
- Associate the value and performance drivers to the critical success factors (CSFs) of the various business areas/groups (based on level of opportunity, priority, and/or importance)

Typical templates that are used:

- Forces and Drivers Map
- Vision, Mission and Goals Map
- Stakeholder Map

Typical BPM CoE roles involved:

- Process Experts/Business Analysts
- Value Experts
- Process Architects

Step 2: Describe Process Goals

Process goals have to be clearly defined, documented, and agreed upon by stakeholders, process owners, and all involved process roles of the organization. Defining the process goals of the organization is the natural continuation from the identification of critical business factors, as those are the main tools—and critical for the goal descriptions—to compare against process goals and plan and prepare for the upcoming design and construction phases of the life cycle. Many BPM CoE organizations are in the habit of working with process goals and, in many cases, it is business as usual to define and document them. Among typical process goals are reducing complexity, aligning processes, identifying duplication, creating new processes by which new business goals are supported, or removing business bottlenecks through automation. Process goals can, however, also link to very multifaceted business innovation and transformation initiatives and therefore be difficult and complex to relate to individual processes. More on how this is done is found in the value-driven process design.

The output of step 2 is consumed by multiple other steps, such as:

- Step 6 to lay the foundation of goals and requirements for the upcoming process planning and design steps, and then moves back again to step 3.
- Step 12 for the purpose of identifying and defining both the high-level requirements as well as the detailed requirements of the entire process landscape of the organization.

Typical tasks that are done within this step:

- Develop the process goals based on the specific critical business factors
- Develop process goals based on the business innovation and transformation initiatives
- Split process goals to specific main, supporting, and management processes
- Define and document process goals
- Relate and connect all of the defined process goals to established business, application, and technology goals.

Typical templates that are used:

- Vision, Mission, and Goals Map and/or Matrix
- Stakeholder Map and/or Matrix
- Process Map

Typical BPM CoE roles involved:

- Process eXperts/Business Analysts
- Process Architects

Value Audit 1:

- Process goals definition and scope
- Determine innovation goals and scope
- Determine transformation goals and scope

Step 3: Choose Building

Similar to software development, for example, building blocks are reusable pieces of content. In BPM, the most common building blocks would be strategic, organizational, process, and technology contexts. The following is an example of typical BPM Building Blocks and thereby reusable aspects that need to be considered again and again (Figure 4).

Choosing the right building blocks for the creation of new business processes or relating to strategy, and linking to organizational context or technology automation are daunting tasks for any BPM CoE organization. These choices should always be based upon review, identification, and documentation of the current baseline

STRATEGIC CONTEXT		ORGANIZATIONAL CONTEXT		PROCESS CONTEXT		TECHNOLOGY CONTEXT	
Strategy	Principles & Rules	Organization	Guidelines & Standards	Business Processes	Process Development	IT Operations	IT Enablement
Vision & Mission	Stakeholder Management	Organizational Structure	Organizational Interaction	Process Models	Process Owner	IT Management	IT Enablement
Market Approach	Business Issues / Problem Chain	Critical Success Factors	Business Governance	Pain Chain	Process Governance	IT Operations	IT Business Model
Strategic Business Objectives	Operating Model	Roles & Tasks	Reward & Motivation	Business Process Execution	Process Performance Indicators	End-user Focus IT Support	IT Documentation
Business Model	Business Value Management	Key Performance Indicators	Program Management	Process Drivers	Process-based Rewards	Software Capabilities / Competencies	IT Standardization
Strategy Map	Value Audits	Change Management	Change Policy	Process Audits	Process Domains	Application Lifecycle Management	IT Integration
Value Map	Value Clusters	Information Need	Business Competency Modelling	Process Policies	IT Process Parameters	Service Orientation Competencies	IT Process Flow
Scorecards	Business Performance Management	Goal Chain	Portfolio Management	Process Measurements	Process Architecture	IT Governance	Process Means / Tools
Enterprise Value Architecture	Business Maturity Models	Training & Education	Organizational Maturity Models	Continuous Improvement	Process Maturity Models	Service Level Agreement	Technology Maturity Models

FIGURE 4

Example of BPM building blocks.

Ref. 5.

(including all of the systems that are already involved with the process landscape) of the organization, and then executing the choices from a perspective of the needed functionality that is required to create new or to re-engineer any existing processes.

The output of step 3 is by step 4.

Typical tasks that are done within this step:

- Identification of relevant building blocks
- Alignment and unification of building blocks across areas
- Review and document current baseline and compare viewpoints of possible solutions

Typical templates that are used:

- Process Map and/or Matrix
- Object Map and/or Matrix
- Service Map and/or Matrix
- Application Service Map and/or Matrix
- Data Service Map and/or Matrix

Typical BPM CoE roles involved:

- Process eXperts
- Business Analysts
- Value eXperts

- Process Engineers
- Process Architects

Step 4: Check for Process Reference Content

Today, most BPM CoE organizations already have a process landscape. The process landscape might not be very well defined or documented, however, and to define the expectations and purpose of both new and existing processes, it is essential to clearly define and document the existing process landscape of the organization. This is achieved through extensive process mapping across all business units, and through meticulous and detailed documentation work. The documentation and mapping task is likely going to require a substantial number of man-hours to allow both process owners and the involved process roles to get an established overview of the "As-Is" situation. It also enables decision makers to make their decisions based on which processes to create and/or reuse (Figure 5).

The output of step 4 is consumed by step 4a (if any process reference content is available) and step 5 (if no currently available process reference content).

Typical tasks that are done within this step:

- Review the existing process portfolio for any available process reference content

Typical templates that are used:

- Information Map and/or Matrix
- Process Map and/or Matrix
- Object Map and/or Matrix
- Service Map and/or Matrix

Typical BPM CoE roles involved:

- Process eXperts
- Business Analysts

Step 4a: Process Reference Content Available

If process content is available for the BPM CoE organization to re-use within the existing process landscape, the process reference content should be clearly identified, reviewed, documented, and prepared for evaluation at the time of analysis and comparison to the existing process landscape. The output of step 4a is consumed by step 4b.

Typical tasks that are done within this step:

- Identify and review the current process reference content
- Document (as needed) and prepare the current process reference content for analysis and comparison

Typical templates that are used:

- Information Map and/or Matrix
- Process Map and/or Matrix

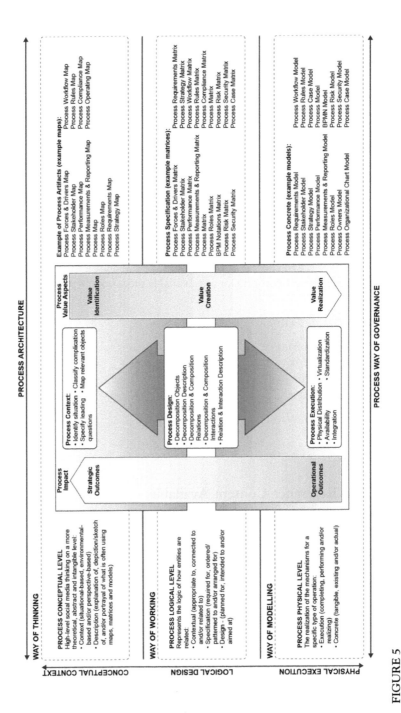

FIGURE 5

Example of a model showing how and when the different parts (maps, matrices, and models) of process reference content is used across the Layered Process Architecture of an organization.

- Object Map and/or Matrix
- Service Map and/or Matrix

  Typical BPM CoE roles involved:

- Process eXperts
- Business Analysts

Step 4b: Define High-Level Process Landscape Based on Process Reference Content

The definition of a high-level process landscape includes using architecture standards and creating relationships between the different process levels used by the organization. The high-level process landscape is often referred to as the Value Chain View, and is a visualization of a process that is used to illustrate how an organization's business units (both primary and supporting) work together to facilitate and execute the organization's business model. The high-level process landscape of an organization is typically used as a tool for setting a standard for how the rest (when diving deeper into the detailed view of the process landscape) of the organization is expected to (and should) use processes. The output of step 4b is consumed by step 4c.

Typical tasks that are done within this step:

- Define the high-level process landscape by defining the objectives and intended content of process areas and process groups (process levels 1–2)
- Define and document the main process areas (process level 1) and process groups (process level 2)
- Define and document the management process areas (process level 1) and process groups (process level 2)
- Define and document the supporting process areas (process level 1) and process groups (process level 2)

  Typical templates that are used:

- Information Map and/or Matrix
- Requirement Map and/or Matrix
- Role Map and/or Matrix
- Owner Map and/or Matrix
- Process Map and/or Matrix
- Object Map and/or Matrix
- Service Map and/or Matrix
- Application Service Map and/or Matrix
- Data Service Map and/or Matrix

  Typical BPM CoE roles involved:

- Process eXperts
- Process Architects

Step 4c: Analyze Match of Process Reference Content

When moving towards the analysis of the process reference content that is available, and when comparing it to the existing process landscape, it is important to draw upon the documentation work done during steps 4a and 4b. Also note that the analysis of all of the processes of the organization is likely to become a very time-consuming process in itself, although much of the work has already been done during the previous review and documentation steps. This analysis and comparison focuses almost exclusively on extracting knowledge, know-how, efficiencies, advantages, and other benefits and nuggets of wisdom that might somehow aid the BPM CoE organization in creating new processes in the future, or to prepare them for process optimization through process reengineering. The output of step 4c is consumed by step 4d. It is important to note, however, that the output of step 4c may (if wanted or deemed required) be consumed directly by step 18 to immediately begin matching existing processes to the available process reference content.

Typical tasks that are done within this step:

- Select the process reference content that *cannot* be used within the currently established process landscape
- Categorize the main, supporting, and management business processes from the process reference content that *can* be used within the currently established process landscape

Typical templates that are used:

- Information Map and/or Matrix
- Process Map and/or Matrix
- Object Map and/or Matrix
- BPM Notations Map and/or Matrix
- Application Service Map and/or Matrix
- Data Service Map and/or Matrix

Typical BPM CoE roles involved:

- Process eXperts
- Business Analysts

Quality Gate 1b:

- Analyze match of process reference content
- Undergo detailed comparison of process reference content to the existing process landscape
- Investigate process requirements, quality goals, and scope definition

Step 4d: Processes That Do Not Match Process Reference Content

Based on the analysis of process during step 4c, there will be a need to collect and gather the processes that do not match the current process reference content. In this regard, it is necessary to thoroughly examine these processes for the purpose of discarding them entirely based on the process goals and the newly defined high-level process landscape, or to prepare them for any reengineering purposes. The output of step 4d is consumed by step 4e.

Typical tasks that are done within this step:

- Collect and gather existing processes that do not match the available process reference content
- Examine and document the processes that do not match the available process reference content

Typical templates that are used:

- Information Map and/or Matrix
- Process Map and/or Matrix
- Object Map and/or Matrix
- BPM Notations Map and/or Matrix
- Application Service Map and/or Matrix
- Data Service Map and/or Matrix

Typical BPM CoE roles involved:

- Process eXperts
- Business Analysts

Step 4e: Understand As-Is High-Level Process Landscape

If no current process reference content is available or if the current process landscape does not match the existing process reference content, it is essential to generate a mutual understanding throughout the organization of the current As-Is high-level process landscape. The output of step 4e is consumed by step 7, yet step 6 is preceded by step 5 that focuses entirely on process planning and design.

Typical tasks that are done within this step:

- High-level process landscape identification and documentation
- Teams must collaborate and spread awareness of the current As-Is process situation
- Examine process requirements and resources needed
- Identify and categorize the main process areas and process groups
- Identify and categorize the management process areas and process groups
- Identify and categorize the supporting process areas and process groups

Typical templates that are used:

- Information Map and/or Matrix
- Process Map and/or Matrix
- Object Map and/or Matrix
- Service Map and/or Matrix

Typical BPM CoE roles involved:

- Process eXperts
- Process Architects

Quality Gate 1a:

- Understand As-Is high-level process landscape
- Determine process specifications and the need for resources and knowledge

Step 5: No Process Reference Content Available

If no current process reference content is available for the organization to further build upon, the output of step 5 is consumed by step 4e.

Typical tasks that are done within this step:

- Examine availability of process reference content
- Research for resources of knowledge, know-how, and firmly established best and leading practices to support the creation and/or reengineering of processes

Typical templates that are used:

- Information Map and/or Matrix
- Process Map and/or Matrix
- Object Map and/or Matrix
- BPM Notations Map and/or Matrix
- Application Service Map and/or Matrix
- Data Service Map and/or Matrix

Typical BPM CoE roles involved:

- Process eXperts
- Business Analysts

In the first phase of the BPM Life Cycle, we focused on the identification of critical business factors, description of process goals, and choosing the correct building blocks for the upcoming design phase. We also put much of our effort on process analysis and checking whether any process reference content was currently available. In the next phase of the BPM Life Cycle, the Design phase, we will begin designing our process solutions through planning, definitions, requirements, and standardization (Figure 6).

PHASE 2: DESIGN—PROJECT REALIZATION AND DESIGN

Business process design is the method by which an organization understands and defines the business activities that enable it to function. Process design is concerned with designing business processes to ensure that they are optimized, effective, meet customer requirements and demands, and support and sustain organizational development and growth. A well-designed process will improve efficiency, deliver greater

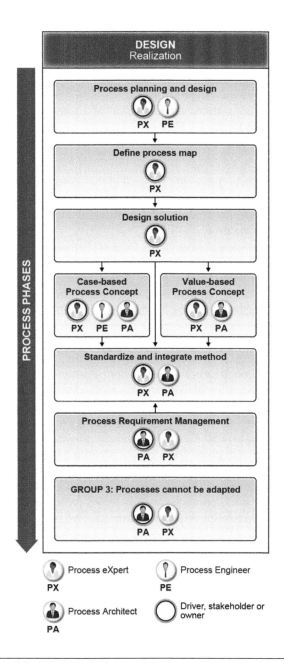

FIGURE 6

The Design Phase of the BPM Life Cycle.

Ref. 7.

productivity, and create more business value.[8] The most common initiatives behind business process design projects are:

- customer and supply chain management;
- operational performance improvement;
- business process integration, standardization, and automation;
- cost reduction; and
- creating new business opportunities.

Business process design typically occurs as an early, critical phase in BPM projects, rather than as an end in itself. The goal of the overall project is to implement business change, whether that change is primarily organizational (improving business operating processes), technical (implementing or integrating software systems), or a combination of the two.

In a process improvement project, the focus of the business process design phase is to streamline the process: to understand and measure the requirements, and to eliminate the risk of losing value through inefficient or inappropriate activities. In a technology implementation project, the focus is on understanding the processes that are being automated, and ensuring that the appropriate technology is selected, configured, and implemented to support them. In both cases, the process design activities can range from modest (e.g., tweak existing processes and look for some quick wins) to aggressive (e.g., identify major opportunities to increase value or drive down costs through radical process improvement or outsourcing). In short, business process design is a tool that can serve many different kinds of projects.

The 2nd phase, the Process Design Phase (see Figure 6), is the phase in which the BPM CoE organization initiates, aligns, arranges, categorizes, defines, determines, as well as quantifies, drafts, outlines, and designs the processes and the process structures. The process design phase considers the identified business requirements and the specific process design considerations for the processes, steps, and activities, as well as events and gateways. Relating requirements and goals to the identified processes applies composition principles and, therefore, process matrices are created to assist project teams in relating the relevant aspects. This phase also includes change management aspects of the defined process innovation and/or transformation. The continuous improvement feedback loop through change management of the BPM Life Cycle, and the likelihood of changes made during this phase, is considered to be medium/high.

Step 6: Process Planning and Design

As a direct continuation from defining and describing the overall process goals, planning and design steps are initiated with the purpose of designing new processes from scratch and/or plan the redesign and reengineering requirements of existing processes. The level of detail in this area is also increased dramatically, as the design process slowly moves away from the high-level process landscape and into a much more detailed process landscape (Figure 7).

The output of step 6 is consumed by step 7.
Typical tasks that are done within this step:

- Determine the need for new main, management, and/or supporting (classification of) processes
- Organize and structure process hierarchy
- Determine and define each required process level
- Gather and categorize process steps, process activities, and events and gateways
- Collect information around process meta objects

Process Workflow Connection Diagram

	STRATEGIC					TACTICAL												OPERATIONAL											
	1	2	3	4	5	6	7	8	9	10	11	12	13	14	15	16	17	18	19	20	21	22	23	24	25	26	27	28	29
1. Strategy (S)	x	x	x	x	x					x				x															
2. Plan (S)	x	x		x						x		x	x	x						x									
3. Forecast (S)	x	x		x							x																		
4. Value Management (S)	x	x	x		x			x			x			x															
5. Budget (S)	x	x		x				x			x							x		x									
6. Strategic Advice (T)	x	x	x	x						x																			
7. Strategic Guidance & Compliance (T)																				x				x			x	x	
8. Monitoring (T)								x	x	x						x	x												
9. Reporting (T)	x								x						x	x	x												
10. Evaluation and/or Audit (T)																x	x												
11. Policy (T)	x	x				x	x				x	x		x	x	x	x												
12. Procedures (T)														x	x	x					x								
13. Measurements (T)							x		x							x	x												
14. Administration (T)		x																											
15. Communication (T)																													
16. Performance Management (T)	x		x				x	x	x					x	x						x								
17. Risk Management (T)		x						x																					
18. Administration (O)																				x									
19. Issue Management (O)									x													x	x		x				
20. Operational Planning (O)																		x							x				x
21. Process Management (O)																		x											x
22. Monitoring (O)									x							x						x	x	x	x	x		x	
23. Reporting (O)									x											x			x	x	x		x	
24. Evaluation and/or Audit (O)									x											x			x	x			x	
25. Measurements (O)							x		x							x				x			x	x		x		x	
26. Procedures (O)									x									x		x							x	x	
27. Operational Advice and/or Support (O)																				x	x								x
28. Operational Guidance & Compliance (O)																				x	x			x	x	x			x
29. Processing (O)																		x			x			x		x			

FIGURE 7

The process workflow connection diagram is a process matrix that shows the connectivity between the services delivered by business processes in the process landscape. This is a very powerful and important tool to use when designing an organization's business processes as it shows how strategic, tactical, and operational service deliverables relate to one another.

Ref. 9.

Typical templates that are used:

- Information Map and/or Matrix
- Process Map and/or Matrix
- Object Map and/or Matrix
- BPM Notations Map and/or Matrix
- Role Map and/or Matrix
- Owner Map and/or Matrix
- Requirement Map and/or Matrix
- Workflow Map and/or Matrix
- Application Service Map and/or Matrix
- Data Service Map and/or Matrix
- Application Rule Map and/or Matrix
- Data Rule Map and/or Matrix

Typical BPM CoE roles involved:

- Process eXperts
- Process Engineers
- Enterprise Architects

Step 7: Define Process Map

When preparing for the design of the process solution, definition of the organization's process maps, matrices, and models is needed to create a foundation upon which to build the organization's future processes. The design foundation also defines criteria for the redesign and/or reengineering of existing processes. The output of step seven is consumed by step 8.

Typical tasks that are done within this step:

- Define process content and the process maps, matrices, and models to be used
- Define relationships between process levels 1–5 and business goals and objectives
- Identify and define business process areas and groups
- Identify and define business processes, steps, and activities
- Identify and define stakeholders, process owners, managers, and roles
- Identify and define the required resources

Typical templates that are used:

- Process Map
- Service Map
- Application Service Map
- Data Service Map

Typical BPM CoE roles involved:

- Process eXperts
- Business Analysts

Quality Gate 2a:

- Process map definition
- Ensure full compatibility with high-level process landscape
- Design process maps

Step 8: Design Solution

Designing the organization's process solution is a huge task in itself, but is fully and extensively supported by the detailed process analysis and documentation done during phase 1. The process solution is designed through an extensive use of detailed process maps, matrices, and models. The process maps, matrices, and models represent information of how the processes relate to the business layer (purpose and goals, value aspects, business competencies, and business services), the application layer (software and data), as well as the underlying technology layer (platform and infrastructure) of the organization. The output of step 8 is consumed by step 9; however, if the need for business cases is present, it would be consumed by step 10, and then consumed by step 11.

Typical tasks that are done within this step:

- Develop and design process maps, matrices, and models
- Develop and design the process meta model to illustrate the connections and relationships between process meta objects and the identified business, application, and technology meta objects

Typical templates that are used:

- Information Map and/or Matrix
- Process Map and/or Matrix
- Object Map and/or Matrix
- BPM Notations Map and/or Matrix
- Role Map and/or Matrix
- Owner Map and/or Matrix
- Requirement Map and/or Matrix
- Workflow Map and/or Matrix
- Application Service Map and/or Matrix
- Data Service Map and/or Matrix
- Application Rule Map and/or Matrix
- Data Rule Map and/or Matrix

Typical BPM CoE roles involved:

- Process eXperts
- Business Analysts

Step 9: Case-Based Process Concept

While designing the process solution, it is of great importance to simultaneously develop a case-based process concept that will serve to illustrate how new processes will function in practice, and how re-engineered processes will support the objectives and goals of the organization. In reality, one may consider a case-based process concept to be constructed much like a business case, although this particular case evolves predominantly around the technical requirements, capabilities, and functionality of both the high level and the detailed process structures that are to be built for the organization. The output of step 9 is consumed by step 11, unless a business case is needed, then the output of step 9 would be consumed by step 10.

Typical tasks that are done within this step:

- Include and document process meta objects
- Include and relate process meta objects to application and technology meta objects
- Create a storyline with illustrations of graphical models that show functionality, principles, and behavior

Typical templates that are used:

- Value Map, Matrix, and/or Model
- Cost Map, Matrix, and/or Model
- Revenue Map, Matrix, and/or Model
- Competency/Business Model Map, Matrix, and/or Model
- Requirement Map, Matrix, and/or Model
- Vision, Mission and Goals Map, Matrix, and/or Model
- Stakeholder Map, Matrix, and/or Model
- Strategy Map, Matrix, and/or Model
- Case Map, Matrix, and/or Model

Typical BPM CoE roles involved:

- Process eXperts
- Process Engineers
- Process Architects

Step 10: Value-Based Process Concept

Much like a case-based process concept, the value-based process concept focuses almost exclusively on the relationship between business processes and the value concepts of the organization. It is typically created to demonstrate how processes relate specifically to each business goal and objective as well as the previously documented value and performance drivers of the organization. The output of step 10 is consumed by step 11.

Typical tasks that are done within this step:

- Relate the value objects, i.e., strategic business objectives (SBOs), critical success factors (CSFs), and performance indicators (KPIs) to the processes
- Sort processes according to the SBOs and CSFs
- Document the connection between process objects and value objects

Typical templates that are used:

- Value Map, Matrix, and/or Model
- Cost Map, Matrix, and/or Model
- Revenue Map, Matrix, and/or Model
- Competency/Business Model Map, Matrix, and/or Model
- Requirement Map, Matrix, and/or Model
- Vision, Mission and Goals Map, Matrix, and/or Model
- Stakeholder Map, Matrix, and/or Model
- Strategy Map, Matrix, and/or Model
- Case Map, Matrix, and/or Model

Typical BPM CoE roles involved:

- Value eXperts
- Process eXperts
- Process Architects

Step 11: Standardize and Integrate

Standardization and integration of the previously designed solution is a necessary step of any BPM project. The definitions have to be clearly documented to categorize which processes can, or should be, standardized, and, in continuation thereof, how they will be integrated. For clear BPM definitions, see the chapter on BPM Ontology. The standardization and integration of the processes are done in the following sequence: output of step 11 is consumed by step 14 and step 15 simultaneously to document the As-Is analysis to prepare for the creation of the To-Be value-driven process design. The output of step 11 is also consumed by step 18 for matching processes to existing reference content.

Typical tasks that are done within this step:

- Identify which processes need to be standardized and/or integrated
- Investigate and thoroughly examine available methods for standardization
- Investigate and thoroughly examine available methods for integration
- Agree on and choose best possible methods for process standardization and integration
- Standardize and integrated chosen processes
- Document changed processes

Typical templates that are used:

- Process Map, Matrix, and/or Model
- Service Map, Matrix, and/or Model
- Operating Map, Matrix, and/or Model
- Information Map, Matrix, and/or Model

Typical BPM CoE roles involved:

- Process eXperts
- Process Architects

Value Gate 2:

- Investigate process standardization opportunities
- Investigate direct process integration opportunities
- Document changed processes

Step 12: Process Requirement Management

Process requirements need to be clearly defined and documented. They are essential and critical information for the purpose of the process design solution, and will contain useful information, such as requirements around:

- Business resources/actors
- Organizational requirements (i.e., does the organization contain process-educated personnel)
- Knowledge of process architecture and process modeling
- Application-layer-specific requirements (i.e., has the process design software been decided upon, does the data support thereof exist, etc.)
- Technology-layer-specific requirements (i.e., does the platform and infrastructure inventory support the automation of processes, etc.)

For the purpose of defining and delivering process requirements for each of these steps, the output of step 12 can be simultaneously consumed by steps 15, 16, 17, and 18.

Typical tasks that are done within this step:

- Identify and categorize process requirements based on resources, business needs and wants, as well as application- and technology-layer aspects

Typical templates that are used:

- Process Map, Matrix, and/or Model
- Requirement Map, Matrix, and/or Model
- Service Map, Matrix, and/or Model
- Application Service Map and/or Matrix
- Data Service Map and/or Matrix

Typical BPM CoE roles involved:

- Process Architects
- Process eXperts
- Value eXperts

Quality Gate 2b:

- Supplier management
- Evaluate and establish
- Categorize suppliers and maintain supply chain design (SCD)
- Manage performance and renew/terminate

Step 13: Processes Cannot Be Adapted

Unadaptable processes that are encountered during the Design phase often require back stepping to step 4d to establish a new or, at the very least, an updated As-Is high-level process landscape. This proactive move enables process owners and decision makers to continuously analyze and plan for the support and requirement of substitute processes that are to be designed and built during the Design and Build phases. The output of step 13 is consumed by step 4d in the Analyze phase because these processes are evaluated as being unadaptable.

Typical tasks that are done within this step:

- Document and compile a list of processes that are expected to be re-engineered and modified to fit with the established process landscape
- Document and compile a list of unadaptable processes
- Eliminate processes that are evaluated as unusable or irrelevant to the established process landscape

Typical templates that are used:

- Process Map, Matrix, and/or Model
- Requirement Map, Matrix, and/or Model
- Information Map, Matrix, and/or Model
- Object Map, Matrix, and/or Model
- Service Map, Matrix, and/or Model

Typical BPM CoE roles involved:

- Process Architects
- Process eXperts

In the second phase of the BPM Life Cycle, we have developed process design solutions to create a strong foundation for business process development to prepare for the upcoming build phase. In the third phase of the BPM Life Cycle, the Build phase (see Figure 8), we turn our attention toward executing upon the previously defined process solution plans and framework based upon the As-Is situation, aiming toward a To-Be value-driven process design. We will be matching existing processes to any available process reference content, and harmonize variants, while documenting changes prior to process release and going live.

PHASE 3: BUILD—FINAL PROJECT PREPARATION

Process models (on all process levels 1–5) are created as flow charts to give a clear, graphical indication of *what* happens *when*.

High-level process models (process levels 1–2)—usually referred to as Value Chain Diagrams (VCDs)—are used to illustrate how primary and supporting (secondary) business units work together to fulfill one or more specific goals. A value chain is then a chain of activities that an organization performs to deliver a product or a service to the customer (whether internal or external).

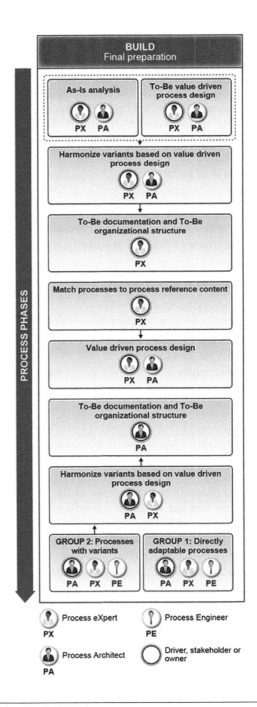

FIGURE 8

The Build phase of the BPM Life Cycle.

Ref. 10.

Business process models (process level 3) are used to demonstrate the activities of an organization or within or around a specific project team (they can also move across multiple business units), such as planning activities, people's actions (what they do), and reactions (internal and/or external outputs) necessary to carry out given tasks within the organization. Creating a business model can, for an example, give the employees of an organization an easy-to-use reference guide that outlines the tasks that they are expected to carry out, including their responsibilities and the steps necessary to complete each task correctly and proficiently.

Business Process Modeling Notation (BPMN) models (process levels 4 and 5) is a standard for business process modeling that provides a graphical notation for specifying business processes in a Business Process Diagram (BPD), based on a flowcharting technique very similar to activity diagrams from Unified Modeling Language (UML). The objective of BPMN is to support business process management for both technical and business users, by providing notation that is intuitive to business users, yet able to represent complex process semantics. The BPMN specification also provides a mapping between the graphics of the notation and the underlying constructs of execution languages, particularly Business Process Execution Language (BPEL).

The primary goal of BPMN is to provide a standard notation readily understandable by all stakeholders. These include the process experts, process engineers, and process architects who create and refine the processes, the technical developers (process engineers and process architects) responsible for implementing them, and the business managers (process owners, process experts, process architects, and business analysts) who monitor and manage them. Consequently, BPMN serves as a common language, bridging the communication gap that frequently occurs between business process design, development, execution, monitoring and optimization.

Regardless of whether a business process model's level (levels 1–5, the higher the more detailed, i.e., levels 4 and 5 are considered BPMN diagrams), the same rules apply to all process models.

A business process, therefore:

1. Has a goal.
2. Has specific inputs.
3. Has specific outputs.
4. Uses resources.
5. Has a number of activities that are performed in some order.
6. May affect more than one organizational unit.
7. Creates value of some kind for the customer (internal or external).

The 3rd phase, the Process Build Phase (see Figure 8), is the phase in which the BPM CoE organization builds, creates, develops, and crafts the processes and the process structures of the organization (see Figure 9). The process build phase takes into account the identified business requirements and the different process design solutions that have been generated for the purpose of process construction.

This phase is where the process models are created. This phase also includes change management aspects of the To-Be process innovation and/or transformation enabled in the value-driven process design. The continuous improvement feedback loop through change management of the BPM Life Cycle, and the degree of changes made during this phase, is considered low/medium.

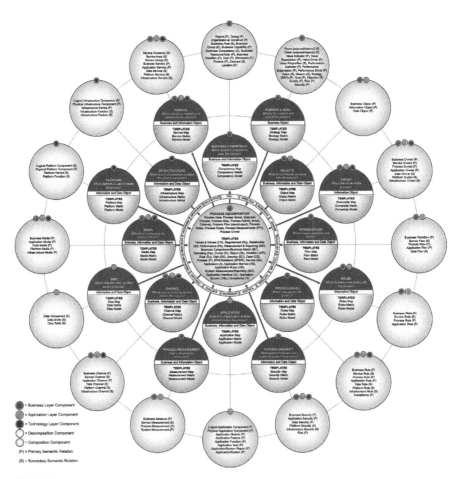

FIGURE 9

The process decomposition and composition model is used to show which meta-objects are combined when building (composing) a business process and which meta-objects are extracted by disassembling (decomposing) a business process. This particular illustration shows intricate detail, as it also connects each specific process-related area with which type of objects (business, information, and data) are used in the creation process. Not only that, it also shows whether the semantic relation between the related meta-objects is primary (required) or secondary (optional).

Ref. 11.

Step 14: As-Is Analysis

The As-Is analysis of the currently developed process design serves as a staging point for creating the To-Be value-driven process design. In today's organizations, the focus on getting the most value out of the process requires understanding the as-is situation and thereby understanding the different capabilities. The output of step 14 is consumed by step 16.

Typical tasks that are done within this step:

- Conduct thorough process analysis across the current process landscape
- Specify which processes should be blueprinted (as-is blueprint) for the build phase
- Put the As-Is situation into BPM Notations
- Identify which challenges correspond to the processes

Typical templates that are used:

- Process Map, Matrix, and/or Model
- Information Map, Matrix, and/or Model
- Object Map, Matrix, and/or Model
- Service Map, Matrix, and/or Model
- BPM Notations Map, Matrix, and/or Model
- Application Service Map and/or Matrix
- Data Service Map and/or Matrix

Typical BPM CoE roles involved:

- Process eXperts
- Process Architects

Step 15: To-Be Value-Driven Process Design

Value-driven process design has but a single focus point; to create and build processes that generate and deliver previously unacquired value to the company and its customers or to enhance already established processes that have been re-engineered to produce even more value than before. The output of step 15 is consumed by step 16.

Typical tasks that are done within this step:

- Align value objects (based on step 10) with the defined process goals
- Sort processes according to the SBOs and CSFs
- Focus on the creation of process designs that put process objects into relationships with value objects across the organization
- Focus on value designs shaped by process structures
- Model the process based on relationships and connectivity between process and value objects
- Identify duplication of processes, business functions, and services
- Review and document current baseline and compare viewpoints of possible solutions

Typical templates that are used:

- Process Map, Matrix, and/or Model
- Information Map, Matrix, and/or Model
- Object Map, Matrix, and/or Model
- Service Map, Matrix, and/or Model
- BPM Notations Map, Matrix, and/or Model
- Value Map, Matrix, and/or Model
- Application Service Map and/or Matrix
- Data Service Map and/or Matrix

Typical BPM CoE roles involved:

- Process eXperts
- Value eXperts
- Process Architects

Value Gate 3:

- Value-driven process design
- Ensure that process designs are focused on continuous value delivery

Step 16: Harmonize Variants Based on Value-Driven Process Design

In the context of Business Process Management, harmonization defines the extent of standards and how they fit together, but it does not attempt to make different standards uniform. Harmonization avoids a one-size-fits-all approach. It makes the trade-off between too many and too few process standards and avoids inconsistencies between standards.[12] The output of step 16 is consumed by step 17.

Typical tasks that are done within this step:

- Identify, assess, and establish process level commonality across the organization
- Identify, assess, and establish process harmonization opportunities across the organization
- Identify, assess, and establish process standardization opportunities across the organization

Typical templates that are used:

- Process Map, Matrix, and/or Model
- Information Map, Matrix, and/or Model
- Object Map, Matrix, and/or Model
- Service Map, Matrix, and/or Model
- BPM Notations Map, Matrix, and/or Model
- Value Map, Matrix, and/or Model
- Application Service Map and/or Matrix
- Data Service Map and/or Matrix

Typical BPM CoE roles involved:

- Process eXperts
- Process Architects
- Value eXperts

Step 17: To-Be Documentation and To-Be Organizational Structure

The To-Be definitions of the process, its structure, and how it relates to the organizational structure (the As-Is as well as the To-Be) is relevant to both the process designs as well as the innovation and transformation potential of the organization. The way this is done is to:

1. Relate it through the process maps and process matrices to processes on all 5 levels:
   a. Process Level 1: Process Areas
   b. Process Level 2: Process Groups
   c. Process Level 3: Business Processes
   d. Process Level 4: Process Steps
   e. Process Level 5: Process Activities (including sub-processes)
2. Adapt the BPM Notations based on the To-Be changes

   The output of step 17 is consumed by step 21.
   Typical tasks that are done within this step:

- Document process direction and organizational structure
- Document high-level To-Be process landscape
- Document detailed To-Be process landscape
- Document process descriptions and technicalities

Typical templates that are used:

- Process Map and/or Matrix
- Organizational Chart Map and/or Matrix
- Service Map and/or Matrix

Typical BPM CoE roles involved:

- Process eXperts
- Enterprise Architects

Quality Gate 3:

- Process documentation and organization
- Establish and develop thorough process definition documentation
- Develop and establish process-oriented organizational structure
- Process report and evaluation

Step 18: Match Processes to Process Reference Content

Matching of existing processes to any available process reference content of the organization is required. This enables process owners and other organizational roles to reduce the number of processes that are used by the organization, and to lessen the chance of overly complex process portfolios in the process landscape. The output of step 17 is consumed by step 15.

Typical tasks that are done within this step:

- Compare existing processes to the process reference content (if any)
- Chose relevant process reference content
- Tailor process reference content
- Agree and align tailor process reference content with own process content

Typical templates that are used:

- Process Map and/or Matrix
- Service Map and/or Matrix
- Object Map and/or Matrix
- Application Service Map and/or Matrix
- Data Service Map and/or Matrix

Typical BPM CoE roles involved:

- Process eXperts
- Business Analysts

Step 19: Processes with Variants

If the initiation of a BPM Life-cycle project has been decided upon and is to be carried out with the intent of updating, reengineering, and/or re-evaluating an already established existing process landscape, processes with different variants will likely already exist in multiple places within the organization. Therefore, it is essential that such processes are identified, accounted for, and re-engineered through process variant harmonization to support the goals of the value-driven process design that has previously been decided upon by the management. In this regard, see step 16. Step 19 is grouped with steps 13 and 20, and relates directly to the process reference content in Phase 1: Analyze. The output of step 19 is consumed by step 16.

Typical tasks that are done within this step:

- Identify and document processes with variants
- Outline their behavior compared to existing processes of the same type
- Catalog a process portfolio of all identified process variants
- Identify duplication (see harmonization and standardization)

Typical templates that are used:

- Process Map and/or Matrix
- Service Map and/or Matrix
- Object Map and/or Matrix

- Application Service Map and/or Matrix
- Data Service Map and/or Matrix

Typical BPM CoE roles involved:

- Process Architects
- Process eXperts
- Process Engineers

Step 20: Directly Adaptable Processes

If the initiation of a BPM Life-cycle project has been decided upon and is to be carried out with the intent of updating, reengineering, and/or re-evaluating an already established existing process landscape, directly adaptable processes simply need to be either customized or re-aligned to support the plans for the value-driven process design. For a value-driven process concept design, see steps 10 and 17. This step is grouped with steps 13 and 19, and relates directly to the process reference content in phase 1. Step 20 output is consumed by step 17.

Typical tasks that are done within this step:

- Identify process variants that can be directly adapted
- Document the process variants that can be directly adapted to fit the defined process landscape
- Catalog a process portfolio of all identified and directly adaptable processes
- Publish directly adaptable processes

Typical templates that are used:

- Process Map and/or Matrix
- Service Map and/or Matrix
- Object Map and/or Matrix

Typical BPM CoE roles involved:

- Process Architects
- Process eXperts
- Process Engineers

In the 3rd phase of the BPM Life Cycle, we went through a series of steps intent on crafting the business processes of the organization. In the 4th phase of the BPM Life Cycle, however, the Deploy/Implement phase (see Figure 10), it is time to prepare for Release and Deployment Management of the business processes and going live. We do this by creating a process-rollout plan, adding rewards and incentives as well as prepare and enable performance measurements.

PHASE 4: DEPLOY/IMPLEMENT—GO LIVE

The 4th phase, the Process Deployment and Implementation phase (see Figure 10), is the phase in which the organization launches, implements, executes, deploys, activates, completes, concludes, and transitions the processes to execution (go live).

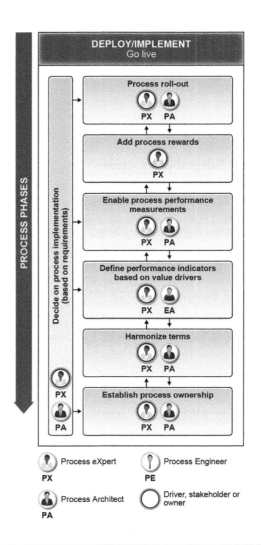

FIGURE 10

The Deploy/Implement phase of the BPM Life Cycle.

Ref. 13.

The Process Release and Deployment Management in the BPM Life Cycle aims to plan, schedule, and control the movement of releases to test in live environments. The primary goal of Release and Deployment Management is to ensure that the integrity of the live environment is protected and that the correct components are released on time and without errors.

Release and Deployment Management aims to build, test, and deliver services to the customers specified by process design by deploying releases into operation, and establishing effective use of the service to deliver value to the customer. As illustrated in Figure 11, process implementation involves multiple aspects from coordination with process owners, change management, to process training.

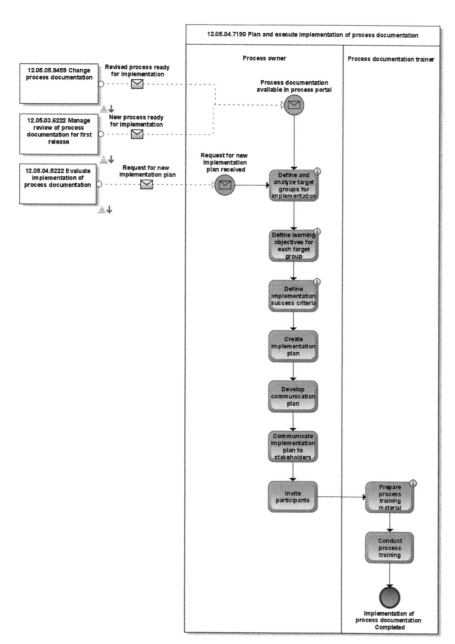

FIGURE 11

Example of a process rollout diagram (Lego Group, Anette Falk Bøgebjerg, Director).

The purpose of Release and Deployment Management is to:

- Define and agree release and deployment plans with customers/stakeholders
- Ensure that each release package consists of a set of related assets and service components that are compatible with each other
- Ensure that integrity of a release package and its constituent components is maintained throughout the transition activities and recorded accurately in the configuration management system
- Ensure that all release and deployment packages can be tracked, installed, tested, verified, and/or uninstalled or backed out, if appropriate
- Ensure that change is managed during the release and deployment activities
- Record and manage deviations, risks, and issues related to the new or changed service, and take necessary corrective action
- Ensure knowledge transfer to enable the customers and users to optimize their use of the service to support their business activities
- Ensure that skills and knowledge are transferred to operations and support staff to enable them to effectively and efficiently deliver, support, and maintain the service, according to required warranties and service levels

Plans for release and deployment will be linked into the overall service transition plan. The approach is to ensure an acceptable set of guidelines is in place for the release into production/operation. Release and deployment plans should be authorized as part of the change management process.

The plan should define the:

- Scope and content of the release
- Risk assessment and risk profile for the release
- Customers/users affected by the release
- Change advisory board (CAB) members that approved the change request for the release and/or deployment
- Team who will be responsible for the release
- Delivery and deployment strategy
- Resources for the release and deployment

Build and test planning establishes the approach to building, testing, and maintaining the controlled environments prior to production. The activities include:

- Developing build plans from the service design package, design specifications, and environment configuration requirements
- Establishing the logistics, lead times, and build times to set up the environments
- Testing the build and related procedures
- Scheduling the build and test activities
- Assigning resources, roles, and responsibilities to perform key activities
- Preparing build and test environments
- Managing test databases and test data

- Software license management

Procedures, templates, and guidance should be used to enable the release team to build an integrated release package efficiently and effectively. Procedures and documents will be required for purchasing, distributing, installing, moving, and controlling assets and components that are relevant to acquiring, building, and testing a release.[14]

Step 21: Decide on Process Implementation (Based on Requirements)

Develop a plan for implementing the processes and the tools in the organization. This plan should describe how to efficiently move from the organization's current state to the release and deployment state. To develop this plan, you need to follow specific project steps.[15] The output of step 21 is consumed by steps 22, 24, 25, and 27.

Typical tasks that are done within this step:

- Set or revise goals
- Identify risks
- Distribute responsibilities and tasks
- Decide when to launch processes and tools
- Plan training and mentoring

Typical templates that are used:

- Process Map and/or Matrix
- Service Map and/or Matrix
- Stakeholder Map and/or Matrix
- Object Map and/or Matrix

Typical BPM CoE roles involved:

- Process eXperts
- Process Architects

Step 22: Process Rollout

During the rollout phase, all areas of change are tested together in the business environment to generate confidence that everything is ready to "go live." During this phase, business users and support teams also receive appropriate training concerning the new processes and the associated systems, organization, and infrastructure.[16] The process rollout should be meticulously executed by using a step-by-step approach and also categorized into levels of importance, preferably based on criteria such as complexity, time, cost, and urgency as well as with clearly defined steps for when the main, supporting, and management process rollouts should occur, and in what sequence. The output of step 22 is consumed by steps 23 and 28.

Typical tasks that are done within this step:

- Process rollout
- Ensure end-to-end process rollout and consistency
- Bring all processes up to target performance
- Business users and process team training
- Test process capability and process adjustment
- Manage issue management and change-request handling
- Implement all the components of the solution

Typical templates that are used:

- Process Map and/or Matrix
- Service Map and/or Matrix
- Object Map and/or Matrix
- Application Service Map and/or Matrix
- Data Service Map and/or Matrix
- Application Rule Map and/or Matrix
- Data Rule Map and/or Matrix
- Compliance Map and/or Matrix

Typical BPM CoE roles involved:

- Process eXperts
- Process Architects

Quality Gate 4:

- Process rollout
- Ensure process quality
- Ensure process coverage

Step 23: Add Process Rewards

Process reward recognition is not just a nice thing to do for the organization or its employees. Process reward recognition is a communication tool that reinforces and rewards the most important process outcomes that people create for your organization. When you recognize people effectively, you reinforce, with your chosen means of process reward recognition, the actions and behaviors you most want to see people repeat. Therefore, process rewards should be defined and created to incite employee motivation for successful implementation, and as rewards for achieving process and value goals. The output of step 23 is consumed by steps 22 and 24.

Typical tasks that are done within this step:

- Establish criteria for what process performance or process contribution constitutes behavior or actions that are rewarded
- All employees must be eligible for the process reward

- Implement process rewards into the process performance model
- Build organizational motivation for chasing process rewards to elevate process performance
- The process reward recognition should occur as close to the performance of the actions as possible, so the recognition reinforces behavior the employer wants to encourage.

Typical templates that are used:

- Value Map and/or Matrix
- Stakeholder Map
- Organizational Chart Map
- Performance Map and/or Matrix

Typical BPM CoE roles involved:

- Process eXperts
- Value eXperts

Step 24: Enable Process Performance Measurements

Process performance measurement is the process of collecting, analyzing, and reporting information regarding the process performance of a group of processes or an individual process. Enabling performance measurements for processes on all measureable levels is an essential behavior of any BPM Life-cycle project and directly links to monitoring, reporting, decision making, as well as process evaluation and audits. The output of step 24 is consumed by steps 23 and 25.

Typical tasks that are done within this step:

- Develop measurement metrics for a process performance model
- Define and relate Process Performance Indicators (PPIs) for process levels 3–5
- Enable Process Performance Reporting and Evaluation
- Identify, categorize, and label Strategic, Tactical, and Operational Process Performance Indicators
- Associate and categorize processes the strategic, Tactical, and Operational Process Performance Indicators to the relevant performance goals/objectives
- Create a Performance Model with decision making and reporting that illustrates the connection and relationship between Strategic, Tactical, and Operational Process Performance Indicators and the business goals and objectives.

Typical templates that are used:

- Process Map and/or Matrix
- Measurement and Reporting Map and/or Matrix
- Performance Map and/or Matrix

Typical BPM CoE roles involved:

- Process eXperts
- Process Architects
- Value eXperts

Value Gate 4a:

- Process performance measurements
- Performance measurement tools efficiency
- Process efficiency evaluation
- Process reporting and evaluation

Step 25: Define Performance Indicators Based on Value Drivers

Establishing direct links between performance indicators and value drivers is essential for both process-modeling and value-modeling perspectives. Therefore, because value drivers indicate value-generating mechanisms, it is important to define performance indicators and let them be based on predefined value drivers. This enables process owners to control and measure the flow of value within the processes on both the high-level and detailed process landscape. The output of step 25 is consumed by steps 24 and 26.

Typical tasks that are done within this step:

- Define, associate, and relate the Process Performance Indicators based on Value Drivers
- Develop value measurements linked to the process performance measurements
- Enable Value based Reporting and Evaluation
- Create a Value Model with decision making and reporting that illustrates the connection and relationship between performance indicators and value indicators.

Typical templates that are used:

- Process Map and/or Matrix
- Performance Map and/or Matrix
- Value Map and/or Matrix

Typical BPM CoE roles involved:

- Value eXperts
- Process eXperts
- Enterprise Architects

Value Gate 4b:

- Process performance indicators establishment
- Number of process targets reached
- Number of process targets obsolete
- Increase/decrease number of process targets

Step 26: Harmonize Terms

The harmonization of process terms across the process landscape has to be continuously evaluated and managed by process owners and teams. Different BPM-oriented organizations and groups today have the tendency to call certain process objects various names, and the same thing goes for the various BPM frameworks, methods, and approaches, such as Six Sigma, Lean, and BPR that use terms in specialized ways. Several business process methodologies have described the use of terms in specific ways. Formal business process languages, like BPML, have semantic definitions that are enforced by the language. Unfortunately, many of these different sources use terms in slightly different ways.[17] We have, therefore, provided basis process terminology and definitions in the BPM ontology chapter. However, it will still be necessary for any organization to tailor these terms, gather additionally needed terms, and establish their own documentation for process terms and definitions to be able to harmonize variants across process groups and process areas to achieve process harmonization (i.e., standardization and integration). The output of step 26 is consumed by steps 25 and 27.

Typical tasks that are done within this step:

- Identify, assess, and establish process-level commonality across the organization
- Identify, assess, and establish process-harmonization opportunities across the organization
- Gather existing process terminology or use the BPM Ontology terminology as a basis to identify relevant terms
- Agree on process terms relevant for the organization
- Ensure process-term harmonization across the organization
- Identify, assess, and establish process-standardization opportunities across the organization

Typical templates that are used:

- Process Map and/or Matrix
- Information Map and/or Matrix
- Service Map and/or Matrix
- Object Map and/or Matrix

Typical BPM CoE roles involved:

- Process eXperts
- Process Architects

Step 27: Establish Process Ownership

As process owners are responsible for the management of processes within the organization, the success of the organization's BPM initiatives depends heavily on implementing good process ownership (see Figure 12). Regardless of the maturity model

Business Architecture: Value Map, Performance Map & Process Map Alignment Worksheet

Business Competency	Strategic Business Objectives	Ownership	Critical Success Factors	Ownership	Key Performance Indicators	Major Business Process and Performance Measures	Ownership	Activity and Performance Measures
						Process:		Process:
						M1.		M1.
						M2.		M2.
						Process:		Process:
						M1.		M1.
						M2.		M2.
						Process:		Process:
						M1.		M1.
						M2.		M2.
						Process:		Process:
						M1.		M1.
						M2.		M2.

Ref. 18.

FIGURE 12

A table tool that can be used to link process ownership with value maps and performance maps.

being applied by an organization, the creation or assignment of process ownership normally occurs one level up from the status quo. However, why is this difficult? Ironically, one of the most neglected areas of process transformation in any kind of change is the definition and assignment of roles and responsibilities. Although there is now a general acknowledgement that people are one of (if not *the* most) critical success factors in any type of business transformation, most organizations are not very accomplished at implementing "people"-oriented changes.[19] In some cases, process owners are current leaders/managers, and in other cases, process owners may be taken from nonleadership positions. Organizational management and structure is an effective tool to use to establish process ownership along with a clear definition of employee requirements and responsibilities. This, at the same time, also incites the need for documenting definitions around process roles, responsibilities, and the who-does-what structure within process-specific teams. The output of step 27 is consumed by step 26.

Typical tasks that are done within this step:

- Specify process ownership responsibility and tasks
- Select process owners
- Implement a process-ownership organization
- Appoint key process roles reporting or working with process owner
- Develop and implement process-improvement initiatives
- Define the process and monitor process performance
- Develop and manage policies and procedures related to the process
- Ensure process adoption, harmonization, standardization, and integration
- Enable process innovation and transformation (link to BPM Change Management and Continuous Improvement)

Typical templates that are used:

- Process Map
- Information Map
- Owner Map and/or Matrix

Typical BPM CoE roles involved:

- Process eXperts
- Process Architects

In the 4th phase of the BPM Life Cycle, we went through a series of steps to execute a successful Release and Deployment Management plan to take the business processes out of the production environment and go live. In the upcoming Run and Maintain phase (see Figure 13), we focus on management of the running process environment in which we will put a lot of effort into monitoring and governing the entire process landscape of the organization.

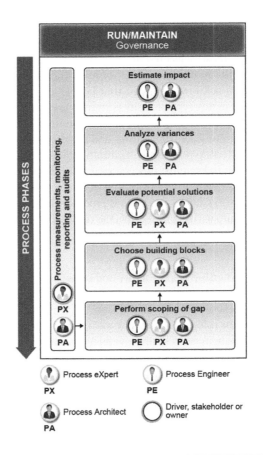

FIGURE 13

The Run/Maintain phase of the BPM Life Cycle.

Ref. 20.

PHASE 5: RUN/MAINTAIN—RUN PROCESSES AND GOVERN PERFORMANCE

The 5th phase, the Process Run and Maintain Phase (see Figure 13), is the phase in which we govern and monitor the active processes that were deployed and implemented during the previous phase. Governance, derived from the Greek verb (kubernáo)—which means to *steer*—is essentially the act of governing what already exists or is in the process of getting developed, deployed/implemented, and/or something that is running.

The *LEADing Practice Way of Process Governance* relates to decisions and guidance that define expectations and direction, grant power, or verify and ensure value identification and creation. It consists of process governance within the entire process life cycle in terms of process analysis, design, construction (build), implementation, and execution (run/maintain), and allows for process monitoring and governance as well as continuous process improvements and optimization disciplines.

The governance phase also includes the many different relationships among the many practitioners in the mentioned phases to ensure that each task enables specific value identification, creation, and realization in achieving the outlined goals. Process governance involves setting standards and priorities for BPM efforts, identifying process governance leaders, and defining BPM project participant roles—all for the purpose of executing and improving upon an organization's process transformation and innovation strategies. The ultimate goal of both business governance and process governance is to both optimize an organization's business processes and make workflow more efficient and effective by implementing and using the built-in continuous improvement concept during phase 6 of the BPM Life Cycle.

As a part of the Continuous Improvement concept, the process governance steps include the establishment of internal BPM or process centers of excellence or competency centers to share process improvement, best practices, as well as leading practices applied within the organization, and spread awareness of the process standards and priorities. Process governance also works to monitor and document both the successes and shortcomings of an organization's operational execution.

In Business Process Management, an additional purpose of governance is to assure (sometimes on behalf of others in terms of stakeholders) that an organization produces the defined pattern of good results, while avoiding an undesirable pattern of bad circumstances. Therefore, the process governance and Continuous Improvement processes and systems are typically administered by a governance body.

Business process governance is often overseen by teams made up of both business and IT professionals. The daily process governance consists of assuring, on behalf of those governed, the desired business innovation, transformation, and value creation while avoiding an undesirable pattern of high cost, process ineffectiveness, and process inefficiency (low performance). Process governance, therefore, consists of the set of governance gates within the life cycle that ensures quality and value aspects within the various phases and tasks.

Step 28: Process Measurements, Monitoring, Reporting, and Audits

Immediately after going live with the processes, it is important to establish an effective way of monitoring and governing the processes while being able to capture real-time data on measurements for the purpose of reporting process performance (see Figure 14) and performing follow-up audits. The output of step 28 is consumed by step 29.

Typical tasks that are done within this step:

- Specify process measurements
- Select real-time process monitoring and governance
- Capture process performance measurements (see Figure 15)
- Document and performance measurement results for reporting and auditing

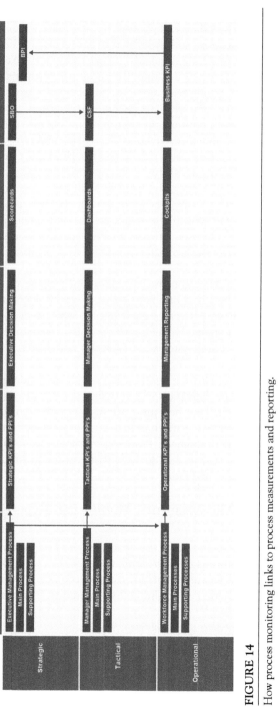

Ref. 21.

FIGURE 14

How process monitoring links to process measurements and reporting.

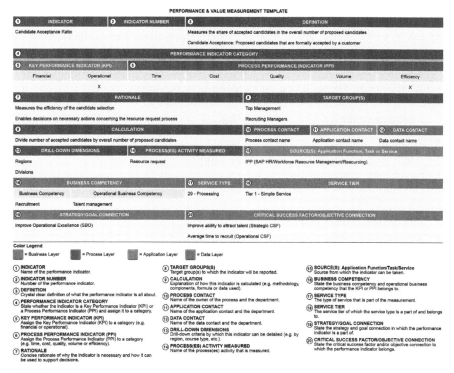

FIGURE 15

An example of a Performance and Value Measurement Template model that can be effectively used to measure process performance.

Ref. 22.

Typical templates that are used:

- Process Map and/or Matrix
- Measurement and Reporting Map and/or Matrix
- Performance Map and/or Matrix
- Role Map and/or Matrix
- Owner Map and/or Matrix
- Application Rule Map and/or Matrix
- Data Rule Map and/or Matrix
- Rule Map and/or Matrix
- Compliance Rule Map and/or Matrix

Typical BPM CoE roles involved:

- Process eXperts
- Process Architects

Step 29: Perform Scoping of Gaps

This includes detailed review, identification, and classification of all running processes in the process portfolio of the organization, and then scoping for performance gaps, irregularities, and other kinds of process performance mishaps and misbehavior. This serves as a staging point for choosing new building blocks to re-engineer existing processes that need to be reconfigured and/or rebuilt. The output of step 29 is consumed by step 30.

Typical tasks that are done within this step:

- Align and associate with defined process goals
- Align with process performance expectations
- Review and document performance gaps

Typical templates that are used:

- Process Map and/or Matrix
- Measurement and Reporting Map and/or Matrix
- System Measurements/Reporting Map and/or Matrix
- Performance Map and/or Matrix
- Role Map and/or Matrix
- Owner Map and/or Matrix

Typical BPM CoE roles involved:

- Process Engineers
- Process eXperts
- Process Architects

Step 30: Choose Building Blocks

As already mentioned in step 3, building blocks are important for the reusability of certain components/aspects. Also in the Run/Maintain phase can building blocks be used, in that the governance and monitoring of value creation is checked. If the value is not realized, alignment of relevant areas between strategic, organizational, process, and technology contexts is initiated. Below in (Figure 16) is an example of typical feedback loops used around business value; among them are business governance, business performance, process monitoring, and IT governance.

In step 30, if business value is not realized as expected, a feedback loop is triggered through either business governance, business performance, process monitoring, and/or IT governance. Building-block concepts are used to enable teams to reuse the artifacts, templates, and models that already have been developed starting in step 3 and through the design, build, and deploy/implement phases. So building blocks from the previously defined process reference content are chosen for the reengineering, process modeling, or process architecture of existing processes to close process performance gaps in Phase 6: Continuous Improvement.

FIGURE 16

Example of the relationship between business value realized, the areas working and focusing on value creation and realization, such as business governance, business performance, process monitoring, and IT governance, and the related building-block groups, that is, strategic, organizational, process, and technology contexts.

Ref. 23.

Therefore, the output of step 30 is consumed by step 31.
Typical tasks that are done within this step:

- Specification of the value and/or performance gaps
- Description of the pain points
- Identification of relevant building blocks
- Choose building blocks from existing process reference content
- Alignment and unification of building blocks across areas
- Review and document possible solutions

Typical templates that are used:

- Process Map and/or Matrix
- Object Map and/or Matrix
- Service Map and/or Matrix

Typical BPM CoE roles involved:

- Process Engineers
- Process eXperts
- Process Architects
- Business Analysts

Step 31: Evaluate Potential Solutions

Evaluating a potential solution is within BPM CoE as much about BPM Governance, BPM Portfolio Management, BPM Alignment, as it is about BPM Change Management. The evaluation for implementing new processes and/or reengineering existing processes is more or less solely based on the scoping of the performance gap, the available building blocks, as well as the value and performance expectations dictated by the process owners and stakeholders.

The output of step 31 is consumed by step 32.

Typical tasks that are done within this step:

- Identify performance gap (link to BPM Governance)
- Specify root cause of performance gap (link to BPM Change Management)
- Identify alternatives and potential solutions (link to BPM Portfolio Management)
- Collect and list advantages and disadvantages of potential solutions (BPM Governance and BPM Change Management)
- Compare and align potential solutions to the existing process landscape (link to BPM Alignment)
- Evaluate and decide upon alternatives, if any are proposed (link to BPM Portfolio Management)

Typical templates that are used:

- Process Map and/or Matrix
- Service Map and/or Matrix
- Performance Map and/or Matrix
- Value Map and/or Matrix
- Operating Map and/or Matrix
- Measurement and Reporting
- System Measurements/Reporting Map and/or Matrix

Typical BPM CoE roles involved:

- Process Engineers
- Process eXperts
- Business Analysts
- Process Architects

Step 32: Analyze Variances

In today's optimized organizations, analyzing process variances is a must-do. This is not only about identifying duplication and a potential for integration, it is also important for the standardization of the various processes that should be similar, but are different. While capturing existing processes in BPMN, performing value-stream mapping and statistical analysis provides critical insight into key factors that help improve business processes. Analyzing traditional business processes does not provide enough information to be able to compare and specify variances. Detailed business process or workflow analysis is needed, in which one examines processes using various techniques, such as BPR, Six Sigma, Lean, providing alternatives to identify duplication, define variances, reduce time and cost, specify steps, waste, and other factors important to the organization when analyzing variances. It is important to remember that process variances differ by variances of a task and in the way the business process flows.

A common business process might exist in multiple variations in an enterprise, due to different legal requirements in different countries, deviations in the supporting IT infrastructure, or differences in the organizational structure. To explore and control such variability,[24] Weidlich and Weske argue that the notion of a main process, the invariant nucleus of all process variants, might be applied, because the degree of variability of process variants might be explored using the notion of a main (core) process. Such a process captures structural and behavioral aspects that are invariant across all process variants. SAP's business process handbook specifies[25] that a business process variant is a fundamental flow variant of a Business Process that uses the same input and delivers the same measurable outcome. The flow of process steps is defined at business process variant level. To keep level consistency it is necessary that each Business Process has at least one business process variant attached. A business process variant should differ from another at least in one of the following:

1. Flow of documents
2. The specific business objects needed
3. Life-cycle schema of the business objects (status and status transitions)
4. Application to Application/Business to Business (A2A/B2B) message choreography or choreography with direct interactions with other Business Processes
5. A business process variant is not just an alternative User Interface (UI)
6. A business process variant is not just another sequence a user decides to perform tasks on the User Interface (UI).
7. Two Business Process Variants differ in the way the business process flows. The difference is so important that the variants are to be considered separately in a business process analysis. The difference is so fundamental that it typically needs to be treated by special software functionality and not just configuration, if implemented in software.

The above clearly illustrates the importance of analyzing, identifying, tracking, and documenting process variances. To test possible solutions, it is important to analyze different process variants in different process scenarios and setups. The output of step 32 is consumed by both steps 33 and 34.

Typical tasks that are done within this step:

- Perform detailed process analysis (main process, flow, roles, tasks, objects, etc.)
- Undertake process performance simulations and report on output
- Specify process variances

- Detailed and thorough testing of new processes
- Detailed and thorough testing of reengineered processes

Typical templates that are used:

- Process Map and/or Matrix
- Service Map and/or Matrix
- Performance Map and/or Matrix

Typical BPM CoE roles involved:

- Process Engineers
- Process Architects

Value Gate 5:

- Evaluate potential solutions
- Investigate opportunities for higher process quality delivery
- Investigate opportunities for higher Return on Investment (ROI)

Step 33: Estimate Impact

Based on acquired process analysis and testing simulations, it is critical to assess the possible impact that either new and/or reengineered processes have upon many different business aspects, but most importantly, what their execution will mean for the value-generating cycle of the organization (Figure 17).

The purpose of the business impact analysis (BIA) is to identify which business units/departments and processes are essential to the survival of the organization. The BIA will identify how quickly essential business units and/or processes have to return to full operation following a disaster situation. The BIA will also identify the resources required to resume business operations. Business impacts are identified based on worst-case scenarios that assume that the physical infrastructure supporting each respective business unit has been destroyed and all records, equipment, etc. are not accessible for 30 days. Please note that the BIA will not address recovery solutions.[26]

The objectives of the BIA are as follows:

- Estimate the financial impacts for each business unit, assuming a worst-case scenario.
- Estimate the intangible (operational) impacts for each business unit, assuming a worst-case scenario.
- Identify the organization's business unit processes and the estimated recovery time frame for each business unit.

The output of step 33 is consumed by step 34.
Typical tasks that are done within this step:

- Document and prepare new processes in a process-testing portfolio (separating them from active processes)

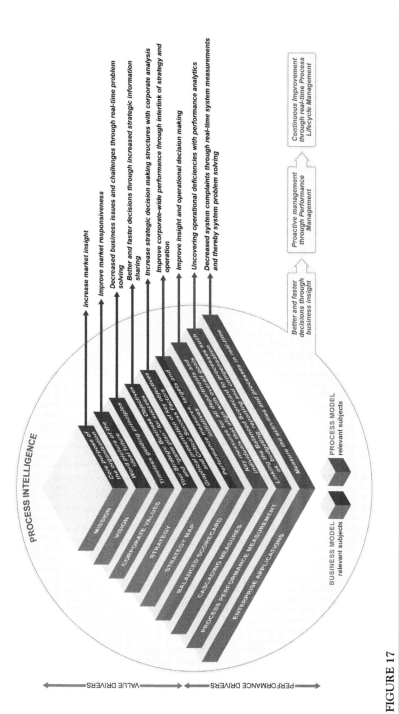

FIGURE 17

How process intelligence should be understood and undertaken by the organization.

Ref. 27.

- Document and prepare the reengineering of existing processes in a process-testing portfolio (move them out of the existing process portfolio temporarily while testing is underway)
- Execute thorough process-testing simulations of both newly created processes as well as reengineered processes

Typical templates that are used:

- Process Map and/or Matrix
- Service Map and/or Matrix
- Performance Map and/or Matrix
- Value Map and/or Matrix
- Operating Map and/or Matrix
- Measurement and Reporting
- System Measurements/Reporting Map and/or Matrix
- Risk Map and/or Matrix

Typical BPM CoE roles involved:

- Process Engineers
- Process Architects

Quality Gate 5:

- Investigate possible business impact and consequences
- Estimate impact on process quality
- Estimate impact on process coverage
- Estimate impact on process goals and scope

During the 5th phase of the BPM Life Cycle, the Run and Maintain phase, we have been focusing mainly on process measurements, monitoring, reporting, and audits. As we enter the last phase of the BPM Life Cycle, the Continuous Improvement phase (see Figure 18), we will be focusing on optimizing processes around prioritized improvement areas, such as the Value Model, Revenue Model, Cost Model, Service Model, Operating Model, and the Performance Model in a collaborative business environment using feedback loops to report on process improvements, requests for changes, and to further manage the process landscape of the organization.

PHASE 6: CONTINUOUS IMPROVEMENT— CONTINUOUSLY OPTIMIZE AND DEVELOP PROCESSES

Business Process Improvement (BPI) is a systematic approach to help an organization optimize its underlying processes to achieve results that are more efficient. The methodology was first documented in H. James Harrington's 1991 book, Business Process Improvement.[28] It is the methodology upon which both Process Redesign and Business Process Reengineering are based (see Figure 18). BPI has allegedly

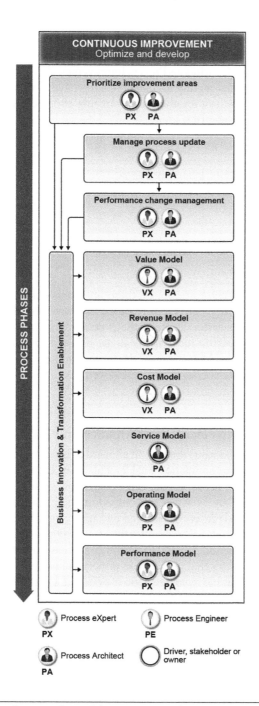

FIGURE 18

The Continuous Development phase of the BPM Life Cycle.

Ref. 29.

been responsible for reducing cost and cycle time by as much as 90% while improving quality by over 60%. In the meantime, the idea and concept of Continuous Improvement (CI) or Continuous Process Improvement (CPI) is applied in multiple areas. Many frameworks, methods, and approaches have some sort of CI and or CPI incorporated in one way or another as an ongoing effort to improve products, services, or processes. To mention some:

- Business process reengineering
- Six Sigma
- Theory of Constraints, Lean, Six Sigma
- Kaizen
- Toyota Production System
- Zero Defect
- Mottainai
- Muda
- Total productive maintenance

There has been some criticism of these approaches, however, and there are claims that these methods are more resource intensive and thereby cost-cutting-focused and that the measures come at the expense of fair labor practices and quality products. This criticism furthermore argue that real continuous improvement governance models would have to consider more than just cost drivers. They would have to incorporate both performance/cost as well as value drivers to link to business transformation and innovation aspects.

Continuous Improvement: Performance and Value Drivers

Performance drivers and value drivers can go hand in hand to specify the link to business innovation and transformation enablement. Even though they are not applied by many organizations, applying both have proven over the years to deliver above-average results. They are what we call outperforming organizations. The first time this was researched and proven was in 1984 by Dutton and Thomas.[30] They measured the results in progress ratios. The number they used represents the cost of production after cumulative production doubles. Dutton and Thomas found that those companies across different industries that apply these principles had the ratio typically around 80%. Thus, if a business has a progress ratio of 80% and it costs $100 to produce a unit after producing 100 units, when cumulative production reaches 200 units, it will cost only $80 to produce the same unit. Formally, for some commodity, if $Cost(t)$ is cost at time t, $d(t)$ is the number of doublings of cumulative output of the commodity in time t, and a is the percent reduction in cost for each doubling of cumulative output (note: $1-a$ is the progress ratio), then we have $Cost(t) = Cost(0)(1-a)^d$.

Some of the known industries that have applied the previously mentioned progress ratios are seen in Table 1.

The core principle here is not only to identify performance/cost as well as value drivers, it is to attach them to a continuous feedback loop and thereby reflect

Table 1 *Industry Table Index*					
Technology	Period	Year 1 Production	Cumulative Production	Cost Index	Progress Ratio
Ford model T auto	1909–1923	15,741	8,028,000	0.290	87%
Integrated circuits	1962–1968	4 million unites	828 million units	0.047	67%
CFC substitutes	1988–1999	100,000 tons	3,871,000 tons	0.690	93%
Scrubbers	1987–1995	65.8 GW	84.3 GW	0.	89%
Photovoltaic	1971–2000	0.1	1451.4	0.042	72%
Magnetic ballasts	1977–1993	29.4 million	629.3 million	0.897	97%
Electronic ballasts	1986–2001	431	350 million units	0.277	88%
Refrigerators	1980–1998	5.1 million	126.3 million	0.556	88%
Freezers	1980–1998	1.8 million	26.1 million	0.374	78%
Clothes washers	1980–1998	4.4 million	104.7 million	0.536	87%
Electronic clothes	1980–1998	2.5 million	61.0 million	0.557	88%
Gas clothes dryer	1980–1998	0.7 million	18.2 million	0.593	90%
Dishwasher	1980–1998	2.7 million	69.7 million	0.450	84%
Room air conditioner	1980–1998	2.4 million	63.3 million	0.478	85%
Selective window coatings	1992–2000	4.8 million m²	157.4 million m²	0.394	83%

(optimization, improvement, and innovation) processes. The purpose of continuous improvement (CI), therefore, is the identification, reduction, elimination, and innovation of suboptimal processes (efficiency). This already goes beyond most approaches that are result/effect-driven and thereby focuses on effectiveness. The emphasis of CI is on incremental, continuous steps rather than giant leaps (Evolution). Continuous Improvements are thereby based on many, small changes rather than the radical optimization project that is more likely handled through a project. The change should come from the operation (the workers themselves) and enable business model changes both in the areas of revenue, value, and service model, as well as the cost, performance, and operating model. Such a feedback loop to the business model domains is more likely to succeed in enabling change. Practically speaking, process improvement is, therefore, an aspect of organizational development (OD) in which a series of actions are taken by a process owner to identify, analyze, and improve existing business processes within an organization to meet new goals and objectives, such as increasing profits and performance, reducing costs, and accelerating schedules. These actions often follow a specific methodology or strategy to increase the likelihood of successful results. Process improvement may include the restructuring of company training programs to increase their effectiveness. Process improvement is also a method to introduce process changes to improve the quality of a product or service to better match customer and consumer needs.

Continuous Business Process Improvement, however, is about taking the cycle of the process optimization phases and steps to another level of detail and efficiency.

Process change requests are received, evaluated, and carried out in support of changing process and/or business objectives and goals, and the simulation and performance measurements are then reported to process owners, stakeholders, and decision makers who are involved with the BPM Life Cycle. This ensures a chain reaction of quality assurance, evaluation, and decision making on behalf of the continuous feedback loop and collaborative work done by all participants involved.

The 6th and final phase of the BPM Life Cycle (see Figure 18), the continuous improvement phase, is the phase in which the processes are managed in terms of their effectiveness, efficiency, incidents/issues, and process change request fulfillments, etc. This is also when the organization improves the existing process operations and evaluates, adjusts, alters, amends, changes, corrects, eliminates, enhances, increases, modifies, optimizes, and/or excludes specific process parts within the process portfolios and landscapes. This phase is all about the link between business process operation and business, and thereby BPM Innovation and Transformation Enablement (see Figure 19). This interlinks with the improvement and optimization of the six business model domains.

Step 34: Prioritize Improvement Areas

Improvement areas have to be defined, documented, and selected through collaborative efforts between business, IT, and technology units of the organization (see Figure 19). As processes are heavily dependent on so many different aspects, it is important to select areas that correlate and align directly with the overall process strategy and the established process goals (Figure 20).

The first step of any process improvement initiative is to take stock of as many organizational processes as possible, because everything is connected to everything else in the value chain from concept to customer. Considering all organizational processes will force the team to think about the interdependencies between individuals, departments, vendors, and customers, all of whom may influence the process.

The next step is to determine which process, if improved, would have the greatest positive impact on the organization (i.e., would most likely contribute to the fulfillment of the organization's goals). There are five steps involved in the selection of choosing which processes to prioritize:

1. *List success criteria:* Success criteria are those measures, ranging from most tangible (e.g., financial measures) to least tangible (e.g., strategic measures), that indicate the larger organization is on the right strategic path. In this case, the organization has determined that hit ratio, combined ratio, and compliance are the three criteria that demonstrate it is performing according to its strategic plan.
2. *Weighted success criteria:* Success criteria are then weighted relative to each other using an index from 0.5 to 1.5, in which 0.5 indicates the criterion has the least weight, and 1.5 indicates the criterion has the most weight. In our example, the organization has deemed new business to be a critical success

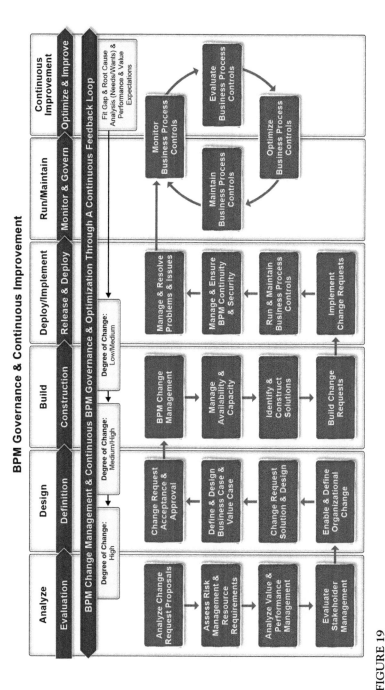

FIGURE 19

A high-level view example of a BPM Governance model that can be used to structure and organize the activities performed and to continuously monitor, govern, and administer the flow of business processes within the organization.

Ref. 31.

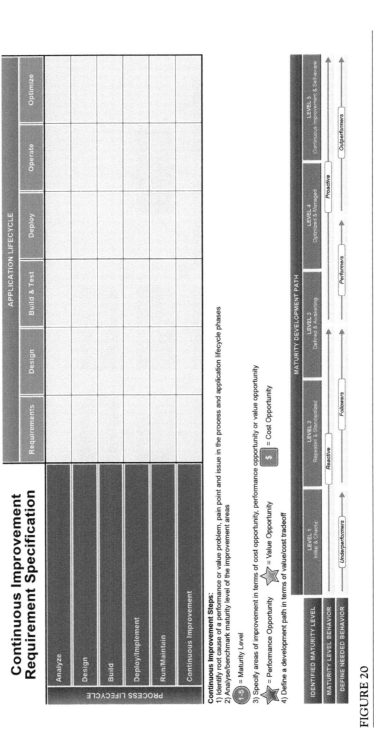

FIGURE 20

An example model of Continuous Improvement and Requirement Specification between the BPM Life Cycle and the Application Life Cycle. This model relates only to automated processes in the process landscape, and will aid the user in identifying the maturity levels as well as performance, value, and cost opportunities associated with processes throughout all six life-cycle phases.

Ref. 32.

factor. As such, the hit ratio (1.5) is the most important strategic measure relative to compliance (1.0) and combined ratio (0.5). They are all important, however; this is simply a relative weighting.

3. *List processes:* List the names of the processes from the process master.
4. *Assign anchors:* A number from 1 to 5 (each, an "anchor") is inserted in each cell indicating the strength of correlation between each process and each success criterion.
5. *Determine score and rank:* The resulting scores, which are the products of the relative weights times the anchors summed across each process, provide a ranking, based on the success criteria, which indicates what specific processes should be given improvement priority. In our example, it has been determined that the state filings process (with a score of 13) most contributes to the fulfillment of the organization's strategic objectives.[33]

The output of step 34 is consumed by step 35.
Typical tasks that are done within this step:

- Define and document steps for improving process structures around each business model domain
- Gather and list advantages and disadvantages for reengineering processes around each business model domain
- Establish process ownership and responsibilities around improvement steps
- Clarify process roles around improvement steps
- Reevaluate and reestablish process goals and requirements around each business model domain

Typical templates that are used:

- Process Map and/or Matrix
- Service Map and/or Matrix
- Information Map and/or Matrix
- Performance Map and/or Matrix
- Value Map and/or Matrix
- Operating Map and/or Matrix
- Measurement and Reporting
- Risk Map and/or Matrix

Typical BPM CoE roles involved:

- Process eXperts
- Business Analysts
- Transformation eXperts
- Process Architects

Quality Gate 6:

- Identify and determine areas to improve upon
- Initiate process quality improvements

- Initiate process coverage improvements
- Initiate process goals improvements
- Update process scope documentation and deliver evaluation report to stakeholders

Step 35: Manage Process Update

Process updates have to be continuously updated and managed by a dedicated process unit/team. This is important because process portfolios are usually quite expansive and cumbersome to manage, so it is essential that a process portfolio is efficiently managed when undergoing regular updates. The output of step 35 is consumed by step 36.

Typical tasks that are done within this step:

- Supervise and execute Change Management

Typical templates that are used:

- Process Map and/or Matrix
- Service Map and/or Matrix
- Information Map and/or Matrix
- Performance Map and/or Matrix
- Operating Map and/or Matrix

Typical BPM CoE roles involved:

- Process eXperts
- Process Architects

Step 36: Performance Change Management

Change management relevant for BPM and how it is handled across the entire BPM Life Cycle is handled in the chapter BPM Change Management. As requirements, the organizations, competitors, or the environment are constantly changing, adapting to outside changes is a challenge faced by nearly all organizations. The changes do not only impact the strategic aspects, the business models, the employees, and the way an organization utilizes technology, but the degree of outside change also influences the organization's ability to maintain control of their work. So while the organization manages the changes befalling the organization, it must also actively manage the change of their business processes. Developing an effective change road map that is integrated into the business process management life cycle and the BPM CoE change and issue management is imperative for the change effectiveness if your initiative is to avoid "the valley of despair" (see BPM Change Management chapter). Purpose and objectives of the BPM Change Management concept are to respond to both process change requests as well as the BPM client's changing requirements while maximizing value and reducing incidents, disruptions, and rework. When executing change management principles for the purpose of managing changes to process performance, it is important to apply both BPM CoE Change Management to the process portfolio, as well as BPM Change Management throughout the life cycle. This must go hand-in-hand with the process reports on performance, their gaps, and suggested solutions and alternatives. It also has to include the expected business impact parameters as well as outline both value and performance expectations. The output of step 36 is consumed by step 37.

Typical tasks that are done within this step:

- Identify performance gaps
- Specify stakeholder value and/or performance expectation (BPM Requirements Management)
- Document improvements
- Planning with link to process portfolio, program, and project management
- Business organizational changes that need to be channeled through the Process Portfolio Management channel
- Investigate BPM Continuous Improvement feedback loop in terms of degree of change (low, medium, or high)
- Clarify value and performance expectations
- Structural changes that need to be channeled through the BPM CoE management; the people-side of change that needs to be channeled through the business change management group

Typical templates that are used:

- Process Map and/or Matrix
- Service Map and/or Matrix
- Information Map and/or Matrix
- Performance Map and/or Matrix
- Value Map and/or Matrix
- Operating Map and/or Matrix
- Measurement and Reporting
- Risk Map and/or Matrix

Typical BPM CoE roles involved:

- Process eXperts
- Transformation eXperts
- Enterprise Architects
- Process Architects

Step 37: Business Innovation and Transformation Enablement

Business Innovation and Transformation Enablement (BITE) principles go hand-in-hand with Performance Change Management described earlier. BITE principles, however, do not only emphasize performance, but also go into detail around suggested process changes and their impact on the organization's value, revenue, cost, service, and operating model as well as the performance model. The output of step 37 is consumed by steps 37a–f, depending on which business model domain the focus is placed. Please note that moving onward to any—or all—of the six different business model domains is not only allowed, but is highly recommended and should be done at all times during phases of process improvement, optimization, and development.

Doing this is also strongly advised because the vast majority of all of the existing and in-use processes in the process landscape plays an important role in the organization. It is often estimated that a significant number of active processes are likely to have a dramatic impact and effect upon the workflow within, execution of, and results delivered by any of the six different business model domains. Therefore, careful precaution and consideration has to be maintained when choosing to eliminate and/or reengineer any of the active processes in the process landscape.

The structure around Business Innovation and Transformation Enablement for the BPM Life Cycle focuses on two directions; the Process Way of thinking (innovation and transformation principles) and the Process Way of working (the sequence of actions taken). The 8 distinct interrogatives that can be used effectively for process analysis, design, construction, and monitoring, as well as for Continuous Improvement are as follows:

1. *Where:* The location/area of the process (i.e., where it is located or resides in the context of the process landscape)
2. *When:* Time of the process (i.e., the timing/time at execution or the length [time consumption] of the process)
3. *Whence:* The source of the process (what exactly is the source of the process, i.e., manual labor sequence, automation through software, etc.)
4. *How:* The manner of the process (how it behaves)
5. *What:* The context of the process (i.e., in which context does it have relevance)
6. *Why:* The reason for the process' existence (i.e., why does it exist, why do we have it/use it)
7. *Who:* Is the process of personal relevance (i.e., does it have an actor)
8. *Whether:* What are the choices, alternatives, and options of the process (i.e., should we choose another path)

The classification form of the 8 distinct process interrogatives can be structured and efficiently organized as shown in the example of Figure 21.

Typical templates that are used:

- Process Map and/or Matrix
- Service Map and/or Matrix
- Performance Map and/or Matrix
- Value Map and/or Matrix
- Operating Map and/or Matrix

Process Innovation Way of Thinking   **Process Transformation Way of Thinking**

BITE Classification Form

Reason	Why	1		1	Where	Location
Options	Whether	2		2	When	Time
Context	What	3		3	Whence	Source
Location	Where	4	Way of Working	4	How	Manner
Manner	How	5		5	What	Context
Source	Whence	6		6	Why	Reason
Time	When	7		7	Who	Personal/actor
Personal/actor	Who	8		8	Whether	Options

FIGURE 21

An example of a model that shows the 8 interrogatives related to process reference content. This particular example also shows the direction of and approach toward Process Innovation and Process Transformation (both of them being a way of thinking and a way of working around processes).

Ref. 34.

- Cost Map and/or Matrix
- Revenue Map and/or Matrix
- Measurement and Reporting
- Risk Map and/or Matrix

Typical BPM CoE roles involved:

- Transformation eXperts

Value Gate 6:

- Business Innovation and Transformation Enablement (BITE) opportunities

Step 37a: Value Model

Process performance changes are closely connected to the organization's value model because all processes are designed to deliver value in one way or another (see Figure 22). In most instances, it is necessary to continuously improve processes by relating them to changes in the value model, such as, for instance, updated or newly defined value drivers and value indicators. The outcome of step 37 is consumed by step 37a.

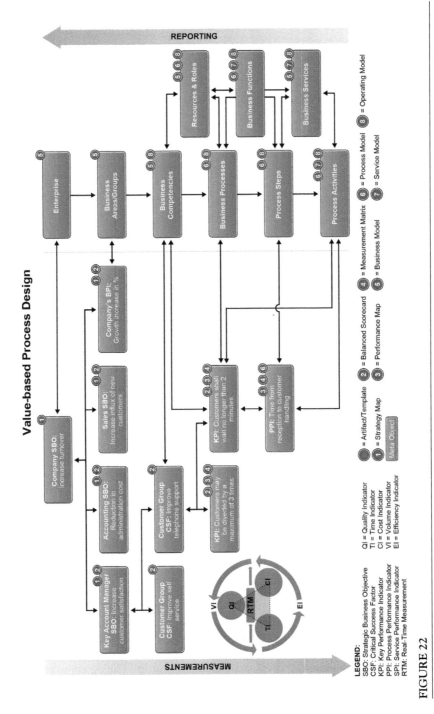

FIGURE 22

An example of a value-based process design in which the business processes of the organization have been designed, constructed, and fully integrated with the organization's value model.

Typical tasks that are done within this step:

- Align and unify all strategic, tactical, and operational processes to the strategic, tactical, and operational key Performance Indicators of the organization
- Include process performance changes to the value flow model
- Relate business processes to process performance indicators and measurements
- Relate process steps and process activities to service performance indicators and measurements
- Relate business processes to business competencies, business resources and roles, and business functions
- Relate process steps and activities to business functions and business services

Typical templates that are used:

- Process Map and/or Matrix
- Service Map and/or Matrix
- Performance Map and/or Matrix
- Value Map, Matrix, and/or Model
- Risk Map and/or Matrix

Typical BPM CoE roles involved:

- Value eXperts
- Business Analysts
- Enterprise Architects
- Process Architects

Step 37b: Revenue Model

When main processes undergo change requests, it is important to realign them with the revenue model, because they are the driving force of processes that are specifically involved with value-generation flows of the organization. The outcome of step 37 is consumed by step 37b.

Typical tasks that are done within this step:

- Optimize and improve main (value-generating) processes in the process landscape
- Focus on communication and analysis around processes that help identify customers, market to those customers, and generate sales to those customers
- Relate business processes, process steps, and process activities to revenue flows
- Relate business process owners, process roles, and process measurement to revenue flows

Typical templates that are used:

- Process Map and/or Matrix
- Service Map and/or Matrix
- Performance Map and/or Matrix
- Value Map and/or Matrix

- Revenue Map, Matrix, and/or Model
- Risk Map and/or Matrix

Typical BPM CoE roles involved:

- Value eXperts
- Business Analysts
- Enterprise Architects
- Process Architects

Step 37c: Cost Model

Processes are an essential part of production facilities regardless of industry, product, or general process practice principles. Creating new processes or reengineering existing processes within the established process portfolio enables organizations to reduce production cost, save time, reduce manpower, and automate previously manual labor through automated processes (see Figure 23). The outcome of step 37 is consumed by step 37c.

Typical tasks that are done within this step:

- Link operational processes to the cost model and cost profiles
- Define cost drivers and opportunities for cost reduction
- Examine cost reduction opportunities in operational processes
- Relate business processes, process steps, and process activities to cost flows
- Relate process roles, process measurement, and process owners to

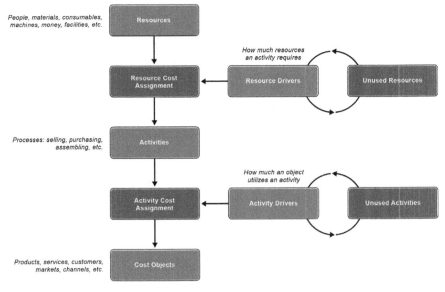

FIGURE 23

An example of how processes relate and integrate with an activity-based costing model.

- High-cost types
- Medium-cost types; and
- Low-cost types

Typical templates that are used:

- Process Map and/or Matrix
- Service Map and/or Matrix
- Performance Map and/or Matrix
- Value Map and/or Matrix
- Cost Map, Matrix, and/or Model
- Risk Map and/or Matrix

Typical BPM CoE roles involved:

- Value eXperts
- Business Analysts
- Enterprise Architects
- Process Architects

Step 37d: Service Model

Business processes deliver business services (Service Provider) to one or more customers (whether internal or external) who then consume the services delivered to them (Service Consumer), thereby making the Service Model and the entire Service-Oriented Architecture landscape of the organization heavily dependent on a stable, reliable, and high-performance process landscape (see Figure 25).

Business services are directly affected by process-change requests and optimizations, because changes in processes will ultimately change the behavior of how services are being delivered by an organization. Therefore, it is essential to continuously update the service models to reflect any changes to existing processes and/or the introduction of new processes to allow the service models to perform at maximum efficiency (see Figure 24). The outcome of step 37 is consumed by step 37d.

Typical tasks that are done within this step:

- Associate and link changes to process steps and activities to business, application, data, platform, and infrastructure services
- Associate and link changes to events and gateways to business, application, data, platform, and infrastructure services
- Associate and link changes to process flow, process roles, and process owners to business, application, data, platform, and infrastructure services

Typical templates that are used:

- Process Map and/or Matrix
- Service Map, Matrix, and/or Model
- Performance Map and/or Matrix

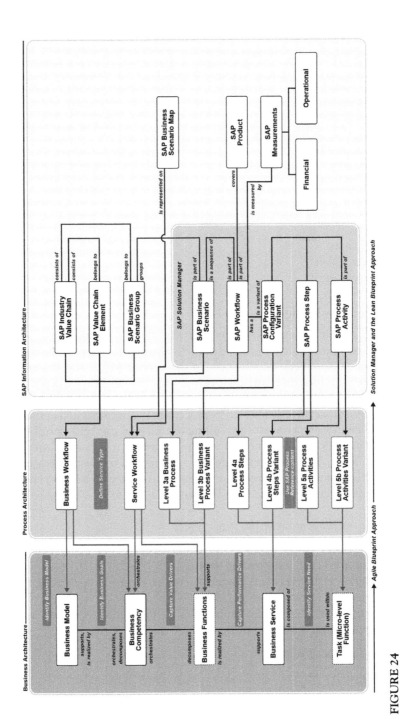

Ref. 36.

FIGURE 24

Example of how process steps (and variants thereof) deliver business services.

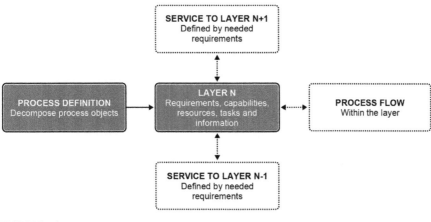

FIGURE 25

An example of a Layered Process Architecture model that shows how the execution of processes delivers services across layers within an organization based on layer requirements.

Ref. 37.

- Value Map and/or Matrix
- Risk Map and/or Matrix

  Typical BPM CoE roles involved:

- Service eXperts
- Business Analysts
- Enterprise Architects
- Process Architects.

Step 37e: Operating Model

The operating model (see Figure 26) focuses on process standardization and integration across the organization, and, because of this, changes made to any of the existing processes of the process portfolio need to be updated with the current operating model to reflect changes made and how services are being delivered as either strategic, tactical, or operational services. The outcome of step 37 is consumed by step 37e.

Typical tasks that are done within this step:

- Investigate opportunities for establishing processes around:
  - *Coordination*—low process standardization but high process integration
  - *Unification*—both high standardization and integration
  - *Diversification*—businesses requiring low standardization and low integration
  - *Replication*—high standardization but low integration

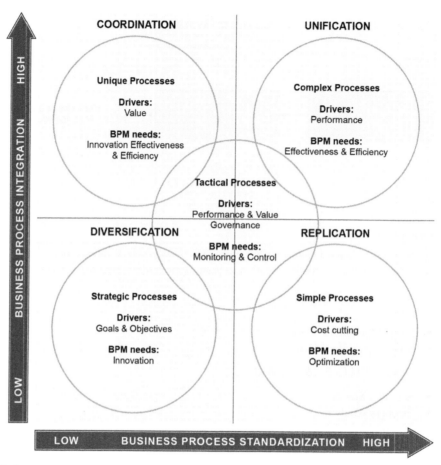

FIGURE 26

An Operating Model focusing on business process integration and business process standardization.

Ref. 38.

- Identify and categorize business processes around
  - business areas and groups
  - business functions
  - business roles and owners
  - resources/actors
  - business competencies
  - business rules and compliance
  - service construct
  - service areas and groups
  - service owners
  - process areas and groups

- process owners
- application/system owners
- data owners
- platform owners
- infrastructure owners

- Associate and connect the process types (i.e., main, management, and support) to
  - business areas and groups;
  - capabilities and functions;
  - business roles and owners;
  - resources/actors;
  - business competencies;
  - business rules and compliance;
  - service construct;
  - service areas and groups;
  - service owners;
  - process areas and groups;
  - business processes;
  - process owners;
  - application/system owners;
  - data owners;
  - platform owners; and
  - infrastructure owners
- Associate each process owner with
  - business and process areas and groups
- Create an Operating Model to illustrate the relationship between process owners and business and process areas and groups

Typical templates that are used:

- Process Map and/or Matrix
- Service Map and/or Matrix
- Performance Map and/or Matrix
- Value Map and/or Matrix
- Operating Map, Matrix, and/or Model
- Risk Map and/or Matrix

Typical BPM CoE roles involved:

- Process eXperts
- Business Analysts
- Information Architects
- Technology Architects
- Enterprise Architects
- Process Architects

Step 37f: Performance Model

Processes are constantly being monitored for performance gaps and issues (see Figure 27), and therefore, changes made to processes must be directly related to the performance model. The outcome of step 37 is consumed by step 37f.

Typical tasks that are done within this step:

- Relate, monitor, and measure strategic, tactical, and operational processes to Strategic Business Objectives (SBOs)
- Relate, monitor, and measure strategic, tactical, and operational processes to Critical Success Factors (CSFs)
- Relate, monitor, and measure strategic, tactical, and operational processes to Key Performance Indicators (KPIs)
- Develop, monitor, and measure Process Performance Indicators (PPIs) around operational processes
- Develop, monitor, and measure Service Performance Indicators (SPIs) around operational processes
- Connect and link process areas, process groups, process measurement, and process owners to
  - Strategic, tactical, and operational Key Performance Indicators (KPIs)
- Connect and link process steps, process activities, and process owners to
  - Strategic, tactical, and operational Process Performance Indicators (PPIs); and
  - Strategic, tactical, and operational Service Performance Indicators (SPIs)

Typical templates that are used:

- Process Map and/or Matrix
- Service Map and/or Matrix
- Performance Map, Matrix, and/or Model
- Value Map and/or Matrix
- Risk Map and/or Matrix

Typical BPM CoE roles involved:

- Process eXperts
- Value eXperts
- Business Analysts
- Enterprise Architects
- Process Architects

CONCLUSION

The organizational requirements of implementing a usable and effective BPM Life Cycle in any organization is a very demanding task in itself. Even more difficult is the need to structure the life cycle in a way that fully, and in a very detailed and explicit manner, revolves around accomplishing not only process-related goals, but

PROCESS/INPUT
Pain Point Situation & Effect Analysis Form

FIGURE 27

The Process/Input Pain Point Situation & Effect Analysis Form is a powerful tool to help monitor, identify, and suggest changes to process pain points.

Ref. 39.

more importantly, business objectives, goals, and strategy. Because, in a nutshell, processes are essentially a sequenced flow of steps and activities that have been specifically designed to achieve a defined business objective and eventually allow for the fulfilment of the strategy of the organization. Thus, processes act as a chain reaction of actions that are indirectly responsible for fulfilling the strategy of an organization, and ultimately, that is the goal.

Most BPM and process life cycles focus almost exclusively on process-oriented solutions and goals, rather than also incorporating business-related challenges. That is where many organizations go about it the wrong way. As mentioned earlier, processes are but a tool to fulfill the goals of the business, and with that in mind, it is important to maintain a strong focus on business objectives and goals when designing the structure and the steps involved with the BPM Life Cycle. Process goals have to serve the needs of the business, and designing a tight collaboration between process objectives and goals, and business objectives and goals, is of the utmost importance.

The work done by the process roles (experts, engineers and architects) in various programs and projects along with their specific tasks always relate to a specific business goal, the roles, tasks, and deliverables that link to the business goals, and can be managed within the process life cycle. This is done through managing the link to strategy on a portfolio, program, and project level, and managing the deliverables/artefacts assigned to the specific roles and their tasks within the process life cycle. As the process management life cycle has already been aligned with BPM Portfolio Management, the key touch points can be highlighted for specific focus on governance and value delivery. This clearly illustrates that the BPM Life Cycle has been specifically designed for creating process solutions that also focus on reaching business objectives and goals as well as solving business issues and challenges (see step 1: "Identify critical business factors", step 2: "Describe process goals" as well as the Business Innovation and Transformation Enablement steps around steps 37a–f).

Going through a detailed and highly analytical design and construction phase to create a useful and effective BPM Life Cycle should be top priority in most organizations. The sheer benefits and many different advantages of doing so far outweigh the number of resources required to complete the production of the life cycle. Let us take a glance at some of the many benefits and advantages you can harvest from creating and using an effective BPM Life Cycle.

Let's start with a few examples of advantages from a **strategic point of view:**

- *Industry and trends:* The identification of industry changes and key external trends can be a great asset for adapting existing processes to meet these changes. Such changes, whether internal or external, should be seen as opportunities and drivers for optimizing existing processes or simply acting as a catalyst for the creation of new processes—not only to adapt to, for instance, a changing market, but certainly also to benefit from new business opportunities and ventures.

- *Understanding and commitment:* A BPM Life Cycle helps to secure a common organizational understanding and commitment of owners, stakeholders, and management teams across organizational boundaries.
- *Proactive organization:* It will help jump start and enable a continuously proactive organization in which all share a common goal—the goal of creating or reengineering processes to reach business objectives and business goals, and thereby realize business strategies.

Advantages from an **organizational point of view:**

- *Ownership, roles, and responsibilities:* Every individual involved with the life cycle is assigned both tasks and responsibilities for carrying out particular objectives. This makes it easier to distribute the appropriate tasks and assignments to the appropriate experts across the organization. Process ownership, stakeholders, and decision makers are also involved in all of the context of the BPM Life Cycle.
- *Communication, collaboration, and feedback loop:* Because ownership, roles, and responsibilities have been placed accordingly, organizational communication across business units and effective collaboration within project teams become much more efficient because everybody knows what's going through regular status reporting, evaluations, audits, and measurements (in terms of process testing and simulation). The feedback loop ensures clear communication about improvements and optimization of existing processes, and also closes bottlenecks and encourages participation and involvement by all parties.

And advantages from a **process-oriented point of view:**

- *Overview and structure:* Creates a single point of reference for all future steps and activities that evolve around process creation and reengineering. The visual landscape and point of reference of the high-level BPM Life Cycle gives everyone involved a clear view of all the steps and activities that are to be done. These range from setting process goals, searching for existing process reference content, adjusting, matching, and/or creating new processes, and inciting high performance and good results through the distribution and assignment of process rewards.
- *Detail and granularity:* It is not only possible, but is highly recommended, to create further levels of detail from the perspective of the high-level view of the BPM Life Cycle. Note that there are literally thousands of tasks involved in all of the steps of the high-level BPM Life Cycle, and all the tasks involved need to be described in detail and with an analytical, determined approach.
- *Process innovation:* It is important to note that the BPM Life Cycle any organization creates should always adhere to innovation principles around processes on all levels. Innovation creates value that was previously unavailable, and process innovation is the key to opening up the gates to new—or better yet—the creation of entirely new markets and/or business opportunities. Process innovation should always be an integrated part of the six different business model domains (i.e., value, revenue, cost, service, operating, and performance models).

- *Process transformation:* Transformation principles have been well-known factors around process change since business process reengineering [40] was first introduced in the early 1990s. Going through a cycle of process reengineering allows for detailed and continuous process optimization and improvements while adhering to process goals and requirements. And, just as with process innovation, process transformation should also always be an integrated part of the six different business model domains (i.e., value, revenue, cost, service, operating, and performance models).

End Notes

1. The BPM Life Cycle Model, LEADing Practice Business Process Reference Content [#LEAD-ES20005BP].
2. See note 1 above.
3. "Document Engineering: Analyzing and Designing Documents for Business Informatics and Web Services", R.J. Glushko and T. McGrath, The MIT Press, (2005).
4. Process Life Cycle Verb Taxonomy Model, LEADing Practice Business Process Reference Content [#LEAD-ES20005BP].
5. BPM Building Blocks Model, LEADing Practice Business Process Reference Content [#LEAD-ES20005BP].
6. Layered Process Architecture, LEADing Practice Process Architecture Reference Content [#LEAD-ES40004BP].
7. See note 1 above.
8. "What is Business Process Design and Why Should I Care?", Jay Cousins and Tony Stewart, RivCom Ltd, (2002)
9. Process Workflow Connection Diagram Model, LEADing Practice Business Process Reference Content [#LEAD-ES20005BP].
10. See note 1 above.
11. Process Decomposition & Composition Model, LEADing Practice Decomposition & Composition Reference Content [#LEAD-ES30001AL].
12. "Standardization or Harmonization? You need Both!", Albrecht Richen and Ansgar Steinhorst, (2008).
13. See note 1 above.
14. "ITIL; A. Guide To Release And Deployment Management", UCISA.
15. "Implementing a Process in an Organization", Rational Software Corporation, (2001).
16. "Process roll-out and nurturing", ProcessNet srl, (2014).
17. "Business Process Change", Paul Harmon, Morgan-Kaufmann, (2003).
18. Value Map, Performance Map & Process Map Alignment Worksheet Model, LEADing Practice Business Architecture Reference Content [#LEAD-ES40002PGBCPSI].
19. K.A. Long, "Process Roles — Who are the Process Owners?" Business Rules Journal, 13, no. 9 (September 2012).
20. See note 1 above.
21. Process Monitoring & Measurements Model, LEADing Practice Business Process Reference Content [#LEAD-ES20005BP].
22. Performance & Value Measurement Model, LEADing Practice Measurement Reference Content [#LEAD-ES20014PG].

23. Business Value Model, LEADing Practice Value Model Reference Content [#LEAD-ES20007BCPG].
24. Structural and Behavioural Commonalities of Process Variants, Matthias Weidlich and Mathias Weske, Hasso-Plattner-Institute, University of Potsdam, German.
25. Business process modeling notation, Jan Mendling, Matthias Weidlich, Mathias Weske, Springer, 2010.
26. "Business Impact Analysis", ISACA.
27. Process Intelligence Model, LEADing Practice Business Process Reference Content [#LEAD-ES20005BP].
28. "Business Process Improvement: The Breakthrough Strategy for Total Quality, Productivity, and Competitiveness", H. James Harrington, McGraw-Hill, (1991).
29. See note 1 above.
30. Treating Progress Functions as a Managerial Opportunity, John M. Dutton and A. Thomas, The Academy of Management Review 9, no. 2 (April 1984): 235–247.
31. BPM Governance Model, LEADing Practice Business Process Reference Content [#LEAD-ES20005BP].
32. Process & Application Lifecycle Continuous Improvement Model, LEADing Practice Lifecycle Management Reference Content [#LEAD-ES30002AL].
33. "Business Process Improvement", Rob Berg, (2008).
34. An example of a Transformation & Innovation Interrogative Model around Business Processes, LEADing Practice Enterprise Transformation & Innovation Reference Content [#LEAD-ES60ETI].
35. Value-based Process Design Model, LEADing Practice Business Process Reference Content [#LEAD-ES20005BP].
36. Service & Process Activity Model, LEADing Practice Process Architecture Reference Content [#LEAD-ES40004BP].
37. Layered Process Architecture Model, LEADing Practice Process Architecture Reference Content [#LEAD-ES40004BP].
38. Process Operating Model, LEADing Practice Process Architecture Reference Content [#LEAD-ES40004BP].
39. Business Process Reference Content: An example of a BPM Continuous Improvement Tool.
40. "Reengineering Work: Don't Automate, Obliterate", Michael Hammer, Harvard Business Review, (1990).

The Chief Process Officer: An Emerging Top Leadership Role

Mathias Kirchmer, Peter Franz, Mark von Rosing

INTRODUCTION

More organizations are establishing business process management (BPM) as a discipline to move their strategies into operational execution with certainty. This is particularly important in the increasingly dynamic and connected business environment. As with any other management discipline, BPM was established through the process of process management. The use of BPM has become a key driver for optimization, cost cutting, effectiveness, and enterprise transformation, especially in an environment of external forces and drivers initiating constant change. As a result, many companies are beginning to develop a dedicated role to lead these initiatives. This emerging top executive role, which manages all process initiatives, is called the chief process officer (CPO).[1] The CPO oversees process management so that it increases performance and ensures value creation[2] by executing the business process strategy across organizational boundaries, such as departments or divisions.

THE EMERGING ROLE OF THE CPO

Process modeling, process optimization, and process innovation have been critical parts of organizations since the Industrial Revolution.[3] Today, with the increasing pace of business change, organizations are experiencing pressure to make continuous process improvements a part of daily operations. Given the increasing importance of processes as the key enablers in the transfer of the business strategy into execution, operational excellence,[4] optimization, and standardization, a top management role has emerged. As with any other important area, good leadership is needed; hence, an appropriate management role is required. In this environment, the ability to rally resources and drive collaboration effectively is vital, especially in diverse organizations, making process leadership not only a management but a C-level imperative.

This new top executive, which we see emerging in various organizations, is the CPO.[5] The title may not always be "chief process officer," but a champion of process is an important executive position at many enterprises. Some process management leaders hold titles such as "chief transformation officer" or "vice president of business process management." However, as the vice president of Gartner Group stated[6]: "Regardless of what the title is, it's for whoever is championing and leading business process improvement."[7]

343

Managing processes appropriately gives an organization the capability to successfully deal with a volatile business environment. The CPO enables the journey of an organization to the next-generation enterprise. He or she develops an integrated view of the organization across organizational boundaries, helping business people to see the power of information technology (IT) and IT people to understand the business challenges.

The transparency created under the leadership of the CPO facilitates other values, including quality and efficiency, agility and compliance, external integration of the company and internal alignment of the employees, and innovation and conservation where appropriate. The result is a lasting competitive advantage, empowered through BPM-enabled transformation under the leadership of the CPO.

The CPO creates a process-centric organization and culture across the more or less functional organization of an existing company; we often refer to this value proposition offering as the "BPM value flow."[8] He or she integrates function-driven and process-driven decision-making and management, as well as enables an end-to-end process view focused on value planning, value identification, and value creation[9] for clients. This overall management approach of the CPO, resulting in company-wide process governance,[10] is shown in Figure 1.

Where do you find such a CPO? In many cases, it is an enlightened chief information officer (CIO) who recognizes that with certain trends,[11] such as "the cloud" or "software as a service," the key assets in the organization are the processes. BPM is the means to get business value out of such technology trends. Some organizations even show that transition openly and move from the CIO role to the "chief process and information officer" (CPIO). Also, a chief operating officer (COO) could become a

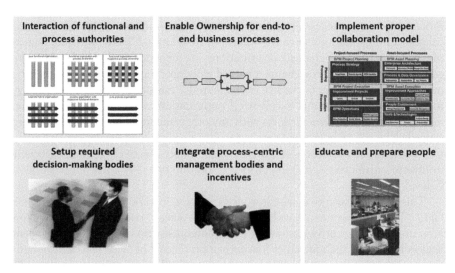

FIGURE 1

Enabling process-centric management of functional organizations.

CPO if he or she recognizes that BPM is more than just efficiency improvement. The role frequently develops on the back of a large business transformation program, with the "transformation director" stepping into this role to create sustainable value. Other organizations need to build the role of a CPO from scratch, co-existing with the CIO and COO. The best solution depends on the specific situation of an organization.

KEY TASKS OF THE CPO

The tasks of the CPO can be directly deduced from the process of process management that he or she owns. Figure 2 shows an overview of the process of process management.[12]

There are five groups of tasks:

- General integration tasks
- Project-related planning tasks
- Project-related execution tasks
- Asset-related planning tasks
- Asset-related execution tasks.

The CPO drives a cross-functional culture in which process owners, process experts, and the various knowledge workers know how they fit into the overall end-to-end process and what that means for their work. The CPO is the overall contact for all process-related topics and provides input in strategic business planning.

The core of the project-related planning task is the management of a BPM strategy. This includes the identification of the high-impact, high-opportunity processes of an organization on which BPM initiatives focus, the identification of required capabilities and capability gaps, as well as the definition of the overall

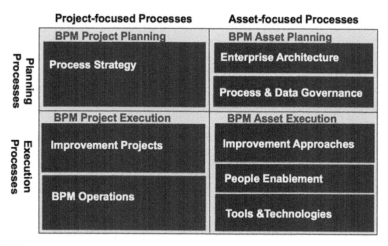

FIGURE 2

Overview of the process of process management.

process management agenda. The process management agenda includes high-level business cases that allow the prioritization of projects.

Project-related execution tasks include the launch and oversight of improvement initiatives, as well as the ongoing BPM operations. Typical operation tasks are the organization of a value-realization approach that enforces the ongoing focus on value, even after the project has concluded, or the procurement of administrative parts of the BPM Centre of Excellence (CoE) as externally delivered managed services.

The organization of an enterprise architecture (EA) approach and the appropriate process governance are key asset-related planning tasks. The governance-related tasks are crucial for a successful BPM discipline. They include the definition of governance-related roles, process owners, and procedures as well as the organization of governance bodies,[13] such as for the process owners to make cross-process decisions.

Asset-related execution tasks include the development of capabilities in various improvement methods, such as a process transformation approach, so that they can be applied in improvement projects. A key task is to organize people enablement initiatives, such as change management (ongoing or as part of a project) or the launch of BPM communities. Last but not least, the direction and oversight for tool- and technology-related assets, such as repository tools, process execution systems, social platforms, and process intelligence tools, comes from the CPO.

POSITIONING OF THE CPO IN THE ORGANIZATION

The positioning of the CPO (or another more relevant name for the role) in an organization depends heavily on the nature of the specific organization. It has to be defined in the context of the existing organizational structure and market dynamics. However, there are several aspects to consider when positioning this role:

- The CPO provides input in the overall business strategy based on his or her cross-functional view and drives the execution of this strategy. The CPO requires appropriate access to the board and the position needs to provide the necessary standing in the organization.
- The CPO works closely with the other process owners, who are in general very senior executives. He or she needs to have the standing and positioning to be successful in this context.
- The CPO leads the BPM core team, which is often a center of excellence. The CPO's positioning needs to give his or her reports the appropriate standing and development perspectives.

These points motivate most organizations to have the CPO role report directly to the management board or at least to another C-level position. This has been confirmed in an empirical research study.[14] It is consistent with our observations working with large and mid-sized organizations around the world.

The typical positioning of the CPO is shown in Figure 3. It also describes the CPO's integration in various governance bodies.

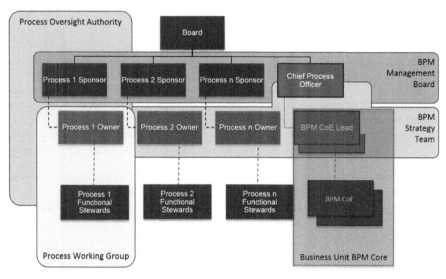

FIGURE 3

Typical positioning of the chief process officer.

The CPO is an emerging role targeting the creation of value by focusing on transferring the business strategy into execution, quickly and with minimal risk. We expect this role to become more and more important in organizations, similar to the rise of the CIO about in the latter part of the 1980s.

CONCLUSION

As organizations respond to the need for greater market responsiveness, they recognize the need for a more robust process management discipline that treats the processes in the organization as an important asset. As with any other major asset, processes need nurturing and caring with the right level of priority. The emergence of a CPO is therefore an inevitable, important enabler in achieving this goal.

End Notes

1. Franz, Kirchmer, *The Chief Process Officer – A Role to Drive Value* (London, Philadelphia: Accenture Whitepaper, 2012-2).
2. Kirchmer, "How to Create Successful IT Projects with Value-Driven BPM," in *CIO Magazine Online* (February 27th 2013).
3. Scheer, *Business Process Engineering – Reference Models of Industrial Enterprises* (Berlin e.a: Springer, 2nd edition, 1995).
4. Kirchmer, *High Performance through Process Excellence – From Strategy to Execution with Business Process Management* (Berlin, e.a: Springer, 2nd edition, 2011).
5. Jost, "Vom CIO zum CPO," *Harvard Business Manager*, (2004): 88–89.
6. Bruce Robertson, Gartner Group Inc. Nov-2013.

7. Morris, *Architect, Design, Deploy, Improve (ADDI) – A BPMS Development Methodology* (Chicago: Wendan Whitepaper, 2014).

8. LEADing Practice Value Modelling Reference Content.

9. Franz, Kirchmer, *Value-Driven Business Process Management – The Value-Switch for Lasting Competitive Advantage* (New York, e.a: McGraw-Hill, 2012-1).

10. Kirchmer, Hofmann, "Value-Driven Process Governance – Wettbewerbsvorteile durch die richtige Processorganisation,". in *IM+io Fachzeitschrift fuer Innovation, Organisation und Management* (Germany, 03/2013).

11. Scheer, "Tipps fuer den CIO: Vom Tekki zum Treiber neuer Business Modelle," in *IM+IO – Das Magazin fuer Innovation, Organisation und Management* (Sonderausgabe, Dezember 2013).

12. Kirchmer M, Franz P, *The BPM-Discipline – Enabling the Next Generation Enterprise. BPM-D Executive Training Documentation* (Philadelphia, London).

13. Kirchmer, Lehmann, Rosemann, zur Muehlen, Laengle, *Research Study – BPM Governance in Practice* (Philadelphia: Accenture Whitepapers, 2013).

14. Ibid.

iBPM—Intelligent Business Process Management

Nathaniel Palmer

The impact of new technologies, the mandate for greater transparency, and the ongoing aftershocks of globalization have collectively removed nearly any trace of predictability within the enterprise environment. In light of this, delivering sustainable competitive advantage can no longer be found through simply scale and efficiency, but rather requires the ability to interpret and adapt in real-time to streams of information flows, make sense of these, rapidly translating these into effective responses designed for precision rather than repeatability. The ability today is best delivery through Business Process Management (BPM). BPM is a discipline involving any combination of modeling, automation, execution, control, measurement, and optimization of business activity flows in support of enterprise goals, spanning systems, employees, customers, and partners within and beyond the enterprise boundaries.

Today, we are in what many see as the third phase of BPM, and what is commonly distinguished as "*Intelligent BPM*" or *iBPM*. The subject of this chapter, iBPM builds upon the previous two generations, yet extends into directions previously out of reach. Among that previously out of reach is what frames the core of the notion of intelligence. Not that BPM previously was dumb, per se, but rather it was blind. Whereas previous generations of BPM offered limited ability to make sense of business activity flows, iBPM System ("IBPMS") are distinguished foremost by a "sense and respond" orientation. In this way we can group and categorize the three phases of BPM in terms of the synergistic combination of three groups of capabilities.

The first phase ("Phase One") offered the ability to separate application from the processes (business logic) that they support, similar to introduction of the relational database systems (RDBMS) and the ability to separate data from applications. The advent of the RDBMS was essential to transforming how business applications were designed and built. In the same way, the introduction the BPMS offered the ability for the first time to manage processes as separate assets, in a similar manner to how we manage data. Just a few years ago, "Phase Two" of BPM introduced new capabilities that support adaptable, goal-driven process models by maintaining the intelligence for how to access information and application resources without having to bind this into a rigid process model. Today, "Phase Three" builds on the first two generations, adding visibility into the process and what is happening in the real-time, as well as through integrated analytics what will likely occur in the near future.

Within the first several years of the market for BPM products being established, applications that addressed these first two phases of capability dominated. Although having added value and offering improved maturity of BPM practice, these approaches also limited the potential market for BPM software. However, for most organizations the vast majority of their business processes is dynamic, not standardized, and thus requires the business systems (e.g., deployed software) that support them to adapt quickly to changes within the business environment. As a business technology, the greatest value of process management software is delivered, not through automation and integration alone, but by introducing a layer between users and existing IT infrastructure to allow business systems to adapt and keep pace with the constant change found in most business environments. Fully realizing the ability offered through orchestration, however, requires the situational awareness necessary to adapt business systems to a changing business environment—the ability to sense and respond. By taking the lid off the black box of automation, Phase Three of BPM offers a framework for continuously validating and refining an understanding of business performance drivers, and adapting business systems accordingly.

To achieve the visibility and feedback to expose what is going on within a process will require a new level of transparency of processes and operations that is sure to present cultural and human factors challenges. However, this is nothing new for BPM. BPM is only slightly about technology. It is, instead, mostly about the business and the people. What is indeed new, however, and at the center of the Phase Three opportunity, is the ability now to adapt systems continuously to match the ever-changing business environment. The model most frequently referenced throughout this chapter, this continuous loop of visibility and adaptability, offers one of the first real leverage points for transforming business through adaptability.

THE EVOLUTION OF INTELLIGENT BPM

To understand the opportunities offered by Intelligent Business Process Management, it is helpful to consider the phases of maturation that solutions have gone through since the late 1990s. Prior to and during technology expansion of the mid- to late-1990s, the management of business processes was typically limited to the repetitive sequencing of activities, with rigid, "hard-wired" application-specific processes set out in documentation and later specified programmatically in custom-coded or conventional Enterprise Resource Planning (ERP) systems. Any more sophisticated degree of workflow management generally imposed a significant integration burden, frequently accounting for 60–80% of the project cost with little opportunity for reuse. Still, integration was typically limited to retrieval of data or documents, similarly hard wired with one-to-one connection points.

These early process management initiatives often focused on integrating and automating repetitive processes, generally within standardized environments. Whether focused on Straight-Through Processing transactions or a discrete process, such as Account Activation, these are applications in which the flow and sequence of activities is predetermined and immutable. The role of exception handling here is to allow human intervention to quickly resolve or correct a break in the flow of an otherwise standard process.

By the end of the 1990s, however, BPM had emerged as an identifiable software segment, a superset of workflow management, distinguished in part by allowing process management independent of any single application. This was enabled by managing application execution instructions separate from process flows, so processes could be defined without limitation to a single application, as well as through support for variable versus hard-wired process flow paths.

The first wave of BPM deployments were typically aimed at bridging the island of automation described above, such as closing gaps in existing ERP deployments. Early BPM solutions were differentiated by integration-centric functionality, such as application adapters, data transformation capabilities, and product-specific process definitions (e.g., an order-to-cash process). Eventually, the introduction of standards, such as Web Services and advances in the development tools within BPM suites, lowered the cost and complexity of data integration. This began to shift the fundamental value proposition of BPM from discrete capabilities to enabling the management of business logic by business process managers, without threatening the integrity of the application logic (the infrastructure that is rightfully managed and protected by IT personnel).

The availability of standards-based protocols significantly lowered the burden on BPM adopters for building and maintaining integration infrastructure, freeing time and resources to focus on process and business performance, rather than being consumed with plumbing issues. Over time, this facilitated a refocus of process management software from that of automation and integration to orchestration and coordination, bringing BPM into the realm of business optimization. The environment in which the modern enterprise operates is dynamic, requiring the business systems that support it to be so as well. This means that systems must be able to easily adapt to changing circumstances of the enterprise. Phase Two of the BPM opportunity was presented through making orchestration a reality—the ability to connect abstracted application capabilities across orchestrated business processes, thereby transforming existing automation infrastructure into reusable business assets. What separates orchestration from automation is presented by a fundamental shift in perspective, from thinking of processes as a flow of discrete steps, to understanding processes in terms of goals and milestones.

FROM AUTOMATION TO ORCHESTRATION: THE REALIGNMENT OF BPM AROUND SERVICE-ORIENTED ARCHITECTURES

Orchestration allows systems to mirror the behavior of the rest of the enterprise environment (one defined in terms of objectives rather than scripts). Over the last decade, orchestration has introduced a visible shift in the axis of business computing. As organizations realize the opportunities presented by orchestration, it offers (arguably mandates) a wholesale rethinking of the role of applications and information systems.

Orchestration has already had a visible impact on the direction of the BPM market, enabled by standards protocols (notably eXtensible Markup Language (XML) and the core Web Services stack of Simple Object Access Protocol (SOAP), Universal Description, Discovery, and Integration (UDDI), and Web Services Description Language (WSDL)); the emergence of Service-Oriented Architectures (SOA) has provided a new level of flexibility and simplicity in resolving integration issues. In fact, it has to such an extent that it almost seems redundant to discuss in the context of the forward-looking perspective of modern BPM.

Indeed, most "adaptability pundits" would find the discussion of SOA as "propeller head" anathema, something only the geekiest techies should worry about. Yet, that is why it is so relevant to the adaptability discussion. Because, previously (e.g., prior to SOA), performing the most basic changes to underlying integration configurations, such as a change in the structure of a document by its sender or the set of information required by the requester, would have required taking running processes and/or systems off line, then having a programmer manually code, test, and deploy each of the changes.

Now we can nearly take for granted that the underlying systems of record are decoupled from how we access them—that access is enabled through a services layer rather than a programmatic interface that requires integration at the code level (i.e., "tightly-coupled"). What SOA provides for BPM and other software environments is a common means for communicating between applications, such that connections do not need to be programmed in advance, as long as the BPM environment "knows" where to find information and how to access it. This is critical to dynamic processes in which the specific information, activities, and roles involved with a process may not be predetermined but identified as the process progresses.

Of course, this does require, however, that the information and infrastructure sought to be accessed is exposed as services. For example, core system capabilities can be exposed as containerized Web services with a WSDL description, able to be invoked by any Web services-compliant application, or increasingly with a representational state transfer (REST)ful[1] interface allowing integration points and data variables to be defined at design time, but resolved at runtime, eliminating the inherent problems of hard-wired integration.

APPLY SOA STRATEGIES TO INTEGRATING UNSTRUCTURED INFORMATION

Although the evolution of SOA has dramatically improved the accessibility of structured information through standardized interfaces, access to unstructured information can be far more challenging. Consider for a moment where customer information resides in your organization. The answer is most likely "everywhere"—records, transactions, profiles, project data, recent news, and other sources of structured and "semi-structured" information (such as correspondence and other documents without uniform representation). For many organizations, it would take years to rationalize all the places where customer data might be found. However, by instead knowing where to find the various instances of each of their data sets and how each is described, they can be left intact yet used for multiple purposes.

Leveraging Content As a Service

Following the same strategy as that which was presented above as being used by SOA for accessing structured information, a relatively new standard called "Content Management Interoperability Services" (CMIS) enables a services approach to "content middleware." CMIS does this by exposing and offering a means to control diverse unstructured document-based information stored within CMIS-compliant content repositories, whether the material is in either internally or externally managed sources. The result is that, as content is captured or otherwise introduced to a process, it can be automatically categorized and indexed based on process state and predefined rules and policies.

This strategy presents a virtual repository of both content and metadata that describes how and where content is managed at various stages of its life cycle such that Metadata are exposed to the system and process nodes where it can be used, but remains invisible to users. Users, instead, are presented with the appropriate content and format based on their identity and the current state of the process.

REALIZING ADAPTABILITY: SHIFTING FROM EVENT-DRIVEN TO GOAL-DRIVEN

The notion of orchestration has changed the role of BPM from that of a transit system, designed to shuttle data from one point to another over predefined routes, to that of a virtual power user that "knows" how to locate, access, and initiate application services and information sources. In contrast with more easily automated system-to-system processes and activities, "knowledge worker" processes characteristic of manual work involve a series of people-based activities that may individually occur in many possible sequences.

This transition in computing orientation can be described as the shift from *event-driven* in which processes are defined in terms of a series of triggers, to *goal-driven* in which processes are defined in terms of specific milestones, outcomes (goals), and constant cycles of adaptations required to achieve them. In event-driven computing, systems respond to a specific event—a request for information is received and the appropriate information is sent, or a process step is complete and so the results are recorded and the next step is initiated. In most cases, the nature of event-driven computing requires explicit scripting or programming of outcomes. In goal-driven processes, however, things are far more complex. A process that has only 20–30 unique activities, a relatively small number for most knowledge-worker processes, may present over 1000 possible permutations in the sequencing of activities. This, of course, presents too many scenarios to hard-code in advance within linear process flows, or to create a single process definition. This fact helps explain the difficulty traditionally faced in the automation of these types of goal-driven processes. Rather, this capability is enabled through the application of goals, policies, and rules, while adjusting the flow of the process to accommodate outcomes not easily identifiable.

Goal-Driven Scenarios

In many cases, each subsequent step in a process is determined only by the outcome and other circumstances of the preceding step. In addition, there may be unanticipated parallel activities that occur without warning, and may immediately impact the process and future (even previous) activities. For these reasons and the others described above, managing goal-driven processes requires the ability to define and manage complex policies and declarative business rules—the parameters and business requirements that determine the true "state" of a process. Goal-driven processes cannot be defined in terms of simple "flow logic" and "task logic," but must be able to represent intricate relationships between activities and information, based on policies, event outcomes, and dependencies (i.e., "context").

Such a case is the admission of a patient for medical treatment. What is involved is in fact a process, yet the specific sequence and set of activities mostly does not follow a specific script, but rather is based on a diagnostic procedure that likely involves applying a combination of policies, procedures, other rules, and the judgment of health care workers. Information discovered in one step (e.g., the assessment of a given condition) can drastically alter the next set of steps, and in the same way a change in "patient state" (e.g., patient goes into heart failure) may completely alter the process flow in other ways. What is needed to successfully execute such a process is either a "super user," who knows both the medical protocols to make a successful diagnosis and the system protocols to know where and how to enter and access the appropriate information, or, alternatively, BPM can exist as the virtual user layer. BPM could provide a single access point for the various roles involved, meanwhile assuming the burden of figuring out where and how access required information. Yet what really differentiates this as a goal-driven system is the ability to determine the sequence of a process based on current context. For example, a BPM system can examine appropriate business rules and other defined policies against the status of a process or activity to determine what step should occur next and what information is required.

Often the flow and sequencing of a goal-driven process is determined largely by individual interpretation of business rules and policies. For example, a nurse who initiates a patient-admitting process will evaluate both medical protocol and the policies of the facility where the health care services are administered. Similarly, an underwriter compiling a policy often makes decisions by referring to policy manuals or his own interpretation of rules and codes. As a result, what may be an otherwise "standard" process will be distinguished by exceptions and pathways that cannot be determined in advance, but at each step each activity must nonetheless adhere to specific rules and policies. For further reading and information on Goal-Driven modelling and scenarios, please see the chapter on Value-Oriented Process Modelling.

PHASE THREE: INTELLIGENT BPM

The first two phases of BPM have laid a solid foundation for enabling adaptable business systems, by allowing business logic (processes, policies, rules, etc.) to be defined and managed within a separate environment, as well as using an open approach to communicating with other systems (Web Services). This has provided a level of adaptability that allows BPM adopters to respond to changes in the operating environment with far greater agility than ever before. This shift towards goal-oriented computing has laid the path for Phase Three BPM, which combines integration and orchestration with the ability to continuously validate and refine the business users' understanding of business performance drivers, and allowing them to adapt business systems and process flows accordingly. The effect of Phase Three BPM is to "take the lid off" what has for years been a black box shrouding automation.

With the third phase of BPM, visibility combines with integration and orchestration to enable business process owners and managers to discover the situation changes that require adaptation. Phase Three of BPM offers a framework for continuously validating and refining an understanding of business performance drivers, and adapting business systems accordingly. This should represent a new and significantly greater level of interest and adoption of BPM software, by attracting organizations seeking to optimize business performance, rather than integrating and automating systems and tasks.

Part of the recent evolution toward iBPMS strategies and technology is the inclusion of more sophisticated reporting capabilities within the BPM environment itself. This is both enabled and in many ways necessitated by the greater flexibility of the architectures introduced with the BPM suites that provide BPM Phase Two capabilities. With these environments, the ability to support nonsequential, goal-driven models is greatly increased, requiring more feedback (reporting) to enable successful execution of this type of less deterministic process models.

With few exceptions, reporting on process events and business performance was previously done only after a process had been executed, or otherwise within a separate environment disjointed from the process. This obviously prevented any opportunity to impact the direction of a process, but was based on a limitation of the management process as well as system and software architectures. Specifically with regard to BPM, process models were most commonly defined as proprietary structures, and in many cases compiled into software. Thus, changes either required bringing down and recompiling an application, or were otherwise limited to discrete points in the process (such as exceptions and yes/no decision points).

Adaptability Begins with Reading Signals

Successful adaptation, to move in the right direction, requires the ability to accurately assess the full and relevant context of status. Indeed, the more flexible and adaptable the systems are, the greater the requirement for visibility. In the same manner, the greater the ability to monitor the signals that define business performance, the more value can be found in the ability to adapt processes and systems accordingly. To illustrate the distinction of orchestration over automation, the metaphor of rail transportation—which moves across a predictable path and direction (quite literally "set in stone") has been used (arguably overused) to illustrate *automation*, contrasted with *orchestration*, described in terms of a car or other personal transportation. The latter offers a vehicle to deliver passengers to a desired destination by understanding the rules of the road and milestones along the way, but does not require scripting every single inch along the way. In fact, it would be nearly impossible to do so given the unpredictability of such factors as traffic and road conditions. Driving through traffic is entirely about *sense-and-respond* in which adaptation is happening real-time—you brake, accelerate, steer left, and so forth. All of these actions are in response to a constant stream of signals and event data.

Thus, what separates personal transportation from rail travel is not only the ability to deviate from the rigidly fixed path, but also the need for visibility. This is an overly simplified, and again arguably overused, metaphor, but it nonetheless offers a tangible concept for why "Intelligent BPM" is indeed a substantively different animal from its predecessor, the currently ubiquitous dumb BPM. The bottom line is that if you cannot see what is ahead of you, you cannot respond accordingly, and prior to achieving the capabilities of "Phase Three BPM," your processes are blind. By way of example, driving a car is an immensely data-driven exercise, even if it is largely tactile and observational data. At least this is the case today, in the absence of widespread adoption of *Google's driverless car*. Yet of course there too, it would be extremely data-intensive and literally data-driven, even if the majority of this data is visible only on a machine-to-machine basis. Similarly, to allow users to drive their process to their self-selected destinations requires access to a rich data environment that connects to the process. As we seek further capability in this area, although it may become more machine and data driven, it may well be that the user increasingly will actually require less ability to see the data as the BPM software "sees."

INTELLIGENT BPM LEVERAGES BIG DATA

Since its inception, IT has been defined by the architecture of the relational database (RDMS). The advances seen in computing, even in the evolution of Internet architecture, were essentially a derivative of the relational database. This has evolved over the years since 1975, and everything from monolithic packaged software to comparatively simple and agile applications have been built on this model. Today, however, we are amidst an inflexion point, moving to the postrelational era, perhaps more aptly named the "Big Data Era."

The intelligence that comes from capturing event data (signal detection), as well as driving greater understanding and innovation through simulation, is a Big Data scenario. This cannot be done with a narrow lens on structured data, nor can it be limited to internal, single-company boundaries (nonetheless organizational or departmental constraints). Successful adaptation requires the ability to manage complex multi-enterprise systems, expanding the window of analysis for strategy beyond the single company or business unit. Through partner value chains, customer interaction, outsourcing, offshoring, peer production, and other extended ecosystems of interdependent entities, Intelligent BPM processes often extend well beyond discrete transactions between suppliers or customers to create the extended enterprise.

This level of collaboration requires standard conventions and mutually understood meaning of data exchanged between stakeholders, but without rigid structure or formalization. In this way, the postrelational shift to Big Data has largely paralleled, and in many ways is driven by, the same conditions and requirements behind adaptability. The movement in both cases is to expand beyond the limits of relational data structures and capture the richer context that defines business events. One of the most frequently discussed Big Data initiatives is *Hadoop*, which is essentially a flat-file document database or file system very reminiscent of the early database hierarchical architecture. It is parallel to the "*NoSQL*" movement, which while it might sound pointedly anti-SQL, actually stands for "Not Only SQL" in the spirit of postrelational flexibility for enabling greater reach and performance than otherwise possible with traditional relational databases.

A core driver behind Big Data is the vast growth of digitized information, in particular that which begins and exists throughout its life cycle in digital format. It's not just that the data volumes are big, but that the broader spectrum of data must be managed differently. The data management goal is no longer about trying to create a monolithic structure, but rather to arrange data in ways such that the semantics—the understanding of the meaning of the data and the interrelationships within it—are accessible.

In an era when an aberrant Tweet can in a matter of minutes cost shareholders millions,[2] it is the meta-context of business events across a spectrum of structured, unstructured, and semistructured information that defines the larger perspective of business activity. The impact of mobile and social capabilities in enterprise systems, as well as external social networks, is having a very real material impact on business. It has become a critical (even if comparatively smaller but clearly growing) piece of the business event stream. It also has advanced the de-materialization of work as well as personal/professional demarcation. Is *LinkedIn* a "work tool" or personal site? Clearly, it is both. Yet for most organizations an increasing amount of work is conducted through otherwise "unsanctioned" channels, such as *LinkedIn*, *Twitter*, and other social sources, offering either the potential wellspring of value-adding business events and event data, or otherwise process "dark matter" outside of the purview of the traditional business IT environment. Social media has allowed not simply individuals, but businesses and brands, to connect directly to consumers. We now have volumes of case studies of missteps and miscalculations with the personae of corporate brands across social networks.

What is less visible, but arguably more important, is the leverage of these tools for successful adaptable business strategy and processes, as we saw with the Proctor and Gamble (P&G) use of social media, in which the company explicitly exploits these channels to engage customers and obtain market advantage. This brings us back to the value of business event management and the speed of adaptation. All business events have an implicit half-life and utility curve. Whatever business you are in, the value represented by the response to an event diminishes over time. In every case, this is based on a utility curve, not a straight line. Responding twice as fast is more than twice as valuable. The faster the response, the greater the business value realized.

Delays in response ("Latency") can be divided into two distinct groups: "Infrastructure Latency," or delay presented by the system in delivering notification of the event, and "Decision Latency," or the period of time between when the business-event data are captured and when it is responded to. For example, the delay between the time from when a customer submits a complaint or (per the scenario above) tweets about a bad experience—from that moment until when it is within an actionable, reporting framework (e.g., when it becomes an actual *signal*), that is Infrastructure Latency.

The time between when the signal is received until the moment someone responds, first deciding then acting, is Decision Latency. Recall the first organizational capability as necessary to foster rapid adaptation offered by Reeves and Deimler, *the ability to read and act on signals of change*, the speed of this is largely a matter of Decision Latency (Figure 1).

Regardless of the specific circumstances involved, the value of the response is greater closest to the moment of the complaint, diminishes over time, and, after a certain period in time, any response is going to be of little value. There is not a single set of hard metrics for all organizations, or all events, but in every case, predictable value is gained from the ability to capture an event. It could be related to a sales opportunity, field maintenance, or terrorist threat; in every case the faster the response, the greater the value.

Faster Adaptation Is Not Necessarily Faster Decisions

It can be assumed that the ability to take action on a specific event will always involve some delay. Yet there is a similar inevitability that the value lost because of that delay will follow a utility curve, not a straight line. Thus, the greatest source of value will always come from faster notification and actionability, rather than simply faster decision-making.

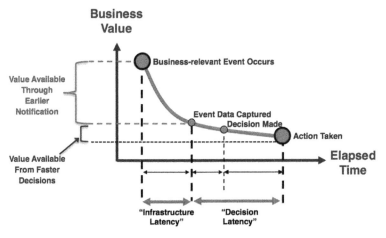

FIGURE 1

Time-based value of business event response.

The value of faster decisions (automating the function of knowledge workers in the decision-making process) offers little value, particularly when compared to the cost of poor decisions made in haste. Because of the greater the delay in notification and actionability, there is greater pressure on making decisions sooner rather than losing further value. Yet the opportunity lies in reducing Infrastructure Latency. By getting actionable information into the hands of knowledge workers sooner, iBPM systems offer a predictable source of business value and clear differentiation from passive systems (i.e., notification only, without the ability to facilitate a response.)

THE VALUE OF SOCIAL MEDIA TO INTELLIGENT BPM

Understanding the time-based impact of business event response illustrates the critical capability and value offered by Intelligent BPM from the ability to move, to signals and actions, to the edge points of interaction. The sooner signals are received and acted on, the tighter the response loop, and the greater the value derived from that business event. Yet this comes not simply as the ability to read events generated from within social media, but also the means or mode through which events are "socialized."

Consider the revolution of *Facebook* in recent years, which was not about enabling me to post stuff about myself for the world to see. That was an established set of capabilities and, frankly, the world hardly needed another outlet for this. If nothing else, *MySpace* sufficiently addressed this, which in 2009 far exceeded *Facebook's* reach and community size. Rather, it was the introduction of the "Like" button, which rapidly transformed the site's orientation (and ultimately that of social networks overall) from self-publishing to collaboration. Within a few months of introducing the Like button, *Facebook* overtook *MySpace* in community size, and soon after sealed its fate altogether.

The "Like" button was (and is) about tapping into an event pipeline and then enriching these events with personal contributions (if nothing else, indicating your like for them). For all intents and purposes, *Facebook* users are tagging that event, adding value to it across its life cycle, just as presented in the notion of the business event management framework. This new model of collaboration has transformed the now decades-old metaphor of threaded discussions. *Facebook* is now the collaboration metaphor for everything from *LinkedIn* to *Salesforce Chatter* to a growing number of iBPMS product vendors. Yet it is not merely a tribute to the success of *Facebook*, which although quite admirable in areas such as the leverage of agile software development methods and speed of community growth, has otherwise been a lackluster example of adaptability (note initial public offering (IPO) struggles and user backlash, which would likely have been largely diminished by following the strategies described in this chapter.)

Rather, the enduring success of the *Facebook Wall* metaphor for collaboration reflects the importance of business events and business event management to

Intelligent BPM and enabling adaptability. The greatest value that social media offers to business processes is the ability to collaborate on events—including but not limited to spontaneous collaboration, but by also tagging and grouping events (e.g., "subscribing") across their life cycle. For further reading and information on social media and BPM, please read the chapter on Social Media and Business Process Management.

The Ability to Mobilize

Reeves and Deimler[3] cite "the ability to mobilize" as a critical organizational practice for enabling adaptability. It was largely presented in the same context as described in the preceding section, specifically for stakeholders to connect and collaborate informally, but surrounding business events. Yet a more literal interpretation is the ability to extend processes to mobile touch-points as a critical precept of Intelligent BPM.

The fact of the matter is that work is already mobile. The iPad, iPhones, and other smartphones and tablets combined are reaching the point of saturation. Mobile is fast becoming the dominant means of personal computing, connected to the cloud and unleashing a flood of big data. This presents a wellspring of new opportunities for engaging customers and empowering knowledge workers, yet they can also quickly overwhelm existing IT resources. Will you be able to evolve your enterprise applications fast enough to keep pace? Probably not. Yet this is where iBPMS is providing the ability to manage the event life cycle across applications, offering both those connection points to existing applications and the ability to manage business events independently.

CONCLUSION

Change remains the one dependable constant in the business environment, yet the speed of change is greater now than perhaps any time before. Where the challenge may have once been simply to keep pace, today the megatrends of Social, Mobile, Cloud, and Big Data collectively have redefined the IT landscape seemingly overnight. Effectively leveraged, these present a wellspring of new opportunities for engaging customers and empowering knowledge workers. Yet few enterprise systems in place today are positioned to support this. Rather, it is what we see with Intelligent BPM and iBPM systems as the ability to support dynamic and adaptive work patterns is what will enable the type of collaborative work needed to thrive on adaptability in a data-driven work.

We conclude with five basic rules of thumb to follow to foster adaptability, to make mobile and cloud work for you today, and future-proof your IT investments for tomorrow. First, begin by considering the goal-driven processes within your enterprise, and consider how current architecture both obstructs and supports these processes (e.g., identify the obstructions to benchmark your need for adaptability.) Next, assess your ability to manage processes as collections of business events, and how to enable a business event management framework to quickly and effectively manage the ability to read and act on signals of change.

The third rule, a critical one, is the leverage of standards. Consider how you will take advantage of certain key standards, notably Content Management Interoperability Services (CMIS), XML Process Definition Language (XPDL), and Business Process Model and Notation (BPMN). You need to know that the assets that you're creating and managing today can be accessible and follow the same evolutionary curve as the systems that you're using to access them. Fourth, you must have the ability to understand social technologies and the means for tagging and adding value to business events and to understand the business event half-life, and why responding to an event in a timely fashion is so critical.

Finally, look at the infrastructure within your organization that is increasingly commoditized, and prioritize where you can leverage cloud and consumerization to offset future upgrades and maintenance costs. Similarly, bring your own device (BYOD) access is making it easy to get mobile devices in the hands of workers—because they're putting them in their own hands. Take advantage of this, and look to leverage Intelligent BPM as a framework for creating, delivering, and managing new capabilities to a larger network of stakeholders and process participants.

End Notes

1. A set of architectural principles by Web services that focus on a system's resources, including how resource states are addressed and transferred over HTTP by a wide range of clients written in different languages.
2. The Twitter feed of the Associated Press reported that Barack Obama had been injured in an explosion at the White House (April 23, 2013).
3. Martin Reeves and Mike Deimler, "Adaptability: The New Competitive Advantage," HBR (July 2011).

Evidence-Based Business Process Management

Marlon Dumas, Fabrizio Maria Maggi

INTRODUCTION

Traditional business process management (BPM) practice has largely relied on rough estimations and manual data gathering techniques when discovering, analyzing, and redesigning business processes. For example, traditional approaches to discovering "as-is" business processes rely on interviews or workshops with managers or process stakeholders, or in situ observation of process work by business process analysts. These techniques are effective when it comes to capturing and conceptualizing the "happy paths" of a process, but they fall short of providing a fully detailed picture thereof, including the numerous exceptions and deviations that generally characterize the performance of the process on a day-to-day basis. Similarly, when performing quantitative analysis, business process analysts generally rely on rough estimations of execution times, error rates, branching probabilities, and other relevant parameters of the process. This may lead analysts to misestimate the actual bottlenecks and sources of defects of the process.

Evidence-based BPM aims at addressing the shortcomings of traditional intuitionistic BPM practices. Evidence-based BPM is the practice of systematically using data produced during the execution of business processes to discover, analyze, and continuously monitor and improve business processes. Evidence-based BPM has garnered significant momentum in recent years, thanks to the widespread adoption of enterprise systems that store detailed business process execution data, as well as advances in data mining techniques and tools.

EVIDENCE-BASED BPM: WHAT FOR?

Evidence-based BPM enables business process analysts and managers (including process owners) to answer a range of questions across the entire spectrum of the BPM lifecycle, but more specifically in the following:

- Process design phase: for example, what will be the impact of a given process redesign decision given what we have observed in the past?
- Process monitoring phase: for example, what is the likelihood that a given case of the process will end up in a negative outcome, or what is the likelihood that we will violate our service-level agreement given the current state of the process and past observations?
- Process analysis: for example, why do certain cases of the process take too long to complete? What are the root causes of deviations with respect to our service-level objectives?

363

Evidence-based BPM relates directly to the operational model of the BPM life-cycle, as it helps analysis to build accurate pictures of the current state of the process (including process models). It is also directly related to the performance model, because it allows analysis to answer key questions related to the performance of the process at present, in the past, and into the future.

For example, in the context of a business process for stock replenishment, specific examples of questions that evidence-based BPM is intended to address include the following:

1. What distinguishes the executions where the stock is replenished on time from those where the stock is replenished too early (overstocks) or too late (out-of-stocks)? In particular, what patterns can be used for early detection of deviant cases leading to overstock or understock?
2. Why do some stock replenishment cases lead to incorrect purchase orders or invoice payments that do not comply with the company policy? Which patterns can be used for early detection of noncompliant cases?

The first of these questions relates to the performance model, while the second one relates to the operational model (focusing on compliance aspects). In this respect, evidence-based BPM is a powerful tool to ensure on a continuous basis the integrity of the process with respect to its performance objectives and compliance rules. This is a highly relevant problem in large organizations where integrity and compliance assurance currently requires significant amounts of manual effort, thus leading to high costs. For example, according to the independent analyst Ponemon Institute, large organizations spend on average USD 3.5 million/year on compliance checking, while the costs of dealing with noncompliance issues (including fines and rectification costs) are much higher, at nearly USD 9.4 million/year.[1]

Evidence-based BPM is supported by a range of techniques to extract knowledge from business process execution logs. These techniques fall under the umbrella of *process mining*.[2] In the rest of this chapter, we provide an overview of process mining techniques, and we discuss by means of case studies how these techniques enable evidence-based BPM in practice.

THE ANSWER: PROCESS MINING

Process mining is concerned with the analysis of collections of event records produced during the execution of a business process. Such event records represent events signaling the start, end, abortion, or other relevant state change of a process or an activity therein, or any other event of relevance to the execution of a process, such as the allocation or deallocation of a process worker to a task, the receipt or dispatching of a message to a process participant, and so on.

In general, the main input of a process mining technique is a business process event log, which is a collection of event records relevant to a given business process. An event log is generally structured (but not necessarily) as a set of traces, where each trace consists of the sequence of events produced by one execution of the process

Table 1 *Extract of a Loan Application*

Customer Identifier	Task	Timestamp	...
13219	Enter loan application	2007-11-09 11:20:10	–
13219	Retrieve applicant data	2007-11-09 11:22:15	–
13220	Enter loan application	2007-11-09 11:22:40	–
13219	Compute installments	2007-11-09 11:22:45	–
13219	Notify eligibility	2007-11-09 11:23:00	–
13219	Approve simple application	2007-11-09 11:24:30	–
13220	Compute installments	2007-11-09 11:24:35	–
...	...	...	...

(i.e., a *case*). As a minimum, an event record contains an identifier of the case of the process to which the event refers, a time stamp, and possibly a number of additional attributes. An example log of a loan application process is sketched in Table 1.

Based on such event logs, process mining techniques extract useful information that allows analysts to gain insights into the process and to formulate and validate hypotheses about the process. The output of process mining can be manifold, ranging from a complete model of the process, to a description of the main (frequent) paths of the process or its deviations, or a diagnosis of the reasons for deviations in a process.

Process mining techniques can be broadly classified into *descriptive techniques* and *predictive techniques*. Descriptive techniques aim at providing insights about the process as it is or as it has been observed in the logs. Predictive techniques aim at predicting how a process as a whole or a specific case of the process will behave in the future under certain hypotheses or conditions.

DESCRIPTIVE APPROACHES

Descriptive process mining approaches can be further classified into the following:

1. *Process performance analytics*, which seek to help analysts to analyze the performance, such as by extracting key performance indicators and uncovering bottlenecks in a business process.
2. *Automated process (model) discovery*, which seeks to automate the work involved in discovering a process that is in use so as to produce a model of the process for documentation and analysis purposes.
3. *Model enhancement*, which seeks to enhance or revise existing process models based on information extracted from the event log.
4. *Deviance mining*, which seeks to help analysts identify and analyze deviations of the business process with respect to normative or desired behavior.
5. *Process variant and outlier identification*, which seeks to help analysts identify and analyze the different variants of a process and to detect isolated cases that stand out with respect to others.

PROCESS PERFORMANCE ANALYTICS

Business process performance analytics refers to a family of techniques that take as input an event log and produce a performance assessment of the process as recorded in the log. Techniques for process performance analytics are widespread and well understood. They are an integral part of mainstream BPM methods and are supported by most commercial BPM tools.

The performance assessments produced via process performance analytics generally include mean values and other descriptive statistics of process metrics (e.g., cycle time, resource utilization), as well as associated graphs, charts, and other visualizations of process performance.[3] More sophisticated tools are able to detect and quantify the impact of bottlenecks and sources of defects in the process and to overlay this information on top of a process model.

Some tools also support *online process performance analytics* (also known as *realtime process performance analytics*), meaning that they continuously recalculate summary statistics of process metrics at runtime. These latter techniques take as input not a full event log, but rather an event stream generated by the information system supporting the business processes under observation. Such online process analytics tools provide dashboards that process managers or analysts can use to continuously monitor the state of the process. Such tools may also provide, in addition to realtime statistics, the ability to inspect specific cases of the process in order to analyze issues as they arise.

AUTOMATED PROCESS DISCOVERY

Automated process (model) discovery techniques take as input an event log and produce as output a process model. These techniques are generally geared towards producing models that capture the *frequent behavior* recorded in the input event log. They can be further classified into approaches that produce procedural models, such as business process model and notation (BPMN)[4] process models and Petri nets, and approaches that produce declarative models, such as a Declare model.[5] The former approaches are detail oriented in that they try to describe the full flow of control between tasks and events in the business process. These techniques produce closed process models—that is, process models in which everything that is not explicitly specified is assumed to be forbidden. Figure 1 shows an example of a business process model in the BPMN notation that could be automatically discovered from the log sketched in Table 1.

On the other hand, declarative approaches are *overview oriented* because they merely try to give a general overview on the process behavior. These approaches describe processes by means of open models—that is, rules that indicate what common behaviors are observed in the event log, without presupposing that other behaviors are not allowed.

As business processes evolve over time, it may be useful to discover not only a model of a snapshot of a business process at a particular point in time, but also to discover how the business process evolves over time. For instance, a business process

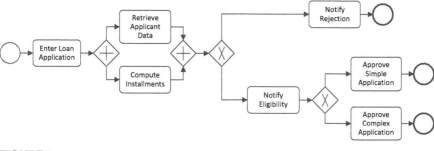

FIGURE 1

Automatically discovered process model in business process model and notation.

for handling insurance claims may be performed in one way when the workload is normal and in a completely different way when the number of claims spikes, such as in case of a natural disaster affecting a large number of customers. A family of process mining techniques known as *business process concept drift discovery* copes with the situation where the process is changing due to periodic or seasonal effects or due to changing environmental conditions. These techniques detect points in time when the observed behavior of the process has changed and provide a description of the changes that the process has undergone.

MODEL ENHANCEMENT

In process mining, model enhancement refers to a group of techniques that take as input an event log and a model and produce as output an enhanced model. Model enhancement techniques can be further classified into *model repair* techniques and *model extension* techniques.

Model repair uses information derived from a log to change an existing (procedural or declarative) process model to better reflect reality. Model repair typically involves two steps. In a first step, called *conformance checking*, the given process model is compared against the event log. In other words, the expected behavior captured in the process model is pitched against the actual behavior observed in the logs. Conformance checking produces as output a set of identified mismatches, where a mismatch is either an event observed in the log that cannot be explained by the process model or (conversely) a step that should occur according to the process model but is not observed in the log. Given the output of conformance checking, the second step in model repair is to add, remove, or modify elements in the process model, so that the resulting (repaired) model has fewer mismatches than the original model.

Model extension, on the other hand, is used to enrich an existing process model with information extracted from a log. A typical example of a model extension technique is *decision mining*, which seeks to automatically discover the branching conditions in a process model from the event log. In other words, given an event log and a process model with decision points (e.g., exclusive decision gateways in BPMN), decision mining techniques discover the conditional expressions that determine when is a given branch of a given decision point taken—for example, that a given branch of a loan application process is taken when the amount of the requested loan exceeds $1000, while the other branch is taken for lower loan amounts.

Other model enhancement techniques are concerned with discovering resource allocation rules, such as that a given approval task in a loan application process is always allocated to the same loan officer who performed an earlier verification task in the same process.

DEVIANCE MINING

Business process deviance mining is a group of process mining techniques that take as input an event log and a specification of expected behavior in the form of rules that the process is expected to fulfill (e.g., compliance rules or process performance objectives). Deviance mining techniques produce as output a diagnostic of deviations in the business process with respect to the given specification. In other words, these techniques aim at identifying (positive or negative) deviations that occur in the input log with respect to the expected behavior described in the input specification. In addition to identifying occurrence of deviations, deviance mining techniques provide a diagnostic explaining why certain cases deviate from the given specification—for example, why certain cases outperform or underperform the given performance objective, or fail to fulfill a given compliance rule. The diagnostic can take different forms, but in any case its purpose is to enable the analyst to identify process improvement opportunities. For example, a common policy in the case of large purchases is that a purchase request and the corresponding payment should be handled by two different people (the "four-eyes principle"). Early detection of deviations with respect to this policy reduces the risk of fraud in such processes.

Starting from the deviations identified via deviance mining, it is possible to discover discriminative rules—that is, rules that discriminate between positive cases (cases that abide to the specification) and negative cases (cases that violate the specification). For example, given a specification stating that every case of a loan application process should be completed in less than 10 days, deviance mining techniques may extract a rule stating that loan applications where the applicant provides incorrect or inaccurate employment data are likely to take more than 10 days to complete. Such insight can help analysts uncover potential causes of undesirable deviations. Deviance mining can also be used to uncover and explain positive deviance, such as explaining what characterizes cases where the customer is served much faster than the norm.

Deviance mining is typically applied in an offline manner to understand the reason for observed deviance. However, deviance mining can also be applied in an online manner, such as in the context of *compliance monitoring*. Several approaches have been proposed to check compliance of an event stream with respect to a compliance model consisting of rules. In this context, compliance rules can be, for example, expressed using some temporal logic and translated into automata that can be used to efficiently monitor the rules at runtime. However, these monitoring approaches are reactive: They allow process stakeholders to identify a violation only after it has occurred rather than supporting them in preventing such violations in the first place. This feature is a key differentiator between these compliance monitoring techniques and predictive monitoring techniques introduced later.

PROCESS VARIANT AND OUTLIER IDENTIFICATION

Techniques for business process variant identification take as input an event log and produce as output a set of variants of the process recorded in the log. For example, given an event log of a loan application process, the output may be three variants of the process: "small loan applications," "large loan applications with mortgage," and "large loan applications without mortgage." These variants correspond to distinct versions of the process that differ in significant ways, such as in terms of the typical sequences of events observed in each variant.

Techniques for process variant identification and analysis usually rely on *trace clustering*, which is a data mining technique in which a set of objects (in this case, the set of traces forming the log) are partitioned into multiple subsets such that each cluster contains similar objects (traces). Each trace cluster produced in this way is a sublog on its own and can therefore be given as input to an automated process discovery technique in order to extract a model of a process variant.

Techniques for *outlier analysis* aim at identifying cases in the process that stand on their own, meaning that they have peculiarities that make them very different from other more common cases. Process mining techniques for outlier analysis also rely on trace clustering. In this context, traces belonging to clusters with a small number of elements are considered to be the outliers. Indeed, such small clusters represent rare behaviors that are sufficiently different from more frequent behavior (represented by larger clusters) to stand apart.

PREDICTIVE APPROACHES

Predictive process mining approaches are geared towards making predictions on the future state or performance of a process. A family of techniques falling in this category is *predictive deviance monitoring*, which is concerned with the early prediction (at runtime) of future deviations in the currently running cases of the process.

Predictive deviance monitoring techniques take as input a stream of events and produce recommendations for process workers during the execution of a case. These recommendations refer to a specific (uncompleted) case of the process and tell the user the impact of a given action on the probability that the case at hand will fail to fulfill the performance objectives or compliance rules. By setting thresholds on such probabilities, users are able to produce streams of warnings and alerts to which they can subscribe in order to monitor the process in real time.

A second family of predictive process mining approaches is *data-driven process simulation*. Data-driven process simulation refers to the practice of simulating a process model by replaying the events in an event log. In other words, rather than manually setting the simulation parameters based on rough estimations or guesswork, the simulation is driven entirely by the log, leading to simulation results that more accurately reflect reality. In the extreme case, the actual process model used for simulation may itself be extracted from the log by means of automated process discovery techniques, in which case both the process model and the stream of events generated during process simulation are designed to closely reflect reality.

Data-driven process simulation allows process analysts to perform "what-if" analysis of the process, in order to determine the potential impact or benefits of a given change to the process on key process metrics (e.g., cycle time). In particular, this technique allows analysts to understand the future performance of a "to-be" process, while taking into consideration historical observations of the process recorded in the log.

CASE STUDIES AND LESSONS IN EVIDENCE-BASED BPM

Several case studies of evidenced-based business process management based on process mining techniques have been reported in the past few years. A compendium of such techniques is maintained in the Website of the Institute of Electrical and Electronics Engineers task force on process mining.[6] In this section, we review a subset of these and other case studies related to automated process discovery, deviance mining, and predictive (deviance) monitoring.

CASE STUDIES IN AUTOMATED PROCESS AND VARIANT DISCOVERY

In *Application of Process Mining in Healthcare: A Case Study in a Dutch Hospital*,[7] analysts sought to obtain information about typical execution paths (i.e., careflows) followed by specific groups of patients in a gynecological oncology process. For these patients, all diagnostic and treatment activities were recorded by a billing system for financial purposes. Filtering and clustering techniques in combination with automated process discovery were then applied to analyze data coming from a group of 627 gynecological oncology patients treated in 2005 and 2006. The outcome of the study confirmed that by using process mining techniques, it is possible to produce understandable models for large groups of patients. The baseline for this analysis was a manually created flowchart for the diagnostic trajectory of the gynecological oncology healthcare process. The results produced using evidence-based analysis were comparable to the flowchart representation, but they provided further details not initially foreseen.

Another related case study has been reported at the hospital of São Sebastião in Santa Maria da Feira, Portugal.[8] The hospital has 300 beds and an in-house IT system used across different departments, recording data about process executions in event logs. In the case study, the execution paths of emergency patients were analyzed for activities related to triage, treatments, diagnosis, medical exams, and forwarding of patients. In this case study, several process mining techniques were adopted, such as the following:

1. Variants and infrequent behavior discovery
2. Performance analysis
3. Deviation mining (to discover discrepancies from medical guidelines)

In *Process Mining to Improve a Service Refund Process*,[9] a service refund process of an electronics manufacturer was analyzed using automated discovery techniques as well as performance and conformance analyses. The study aims at identifying the cause of some inefficiencies and too-long throughput times in the process, starting from concrete questions and problems coming from inspections and customer complaints and using the data collected in the event logs recorded by a service platform. Valuable insights have been derived from the discussion of the results of the data analysis with process managers.

In *Process Mining to Compare Procure-to-Pay Processes in Different Countries*,[10] a case study is discussed conducted in collaboration with AkzoNobel, the largest global paint and coatings company and a major producer of specialty chemicals headquartered in Amsterdam, the Netherlands, with operations in more than 80 countries. The analysis with process mining techniques revealed what was really happening in the different local procure-to-pay processes and has allowed process managers to get actionable insights on how to improve the process. Specifically, this study allowed management to

1. Obtain insights about cases in which the "first time right" principle was not realized
2. Compare the processes executed in different countries to identify process variants and best practices that can be adopted on the corporate level
3. Realize a compliance control to execute in accordance with corporate guidelines

CASE STUDIES IN DEVIANCE MINING

An increasing number of deviance mining case studies have been reported in recent years. One such case study in a large Australian insurance company was reported.[11] In this case, a team of analysts sought to find the reasons why certain simple claims, which should normally be handled within a few days, were taking substantially longer to be resolved. In other words, they needed to understand the difference between "simple quick claims" that were handled in less than X days and "simple slow claims" that took longer to be handled. They used a technique known as delta analysis, which consists of discovering one process model from each partition of an event log and comparing these models. In this case, one model was discovered for "simple slow claims" and another for "simple quick claims," and the resulting models were manually compared. It was found that certain paths and cycles were more frequent for slow claims than for quick claims, and that two activity metrics distinguished slow versus quick claims, namely "an average number of occurrences of a given activity X (per case)" and "percentage of cases where a given activity X appears at least once." By calculating these metrics for each activity, the team traced the sources of delays to specific activities.

A similar idea was applied by Sun et al.[12] in the context of software defect handling processes in a large commercial bank in China. The authors took a log of more than 2600 defect reports of four large software development projects and examined the differences between defect reports that had led to a correct resolution (normal cases) versus those defect reports that had led to complaints by users (anomalous cases). The team defined a number of features to distinguish between normal and anomalous complaints, including the "number of occurrences of a given activity X in a case" (for each possible activity X) and the "number of occurrences of activity B after an activity A." Because there are many such combinations (A,B) and to avoid having a too-large number of features, the authors employed a discriminative item-set mining technique to identify the most relevant such pairs (A,B). Based on the resulting features, the authors constructed a decision tree that classified cases into "normal" and "anomalous." Finally, from the decision tree they extracted a set of seven rules that explained the majority of the anomalous cases, thus leading to potential improvement ideas.

In A *Process Deviation Analysis: A Case Study*,[13] instead of using item-set mining and a decision tree for discriminating between normal and anomalous cases, the authors proposed a methodology based on association rule mining. The proposed methodology is applied to a real-life case study pertaining to a procurement process in a European financial institution.

Another case study showing the potential of deviance mining, this time in the healthcare domain, was reported by Lakshmanan and Wang.[14] Here, the team applied deviance mining techniques to understand the differences between cases leading to positive clinical outcomes versus those leading to negative outcomes in the process of treatment of congestive heart failure at a large US-based healthcare provider. In this case, the team employed a combination of delta analysis (as in the Australian insurer case study mentioned above) with sequence mining techniques. Specifically, the authors used sequence mining to detect typical sequences of activities (e.g., activity B occurring sometime after activity A) that were common for positive outcomes but not common for negative ones, or vice versa. The observations made using sequence mining were complemented with additional observations obtained by comparing a process model discovered from cases with positive outcomes with the model obtained for cases with negative outcomes. In this way, the authors extracted a number of pathways and patterns that discriminate between positive and negative cases.

Another case study reported by Bose and van der Aalst,[15] applied a technique for extracting patterns that discriminate between event traces associated with malfunctions (versus normal traces) in components of remotely monitored X-ray machines. The techniques they employed fall under a wider family of techniques known as discriminative sequence mining techniques,[16,17] which, in a nutshell, allow one to extract sequential patterns that discriminate between multiple classes of sequences (e.g., sequences leading to normal outcome vs. sequences containing deviations).

CASE STUDIES IN PREDICTIVE MONITORING

Case studies of predictive process monitoring in the field of transportation and logistics have been reported.[18,19] These case studies showed how predictive process monitoring can be used to explain and predict "late show" events in a transportation process. Here, a "late show" refers to a delay between expected and actual time of delivering the goods to a carrier (e.g., airline). In this case study, standard statistical techniques are used to find correlations between "late show" events and external variables such as weather conditions or road traffic. The uncovered correlations are then used to define complex event processing rules that detect situations where "late show" events are likely to occur.

A challenge for predictive process monitoring in this setting is that transportation processes are generally not "case based" because goods emanating from different customers are often aggregated and unaggregated at different points in the process. In other words, multiple "cases" of a transportation process will typically merge and split at runtime; thus, delays affecting one delivery might end up affecting others.

CONCLUSION

Evidence-based business process management based on process mining has gained significant momentum in recent years, as evidenced by numerous reported case studies in various fields. Also, over the past few years, an increasing number of tools supporting process mining have emerged and reached various levels of sophistication, including Disco by Fluxicon,[20] QPR Process Analyzer,[21] Perceptive Process Mining,[22] and the open-source ProM toolkit.[23] In parallel, methods for applying process mining have emerged, such as van der Aalst's L* method.[24]

Moving forward, we foresee the emergence of more sophisticated process mining methods capable of handling larger, more heterogeneous, and noisy datasets with high levels of accuracy. Equally or more importantly, though, we foresee the emergence of evidence-based business process governance methods, allowing managers to effectively set up and steer evidence-based BPM initiatives in large organizations, so that evidence-based BPM becomes part of the organization's management culture. This will bring BPM to the level of modern marketing approaches, which are often data driven. In an ideal evidence-based organization, every business process redesign decision will be made with data, backed by data, and continuously put into question based on data.

End Notes

1. Ponemon Institute, "The true cost of compliance," *Benchmark Study of Multinational Organizations*, (January 2011). http://www.tripwire.com/tripwire/assets/File/ponemon/True_Cost_of_Compliance_Report.pdf.

2. W.M.P. van der Aalst, *Process Mining—Discovery, Conformance and Enhancement of Business Processes* I–XVI (Springer, 2011), 1–352.

3. M. zur Mühlen and R. Shapiro, "Business process analytics," in *Handbook on Business Process Management 2*, (Springer, 2010), 137–157.

4. BPMN (Business Process Model and Notation) is a standard process modeling notation defined by the Object Management Group (OMG)–http://bpmn.org/.

5. W.M.P. van der Aalst, Maja Pesic, and Helen Schonenberg, "Declarative workflows: balancing between flexibility and support", *Computer Science—R&D* 23 no. 2 (2009): 99–113.

6. http://www.win.tue.nl/ieeetfpm/doku.php?id=shared:process_mining_case_studies.

7. R.S. Mans, H. Schonenberg, M. Song, W.M.P. van der Aalst and Piet J. M. Bakker, "Application of process mining in healthcare—A Case Study in a Dutch Hospital," in *BIOSTEC (Selected Papers)*, (2008), 425–438.

8. A. Rebuge and D.R. Ferreira, "Business process analysis in healthcare environments: a methodology based on process mining," *Information Systems* 37, no. 2 (2012): 99–116.

9. Fluxicon, "Process mining to improve a service refund process," http://fluxicon.com/blog/2012/11/case-study-process-mining-to-improve-a-service-refund-process/, (retrieved on 28 05 2014).

10. Fluxicon, "Process mining to compare Procure-to-Pay processes in different countries," http://fluxicon.com/blog/2012/11/case-study-process-mining-to-compare-procure-to-pay-processes-in-different-countries/, (retrieved on 28 05 2014).

11. S. Suriadi, M.T. Wynn, C. Ouyang, A.H.M. ter Hofstede, and N.J. van Dijk, "Understanding process behaviors in a large insurance company in Australia: a case study," in *Proc. of the International Conference on Advanced Information Systems Engineering (CAiSE)*, (Springer, 2013), 449–464.

12. C. Sun, J. Du, N. Chen, S.-C. Khoo and Y. Yang, "Mining explicit rules for software process evaluation," in *Proc. of the International Conference on Software and System Process (ICSSP)*, (ACM, 2013), 118–125.

13. J. Swinnen, B. Depaire, M.J. Jans and K. Vanhoof, "A process deviation analysis—a case study," in *Proc. of Business Process Management Workshops*, (Springer, 2011), 87–98.

14. G.T. Lakshmanan, S. Rozsnyai, F. Wang, F., "Investigating clinical care pathways correlated with outcomes," in *Proc. of the International Conference on Business Process Management*, (Springer, 2013) 323–338.

15. R.P.J.C. Bose, W.M.P. van der Aalst, "Discovering signature patterns from event logs", in *Proceedings of the IEEE Symposium on Computational Intelligence and Data Mining (CIDM)*, (IEEE, 2013) 111–118.

16. D. Lo, H. Cheng, J. Han, S.-C. Khoo and C. Chengnian, "Classification of software behaviors for failure detection: a discriminative pattern mining approach," in *Proc. of the International Conference on Knowledge Discovery in Databases (KDD)*, (2009) 557–566.

17. X. Xing, J. Pei and E.J. Keogh, "A brief survey on sequence classification," *SIGKDD Explorations* 12 no. 1 (2010) 40–48.

18. A. Metzger, R. Franklin and Y. Engel," Predictive monitoring of heterogeneous service-oriented business networks: the transport and logistics case," in *Proc. of the SRII Global Conference*, (2012), 313–322.

19. Z. Feldman, F. Fournier, R. Franklin and A. Metzger," Proactive event processing in action: a case study on the proactive management of transport processes," in *Proc. of ACM International Conference on Distributed Event-Based Systems (DEBS)*, (ACM, 2013) 97–106.
20. http://www.fluxicon.com.
21. http://www.qpr.com.
22. http://www.perceptivesoftware.com/products/perceptive-process/process-mining.
23. http://promtools.org.
24. W. M. P. van der Aalst, Ibid.

Social Media and Business Process Management

Henrik von Scheel, Zakaria Maamar, Mona von Rosing

INTRODUCTION

As with the internet itself, social media has come to stay and is fundamentally affecting the way organizations are interacting, both internally and externally. However, when organizations adopt social media initiatives, they will not achieve its full potential unless the changes are integrated with both its operational processes and its approach to continuous improvement. Exploiting social media by making the requisite connections to the Business Process Management (BPM) Center of Excellence (CoE) interaction and feedback loop enables the creation of customer-centric process design, as well as providing access to stakeholder input about the maturity of BPM processes related to customer services, which again drives process-improvement decisions. This chapter will discuss the changing market around social media as well as how Socially Oriented Process Modeling can be used effectively to enable business model renewal, service improvements, customer performance focus, as well as address critical debates about whether to automate certain processes or keep them manual.

THE DIGITAL MIND-SET IS CHANGING

We live in a "connected world" and organizations can no longer ignore this nor take it for granted. What many organizations are not realizing is that we are not in a shifting technical period, nor in a business or economic shift. We are experiencing a major cultural shift, and that shift affects technology, business, and economies. It is a revolution that is creating a "digital mind-set" that is fundamentally transforming and affecting the way organizations are doing business, and it is vital to their survival that they understand these changes. A digital mind-set is different from the transactional mind-set that it is supplanting. A digital mind-set is open, connected, participating, selective, and controlling. It is fundamentally a very different way of thinking and working, in which the digital mind-set builds followers, from embracing one and becoming a "friend," whereas the transactional mind-set is looking for suspects who they can turn into prospects and will love you only if you become or have the potential to become a customer (Figure 1).

In the digital mind-set the person can be the user, consumer, community member, participant, producer, as well as customer, all at the same time. The important aspect is that such a mind-set operates in an open, connected, and participating

Digital Mindsets

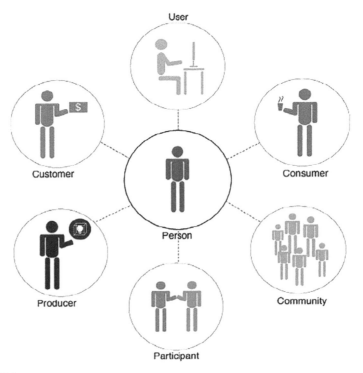

FIGURE 1

The digital mind-sets.

way. Although not everyone is open or even supportive to such a mind-set, as the internet in its very nature is open and connected such that it sees things that are hidden or obscured as "damaged," which it seeks to repair by bringing into the open the entities, for example, people/persons who successfully "interact" in the internet naturally pursue the most openness, connectedness, and participation.

It can be argued that few of us treat others as we want to be treated; most of us look for short cuts and manipulatively clever tricks that can fool people into buying. So why is such a digital mind-set so good for business? Because, when organizations have a digital mind-set, they are more connected and they can more quickly solve problems.

As discussed in the earlier chapters, some of the Global University Alliance research has revealed a difference between outperforming and underperforming organizations. One of those differences is that outperforming organizations have empowered employees to communicate more effectively through many tools, including social media channels and technology.

SOCIAL MEDIA ARE RESHAPING BUSINESS

Traditional business models, particularly in large organizations, have had, as one common characteristic, careful limitation of direct contact between those within the organization and those outside. Only certain specific individuals (most frequently in roles such as sales, customer service, and field consulting) are designated as "customer-facing" personnel. Organizations further limited outside access to internal employees through filtering mechanisms such as publishing only a main switchboard number (whether routed through a live receptionist or an interactive voice response system), generic mailing, or email addresses such as "sales@" or "info@".

As discussed in the chapter on "outperformers and underperformers", success is based on doing what the outperformers know: being successful means constantly changing. And, therein lies the irony—to be successful you have got to change something...and something that must be changed must be something that has allowed you to be successful up to now ("we don't change a winning team"). However, where do you start? What needs to change? We all know that aspects of a process and activities need to be changed. Nevertheless, this is not the start of the journey. So the real question remains, what needs to change? Now, combine that reality with day-to-day business challenges such as: entry of new competitors, rising price of doing business, new technologies, evolving customer expectations, changing consumer demands, and your team's desire to better interact. Today, many organizations have "satisfied" customers and a sound business model, and they are confident that social media will have a nominal impact on their organizations. It is apparent, however, that social media have already had an impact on customers' daily lives and are here to stay, and, therefore, this confidence is both falsely held and ultimately likely dangerous for those that hold the view. We are still very early in the social media era, however, and some changes are already evident in the market. The question is not whether your organization is adapting any abilities around social media. The real question is to what extent are your customers or even your competitors already doing it. The only way to find out is to start watching your environment for the influence these changes will bring to your business. Moreover, here is the second irony, watching for the impact of social media requires that you employ social media.

We see that social media have the ability to change the Business Model in the following areas (Figure 2):

- From selling to connecting with customers
- To create a new era of brand management that recognizes the role and nature of bonding, advantage, performance, relevance, and presence
- From large campaigns to small and rapid actions
- From controlling the message to transparency
- From hard to reach to available everywhere

Social and mobile business is affecting most organizations in different ways, but some will be more impacted than others. Some organizations don't even realize it.

The following are five clear examples in which we see the impact of social media on business models in various industries:

1. **Organizations that own assets and make them available to consumers for rent.** For example, hospitality and car rental companies face new competition from peer-to-peer models. In New York, hotels now compete against 10,000 rooms, apartments, and even spare couches offered by consumers in social media communities.

2. **For most consumers, the car is one of the most expensive assets owned**; yet the average consumer uses their car just 8% of the time. It is this low utilization that is leading some to offer their cars for rent. In addition, as consumers get access to the cars they need when they need them, ownership becomes less attractive. One study found that people who use car-sharing services were 72% less likely to buy or lease a car in the future.

3. **Companies that facilitate business between consumers.** If you are in the business of earning fees to take something from one customer and get it to another customer, social business models will challenge your business. We are not referring to eBay or Craigslist—they already are the standard for Peer-to-Peer (P2P) disintermediation and reintermediation, having taken a big piece of the newspapers' classified ad business; rather we are referring to applications that allow consumers to hail cabs, provide job search tools, and so on.

4. **Financial business model.** Look at banks, which take money from savers and lend it to borrowers. Today, savers get little, but this is not the case for folks lending money on Prosper and LendingClub. Although the risks are greater,

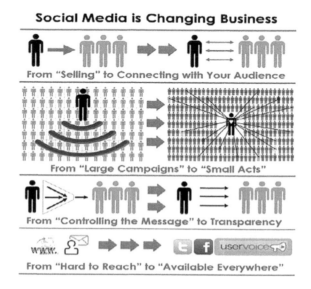

FIGURE 2

Social media are changing business.

the rewards are as well. Although the regulatory hurdles for being a "bank" are high, companies are able to skirt the regulations and bring down costs to consumers and provide new services with capabilities such as "mobile wallets", P2P money transfer, and P2P lending models.

5. **Business models that manufacture durable goods.** Younger consumers are less interested in obtaining drivers' licenses and prefer to meet friends online and seek to decrease the miles they drive as a means to save the environment. It is clear that P2P and sharing business models will affect the auto business (and related industries such as auto parts and auto insurance).

For both hotels and cars, more supply means lower costs for consumers and less revenue for providers. In addition, the new social business competition has a vastly different cost structure from traditional providers. The social media rental rooms, couch surfing, rental sharing, or used CD, games, or book sales do not need to purchase, own, or maintain assets, resources, and locations the same way the traditional business models do.

All the aforementioned changes to the assumptions and conditions of the affected business models reflect how and why organizations should rely on their social networks referred to as customer, supplier, competitor, and partner. These four networks are established based on the interaction circles, which show the "social" or communications distance to be overcome when interacting, which define the environment of a company (Figure 3).

- Scenario 1. A company uses a customer social network to contact a customer's "friends" to disseminate information on products and services and, hence, boost sales.

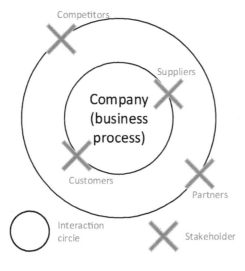

FIGURE 3

Interaction circles (From Badr & Maamar, 2009).

- Scenario 2. A company uses a supplier social network to establish the reliability of a supplier, as perceived by other parties (e.g., customers and suppliers) that have dealt with this particular supplier in the past.
- Scenario 3. A company uses a competitor social network to work with competitors, and partners of competitors, to establish standards and common norms.
- Scenario 4. Finally, a company uses a partner social network to identify the individuals and groups with which it can join forces to tackle complex initiatives.[1]

Modern business strategy and models must expect and can exploit the fact that well-informed consumers will have more access to information in real time and can avail themselves of new social and mobile business models that save money. Social and mobile-centric business models have a way of empowering consumers so they can make better decisions. The introduction of these changes will mean that many organizations will have to scramble to keep up with lean new competitors and consumers' rapidly changing technology habits and sharing behaviors.

When changes occur in a business model, this means that, fundamentally, the organization must change their services and processes as well. A social media strategy that is supported by an organization that is able to rapidly alter business processes, listen to, identify, and manage risks early on, and generate sales opportunities, will be an effective one. Therefore, innovating and transforming one's process models is, in social media, the cornerstone for adapting the organization to a new service and value to the customer.

Consider how social media can impact the following operational and management processes. These provide good examples of how operational processes can be changed to take advantage of social media:

- **Purchase requisition to goods received.** Quality issues in goods received may immediately trigger an interaction between customer and supplier via a blog or other method to discuss how to best address the issues.
- **Order-to-delivery.** Use of online "Process communities" can help align all resources and people involved in a particular scenario and, through a focus on customer-centric metrics, such as low delivery variance, enhance delivery performance.
- **Human resources.** Recruitment processes can be enriched through social media. Consider the use of sites such as LinkedIn as part of the hiring process. Companies that develop software might look to recruit those most involved in forums or developing apps based on the company's application program interface. Blogs can highlight talent in particular areas as well.
- **Marketing.** By finding out what customers and prospects are saying about your products or those in your market space, you can enhance and target marketing efforts. Facebook, Pinterest, and other sites offer new ways to drive traffic and interest in products and services. Online focus groups can be conducted via online social media sites. Mini-surveys on a company's Facebook page often elicit responses that can rapidly close the feedback loop, making for effective marketing.
- **Customer service.** As never before, people are saying what they think in social media. Monitoring and engaging with customers using these tools can help drive customer centricity and customer loyalty. Engage your customers wherever they are speaking out, from Yelp to Tripadvisor to Facebook.

- **Research and development**. Instead of formulating product direction in a vacuum, one electronics company that produces accessories started listening to early iPad owners speaking out on social media and let that drive their product strategy, with very strong results.
- **Operational processes** can be enhanced and supported by strategic engagement with social media, both inside and outside the company.

ENABLING CUSTOMER-CENTRICITY

The most important aspect of social media is understanding the social consumer decision life cycle journey. As discussed, the traditional consumer decision funnel is changing because it is outdated or not applicable in the world of social media. The graphical model in Figure 4 below describes the consumer decision life-cycle journey. This model was introduced by Henrik von Scheel and Prof. Mark von Rosing in November 2003, based on a "consumer influencer decision making cycle in e-Commerce" model developed with IKEA and Google, which uniquely combines specific defined online consumer persona behaviors with the traditional marketing purchase funnel to support a traditional customer journey and a distinct online purchase funnel. The model shows the states a consumer goes through within the cycle as they determine whether to purchase something, what an organization can do to act on the decision as an influencer, and how the two are connected.

This model contrasts with the pure version of the more traditional purchase funnel developed to map the consumer journey from the time they are initially aware of a brand or product to the point of action or purchase. This staged process is summarized as:

- **Awareness**. The customer is aware of the existence of a product or service
- **Interest**. Actively expressing an interest in a product group
- **Desire**. Aspiring to a particular brand or product
- **Action**. Taking the next step towards purchasing the chosen product

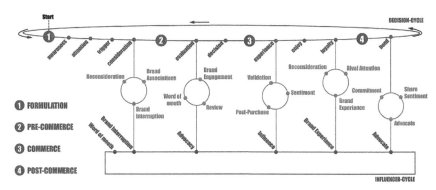

FIGURE 4

Consumer decision life cycle.

Today's consumers take a much more complex and more iterative path that extends through and beyond purchase. The classic funnel shows an ever-narrowing array of decisions and choices until purchase, when in fact the social, connected, and channel-surfing customer today often is expanding the set of choices and decisions after their initial consideration.

Just as important, the consumer decision life cycle treats the post-purchase process with the same level of importance as the prepurchase journey. It's a simple concept, really, but it adds significantly to the insight that can be gained as to how to engage consumers and the implications for organization design, including business process design, because this visually highlights and isolates the most important aspects of the journey in this new paradigm:

- **Consider**. What brands/products do consumers have in mind as they contemplate a purchase?
- **Evaluate**. Consumers gather information to narrow down their choices.
- **Buy**. Consumers decide on a brand and buy it.
- **Post-purchase**. Consumers reflect on the buying experience, creating expectations/considerations that will inform a subsequent purchase.
- **Advocate**. Consumers tell others about the product or service they bought.

The funnel model also ignores and the consumer decision life cycle journey exposes the role that influencers play in modern consumer behavior, a reality that must be reflected in modern business design and managed through BPM capabilities. This visualization of the journey helps focus conversations on where to invest time, money, and attention, where the opportunities are, what sorts of people and processes you need to deliver on them, where you are weak and your competitors strong. The consumer decision journey approach helps clarify the issues that are undermining a brand, or where a brand has an opportunity to grow. What part of the consumer decision journey is critical to a brand? Social media provides organizations with a wealth of information on their customers. Although social media and BPM can definitely enable customer centricity, the long-term success for organizations will depend on the enterprise-wide social media monetization strategy and the agility of internal business processes.

Social media complemented by agile business processes can definitely aid in creating "customer-centric" organizations. These organizations will be able to successfully attract and retain customers, align and position their offerings in line with customer requirements, effectively optimize their marketing strategies, and will find ample opportunities for improved customer experience and enhanced customer relationship management.

LESSONS LEARNED AROUND SOCIAL-ORIENTED PROCESS MODELING

The customer acquisition process consists of identifying potential prospects, qualifying them, and converting them to live customers.

Organizations can observe customer patterns and behaviors on social media platforms by using the right tools and technologies, and identifying potential prospects. Structured analysis and aggregation can help in customer profiling and segmentation. Subsequently, targeted marketing campaigns and customer dialog can help in customer qualification and acquisition. However, all of this can be done only if business processes are developed and deployed to provide these capabilities and only if they have been integrated into the other business processes to align with an overarching strategy, a fact that of necessity means the adoption of BPM.

An example of where this transition has been made and the necessary capabilities developed includes as an example, UBS Bank. This organization launched a new credit card with special features and a preapproved credit limit targeting students. To reach potential customers, it could then look at the basic profile information of students on Twitter. This is the first level of customer segmentation. At the next level, UBS can now examine the tweets posted by the target prospects. Let's explore what this means by assuming that a couple of these prospects are tweeting about their need for a credit card that offers a minimum level of interest. If the bank is able to detect this, a process can be triggered to facilitate customer conversion, by initiating a social media-centered marketing campaign, which sends customized information to the prospects about specific credit card products. Such a campaign is much cheaper than traditional campaigns to establish and develop a new credit card product. Based on the interest and response from target customers, subsequent steps of the business process can be orchestrated to facilitate customer acquisition through target marketing campaigns, by improving prospect qualification, through new approaches to customer relationship management, and by creating process flows that reflect and leverage the properties of social media. These approaches are discussed in the remainder of this chapter.

TARGET MARKETING CAMPAIGNS WITH SOCIAL MEDIA

Figure 5 shows the possible interaction between platforms in a targeted social media campaign strategy that:

- Changes the flow of process, information, and services to **reach** more people
- Keeps the followers **informed**
- Allows people to **sample/put** together their wishes and wants
- Offers product and/or services to be **sold** to the customer
- Has content/information that customers can pass along to **involve** their connections/friends

Business processes that use customer patterns and behaviors on social media platforms mixed with analytical data from previous purchases as an input to trigger the right marketing campaigns, can prove very effective. Using a portfolio of social media platforms with applicable processes can integrate these prospects into processes that can efficiently convert them into new customers.

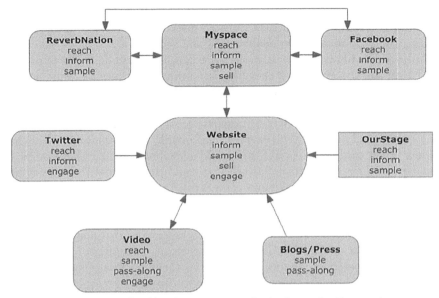

Reach: twitter, video, blogs/press, myspace, facebook, reverbnation, ourstage

Inform: twitter, myspace, facebook, reverbnation, ourstage, website, e-mail

Sample: myspace, facebook, reverbnation, ourstage, website, video, blogs/press

Sell: myspace, website

Pass-along: video, blogs/press

Engage: video, twitter, website/artist blog

FIGURE 5

Social media platforms enabling a marketing campaign.

IMPROVING THE PROSPECT QUALIFICATION PROCESS

A well-defined business process, the collection of data, and performance measures for prospect qualification are important aspects of customer acquisition. Partial/ complete automation of the steps in this process can be achieved by leveraging the power of a process flow, steps, and activities with business rules defined in accordance with an organization's business objectives.

CUSTOMER PROFILE DATA FOR PROCESS (SIMPLIFICATION)

One of the key benefits of social media platforms is the availability of customer profile information in the public domain. Additional customer profile data can be collected from these platforms by using analytical tools. This customer profile data can provide vital information for use in defining, optimizing, and simplifying the steps in the customer acquisition process, thus playing a significant role in identifying where the proactive or reactive process should be set up to influence the decision life cycle. Configuration and execution of process steps based on the kind of customer profile information can significantly reduce customer acquisition costs.

CUSTOMER NOTIFICATIONS FOR PROCESS (VISIBILITY)

One of the most important aspects of customer acquisition is continuous interaction and communication on the status and progress of the customer acquisition process. Process notification steps can be configured to provide customized customer communications based on the status of the requests, and sent to customers via channels like Twitter, blogs, direct messages, texts, and so on. These processes and the information they generate, however, need to be integrated into other aspects of the business operation.

ALTERNATIVE CHANNELS FOR SALES

Social media platforms are already being used as alternative sales channels for initiating specific customer requests, by extending the existing process and systems to include the social media platforms as input channels for initiating the sales process. A process-based solution for channel unification can also be considered.

SELECTION OF THE RIGHT OFFERING/SOLUTION

Customer patterns and behaviors on social media platforms can be effectively used as key decision variables in predefined business processes to aid in the selection of the right offering/solution for customers. In addition to specific data provided by customers, social media analytics can be leveraged to provide recommendations to customers on the best solutions for their requirements, provided the insight gained about patterns and behaviors can be communicated to, and exploited by, the design, production, distribution, service, and other arms of the enterprise.

SOCIAL MEDIA AND BPM FOR CUSTOMER SERVICING

The customer-servicing process consists of understanding and working on the customers' requirements/requests to address their specific needs. Social media platforms provide a wealth of information on customer expectations, preferences, and most importantly, real-time updates on changing customer needs. Customer expectations revealed on social media are an invaluable resource for organizations striving to be customer-centric. Processes can be orchestrated to connect with the customer, and to validate whether these changing customer expectations and preferences should be factored in to service their requests.

In a case within Vodafone, for example, they found a situation in which a customer had subscribed to a prepaid plan, and, unfortunately, errors occurred in billing. The customer was unable to reach the Customer Care section of Vodafone and understandably was upset and frustrated that he was unable to get a satisfactory explanation for the erroneous billing, and tweeted his dissatisfaction. Vodafone has active listening agents who read the Twitter or Facebook messages, and contacted the dissatisfied customer to help resolve the billing issue. Because of this, Vodafone was able to intercept the problem and initiate a process to recover the situation. Once the process is initiated, internal systems and resources work collaboratively to ensure that either a response is provided in the form of an acknowledgment, a clarification is provided, or the issue is resolved. This integration of social media-based processes properly integrated with internal systems turned what could have been a difficult experience into a constructive customer experience.

Every interaction a customer has with an organization is a "Moment of Truth" – the possibility of an experience which can be positive, negative, or neutral. On the one hand positive experiences usually translate into repeat business and customer loyalty, and referrals, recommendations or reviews on several channels. Hence the organization can initiate processes to further enhance and strengthen customer relationships through dialog, cross-selling/up-selling other products and services. On the other hand, negative experiences can result in negative reviews and feedback through these channels, or termination of the business relationship with an organization. Here the organization should track these experiences and then trigger the process of raising a customer service ticket to address the specific customer concern. Once triggered, internal systems, people, and resources are aligned to execute the processes.

There are, however, many other ways in which BPM along with social media can be leveraged for customer servicing such as: change request initiation; enriched customer profile data; sustained focus on operational efficiency; service request initiation (complaint/query/feedback and customer notifications) for process and filtration and prioritization of requests.

CUSTOMER RELATIONSHIP MANAGEMENT

The process of Customer Relationship Management (CRM) involves listening to customers, providing satisfactory responses (as applicable), advice, recommendations (as required), and, most importantly, continuously engaging with customers. Social media provide several opportunities for organizations to observe, listen, and communicate with their customers, creating new relationships and nurturing existing ones through meaningful dialogs. Based on the kind of interaction, several organizational processes can be initiated, modeled, created, modified, or decommissioned as needed.

The social CRM process and environment is set out in Figure 6. In this figure, we see communities interacting through social media that are subject to ongoing and active monitoring using listening tools, which are then able to pass the results into the CRM environment.

Social CRM Process

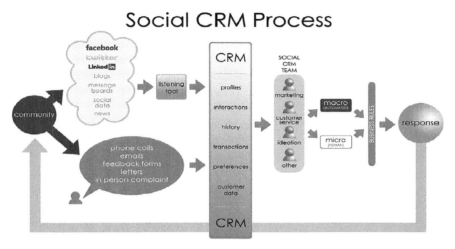

FIGURE 6

Components of social customer relationship management (CRM).

Although these processes augment the more traditional and passive channels, such as telephone, email, or letters, they also support new social media channels.

A CRM business process is among the multiple business processes in a company that could be designed from a social perspective. In "The Network-Based Business Process" by Ejub et al.,[2] the authors develop an approach to design social business processes. The three components that define a process are task, person, and machine. A task is a work unit (e.g., deliver report) that constitutes, with other tasks, a business process and that a person and/or machine execute. Execution is either manual (i.e., person only), automatic (i.e., machine only), or mixed (i.e., person and machine). Because the variety of interactions occur during the completion of business processes, it becomes possible to map some of these interactions onto specific social relations between these three components. Indeed, tasks are put together to form processes, persons collaborate on complex tasks, and machines replace each other in the case of failure. These examples offer a glimpse into the social relations that business process management systems exhibit and, hence, can be captured. Although Ejub et al. acknowledge that tasks and machines cannot "socialize" (in the strict sense), combining tasks and machines presents a lot of similarities with how people behave daily. Supporting the importance of socializing tasks and machines, Tan et al. state that "...*Currently, most social networks connect people or groups who expose similar interests or features. In the near future, we expect that such networks will connect other entities, such as software components, Web-based services, data resources, and workflows. More importantly, the interactions among people and nonhuman artifacts have significantly enhanced data scientists' productivity*".[3] Examples of social relations between business process components include coupling, interchange, delegation, and partnership. The different social relations are used for developing a configuration network of tasks, a social network of persons, and a support network of machines.

SOCIAL MEDIA PROCESS FLOW

When remodeling processes to align them to the chosen social media strategy, we see many organizations faced with challenges of understanding not only how to change manual processes, but also the importance of automated processes and the ability of automated learning and sophisticated decision rules within the process. The realignment of users sets up process flows, defines decision points within each flow, and connects to touch-point systems to capture events at those decision points. The **system** can then be used to automatically correlate event outcomes with the new social media channels, offers, customer attributes, and other factors. In addition to that, the social media process flow should include standard campaign measurements and reporting. Decision rules within the process can incorporate and link to multiple goals, each assigned a relative weight, and multiple business choices, each assigned a value toward reaching each goal. The system scores each choice by adding up the value it contributes to each goal, adjusted for the probability that the customer will accept that choice if offered. Users within the process of the customer interaction can also weigh goals differently for different customer segments: for example, retention might be more important for high-value customers, whereas cost reduction could be a priority for customers who are less profitable. The same goal definitions can apply to multiple decisions, reducing work, and ensuring consistency throughout the process.

We can, therefore, derive the following important aspects for success in social media process flow modeling:

1. Define specific goals for the social media process flow
2. Different flows involved, such as the response information and service flow
3. Roles involved in terms of "who does what"
4. The various services and their actual delivery of value to customers
5. The platforms that are used to enable parts of process automation
6. From a process-technology point of view, processes are automated with dedicated technology, which considers infrastructure aspects, for example, the process rule engine resides on infrastructure components and infrastructure services support the platform services

Figure 7 illustrates a basic view of such a Social Media Process Flow.

In addition to developing a social media process flow, do we recommend developing a posting interaction response? This can, among others, include some of the following considerations:

1. How can the posting response create customer value? Organizations realize that customer value creation is subject to the relationship between business processes and their resources, tasks, events, and the service they deliver.
2. Include interaction and response rules, including time frame and tone for response
   - response handling
   - tone of response
   - response content structure
   - Social media Frequently Asked Questions and expected issues and answers

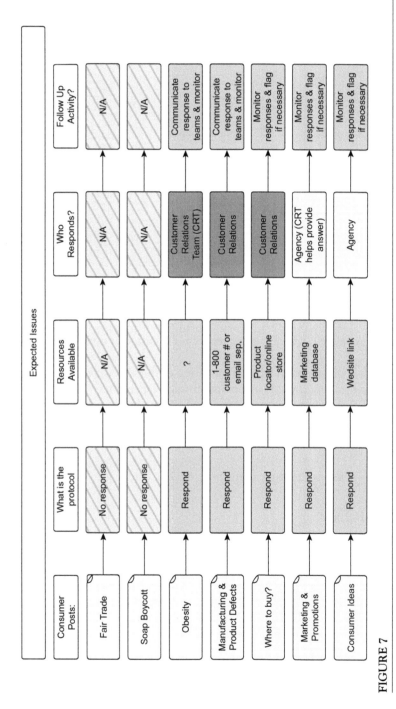

FIGURE 7

Overview of the social media process flow.

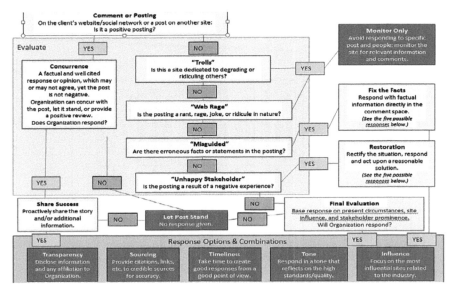

FIGURE 8

Overview of interaction response and combination.

3. Make sure the comment policy is integrated into the customer interaction processes
4. Identify which applications and data are involved in the various processes
5. Ensure process measurement and process monitoring capabilities
6. Enable the different technology media involved and used within the process
7. The various social media customer channels, for example, portal, business-to-customer, and business-to-business commerce need to be applying the same posting response

The illustration of such a posting interaction response can be seen in Figure 8.

CONCLUSION

The outperforming organizations investing in social media, both internally and externally, did this through mobile technology, cloud technology, data analytics, as well as new service constructs and knowledge workers. For most organizations, the initial promise of social media is therefore about customer interaction, customer/market data, brand, reach, profit, as well as the possibility of employee self-service and automation. The Global University Alliance analysis revealed that the promise of social media enables for most the following benefits:

- **Cost:** Content-rich social media are free, and can be accessed in an automated and repeatable way. This means that social media are less expensive than traditional customer research.

- **Accuracy**: Given the advances in analytics and intelligence technology, we should be able to accurately identify consumer's preferences, behaviors, and patterns, what customers are discussing, and the emotional disposition of those conversations. This means that social media will tell us more about online consumer persona behaviors, the online purchase funnel, and the customer journey, as well as create insight into the general purchase funnel, evolving social media into an automated proactive intelligence with more accurate information to enable informed decisions.
- **Relevance**: So much content is available on the web that one can find narratives on almost any topic or perspective. This means that social media enable specific views, trends, and content. Gathering and customizing data to make your information relevant and stand out is a unique opportunity.
- **Representativeness**: Given the census-like approach to collecting content from the web, any analysis should be a more accurate representation of market experiences than other methods—so extensive sampling or weighting will not be as necessary.
- **End-to-end flow**. Today, it is all about easy access and delivering on time. This requires a rethinking of how to identify, create, innovate, and manage an end-to-end service, information, data, and process flow.

Socially Oriented Process Modeling can be used effectively, internally and externally, to share solutions within an organization and to reach out to customers who talk about the business in their own social media interactions, facilitating new processes, and process changes. It can help solve critical debates about whether to automate certain processes or keep them manual. It is both a stand-alone tool in the BPM toolbox and an asset for improving existing BPM technology. Fundamentally, Socially Oriented Process Modeling is a powerful asset for a process-driven organization that will manifest itself in new and currently unforeseen ways. The organizations that embrace social media and BPM concepts will have some of the most developed process capabilities in their fields, and will be the most resilient in the face of change. However, Social Media will not achieve their full potential in an organization unless they are integrated both strategically and with operational process improvement. We have demonstrated how to apply social media and BPM to enable customer centricity. **Some of the critical success factors include:**

- Requirements needed to address the Social Media Strategy
- Processes that will be affected by the Requirements (these are likely to be new processes)
- Where new processes may affect workflow
- The preferred use of the Social Media Applications
- Information/Data that will be exchanged. This could be in the form of advertising content going to the Social Media Application or consumer feedback coming from a Social Media Application.
- Who is responsible for Social Media Application(s) that will be used and monitored to achieve the Social Media Strategy

- Updates to the point-of-sale application to direct consumers to the organization's Social Media presence
- The types of Measurements used to determine success of any new Social Media Strategy

End Notes

1. Y. Badr and Z. Maamar, "Can Enterprises Capitalize on Their Social Networks? Cutter IT Journal," *Special Issue on Measuring the Success of Social Networks in the Enterprise*, 22 no. 10 (October 2009).
2. K. Ejub, F. Noura, M. Zakaria, L. Alfred, P. Aldina, and Z.S. Quan, "The Network-Based Business Process," *IEEE Internet Computing*, 18, no. 2 (March/April 2014).
3. W. Tan, M.B. Blake, I. Saleh, and S. Dustdsar, "Social-Network-Sourced Big Data Analytics," *IEEE Internet Computing*, 17, no. 5 (September/October 2013).

BPM and Maturity Models

Henrik von Scheel, Gabriella von Rosing, Krzysztof Skurzak, Maria Hove

INTRODUCTION

For organizations to perform well in a global competitive world, it is important to identify the competitive advantages from which they can benefit. Models to assess the status of one's capabilities and identify improvement opportunities, and, in particular, maturity models that can help organizations assess their current capabilities in a structured way to implement changes and improvements, have become essential. A maturity model can be described as a structured collection of elements that describe certain aspects of capability maturity in an organization. A maturity model may provide, for example:

- a situational analysis of one's capabilities
- a place to start
- the benefit of a community's prior experiences
- a common language and a shared vision
- a framework for prioritizing actions
- a way to define what improvement means for your organization.
- as a benchmark for comparison and as an aid to understanding.

In this section, we will focus on maturity models, what they are, their historic development, how they can be used, and when business process management (BPM) can use maturity concepts. This includes a detailed BPM maturity self-assessment, a benchmark among the various aspects that are related to the BPM maturity context as well as a BPM maturity development path.

HISTORIC DEVELOPMENT OF MATURITY MODELS

Maturity models are used in multiple areas ranging from Software,[1] Organizational Project Management Maturity,[2] People Capability Maturity Model,[3] Portfolio, Program and Project Management Maturity,[4] to concepts like E-learning Maturity.[5] Maturity Models have existed for close to 40 years and are therefore not a new way of evaluating the maturity level of a business. Although maturity models for the most part are attributed to Carnegie Mellon University Software Engineering Institute[6] this is not really correct. The first published maturity model was developed by Richard L. Nolan, who in 1973 published the Stages of Growth model for IT organizations. It didn't take more than 6 years for Philip B. Crosby to publish his 1979 book, Quality is Free,[7] the Quality Management Maturity Grid (QMMG), which is an organizational maturity matrix. The QMMG is used by a business or organization as a benchmark of how mature are their processes, and how well they are embedded in their culture, with respect to service or product quality management. The staged structure of the framework is based on total quality management (TQM) principles that have existed for nearly a century. The work of Frederick Taylor and Frank Gilbreth on "scientific management" and time and motion studies in the early 1900s eventually led to the new discipline of industrial engineering.[8] In the 1930s, Walter Shewhart, a physicist at AT&T Bell Laboratories, established the principles of statistical quality control. These principles were further developed and successfully demonstrated in the work of such authorities as W. Edwards Deming[9] (1986) and Joseph M. Juran[10] (1988).

In recent years, the TQM concepts have been extended from manufacturing processes to service and engineering design processes. The software process[11] can be defined as a set of activities, methods, practices, and transformations that people use to develop and maintain software and the associated products. As an organization matures, the software process[12] becomes better defined and more consistently implemented throughout the organization. This, in turn, leads to higher-quality software, increased productivity, less rework, and improved software project plans and management. Crosby describes five evolutionary stages in adopting quality practices. As seen in Table 1, the quality management maturity grid applies five stages to six measurement categories in subjectively rating an organization's quality operation.

Table 1 The Quality Management Maturity Grid (QMMG)

	Stage 1: Uncertainty	Stage 2: Awakening	Stage 3: Enlightenment	Stage 4: Wisdom	Stage 5: Certainty
Management understanding and attitude	No comprehension of quality as a management tool. Tend to blame quality department for "quality problems."	Recognizing that quality management may be of value but not willing to provide money or time to make it all happen.	While going through quality improvement program, learning more about quality management; becoming supportive and helpful.	Participating. Understand absolutes of quality management. Recognize their personal role in continuing emphasis.	Consider quality management as an essential part of company system.
Quality organization status	Quality is hidden in manufacturing or engineering departments. Inspection probably not part of organization. Emphasis on appraisal and sorting.	A stronger quality leader is appointed but main emphasis is still on appraisal and moving the product. Still part of manufacturing or other.	Quality department reports to top management, all appraisals are incorporated and manager has role in management of company.	Quality manager is an officer of company; effective status reporting and preventive action. Involved with customer affairs and special assignments.	Quality manager on board of directors. Prevention is main concern. Quality is a thought leader.
Problem handling	Problems are fought as they occur; no resolution; inadequate definition; lots of yelling and accusations.	Teams are set up to attack major problems. Long-range solutions are not solicited.	Corrective action communication established. Problems are faced openly and resolved in an orderly way.	Problems are identified early in their development. All functions are open to suggestion and improvement.	Except in the most usual cases, problems are prevented.
Cost of quality as % of sales	Reported: unknown Actual: 20%	Reported: 3% Actual: 18%	Reported: 8% Actual: 12%	Reported: 6.5% Actual: 8%	Reported: 2.5% Actual: 2.5%
Quality improvement actions	No organized activities. No understanding of such activities.	Trying obvious "motivational" short-range efforts.	Implementation of a multi-step program (e.g., Crosby's 14-step) with thorough understanding and establishment of each step.	Continuing the multi-step program and starting other pro-active/preventive product quality initiatives.	Quality improvement is a normal and continued activity.
Summary of company quality posture	"We don't know why we have problems with quality."	"Is it absolutely necessary to always have problems with quality?"	"Through management commitment and quality improvement we are identifying and resolving our problems."	"Defect prevention is a routine part of our operation."	"We know why we do not have problems with quality."

The QMMG is credited with being the precursor of all maturity models. In August 1986, the Software Engineering Institute (SEI) at Carnegie Mellon University, with assistance from the MITRE Corporation, began developing a process maturity framework that would help organizations improve their software processes. This effort was initiated in response to a request to provide the federal government with a method for assessing the capability of their software contractors. In June 1987, the SEI released a brief description of the software process maturity[13] framework and, in September 1987, a preliminary maturity questionnaire. Based on experience in using

Subject and Reference	Approach
Quality Management Maturity Grid (Crosby, 1979)	Grid, 6 issues, detailed description at each level
R&D Effectiveness Audit (Szakoryi, 1994)	Grid, 10 issues, detailed description at each level
Quality Management Process Maturity Grid (Crosby, 1996)	Grid, 5 issues, captions describing performance at each level
Technical Innovation Audit (Chiesa and others, 1996)	Grid, 8 areas, 23 issues, detailed descriptions at each level
Product & Cycle Time Excellence (McGrath, 1996)	Grid, 10 issues, detailed description at each level
Design Maturity Model (Fraser & Moultrie, 192001)	Grid, 5 areas, 21 issues, detailed descriptions and captions
Product & Cycle Time Excellence - Mark 2 (McGrath, 2002)	Grid, Revision of earlier model
Collaboration Maturity Model (Fraser & Gregory, 2002)	Grid, 7 issues, detailed descriptions and captions
Design Atlas - Design Capability (Design Council, 2002)	Grid, 5 areas, 15 issues, detailed descriptions at each level
Supplier Relationships (Macbeth & Ferguson, 1994)	Grid / Likert Hybrid, 9 issues, brief descriptions at 3 levels plus 7 point scale
Continuous Improvement in NPD (Caffyn, 1997)	Global levels defined, 6 core abilities, 10 key behaviors
ISO 9004 (EN ISO 9004, 2000)	Global levels defined, 5 questions, 11 issues
Project Management Maturity (Dooley and others, 2001)	Likert style questionnaire, 15 areas, 85 issues, no descriptions of performance
Software CMM - Staged Maturity Levels (Pauk and others, 1993)	CMM Style
Agility (change proficiency) Maturity Model (Dove, 1996)	CMM Style
Usability - Human Factors Maturity (Earthy, 1998)	CMM Style
CMMI - Continuous Capability Levels (Shrum, 2000)	CMM Style
Free (collaboration) Capability Assessment Framework (Wognum & Faber, 2000)	CMM Style

FIGURE 1

Overview of various maturity model concepts.[14]

the software process maturity framework and the maturity questionnaire for diagnosing problems and improving processes, the SEI[15] formalized the concepts as the Capability Maturity Model for Software[16] (Software CMM[17]). Version 1.0[18] of the model was published in 1991.[19] Version 1.1[20] was released in 1993.[21] The Software CMM[22] was then retired in favor of the CMM Integration (CMMI[23]) model. CMMI was developed by the CMMI project, which aimed to improve the usability of maturity models by integrating three different models into one framework.

The project consisted of members of industry, government, and the Carnegie Mellon Software Engineering Institute[24] (SEI). The main sponsors included the Office of the Secretary of Defense (OSD) and the National Defense Industrial Association.[25] CMMI currently addresses three areas of process interest:

- Development—addresses product and service development
- Acquisition[26]—addresses supply chain management, acquisition, and outsourcing
- Services[27]—addresses guidance for delivering services.

However, as shown in Figure 1, whereas the CMM/CMMI evolved and matured, so did many of the other maturity model approaches; e.g., Agility, Usability of Human Factors, as well as Continuous Capability Levels and Free (collaboration) Capability Assessment maturity models emerged.

From the described Quality Management Maturity Grid from Crosby emerged not only the maturity models but numerable other Grid approaches, such as Research and Development, Product Cycle,[28] Continuous Improvement levels and approaches, as well as Project Management Maturity. As it many times happens one model and framework inspires the work and content of another standards and frameworks in related engineering and/or management areas and disciplines.

THE DIFFERENT STAGES OF MATURITY MODELS

In the software process maturity framework,[29] Humphrey identified five maturity levels that, even though they are based on the idea of Crosby, are claimed to describe successive foundations for process improvement and defined an ordinal scale for measuring the maturity of an organization's software processes. The descried concepts underlying maturity levels have remained stable through the evolution of the Software CMM. In discussions of this early work, Bill Curtis, Humphrey's[30] successor as director of the Process Program, identifies the focus on identifying and managing project commitments and managing to a plan as one of the few differences between maturity models and Crosby's maturity grid. It also reflects Beer, Eisenstat, and Spector's (1990) observation that senior managers create a climate for change in successful change programs, but this change needs to start at the grass roots level rather than top-down.

The general idea with the maturity or grids levels is to provide possible improvement priorities or define levels of possible development—guidance for selecting levels of improvement activities:

- At **Level 1**, the initial level, the stage is typically characterized as ad hoc, not recognized, informal, uncertainty, occasionally even chaotic, and no formal approach. Few activities are defined, and success depends on individual effort and heroics. The challenge with the first stage activities is that it is difficult to predict performance and value realization or learn from experience when everything is new and unique. In nearly all the maturity or grid approaches, the first level is more defined by the failure to satisfy the requirements for Level 2.

- At **Level 2**, which is more the repeatable level, basic, initial efforts, regression, and repeatable activities are established to track cost, schedule, and functionality. The necessary process discipline is in place to repeat earlier successes on projects with similar experience. The focus at Level 2 does not explicitly include operational activities, because the major problems Level 1 organizations face are for the most part managerial, not operational, problems. Operational activities are planned and tracked at Level 2, but they are not described in detail—or even listed in most versions of the different models.
- At **Level 3**, the awakening and defined level, both strategic (management) and operational activities are documented, standardized, and integrated into a set of standard competencies for the organization. Programs, portfolio, and projects use an approved, tailored version of the organization's set of standard approaches, methods, and processes. The operational processes are first explicitly addressed at Level 3, but they must be implemented at Level 1 if the organization is, for example, developing a product, creating quality management, or building software, even if those engineering processes are informal, ad hoc, and inconsistently performed. The emphasis of Level 3, however, is more centered on organizational learning via competency and process definition and improvement.
- At **Level 4**, the wisdom, enlightenment, excellence, improvement integrated, and/or managed level, detailed measures of the process, and product quality are collected. Both the competencies and activities, and thereby process and products, are quantitatively understood and controlled. This implies statistical thinking[31] and evidence-based management,[32] although these terms were not used in the early formulations of the different models. It also should be noted that measurement and analysis could occur at all levels of the models, although it comes to the forefront in Levels 4 and 5.
- At **Level 5**, the certain, collaborative, enterprise-wide integration, continuous improvement, culturally embedded, best in class, mastered as well as institutionalized or optimized level, should be enabled by feedback from the competencies, activities, and processes, and from piloting innovative ideas and technologies. Applying statistical and analytical thinking enables the organization to understand their competencies as well as their process and activities and confirm when measurably significant differences occur in performance.

As shown in Figure 2, the basic level approaches are all based upon and further developed from the one grid approach developed by Crosby. Most of them have five levels/stages, and the ones that have less or even more have split some of the stages or joined them, but the biggest difference is the focus of the subjects and areas, e.g., Quality Management, R&D Effectiveness, Technical Innovation, Excellence, Design, Change, Project Management, and/or Relationship Management.

Subject and Reference	Maturity Levels						Approach
Quality Management Maturity Grid (Crosby, 1979)	Level 1 Uncertainty	Level 2 Awakening	Level 3 Enlightenment	Level 4 Wisdom	Level5 Certainty		Grid 6 issues, detailed description at each level
R&D Effectiveness Audit (Szakoryi, 1994)	Level A Not recognised	Level B Initial efforts	Level C Skills	Level D Methods	Level E Responsibilities	Level F Continuous Improvement	Grid 10 issues, detailed description at each level
Quality Management Process Maturity Grid (Crosby, 1996)	Level 1 Uncertainty	Level 2 Regression	Level 3 Awakening	Level 4 Enlightenment	Level 5 Certainty		Grid 5 issues, captions describing performance at each level
Technical Innovation Audit (Chiesa and others, 1996)	1	2	3	4			Grid 8 areas, 23 issues, detailed descriptions at each level
Product & Cycle Time Excellence (McGrath, 1996)	Stage 0 Informal	Stage 1 Functionally focused project managed	Stage 2 Cross functional project management	Stage 3 Enterprise wide integration of prod. dev.			Grid 10 issues, detailed description at each level
Design Maturity Model (Fraser & Moultrie, 192001)	Level 1 None	Level 2 Partial	Level 3 Formal	Level 4 Culturally embedded			Grid 5 areas, 21 issues, detailed descriptions and captions
Product & Cycle Time Excellence - Mark 2 (McGrath, 2002)	Stage 0 Informal Management	Stage 1 Functional Excellence	Stage 2 Project Excellence	Stage 3 Portfolio Excellence	Stage 4 Collaborative		Grid Revision of earlier model
Collaboration Maturity Model (Fraser & Gregory, 2002)	Level 1 None	Level 2 Partial	Level 3 Formal	Level 4 Culturally embedded			Grid 7 issues, detailed descriptions and captions
Design Atlas - Design Capability (Design Council, 2002)	Level 1	Level 3	Level 4	Level 5			Grid 5 areas, 15 issues, detailed descriptions at each level
Supplier Relationships (Macbeth & Ferguson, 1994)	Level 1 Adversarial	Level 2 Transitional	Level 3 Partnership				Grid / Likert Hybrid 9 issues, brief descriptions at 3 levels plus 7 point scale
Continuous Improvement in NPD (Caffyn, 1997)	Level 1 Natural or background CI	Level 2 Structured CI	Level 3 Goal oriented CI	Level 4 Proactive, autonomous CI	Level 5 Full CI capability		Global levels defined 6 core abilities 10 key behaviors
ISO 9004 (EN ISO 9004, 2000)	Level 1 No formal approach	Level 2 Reactive approach	Level 3 Stable formal system approach	Level 4 Cont. improvement emphasized	Level 5 Best in class performance		Global levels defined 5 questions, 11 issues
Project Management Maturity (Dooley and others, 2001)	1	2	3	4	5		Likert style questionnaire 15 areas, 85 issues, no descriptions of performance
Software CMM - Staged Maturity Levels (Pauk and others, 1993)	Level 1 Initial	Level 2 Repeatable	Level 3 Defined	Level 4 Managed	Level5 Optimizing		CMM Style
Agility (change proficiency) Maturity Model (Dove, 1996)	Level 1 Accidental	Level 2 Repeatable	Level 3 Defined	Level 4 Managed	Level5 Mastered		CMM Style
Usability - Human Factors Maturity (Earthy, 1998)	Level X Unrecognised	Level A Recognised	Level B Considered	Level C Implemented	Level D Integrated	Level E Institutionalized	CMM Style
CMMI - Continuous Capability Levels (Shrum, 2000)	Level 0 Not performed	Level 1 Performed	Level 2 Managed	Level 3 Defined	Level 4 Qualitatively Managed	Level 5 Optimizing	CMM Style
Free (collaboration) Capability Assessment Framework (Wognum & Faber, 2000)	Level 2 Repeatable	Level 3 Defined	Level 4 Managed	Level 5 Optimizing			CMM Style

FIGURE 2

Historic development of the maturity grids and models.[33]

THE MISSING PARTS OF THE MATURITY MODELS

Although the adoption rate of the mentioned models is high, the one that is most developed and adopted is the discussed CMM and then CMMI. The last years, however, have seen the CMMI approach/models heavily criticized both in theory[34] as well as in practice. In the following, we summarize the criticism, which is in six main areas:

1. The CMM/CMMI model is based on the experiences of large government contractors and of Watts Humprey's own experience in the mainframe world. It does not represent the successful experiences of many software companies

that, as a matter of fact, would be judged to be a "Level 1" organization by the CMM/CMMI levels. For example, the CMM or CMMI for software development[35] was arguably irrelevant to successful software development and therefore criticized for the applicability of the narrow capability view. For some of the most successful software companies like Microsoft, IBM, Apple, Oracle, Google, Softbank, SAP, CSC, Yahoo, Software AG, and Symantec. Though these companies may have successfully developed their software, they would not necessarily have considered or defined or managed their processes as the CMM/CMMI described as level three or above, and so would have fit Level 1 or 2 of the model.[36] This did not change the successful development of their software. As CMM/CMMI is not built on empirical research, but rather is built on experience, the experience/best practice would somehow have to build on the industry leaders to be a foundation of best practice standardization, which the CMM/CMMI is not.

2. CMMI ignores the importance of people involved with the process by assuming that processes can somehow render individual excellence less important. For this to be the case, people/team tasks would somehow have to be included in the process itself, which the CMMI does not address.

3. CMMI does not effectively describe any information on process dynamics, which confuses the study of the relationships between practices and levels within the CMMI. The CMMI does not perceive or adapt to the conditions of the combined capabilities of an organization. Arguably, most, and perhaps all, of the key practices of the CMMI at its various levels could be performed usefully at Level 1, depending on the particular dynamics of an organization. Instead of modeling these process capability dynamics, the CMMI merely satisfies them.

4. CMMI's focus is only on process capability, which is only one side of the coin, for a company can not separate one's capabilities from the relationship of another related capability that are connected. Therefore, a company should not only look at its capability maturity model of one area, but rather look at its related Enterprise Maturity. However, CMMI does not address this.

5. CMMI reveres the institutionalization of process for its own sake. This guarantees nothing, and in some cases, the institutionalization of processes may lead to oversimplified public processes, ignoring the actual successful practice of the organization. For one cannot look at a process in itself, without taking into consideration which other capabilities are attached to the process and activity. To consider which other capabilities are attached to the process and its activity, other capability maturity models would have to be interlinked with and measure the process capabilities, which the CMMI does not address. Therefore, a process maturity model would have to consider the related aspects to the process, which gives it context. This includes the purpose and goal, the organizational context (competencies

and business function), the roles, owners, flows, rules, compliance aspects, automated pieces (applications), measures, channels, media, platform, infrastructure, and the services delivered.

6. CMMI encourages the achievement of a higher maturity level with all aspects, in some cases by displacing the true mission, which is improving the process and overall competency in lowering the cost and increasing the revenue. In most cases, the cost to achieve a higher maturity level would be far greater than the possible gain. This may effectively "blind" an organization to the most effective use of its capabilities and resources.

This narrow focus makes CMMI limited in real essential improvement that a BPM maturity model would need.

BPM MATURITY MODEL

From the above discussion, we will in this section illustrate of which components a BPM Maturity Model should consist. These components include Business Process levels, their description, and the areas that give context to BPM maturity. We will then exemplify a BPM maturity benchmark and a BPM maturity development path.

MATURITY LEVELS

Business Process Maturity: Level 1

The organization's process portfolio and initiatives are functionally oriented and exist in multiple instances. The process initiatives are typically characterized as ad hoc in terms of specific for only one or a few business units/departments, thereby organizationally siloed, not fully recognized, or adaptable by others. The process solutions are thereby more department or business-unit centric, occasionally coordinated with others and sometimes even jointly developed. Such coordination and joint development are initial and, therefore, from an enterprise perspective the process strategy is unorganized and partly chaotic in having no formal process approach. Few cross-enterprise process strategies, developments, and improvements are defined, and success of these solutions depends on few individual heroic departments coordinating or a process Center of Excellence (CoE) effort. The challenge with the first stage is that, with multiple process solutions/instances, it is difficult to predict joint value creation or performance. At this stage, it is more difficult to learn from experience when everything is done initially in silos and, if done jointly, it is for the most part new for each business unit/department. In nearly all the maturity or grid approaches, the first level is therefore defined by the failure to satisfy the requirements for Level 2.

Business Process Maturity: Level 2

The repeatable level is the level in which basic process standardization efforts and repeatable joint process development initiatives (workflow, programming, upgrades, blueprints, etc.) are established to track process development cost, schedule, and functionality. The necessary process CoE disciplines are in place to repeat earlier successes in areas/projects with similar experience. The focus at Level 2 does not explicitly include operational process system merger activities, because the major problems Level 1 organizations face are multiple process managerial problems (e.g., process solution development definition, development planning, value identification, performance measurements, initiatives, and joint reporting in process solutions), and not operational system problems. Joint operational process solution initiatives are planned and tracked at Level 2, but they are not described or executed in detail.

Business Process Maturity: Level 3

The defined and awakening level, around both management (strategic and tactical level) and operations, have a common documented process. The Level 2 standardizations around process are thereby documented and integrated into a set of standard joint process developments and joint competencies for the organization. Process joint development programs, portfolio, and projects use an approved, tailored version of the organization's set of process/solution framework, method, and approaches. The operational multi-instance challenges and possible process single-instance strategies and/or initiatives are first explicitly defined and thereby addressed at Level 3. Nevertheless, they must be implemented at Level 1 if the organization is, for example, developing a process single-instance product, creating quality management, or building tools, even if those initiatives are informal, ad hoc, and inconsistently executed. The emphasis of Level 3, however, is centered more around organizational learning of their pain points, challenges, goals, competencies, process definition, and improvements of the standardized processes.

Business Process Maturity: Level 4

At the management level, process/solution excellence is managed across the organizational boundaries. The detailed system measures of the processes are collected in joint cockpits, dashboards, and scorecards, and are optimized and managed. Both the process strategy and competencies, and thereby the process initiatives, are quantitatively understood, monitored, controlled, and managed. This implies statistical thinking[31] and evidence-based management[32] about the process initiatives. It also should be noted that process measurement and analytical abilities could occur at earlier phases (Levels 1, 2 or 3), although it comes as full crossdiscipline to the forefront at Levels 4 and 5, when the process solution is optimized for joint enterprise performance and value creation.

Business Process Maturity: Level 5

The organization becomes process centric in terms of collaborative developments, enterprise-wide integration and, most important, continuous improvement becomes culturally embedded in the organization. The continuous process improvements support the business differentiation which the organizations are pursuing. On this maturity level, the continuous improvement of the process portfolio is enabled by feedback from the business competencies and their functions, tasks, and services. Applying strategic and analytical thinking enables the organization to understand its expert competencies as well as its processes and the activities that enable their processes. The organization optimizes and develops its processes when and where measurable significant differences in performance and value creation occur.

In Figure 3, we see how the levels are put together with an example of a maturity journey and the statistical Ease of Adoption curve, together with the Return on Investment (ROI) curve:

As we described earlier, CMMI reveres the institutionalization of process for its own sake. This guarantees nothing, and in some cases, the institutionalization of processes may lead to an oversimplified view, ignoring the successful practice of the organization and its process context. For one cannot look at a process itself, without taking into consideration other capabilities that are attached to the process and activity. As the organization progresses and ascends through each phase of maturity, the achievement of its critical success factors must also evolve. Leading organizations take a balanced approach to managing their different critical success factors and what makes them unique. Managed together, they represent the framework from which BPM competencies are built. This includes multiple factors.[37]

To consider what other capabilities are attached to the process and activity, other capability maturity models would have to be interlinked and used to measure the process capabilities. Therefore, a BPM maturity model would have to consider the related aspects of the process that give it context. This includes the purpose and goal, the organizational context (competencies and business function), the roles, owners, flows, rules, compliance aspects, automated pieces (applications), measures, channels, media, platform, infrastructure, and the services delivered. Therefore, the BPM maturity model would have to include the context of the maturity benchmark question that enables one to place it into a maturity level. In Figure 4 is an example of a BPM Maturity Model with related context for BPM maturity assessment.

In the following, we have listed the various aspects relevant for BPM maturity. The questions and the list do not claim to be complete, but more illustrative and representative for how such a BPM maturity benchmark works, and the questions that lead to placement of the organization into a maturity level (Table 2).

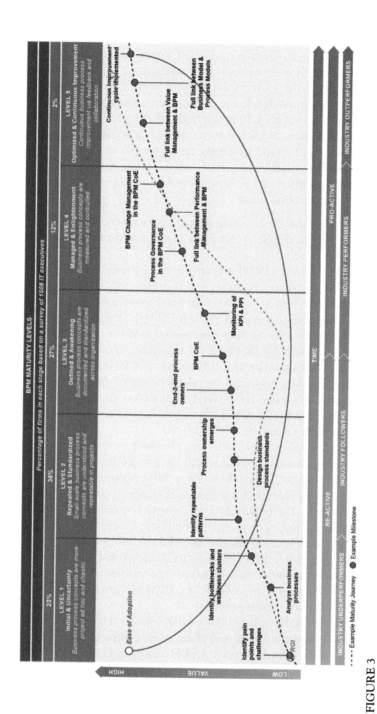

FIGURE 3

Example maturity journey and the statistical Ease of Adoption and Return on Investment (ROI) curve.[38]

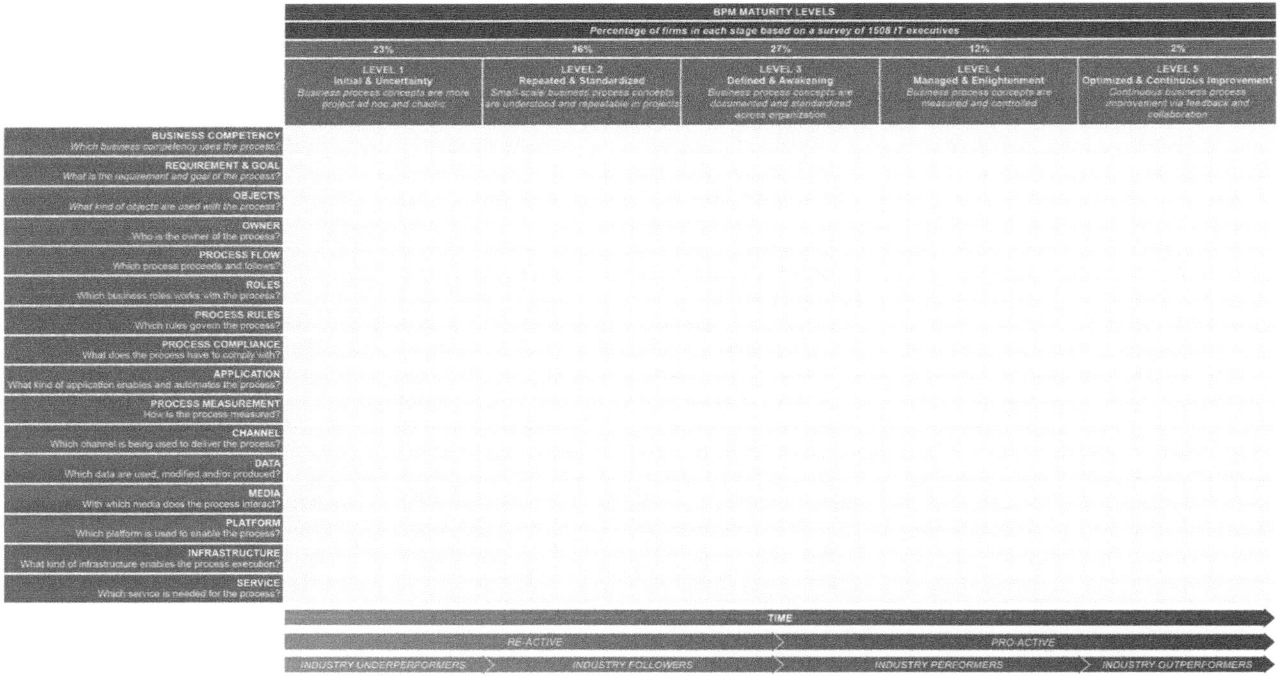

FIGURE 4

An example of context for a business process management (BPM) maturity assessment.[39]

Table 2 *The Business Process Management (BPM) Maturity Self-Assessment*

		Process Maturity Levels Over Time			
	Level 1 **Initial and Uncertain**	**Level 2** **Repeated and Standardize**	**Level 3** **Defined and Awakening**	**Level 4** **Managed and Enlightenment**	**Level 5** **Continuous Improvement**
Process	The organization's process portfolio and initiatives are functionally oriented and exist in multiple instances. The process initiatives are typically characterized as ad hoc in terms of specific for only one or a few business units/departments, thereby organizationally siloed, not fully recognized or adaptable by others. The process solutions are thereby more department- or business-unit centric, occasionally coordinated with others and sometimes even jointly developed. Such a coordination and joint development are initial and therefore from an enterprise perspective the process strategy is unorganized and partly chaotic in having no formal process approach. Few cross-enterprise process strategies, development, and improvements are defined, and success of these solutions depends on few individual heroic departments coordinating or a process center of excellence (CoE) effort. The	The repeatable level is the level at which basic process standardization efforts, and repeatable joint process development initiatives (workflow, programming, upgrades, blueprints etc.) are established to track process development cost, schedule, and functionality. The necessary process CoE disciplines are in place to repeat earlier successes in areas/projects with similar experience. The focus at Level 2 does not explicitly include operational process system merger activities, because the major problems Level 1 organizations face are multiple-process managerial problems (e.g., process solution development	The defined and awakening level, both around management (strategic and tactical level) and operations, has a common documented process. The Level 2 standardizations around process are thereby documented and integrated into a set of standard joint process developments and joint competencies for the organization. Process joint development programs, portfolio, and projects use an approved, tailored version of the organization's set of process/solution framework, method, and approaches. The operational multi-instance challenges and possible process single-instance strategies and/or initiatives are first explicitly defined and thereby addressed at Level 3. Nevertheless, they must be implemented at Level 1 if the organization is, for example, developing	At the management level, process/ solution excellence is managed across organizational boundaries. The detailed system measures of the processes are collected in joint cockpits, dashboards, and scorecards and are optimized and managed. Both the process strategy and competencies, and thereby the process initiatives, are quantitatively understood, monitored, controlled, and managed. This implies statistical thinking[429] and evidence-based management[430] about the process initiatives. It also should be noted that process measurement and analytical abilities could occur	The organization becomes process centric in terms of collaborative developments, enterprise-wide integration and, most important, continuous improvement becomes culturally embedded in the organization. The continuous process improvement supports the business differentiation that the organizations are pursuing. On this maturity level, the continuous improvement of the process portfolio is enabled by feedback from the business competencies and their functions, tasks, and services. Applying strategic and analytical thinking enables the organization to understand its

	challenge with the first stage is that with multiple process solutions/instances, it is difficult to predict joint value creation and/or performance. At this stage it is furthermore difficult to learn from experience when everything is done initially in silos and if done jointly, it is for the most part new (for each business unit/department). In nearly all the maturity or grid approaches the first level is therefore more defined by the failure to satisfy the requirements for Level 2.	definition, development planning, value identification, performance measurements, initiatives, and joint reporting in process solutions), and not operational system problems. Joint operational process solution initiatives are planned and tracked at Level 2, but they are not described or executed in detail.	a process single-instance product, creating quality management, or building tools, even if those initiatives are informal, ad hoc, and inconsistently executed. The emphasis of Level 3, however, is centered more around organizational learning of their pain points, challenges, goals, competencies, process definition, and improvements of the standardized processes.	at earlier phases (Levels 1, 2, or 3), although it comes as full cross-discipline to the forefront at Levels 4 and 5, when the process solution is optimized for joint enterprise performance and value creation.	expert competencies as well as its processes and activities that enable their processes. The organization optimizes and develops its processes when and where measurable significant differences in performance and value creation occur.
Business competency	Business competencies share only sporadic and ad hoc relation to business processes, and knowledge of this relation is not shared across business units, making the relation entirely silo-based. Furthermore, business competency potential is neither fully recognized nor adaptable to changing business requirements.	Business competencies and their connection to the business processes across business units is now part of basic standardization projects and initiatives. Successes from earlier initiatives have now become repeatable in future process-oriented projects and development initiatives.	Business competencies are now being defined and documented in detail. This knowledge is shared across organizational boundaries at the strategic, tactical, and operational management levels, and is centered around the learning of how competencies can be used within the existing process portfolio in future process-oriented projects and development initiatives.	All business competencies of the enterprise now share a direct relationship to all of the business processes across the organizational boundaries. Business competencies and their relation to business processes are now fully understood, managed, controlled, and monitored during process-oriented projects and development initiatives.	Business competencies play a significant role within the collaborative feedback loop of continuous business process improvement and optimization projects and initiatives. The relation between value-creating business processes, and business competencies of the organization help build business differentiation on the market.

Continued

Table 2 The Business Process Management (BPM) Maturity Self-Assessment—Cont'd

	Process Maturity Levels Over Time				
	Level 1 Initial and Uncertain	Level 2 Repeated and Standardize	Level 3 Defined and Awakening	Level 4 Managed and Enlightenment	Level 5 Continuous Improvement
Purpose and goal	Few to no value-centric aspects of what can, or does, give the business processes purposes and goals—in terms of both forces (external and internal), drivers (external and internal), value propositions, performance indicators, strategy, goals, objectives, and quality thereof—exist as concepts in the organization. Value-centric aspects such as these often remain locked in silos, and are rarely shared across organizational boundaries. Furthermore, the aforementioned value aspects are rarely, if ever, linked to processes, and, if so, only applied in an ad hoc manner during process-oriented projects and initiatives within each individual business unit of the organization.	Some value-centric aspects around that which gives the business processes a purpose and a goal—in terms of forces (external and internal), drivers (external and internal), value indicators, value propositions, performance indicators, strategy, goals, objectives, and quality thereof—have become repeatable due to successful integration in previous process-oriented project initiatives that have been performed within individual business units. These successes are shared across organizational boundaries, and some of these value-centric aspects around the business processes of each business unit are now standardized and allow for repeatable development initiatives during process-oriented projects and initiatives.	Most value-centric aspects around the purpose and goals of business processes—such as forces (external and internal), drivers (external and internal), value indicators, value propositions, performance indicators, strategy, goals, objectives, and quality thereof—are explicitly defined across the organizational boundaries of all the business units, and share a common documentation point of reference at the strategic, tactical and operational levels within the organization.	All value-centric aspects around the purpose and goals of business processes—such as forces (external and internal), drivers (external and internal), value indicators, value propositions, performance indicators, strategy, goals, objectives, and quality thereof—are quantitatively understood, controlled, monitored, measured, and managed across organizational boundaries of the enterprise.	The enterprise-wide organization has become purpose- and goal-centric—in terms of forces (external and internal), drivers (external and internal), value indicators, value propositions, performance indicators, strategy, goals, objectives, and quality thereof—around the continuous improvement of business processes. The development, improvement, and optimization of business processes around value-adding aspects is now the central focus in process-oriented project initiatives across the enterprise. This development is supported by a collaborative feedback loop of the organization at the strategic, tactical, and operational levels.

Objects (business, information and data)	Business information and data objects exist only in silos and—apart from data objects—share little to no coherency nor affiliation with the business processes of the organization. In the case that business and/or information objects are part of a business process, its participation is largely initial and sporadic in context.	Business information and data objects are gradually being implemented across business processes in the organization. This allows for repeating earlier development successes and makes room for basic standardization upon implementation across business units.	Business information and data objects are now being addressed and explicitly defined for use in process-oriented projects and initiatives. Furthermore, the objects share a common set of documentation standards across the strategic, tactical, and operational management levels across organizational boundaries.	All business information and data objects are now being individually mapped and related to all process-centric meta objects during process-oriented projects and development initiatives. This allows for a much higher degree of object management and control as well as continuous object governance and monitoring.	Business information and data objects are a central part of business process development and optimization during process-oriented projects and initiatives across organizational boundaries. Furthermore, the collaborative environment across all business units becomes "object"-centric during process modeling in a continuous effort to improve organizational business processes.

Continued

Table 2 The Business Process Management (BPM) Maturity Self-Assessment—Cont'd

	Process Maturity Levels Over Time				
	Level 1 Initial and Uncertain	Level 2 Repeated and Standardize	Level 3 Defined and Awakening	Level 4 Managed and Enlightenment	Level 5 Continuous Improvement
Process owner	Few to no process owners exist around the current process portfolio within each individual business unit. For the process owners that do exist, their responsibilities and accountability remains largely ad hoc and their roles are neither fully understood nor recognized during process-oriented projects and initiatives.	Process ownership is being established across the organizational boundaries, which allows for the repetition of earlier successes from previous process-oriented projects and initiatives. This allows for a basic standardized incorporation of process ownership in both new and existing projects and initiatives.	Process ownership has become explicitly defined and is fully standardized and incorporated in process-oriented projects and initiatives across the organizational boundaries. The role and purpose of process ownership is fully documented and shared across the strategic, tactical, and operational levels of the enterprise.	Process ownership and their relation to the other owners—such as the business, service, application, data, platform, and infrastructure owners—is being managed across the enterprise. Their role and responsibility is fully understood and controlled and their results are monitored and measured during process-oriented projects and initiatives.	Process ownership—including their collaboration with the other business services, application, data, platform, and infrastructure owners of the organization—play fundamental roles within the enterprise when it comes to the development and optimization of both new as well as existing business processes across the organizational boundaries. They play a key role in the collaborative feedback loop around the continuous improvement of business processes.

Process flow	Process flows are the natural part of all business processes in the respective business units, although they exist only in silos. Thus, knowledge of them is not shared across organizational boundaries (i.e., between business units).	Process flows have become an increasingly larger part of basic business process standardization across organizational units, and are now used in repeatable process-oriented projects and development initiatives.	Process flows are now being defined and documented in detail. This information is shared across all organizational units and on the strategic, tactical, and operational management levels of each business unit.	Process flows have become quantitatively understood, monitored, controlled, and are being managed across organizational boundaries. They also share a direct relationship to all other flows of the organization, such as the business work flows, service flows, other process flows, application flows, as well as data flows.	During process-oriented projects and development initiatives, process flows play a significant role in the collaborative feedback environment because of their direct relation to all other flows of the organization, such as the business work flows, service flows, other process flows, application flows, as well as data flows. They also represent an important aspect of continuous business process improvement initiatives across organizational boundaries.

Continued

Table 2 *The Business Process Management (BPM) Maturity Self-Assessment—Cont'd*

	Process Maturity Levels Over Time				
	Level 1 Initial and Uncertain	Level 2 Repeated and Standardize	Level 3 Defined and Awakening	Level 4 Managed and Enlightenment	Level 5 Continuous Improvement
Process roles	Process roles largely work ad hoc on an initial basis during all process-oriented projects and initiatives. Their role, responsibilities, and overall purpose within the organization are not fully recognized nor understood. Their work is also only carried out in silos—and the result is knowledge that is retained and static, and not shared across business units nor across organizational boundaries.	Process roles are now being established across all business units, as earlier successes from process-oriented projects and development initiatives allow for being repeated in new projects and initiatives. Process roles have also become part of basic business process standardization initiatives across business units.	Process roles have become explicitly defined and are fully standardized and incorporated in process-oriented projects and initiatives across the organizational boundaries. The role and purpose of process ownership is fully documented and shared across the strategic, tactical, and operational levels of the enterprise.	Process roles and their relation to the role owners—such as the business services, application, data, platform, and infrastructure roles—are being managed across the enterprise. Their role and responsibility is fully understood and controlled and their results are monitored and measured during process-oriented projects and initiatives.	Process roles—including their collaboration with the other business services, application, data, platform, and infrastructure roles of the organization—plays fundamental role within the enterprise when it comes to the development and optimization of both new as well as existing business processes across organizational boundaries. They play key roles in the collaborative feedback loop around the continuous improvement of business processes.

Process rules	The process rules of each individual business unit share no relation or connection to the other rules of organization (i.e., business, service, application, data, platform, and infrastructure rules). This makes the process rules function only in silos, and their influence upon other business units is not fully understood.	Process rules share little to no connection to the other rules of the organization (i.e., business, service, application, data, platform, and infrastructure rules), but previous successful business process implementation initiatives allows for repetition. Process rules are now a natural part of business process standardization across organizational boundaries.	Process rules and their connection to business, service, application, data, platform, and infrastructure rules have become explicitly defined and documented for future development and implementation projects. Their definitions and the documentation thereof allow for knowledge sharing and use across organizational boundaries in all process-oriented projects and initiatives.	Process rules and their relation to business, service, application, data, platform, and infrastructure rules are now being efficiently managed, controlled, and monitored across organizational boundaries.	Process rules have become a central part of all process-oriented development and continuous improvement initiatives across all organizational business units. They also represent an important aspect of the enterprise-wide collaborative feedback loop.
Process compliance	Process compliance is entirely silo-based and shares no relation to any other form of compliance, regardless of which business unit of which the associated business process is a part.	The successful implementation of process compliance during earlier process-oriented projects and initiatives allows for basic process compliance standardization across organizational boundaries.	Process compliance is now standardized, defined, and fully documented. Process compliance is furthermore being addressed during all process-oriented projects and development initiatives across organizational boundaries.	Process compliance now shares a direct connection to business, application, data, platform, and infrastructure compliance. These connections are now fully understood, and their usability is managed, controlled, and monitored during all process-oriented projects and development initiatives.	Process compliance, along with process rules, have become a central part of all process-oriented development and continuous improvement initiatives across all organizational business units. They also represent an important aspect of the enterprise-wide collaborative feedback loop.

Continued

Table 2   *The Business Process Management (BPM) Maturity Self-Assessment—Cont'd*

	Process Maturity Levels Over Time				
	Level 1 **Initial and Uncertain**	**Level 2** **Repeated and** **Standardize**	**Level 3** **Defined and Awakening**	**Level 4** **Managed and** **Enlightenment**	**Level 5** **Continuous** **Improvement**
Application	Logical and physical application components as well as application modules, features, functions, tasks, and system reports support the execution of business processes, although only in silos, and performance and implementation knowledge is not shared across organizational boundaries.	Using logical and physical application components as well as application modules, features, functions, tasks, and system reports to successfully implement and run business processes is not repeatable across organizational boundaries and allows for basic business process standardization.	Logical and physical application components as well as application modules, features, functions, tasks, and system reports are now being clearly defined and documented across organizational boundaries. Knowledge sharing happens across the strategic, tactical, and operational management levels across business units.	Logical and physical application components as well as application modules, features, functions, tasks, and system reports share a direct connection to all business processes, and are managed, controlled, and monitored during all process-oriented projects and development initiatives.	Logical and physical application components as well as application modules, features, functions, tasks, and system reports and their connection to business processes have become a part in collaborative feedback loop of continuous business process improvement and optimization across organizational boundaries.

Process measurement	Process measurements are carried out largely sporadically and only in an ad hoc manner. Process measurement results and reporting is also entirely silo-based, which prevents knowledge sharing across business units.	Drawn from the successes of previous execution and implementation, process measurements are now being done on all executed business processes and allow for basic standardization across organizational boundaries.	Process measurements are explicitly defined and documented for how they should measure executable business processes. Process measurement results and reporting happen across business units to enhance organizational learning.	Process measurements are being efficiently managed, controlled, and monitored in correspondence to relevant business measures, service measurements, as well as system measurements, and reporting is afterward delivered to all relevant process owners and stakeholders.	Process measurements are used as a central part in the collaborative feedback loop of continuous business process improvement across organizational boundaries. The process measurement results in combination with business measures, service measurements as well as system measurements allow for a much higher degree of knowledge-based business process development and optimization during process-oriented projects and initiatives.

Continued

Table 2 *The Business Process Management (BPM) Maturity Self-Assessment—Cont'd*

	Process Maturity Levels Over Time				
	Level 1 Initial and Uncertain	Level 2 Repeated and Standardize	Level 3 Defined and Awakening	Level 4 Managed and Enlightenment	Level 5 Continuous Improvement
Channel	Business, service, application, data, platform, and infrastructure channels are used only sporadically and largely ad hoc during business process execution. They are used only in silos, thus preventing knowledge sharing across organizational boundaries.	Business, service, application, data, platform, and infrastructure channels have become standardized and are now repeatable due to earlier successful implementations in process-oriented projects and development initiatives.	Business, service, application, data, platform, and infrastructure channels are defined and documented in detail across organizational boundaries on the strategic, tactical, and operational management levels and are central to knowledge sharing and learning across the enterprise.	Business, service, application, data, platform, and infrastructure channels are directly related to all business process operations and are managed, controlled, and monitored across organizational boundaries during process-oriented projects and initiatives.	All business process operations make use of business, service, application, data, platform, and infrastructure channels in the collaborative feedback loop during process-oriented projects and development initiatives. They also represent an important aspect of supporting the continuous improvement and optimization of existing business processes.
Data	Data components, entities, and tables are used actively throughout all business process operations, although only in silos (i.e., in single business units), preventing knowledge spread throughout the organization.	Data components, entities, and tables are being utilized across organizational boundaries during business process implementation. The data components, entities, and tables are fully understood, and are now repeatable for standardization projects around business process implementation.	Data components, entities, and tables have become clearly defined and documented across all strategic, tactical, and operational management levels to help support organizational learning around business process operations.	Data components, entities, and tables have a direct relationship to all relevant process objects, and their purpose is fully understood across the organizational business units.	The organization has become explicitly data-centric and data-driven in the collaborative feedback loop during business process implementation, development, and improvement projects and initiatives. Data aid in supporting business differentiation and support enterprise-wide integration.

Media	The use of business, application, data, platform, and infrastructure media during business process operations often occurs ad hoc and delivers performance on an initial basis. The usage also only happens in silos, so knowledge is never shared among business units.	Business process operations during implementation phases make use of business, application, data, platform, and infrastructure media under more standardized yet basic circumstances.	Business, application, data, platform, and infrastructure media have now been explicitly defined and documented in how they support business process operations and development, and the knowledge thereof is shared across organizational boundaries for increased strategic, tactical, and operational management agility.	Business, application, data, platform, and infrastructure media relate to all relevant process objects, and support business process execution across organizational boundaries. The use of media is fully understood by the organization. They are also managed, controlled, and monitored across the enterprise.	All business process operations make use of business, application, data, platform, and infrastructure media in the collaborative feedback loop during process-oriented projects and development initiatives and are of high importance in the support of continuous business process improvement and optimization.
Platform	Logical and physical platform components as well as platform devices and functions effectively support the development and execution of business process operations, although their use is largely ad hoc and occurs only in silos within the organization.	Logical and physical platform components as well as platform devices and functions support implementation of standardized business process developments and installments.	Logical and physical platform components as well as platform devices and functions are being clearly defined and documented across the organization to support organizational learning of business process operations and development.	Logical and physical platform components as well as platform devices and functions are efficiently managed and controlled across organizational boundaries. The platform objects are also directly related to all relevant process objects.	Logical and physical platform components as well as platform devices and functions serve as important aspects to support the continuous business process improvement and optimization during the collaborative feedback loop.

Continued

Table 2 *The Business Process Management (BPM) Maturity Self-Assessment—Cont'd*

	Process Maturity Levels Over Time				
	Level 1 Initial and Uncertain	Level 2 Repeated and Standardize	Level 3 Defined and Awakening	Level 4 Managed and Enlightenment	Level 5 Continuous Improvement
Infrastructure	Logical and physical infrastructure components as well as infrastructure devices, functions, and features effectively support the development and execution of business process operations, and help support the organization in doing so through networking capabilities.	Logical and physical infrastructure components as well as infrastructure devices, functions, and features aid the platform components in supporting the implementation of standardized business process developments and operations.	Logical and physical infrastructure components as well as infrastructure devices, functions, and features are being clearly defined and documented across the organization to support organizational learning of business process operations and development.	Logical and physical infrastructure components as well as infrastructure devices, functions and features are efficiently managed and controlled across organizational boundaries. The infrastructure objects are also directly related to all relevant process objects.	Logical and physical infrastructure components as well as infrastructure devices, functions, and features serve as important aspects to support the continuous business process improvement and optimization during the collaborative feedback loop.
Service	Business processes are directly supported by application, data, platform, and infrastructure services; however, they share no connection to the business services of the organization. Service delivery of executed business processes are neither measured nor controlled, and appear largely ad hoc and initial in their behavior.	Application, data, platform, and infrastructure services are used to support basic business process standardization across organizational boundaries due to the repetition of earlier successes in previous process-oriented projects and development initiatives.	Application, data, platform, and infrastructure services have been defined and documented in detail to support and enhance organizational learning of their function and purpose around business process operations and development.	Business, application, data, platform, and infrastructure services are now all directly related to all relevant process flows. Their function and purpose is fully managed, controlled, and monitored across organizational boundaries of the enterprise.	Business, application, data, platform, and infrastructure services are used as a central part in the collaborative feedback loop across organizational boundaries. The services also aid in supporting the organization during continuous business improvement and optimization.

FROM MATURITY LEVEL ASSESSMENT TO MATURITY BENCHMARK

A BPM Maturity level assessment is essentially a way of describing the extent to which a process or function exists in context with the rest of the organization. This is important because the process activities and their context are the relationships that relate to the:

- Effective way of working
- Efficient operation
- Consistent performance
- Reliable value creation and realization.

Since the early 1990s, to develop new strategic direction and improve performance, organizations have analyzed their As-Is situation to find out what they need to change to reach the desired To-Be stage. Once the organization has finished the BPM maturity self-assessment and understand its BPM maturity of its As-Is situation, we have found that various organizations spend a tremendous amount of time, resources, and money to understand and benchmark the different aspects. We have, therefore, developed a standard BPM maturity benchmark that enables comparison of the different areas against one other. Given an immediate overview of the specific maturity level of the different areas and where the lowest maturity within an area is, this enables us to see the weakest maturity and how it impacts the other areas. In Figure 5, an example of such a BPM Maturity Benchmark is illustrated.

Organizations and people want to know the maturity and benchmark against the various functions related to processes for two main reasons. The first is to establish a baseline, that is, Where are we now? The second is to understand the potential for improvement and development. If the self-assessment generates a maturity value of less than 4 or 5, one could say that hope exists for improvement and development. Likewise in a benchmarking exercise if the various maturity assessments against each other reveal a huge gap, an organization can assume that hope exists for improvement and development. It is, however, vital to understand that such a benchmark cannot answer the following important questions:

- What should the maturity value be for this process in our organization now?
- What could a possible maturity development path look like?
- Which areas are impacted and improve when increasing the maturity in this specific area?

In addition to the above, one of the greatest challenges in such a process is the impact to the business in terms of the impact to the operating model, performance, and cost model as well as the service, value, and even revenue model. This is seen as very relevant because the various context areas assessed impact on the business

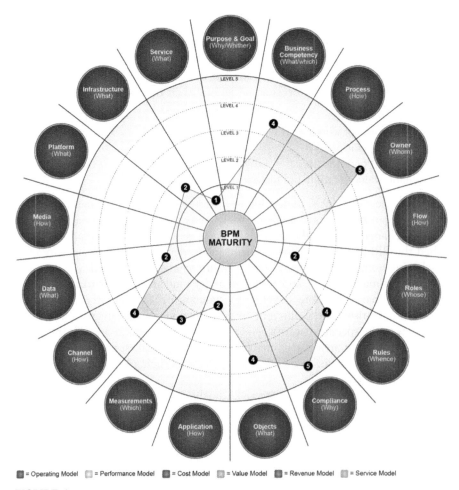

= Operating Model   = Performance Model   = Cost Model   = Value Model   = Revenue Model   = Service Model

FIGURE 5

Example of a business process management (BPM) maturity benchmark.[40] (For interpretation of the references to color in this figure legend, the reader is referred to the online version of this book.)

in different ways. In Figure 6 is an example of a BPM maturity development path that specifies the existing maturity, which in this example is level 1, the identified impacted business aspects. In this example, the impacted business aspects of low maturity affect the revenue model, the value model, as well as the daily performance model. In addition, the time frame for development through the maturity levels is specified.

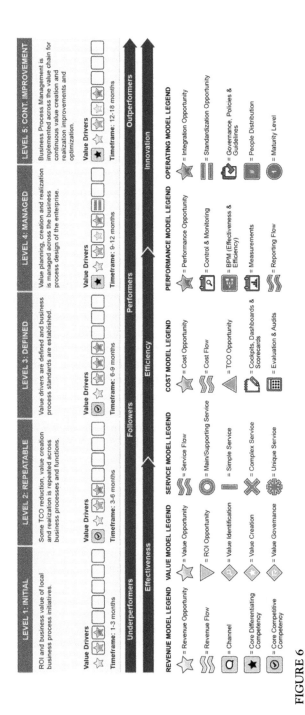

FIGURE 6

Example of a business process management (BPM) maturity development path complete with value drivers and time line for each maturity level.[41]

(For interpretation of the references to color in this figure legend, the reader is referred to the online version of this book.)

Such a specific development path is seen as vital for any organization, especially because this is one of the weak points of general maturity models, for example, CMMI. General maturity models encourage the achievement of a higher maturity level in all aspects. We see this as wrong, and actually more hurtful of the development of the organization than helping it. An organization will and needs to have different levels of maturity in its various areas. Although, for example, core-differentiating aspects and the value-creating aspects of an organization need to be at maturity levels 4 and 5. However, the nondifferentiating, noncompeting aspects of the organization should not be at maturity level 4 or 5, as the cost to achieve a higher maturity level than 3 would be far greater than the possible gain. The best maturity could be level 2 at which it needs to be repeated and standardized; anything higher might not have the cost/value trade-off. Such a cost/value trade-off obviously needs to be closely analyzed by the organization, and this is exactly what the BPM maturity development path is about.

CONCLUSION

In this section, we have focused on maturity models, what they are, their historic development, how they could be used, and when BPM can use maturity concepts. We illustrated a detailed BPM maturity self-assessment, a benchmark among the various aspects that are related to the BPM maturity context, as well as a BPM maturity development path, all to enable hands-on practical guidance, assess one's maturity, and develop it. Without such a BPM Maturity assessment and a connected benchmark, the journey to BPM maturity will be difficult and frustrating. What we have provided here is a starting point for organizations to map out their development journey ahead of time and determine the proper number of rest stops along the way to the ultimate destination, which may or not be level 5. We believe this is the start of a great journey, and we wish you luck with your maturity development journey.

End Notes

1. CMMI for Software Development. CMMI-DEV. Carnegie Mellon University Software Engineering Institute.
2. Organizational Project Management Maturity Model (OPM3®) – Third Edition, 2013, Project Management Institute: http://www.pmi.org/PMBOK-Guide-and-Standards/Standards-Library-of-PMI-Global-Standards.aspx.
3. Curtis B., Hefley W. E., and Miller S., *People Capability Maturity Model*. CMU/SEI-95-MM-02 (Pittsburgh: Carnegie Mellon University, Software Engineering Institute, 1995). Available at: http://www.sei.cmu.edu/cmmi/tools/peoplecmm/.
4. http://www.p3m3-officialsite.com/nmsruntime/saveasdialog.aspx?lID=456&sID=166.
5. http://www.utdc.vuw.ac.nz/research/emm/.
6. Humphrey W. S., *Characterizing the Software Process: A Maturity Framework*. CMU/SEI-87-TR-11 (Pittsburgh: Carnegie Mellon University, Software Engineering Institute, 1987).

7. Crosby P. B., *Quality is Free*, (New York: McGraw-Hill, 1979).

8. Hays D. W., "Quality improvement and its origin in scientific management," *Quality Progress* 27, no. 6 (May 1994): 89–90.

9. Deming W. E., *Out of the Crisis* (Cambridge, MA: MIT Center for Advanced Engineering Study, 1986).

10. Juran J. M., *Juran on Planning for Quality* (New York: Macmillan, 1988).

11. Emam K. and Goldenson D. R., (1999), An empirical review of software process assessments. NRC/ERB-1065 (NRC 43610). National Research Council Canada, Institute for Information Tech.

12. Humphrey W. S., *Managing the Software Process* (Reading, MA: Addison-Wesley, 1989).

13. Paulk M. C., Humphrey W. S., and Pandelios G. J., "Software process assessments: issues and lessons learned," in Proceedings of ISQE92, Juran Institute, March 1992, 4B/41–58.

14. LEADing Practice Maturity Reference Content [#LEAD-ES60003AL].

15. Kasse, Konrad M. D., Perdue J. R., Weber C. V., and Withey J. V., *Capability Maturity Model for Software*. CMU/SEI-91-TR-24 (Pittsburgh: Carnegie Mellon University, Software Engineering Institute, 1991).

16. Paulk M. C., Curtis B., Chrissis M. B., and Weber C. V., *Capability Maturity Model for Software, Version 1.1*. CMU/SEI-93-TR-24 (Pittsburgh: Carnegie Mellon University, Software Engineering Institute, 1993a).

17. Paulk M. C., Weber C. V., Curtis B., and Chrissis M. B., *The Capability Maturity Model: Guidelines for Improving the Software Process* (1995a).

18. Capability Maturity Model Version 1.0. CMU/SEI-94-HB-04 (Pittsburgh: Carnegie Mellon University, Software Engineering Institute).

19. Paulk M. C., Humphrey W. S., and Pandelios G. J., Software Process (1992).

20. Paulk M. C., Weber C. V., Garcia S. M., Chrissis M. B., and Bush M. W., *Key Practices of the Capability Maturity Model, Version 1.1*. CMU/SEI-93-TR-25 (Pittsburgh: Carnegie Mellon University, Software Engineering Institute, 1993b).

21. Paulk M. C., Curtis B., Chrissis M. B., Averill E. L., Bamberger J., T. C. Kasse, M. D. Konrad, J. R. Perdue, C. V. Weber, and J. V. Withey. 1991. *Capability Maturity Model for Software*. CMU/SEI-91-TR-24. Pittsburgh: Carnegie Mellon University, Software Engineering Institute.

22. SEI, *Process Maturity Profile: Software CMM 2005 End-Year Update* (Pittsburgh: Software Engineering Institute, Carnegie Mellon University, 2006).

23. Chrissis M. B., Konrad M. D., and Shrum S., *CMMI: Guidelines for Process Integration and Product Improvement*, second ed. (Boston: Addison-Wesley, 2006).

24. Humphrey W. S. and Sweet W. L., (1987b), A Method for Assessing the Software Engineering Capability of Contractors, Carnegie Mellon University, Software Engineering Institute, CMU/SEI-87-TR-23, September.

25. DOD, "Excerpts from Fall 1987 Report of the defense science board task force on military software," *ACM Ada Letters*, (July/August, 1988): 35–46.

26. SEI, *CMMI for Acquisition, Version 1.2*. CMU/SEI-2007-TR-017 (Pittsburgh: Carnegie Mellon University, Software Engineering Institute, 2007).

27. SEI, *CMMI for Services, Version 1.2*. CMU/SEI-2009-TR-001 (Pittsburgh: Carnegie Mellon University, Software Engineering Institute, 2009).

28. Gallagher B. P., Phillips M., Richter K. J., and Shrum S., CMMIACQ: Guidelines for Improving the Acquisition of Products and Services (Boston: Addison-Wesley Professional, 2009).

29. Paulk M. C., (2008), A taxonomy for improvement frameworks. World Congress for Software Quality, Bethesda, MD, 15–18 September.
30. Humphrey W. S., "Three process perspectives: organizations, teams, and people," *Annals of Software Engineering* 4, (2002): 39–72.
31. Britz G., Emerling D., Hare L., Hoerl R., and Shade J., *Statistical Thinking*. A Special Publication of the ASQC Statistics Division (Spring, 1996).
32. Pfeffer J. and Sutton R. I., *Hard Facts, Dangerous Half-Truths, & Total Nonsense: Profiting from Evidence-Based Management*. (Boston: Harvard Business School Press, 2006).
33. See note 14 above.
34. Besselman J. J., "A collection of software capability evaluation (SCE) findings: many lessons learned," in Proceedings of the Eighth Annual National Joint Conference on Software Quality and Productivity, Arlington, VA, March 1992, 196–215.
35. Krasner H., (2001), "Accumulating the body of evidence for the payoff of software process improvement – 1997," in *Software Process Improvement*, eds. Hunter R. B., and Thayer R. H., (New York: IEEE Computer Society Press, 2001), 519–539.
36. Austin, R. D., *Measuring and Managing Performance in Organizations* (New York: Dorset House Publishing, 1996).
37. "BPM Maturity Model is Important for Long Lasting BPM Success," Michael Melenovsky and Jim Sinur from http://www.brcommunity.com/b325.php.
38. See note 14 above.
39. See note 14 above.
40. Ibid.
41. Ibid.

The BPM Way of Modeling

Mark von Rosing, Henrik von Scheel, August-Wilhelm Scheer

INTRODUCTION

Part IV provides practical and essential guidance to the "*Way of Modeling*" with and around business process concepts. Part IV outlines the approach the practitioner follows to apply principles for representing process and making an objective assessment of the possible. By using decomposition and composition modeling techniques within the different layers, for example, business, application, and technology, the approach provides you, the practitioner, faced with real world challenges, a uniform and structured description of the model objects and artifacts within one or more different types of models.

Identifying and classifying the different objects, for example, business information and/or data, is not always easy, relating such to the process and/or service model as well as the execution and realization of such into application software solutions is also quite complex. The ways to model one's process models both in terms of EPC-Event-Driven Process Chain from ARIS (Software AG), with examples of information and process models, BPNM, to value-oriented process modeling, and sustainability modeling, is the focus of Part IV.

Business Process Model and Notation—BPMN

Mark von Rosing, Stephen White, Fred Cummins, Henk de Man

INTRODUCTION

This chapter is intended to provide an overview and introduction to the Business Process Model and Notation (BPMN). We will describe BPMN and its historic development. In addition, we will provide the general context and usage of BPMN, layered upon the technical details defined in the BPMN 2.0 Specification. The basics of the BPMN notation will be described—that is, the types of graphical shapes, their purpose, and how they work together as part of a Business Process Model/Diagram. Also discussed will be the different uses of BPMN diagram types, including how levels of precision affect what a modeler will include in a diagram. Finally, the value in using BPMN as a standard notation will be defined.

It is vital to note that because both main authors and the additional four authors all officially work with the Object Management Group (OMG) to develop standards, this chapter and its content be based on the official OMG BPMN specification.[1]

WHAT IS BPMN?

Business Process Model and Notation (BPMN) is a standard for business process modeling that provides graphical notation for specifying business processes in a Business Process Diagram (BPD),[2] based on traditional flowcharting techniques. The objective of BPMN is to support business process modeling for both technical users and business users, by providing notation that is intuitive to business users, yet able to represent complex process semantics. The BPMN 2.0 specification also provides execution semantics as well as mapping between the graphics of the notation and other execution languages, particularly Business Process Execution Language (BPEL).[3]

BPMN is designed to be readily understandable by all business stakeholders. These include the business analysts who create and refine the processes, the technical developers responsible for implementing them, and the business managers who monitor and manage them. Consequently, BPMN serves as a common language, bridging the communication gap that frequently occurs between business process design and implementation.

THE HISTORIC DEVELOPMENT OF BPMN

In 2001, the process-modeling marketplace was fragmented with many different modeling notations and viewpoints. It was in this context that members of Business Process Management Institute (BPMI), many of whom represented companies that contributed to the fragmented market, began discussing the idea of standardizing business-oriented techniques for visually representing process components and aligning the notation with an executable process language. The BPMN 1.0 specification was released to the public in May 2004. With this, the primary goal of the BPMN specification was to provide a notation that is readily understandable by all business users, from the business analysts that create the initial drafts of the processes, to the technical developers responsible for implementing the technology that will perform those processes, and finally, to the business people who will manage and monitor those processes. BPMN 1.0 was also supported with an internal model that was mapped to executable BPEL4WS.

It was February 6, 2006, when BPMI was subsumed by the OMG, who has since maintained and developed the BPMN standard. The BPMN 1.1 version was published in January 2008[4] and a year later version 1.2[5] was published. Work on the well-known version 2.0 took another two years, and it was published in January 2011.[6] This international standard represents the amalgamation of best practices within the business modeling community to define the notation and semantics of collaboration diagrams, process diagrams, and choreography diagrams. In doing so, BPMN will provide a simple means of communicating process information to other business users, process implementers, customers, and suppliers.

Another goal, but no less important, is to ensure that the models created by BPMN are executable. BPMN 1.x provided mappings to Extensible Markup Language (XML) designed for the execution of business processes, such as Web Services Business Process Execution Language (WSBPEL). The ability to execute BPMN via BPEL (BPEL, also known as WS-BPEL) breathed life into model-driven process execution. In essence, the equation Application = Computation + Coordination has become reality with network-addressable computation being provided by Web Services and BPMN graphically depicting the coordination logic. BPMN 2.0 provided its own execution semantics in addition to an updated mapping to BPEL. Thus, new process engines can directly execute BPMN models without the potential behavioral restrictions that might result in the complex mapping of the more free-form BPMN to the more structured BPEL.

Some of the main changes that the BPMN versions 2.0 brought with them are among others:

- The addition of a Choreography diagram.
- The addition of a Conversation diagram.

- Noninterrupting Events for a Process.
- Event Subprocesses for a Process.

The major technical changes include:

- A definition of the process execution semantics.
- A formal metamodel as shown through the class diagram figures.
- Interchange formats for abstract syntax model interchange in both XML Metadata Interchange (XMI) and XML Schema Definition (XSD).
- Interchange formats for diagram interchange in both XMI and XSD.
- Extensible Stylesheet Language Transformations (XSLT) between the XMI and XSD formats.

Other technical changes include:

- Reference Tasks are removed. These provided reusability within a single diagram, as compared to Global Tasks, which are reusable across multiple diagrams. The new Call Activity can be used to reference a Global Task or another Process to be used within a Process (instead of Reference Tasks).

Because of the version 2.0 updates, the number of elements more than doubled from 55 elements to 116. Many of these new elements were applied to modeling interactions between processes and/or entities, such as the new choreography diagram.

BPMN 2.0.2, released in December 2013,[7] included only minor modifications in terms of typo corrections and a change in clause 15.

THE BPMN NOTATIONS/SHAPES

A major goal for the development of BPMN was to create a simple and understandable notation for creating Business Process models, while providing the semantics and underlying mechanisms to handle the complexity inherent in Business Processes. The approach taken to handle these two conflicting requirements was to organize the graphical aspects of the notation into specific categories. This provides a small set of notation categories so that the reader of a BPMN diagram can easily recognize the basic types of elements and understand the diagram. The various basic BPMN shapes are shown below (Tables 1–6).

Within the basic categories of elements, additional variation and information can be added to support the requirements for complexity without dramatically changing the basic look and feel of the diagram. In the following sections, we will illustrate how the BPMN shapes are used in various end-to-end BPMN models.

Table 1 *BPMN Task Description*

BPMN 2.0.2	Task Description
None	No special task type is indicated.
User Task	A User Task is a typical "workflow" task in which a human performer performs the task with the assistance of a software application and could be scheduled through a task list manager of some sort.
Manual Task	A Manual Task is a task that is expected to be performed without the aid of any business process execution engine or application.
Service Task	A Service Task is a task that uses some sort of service, which could be a web service or an automated application.
Receive Task	A Receive Task is a simple task that is designed to wait for a message to arrive from an external participant (relative to the process).
Send	A Send Task is a simple task that is designed to send a message to an external participant (relative to the process).
Script	A Script Task is executed by a business process engine. The modeler or implementer defines a script in a language that the engine can interpret. When the task is ready to start, the engine will execute the script. When the script is completed, the task will also be completed.

Table 1 *BPMN Task Description—Cont'd*

BPMN 2.0.2	Task Description
Business Rule	A Business Rule Task provides a mechanism for the process to provide input to a Business Rules Engine and to get the output of calculations that the Business Rules Engine might provide. The input/output specification of the task will allow the process to send data to and receive data from the Business Rules Engine.
Sub-Process	A Sub-Process is a type of activity within a process, but it also can be "opened up" to show a lower-level process. This is useful for process decomposition or general process organization.
Call Activity	A Call Activity is a type of activity within a process. It provides a link to reusable activities: for example, it will call a task into the Process (see upper figure on the left) or another Process (see lower figure on the left).

Table 2 *BPMN Flow Description*

BPMN 2.0.2	Flow Description
Sequence Flow	A Sequence Flow is represented by a solid line with a solid arrowhead and is used to show the order (the sequence) in which activities will be performed in a process or choreography diagram.
Message Flow	A Message Flow is represented by a dashed line with an open arrowhead and is used to show the flow of messages between two separate process participants (business entities or business roles) that send and receive them.
Association	An Association is represented by a dotted line, which may have a line arrowhead on one or both ends, and is used to associate text and other artifacts with flow objects.
Data Association	A Data Association is represented by a dotted line with a line arrowhead and is used to associate data (electronic or nonelectronic) with flow objects. Data Associations are used to show the inputs and outputs of activities.

Table 3 *BPMN Marker Description*

BPMN 2.0.2	Markers Description
↻ Loop Marker	A Loop Marker is used to represent an activity that will be executed multiple times until the condition is satisfied. The condition can be validated either at the start or end of the activity.
||| Parallel Multiple Instance Marker	A Parallel Multi-Instance Marker is used to represent an activity that can be executed as multiple instances performed in parallel. The number of instances will be determined through a condition expression that is evaluated at the start of the activity. All the instances will start in parallel and each instance can have different input parameters. The activity, as a whole, is completed after all the instances are completed. However, another expression, if it becomes true, will stop all instances and complete the activity.
☰ Sequential Multiple Instance Marker	A Sequential Multi-Instance Marker represents an activity that is similar to a Parallel Multi-Instance activity, but its instances will be executed in sequence. The second instance will wait until the first instance is completed and so on.
∼ Adhoc Marker	The Adhoc Marker is a tilde symbol and used to mark a Sub-Process for which the normal sequence patterns are relaxed and its activities can be performed in any order at the discretion of the users. Tasks can start any time without any direct dependency on other tasks.
Text Annotation Annotation Marker	An Annotation Marker is a mechanism for a modeler to provide additional text information (i.e., notes) for the reader of a BPMN diagram. Annotations can be connected to other objects through an Association (see above).

Table 4 *BPMN Data Object Description*

BPMN 2.0.2	Data Description
📄 Data Object	A Data Object represents the data that are used as inputs and outputs to the activities of a process. Data Objects can represent singular objects or collections of objects.
📄 Data Input	A Data Input is an external data input for the entire process. It is a kind of input parameter.

Table 4 *BPMN Data Object Description—Cont'd*

BPMN 2.0.2	Data Description
Data Output	A Data Output is the data result of the entire process. It is a kind of output parameter.
Data Store	A Data Store is a place where the process can read or write data (e.g., a database or a filing cabinet). It persists beyond the lifetime of the process instance.
Collection of Data Objects	A Collection of Data Objects represents a collection of data elements related to the same data entity (e.g., a list of order items).

Table 5 *BPMN Event Description*

BPMN 2.0.2	Event Description
Event: Start	Start Events indicate the instance or initiation of a process or an Event Sub-Process and have no incoming sequence flow. A Process can have more than one Start Event, but an Event Sub-Process only have one Start Event.
Event: Event Sub-Process non-interrupting	Non-interrupting Start Events can be used to initiate an Event Sub-Process without interfering with the main process flow.
Event: Intermediate and Boundary	Intermediate Events indicate something that occurs or may occur during the course of the process, between Start and End. Intermediate Catching Events can be used to catch the event trigger and can be in the flow or attached to the boundary of an activity. Intermediate Throwing Events can be used to throw the event trigger.
Event: Boundary non-interrupting	Non-interrupting Boundary Events can be attached to the boundary of an activity. When they are triggered, flow will be generated from them, but the source activity will continue to be performed.
Event: End	The End Event indicates where a path in the Process will end. A Process can have more than one end. The Process ends when all active paths have ended. End Events have no outgoing sequence flows.

Continued

Table 5 BPMN *Event Description*—*Cont'd*	
BPMN 2.0.2	**Event Description**
Message (receive)	Receive messages to start a Process or in the middle of a Process, either in the flow or attached to the boundary of an activity.
Message (send)	Send messages in the middle or at the end of a Process path.
Timer (catch)	A Timer Event is always of catch type and used to signify waiting for a specific time condition to evaluate to true, which will start a Process, start an Event Sub-Process, wait in the middle of a flow, or wait as a Boundary Event.
Escalation (catch)	An Escalation Event handles escalation conditions, triggering the start of an Event Sub-Process or a Boundary Event.
Escalation (throw)	A throw Escalation Event will cause the escalation conditions that will trigger the catch Events.
Link (throw and catch)	A Link Event has no significance related to how the Process is performed, but it facilitates the diagram-creation process. For example, you can use two associated links as an alternative to a long sequence flow. There is a throwing Link Event as the "exit point," and a catching Link Event as the "entrance point," and the two events are marked as a pair.
Error (catch)	A catch Error Event is used to capture errors and to handle them. This event can only be used as the start an Event Sub-Process or as a Boundary Event. These events can catch errors thrown by the throw Error Events or errors thrown by a BPM system or services used by the Process.

Table 5 *BPMN Event Description—Cont'd*

BPMN 2.0.2	Event Description
 Error (throw)	A throw Error Event is used to set an error to be handled. This event can only be used as an End Event (i.e., never as an Intermediate Event).
 Cancel (catch)	Cancel Events can only be used in the context of the transactions. The catch Cancel Events are used as Boundary Events for the transaction Sub-Process, and will trigger the roll back of the transaction (i.e., the Activities of the Sub-Process).
 Cancel (throw)	Cancel Events can only be used in the context of the transactions. The throw Cancel Events are only used within a transaction Sub-Process.
 Conditional (catch)	Conditional Events are used to determine whether to start (or continue) only if a certain condition is true. Like the Timer Event, the Conditional Event can only exist as a catching event. They can be used at the start of a Process or an Event Sub-Process, in the middle of the flow, or as a Boundary Event.
 Compensation (catch)	A Compensation Event is used to handle compensation in the process. The catching Compensation Event can be triggered as an Event Sub-Process Start Event, or as a Boundary Event.
 Compensation (throw)	A Compensation Event is used to handle compensation in the process. The throwing Compensation Event can be used in the middle or end of a Process path.
 Signal (start)	Catching Signal Events are used for receiving signals. They are a generic, simple form of communication and exist within pools (same participant), across pools (different participants), and across diagrams. They can be used at the start of a Process or an Event Sub-Process, in the middle of the flow, or as a Boundary Event.
 Signal (end)	Throwing Signal Events are used for sending signals. They are a generic, simple form of communication and exist within pools (same participant), across pools (different participants), and across diagrams. They can be used in the middle or end of a Process path.

Continued

Table 5 *BPMN Event Description—Cont'd*

BPMN 2.0.2	Event Description
Multiple (catch)	The Multiple Event is used to summarize several event types with a single symbol. The event is triggered if any one of those types is satisfied. They can be used at the start of a Process or an Event Sub-Process, in the middle of the flow, or as a Boundary Event.
Multiple (throw)	The Multiple Event is used to summarize several event types with a single symbol. When this is event is reached, then all the event types are thrown. They can be used in the middle or end of a Process path.
Parallel Multiple (catch)	The Parallel Multiple Event is used to summarize several event types with a single symbol. The difference between this event and the Multiple Event is that the Parallel Multiple is only triggered if *all* of those types are satisfied. They can be used at the start of a Process or an Event Sub-Process, in the middle of the flow, or as a Boundary Event.
Terminate (throw)	The Terminate End Event is the "stop everything" event. When a Terminate End Event is reached, the entire process is stopped, including all parallel activities.

Table 6 *BPMN Gateway Description*

BPMN 2.0.2	Gateway Description
Gateway	Gateways are used to control how process paths converge and diverge within a process.
Exclusive Gateway	The Event Gateway, when splitting, routes sequence flow to only one of the outgoing branches, based on conditions. When merging, it awaits one incoming branch to complete before continuing the flow. The Gateway can be displayed with or without the "X" marker, but the behavior is the same.
Inclusive Gateway	The Inclusive Gateway, when splitting, allows one or more branches to be activated, based on conditions. All active incoming branches must complete before merging.

Table 6 BPMN *Gateway Description—Cont'd*	
BPMN 2.0.2	**Gateway Description**
⊕ Parallel Gateway	The Parallel Gateway, when splitting, will direct the flow down all the outgoing branches. When merging, it awaits in all the branches to complete before continuing the flow.
◈ ◇ Event-based Gateway	The Event Gateway is always followed by catching events or receive tasks. The flow of the Process is routed to the subsequent event/task which happens first. When merging, it behaves like an Event Gateway. This Gateway can be configured such that it can be used to start a Process, based on the first event that follows it (see the lower figure on the left).
⊕ Parallel Event-based Gateway	The Parallel Event Gateway is only used for starting a Process. It is configured like a regular Event Gateway, but *all* of the subsequent events must be triggered before a new process instance is created.
✳ Complex Gateway	The Complex Gateway defines behavior that is not captured by other gateways. Expressions are used to determine the merging and splitting behavior.

BPMN DIAGRAMS

Business Process Modeling is used to communicate a wide variety of process configurations to a wide variety of audiences. Thus, BPMN was designed to cover many types of modeling and allow the creation of end-to-end Business Processes. The structural elements of BPMN allow the viewer to be able to easily differentiate between sections of a BPMN Diagram. There are three basic types of submodels within a BPMN modeling environment:

1. Processes (*Orchestration*), including:
    a. *Private non-executable* (internal) Business Processes.
    b. *Private executable* (internal) Business Processes.
    c. *Public* Processes.
2. Choreographies.
3. Collaborations, which can include Processes and/or Choreographies.
    a. A view of Conversations.

TO POINT (1) PRIVATE (INTERNAL) BUSINESS PROCESSES

Private Business Processes are those internal to a specific organization. These Processes have been generally called workflow or BPM Processes (see Figure 1). Another synonym typically used in the Web services area is the *Orchestration* of services. There are two types of *private* Processes: *executable* and *non-executable*.

FIGURE 1

Example of private process.

An *executable* Process is a Process that has been modeled for being executed according to the defined BPMN execution semantics. Of course, during the development cycle of the Process, there will be stages in which the Process does not have enough detail to be "executable."

A *non-executable* Process is a *private* Process that has been modeled for documenting Process behavior at a modeler-defined level of detail. Thus, information needed for execution, such as formal condition expressions are typically not included in a *non-executable* Process.

If a swim lanes-like notation is used (e.g., a Collaboration, see below) then a *private* Business Process will be contained within a single Pool. The Process flow is therefore contained within the Pool and cannot cross the boundaries of the Pool. The flow of Messages can cross the Pool boundary to show the interactions that exist between separate *private* or *public* Business Processes.

PUBLIC PROCESSES

A *public* Process represents the interactions to and from another Process or *Participant* (see Figure 2). Only those Activities and Events that are used to communicate to the other *Participants* are included in the *public* Process. These Activities and Events can be considered the "touch-points" between the participants. All other "internal" Activities of the *private* Business Process are not shown in the *public* Process. Thus, the *public* Process shows to the outside world the Message Flows and the order of those Message Flows that is needed to interact with that Process. *Public* Processes can be modeled separately

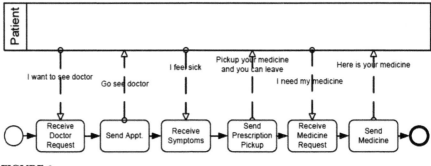

FIGURE 2

Example of public process.

or within a Collaboration to show the directional flow of Messages. Note that the *public* type of Process was named "abstract" in BPMN 1.2 (2009 release).

COLLABORATIONS

A Collaboration depicts the interactions between two or more business entities. A Collaboration usually contains two or more Pools, representing the *Participants* in the Collaboration. The Message exchange between the *Participants* is shown by a Message Flow that connects two Pools (or the objects within the Pools). The Messages associated with the Message Flows can also be shown graphically. The Collaboration can be shown as two or more *public* and/or *private* Processes communicating with each other (see Figure 3). Or a Pool MAY be empty, a "black box." Choreography elements MAY be shown "in between" the Pools as they bisect the Message Flows between the Pools. All combinations of Pools, Processes, and a Choreography are allowed in a Collaboration.

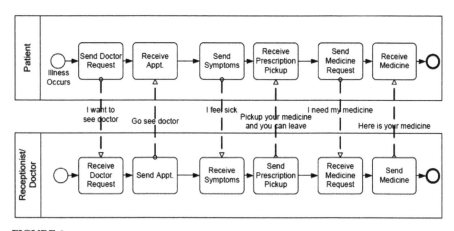

FIGURE 3

Example of a Collaboration.

TO POINT (2) CHOREOGRAPHY

A self-contained Choreography (no Pools or *Orchestration*) is a definition of the expected behavior, basically, a procedural contract between interacting *Participants*. Although a normal Process exists within a Pool, a Choreography exists between Pools (or *Participants*).

The Choreography looks similar to a *private* Business Process because it consists of a network of Activities, Events, and Gateways (see Figure 4). However, a Choreography is different in that the Activities are interactions that represent a set (one or more) of Message exchanges, which involves two or more *Participants*. In addition, unlike a normal Process, no central controller, responsible entity, or observer of the Process exists.

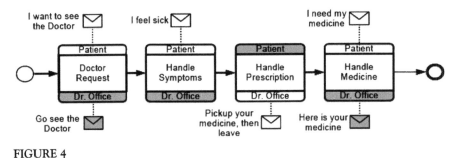

FIGURE 4

Example of a Choreography.

TO POINT (3) CONVERSATIONS

The Conversation diagram is a particular usage and an informal description of a Collaboration diagram. However, the Pools of a Conversation diagram usually do not contain a Process, and a Choreography is usually not placed between the Pools of a Conversation diagram. An individual Conversation (within the diagram) is the logical relation of Message exchanges. The logical relation, in practice, often concerns a business object(s) of interest, for example, "Order," "Shipment and Delivery," or "Invoice."

Thus, the Conversation diagram is a high-level modeling diagram that depicts a set of related Conversations that reflect a distinct business scenario Table 7. For example, in logistics, stock replenishments involve the following type of scenarios: creation of sales orders, assignment of carriers for shipments combining different sales orders, crossing customs/quarantine, processing payment, and investigating exceptions. Thus, a Conversation diagram, as shown in Figure 5, shows Conversations (as hexagons) between *Participants* (Pools). This provides a "bird's eye" perspective of the different Conversations that relate to the domain.

Table 7 *BPMN Conversation Description*	
BPMN 2.0.2	**Conversations Description**
⬡ Conversation	A Conversation defines a set of logically related Message Flows. When marked with a (+) symbol it indicates a Sub-Conversation, a compound conversation element.
⬡ Call Conversation	A Call Conversation is a wrapper for a globally defined, re-usable Conversation or Collaboration. A call to a Collaboration is marked with a (+) symbol.
═══════ Conversation Link	Connects Conversations and Participants.

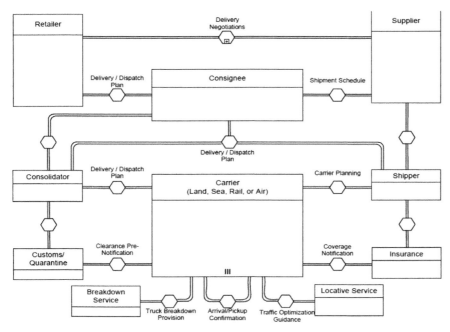

FIGURE 5

Example of a conversation diagram.

BPMN USAGE

We have just illustrated the three basic BPMN models of Processes—*private* Processes (both *executable* and *non-executable*), *public* Processes—Collaborations (including Conversations), and Choreographies. Within and between these BPMN sub-models, many types of Diagrams can be created.

The following are examples of Business Processes that can be modeled:

- High-level *non-executable* Process Activities (not functional breakdown).
- Detailed executable Business Process.
- As-is or old Business Process.
- To-be or new Business Process.
- A description of expected behavior between two or more business Participants—a Choreography.
- Detailed *private* Business Process (either *executable* or *non-executable*) with interactions to one or more external *Entities* (or "Black Box" Processes).
- Two or more detailed *executable* Processes interacting.
- Detailed *executable* Business Process relationship to a Choreography.
- Two or more *public* Processes.
- *Public* Process relationship to Choreography.
- Two or more detailed *executable* Business Processes interacting through a Choreography.

One of the benefits of BPMN, among others, is that it has the flexibility to allow the development of all the above examples of business processes. However, the ways that different submodels are combined within a specific tool is a choice of the vendors and can vary quite a bit.

DIAGRAM POINT OF VIEW

Because a BPMN diagram may depict the processes of different participants, each participant could view the diagram differently. That is, the participants have different points of view regarding how the processes will apply to them. Some of the activities will be internal to a participant (that is, they are performed by or under control of that participant) and other activities will be external to that participant. Each participant will have a different perspective as to which are internal and external. At run time, the difference between internal and external activities is important in how a participant can view the status of the activities or troubleshoot any problems. However, the diagram itself remains the same. Figure 3, above, displays a business process that has two points of view. One point of view is of a patient, the other is of the doctor's office.

The diagram may show the activities of both participants in the process, but when the process is actually being performed, each participant will only have control over their own activities. Although the diagram point of view is important for a viewer of the diagram to understand how the behavior of the process will relate to that viewer, BPMN will not currently specify any graphical mechanisms to highlight the point of view. It is open to the modeler or modeling tool vendor to provide any visual cues to emphasize this characteristic of a diagram.

UNDERSTANDING THE BEHAVIOR OF DIAGRAMS

So far, we have mentioned how sequence flows are used within a process. To facilitate the understanding of process behavior, we employ the concept of a *token* that will traverse the sequence flows and pass through the elements in the process. A *token* is a theoretical concept that is used as an aid to define the behavior of a process that is being performed. However, modeling and execution tools that implement BPMN are NOT REQUIRED to implement any form of *token*.

Process elements can be defined by describing how they interact with a *token* as it moves through the structure of the Process. A Start Event generates a *token* that MUST eventually be consumed at an End Event (which MAY be implicit if not graphically displayed). The path of a *token* should be traceable through the network of Sequence Flows, Gateways, Events, and Activities within a process.

Note: A *token* does not traverse a Message Flow since it is a Message that is passed down a Message Flow (as the name implies).

BPMN EXAMPLE

The following is an example of a manufacturing process from different perspectives (Figures 6–8).

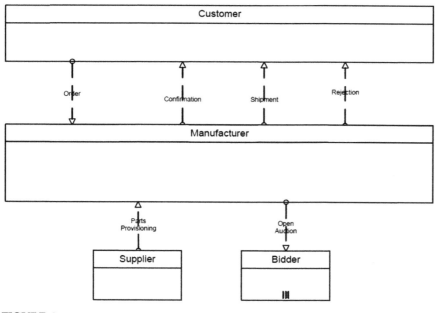

FIGURE 6

An example of a Collaboration diagram with black-box Pools.

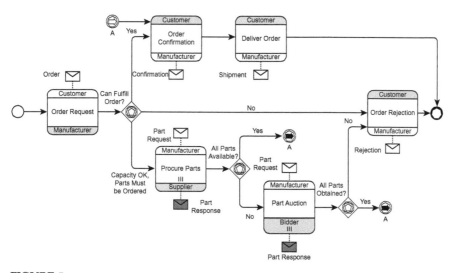

FIGURE 7

An example of a standalone Choreography diagram.

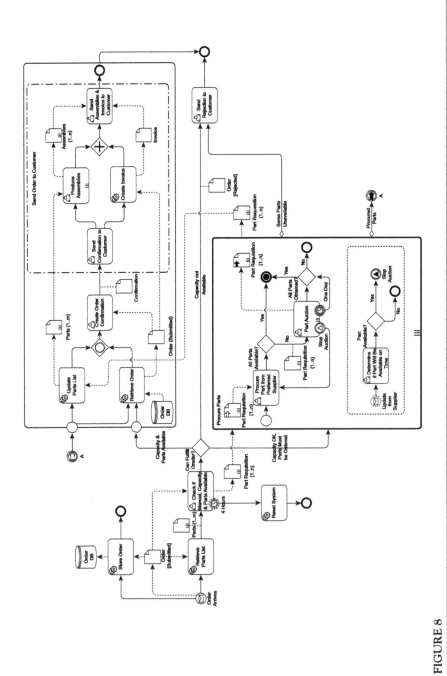

FIGURE 8

An example of a standalone Process (Orchestration) diagram.

BPMN CAVEATS

The focus of BPMN is to enhance primary process modeling capabilities. It does not attempt to model other business models, such as organization, strategic direction, business functions, rules/compliance aspects, etc. Therefore, it is vital to understand that other types of modeling done by organizations outside the primary process purposes are out of scope for BPMN, but they all fit within larger BPM solutions. Below is therefore a specification of modeling principles and concepts excluded from BPMN:

- The linking of business strategies, critical success factors, and value drivers to processes.
- The relation between organizational structures, including business competencies, capabilities, and resources to processes.
- Functional breakdowns of business functions into process tasks.
- Arrangement of business objects such as product, machine, warehouse, and so on, throughout the process models.
- Specification of information objects and thereby information flow within the process models.
- The ability to illustrate or model business measurement, that is, Key Performance Indicators or Process Performance Indicators (PPIs) within the process.
- Data models, whereas BPMN shows the flow of data (messages), and the association of data artifacts to activities, it is not a data model or even a data flow diagram.
- Even though the data objects are specified within the process, real-time process monitoring in terms of Scorecards, Dashboards, and/or Cockpits.
- The support for Business Rules Modeling, in terms of business rules, rule script, flow rule, decision table, report, and thereby decision-making support.
- The ability to run process ownership gap analysis, that is, to both process and processes rules or process measurements.

So although we realize that many BPM teams wish the ability to relate process models to other vital aspects of enterprise modeling, that is, business modeling, value modeling, performance management, and enterprise architecture (e.g., business architecture, allocation/information systems architecture, and technology architecture). The scope of BPMN does not provide such modeling capabilities, but a robust BPM modeling environment could provide the linkages between the various BPM modeling domains.

THE FUTURE OF BPMN

At some point, the OMG will update BPMN to version 3.0. Although some discussions have occurred on this topic, no certain timeline exists as to when this will happen. BPMN versions 1.0 and 2.0 did not cover the wide landscapes and complexities that exist in the process-modeling domain. Thus, certain topics and capabilities could and should be addressed in BPMN 3.0. However, note that the material presented in this section is solely the opinion of the authors of this chapter. The OMG membership, which does include the authors, will determine what will be included in the next version of BPMN.

FULFILLING THE BPMN VISION

In a presentation introducing BPMN to the Business Process Management Initiative (BPMI) in April 2002, the following statement was made: "The BPMN will provide businesses with the capability of understanding their internal and external business procedures with graphical notation and will give organizations the ability to communicate these procedures in a standard manner."

Business Process types cover a wide range that is required for normal operations of most organizations. In the first two versions of BPMN, the standard has focused on more controlled, prescriptive types of internal processes as well as external processes modeled through Collaboration, Conversation, and Choreography. Nevertheless, BPMN does not yet have the built-in capabilities to easily model the entire range of process types that organizations require to run their businesses.

To fulfill this vision, BPMN eventually must be able to cover the entire range of processes that occur in the real world. This range is bounded on one side by very structured processes and on the other side by very unstructured (ad hoc) processes (see Figure 9). Potential work is available on both ends of the spectrum.

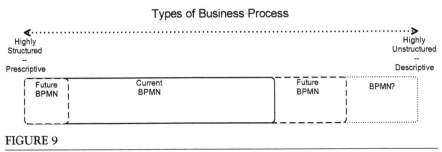

FIGURE 9

A diagram representing the range of process types that are performed by organizations.

There are different areas where future work can be applied to BPMN, including:

- Collaboration, Choreography, and Conversation.
- Metamodel changes.
- Implementation Level Modeling.
- Case Management.

We don't expect much work to be done on Collaboration, Choreography, or Conversation. More vendor/customer experience and feedback is required.

In terms of metamodel work, the following could be applied:

- Various extensions could be added.
- Separate ad hoc processes for better case management support.
- Inherent support for element substitution.
- Allowing different levels of detail or local variations of detail based on single model.

The next two sections discuss the two other major topics that could be added to the BPMN standard.

IMPLEMENTATION LEVEL MODELING

This type of modeling involves highly structured diagrams and fits on the left side of Figure 9 (above). BPMN allows multiple levels of process detail through sub-processes and tasks. But tasks are the lowest level of detail that can be modeled in BPMN. However, some BPM tools provide modelers of executable BPMN models with additional modeling capabilities for modeling the execution details of tasks, which are provided by the services that implement the tasks. These details include the sequence of steps or user interface screens in a service (sometimes called screen flow).

Thus, a process-like level of modeling exists at the service or implementation level. The layout of these models looks very similar to standard BPMN processes, but they are not, at this point, BPMN processes. They have slightly different semantics and visualizations. Figure 10 shows how a BPMN user task could be broken down to an implementation flow.

Some of the characteristics of service flow models include (for example):

- No Lanes. They exist fully within the lane of their parent task.
- Only one Start Event. This Start Event does not have a trigger. Control is always passed from the parent task.
- There are no parallel paths.
- Gateways are allowed.
- They can nest lower level service flow models.
- Semantics of the user events in a service level.
  - They do not interrupt activity in normal sense.
  - They represent a normal completion of the activity.
  - For example, through the clicking of a screen button.
  - User Event notation: User (like a User Task) or a button icon.

Given that modeling tools already exist that provide modeling at the implementation level, this type of diagram could easily be built into the BPMN standard.

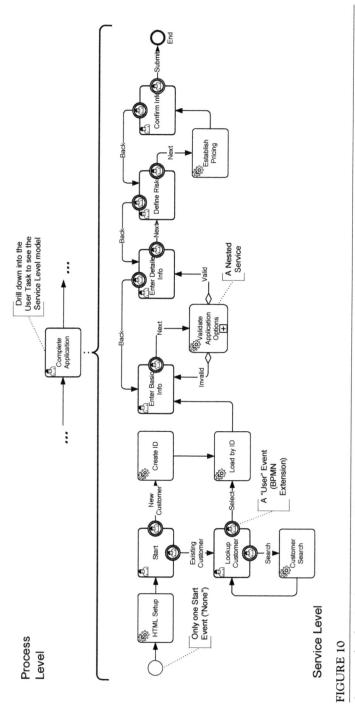

FIGURE 10

An example of an Implementation Level Diagram.

CASE MANAGEMENT MODELING

Case Management is a hot topic in BPM. This type of modeling involves highly unstructured diagrams and fits on the right side of Figure 9 (above). However, not all businesses have the same understanding of what Case Management is or how it works. Sometimes a case involves mainly straight-through prescriptive processes, with some trouble-shooting. However, most of the time a case involves mainly free-form descriptive processes.

BPMN 2.0 has incomplete support for Case Management (unstructured) Processes. BPMN mainly defines "Structured" Processes—those processes that have a well-defined sequence flow. But BPMN does provide for "Unstructured" Processes—The Ad Hoc Sub-Process. However, additional descriptive process types and behavior are required to fully handle all the unique aspects of unstructured processes.

When BPMN 1.0 was first developed, there was an understanding that descriptive processes were an important part of the process landscape. However, the initial focus of BPMN was to create a business process modeling language for business people that could also be executed by the available BPMSs. The Ad Hoc Process was included in BPMN as a placeholder that provides many of the capabilities required for modeling descriptive processes. It is expected as BPMN evolves, the Ad Hoc Process will also evolve to handle all Case Management Process requirements, which include:

- No predefined sequence flow exists.
- Activities can occur in any order or any frequency.
- But some sequence flow and data flow can be shown.

  Unstructured Processes have additional requirements, such as:

- Milestones—e.g., a Case state life cycle.
- New types of events.
- For example, the Case state (life cycle) changes, document updates, and so on.
- Preconditions, dependencies.
- Activities that can be started manually or automatically.
- Activities that are optional.
- Activities that can be repeated.

Figure 11 displays some potential notational updates to BPMN elements that would allow the standard to provide the modeling of more sophisticated unstructured processes.

The OMG has been developing a Case Management Modeling Notation (see the CMMN Chapter) standard. It is focused on a specification for tools that specialize in free-form Case Management behaviors. Because both CMMN and BPMN provide modeling, the authors believe that the best course is that the OMG consolidate the two specifications in the next update to BPMN (version 3.0).

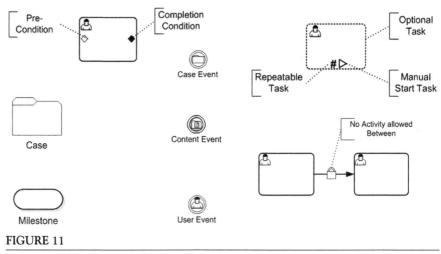

FIGURE 11

Potential notation updates for BPMN 3.0.

CONCLUSIONS

This chapter provides an overview and introduction to the Business Process Model and Notation (BPMN), what it is, and how it is used. We illustrated the primary goal of BPMN and how it provides a standard notation readily understandable by various stakeholders. Further, through its model types, BPMN provides the flexibility to integrate various views from business to technical perspectives. However, as we talk with many organizations about how BPMN can and cannot be used, we have discovered that BPMN has been, by choice, constrained to support only the concepts of modeling applicable to traditional business processes. Therefore, extended business process modeling aspects such as linking processes to business goals, the ability to do Value-Oriented Process Modeling, defining relationships between business competencies and processes, specifying measurements and reporting aspects, or defining rule sets (business, application, etc.), while all relevant, are not the focus of BPMN. It was, however, more vital to have a standard in the marketplace that enables all to have a common platform, than having the ability to do extended business process modeling. It is the start of a great journey, one that enables organizations and BPM teams around the world to analyze, design, build, and implement their processes. More will come!

End Notes

1. Object Management Group, "BMI Standard Specification 2.0.2," (2013), http://www.omg.org/spec/BPMN//2.0.2/PDF.
2. Simpson S., "An XML Representation for Crew Procedures, Final Report NASA Faculty Fellowship Program (Johnson Space Center)," (2004).

3. White S., *"Business Process Modeling Notation v1.0." for the Business Process Management Initiative (BPMI)* (May 2004).

4. Object Management Group, "BMI Standard Specification 1.1," (2008), http://www.omg. org/spec/BPMN/1.1/.

5. Object Management Group, "BMI Standard Specification 1.2," (2009), http://www.omg. org/spec/BPMN/1.2/.

6. Object Management Group, "BMI Standard Specification 2.0," (2011), http://www.omg. org/spec/BPMN/2.0/.

7. Object Management Group, "BMI Standard," http://www.omg.org/spec/BPMN/2.0.2/.

Variation in Business Processes

Mark von Rosing, Jonnro Erasmus

INTRODUCTION

During business processes analysis and development, we are often confronted with the criticism that we introduce additional administration and stifle the creativity of those who play a part in the process. As analysts and architects, we naturally oppose this notion in our quest for simplicity and optimal solutions. With good reason too; enterprises are complicated, and it is not uncommon to encounter hundreds of business processes, categorized into dozens of process groups and several process areas.[1] Such decomposition may lead to thousands of process activities and tasks, quickly becoming a managerial burden. This makes it easy for us to make the argument for standardization, because allowing every business unit or competency area to have its own variation of common processes will exponentially grow those numbers.

Yet we know that variation exists, and the goal of business process modeling is to capture things that reflect reality. For example, the way quality management is performed in manufacturing operations differs quite significantly from the way it is done in accounting. Although these business processes have similar goals and contribute towards the overall quality targets of the enterprise, the techniques applied and skills required are so different that we do not even consider these the same processes. Manufacturing applies techniques like statistical process control and is concerned with concepts such as sample sizes, whereas accounting relies more heavily on checks, balances, and audits. Clearly, these two very different practices should not be unified and standardized, as that will decrease value while cutting very little cost. In fact, the decision to allow variation in business processes is always a trade-off between value to the enterprise and the potential to decrease costs.

This chapter explores the phenomenon of variation in business processes. It explains what process variance is and how to identify it. Much of the discussion is related to the need for business process variation and how much is enough. Some examples are provided on how to model and manage process variance and how to relate it to the business model and strategy. Finally, the benefits, and typical pitfalls when modeling and managing process variance, are explained to give insight into how variance should be handled and what to avoid.

BUSINESS PROCESS VARIANCE: WHAT IS IT?

According to ISO9000:2005, a process is quite simply a set of activities that transforms inputs into outputs.[2] However, even though the activities performed may be the same, various other factors influence how those activities are actually performed. The most obvious factors that cause such variation are unequal quality of input or the ability of the role players in the process. Factors that are more difficult to detect and define are influences such as the motivation of practitioners or poorly defined interdependencies between business processes. In reality, slight differences in the way business processes are executed are always present, though it may be at a level of detail that does not lend itself to concern.

Variation in process performance prompted the pioneering research of Frederick Winslow Taylor on scientific management. He improved industrial efficiency by performing work studies and providing detailed instructions to standardize the work.[3] Yet, by studying what is normal, we will remain merely normal, and, in many cases, the outliers or nonstandard data points inspire the inquiry.[4] It is not in the interest of a modern business to remain normal, but rather to become an outlier and differentiate itself from its competitors. In fact, those differentiating capabilities offer superior value to customers that give businesses their competitive advantage.[5]

Variations of business processes occur in different ways. The example given above, showing how different quality is managed within the manufacturing and accounting domains of a business, represents the type of variation that can be found in any enterprise. Most processes are variations of the basic themes in business, such as governance, resource management, product realization and service delivery.

Systems Applications Products (SAP) define process variances the following way[6]: "A Business Process Variant is a fundamental flow variant of a Business Process which uses the same input and delivers the same measurable outcome." The flow of process steps is defined at Business Process Variant level. To keep level consistency, it is necessary that each business process has at least one Business Process Variant attached. The SAP modeling handbook proceeds by stating that a Business Process Variant should differ from another at least in one of the following ways:

- Flow of documents;
- Business objects needed;
- Life cycle schema of the business objects (status and status transitions);
- Application to Application/Business to Business (A2A/B2B) message choreography or choreography with direct interactions with other business processes.

The SAP handbook also offers the following characteristics of business process variants:

- A business process variant is not just an alternative user interface (UI);
- A process variant is not just another sequence of tasks that a user decides to perform on the UI;
- Two business process variants differ in the way the business process flows. The difference is so important that the variants are to be considered separately in a business process analysis.[7]

Thus, variance is a challenge within BPM, information management, and operations management, effecting entire end-to-end flows of processes, information, and services. To illustrate this, consider the following scenario: finance, people, and raw materials are all types of resources consumed and managed in the business, through the processes of financial management, human resource management, material management, and production/operation. It is very difficult to identify commonality, partly because the processes have different purposes, roles, and so on. At the other extreme, however, we find those business processes serve the same purpose and seem identical, except for the finest of details. These processes are typically found in the same business area and can therefore truly be considered variances of each other. To illustrate, consider the differences in how engineers perform failure analysis for two different pieces of equipment. Failure analysis is a well-documented industry standard, but for the equipment specialists the differences are huge.

These two extremes help us distinguish between what are typically considered separate processes and what we consider business process variances. Both of these, though, are controlled variations. The differences in how the different competencies and people perform quality management and failure analysis are understood and acknowledged. Variation can also be uncontrolled, in which the state of the business has an impact on the processes, for example, emergency state as opposed to normal operation.

COMPLICATIONS AND CHALLENGES

Although it is very important to be able to define process variances, many organizations suffer under the phenomenon of having too much variation. Typically, this happens when the various business units are allowed to specify how unique they are during process development and mapping. This leaves the organization with too much variation, resulting in increased cost and complexity of operation. Even more debilitating is when such processes are used in blueprints for information systems and are implemented into customer relationship management (CRM), enterprise resource planning (ERP), supply chain management (SCM), security risk management (SRM), and/or mobile solutions. Not only are high cost and complexity built into the business processes, but now also into the information systems of the organization.

Some vendors offer standard reports on variances of work. These reports enable organizations to identify where they have too many variances and perhaps even duplication or unnecessary processes. These variances in work processes occur when the total costs charged to a job or schedule do not equal the total costs relieved from a job or schedule. Oracle provides the following usage, efficiency, and standard cost adjustment variance calculations in transactions[8]:

- Material Usage Variance;
- Resource and Outside Processing Efficiency Variance;
- Move-Based Overhead Efficiency Variance;
- Resource-Based Overhead Efficiency Variance;
- Standard Cost Adjustment Variance.

Variance is a known pitfall and issue of business process modeling and management, so much so that the ERP vendors officially ask their customers to "Define

Reasons for Variances." For example, SAP asks customers to define the reasons for any variance that occurs and to document this variance.[9] The official action is to "define the possible causes for variation that could occur in your company." Such variances might be any of the following[10]:

- Scrap on a quantity basis;
- Excess consumption of activities;
- Longer execution time;
- Other resource, and so on.

Anyone following that recipe will end up with multiple variations, which has also been evident of the high level of ERP system customization, not realizing that there might be a variation because of duplication of business function, roles, services, and so forth. Another missing aspect is the lack of ability to identify aspects in which the organization is unique and not unique. Therefore, as with most aspects of business process modeling and management, no simple recipe exists to model and manage business process variance. It depends on what is expected from the modeling and management effort. Business processes are developed, modeled, and managed for different reasons, and different stakeholders have different expectations. For example, the manager of an engineering department may be entirely aware of the differences between failure analysis for mechanical and that for electronic components, but does not consider the differences of enough significance to warrant separate processes. For the engineers who design and develop the mechanical and electronic products, those differences are of the greatest significance and may even be the unique value that a specific group or team contributes to the organization. The difference between the two variations of the failure analysis process does not necessarily have to lie in the steps carried out, but can be in the type of information used or how the results are captured and presented. Both those cases are from the perspectives within the process, however. Tsikriktsis and Heineke found that customer satisfaction is significantly affected by inconsistency in process, especially when the average service quality is low.[11] Clearly then, allowing variation is a decision best taken with care.

This example is meant to serve the purpose of showing how different expectations will inform the decision to allow business process variation and how much to allow. Again, the basis for decision returns to the business model of the organization. It has been shown that most organizations, especially highly successful organizations, have more than one business strategy concurrently in effect, in an effort to maintain its competitive advantage.[12] The model that is concerned with delivering unique value to customers will most likely embrace business process variance in the parts of the organization that creates that value. The business model that drives cost cutting will drive for standardization and simplification when possible.

Embracing variation does not acquit us from the burden to manage the business processes. In fact, allowing more than one version of a business process to exist inherently increases the complexity in the business. More problematic though, it becomes important to identify and clearly define the similarities and principles that must be maintained in all versions of a process. It is also easy to extend the thinking toward a scenario in which the differences between two variations of a business process become so pronounced that it is difficult to explain why they are considered variations of the same process. Clearly then, the decision to allow variations of a business process to exist should be taken very carefully and should support business goals and objectives.

To make informed decisions regarding business process variation, the problem has to be understood. To summarize, four main challenges deal with business process variation:

- Deciding when and how much variation to allow;
- Defining and justifying business process variances;
- Capturing business process variation without introducing unnecessary complexity and ambiguity; and
- Managing business process variances.

SOLUTION DESCRIPTION

Business analysts and architects will naturally oppose allowing variation in business processes. It will seem like it makes the solution more complicated or even suboptimal. Instead, business process variance should be seen as an opportunity for the processes to more accurately reflect reality. More importantly, process variance is a way to capture techniques, knowledge, or other intricacies that are unique to a certain business competency or practitioner. Those details can be compared to the standardized process to identify that which creates the unique value to the business. Thus, business process variance is not only a viable option for an organization to identify its own unique value enablers, but also to exploit those enablers and hopefully build on them.

When Should Variation Be Allowed and How Much Is Enough?

We have established that variation in business processes introduces performance, modeling, and management challenges. Thus, we require guidance on when business process variance is desirable and how much should be allowed. What helps here is to find out when the organization should allow for uniqueness and thereby high variability, or when the level of standardization should be high and variation minimal. The challenge is that this information will not be found in the process itself, but rather in the business model showing the relevant business competencies being identified and calling upon their respective processes.[13] By exercising its business competencies, the business delivers value internally and externally, for example, value is delivered through business tasks, business functions, and services within a competency to those that benefit from the value created. Competencies may be essential to compete, in which case they are described as *core-competitive*; or they may differentiate the business from its customers, in which case they are core-differentiating. The majority of competencies are simply necessary for the functioning of the business, and these are commonly referred to as *non-core* competencies. The ability to categorize competencies as either *core-differentiated*, *core-competitive*, or *non-core* is missing within contemporary process modeling and process architecture practice. The inability to identify competencies is the very reason why process experts and process architects have no insight as to which processes are a part of an organization's competitive aspects and which are not. This is also why they are not able to take into consideration the process variances in terms of where they should be, where they create value and where they should not be.

The link between the organization's competencies and process execution provides the means of identifying ways to appropriately standardize variances and thereby reduce cost, improve the effectiveness and efficiency of operations, or conversely to support value creation and thereby revenue growth. Without this context, there is no means to judge the "goodness" of a particular process or process variance design. For example, if it is not possible to detect that a process contributes value, it is best not to have any variances as it should be done is the cheapest way possible. Figure 1 shows a summary of the concepts for categorizing the three domains of business models, the competencies that enable the business models, and the type of practice standards that correspond to the different competencies.[14]

For noncore competencies it makes sense to adopt standard best practice, in an effort to optimize operations and minimize cost. Similarly, industry best practice may be adopted for core-competitive competencies, because the business only aims to compete effectively with its competitors and maximize its performance. However, to drive growth in revenue and value, new products and services have to be developed to give the business a competitive advantage. By its nature, an advantage requires something that is not offered elsewhere, thus the business strives toward developing and nurturing core-differentiating competencies. However, applying such differentiating competencies in a standardized business process will at best result in high performance, but not in differentiating value. As shown in Figure 1, true differentiating competencies

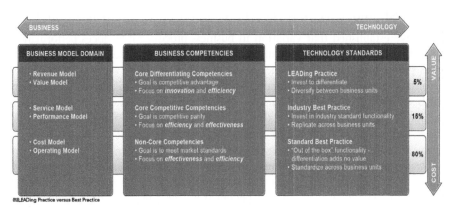

FIGURE 1

When to apply LEADing industry and best practice.[15]

typically compose a very small portion of the business, though it may be a much larger percentage in truly innovative enterprises. Therefore, in the relatively limited cases in which a business aims to offer unique or even market-leading products and services, it is crucial for the business to appreciate and embrace variation in the business processes that produce the characteristics that make the offering superior.

The challenge we see in most organizations is actually relating the business competencies to the processes. Table 1 illustrates how to link traditional process aspects with business competencies and Table 2 provides a step-by-step guide how to do it.

Table 1 *The Possible Linkage between Process and Competencies*

		What Specification:					Who/Whose Specification:		
	Process #	Business Process Area	Process Groups	Business Process	Process Steps	Process Activities	Stakeholder Involved	Process Owner	Roles/ Involved
Business competency 1	#								
Business competency 2	#								
Business competency N	#								

Table 2 *A Table Showing that Process Objects Relate to Business Competency and the Tasks Associated with It*

Business Competency: An Integrated and Holistic Set of Interconnected Knowledge, Skills, and Abilities, Related to a Specific Set of Resources (Including Persons and Organizations) that, Combined, Enable the Enterprise to Act in a Particular Situation

Rules	(D) Process relates to Business Competency.
Tasks	• Identify in the business model or an operating model which business competencies are core-differentiated. • Identify in the business model or an operating model which business competencies are core-competitive. • Identify in the business model or an operating model which business competencies are non-core. • Associate and tie the business competencies to the business processes. • Associate and tie the business competencies to the process steps of the business process. • Associate and tie the business competencies to the process activities of the business process. • Associate and tie the business competencies to the stakeholders involved in the business process. • Associate and tie the business competencies to the process owner of the business process. • Associate and tie the business competencies to the managers involved in the business process. • Associate and tie the business competencies to the roles/resources involved in the business process.

Table 1 shows all the aspects that can be linked to a competency, including stakeholders, managers, process owners, and roles that are in a business competency area. The process–business competency matrix captures all aspects that can be linked between a business competency and business processes. See Table 2 for the semantic rules for this mapping and the tasks to establish the relationship.

It is important to note that the business competency type, that is, core-differentiated, core-competitive or non-core, needs to be derived directly from a business model, operating model, or a business competency matrix.[16] Figure 2 shows an example of an Oil and Gas business model showing the business competencies and the typical aspects of a business model, including the following[17]:

- The Business Competency Areas;
- The Business Competency Groups;
- The various Business Competencies.

This Oil and Gas Petroleum Engineering business model will be used to show the different options for modeling business process variance. The Technical Quality Control business competency will be used, because it was identified to be core-competitive with high-value potential, but poor performance. In addition to that, it needs to be standardized and needs evaluation and audit aspects. It is exactly such a case in which process variances and the people involved need to be identified to reduce unnecessary complexity and ensure high performance and value realization.

Defining and Justifying Business Process Variance

Once it has been determined when and how much variance will be allowed, these decisions should be documented to ensure that the rationale is captured. Furthermore, the variances that will be allowed should be defined to ensure that the business process modeling stays in line with the intention. Table 3 shows a matrix that may be used to document the decisions and define the variances to be developed.

As previously explained, process variances are justified by linking the process to a core business competency. Table 3 also allows business competency variances to be defined and justified and the number of variances that will be created. To ensure consistency in the way variances are identified, justified, and defined among different team members, Table 4 provides some rules and tasks to be followed by the business analysts, architects, and subject matter experts. These rules are similar to the reasons for process variance listed in Section 3 of this chapter.

Once a process or competency variant has been justified, the steps listed in Table 4 may be followed to complete Table 3. This will help that the necessary information for each variant is properly captured, resulting in consistency and repeatability in the business process modeling. Such a completed table will be an invaluable input into the modeling of business process variance.

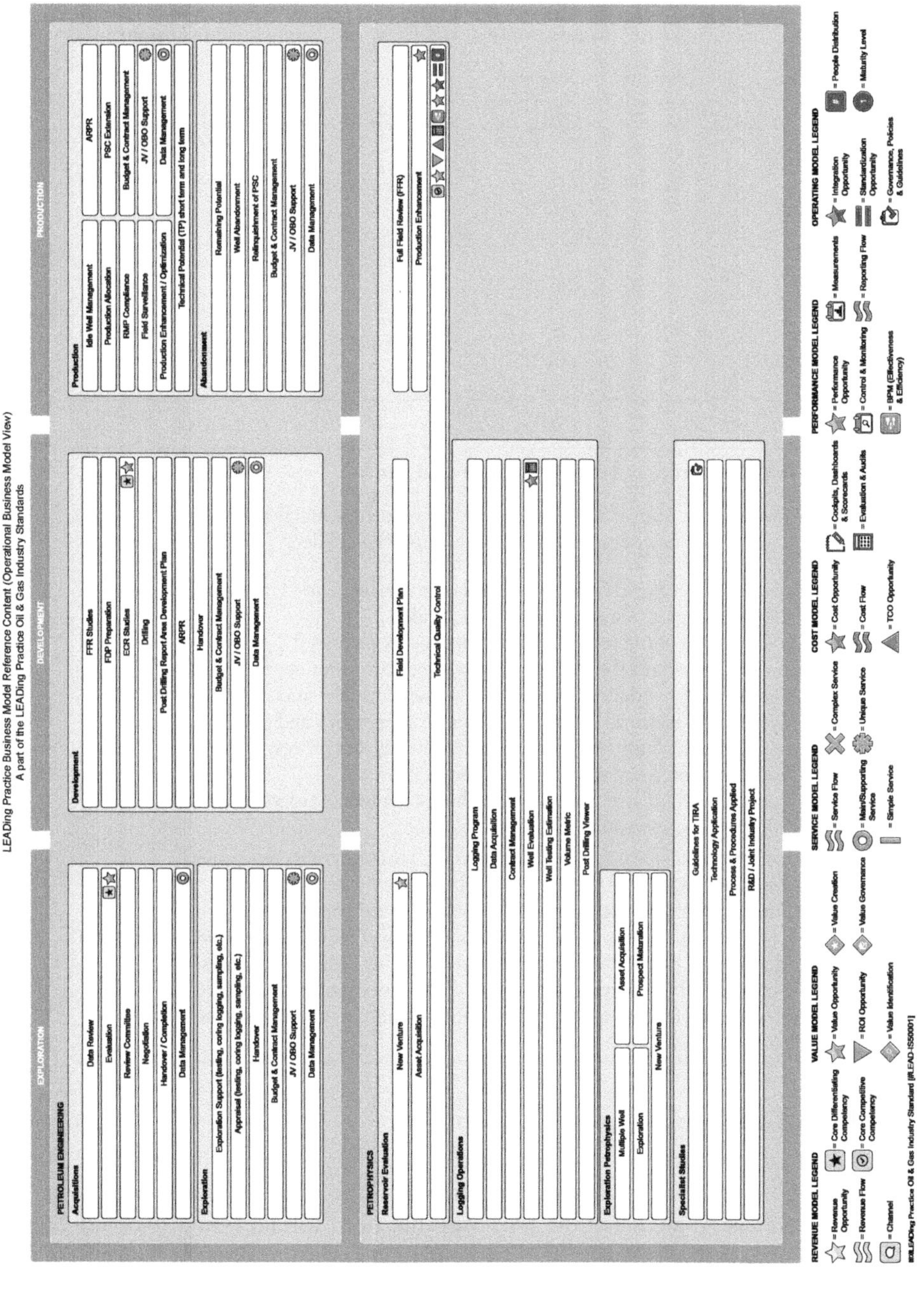

FIGURE 2

Example of Oil and Gas Petroleum Engineering business model.

Table 3 Business Process Variance Matrix

Process Variance Matrix	Variance #	Where Specification: (Business Model Relevant)			What Specification: (Process Model Relevant)		
		Business Competency Area	Business Competency Group	Business Competency	Business Process	Process Steps	Process Activities
Variance 1 List reason for variance	#						
Variance 2 List reason for variance	#						
Variance N List reason for variance	#						

Table 4 Example of Process Variance Rules and Tasks

	Process Variances: A Matrix Used by an Enterprise to Indicate Where They Have Variances and Indicate Why They Have Them
Rules	Process variance should be allowed based on the rules defined in the organization. The following are some examples of such rules: • The function of the resource varies (competency relevant). • Resource-based overhead efficiency variance (competency and process relevant). • Material-usage variance (competency and process relevant). • Move-based overhead efficiency variance (competency and process relevant). • Standard cost adjustment variance (competency and process relevant). • Processing-efficiency variance (process relevant). • Process policy, rule, and process compliance variance (process relevant). • Process-execution variance (process relevant).
Tasks	1. Identify and categorize the variance to the business competency areas. 2. Associate and tie the variance to the business competency groups. 3. Pinpoint the variances relevant for the business competencies. 4. Relate variances relevant for the business competencies to the business processes. 5. Identify and categorize the variance-only specific business processes. 6. Decompose business process variance to process steps and process activities. 7. Identify and categorize the variance only specific to process steps and process activities.

Modeling of Business Process Variance

Once the business process has been linked to the business competencies, classified as core-differentiated, core-competitive, or non-core, business process development relies on modeling the processes that need variances and standardize those that need more repetition. This modeling takes on different forms to achieve different critical success factors and business objectives. This is important, because the most appropriate way business process variances are captured and modelled also depends on the purpose. The following three options, or combinations thereof, can be considered:

1. Distinctive business process maps, diagrams, or models;
2. Separate processes with a master-and-variant type relationship; or
3. Single process with variances at the lower levels, such as activity or task variances.

These three options differ mostly at the level of detail at which the variation is captured. Variation in business processes can also entirely be removed from the process itself by capturing the differences in documents that accompany and support the process. Admittedly, this will lead to the desirable scenario in which only one business process model or document exists for each process, but simply delegates the burden to the domain of documentation management. This approach will also inevitably lead to unnecessarily complicated documents; therefore, this approach is not recommended here. These three listed options are briefly discussed to illustrate the differences.

Distinctive Processes

Creating new, distinctive business processes can be considered the most extreme measure for dealing with business process variations. Essentially, it eliminates the need for any special consideration of process variance, by rather increasing the number of business processes. It should also be noted that such distinct variances can be created at any level of decomposition. Business competencies or even competency groups may be variations of each other. In fact, it is common for organizations to establish new competencies as variations of current competencies, to develop new, specialized, or innovative products or services. It is very common for organizations to create new competency and process variants, then later consolidate to cut costs and standardize.

Figure 3 shows the Technical Quality Control business process of the Oil and Gas Petroleum Engineering business model. Four separate and specialized process steps are shown, with their own activities for failure analysis for different types of mechanical equipment.

These process steps may initially have come from a single failure analysis process, but now represent four distinct activity flows, with no dependencies or relationships actively maintained. The obvious result of such a separation is that eventually these processes may have nothing in common. Conversely, though, the possible benefit is that the unique details, such as process activities, skills, knowledge, and information can easily be captured.

Master-and-Variant Processes

If there is a desire to maintain commonality between different process variants, or at least traceability back to the master process, it is advisable not to create distinct process maps, diagrams, or models. Maintaining such relationships in documents is a laborious task and business process modeling methodologies and tools do not typically support it. Instead, the master process and its variants should be seen as

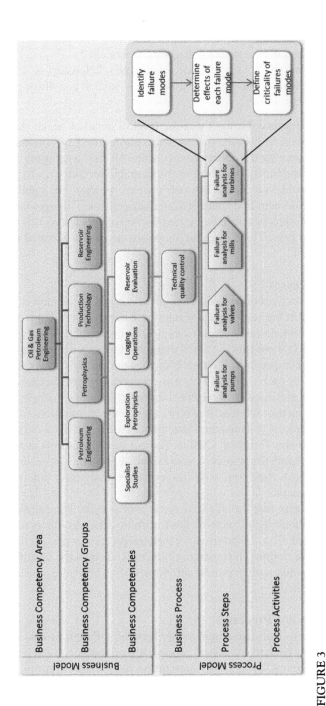

FIGURE 3

Breakdown of processes by failure analysis.

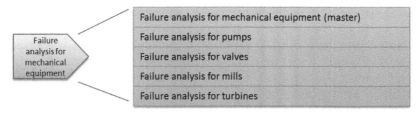

FIGURE 4

Master process with variants.

a single unit, with multiple stakeholders. In document format, the master and its variants will typically occupy a single document, with sections for the variants. Figure 4 shows a very simple illustration of how this configuration can be modeled for the same failure analysis process used previously.

When accessing the details of the failure analysis process, several options are presented. The user then has the option to access the details of the master process or any of its variants. Admittedly, this approach still does not force commonality between the process variances, but at least the traceability to the master process is very clearly maintained. Representing this type of business process with variants in a document format will ultimately result in a substantial document with sections for each of the variances.

Lower Level Variances

The final approach presented aims to maintain commonality of at least the process activities, or any lower level details of the process. Thus, traceability and alignment between the master and variance processes are maintained by essentially forcing the use of common process activities or tasks. This approach then only allows for differences in the inputs, outputs, controls, and mechanisms involved in the process. Figure 5 shows a very simple example of the lower level details of the same failure analysis process.

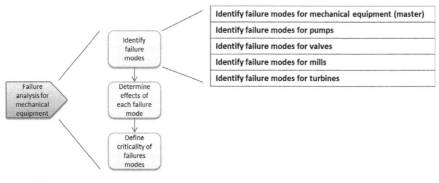

FIGURE 5

Common process with variation on activity level.

Only one process is shown with a definitive set of activities. When attempting to access the details of the first activity, the user is presented with a menu of options, corresponding to the application of the failure analysis process to different types of equipment. When selecting one of the options, the user may be presented with tasks that are more detailed or perhaps with the inputs, outputs, controls, and mechanisms for that specific application of the activity. This approach suffers when presenting business processes in document format. Each process step or activity is accompanied by a matrix to show the different inputs, outputs, mechanisms, and controls of the variants.

Managing Business Process Variances

The three approaches to capturing and modeling business process variance unsurprisingly result in varying degrees of managerial burden. Simply put, the amount of administrative control necessary is proportional to the amount of content created and the need for accurate traceability. The first approach, in which distinctive processes are created, results in the most architectural content, but does not really lend itself to maintaining traceability between the processes. A generic master process may obviously be documented, but its relationship to the variant processes can at best be a text-based reference. The other two approaches are better suited to maintaining traceability to the master process. The second approach, in which variants of the master process are created, will result in significantly more business processes, but at least commonality is encouraged by keeping the processes together in the model. The third approach will result in the fewest business processes and least content to manage, but is very difficult to capture in document format.

When considering management of the complete process life cycle, the need for different approaches for different processes is further enforced. Figure 6 shows how the various business models drive the value life cycle, which in turn drives the process life cycle.

The value and revenue models target innovation and align to the analysis and design phases of the process lifecycle. Thus, in the context of business process variance, business value, and revenue creation will drive the identification of unique variations in process and how those variations deliver value to the business. Innovation will eventually make way for a focus on efficiency and effectiveness, once a product or service reaches its midlife. Thus, the performance and service models will drive business process improvement and standardization. Eventually then, cost and operating models will be introduced to drive optimization and simplification. Thus, the management of business process variance is not only dependent on the business model and strategies, but also on the life cycle of the specific process and its resulting product or service. Early in the life cycle, when innovation is encouraged and freedom is sought, variation should be allowed. When the innovation delivers value, the core-differentiating competencies should be captured and treated as recognized business process variances. This approach ensures that the

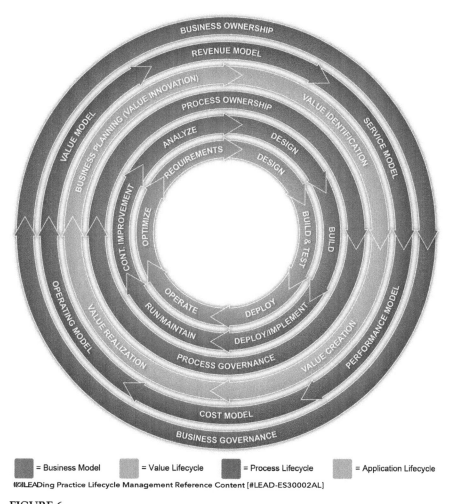

FIGURE 6

Business models and life cycle alignment.[18]

justification for the variance is captured to enable informed management thereof later in the process life cycle.

Regardless of the life-cycle phase of a process, it should be measured and managed. The process performance indicators will typically be associated to individual variants, to allow for comparison of the process variants. The more business process variance exists, the more management effort is necessary, because effectively the amount of architectural content is increased. As with all business processes the documentation, configuration, and interfaces of all variants must be managed. This task is significantly more difficult though; not only must alignment be maintained between the actual processes, the documentation that describes it and what is expected of the process, but also traceability and commonality to the master process, if one exists. This requires establishment and maintenance of an additional relationship within the process content and appreciable attention from business process management.

COST CALCULATION OF PROCESS VARIANCES

The ability to calculate the cost of process variances is an important aspect for BPM, Information Management, and Operations Management. The typical information solution vendors like SAP[19] or Oracle have standards to calculate cost of process variances. Oracle lists the following ways to calculate cost of process variances[20]:

1. *Material Usage Variance*: The difference between the actual material issued and the standard material required to build a given assembly, calculated as follows:

   Standard material cost × (*quantified issued* − *quantified required*)
   Such a variance occurs when an organization over- or underissues components or uses an alternate bill.

2. *Resource and Outside Processing Efficiency Variance*: The difference between the resources and outside processing charges incurred and the standard resource and outside processing charges required to build a given assembly, calculated as follows:

   (*applied resources units* × *standard or actual rate*) − (*standard resource units at standard resource rate*)
   This variance occurs when you use an alternate routing, add new operations to a standard routing during production, assign cost resources to No-direct charge operations skipped by shop floor moves, overcharge or undercharge a resource, or charge a resource at actual.

3. *Move-Based Overhead Efficiency Variance*: Move-based overhead efficiency variance is the difference between overhead charges incurred for move-based overheads (overhead basis of Item or Lot) and standard move-based overheads required to build a given assembly, calculated as follows:

   applied move-based overheads − *standard move-based overheads*
   This variance occurs when you use an alternate routing, add operations to a standard routing during production, or do not complete all the move transactions associated with the assembly quantity being built.

4. *Resource-Based Overhead Efficiency Variance*: Resource-based overhead efficiency variance is the difference between overhead charges incurred for resource based overheads (overhead basis of Resource units or Resource value) and standard resource-based overheads required to build a given assembly, calculated as follows:

   applied resource-based overheads − *standard resource-based overheads*
   This variance occurs when you use an alternate routing, add new operations to a standard routing during production, assign cost resources to No-direct charge

operations skipped by shop floor moves, overcharge or undercharge a resource, or charge a resource at actual.

5. *Standard Cost Adjustment Variance*: Standard cost adjustment variance is the difference between costs at the previous standards and costs at the new standards created by cost update transactions.

cost of previous standards – cost of new standards

The following are some of the challenges doing cost calculations of process variances:

- The cost of the process variances can only be calculated if all the numbers exist before and after. Many organizations do not measure what they had, or they did not measure it the same way.
- The cost of calculating the cost of variances is very time and resource consuming. In other words, it is very costly to identify high-cost and inefficient process variances.
- To determine variances between production and planning involves not only the process but also the information flow. Although such an analysis has huge potential, it can be very time-consuming.
- The ability to show the causes of the variances and assign the variances to different variance categories depending on the cause.
- All of the above ways of evaluating cost of process variances do not really identify the specific process that is the root cause for the high cost and inefficient process variances. They only identify the high cost of doing it in a different way.

LESSONS LEARNED

For business process variance to deliver value to the enterprise, it is crucial to properly plan how it will be modeled and managed. As explained, variance introduces significant additional content and complexity to the business process landscape, resulting in increased management burden. Furthermore, it is important to consider whether the business process management function is up to the task of handling the increased burden. Ultimately, it is always a trade-off between more accurate representation of the core-differentiating competencies and increased complexity in the business processes.

The best approach is to introduce as little variation as possible and to make sure it is in the core business. If it is found that only the skills, knowledge, information, or tools differ between process variants, it should be entirely adequate to only have variances at process activity level. This will ensure that the desired commonality between the process variants is maintained and the amount of new content is minimized. Alternatively, if the business is targeting innovation and wants to allow its practitioners more freedom, it is probably more appropriate to create completely distinct and separate processes. Either way, the business processes should be formalized and documented, even if only at a low level of detail, to gain the wide-ranging benefits thereof.

CONCLUSION AND SUMMARY

Business process variance should be seen as a viable way of allowing small differences in the way the core business functions are performed. It is advisable to only introduce variation in those business processes that represent the core-differentiating competencies of the organization. This will allow an enterprise to develop its own practice and deliver unique value to clients and other stakeholders. For non-core and core-competitive competencies, best practice and industry best practice should suffice.

Business process variance can be modeled three different ways, depending on what is expected thereof. If the aim is only to capture slight differences in the inputs, outputs, controls, and mechanisms of processes, it will be adequate to only create variances at the process activity or task levels. However, if the actual steps of the variant processes are different, true process variances can be used by presenting all the variances together in a single model or document or separate distinct processes may even be developed.

The modeling approach taken has a major impact on the management of the business processes and variances. When certain commonality between the master process and its variants is important, additional business process management techniques are necessary to maintain this traceability. This will require that a great deal of attention is given to establishing and maintaining the traceability links between the variants. Separate and distinct processes introduce more process content, but standard business process management is applied because traceability to the master process is unnecessary.

When introducing process variance, caution should be taken and the amount of variation should be minimized. If the development and modeling is not sufficiently controlled, the amount of additional and unnecessary content will very quickly become unmanageable. However, if it is done well, it is an excellent way for organizations to acknowledge and embrace their unique value enablers, without losing out on the many benefits of business process modeling and management.

End Notes

1. Dijkman R., La Rosa M., and Reijers H. A., "Managing large collections of business process models – current techniques and challenges," *Computers in Industry* 63, no. 2 (2012): 91–97, doi:10.1016/j.compind.2011.12.003.
2. *Quality Management Systems – Fundamentals and Vocabulary*, International Standard (Switzerland: The International Organization for Standardization, 2005).
3. Stephanie C. Payne, Satoris S. Youngcourt, and Watrous K. M., "Portrayals of F. W. Taylor across textbooks," *Journal of Management History* 12, no. 4 (2006): 385–407, doi:10.1108/17511340610692752.
4. Jason W. Osborne and Overbay A., "The power of outliers (and why researchers should ALWAYS check for them)," *Practical Assessment, Research & Evaluation* 9, no. 6 (March 2, 2004), http://pareonline.net/getvn.asp?v=9&n=6+.
5. Woodruff R. B., "Customer value: the next source for competitive advantage," *Journal of the Academy of Marketing Science* 25, no. 2 (March 1997): 139–153, doi:10.1007/BF02894350.

6. Rosenberg A., Business Processes Variants – SAP Modeling Handbook – Modeling Standards – SCN Wiki (January 4, 2014), http://wiki.scn.sap.com/wiki/display/ModHandbook/Business+Processes+Variants.

7. Rosenberg B., Processes Variants – SAP Modeling Handbook – Modeling Standards – SCN Wiki.

8. Work in Process Standard Cost Variances (Oracle Cost Management), accessed August 13, 2014, http://docs.oracle.com/cd/A60725_05/html/comnls/us/cst/stdvar01.htm.

9. Define Reasons for Variances – Process Order – SAP Library, accessed August 13, 2014, http://help.sap.com/saphelp_46c/helpdata/en/a9/e264b20437d1118b3f0060b03ca329/frameset.htm.

10. Ibid.

11. Tsikriktsis N. and Heineke J., "The impact of process variation on customer dissatisfaction: evidence from the U.S. Domestic Airline Industry," *Decision Sciences* 35, no. 1 (February 2004): 129–141, doi:10.1111/j.1540-5414.2004.02483.x.

12. David J. Teece, "Business models, business strategy and innovation," *Long Range Planning* 43, no. 2–3 (April 2010): 172–194, doi:10.1016/j.lrp.2009.07.003.

13. LEADing Practice Competency Modeling Reference Content (LEAD-ES20013BC).

14. Ibid.

15. Ibid.

16. Ibid.

17. LEADing Practice Business Model Reference Content (LEAD-ES20004BC).

18. LEADing Practice Lifecycle Management Reference Content, Standard (LEADing Practice, n.d.), accessed August 7, 2014.

19. http://help.sap.com/saphelp_45b/helpdata/en/90/ba667e446711d189420000e829fbbd/content.htm.

20. Work in Process Standard Cost Variances (Oracle Cost Management).

Focusing Business Processes on Superior Value Creation: Value-oriented Process Modeling

Mark von Rosing, Mathias Kirchmer

INTRODUCTION

In this chapter, we will focus on Value-oriented Process Modeling, both in terms of what it is, how it is applied, as well as when it can be applied. This includes Value-oriented Process analysis, design, implementation, and governance considerations; enabling organizations with the ability to interlink value engineering,[1] modeling, and architecture concepts with process aspects.

VALUE IS A DIFFERENT KIND OF CONCEPT FOR PROCESS TEAMS

Value planning, value identification, value creation, and value realization are not necessarily methods and approaches that are used by process teams today. However, the Global University Alliance[2] research around value modeling concepts has revealed that most organizations differentiate about 5% of their business competencies and have about 15% of their business competencies in the areas of core-competitive aspects. Competing head to head with the rest of the industry, the rest of the organization's business competencies are non-core and, thereby, commodity. This is very relevant for process modeling, as about 80% of the processes are commodity processes that do not add to the differentiation or competitiveness of the organization. A value-oriented process design and implementation considers this by focusing innovation and optimization initiatives, as well as company-specific software development, on the 20% high-impact processes, whereas commodity processes are designed based on industry reference models and implemented as far as possible through standard software. Design and implementation of processes target systematically on creating business value.

The chapter describes an approach to such a value-oriented segmentation, design, and implementation of businesses processes—transferring strategy into execution, at pace with certainty. The approach is explained using case examples.

Targeting Value

Organizations have to master the permanent change in our business environment if they want to survive in the intermediate and long term. Dealing successfully with a volatile business environment, in general, means continuously "leveraging people to build a customer-centric performance-based culture."[3] Therefore, it is not only important to have a good strategy, hence to know *what* to do, but, in many organizations, the key challenge is about *how* to execute the strategy. To overcome this challenge, more and more organizations establish a value-oriented Business Process Management (BPM)[4] concept with a consequent process orientation across the company. This management discipline is about moving strategy into execution quickly with low risk. It enforces in particular a customer and performance focus, because business processes deliver, by definition, a result of value for a client outside the process. A key component of such a BPM discipline is a structured value-oriented design of processes realizing the business strategy of an organization.[5,6]

This chapter presents an approach for business process design and implementation that meets those requirements of targeting value. It is both focused on executing the strategy of an organization and on being as resource efficient as possible. The result is a practical and effective approach to process design and implementation. The typical results of this approach embedded into BPM are transparency throughout an organization's processes, which enables achievement of quality and efficiency, agility and compliance, external integration and internal alignment, as well as innovation and conservation.

Research has shown that organizations compete with only about 5% of their processes, and another 15% are important processes supporting their competitive advantage. This means that 80% of the business processes are commodity processes, which can be carried out according to industry standards or common industry practices. An industry average performance is sufficient. Sophisticated improvement approaches or even innovation initiatives targeting higher performance are not delivering real additional business value. Hence, process innovation and optimization initiatives have to focus on the 20% high-impact processes, whereas other business processes can be designed and implemented using existing industry common practices. Results are highly organization-specific business processes in which competitive advantages and processes are delivered following industry common practices when these are sufficient.

Targeting value systematically requires the appropriate segmentation of processes as basis for a differentiated design and implementation approach.[7] Process models developed during the process design need to reflect the requirements of those different process segments and the importance of the resulting business processes for the strategy of an organization. Different levels of sophistication regarding the improvement approaches are necessary.

The following process implementation, including the appropriate software support, is executed according to the process design based on the identified process segments. The value-oriented design leads often to different approaches to procure required enabling software. Highly organization-specific processes often require an individual development of software. Processes designed based on industry standards[8] lead in most cases to the use of standard software packages.

A value-oriented approach to design and implementation of processes enables organizations to use resources when they provide best value during design and implementation initiatives. People who are highly qualified in sophisticated process design and implementation methods, for example, focus on high-value areas. They can systematically target value as well as reduce the risk of project failure. They focus on moving the organization to the next level of performance, including the right degree of digitalization. This requires, in general, an "enlightened" Chief Information Officer (CIO),[9,10] who moves away from being a technical expert to becoming a driver of innovation and performance. The approach allows such a CIO to transition into a Chief Process Officer.[11]

The approach has been developed based on practical experience in large and mid-size organizations, mainly in the USA, South America, Japan, India, and Europe. It has been combined with academic research regarding value-oriented design and implementation methodologies, especially the LEADing practice value reference content.[12]

Segmentation of Business Processes

A business strategy needs to be operationalized to use it to drive process design and implementation. This is done by deriving strategic value drivers of an organization from its strategy. Those value drivers describe necessary achievements to make the strategy happen. The degree of realization of a value orientation is measured through key performance indicators (KPIs). A business process assessment based on the impact of a business process on strategic value drivers is the basis for the segmentation of processes into high-impact and commodity processes.[13,14] This process assessment is the key tool to align business strategy with process design and implementation. It enables the desired value-oriented approach and makes it part of a BPM discipline to transfer strategy into execution.

The value drivers are derived from the business strategy of the organization using value-driver-tree models (value-driver trees). This is a way of transferring the strategic intension of an organization into operational value-oriented business targets. An example for such a value-driver tree is shown in Figure 1. The value drivers themselves can again be weighted to focus the segmentation on the most important value drivers.

In practice, a three-step approach to developing a value-driver tree has proven successful. The strategy delivers the business priorities showing the overall direction toward which a company has to move. These priorities are decomposed into strategic objectives describing the key components of a business priority. Then one or several value drivers are identified for each objective, hence the operational achievements that make this objective happen.

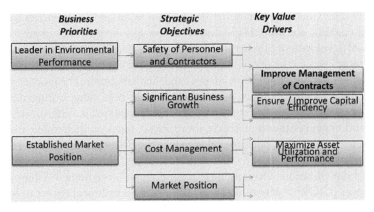

FIGURE 1

Value-driver tree (excerpt).

For a full-value-driver tree and reference content that can be used by organizations, please see the Value Tree.[15]

The business processes of an organization are then evaluated based on their total impact on the specific value drivers. The results are two segments of business processes: high-impact and commodity processes. "High-impact" processes are the ones that are key to make the business strategy of the organization happen: the "competitive" processes and supporting core processes. They are the most important link of business strategy to execution. This approach is visualized in Figure 2.

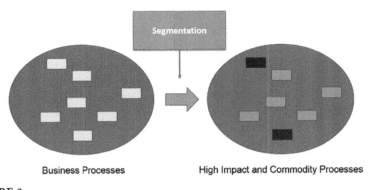

FIGURE 2

High impact and commodity processes.

The value drivers can be weighted by their importance. Minor changes and adjustments in strategy can then be reflected through adjustments of those weights. Larger strategy changes result in different or additional value drivers. This update of value drivers and their weights enables an agile adjustment of process priorities to updated strategies reflecting changing business environments.

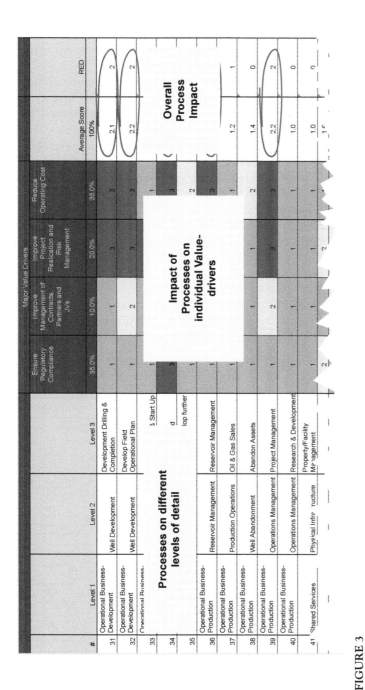

FIGURE 3

Process assessment matrix (excerpt).

For each process, it has to be defined if it has no (0), low (1), medium (2), or high (3) impact on each of the value drivers. Then the overall impact is calculated in a process assessment matrix by multiplying impact with the weight of the appropriate value driver and calculating the total of all impacts of a process. An example of a process assessment matrix is shown in Figure 3.

The high-impact processes have then to be evaluated based on general industry practices, for example, through benchmarks or purely qualitative evaluations. In those ways, you identify the high-impact "high-opportunity" business processes. Improvements have the biggest value potential, because the processes have a high impact on the strategy, but they currently perform only in, or even below, the industry average of these processes.

Practice experience with different companies has shown that the processes should be identified on a level of detail so that 150–200 process definitions describe the entire organization. This is often referred to as "level 3" (L3). This level is detailed enough to obtain differentiated results, but high level enough to avoid to high work efforts. Using the results of the process assessment matrix, the 20% of the processes that are classified as high impact can be identified. The others are considered the commodity processes.

In practice, a "gray" area of processes could be in either group. Hence, approximately 20% of the processes are in the high-impact segment. This issue has to be resolved in a case-by-case basis reflecting the specific situation of an organization, its business strategy, and the overall business environment in which it works (see Figure 4).

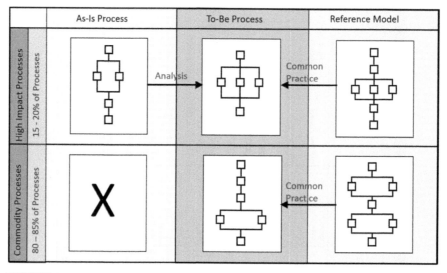

FIGURE 4

Conceptual view of the value-oriented process approach.

Value-oriented Design

The high-impact processes (or at least high-impact, high-opportunity processes, if further prioritization is necessary, say, due to budgets) are subject to detailed process innovation and optimization activities focusing on the previously identified value drivers. The degree of achievement is measured through KPIs that relate to the identified value drivers. The check of the quality of a process design through KPIs can be used in agile or top-down waterfall design approaches. Depending on the specific process and the culture of the organization, both approaches or a combination of both can be relevant.[16] The design approach uses formal modeling methods like Event-driven Process Chains (EPC), the Business Process Modeling Notation (BPMN) or VDML—Value Delivery Modeling Language to model the value and the activities and thereby facilitate the integration of process design and implementation.

Product and market-oriented design approaches have been proven effective, because they link processes with their value drivers to the offerings a client is looking for. The product and market-oriented design supports an integrated product (offering) and process innovation. Such an approach is especially important for the processes that are highly relevant for the strategic positioning of an organization, hence the top 5%. To identify these business processes, another segmentation of the high-impact processes is required distinguishing between strategic and nonstrategic high-impact processes. The focus is on high-impact strategic processes. These are perfect targets for innovation initiatives. As an example, a compressor company may deliver "compressed air as a service" instead of just selling compressors. Offering as well as related sales, delivery, and maintenance processes change simultaneously, reflected in the integrated value-oriented design.

Also new technologies, especially information technologies (IT) relevant for specific processes, have to be evaluated in a business-driven way. You can, for example, model different process scenarios representing various degrees of automation. The best scenario is chosen based on the expected value of the relevant KPIs.

For all high-impact processes, techniques like process model-based simulations and animations are helpful to come up with best-suited design solutions based on KPIs. Often even the transparency created through those information models is sufficient by itself to discover relevant improvement or even innovation opportunities.

Traditional improvement methods like Lean or Six Sigma[17] can be applied in selected cases. However, these approaches do not generally support focused innovation or a full-blown optimization of processes, including automation opportunities. Hence, they are more targeted to bringing less-strategic, people-intensive processes to better efficiency, in most cases resulting in cost or time reductions.

The starting points for the design of the 80% commodity processes are industry or functional reference models. These models are available, for example, through industry organizations or consulting and software companies. In many cases, they are already developed using standard modeling methods. The industry common practices reflected in those models are only adjusted to the specific organization when this is absolutely necessary, for example due to legal requirements in country subsidiaries or specific logistics requirements through the product.

The process design work focuses on "making the industry standard happen." If process areas are identified when the industry standard cannot be applied, for example, due to product specifics, only those areas will be designed in a company-specific way, keeping the adjustments as close to the industry standard as possible. Process solutions can here often be found through a simple application of the mentioned traditional improvement methods like Lean and Six Sigma, because a pure efficiency focus is in most cases justified here. However, it is important to keep in mind that it is, in general, not worth improving above industry average performance.

This value-oriented process design approach is visualized in Figure 5. It shows that, also for the design of high-impact processes, reference models can be used as an input. Nevertheless, this is only one component of getting all information together to come up with real innovative and optimized solutions regarding the KPIs and the value drivers to which they relate.

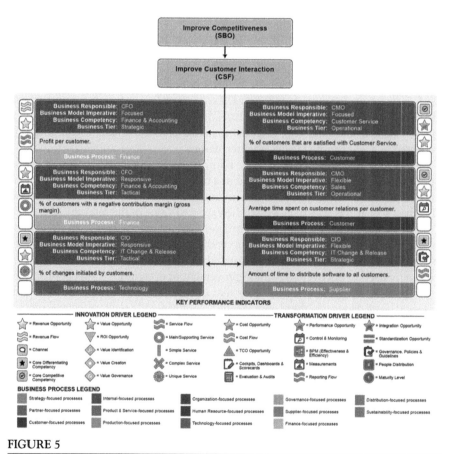

FIGURE 5

Value oriented process modeling.[18]

In both cases, process models are developed until the level of detail that still provides relevant business information through the design. The decomposition of the function "Enter Customer Order" into "Enter First Name", "Enter Last Name", and so on, would from a business point of view not add any additional relevant content (but may be necessary later for the development of software). When reference models are used, this can mean that in areas in which the design deviates from the initial industry model a higher level of modeling detail is required than in other "standard" areas.

Both high-impact and commodity processes are part of overlying end-to-end business processes. Process interfaces in the underlying detailed processes reflect this overall context and make sure that the various process components or subprocesses fit together. Hence, during the process improvement work cause-and-effect considerations have to take place to avoid fixing issues in one area while creating new ones in other processes.

Value-oriented Process Modeling

The value-oriented process modeling concepts require more consideration to the design and modeling aspects than traditional process design and modeling. For the most part, because Value-oriented Process Modeling needs a formalized breakdown of strategic business objectives (SBOs) into critical success factors (CSFs), with their associated KPIs and process performance indicators (PPIs), only then, the right measurements can be put in place in a manner that ensures that they are integrated and strategically aligned. They then can be linked to the proper responsible decision-making bodies, in a way that they allow performance improvement to occur. This brings support to this complex task by providing the discussed value tree, as shown in Figure 6, a taxonomy of the previously mentioned value indicators and

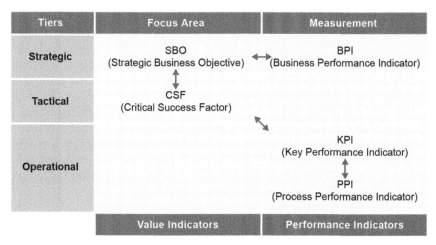

FIGURE 6

Value indicators and performance indicators.[19]

performance indicators and how they relate to each other.[20] Enabling organizations to categorize and classify their value indicators and performance indicators according to the enterprise tiers, focus areas, and existing measures.

Many organizations realize that traditional process design does not consider the value-oriented aspects of one's organization. Executives who ask themselves what it takes to move from traditional process design to value-oriented process design have to consider the strategic role that value-oriented aspects play in their organization, but also how and when to apply the concepts. The ability to succeed with one's value-oriented initiatives is directly related to the ability to connect the defined value drivers (SBOs and CSFs) and the performance drivers (KPIs and PPIs), as well as how the organization applies them to their competencies, processes, and services.

As illustrated in Figure 5, the core aspects of Value-oriented process modeling are therefore about linking the various aspects together; this includes:

1. Value drivers (SBOs and CSFs)
2. Performance drivers (KPIs and PPIs)
3. Organizational components (relevant Business Competencies)
4. The responsible person
5. The relevant business tier, that is, strategic, tactical, or operational
6. The appropriate and related process that links to all above points
7. Specification of the innovation and transformation aspects

Once the process has been sorted according to the value-oriented aspects, the organization now fully understands the value of their process investments, the relationship to their organizational components (relevant business competencies), the responsible persons or owners involved, and thereby also a link to evidence-based decision making.

Value-oriented process modeling, in addition, enables a whole new way of interlinking to the enterprise innovation and transformation aspects. This thereby enables not only Value-oriented process analysis, design, building, and implementation, it ensures that the business innovation and transformation happens alongside the progression. The link to innovation and transformation, however, prerequisites that all the processes involved need to be mapped to the value and performance indicators. The reason this is so vital is that, as illustrated in Figure 7, different strategies will have different critical success factors, all supporting the same strategy. To ensure consistency of value-oriented process modeling and to make sure that the strategies are executed, all relevant processes must be included. If not, it will be a siloed view of strategy execution. That is good enough for value-oriented process *design*, but not good enough for full value-oriented process *modeling*, which must include aspects of innovation and transformation.

Value-oriented Implementation

The organization-specific process models for high-impact business processes are, in general, implemented using people and highly flexible next-generation process

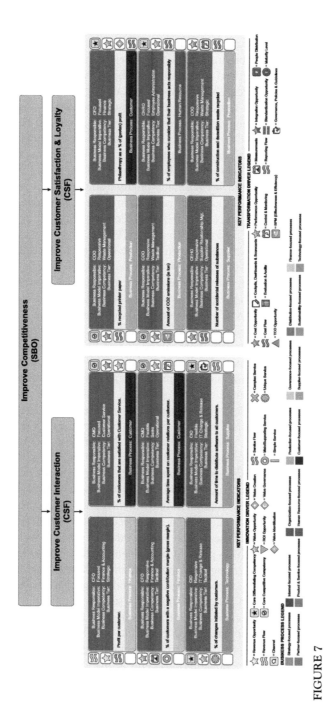

Value-oriented process modeling and the link to common strategy but different value and performance indicators.[21]

automation engines. The implementation requires in most cases the development of specific application software components. The process models reflecting the optimized KPIs regarding the relevant value drivers are the entrance points for the more detailed modeling of the underlying software. They enable a consistently value-oriented process implementation and automation. At this point, the modeling method can change, for example, to the Unified Modeling Language (UML), reflecting the desired software structure to support the high-impact processes. In addition, the work-flow engine of next-generation process automation engines can be configured based on those models, depending on the underlying modeling repository and execution technology even automatically or semi-automatically. The integration between process modeling and execution tools can be extremely beneficial in this situation, especially because it enables the flexible value-oriented adjustment of processes.

The overall architecture of such next-generation process automation environments is often referred to as Service-oriented Architecture (SOA). In such architecture, the "execution software" and the "process logic" (work flow) are separated.[22,23] Hence, the developed process models can on one hand be used to configure the work flow and on the other hand to develop the software services that are not available in existing libraries. Existing software services may include detailed process reference models that can be re-used in the process design. This architecture of next-generation process automation environments is visualized in Figure 8.

The key advantage of such architecture is the high degree of flexibility in adjusting process flows and functionality. This can be crucial for a company looking for agility and adaptability. The main disadvantage is the effort for providing the appropriate governance while running such an environment, as well as information modeling efforts in the building phase.

The process models of the commodity processes are used to select or at least evaluate preselected "traditional" software packages like Enterprise Resource Planning (ERP) systems, Supply Chain Management (SCM), or Customer Relationship Management (CRM) systems. These can become part of the overall next-generation architecture, representing one software component. Then those models from the process design are used to drive a process-oriented implementation of the software packages across the various organizational units involved in the business processes in scope.[24,25] Ideally, one uses already industry-specific software-reference models during the process design. This means one procures the reference models to be used from the software vendor. If this is possible, one benefits from the "business content" of the software and minimizes design and modeling efforts. Using other industry reference models (different from the software-based model) may lead to design adjustments and with that to rework, once the software is selected.

Figure 9 shows the architecture of such traditional software. Here, process definition and software functionality are linked in a static way. This means the software more or less dictates how a process has to be executed (allowing only predefined variants through the software configuration). This is fine for commodity processes, but often causes issues in strategic high-impact processes that need to be company specific. Consequently, we have used another implementation approach for those strategic processes. However, in some cases it is also possible to develop add-on

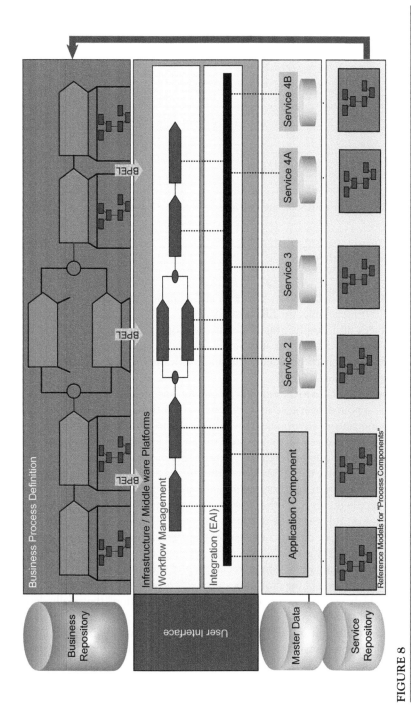

FIGURE 8

Next generation process automation.

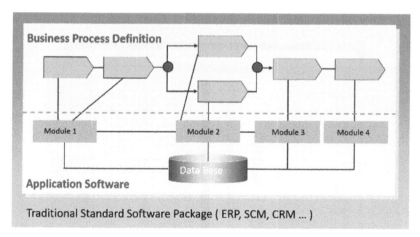

FIGURE 9

Traditional software architecture.

software to support high-impact processes and integrate them into the larger soft-ware package, for example, the ERP system.

Advantages and disadvantages are just the opposite as explained for next-generation process automation approaches. Hence, in practice, a combination of both implementation technologies and approaches is in most cases the solution that delivers best value.

The process interfaces in the different process models guide the software integration. This can be supported from a technology point of view through appropriate enterprise application integration environments—in general, included in SOA environments. Such software or middle-ware tools reduce the efforts for interface development to a necessary minimum. Their efficient use is again driven through the appropriate process models, specifically, the integration of the various process components.

The implementation of processes includes as a main component the prepara-tion of the people involved for the new work environment. They have to learn new manual processes and how to use the automation technologies in the specific process context. The necessary change management is carried out using the same process design as a basis that was used to drive the development and configuration of the IT components. Information, communication, and training are supported through the information models of the process design.[26,27] The integrated implementation of people- and IT-based processes leads to a "digital organization" that really delivers additional business value.

The implementation of the business processes can again be based on an agile approach, developing several "intermediate" prototypes or a top-down waterfall approach. In most cases a combination of both is best suited, because this avoids a possibly "endless" number of development cycles created by agile development or developments getting stuck on their way top–down of waterfall development models.[28]

The results are end-to-end business processes based on a value-oriented process design and an appropriate integrated automation. The approaches provide the necessary flexibility by which they deliver real business value and the required efficiency when possible.

Value-oriented Process Governance to Sustain Value

Once business processes have been designed and implemented targeting business value, the results need to be sustained and governed. To control one's business processes, especially the high-impact processes, if the KPIs remain in an acceptable range, adjust design or implementation as necessary. In addition, changes in business strategy need to be reflected. Therefore, the value-oriented design and implementation approach needs to be part of the larger BPM concept and discipline, the management discipline focused on moving strategy to execution, quickly, and at low risk. This BPM discipline is established through an appropriate "process of process management" in the BPM Center of Excellence (see the BPM CoE chapter) that manages the work, monitoring, and continuous improvement through the life cycle (see the BPM life cycle chapter).

Providing appropriate process governance is especially important to make BPM Governance a reality and keep processes focused on creating value (see the BPM governance chapter). This means that the process ownership, accountability, and responsibility, as well as a mechanism to take decisions and execute resulting actions across organizational boundaries, are defined.[29,30] In many successful organizations, the "process of process management" is owned and focused on value by a chief processes officer (CPO) and operationally managed by a BPM Center of Excellence (CoE) with various operational BPM roles (see the BPM roles chapter). Business processes require roles like process owners and supporting operative roles to be kept on target over time. These roles can be decentralized in business units or centralized, project-based, or permanent, in-house or out-sourced.

The approach of value-oriented process modeling allows an organization to move its strategy systematically into execution. It aligns the modeling and implementation efforts with the strategic direction of the organization after which the value-oriented process governance starts.

First experiences with real live companies showed that this approach helps on one hand to dramatically reduce process design and implementation times due to the efficient handling of commodity processes. Companies estimated more than 50% savings in time and effort. On the other hand, it enables real strategic advantage though the innovation and optimization of high-impact process areas based on the KPIs and the related strategic value drivers. To sustain the value creation and realization in the process execution, the following aspects illustrated in Figure 10 need to governed.

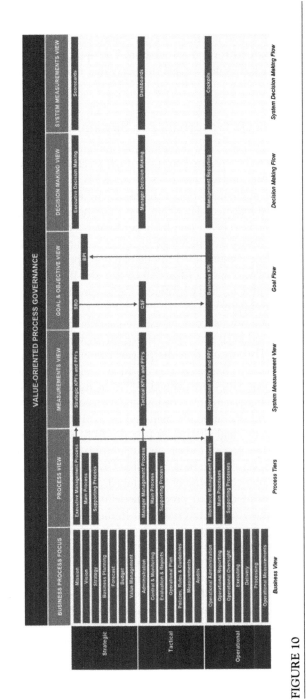

FIGURE 10

Example of a value oriented process governance.[31]

CONCLUSION

In this chapter, we have elaborated on what value-oriented process modeling is and how it differentiates to the traditional process analysis, process design, process implementation, and process governance considerations. We furthermore illustrated practical examples on who applies value-oriented process modeling and how it enables the link to innovation and transformation. It enables organizations with the ability to address their processes as core enterprise assets in a whole new way.

End Notes

1. Elzina G., Lee, *Business Engineering* (Norwell: Springer, 1999).
2. http://www.globaluniversityalliance.net/.
3. Mitchel R., van Ark, *The Conference Board – CEO Challenge 2014: People and Performance, Reconnecting with the Customer and Reshaping the Culture of Work. The Conference Board Whitepaer, New York, e.a. 2014* (2014).
4. Stary, *S-BPM One – Scientific Research. 4th International Conference, S-BPM ONE 2012, Vienna, Austria, April 2012, Proceedings* (2012).
5. Rummler R., Rummler, *White Space Revisited – Creating Value through Processes* (San Francisco: Wiley, 2010).
6. Burlton, "Delivering Business Strategy through Process Management," in *Handbook on Business Process Management 2 – Strategic Alignment, Governance, People and Culture* ed. J. Vom Brocke, M. Roemann (Berlin, New York, e.a.: Springer, 2013).
7. Hendrickx H. H. M., Daley S. K., Mahakena M., and von Rosing M, *Defining the Business Architecture Profession* (IEEE Commerce and Enterprise Computing, September 2011), 325–332.
8. Scheer, ARIS – Business Process Frameworks, 2nd ed. (Berlin, e.g.: Springer, 1998).
9. LEADing, *The Leading Practice Value Reference Content #Lead-ES20007BCPG – A Value Ontology and Value Semantic Description – Views, Stakeholders and Concerns. Version: Lead 3.0* (Leading Practice publication, 2014).
10. Scheer, "Tipps fuer den CIO: Vom Tekki zum Treiber neuer Business Modelle," in *IM+IO – Das Magazin fuer Innovation, Organisation und Management* (Sonderausgabe, December 2013).
11. Franz K., *Value oriented business Process Management – The Value-Switch for Lasting Competitive Advantage* (New York, e.a.: McGraw-Hill, 2012).
12. http://www.leadingpractice.com/enterprise-standards/enterprise-modelling/value-model/.
13. Kirchmer F., *The BPM-Discipline – Enabling the Next Generation Enterprise* (London, Philadelphia: BPM-D Executive Training Documentation, 2014).
14. Kirchmer, "Value oriented Design and Implementation of Business Processes – From Strategy to Execution at Pace with Certainty," *Accepted for publication in: BMSD'14 Proceedings* (Luxembourg, June 2014).
15. http://www.leadingpractice.com/wp-content/uploads/2013/05/LEAD-Value-Reference-Framework-Enterprise-Value-Tree.pdf.
16. Morris, *Architect, Design, Deploy, Improve (ADDI) – A BPMS Development Methodology* (Chicago: Wendan Whitepaper, 2014).
17. George, *The Lean Six Sigma Guide to Doing More with Less – Cut Costs, Reduce Waste, and Lower your Overhead.* (New York, e.a.: McGraw-Hill, 2010).

18. Value & Performance Management Model, LEADing Practice Value Model Reference Content #LEAD-ES20007BCPG.

19. Ibid.

20. Taken from the Value Model Reference Content (Enterprise Standard ID# LEAD-ES20007BCPG), http://www.leadingpractice.com/enterprise-standards/enterprise-modelling/value-model/.

21. See note 18 above.

22. Kirchmer, *High Performance through Process Excellence – From Strategy to Execution with Business Process Management*, 2nd ed. (Berlin, e.a.: Springer, 2011).

23. Slama N., Enterprise BPM – Erfolgsrezepte fuer unternehmensweites Prozessmanagement. (Heidelberg: dpunkt.verlag, 2011).

24. Kirchmer, 1999a. *Business Process Oriented Implementation of Standard Software – How to achieve Competitive Advantage Efficiently and Effectively*, 2nd ed. (Berline, e.a.: Springer).

25. Kirchmer, "Market- and Product-oriented Definition of Business Processes," in *Business Engineering* ed. D. J. Elzina, T. R. Gulledge, C-Y. Lee (Norwell: Springer, 1999b).

26. Kirchmer, *High Performance through Process Excellence – From Strategy to Execution with Business Process Management*, 2nd ed. (Berlin, e.a.: Springer 2011).

27. Franz K., *Value oriented business Process Management – The Value-Switch for Lasting Competitive Advantage* (New York, e.a.: McGraw-Hill, 2012).

28. Morris, *Architect, Design, Deploy, Improve (ADDI) – A BPMS Development Methodology* (Chicago: Wendan Whitepaper, 2014).

29. Kirchmer H., "Value oriented process Governance – Wettbewerbsvorteile durch die richtige Processorganisation," in *IM+io Fachzeitschrift fuer Innovation, Organisation und Management* (Germany, March, 2013).

30. Kirchmer, "How to create successful IT Projects with Value oriented BPM," in *CIO Magazine Online*, (February 27, 2013).

31. See note 18 above.

Sustainability Oriented Process Modeling

Gabriella von Rosing, David Coloma, Henrik von Scheel

INTRODUCTION

Sustainability is becoming a part of organizations and thus strategy, branding, and customer orientation and all of their processes. Executives, managers, business analysts, process experts, process architects, and process owners are a few types of profession that have an interest in sustainability and how it relates to business process management (BPM). Sustainability, achieving endurance of systems and processes, is one of the most relevant challenges that organizations and societies need to address. The ability to meet this challenge is hindered by the complexity of integrating sustainability into the strategy, the business model, and the different business functions that will execute the strategy. The 5 years of research work by the Global University Alliance on Enterprise Sustainability, which resulted in the development of an enterprise standard in terms of an enterprise sustainability reference content[1] and how it relates to BPM, is presented in this chapter. Areas touched by and of concern in sustainability oriented process modeling, including process design and operations, the link to strategy, and flows, roles involved, relevant rules, and compliance aspects as well as process automation, measurements, and reporting are discussed.

SITUATION, COMPLICATIONS, AND THE MAIN QUESTIONS

Since the publication of *The Limits of Growth*, sustainability has been a growing issue in the global agenda. Other significant landmarks are the publication of *Our Common Future* by the World Commission for Environment and Development, the Rio Earth Summits of 1992 and 2012, and the Kyoto Protocol (1997).

During this time, the world has seen some formidable environmental challenges, such as

- Ozone layer depletion, avoided thanks to the ban on chlorofluorocarbons
- The climate change challenge, still to be resolved
- The Fukushima, Three Mile Island, and Chernobyl nuclear disasters.
- Oil spills such as the Deepwater horizon rig and the *Exxon Valdez* tanker
- Waste and pollution threats as the Great Pacific garbage patch

- Deforestation and desertification
- The depletion of fisheries and the destruction of biodiversity

This range of problems presented poses tremendous challenges to humanity as the environmental services on which we rely on are severely compromised. Simultaneously, nongovernmental organizations (NGOs) have arisen as prominent players in the global arena by reacting against some of the most questionable facets of the pursuit of indefinite economic growth in a closed system. This in turn has given rise to promotion of the idea that economic development has to come about in ways that respect the rights and needs of workers and communities as well as alleviating negative side effects to other third parties. This mindset has resulted in the surge of the idea of corporate social responsibility.

In view of this, two relevant concepts have emerged. The first is the idea of sustainable development, popularized in the *Our Common Future* report by the World Commission for Environment and Development, which describes it as the "development that meets the needs of present generations without compromising the ability of future generations to meet their needs."

As an extension of this concept, the second one is the Elkington's *Triple Bottom Line*, which asserts that business performance has to deliver value in three key areas: economic, environmental, and social. Any outcome that fails to accomplish positive impacts in all three criteria will be clearly unsustainable in the long term.

This situation makes paramount the role of businesses in finding solutions, because they are the main agents that supply products and services to our society.

In the face of these demands, the data show that the time is ripe for solutions and the value of achieving more sustainable performance. Data from the International Organization for Standardization show[2] that in 2009 223,149 organizations were certified with ISO 14,001 from 159 countries, far from the 4433 organizations in 1997. Also, the need for sustainable management solutions was clearly shown by a Forrester Research study[3] that estimated that the global sustainability consulting market was worth $2.7 billion US in 2010 and that it would grow to $9.6 billion by 2015.

From the executive viewpoint, a United Nations Global Compact study[4] revealed that 93% of 766 global chief executive officers (CEOs) surveyed believed that sustainability was critical to the future success of their organizations. However, in this same study 49% of CEOs cited complexity of implementation across functions as the most significant barrier to implementing an integrated, organization-wide approach to sustainability, whereas competing strategic priorities was second, with 48% of respondents.

CONDITIONS, CIRCUMSTANCES, AND COMPLEXITY

Strong social and business demand for wide sustainability creates a scenario in which organizations, public and private, feel more pressure to improve in sustainability performance to achieve:

- Cost efficiencies, in which eco-efficiency is taking an increasing role as it delivers a reduction in raw materials and energy consumption, in greenhouse and other taxed emissions and waste
- Easier accommodation to stricter environmental standards and regulations, whether governmental or voluntary
- Exploitation of business opportunities in the form of new products and services or new revenue streams brought about by the monetization of emission rights, sale of by-products, or license of know-how on sustainability. Here, we can find some new products and services such as electric and hybrid cars, renewable energy projects, and smart grids and cities
- Radical transformation of those business models most affected by sustainability concerns, such as logistics, oil, power, mining, and forest products, among others
- Improved reputation as well as proactive response to customer and stakeholder requirements of environmental- and community-friendly products, services, and processes

Currently, there are several approaches to environmental and social responsibility (ISO 14,001, EMAS (Eco-Management and Audit Scheme), GRI (Global Reporting Initiative), ISO 26,000, etc.). Unfortunately, their focus is narrow because they seek only specific aspects of sustainability in organizations, addressing areas such as reporting, communication of impacts to stakeholders, process controls, compliance, or performance improvement, but typically only an environmental or social context. When any of these approaches takes on the larger view, it is at best addressed in a partial and restricted way. Then, wider opportunities for sustainable value creation remain mostly untouched because of a lack of integration of those considerations in the organization's (or indeed, the enterprise's) overall operations.

THE MAIN QUESTIONS COVERED

To deal with these primordial challenges, we propose a sustainability oriented process modeling framework as a response to the need for innovative and transformed strategies, business models, processes, and various end-to-end process flows to achieve drastic improvement not only in the economic value area but also in the environmental and social areas.

Here, BPM is an especially powerful approach to sustainability problems, because it implies the achievement of an organization's objectives through the improvement, management, and control of essential processes.

The sustainability oriented process modeling concept brings a unified way of thinking, working, modeling, governing, implementing, and training to organizations willing to implement sustainability.

- A *way of thinking* is provided because it articulates the definitions and guiding principles to capture, design, plan, and structure process-relevant objects and artifacts to understand problems and bring about solutions to different process domains.

- A *way of working* is supported, as the sustainability oriented process modeling principles, structuring the tasks to be performed in the development and implementation of process initiatives.
- A *way of modeling* is supplied as the sustainability oriented process modeling principles allow the description of the relevant process entities and relationships in the business sustainability domain so that solutions can be communicated to diverse stakeholders with different sustainability views and business concerns, and insights can be elicited.
- A *way of implementing* is provided so that appropriate paths of process transformation are made available.
- A *way of governing* is enabled by defining the expectations, intent, authority and responsibilities, and performance and sustainable process architecture to ensure value identification and creation.
- A *way of training* employees involved in sustainability management is brought about in the BPM certificate of excellence (CoE) and process owners and the rest of the organization.

THE ANSWER

The solution proposed to face these challenges is an integrated approach in the form of sustainability oriented process modeling principles that allows organizations to incorporate that triple-faceted concept of sustainability value into the business model, link it to the strategy, and develop the right performance measures as well as integrate it with its competencies and processes.

These sustainability oriented process modeling principles emerge from the Global University Alliance article entitled "Initial thoughts on a sustainability framework," written in 2009 by Mark von Rosing, Maria Hove, and Henrik von Scheel. It tried to tackle the complexity cited by executives as the main barrier to transitioning to more sustainable business models. By easing the transformation of the business processes from a sustainability point of view, it can be a powerful enabler.

THE WAY OF THINKING AROUND SUSTAINABILITY ORIENTED PROCESS MODELING

The way of thinking articulates the sustainability oriented process modeling principles by defining its scope and underlying principles. It deals with a set of objects and elements so that they can be properly identified, described, and further developed as needed:

- External sustainability drivers and forces, as well as stakeholders and their requirements
- Mission, vision, goals, and value drivers
- Strategy, cost, operating, service, revenue, value, and performance models
- Sustainability processes and workflows, as well as their rules
- Overall governance and compliance
- Competencies and other relevant business and sustainability objects
- Organization chart, sustainability roles, and ownerships
- Performance measures and reporting, balanced scorecard, and governance
- Sustainability media and channels
- Objects needed in the infrastructure, application, and data layers below the sustainable business and process layers

We define, as many others in the market, sustainability in reference to three key focus areas (economic, environmental, and social), that have to be addressed in the business model through processes and resources that strive to reach eco-efficiency, social responsibility, and well-balanced growth goals (Figure 1).

The economic sustainability focus area has to attend to economic value creation, so that an effective and efficient use of economic resources brings economic success to the organization and prosperity to the society.

Environmental sustainability is about the wise use of natural resources, in the sense that they are preserved to meet the future needs of the organization and society. Here, cardinal notions and tools such as the ecological footprint, life cycle assessment, and ecological cost accounting, among others, are used.

The environmental area would be incomplete if no room were allowed for respect for other living forms besides the carrying capacity considerations. Here, biodiversity preservation, pollution prevention, and animal rights are to be considered.

Finally, the social sustainability focus area deals with conducting the business operations in a form that respects people inside and outside the organization, and tries to avert avoidable negative impact to third parties.

SUSTAINABILITY ORIENTED PROCESS MODELING: THE WAY OF WORKING

Steps to sustainability principles within BPM include:

1. Understanding the organization's sustainability personality
2. Building and transforming the BPM CoE and organization's culture toward sustainability
3. Developing the organization's business model
4. Developing the sustainability's life cycle
5. Building the organization's sustainability maturity model

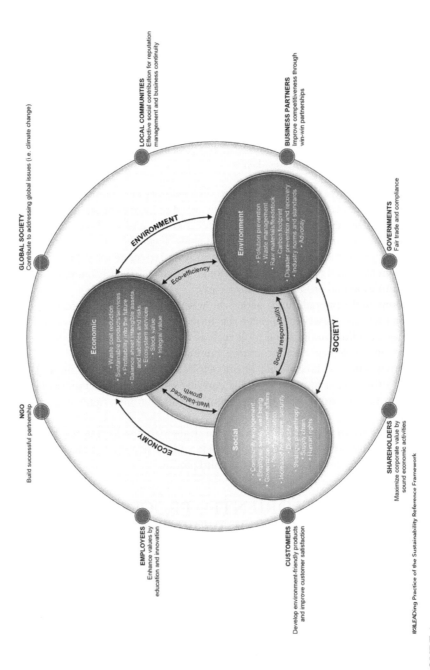

FIGURE 1

Business model for sustainability.[5]

6. Developing the sustainability value model
7. Developing the sustainability revenue model

Details of these steps are provided below.

Understanding Your Organization's Sustainability Personality

The first step in the path to sustainability is to understand what the organization's personality is with regard to sustainability. That personality is derived from two dimensions: the attitudes and intentions toward sustainability and the activities and initiatives.

If the organization has initiated some sort of evolution toward sustainability, four sustainable personalities can be identified:

- Sustainability awareness, with low levels of both initiatives and intentions. Here, the organization probably has put in place some initial, unstructured measures
- Sustainability understanding, in which the initiatives level remains low but intentions have grown to higher levels. In this personality the organization has initiated sustainable strategies, policies, and initiatives
- Sustainability acceptance, with a high level of initiatives but a low level of intentions. Here, the organization would have implemented sustainable portfolio and performance management
- Sustainable commitment, in which the organization has both high intentions and initiatives levels. The sustainability is integrated in the strategy, sustainable innovation is developed, and there are aggressive sustainable goals and impacts

Building and Transforming the BPM CoE and Organization's Culture Toward Sustainability

To climb up the attitude ladder from compliance to leadership, the organization needs to provide motivation to create engagement. Therefore, the next step is to build within the BPM CoE a business case for sustainability that articulates an understanding of the business value at stake for the organization as well as the external forces and drivers of change that can affect the business process operating context.

Developing the Organization's Business Model

This phase in the road to sustainability provides the definition of the business model. Here, it is described in a hierarchical top-down way cascading into more detail. Thus, decomposition of the business model is broken down into the deeper and more concrete layers of competency groups, sustainable competencies, competency elements, process categories, process groups, processes, and activities.

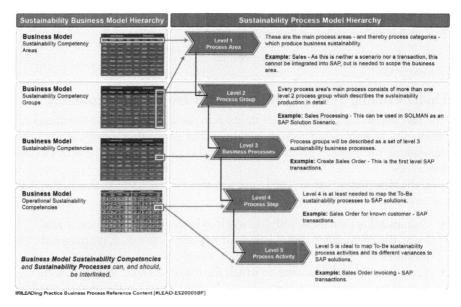

FIGURE 2

The sustainability business model to process model hierarchy.

In addition to the cascading detail of the business model, scenarios are elaborated that describe the processes needed to achieve a sustainability outcome (Figure 2).

Developing the Sustainability's Life Cycle

The subsequent point in the path to sustainability is to establish the organization's life cycle through which the transformation is to be carried out.

The sustainability lifecycle is based on the LEADing[1] practice life cycle model whose graphical representation is provided in Figure 3. It ensures that the different business model domains (service, revenue, cost, operating, value, and performance models) are addressed through a set of life cycles.

Following and exploiting these life cycles allows innovation and transformation of the sustainable business with a series of phases at the business process level and the applications level that support them, along with their required governance and value management.

The process life cycle corresponds to the sustainability personality. The analysis phase corresponds with the awareness personality, the design phase with understanding, implementation with acceptance, and continuous improvement with commitment.

This life cycle delivers alignment at the strategic, organizational, technological, and process levels.

---

[1] LEAD stands for Layered Enterprise Architecture Development.

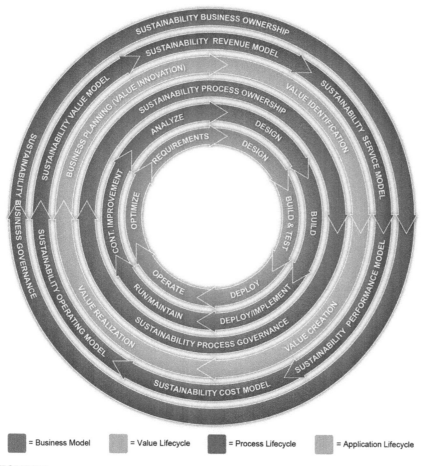

FIGURE 3

Business process management life cycle.[6]

Building the Organization's Sustainability Maturity Model

A tool is needed to guide evolution toward higher sustainability. Here, a sustainability maturity model (Figure 4) provides a benchmark tool against which the organization's status on the path to sustainability can be understood and from which guidelines and a roadmap to prioritize actions to evolve can be derived, as well as critical success factors (CSFs) and measurements produced.

The sustainability maturity model establishes five levels:

1. Recognize. First green processes come up, but in an ad hoc, poorly formalized, and uncontrolled manner.

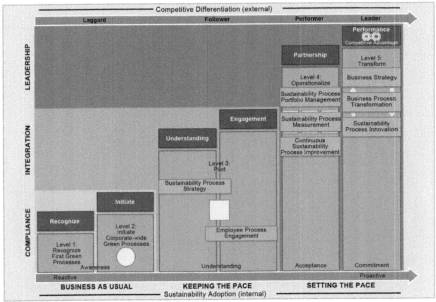

FIGURE 4

Maturity levels and personality profiles.[7]

2. Initiate. Sustainability processes are defined so that they become repeatable and consistent, although with room for improvement in rigor. Here, most initiatives seek compliance to rules or are "me too" respectable but unsound motivations.
3. Pilot. A sustainability strategy is established as well as standard sustainability processes and consistency in sustainability is achieved. The organization personality here evolves from awareness to understanding and starts to acknowledge the competitive importance of sustainability.
4. Operationalize. At this point, organization-wide sustainable portfolio management is set up while controlling the green sustainability initiatives and establishing sustainability capabilities.
5. Transform. In this stage, the organization focuses on improving sustainable innovation as sustainability is fully integrated into the business strategy.

Developing the Sustainability Value Model

The next activity in the sustainability transformation is elaboration of the sustainability value model, in which the different value viewpoints are considered from the triple bottom line perspectives.

The value model describes the external and internal value drivers, the value proposition, and expectations while translating the business strategy into strategic business objectives (SBOs) and CSFs.

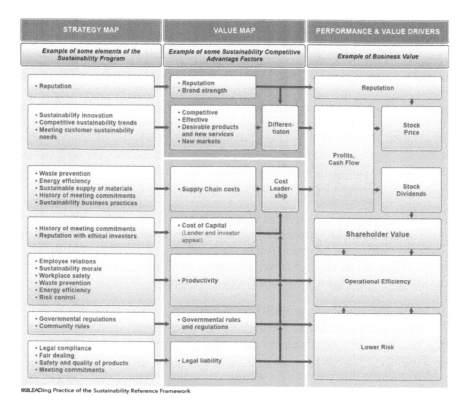

IIOILEADing Practice of the Sustainability Reference Framework

FIGURE 5

Relation among elements in sustainability, competitive advantage factors, and value drivers.[8]

One tool also used is selection of the competitive strategies (cost leadership, differentiation, or focus) that result in uniqueness and competitive advantages. Here, some considerations have to be made because current studies show that in our times, instead of choosing among exclusive strategies, some organizations are using blended strategies with successful results.

In creating these competitive advantages, construction of a sustainable balanced scorecard and a strategy map is essential because it helps to understand which pivotal competencies participate in the causal relationships among key sustainability value drivers.

In Figure 5 a map of the relations among sustainability strategy elements, value levers, and performance is provided.

The sustainability oriented process modeling concepts require more consideration of the value management discipline, because the two other sustainability value areas (environmental and social) have to be addressed in addition to the economic one.

Here, as described in the chapter on Value-Oriented Process Modeling, value management requires a formalized breakdown of (SBOs) into (CSFs), their associated key performance indicators (KPIs), and process performance indicators (PPIs). Only then can the right measurements be put into place in a manner that ensures that they are integrated and strategically aligned as well as linked to the proper sustainability owners and decision-making bodies so that they allow performance improvement to occur. This brings support to this complex task by providing a green BPM value tree, a taxonomy of the previously mentioned value indicators.

Many organizations realize that traditional process design does not consider the sustainability aspects of one's organization. Executives who ask themselves what it takes to move from traditional process design to sustainability oriented process design have to consider the strategic role that sustainability has in their organization, but also how and where to apply the sustainability concepts. The ability to succeed with one's sustainability initiatives is directly related to the ability to connect the defined sustainability value drivers (SBOs and CSFs) and the sustainability performance drivers (KPIs and PPIs), as well as how the organization applies them to their competencies, processes, and services.

As illustrated in Figure 6, the core aspects of sustainability oriented process modeling are about linking the various aspects together:

1. Sustainability value drivers (SBOs and CSFs)
2. Sustainability performance drivers (KPIs and PPIs)
3. Organizational components (relevant business competencies)
4. The responsible person
5. The relevant business tier, i.e., strategic, tactical, or operational
6. The appropriate and related process that links to all five points
7. Specification of aspects of innovation and transformation

Once the right metrics are available, the value management life cycle can be operated—with the value planning, identification, creation, and realization phases—so that organizations can understand the value of their sustainable investments and impacts.

Then decisions can be properly made because their impact on sustainability is understood. These decisions encompass areas such as operational efficiency, risk management, market positioning, innovation, human capital development, community acceptance, supply chain management, access to resources, access to capital, and corporate governance.

Developing the Sustainability Revenue Model

Once value implications are understood, it is the time to describe revenue generation through the revenue model. This model defines how the organization makes money thanks to its value proposition and pricing model.

A sustainable business can generate income from sources other than the usual sales of goods and services, from other revenue opportunities such as the sale of by-products, emission rights, sustainable technologies, and process management know-how, among many others.

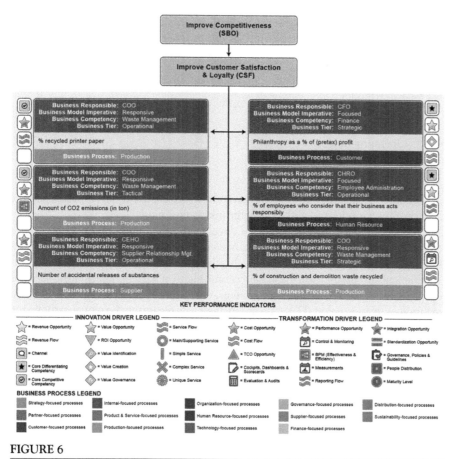

FIGURE 6

Example of sustainability oriented process modeling.[9]

In addition, a sustainable organization will increase in sales because of the increased appeal of sustainable products and services and the reputation effects (over price premiums and volume) of a sustainable brand.

A sustainable revenue model has to be linked to the development of a sustainable brand as well as sustainable marketing and communications to make customers and stakeholders aware of its sustainable performance.

SUSTAINABILITY ORIENTED PROCESS MODELING: WAY OF MODELING

As illustrated in Figure 6, sustainability oriented process modeling enables modeling of innovation and the transformation components within the business. Once the way of working is defined, the objects and their relationships can be modeled with the detail and techniques necessary to facilitate their deployment in the different layers. This can be modeled with the following aspects:

Innovation drivers
- Revenue model
- Value model
- Service model

Transformation drivers
- Operating model
- Cost model
- Performance model

Because of space limitations, we have chosen to focus on developing a sustainable operating model and within it, interlinking cost model concepts.

The sustainable operating model is developed, describing how the organization uses its resources and delivers performance and value across business competencies, functions, process, organization and technology.

Efficient sustainable execution has become highly reliant on information technology (IT) because the alignment of strategy, organization, and processes depends on technology. Nevertheless, IT has an ambivalent role regarding the global carbon footprint. Information technology is the cause of 2% of global CO_2 emissions with estimations of rapid growth,[10] but it has a huge potential because of its role as an enabler of efficiencies that can reduce the carbon footprints of the other 98% of emissions.

There are seven sustainable competency areas in which IT-enabled solutions can produce efficiencies (Table 1):

1. Energy and carbon. Here, the consumption of energy and the carbon emissions can be tracked and reported so that they can be reduced by a combination of initiatives in areas such as energy savings, energy mix optimization, carbon abatement initiatives, and carbon trading
2. Product safety and stewardship. These solutions empower products and services that are compliant and safe, and are designed with sustainable criteria that facilitate recycling and reuse and a low life cycle environmental footprint
3. Sustainable supply chain. Visibility throughout the supply chain can be warranted so that procurement, logistics, operations, assets, and product life cycle management activities can be optimized, and suppliers that most support the sustainability objectives can be selected
4. Environment, health, and safety. Here, the environmental performance and issues regarding the occupational health of workers, industrial hygiene and safety, and emergency management issues are addressed
5. Sustainable workforce. With these solutions, the organization can enforce and ensure compliance with labor rights and respect for diversity—both inside and outside the environment—and properly manage talent
6. Information technology infrastructure, further developed below
7. Sustainability performance. This covers the capabilities to manage performance on sustainability

Table 1 *Sustainable Competency Areas Supported by Information technology (IT) Solutions (SAP Example)*

Energy & Carbon	Energy-efficient Assets		Energy Management	Carbon Management		Smart Grids	
Product Safety & Stewardship	Product Compliance	Material & Product Safety	Recycling & Re-use	Recall Management	Environmental Footprint	Sustainable Design	
Sustainable Supply Chain	Procurement	Traceability	Commodity Trade & Risk Management		Resource Optimization	Supply Chain Optimization	
Environment, Health & Safety	Environmental Performance	Occupational Health		Industrial Hygiene & Safety		Emergency Management	
Sustainable Workforce	Labor Compliance & Rights		Diversity			Talent Management	
IT Infrastructure	Availability, Security, Accessibility & Privacy			Sustainability Oriented IT			
Sustainability Performance Management	Assured Reporting/Compliance		Benchmarks & Analytics	Strategy & Risk		Financial Performance	

In mixing the operating model, one can develop a sustainability cost model. It describes the costs incurred in operating the organization so that the service and revenue models are supported. Also, at this time the route for the transformation is developed, depending on the objectives and constraints of the organization. Three different transformation paths can be selected depending on the intent of the organization.

- Revolutionary approach, a big bang strategy that wants to achieve maximum improvement in the shortest time span. It is a high-cost bet that can bring fast and radical improvement but at a high risk and high disruption over daily operations
- Step-by-step approach, in which improvement is produced project by project. It delivers cost savings with lower risks but in a slower fashion. Here, dependencies between projects may not be properly addressed
- Evolutionary approach, in which improvement is tackled in a process-by-process mode. This approach mitigates risks but realization of benefits is slow

SUSTAINABILITY ORIENTED PROCESS MODELING: WAY OF IMPLEMENTING

This realm of the sustainability oriented process modeling framework is tackled mainly through a sustainability performance model that allows translation of the vision and strategy into performance measures and balanced scorecards as well as other constructs as policies, codes of conduct, and reporting and responsibility lines.

Specific reporting guidelines need to be developed so that auditability and transparency to third parties is ensured. For more information, we reference the process implementation and deployment chapter.

SUSTAINABILITY ORIENTED PROCESS MODELING: WAY OF GOVERNING

In this part, an approach to sustainability governance and continuous improvement is developed. A sustainability board is established and sustainability owners are defined and mapped.

Stakeholders and their concerns and requirements are also described and mapped. Special attention to them should be given in addressing sustainability, because the nature of the subject implies more complexity than in other domains. Therefore, the needs of the supply chain actors (suppliers, customers, channels, and partners), employees, investors and lenders, governments, communities, and NGOs have to be carefully defined and considered. For more information, we reference the BPM governance chapter.

BENEFITS OF COMBINING BPM AND SUSTAINABILITY ORIENTED PROCESS MODELING

The benefits of combining BPM and sustainability oriented process modeling are multiple. Some of the concepts evolve the organization's sustainability maturity in that it enables the organization to:

- Understand the sustainability personality and transform its culture
- Develop the business model concepts around sustainability
- Establish the sustainability life cycle that aligns the different elements
- Progress toward sustainability with the help of a maturity tool
- Define the sustainability value, revenue, operating, performance, and cost models, as well as ensure green IT processes
- Build a sustainability governance model, including a board

The proposed approach to sustainability and BPM results in technical and business advantages to the applying organizations. Because executives cite complexity as the main barrier in transitioning to more sustainable business models, the sustainability oriented process modeling principles covered can enable benefits:

- Business value aspects:
  - Improved responsiveness and agility, including the ability to change business processes and business model in response to a changing environment
  - Improved innovation in products, services, processes, and business model

- Integrated stakeholder management requirements in the business processes
- Reduced costs and increased employee and resource productivity
- Reduced risk and improved compliance to regulations and internal policies
- Improved quality
- Reduced waste and nonvalue-added activities
- Improved performance and control over processes
- Improved coordination
- Improved reputation
- Technical value aspects that result in diminished costs of implementation and operation of business processes:
  - Improved efficiency of processes
  - Component and process reuse, with lowered implementation time-to-market
  - Improved coordination among functions
- Better application integration
- Environmental value aspects:
  - Lower ecological footprint, with less energy and materials consumption and greenhouse gases emission
  - Lowered pollution levels
  - Enhanced product safety and traceability
  - Biodiversity preservation
- Social aspects:
  - Social rights of labor and communities respected
  - Improved diversity in workforce
  - Improved occupational health and safety

CONCLUSIONS

In this chapter we have deliberated on the various aspects of sustainability and BPM. Because of space constraints, not all aspects could be covered that are needed for BPM and sustainability oriented process modeling and all of the tasks and artifacts to achieve the right way of thinking, working, modeling, implementation, and governance.

We focused on the definition of sustainability that encompasses economic, environmental, and social value, why it is needed, the relevance to the business model and the process model, and a guided step-by-step approach to sustainability oriented process modeling, including strategy, competencies, value, performance, measurement, and reporting, all linked to processes.

End Notes

1. The LEADing Practice Enterprise Sustainability Reference Content (LEAD-ES20018AL).
2. International Organization for Standardization (ISO), "The ISO Survey 2009,".

3. "Capitalizing on the Sustainability Consulting Services Opportunity," *Forrester Research*, (October 2010).
4. Accenture CEO Study (2010, 2011, 2012), "A New Era of Sustainability," (UN Global Compact).
5. Source: www.LEADingPractice.com
6. LEADing Practice Business Process Reference Content #LEAD-ES20005BP.
7. LEADing Practice Maturity Reference Content #LEAD-ES60003AL.
8. LEADing Practice Value Architecture Reference Content #LEAD-ES40003PG.
9. LEADing Practice Business Process Reference Content #LEAD-ES20005BP.
10. McKinsey & Company, "Pathway to a Low-Carbon Economy: Version 3 of the Global Greenhouse Gas Abatement Cost Curve," (2009): 7.

Information Modeling and Process Modeling

Hans-Jürgen Scheruhn, Mark von Rosing, Richard L. Fallon

INTRODUCTION

Business process modeling, the activity of recording and representing the processes of an enterprise, is an important part of information modeling, which is the recording and depiction of the persistent and future arrangement of information assets of an organization in a structured or formal manner. Information modeling is often incorrectly understood to be concerned only with data modeling. In reality, information modeling is composed of not only data modeling but also other aspects such as process modeling as well as value- or service-oriented modeling. The resulting information models, covering the strategic, tactical, and operational tier, can ultimately form a single integrated enterprise information model (see Figure 1). The message of this figure is that there must be integration of the strategic, tactical, and operating information models as well as integration into all phases of the business process life cycle. The information models and the record of their content fulfill the purpose of mapping not only the dynamic aspects of the business processes and data flows within an organization, but also the static characteristics of the information space on which the dynamic (time-dependent) aspects build.[1] The purpose of these models is varied; among other things, they provide a record of the information assets of the enterprise, the idea of creating a shared understanding of the business, and thus are important in problem solving and executing change.

Business process modeling tools should be used to depict current business processes ("as-is" modeling) as well as to develop the design of the new business process blueprint[2] ("to-be" modeling). Interlinking the business and application layers and their information meta objects can be organized and their content represented using a range of current information modeling techniques. These models apply concepts already discussed in the Extended Business Process Model and Notation (xBPMN) in Chapter[3], event-driven process chain (EPC), Unified Modeling Language (UML), information engineering (IE), and entity-relationship (ER) modeling, among others. We will then provide evidence via a case study of how these different modeling techniques complement each other through practical examples of their use.

INTENDED AUDIENCE

This topic is interesting to individuals who use only one of these information modeling techniques in their daily work, or professionals seeking to gain insight into how these modeling techniques can be put into practice in a real-world situation.

511

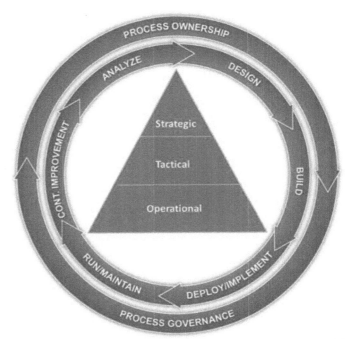

((©)LEADing Practice Business Process Reference Content [#LEAD-ES30002AL]

FIGURE 1

Process life cycle and enterprise tiers.[4]

The models in the section "The Answer" show how each of the different modeling techniques can in fact complement each other and thus provide a set of integrated enterprise information models that contain all aspects of the business process that has been modeled.

PROCESS LIFE CYCLE

The view of a process life cycle is not new. Several authors[4,5–8] have looked at the problem of defining these cycles and proposed a number of different approaches; for example, Verner proposed a process life cycle containing seven individual stages to an iteration:

Analyze→Design→Build/Develop→Deploy→Operate→Maintain/Continuous Improvement.

However, for our working examples we will use the definition of the process life cycle (see Figure 2) as defined by the LEADing Practice framework[9] because the LEAD standards offer a paradigm shift in the goal of producing a truly open all-encompassing standard (LEAD standards include interfaces to other frameworks, methods, and approaches such as TOGAF, Zachman, FEAF, ITIL, Prince2, COBIT,

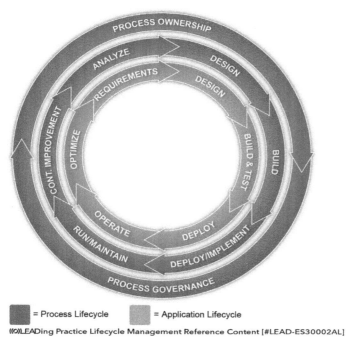

FIGURE 2

Process life cycle with the application life cycle.

and DNEAF).[10] For our working examples, we will use the definition of the process life cycle discussed in the chapter "BPM Life Cycle."

The diagram above (Figure 2) illustrates the cyclical nature of the process and application life cycle.

Analyze (and Discover)

The goal of process analysis is to detect implicit knowledge that exists in the organization about existing or as-is processes and make this knowledge available in an as-is model so as to organize and represent this knowledge.[11] Thus, the analysis phase and documentation are the first steps in providing a complete discovery of existing (as-is) business processes, closely followed by the capture, decomposition,[12] and documentation of all relevant related information objects, properties, and relationships. This procedure is commonly known as business process analysis (BPA).[13]

Above all, the processes, together with the related dynamic and static business structures, should ultimately support and execute the strategic business objectives and critical success factors of the organization. Thus, these strategic aspects are a part of the business direction and therefore value expectations and business requirements that have to be considered in the analysis and organizational design of the associated strategic information objects and their relationships to the processes. The connection between these objects and the processes must be both identifiable and verifiable. This connection occurs only through each of the members of the array of integrated and holistic sets of related knowledge, skills, and abilities that, combined, enable the enterprise to act in its environment—the enterprise's competencies. These competencies are important in executing the structured analysis of a process because they provide the context in which to judge the optimization criteria to be used when designing a process, whether centered on value maximization or cost minimization. It is therefore critical to distinguish at an early stage between core competitive, core differentiating, and non-core competencies and thereby the related processes.[14,15] Core competitive competencies and all related processes are essential for an enterprise to compete and core differentiating competencies and all related processes are those that differentiate the business to its customers. In both cases, the processes involved are the tasks that create value, whereas anything that is non-core but that must be done should be done for as little cost as possible.

For a correct and complete analysis of a business process (as-is model), all relevant information objects and their relationships to each other must be identified and documented. This includes consideration of value and business process flow, business competency, service, and data flow. In addition to the dynamic flows, the enclosing static (hierarchical) structures (value, competency, service, process, application, and data) should also be considered. In the case of any of these, the process expert or process engineer must make a thorough decomposition and analysis of the business process. Decomposition is the procedure by which the objects are broken down into their simpler forms. For example, a business process is decomposed into one or more process step(s), whereas a process step is decomposed into one or more process activities(s) and a process activity is decomposed into one or more transaction(s). The result of several successful iterations of the discover/analyze cycle is the completed as-is model.

The manual process of analyzing, decomposing, and documenting business processes from a previous successful run of a process life cycle (assuming process maturity greater than "3" or "standardized") can also be assisted using tools such as SAP Reverse Business Engineering and SAP Solution Manager or ARIS Process Performance Management. However, some tools provide only part of the information required about the processes' state and the relationships between the relevant objects. These tools are even less successful when determining process flows with business rules as well as static structures and hierarchies needed to obtain a full understanding of their design and properties, and lead to incomplete designs that often do not work as needed.

Design

In this phase the new business process flow and business process structures (to-be status) are designed.

Depending on the scope of the project, the design work can involve anything from altering the complete process flow to adding and/or deleting business processes, or just to small changes in basic behavior. A similar range of the scope of change can occur with the information objects and the related dynamic and static structures contained within each of the business processes. This is relevant because the information model must be created throughout the end-to-end process flows. Therefore, output/product of this phase is the successful composition of the new to-be design, captured in a model.[16]

Build

The process build phase is concerned with applying the to-be models defined within the process design phase, including all related dynamic and static structures, to create the operating system (manual or automated).

In a purely manual situation, the build phases are addressed through work design, training, and the preparation of documentation. In an automated environment build, the activity may include programming, configuration, or other work within the software that performs or enables the work. Obviously, in many cases both types of work will be required and must be coordinated to complete the build to achieve the results that are required from the new operations.

Depending on the size and scope of the software-oriented build and the quality of the process models produced in advance, a so-called model-driven design can be used.[4,17] However, more comprehensive process models and methods are required when deploying enterprise and Web/restful services than are the case for implementing or customizing corporate standard software. In the latter case, for example an ERP system, partial automation can also be obtained through such tools as SAP Solution Manager and SAP Business Workflow or BPM systems such as SAP BPM or Software AG webMethods support.

The needs of the business analysts who have produced the specification of the to-be business and the technical application developers who implement the system are not always the same.[18] The challenge and problems associated with producing a successful combined system of work that fully implements the to-be models must therefore lie in collaboration between the members of these two groups. Part of the problem is finding balance between the parts of the work that should be done by machine and those best done by humans, and how best to establish the interface between the two; often the problems are related to matters of precision, which, with BPM and automated business processes, can lead to implementation that does not accurately fulfill the business requirements. When considered in total, the result is the description of a system of work in which human work is efficiently and effectively enabled by the roles and capabilities of the applications. Often attempts at a solution to this problem try to use UML diagrams. However, these are more suited to technical designers and less to business analysts, and they suffer from the fact they do not capture the information needed to provide a complete solution to this problem. In the section on the UML model, we detail a to-be example based on UML class diagrams.

Deploy/Implement

This is the phase where processes based on the to-be models are put into effect to be used by the business. The process models and the information models within them can be a basis for testing and can be used to offer a high level of support during the implementation phase.

Run/Maintain (Monitoring)

This phase is concerned with the successful operation of business processes and their enablers in a production environment. During this phase, efforts must be made to guard the process to ensure its operations remain consistent with the design objectives. Without oversight, the process may be sub-optimized or otherwise modified in ways that needlessly increase cost or reduce value. This is the main task of the process-monitoring phase, which is the final phase and ultimately is the input to the analysis phase in the next iteration of the cycle. Whereas the analysis phase is concerned with determining possible weaknesses of the dynamic and static structures of the business processes and their interrelation, the monitoring phase is concerned solely with one aspect: measurement of process performance indicators (PPIs) together with time, cost, and quality to verify the status of the process. The Gartner group quoted by Verner[19] coined the term "business activity monitoring" to describe the ability to produce real-time performance indicators to assess speed and effectiveness of business operations.

Continuous Improvement

Once the new business processes are operational, ongoing work is necessary to verify whether the intended goals have been met through a continual effort to learn from and improve on the design of the process to achieve its design goals. These efforts can seek evolutionary change or may involve innovative change to the design.

Continuous improvement is a key aspect of BPM whereby feedback from the process and the customer are evaluated against design goals.

PROCESS ATTRIBUTES

Process Flow and Process Resources

A process flow consists of a set of connected process activities organized into a stream, sequence, course, succession, series, or progression, all based on the process input/output states, in which each process input/output defines the process flow that together performs a behavior. These process activities may connect to static resources, including business objects of various types, and to roles.

Process resources such as roles, which are represented as pools or lanes in BPM notation (BPMN) process or collaboration models, have an important role in describing work, in that they signify the allocations of responsibility and thus require consideration in the analysis and design of the work.

For transactional and tacit work, process resources may be either human or automated via software applications.[20] Resource allocation can be useful in showing where one system connects resources to another or where there is an exchange between roles. In our business process model examples, we have identified the following resources:

- Enterprise organization (e.g., sales and distribution, marketing department, warehouse employee, etc.)
- System organizational units of ERP (e.g., client, company code, sales area, etc.)
- Information cubes (e.g., purchase order), dimensions (e.g., time, material, unit)
- Business objects of ERP (e.g., SAP purchase order BUS 2012)
- External Web services (Break Even Point)
- Data entities (e.g., customer master file, condition master, customer order)

Data Flow

For the analysis to be sound, data flow needs to be viewed separately from the process flow. A deficiency of BPMN is that it considers just the process flow and does not consider and integrate into a holistic model the separate flows of the business and information objects. Also, BPMN does not recognize that the assignment of business objects or information cubes to process activities may occur and that exposing how, where, and who views static data, information, or data flow is also useful in showing where business data structures are used in the process flow and how they change states.

Process Automation (Application)

Process automation may be supported through a number of means including a specialized BPM engine. To provide a complete solution any tool used to manage processes requires the specification of the process and data flows, together with their association with the above resources.

WHY THE SUBJECT IS IMPORTANT AND THE PROBLEMS AND CHALLENGES IT WILL SOLVE

A major problem for business process professionals is the volatile environment in which they must drive change through the business process improvement life cycle. The volatility of these conditions is highlighted by the fact that "If there is one constant in the market, it is that things are always changing faster and are more dynamic,"[21] thus enforcing the idea that organizations and enterprises are under continuous pressure when optimizing their business processes and thus have to constantly play catch-up with their competitors.

Optimization of business processes most commonly stems from the need to solve three main business problems/strategies:

1. Those that pertain to productivity enhancement
2. Market expansion
3. The creation of new markets[22]

The goal of optimizing business processes can also be one of pure optimization, by reducing time and costs and improving quality within the organization.

The interrelations between these and other strategies or strategic goals are depicted as cause-and-effect chains within balanced scorecards being addressed within the examples of the to-be models.

In a report by the Gartner Group,[23] one of the four usage scenarios driving the purchase of BPM Suites was the "Support for a continuous process improvement program," which highlights recognition of the need to optimize business processes. This change is important to enable an enterprise to overlay its application assets with a business-level representation of the end-to-end processes that are then supported by the software assets. This allows the enterprise to see and assess how applications contribute capability and enable the business. The model-driven approach is seen as one of the best ways to enable business and IT professionals to manage and change processes collaboratively to achieve these improvements. Although process-centric models have a critical role in this work, these models must be both complemented by and connected to other applicable information models. Collectively, this approach creates a unified set of models that can provide a complete picture of all phases of the process life cycle. The result is a portfolio of business-oriented models that foster a shared understanding as to how best to pursue business process management objectives.[24]

There has been a significant rate of failure of many BPM projects. The size and cost[25] of these failures expose the correlation between the need for improvement of process and information models and the need for successful completion of the BPM projects. The fact that these models must cross all levels and hierarchies of an organization creates a high level of complexity, with the consequence that many levels of decomposition/composition are required to produce useful and consistent information models,[3] and which therefore can be controlled. Often the reason for failure of the BPM projects lies with the problem that the initial process requirements were not correctly understood, formulated, or communicated throughout the design process.[26] Again, this highlights the need for methods of representation to empower the business process engineer, together with the tools and infrastructure engineers, and other contributors and stakeholders, to achieve greater success.[27]

INFORMATION MODELS WITHIN AS-IS AND TO-BE MODELS

Among the many challenges associated with process modeling, process engineering, and process architecture, questions about how to produce quality as-is and to-be process models are of great concern. The answer to these challenges is not easy because BPM and BPMN do not consider a process in its full context; it is extremely difficult to repeatedly determine the scope, level, and quality standard for processes.

Figure 3 illustrates the architectural layers that are relevant to the analysis, specification, and management of process, e.g., process modeling, as well as relevant to the context of the process architecture. This figure shows the process layer as enabled by the behavior and features of the objects in the application layer, which in turn provides access to the persistent data structure of the data layer. In addition,

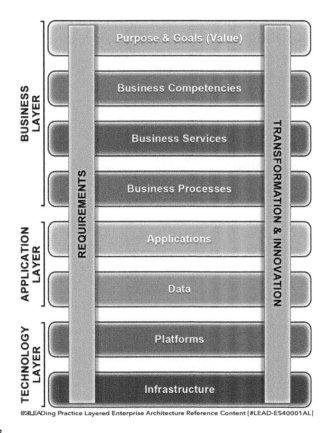

FIGURE 3

Architectural layers.

the figure shows that the need for a process to produce value, and thereby support the enterprise strategy, may only be achieved through the objects within the competency and service layer. It is the services that expose the value of the processes and the competencies that organize, contextualize, and align the processes and services to the enterprise view of value. Enterprise processes and therefore enterprise process models must be designed within and connect to this context and to the relevant objectives that reside in each. By working in this manner, we are exercising the principles behind the objects that ensure that the object of interest, in this case a process, is completely and fully defined. Furthermore, the value in assigning the objects across the layers is that within the layers the various stakeholders who have concerns about the objects view them.

It is important when defining the contextual, conceptual, logical, and physical aspects[28] it relates to a specific way of modeling process aspects of object clustering to define the correct levels of hierarchy. In our example organization, we have assigned four levels, as shown in Figure 4.

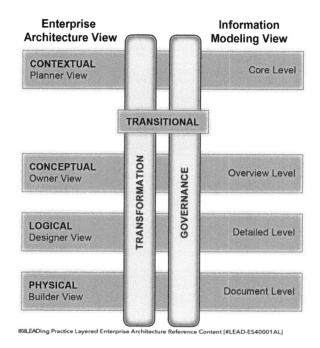

FIGURE 4

Conceptual and logical object clustering hierarchy levels.

The levels and views in Figure 4 should be understood in the following ways [29]:

- Contextual models are the perspective of the planners of the enterprise, and in creating the link between process and information models this is a core level.
- Conceptual models are the perspective of the owners of the enterprise, and in creating the link between process and information models this is the overview level.
- Logical models are the perspective of the designers of the enterprise, and in creating the link between process and information models this is the detailed level.
- Physical models are the perspective of the builders of the enterprise, and in creating the link between process and information models this is document level.

What differentiates the views and levels are not only the details, but in reality the specific models used or developed within them and subsequently different contexts in terms of purpose and goals from the models. The reason this is so important is that the different levels all have different value potential, e.g., purpose and goals, and as a result the different views and levels have their specific transformation potential and governance concept that need to be explored and interlinked throughout the layers (Figure 4). Decomposition and composition happen through the relevant objects across the views and levels and their models, an abstraction that represents and considers the process and information as a whole. As illustrated in

Figure 3, an enterprise should be considered as a whole which subsequently includes the views and models that capture the:

- Business layer, such as the resources, roles, value aspects, enterprise capabilities, functions, and services
- Application layer, representing the automated processes and thereby the application components, application modules, tasks, application services, and data components, data objects, data entities, data tables, and data services
- Technology layer, such as the platform components, platform function, platform devices, and platform services, as well as the infrastructure components, infrastructure functions, infrastructure devices, and infrastructure services

In addition to the views and levels discussed, aspects important for both information modeling and process modeling are the subject of tagging and thereby classification and categorization. Processes, information objects, and services can be tagged according to their strategy, tactics, and operational tiers. Figure 5 illustrates an example of the enterprise tiers and relevant process areas.[30]

As illustrated in Figure 5, the enterprise tiers represent tagging possibilities that link the processes, goal and objective view, decision making, and system measurement and reporting view. Therefore, classifying the process links to multiple aspects needed in the information models:

- Strategic aspects: This tier affects the entire direction of the firm. An example is the mission, vision, strategic business objectives (SBOs), and specific business performance indicators (BPIs) and business plans. The strategic tier has the long-term, complex decisions made by executives and senior management and the measurement reporting view is used for the most scorecards.
- Tactical aspects: The aspects at this tier are more medium-term, less complex decisions made mostly by middle managers. They follow from strategic decisions and aim to meet the critical success factors. The way to do this is for governance, evaluation, reports, control and monitoring and the measurement reporting view which is used for most dashboards.
- Operational aspects: At this tier day-to-day decisions are made by operational managers and are simple and routine; the measurement reporting view used is for the most cockpits.

As-Is Modeling

The purpose of as-is modeling is to explore and capture how the processes are performed today. This provides a baseline for describing the business.

Determining the Hierarchy Level

The following section describes a suitable procedure for determining the level within the hierarchy that is applicable to the analytical work being performed, the so-called decomposition or composition level of the information objects.[31]

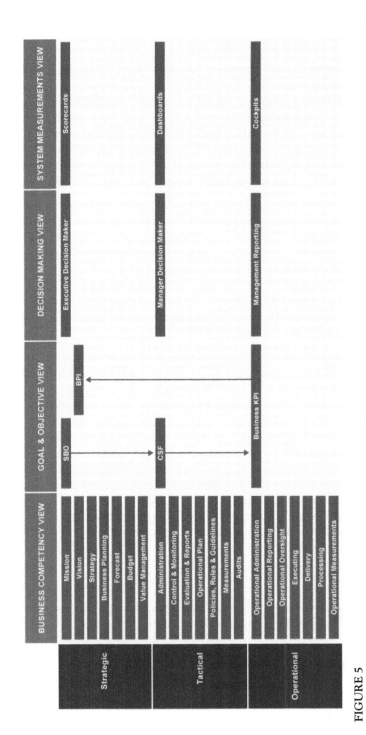

FIGURE 5

Example of enterprise tiers.

Various alternative views exist of the approach to this particular problem. Figure 6 presents the principle variations: the supply chain operations reference model (SCOR)[32] and the American productivity and quality center (APQC).[33] As shown in the figure, each framework attempts to describe and populate the various levels of detail of process with authoritative process inventories. They alternatively provide for four or five levels of process decomposition. On the other hand, the SAP Business Blueprint Solution Manager (in the current version 7.1), which must implement these processes, has support only for three process levels. Unification is therefore not possible without finding another way to approach the problem.

Another related challenge is that when other models are being used, these models must also be consistent with and align with the applicable process model structure. For example, for the models used to describe an enterprise to be unified, it is critical that there be a method to connect horizontally, i.e., within the same level, an information object such as resources (Business Competency layer of Figure 3) to relate in a logical and coherent way with an information object from the process layer, e.g., a process activity.

A possible solution to this problem is to find and establish horizontal and vertical connections between the objects of interest so as to place the various concepts in layered structures to link the leading process layer structure from "above" to all other applicable layers while simultaneously consolidating/integrating them with their respective data layer from "below". Looking at the intersection of the different frameworks in Figure 6, it makes sense for the processes and all other layers to be set initially to three levels with a default going downward, e.g. Level 1–Business Process, Level 2–Business Step, and Level 3–Process Activity (ref. LEAD column in Figure 6). Process activities access data entities (Data layer) on the same level (horizontal navigation), with the result that finally the data table (data layer) appears (vertical navigation) at Level 4, where the associated key (used to establish and identify relations between tables), foreign keys (establish and enforce a link between

Levels of Hierarchy	APQC PCF	LEAD	SAP SolMan	SCOR
	1. Category	Process Area		
	2. Process Group	Process Group		
	3. Process	1. Business Process	1. Szenario	1. Level 1 2. Level 2
	4. Activity	2. Process Step	2. Process	3. Level 3
	5. Task	3. Process Activity	3. Process Step	4. Level 4
		4. Transaction / PPI		

FIGURE 6

Comparison of the different levels of hierarchy of the process layer.

two tables), and descriptive attributes are found. These attributes are then accessed by transactions (process layer) on Level 4, representing a defined (committed) status of data input and output, creating a spine.

Another important factor that indicates the positioning of transactions at Level 4 is that performance indicators (value layer) must use this level to determine the achievement of strategic business objectives. In all other layers, this performance indicator appears on the same Level 4, e.g. Business Compliance, Service Level Agreements, Process Performance, IT Governance.

Meta Information Objects Within Information and Process Modeling

To answer the question of how to model the business and application layer meta objects, we begin by providing two summaries (Figures 7 and 8). In each case, object mapping is based on the use of four business layers (whereby components are distinguished by their contribution to value,[34] competency,[35] service,[36] and process[37]) and two application layers (which classify the components as to whether they are part of application structure[38] and behavior, or data[39]). These are brought together in a matrix. The layers are classified side by side in six columns to set all objects to a coherent set of categories or layers, and then into a hierarchy of levels (Levels 1–4) to distinguish between their areas of contribution.

Looking further, Level 3 contains the data media or data objects representing data entities and dimensions (application layer). The latter connects directly to Level 2 above, together with the information cubes. From the service group (service layer) on Level 2, individual business services connected to business objects on Level 3 can be refined (Figure 7). These in turn are used with the business objects (application layer) to encapsulate process activities and events (process layer) and the data entities (application layer) on the same level (horizontal).

To complete the picture from a business perspective, the organizational structure of the enterprise (competency layer) must now be included in and distributed across the layers. These can be seen in Levels 1–3. The business areas consist of business groups; business roles are thus assigned to both business areas and business groups (competency layer). When more than three levels of enterprise hierarchies exist, it is useful to divide these into the context of three separate process levels. At Level 3 only business roles are used.

The so-called (by SAP) system organizational unit structure of the ERP application (application layer) should be modeled on the similar-sounding but different internal departmental structure. In contrast to the organizational structure for employees in the enterprise, this structure contains the mapping of external customers and suppliers, services, stock flow, cash inflows/outputs, etc., with a process activity. The system organizational units also constitute a hierarchy of several levels. A process activity on Level 3 of the process layer can access any level in the hierarchy of the system organization. All SAP Solution Manager "compatible" information objects are highlighted blue in Figure 7.

Information Meta Objects Mapping

Layer	Business Layer				Application Layer (ERP, BI, InMemory, Mobile, SOA)	
Level of Decomp.	Value	Competency	Service	Process (BPMN)	Application	Data
1	Vision					Information Object
1	Mission					Information Object
1	Strategy					Information Object
1	Goal					Information Object
1		Business Area	Service Area	Business Process	Application Module	Information Object
1		Organizational unit		Pool	Organizational Unit	Information Object
2	Strategy					Information Object
2	Goal					Information Object
2		Business Group	Service Group	Process Step/Sub Process	Application Module	Information Object
2		Organizational unit		Lane	Organizational Unit	Information Object
2		Revenue/CostFlow		Revenue/CostFlow		Information Object
2		Information Cube		Lane	Information Cube	Information Object
2				Service Group(Flow)		Information Object
3	Strategy					
3	Goal					
3	Objective					Information Object
3		Business Object	Business Service	Process Activity	Application Function / Business Object	Information Object
3				Screen	Transaction Code	Information Object
3				Lane	System Organizational Unit	Data Entity
3				Events	Business Object	Data Entity
3				Lane	Business Object	Data Entity
3				Lane	Dimension	Data Entity
3				Data Object	Data Entity	Data Media
3		Business Roles	Services Roles	Lane	Data Object	Data Entity
3		Business Rules	Service Rules	Process Rules	Application Rules	Data Rules
3					Application Rules	
4	Performance Indicator	Business Compliance	Service Level Agreement (SLA)	Process Performance Indicator (PPI)	IT Governance / System Measurements	Fact Table
4						Customizing Data Table
4				Transaction	Application Task	Master Data Table
4						Transaction DataTable
4						Key
4						Foreign Key
4						Describing Attributes

FIGURE 7

Mapping meta objects.

Typical decomposition structures of the meta objects are found when navigating vertically downward; correspondingly, the compositions are found when navigating vertically upward. For example, a business area on Level 1 can be aligned horizontally against a business process or an application module, whereas a business area on Level 1 can be refined into a business group on Level 2. A business process consists of process steps or sub-processes. Information meta objects that have a vertical assignment to an underlying level can be aligned to the lower right side to an additional symbol that branches into one of the more appropriate models of the underlying layer shown within Figure 7. Organizational unit (competency layer) may appear in the processes at Level 1 as BPMN pools (process layer) or in the lower hierarchy Level 2 as BPMN lanes. All system organizational units are assigned to Level 3. Their keys and foreign keys such as sales organization are assigned to Level 4.

As the engine that informs, influences, and drives all other behavior, vision, mission, strategy, and goal are assigned to the value layer at Level 1. Because they may be constrained by these larger factors, strategy and goal again appear at Levels 2 and 3. The value layer is not going to be implemented but realized, shown as information objects in the matrix of Figure 7. The same applies to the revenue/cost flow as well as the group services on Level 2 of the competency and service layer. Business services, however, are considered on Level 3, as methods of business objects. Their implementation is completed as a process activity (process layer) or application function (application layer). Finally, process activities may appear as collapsed sub-processes in BPMN diagrams at Level 2.

Information cubes (application layer) exist only on Level 2 to support the field of business intelligence. Information cubes consist of dimensions on Level 3 and fact tables on Level 4 of the data layer. On Level 4, the data layer contains master, transaction, and customizing tables as well as their associated keys, foreign keys, and descriptive attributes. The corresponding attributes feed (horizontally), e.g., the PPI of the process layer or the SLA of the service layer.

Business rules culminate in our example in process or application rules; responsibility for the integrity of the data rules (e.g., entity and referential integrity) lies with the database management system. Service rules will not be considered further in our example.

Level 3 of the process layer contains items that are considered resources, respectively lanes of processes: system organizational units, business objects, dimensions, data entities, and roles. In xBPMN, data objects represent information objects and are interpreted within our example as data media (document) on Level 3 representing data entities at Level 3 or a data table on Level 4.

The information meta objects in fact have many more relationships than previously mentioned within this hierarchy; all relationships are shown in the following models in Figure 8, in which exactly one layer and one level are identified. The respective models represent more than one layer or more than one Level (e.g., hierarchical models) and therefore its information meta objects from Figure 7 can appear multiple times.

Information Models Mapping

Level of Hierarchy	Business Layer — Value	Competency	Service	Process	Application	Application Layer — Data
1	Balanced Scorecard; Objective Diagram	Organizational Chart (Business)	Function Tree	BPMN Process Diagram (Business)	Value Added Chain Diagram; Function Allocation Diagram (level 0); Function Allocation Diagram	
2	Balanced Scorecard; Objective Diagram	Organizational Chart (Business)	Function Tree	BPMN Process Diagram (Business)	Value Added Chain Diagram; Function Allocation Diagram	
3	Balanced Scorecard; Objective Diagram	Organizational Chart (Business); Business Vocabulary; Accounting Model	Function Tree; UML Class Diagram	E-Business Scenario Diagram; BPMN Collaboration Diagram (Business Rules)	eEPC; BPMN Process Diagram (Application); Function Allocation Diagram	Data Warehouse Structure Diagram (Information Cube); Organizational Chart (Application); BPMN Process Diagram (Data); Information Engineering; ERM; Document Flow
4	KPI Allocation Diagram; KPI Allocation Diagram	KPI Allocation Diagram	KPI Allocation Diagram	KPI Allocation Diagram	KPI Allocation Diagram; Screen Diagram (Mobile)	Data Warehouse Structure Diagram (Dimension); Data Warehouse Structure Diagram (Fact Table); Attribute Allocation Diagram

FIGURE 8

Mapping information models.

The balanced scorecard (value layer) for the organization should not only exist on Level 1 but should also be included (cascaded) to Level 2 as departmental balanced scorecards and therefore exist for each individual department (Business Group). On Level 3 we can find an employee balanced scorecard. In addition to the external customer/supplier relationship at Level 1, the related cause-and-effect chains on Level 2 should also depict the internal relationship among all departments (Business Groups). The objective diagram on Level 1 shows an objective hierarchy for each of the four perspectives of the balanced scorecard of the enterprise (Level 1) and its departments (Level 2), whereas Level 2 connects the strategic objectives (goals) of the departments of the balanced scorecard to the corresponding process steps. Via key performance indicator (KPI) allocation diagrams on Levels 3 and 4, the goals are connected to objectives that are later connected to their KPIs.

The organizational structure (competency layer) includes three levels; the corresponding department hierarchy can be mapped into a single organizational chart or broken down into hierarchies over these three levels. The individual departments are identified for reasons of simplification in our example as cost centers. Using the standard accounting model, the individual transactions will be booked according to the rules of accounting on Level 3. The KPI allocation diagram on Level 4 is used to measure business compliance.

Value-added chain diagrams describe Levels 1 and 2 of the application layer (Figure 8). Level 2 can also be represented by either an xBPMN process diagram or an e-business scenario diagram (process layer). On Level 3 both EPC and xBPMN process diagrams are used in the application layer. The connection to the business objects is represented through an UML class diagram (service layer). The KPI allocation diagrams on Level 4 cover the measurement of the service level agreements and process performance indicators (process layer).

The lowest level of the application and data layer (Level 4) covers the screen diagram and the attribute allocation diagram. The requirement and importance of fully integrating mobile workplaces into an organization's business processes is paramount in today's mobile society.[40] The key, foreign key, and attributes that describe the transactions of a screen and documents, and system organizational units are mapped to the attribute allocation diagram. The KPI allocation diagrams map the values of KPI (IT Governance) that have been identified with the fact table.

On Level 3 the data layer contains a document flow diagram, an ERM, and an information engineering model. The data warehouse information cubes are represented as star schema on Level 2, as dimensions on Level 3, and as fact tables on Level 4 of the data layer. One BPMN process diagram (data) specifies and collects the assignments of the data entities (data layer) and one BPMN process diagram (application) the system organizational units (application layer) of the function allocation diagrams, showing the process models in different complementary views for demo company Global Bike inc. (GBI).[41]

EXAMPLE AS-IS MODEL (SALES AND DISTRIBUTION)

Business Process Model and Notation Model

Business process model and notation (BPMN) is a standard for graphical representation of business processes that provides a means for specifying business processes.[42] The objective of BPMN is to support business process management for both technical users and business users.

During the categorization of information models, the information meta objects have an important part in the analytic process, depending on whether the objects are types (like "employee") or instances of types (like "Sales Person 1"). The enterprise information model can be used to depict many different types of organization: for example, for a specific branch of an organization or an entire enterprise (consisting of several organizations), or for only one specific organization. The enterprise information model usually also depicts the actors (subjects) within the organization, including the entire organizational chart (usually with employee name, position, department, etc.), which can be defined either by so-called type or instance level, or sometimes mixed together. In comparison, the enterprise objects (customer, supplier, material, etc.) and services (quotation provision, sales order provision, etc.) are generally assigned only as types to a model. Eventually, during the execution phase of a single business process, only instances of all objects remain. Figure 9 shows an example of a fragment of BPMN diagram in which both types (e.g. "create sales order") and instances of types (e.g. "Sales Person 2") are used.

The BPMN collaboration diagram in Figure 9 records the as-is status of a typical sales and distribution process at Level 3 (process activity). What are expressed and can be seen are the process and the data flows of the data objects and actors involved within the operating organization. The upper black box includes activities of external customers and the exchanged documents (data objects). Both pools are located at the hierarchy Level 1, the departmental three (only "Marketing" is visible in Figure 9) lanes of the GBI on Level 2, and the seven (only three of them are visible in Figure 9) role lanes at Level 3. This allows the process to be assigned on Level 3 and thus go through many hands. The occurrence of various intermediate events wait until the process terminates; until then, numerous data objects flow back and forth between the various process activities.

The data objects flow at Level 3 can be defined by the logical/physical procedures of the organization, which require the fulfillment of certain conditions or an allocation of certain resources. The document flow in Figure 10 shows how individual documents from left to right reference each other; thus, in our example, customer payment, customer invoice, and outbound delivery are all based on a sales order. Documents such as goods issue or customer payment are required to maintain certain business compliance such as the HGB (Handelsgesetzbuch, the German commercial law) or USGAP (United States General Accounting Principles).

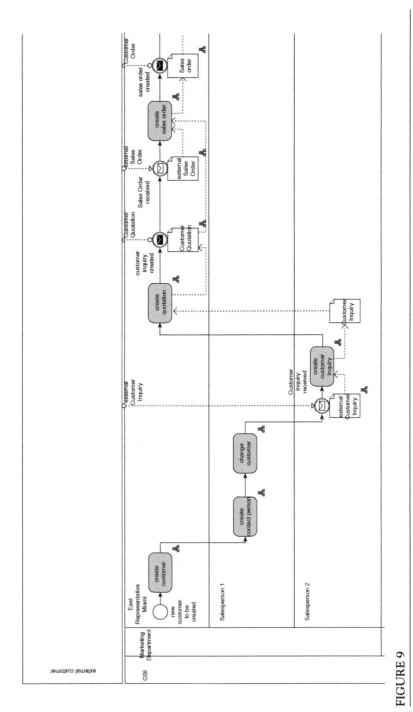

FIGURE 9

Business process model and notation collaboration diagram with process and information flow and organizational lanes (Level 3).

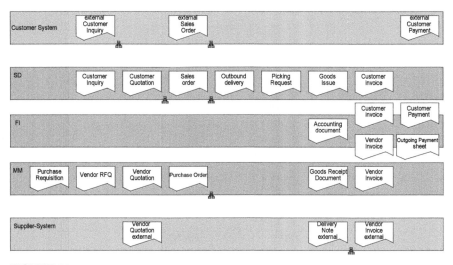

FIGURE 10

SAP document flow (Level 3).

The accounting sales model presented in Figure 11 represents the set of documents from the document with the double book entry activity necessary to execute a complete customer payment. Once the ware leaves the company, there is an effect on the balance, inasmuch as the value of the ware is missing. At the same moment, an account accrues to the customer who requested the material. A goods issue records the decreasing of material in the inventory and discharges the real account in finance. The debtor bill creates an account for the debtor. Then, in-payment bill balances the debtor bill and money gets transferred to the bank account.

Event-driven Process Chain Model

Event-driven Process Chain (EPC) diagrams are another approach to expressing business process work flows.

As shown in Figure 10, for the flows to be truly unified, three different functional areas (data objects systems within SAP) must be integrated: the customer system, sales and distribution (SD), and financial (FI) system; the external sales order should ultimately be stored as a sales order in the SD system. Because the two systems are not physically connected, until this occurs there will be a data discrepancy/media disruption between the two data objects. This is evident on the EPC in Figure 12, which depicts the processing through time from top to bottom. What the model shows is that the data (data object "sales order") of the incoming document "external sales order" must be entered manually by East Representative Miami in the screen mask VA01 Order create. This is shown

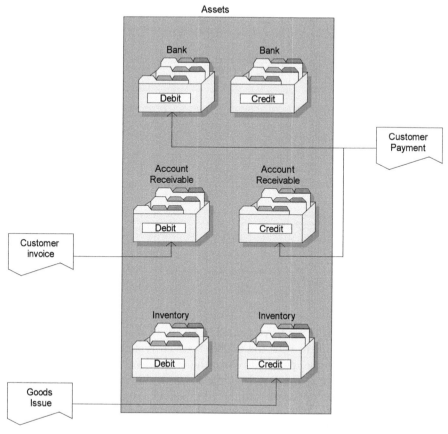

FIGURE 11

Accounting model sales/financial impact (Level 3).

on a more detailed level in Figure 13, where purchase order number is recognized as a foreign key attribute for the hierarchies on Level 4 of the model, thus providing the exact reference to the existing purchase order number of the customer.

The enterprise information models also include its customers and suppliers, such that all attributes on Level 4 refer to a unified data model (a portion of which is presented in Figure 14) on Level 3.

The focus of the BPMN process model in Figure 15 is on a portion of the persistent integration (data read/write) of the recorded sales process with the appropriate master (e.g., customer, material, and condition) and transaction data (e.g., sales order, goods issue, etc.) on Level 3 at the GBI (Level 1) in marketing (Level 2). The data are implemented and nested in Level 3 over overlapping

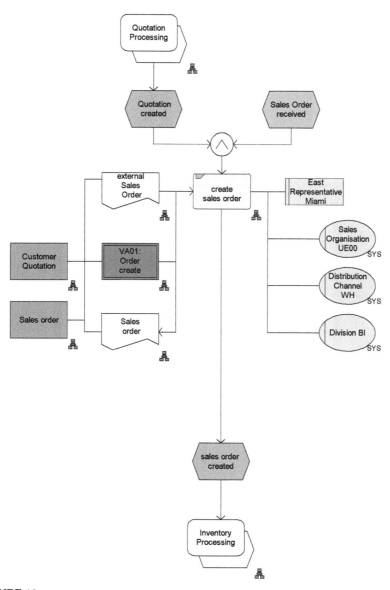

FIGURE 12

Event-driven Process Chain "create customer order" with documents, data entities, SAP screens, position and SAP system organizational units (Level 3).

lanes and are not included in this figure. Figure 15 shows that when a new customer is identified, a business process is performed to assign first the customer master data that are in turn associated with the condition master. The condition master overlaps in the upper part with the material master (not visible in the

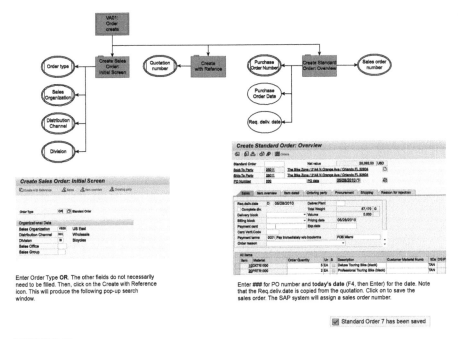

FIGURE 13

SAP screen diagram "VA01 order create" (Level 4).

FIGURE 14

Fragment of entity–relationship (ER) model customer order (Level 3).

figure); therefore, creation of the first transaction data such as customer inquiry also means that material or a combination of materials, customers, and condition master (see overlap) data is generated. Many other transaction data are based on this combination.

Entity–Relationship (ER) Model

The ER model is a method for describing the persistent data or information aspects of a business domain using properties of the data.

The fragment of the ERM associated with the example (Figure 14) shows the dependencies between the customer master data and different transaction data. A sales order leads to at least a (partial) delivery; one or more outbound deliveries

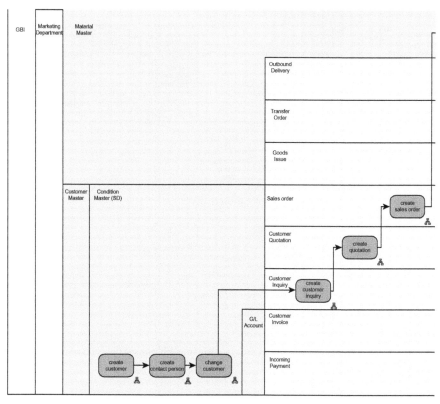

FIGURE 15

Business process management notation process diagram with process flow and data lanes (Level 3).

are created from a single sales order, whereas a (collective) delivery is associated with at least one sales order. The corresponding key or foreign key and descriptive attributes (Level 4) are not visible in this view; however, the input/output attributes (Figure 13) are shown via a 1:1 relationship, with the exception of system organization objects that are defined by customizing data entities.

The BPMN of Figure 16 shows the same process on Level 3 at the GBI (Level 1) in marketing (Level 2), this time as a function of the instances of the organizational units hierarchy of the involved system—which can exist at Level 3—similar to the BPMN collaboration diagram in Figure 15. The system organizational units are shown in Figure 16 as nested but not overlapping lanes (not visible in the example figure), which are all on the same Level 3. The system organizational units covering four extra levels are exposed within their own hierarchy in Figure 16. On the first two levels of this separate hierarchy, the company code

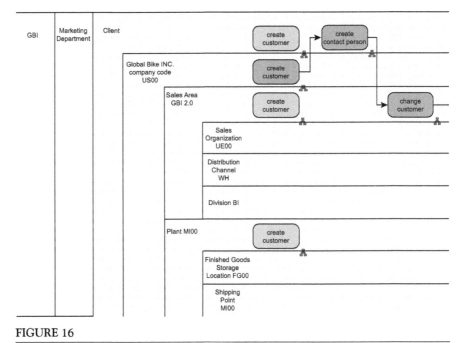

FIGURE 16

Business process management notation process diagram with process flow and system organizational unit lanes (Level 3).

US00 is assigned to the client GBI and consists of the Sales Area GBI 2.0 plus the Plant MI00, etc. A customer can be created as a "general customer (Client)", as a "sales area customer", as a "company code customer "or can be assigned to a delivery plant (plant MI 1000).

To-Be Modeling

Models can be used to describe or capture the current behavior and structure of the business. They can also be used to express possible future ways of doing business, which can then be developed. These to-be models allow decision makers to develop a shared understanding regarding how to do business and to consider design trade-offs, just as one would do with a more tangible product such as a house, a car, a toaster, or an item of clothing.

EXAMPLE OF TO-BE (BPMN) MODEL (MATERIALS MANAGEMENT)

Process automation typically focuses on the to-be status, in this case for materials management. The BPMN collaboration diagram for the purchasing process

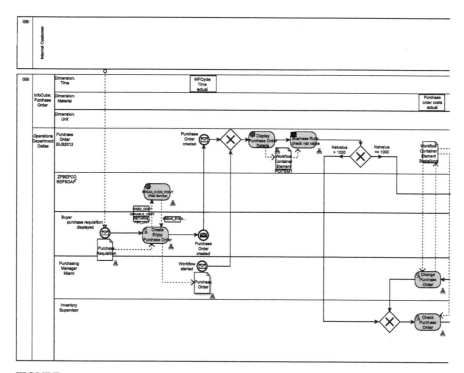

FIGURE 17

Business process management notation collaboration diagram "Purchasing Process" with process and information flow (Level 3).

in Figure 17 includes three pools, above the internal customers (black box, i.e., it not possible to see inside), below the external supplier (which is all expressed as a black box), and in the middle of the purchasing process at Level 3. The left frame for the middle and upper pool depicts the organization GBI at Level 1, which can be found next to the internal customer and the Operations Department Dallas as a lane on Level 2. These use the info cube "Purchase Order" with the three dimensions of time, material, and unit, which are also designated with lanes on Level 3. The buyer, purchasing manager Miami, and inventory supervisor use the SAP Business Object 2012 (Business Order) and the Web service Break Even Point (BEP) (both on Level 3). After displaying a purchase requisition the process is started, e.g., from a mobile work place (terminal), by the buyer. Once the break-even point has been calculated automatically, the buyer generates a purchase order. The consequence of this process is that at a predefined time, an event is automatically generated that starts a business rule, which ultimately forwards a decision to increase the inventory limits to the inventory supervisor. Alternatively, the Purchasing Manager Miami can start the workflow manually. Upon completion of the workflow, both the workflow order cycle time and the number of traversed workflows measured can then be found as PPI on Level 4. The data object flows are displayed, as well as the business documentation together with such values as purchase requisition and purchase order (see SAP Document Flow in Figure 10) technical data object flows such as the so-called workflow container flow.

Unified Modeling Language Model

The UML class diagram (Figure 18) shows a section of the business object BUS 2012 on Level 3. It displays the component together with its attributes and methods: the automated receive activity "Display Purchase Order Details ()", the user task "Change Purchase Order ()", the "Create Enjoy Purchase Order()", and the send task "Display Object ()" used by three different roles and therefore shown in three separate lanes in Figure 17. The attributes of the UML class diagrams are integrated on Level 4 with keys, foreign keys, and attributes.

Note. The UML class diagram needs to be expanded for use in Web and enterprise services.

Star Scheme

The use of the so-called star scheme or star schema is a design strategy to improve access to data for the purpose of generating complex reports. The data structure separates business process data into facts that hold the measurable quantitative data about a business, and dimensions that are foreign keys related to the fact data. This information is held in what is often referred to as a data warehouse or data mart; data are held for the purpose of reporting or analytics, so-called online analytic processing, as opposed to online transaction processing, in which data are optimized for transaction processing.

In the following example, and building on the case example, the information cube Purchase Order presented in Figure 19 is located on Level 2. It contains the three dimensions "Time", "Material" and "Unit" referring to Figure 17.

Information Engineering

Information engineering (IE) is an architectural method for planning, analyzing, designing, and implementing persistent data structures in an enterprise. Its aim is to enable an enterprise to improve the management of its resources, including capital, people, and information systems, to support the achievement of its business vision.

Purchase Order BUS2012
Purchase Order Number
Account Number of Vendor
BAPIMEPOHEADER
BAPIEKKO
BAPIEKPO
BAPIPARA
BAPIMEPOITEM
BAPIMEPOITEM
Display Purchase Order Details()
Create Enjoy Purchase Order ()
Display Object()
Change Purchase Order()

FIGURE 18

UML class diagram for SAP business object BUS 2012 (Level 3).

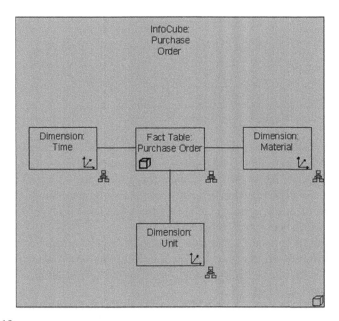

FIGURE 19

Information cube Purchase Order (Level 2).

The IE model (Figure 20) at Level 3 shows how it is possible using an in-memory database at Level 4 to accelerate access to the relevant information cube: for example, sales and distribution data. The customer and product (material master) attributes views, as well as the data foundation, include data entities used by extract–transfer–load of the

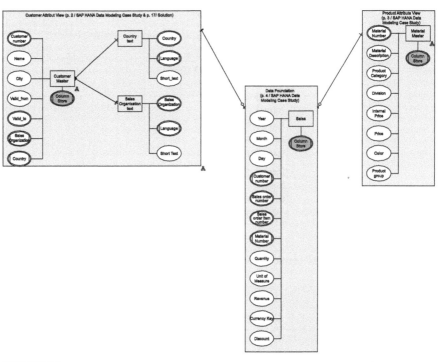

FIGURE 20

SAP High-Performance Analytic Appliance (HANA) data model analytical view (Level 3).

master and transaction data, such as material master or sales from the data warehouse, which are stored subsequently and used via column store in the in-memory database.

Current practice has evolved so that data are now stored separately in two different systems, and evolving strategy is looking toward the future and has everything implemented in one system, whereby the multiple views are combined with one primary key for the customer or material.

The details of how such a fact table (Figure 19) can be organized and its related components are shown in Figure 21. The four PPI pairs—each of as-is (actual) and to-be (plan) status—correspond to the objectives of the four perspectives of a balanced scorecard, e.g., Figure 22.

The objective diagram on Level 2 (Figure 23) shows the breakdown of the strategic objective "improve purchase order process" for the Check Purchase Order process step on the three process dimensions: quality management target, time target, and ABC target (not relevant here). These dimensions are not to be confused with the dimensions of the information cube. Arranging the strategic objective leads into a hierarchy for a KPI allocation diagram (value layer of Figure 8) on Level 3 (not shown for reasons of space), which then leads by another hierarchy to Level 4 and subsequent horizontal navigation to the data layer (Figure 8) branches in the fact table shown (Figure 21).

Level 2 depicts the process step Check Purchase Order, which can also be navigated horizontally into the e-business scenario map (Figure 24). This is shown with

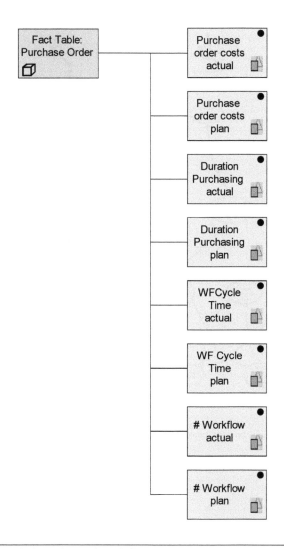

FIGURE 21

Fact table Purchase Order with PPIs (Level 4).

(internal) customers to the right, together with the (internal) suppliers to the left. The process flow extends from top to bottom. Also evident in this diagram is the revenue/cost and business service group flow and the document flow, which are actually a deeper level, at Level 3. This historically grown property is characteristic of the e-business scenario diagram during the document flow from right to left, e.g., from the purchasing department to the external supplier as a purchase order, or from left to right, e.g., from the supplier to the FI department as an external vendor invoice. The net cash flow may show only the (internal) customers toward the (internal) suppliers. In this case, they roughly correspond to the costs of the three pictured internal departments and the difference of the incoming moving/standard price minus the

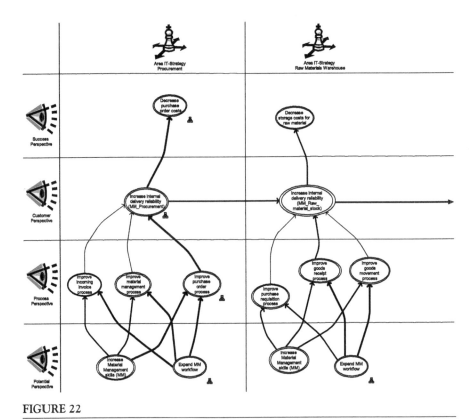

FIGURE 22

Department balanced scorecard cause-and-effect chain procurement (Level 2).

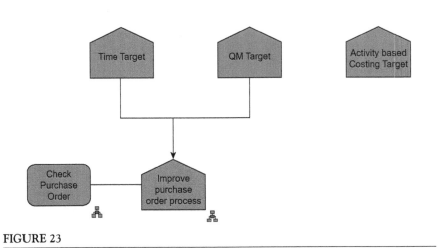

FIGURE 23

Objective diagram of process perspective of purchase department (Level 2).

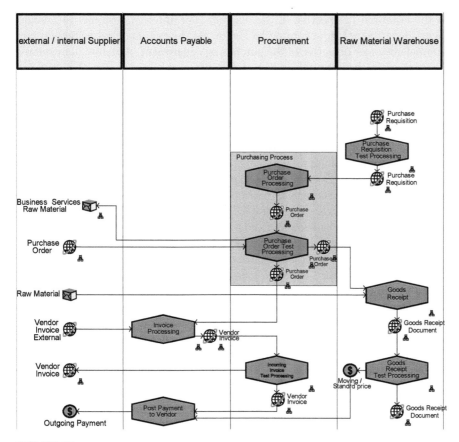

FIGURE 24

e-Business scenario diagram fragment (Level 2).

actually flowing externally outgoing payments. The services that are to be provided in return business services, e.g., to the purchasing department and another internal supplier such as an IT department run counter to the net financial flow. The BPMN shown in the Figure 17 collaboration diagram Purchasing Process (gray shaded) includes both the process Create Purchasing Order referring to RFQ and Check Purchase Order.

Balanced Scorecard Cause-and-Effect Chain

Alternatively, it is possible to navigate horizontally from the objective diagram in Figure 23 via the process objective "Improve Purchase Order Process" into the corresponding department balanced scorecard cause-and-effect chain (Figure 22). In the example considered, the two areas of procurement and raw material warehouse are managed as cost centers. Furthermore, a procure-to-stock scenario is assumed. The strategy is based on an expansion of the existing IT resources (materials management (MM) skills and workflow system), which is also reflected in the Potential Perspective of the diagram. The internal customer of procurement (department) is, according to Figure 24, the raw material warehouse and internal customer objective of the purchasing department, therefore, for example, an increase in the internal delivery reliability as a consequence of its internal customers, so the range of raw material warehouse is all a part of the flow. Ideally, a cost savings to the department occurs and supports the goals of the business in question and its customers, represented by a connecting line from the left to the right cause–effect chain. Another horizontal line connecting to the right emphasizes this point, where the warehouse must support the goals of its internal customer (e.g., production or sales and distribution receiving "finished goods"). Over a two-step hierarchical jump of the strategic objective, the model user vertically navigates to Level 4, where by horizontal navigation, he ultimately gets to the fact table (Figure 21) and can assign one KPI couple (actual/plan) to each of the four perspectives of the balanced scorecard.

In Figure 22 we assumed the internal customer of the finished goods warehouse department, seen as an internal supplier, could possibly be the sales and distribution department as mentioned above. We also found in Figure 24 that for every department, internal suppliers exist. If we have a closer look at the sales and distribution department balanced scorecard in Figure 25, we can see another internal supplier of the sales and distribution department: the human capital management department. Its supplier is the internal/external job market. The characteristics of the internal/external job market finally are its objectives on the potential perspective: increase general education and increase national culture. The cultural aspects might have an important role in the success of BPM in the future.[43]

LESSON LEARNED

As we have highlighted, business process modeling is a key element when aligning business processes with the requirements of an organization. With the right methodology and appropriate artifacts, it is possible to provide a clear, complete, accurate, and actionable framework for information and process modeling.

WHAT WORKED

Business process management notation process models must be complemented by and extended with information models aspects for several reasons:

1. Information modeling aspects within the process are important in any ERP implementation projects, primarily to streamline the execution of the business process and to support all report requirements
2. Reporting requirements can stem from different information aspects in an end-to-end process flow
3. Integration of more information objects of the business world (i.e., mission, vision, strategy, objectives/requirements engineering)
4. Integration of three enterprise tiers (strategic, operational, and tactical)

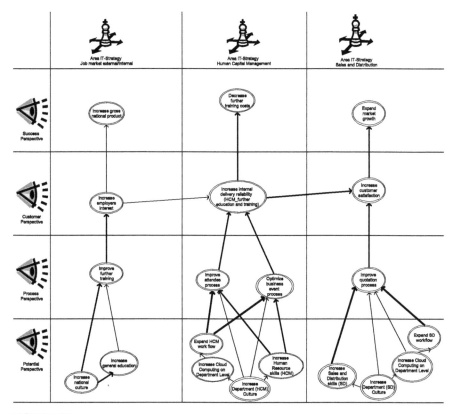

FIGURE 25

Department balanced scorecard cause-and-effect chain Human Capital Management (Level 2).

5. Performance management in an organization can be:
    a. Strategically related—measuring performance against a strategic plan
    b. Tactically related—enabling oversight, governance, evaluation, and audits
    c. Operationally related—measuring operational related activities
6. The information system will also need to be able to respond to strategic, tactical, and operational requirements, and operational requirements simultaneously
7. Different levels of abstraction (from overview to detailed level of composition/decomposition)
8. Identification and cascading of internal customer/supplier relationships (i.e., procurement/warehouse/employee)
9. Integration of dynamic (time dependent) and static information models (i.e., organizational chart, ERM)
10. Identification of more BPMN resources (i.e., system organizational units, business objects, or information cubes)

11. Integration of business compliance (HGB, USGAP)
12. Integration of types and instances (such as process activities versus business department names)
13. Integration of old but content-rich information model types (EPC) with new but content-poor (BPMN) ones
14. The integrated end-to-end flow should take business, application, and technology layered requirements into consideration, thus aligning end-to-end flow process automation potential with requirements across the layers
15. Different views/layers (i.e., business and application)
16. System integration should address all of these stakeholder requirements to ensure that the correct information is available to all areas when business processes execute and afterward.
17. All related objects, in terms of business objects, information objects, and data objects, should be derived automatically in the process.
18. The purpose of the designed and integrated end-to-end flow is to maximize the level of automation by which associated business, information, and data objects in the flow through the information system are derived when a business process is executed
19. Rules are applied within the process as well as information models as traditional rule sets, rule scripts, and flow rule sets
20. Transformation potential is identified in the various process and information models. Exploiting the full innovation as well as transformation potential of the opportunities must consider both process and information models

This extension can only happen within a well-elaborated enterprise information model architecture using four or more levels of composition/decomposition, which can be found in APQC, SCOR, and other frameworks. The challenge is to transfer these levels to layers other than processes, e.g., value, competency, or application. Once this has been defined, horizontal (to get a different view) and vertical navigation (to get a more/less detailed view) between different information model and object types within one single integrated enterprise information model are possible.

This integrated enterprise information model supports the entire process life cycle from Analyze to continous improvement.

WHAT DID NOT WORK

Pure BPMN collaboration or BPMN process diagrams are not sufficient to provide all of the information needed for a successful business process implementation. The integrated enterprise information model does not yet support complete model-driven implementation. With existing BPM tools fewer than 50% of the information models (e.g., with ARIS Netweaver for SAP, SAP Solution Manager,[44] SAP Business Workflow, iGrafx, or SAP BPM) can be implemented. The reason for this deficiency is that existing tools focus on specific tiers, views, levels, model types, or information objects, and have missing or limited interfaces between the different conceptual spaces in which they reside, considering only narrow aspects of the total problem, such as focusing on automation or on transformational work, without fully capturing other forms of work.

CONCLUSIONS
Findings and Summary

In this chapter, we have elaborated on the need to interlink the process models with information model aspects and have shown how it would be done. To increase the level of understanding we have provided a comparison of the different hierarchies for the process layer. We have demonstrated how it is possible to align the different levels against each other for a number of different frameworks: APQC PCF, LEAD/ GBI, SAP Solution Manager, and SCOR (Figure 6).

Through our analysis we identified the problem of determining when using multiple information models whether it is possible to map the layers from one information model to another, e.g., LEAD to SAP solution manager, and retain a consistent process model structure. As a solution, we proposed the idea of making horizontal (layers) or vertical (levels) connections of the leading process layer structure from "above" to all the other layers, with simultaneous consolidation/integration with the data layer from "below".

The result of this solution is the matrix (Figure 7) showing how we can map business and application layer meta objects over four business layers and two application layers, whereby the layers are classified side-by-side in six columns. This allows us to detail the relationship of meta information objects to each other in different layers (horizontal integration) on different levels (vertical integration). Moreover, the meta information objects are associated with each of one or more of the specific layers (1–6) and one or more of the specific hierarchy levels (Levels 1–4), thus allowing for horizontal or vertical navigation in the matrix for each of the information meta objects.

In reality, the information meta objects have many more relationships than are detailed within the meta object mapping (Figure 7); thus, we have also provided a map of the information models (Figure 8) in which exactly one layer and one level are identified. The resulting models represent more than one layer or more than one level (e.g., hierarchical models), and therefore the information meta objects from Figure 7 can appear multiple times.

We have then taken our mapping matrices and, using a case study as detailed in Section "Process life cycle", provided validation of how they can be effective in producing business and application information models. The case study and examples detailed identify how it is possible, using our matrices and methods identified by the LEADing Practice together with a range of different modeling techniques (BSC, BPMN,[45] EPC, UML, and ER modeling), to produce useful as-is and to-be process models.

The business and application information models that we have provided detail the following:

- Integration of document flows (Figure 10) required for compliance and adherence to regulations
- Integration of user interfaces (Figure 13)
- Integration of system organizational units (second organization) (Figure 12)

- Integration of keys, foreign keys (media break), and describing attributes
- Integration of BI (three tiers), information cubes (Figure 19), dimensions, and fact tables (Figure 21)
- In-memory (SAP HANA) analytical view (Figure 20)
- Integration of enterprise services and Web services (Figure 24)
- Enterprise and department balanced scorecard cause-and-effect chains (Figures 22 and 25)

These process models identify how using meta object (Figure 7) and information models (Figure 8), matrices, and the initial ideas of the LEADing Practice have improved the quality of the process models by providing extended information modeling. Thus, we have been able to identify:

- Visible connection of strategic objectives and business processes
- Internal customer supplier relationship interfaces to other departments (flow of money, services)
- Integration of three process dimensions (quality, time, and costs)
- Integration of process and data flow

Our models demonstrate how it is possible to integrate six layers (20 model types and 38 information objects) (Figures 7 and 8) and provide information models that also show how composition/decomposition can provide relevant information over four levels of six layers showing both vertical and horizontal integration/navigation. To date, the authors are not aware of another solution using such a step-by-step repeatable description that enables one to build the information models into the process landscape with a high level of detail in as-is and to-be process models.

Finally, our matrix and working examples use the definition of the process life cycle and frameworks as described in the BPM Life Cycle chapter. It can also be found as enterprise standards[46] that are flexible, agile, and highly customizable. A further benefit in using the LEADing Practice standards is that they interlink to other frameworks, methods, and approaches such as TOGAF, Zachman, FEAF, ITIL, Prince2, COBIT, DNEAF, and many others,[47] and thus provide a powerful integrated BPM framework and enterprise architecture framework.[48]

End Notes

1. Hommes B and Van Reijswoud V, "Assessing The Quality of Business Process Modelling Techniques." in *Proceedings of the 33rd Annual Hawaii International Conference on System Sciences* 1, (IEEE, 2000), 10.
2. Bosilj-Vukšić V and Ivandić-Vidović D, "Business process change using ARIS: The case study of a Croatian insurance company. Management," *Journal of Contemporary Management Issues* 10, (2005): 77–91.
3. LEADing Practice, *The LEADing Practice eXtended BPMN Standard.* Available at: http://www.leadingpractice.com/wp-content/uploads/2013/10/LEADing-Practice-XBPMN.pdf, accessed October 14, 2014.
4. Scheruhn H, Ackermann D, Braun R, and Förster U, "Repository-based implementation of Enterprise Tiers: A study based on an ERP case study," in *Human-Computer Interaction. Users and Contexts of Use*, (Springer, 2013), 446–455.

5. Verner L, "The Challenge of Process Discovery," *BPM Trends*, (BPTrends, May, 2004). Available from: www.bptrends.com.

6. Rosenberg A, von Rosing M, Chase G, Omar R et al., *Applying Real-World BPM in an SAP Environment*, (Galileo Press, 2011).

7. Ko R. K, "A Computer Scientist's Introductory Guide to Business Process Management (BPM)," *Crossroads, the ACM student magazine* 15, no. 4 (2009): 4.

8. von Rosing M, Subbarao R, Hove M, and Preston T. W, "Combining BPM and EA in complex IT projects: (A business architecture discipline)." *Commerce and Enterprise Computing (CEC), 13th IEEE Conference on Commerce and Enterprise Computing*, (IEEE, 2011), 271–278.

9. von Rosing M, "Crash Course with the LEAD Frameworks," *Methods and Approaches.* Available at: http://www.leadingpractice.com/wp-content/uploads/2013/10/Crash-Course-to-LEAD-3.0.pdf, accessed May 20, 2014.

10. LEADing Practice, *Welcome to LEADing Practice.* Available at: http://www.leadingpractice.com/, accessed May 21, 2014.

11. Weilkiens T, Weiss C, and Grass A, *OCEB Certification Guide: Business Process Management-Fundamental Level*, (Elsevier, 2011).

12. LEADing Practice, *Decomposition & Composition Reference Content.* Available at: http://www.leadingpractice.com/enterprise-standards/enterprise-engineering/decomposition-composition/, accessed May 21, 2014.

13. Weilkiens op. cit.

14. Hommes B and Van Reijswoud V, "Assessing the quality of business process modelling techniques," *Proceedings of the 33rd Annual Hawaii International Conference on System Sciences* 1, (IEEE, 2000), 10.

15. LEADing Practice, *The LEADing Practice eXtended BPMN Standard.* Available at: http://www.leadingpractice.com/wp-content/uploads/2013/10/LEADing-Practice-XBPMN.pdf, accessed May 14, 2014.

16. http://www.leadingpractice.com/enterprise-standards/enterprise-engineering/decomposition-composition/, accessed May 21, 2014.

17. The Representation of the Business Process Captured in the Model is Implemented Directly from the Properties and Relationships of the Components Portrayed in the Model.

18. Verner L. op. cit.

19. BPM, "The Promise and the Challenge", Laury Verner, 2004.

20. Mertens P, Bodendorf F, König W, Picot A et al., *Grundzüge Der Wirtschaftsinformatik* (Springer, 2005).

21. von Rosing M, Subbarao R, Hove M, and Preston T. W, "Combining BPM and EA in complex IT projects: (A business architecture discipline)," *Commerce and Enterprise Computing (CEC), 13th IEEE Conference on Commerce and Enterprise Computing*, (IEEE, 2011), 271–278.

22. van Rensburg A, "Principles for modelling business processes," *Industrial Engineering and Engineering Management (IEEM)*, (IEEE, 2011), 1710–1714.

23. Sinur J and Hill J.B, "Magic quadrant for business process management suites," *Gartner RAS Core research note*, (Gartner, 2010), 1–24.

24. Fallon RL and Polovina S, "REA analysis of SAP HCM; some initial findings," *Dresden, Germany: ICFCA 2013: 11th International Conference on Formal Concept Analysis*, 2013.

25. Ko R. K, "A computer scientist's introductory guide to business process management (BPM)," *Crossroads, the ACM student magazine* 15, no. 4 (2009).

26. Karagiannis D and Kühn H, "Metamodelling platforms," *Proceedings of the Third International Conference EC-Web*, (Berlin, Heidelberg: Springer-Verlag, 2002),182.

27. van Rensburg A, "Principles for modelling business processes," *Industrial Engineering and Engineering Management (IEEM)*, (IEEE, 2011), 1710–1714.

28. John A. Zachman, Henrik von Scheel, and Mark von Rosing, "The focus of Enterprise Architecture," *The Complete Business Process Handbook*, (Morgan Kaufman, 2014).

29. John A. Zachman, Henrik von Scheel, Mark von Rosing. "The focus of Enterprise Architecture," *The Complete Business Process Handbook 2*, (Morgan Kaufman, 2014).

30. LEADing Practice—Categorization & Classification Body of Knowledge, 2014.

31. LEADing Practice, *Decomposition & Composition Reference Content*. Available at: http://www.leadingpractice.com/enterprise-standards/enterprise-engineering/decomposition-composition/, accessed May 21, 2014.

32. https://supply-chain.org/f/SCOR-Overview-Web.pdf.

33. http://www.apqc.org/.

34. Business Objects that Capture the Scope and Value of the Business.

35. Business Objects that Capture and Describe the Essential Organizations Skill And Knowledge Needed to Fulfil the Scope And Purpose of the Business.

36. Business Objects that Realize Behaviour.

37. Business Objects Necessary to Execute Work and Create Value.

38. Business Objects Necessary to Describe the Structure and Behaviour of Software that Enables Work.

39. Business Objects Necessary to Describe the Persistent Information Used within the Software.

40. Gumpp A and Pousttchi K, "The 'Mobility-M'-framework for application of mobile technology in business processes." *INFORMATIK 2005-Informatik LIVE—Jahrestagung der Gesellschaft für Informatik e V (GI) 2*, 2005, 523–527.

41. Scheruhn H, Sicorello S, Weidner S, Repository-based ERP case studies: A study about chances and benefits of agile case study development in Witold Abramowicz, John Domingue, Krzysztof Wecel (Eds.): *Business Information Systems Workshops—BIS 2012 International Workshops and Future Internet Symposium, Vilnius, Lithuania, May 21–23, 2012 Revised Papers*. Springer 2012.

42. http://www.bpmn.org/.

43. Zhao F, Scheruhn H and von Rosing M, "The Impact of Culture Differences on Cloud Computing Adoption" In: *Human-Computer Interaction*, (Springer 2014), 776–785.

44. Scheruhn H, Ackermann D, Braun R and Förster U, "Repository-based implementation of Enterprise Tiers: A study based on an ERP case study," In: *Human-Computer Interaction. Users and Contexts of Use*, (Springer, 2013), 446–455.

45. LEADing Practice, *The LEADing Practice eXtended BPMN Standard*. Available at: http://www.leadingpractice.com/wp-content/uploads/2013/10/LEADing-Practice-XBPMN.pdf, accessed May 14, 2014.

46. APQC and von Rosing M, "Crash Course with the LEAD Frameworks," *Methods and Approaches*. Available at: http://www.leadingpractice.com/wp-content/uploads/2013/10/Crash-Course-to-LEAD-3.0.pdf, accessed May 20, 2014.

47. LEADing Practice. *Interconnects with Existing Frameworks*. Available at: http://www.leadingpractice.com/about-us/interconnects-with-main-existing-frameworks/, accessed May 26, 2014.

48. LEADing Practice. *Welcome to LEADing Practice*. Available at: http://www.leadingpractice.com/, accessed May 21, 2014.

The BPM Way of Implementation and Governance

Mark von Rosing, Henrik von Scheel, August-Wilhelm Scheer

INTRODUCTION

Most process initiatives today include some sort of business process automation, whereas implementation and governing of complex processes in this complex setting can be a daunting thing.

The reality is that 72% of process automation (IT) projects fail to deliver on time, on budget, or on value.[1] Most IT projects fail during the implementation/deployment phase.[2] Research indicates that only 25% of failed process automation (IT) projects occur because of unsolvable technical issues, whereas 75% of all failures are due to a complex mixture of problems including missing process leadership, missing employee process skills, bad communication and so on. This clearly suggests at least part of the gap is between the "as-is" process landscape, the "to-be" process design, and the actual business transformation sought in and through the process implementation.

In Part V, we focus on the "Way of Implementing" and "Way of Governing", spanning from agile way from process design, to process implementation, BPM change management, process outsourcing, holistic process governance, project, program, portfolio, and BPM Governance as well as BPM Alignment.

We will outline the "Way of Implementing" or the approach, you, the practitioner, follow to apply the way of working and modeling into the physical and thereby the process execution and concrete relevant aspects. In the "Way of Governing," we outline the approach the practitioner follows to steer and govern what exists. It consists both of a holistic BPM Governance approach as well as a separate governance process that spans across the BPM Life Cycle, for example, process analysis, process design, process implementation, and run, monitor, and optimize the existing process.

End Notes

1. The Standish Group, CHAOS (2009)
2. Trad, Antoine; Kalpi, Damir & Trad, Hiam, The Selection and Training Framework for Managers in Business Innovation Transformation Projects, (June 2013)

Applying Agile Principles to BPM

Mark von Rosing, Joshua von Scheel, Asif Qumer Gill

INTRODUCTION

The term "Agile" has attracted significant attention across industry and academia.[1] Agile is not new. The history of agile concepts can be traced back to the 1930s. It has its foundation in iterative and incremental approaches. Many ways exist in which agile concepts can be applied across various disciplines and industry verticals, such as agile software development, agile project management, agile supply chain, agile manufacturing, agile service management, agile enterprise, and the list goes on. Similarly, agile concepts can also be applied to business process management (BPM) planning, analysis, architecture, design, implementation, operation, monitoring, and improvement. However, before jumping on the bandwagon of Agile BPM, it is important to understand what is meant by "Agile." What are the building blocks or principles underlying agile? What does it mean to use agile principles? What is the difference between agile and traditional non-agile ways of working? Why do we need to be agile? How is an Agile BPM capability established? The purpose of this chapter is to provide the precise and practical answers to these fundamental questions. This chapter is organized as follows. Firstly, it describes the agile thinking and its origin. Secondly, it describes the agile characteristics, values and principles. Thirdly, it describes the agile practices or ways of working. Fourthly, it describes the difference between the agile and traditional ways of working. Fifthly, it describes the application of agile ways of working to BPM and defines the Agile BPM. Sixthly, it discusses how to establish an Agile BPM capability by using the agility adoption and improvement model. Finally, it concludes the chapter with key take away points.

WHAT IS AGILE?

Although the basic "agile" term comes from the Latin word *agilis* and means to drive, do, and see. The basic meaning of agile is to move quickly, lightly, and easily. In the 1930s, the automobile industry introduced the first agile concepts through the introduction of optimization concepts and work splitting. Further, agile concepts have been applied within the lean manufacturing/lean consumption paradigms. With Agile's growing popularity, other industry segments started realizing that agile principles are not limited to any specific industry segment or functional group. Most relevant to this discussion, over the past decade the software industry has successfully adopted agile principles, and Agile has become a popular software project and product development methodology. Agile methods and practices can be traced back to the incremental software development methods as far back as 1957[2] before falling out of favor for the heavyweight waterfall method. More recently, the agile movement began to come back when, in 1974, a paper by E. A. Edmonds introduced an adaptive software development process.[3] Concurrently and independently, the same methods were developed and deployed by the New York Telephone Company's Systems Development Center under the direction of Dan Gielan. Also in the early 1970s, the concepts of Evolutionary Project Management (EPM), which has evolved into Competitive Engineering, got their start. These were followed with the so-called lightweight agile software development methods, which evolved in the mid-1990s as the carminative reaction against the waterfall-oriented methods, which were characterized by their critics as being heavily regulated, regimented, and micromanaged, and having overly incremental approaches to development. Proponents of these newer, lightweight agile methods contend that they are returning to development practices, which were present early in the history of software development.[4] Compared to traditional software engineering, agile development is mainly targeted at complex systems and projects with dynamic, "undeterministic", and nonlinear characteristics, in which accurate estimates, stable plans, and predictions are often hard to get in early stages, and big upfront designs and arrangements will probably cause a lot of waste, that is, not economically sound. These basic arguments and precious industry experiences learned from years of successes and failures have helped shape agile's flavor of adaptive, iterative, and evolutionary development.[5]

Early implementations of agile methods include Rational Unified Process (1994), Scrum (1995), Crystal Clear, Extreme Programing (1996), Adaptive Software Development, Feature Driven Development (1997), and Dynamic Systems Development Method (DSDM) (1995). After the Agile Manifesto[6] was published in 2001,[7] these have since been referred to collectively as "agile methodologies."

Although Agile is now being applied and discussed around software development, the core of Agile is also about the ability to structure organizations in such a way that they can embrace change and adapt quickly to service the customers in their ever-changing needs. However, taking a big-bang approach to Agile is not really a viable option for many organizations, as most successful adoptions of Agile are tailored to the strengths and limitations of the specific organization.

Like any other change, Agile adoption is not always welcomed right away and faces resistance. Organizations observe many types of frictions that reduce the momentum during Agile implementation. These frictions absorb energy because of the resistance at various levels. Friction is not a fundamental force but occurs because of the turbulence caused by the change. Three main types of frictions apply to the strategy linkage, organization, processes, and technical agility. In this way, Agile is referred to as a mindset, change, flexibility, nonfunctional requirement (link to strategy and goals), culture, and the ways of working, approach, or philosophy. This section discusses the basic definition of agility and introduces the agile features—the characteristics, values, principles, and practices of which Agile is composed.

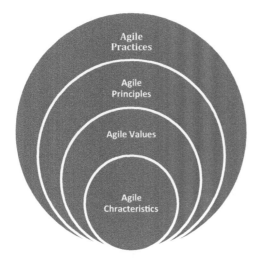

FIGURE 1

What is agile?

Figure 1 shows the conceptual relationship between agile features. At the core, and by far the most critical to the nature of Agile, are its characteristics; slightly less important are the values that are employed when Agile is practiced. This is followed by the agile principles that guide how Agile is applied, and then finally are the agile practices that form the basis for work within an agile setting.

Qumer and Henderson-Sellers (2008) provide the following precise definitions of agility and agile methods:

"Agility is a persistent behavior or ability of a sensitive entity that exhibits flexibility to accommodate expected or unexpected changes rapidly, follows the shortest time span, uses economical, simple and quality instruments in a dynamic environment, and applies updated prior knowledge and experience to learn from the internal and external environment."[8]

"A software development method is said to be an agile software development method when a method is people focused, communications oriented, flexible (ready to adapt to expected or unexpected change at any time), speedy (encourages rapid and iterative development of the product in small releases), lean (focuses on shortening time frame and cost and on improved quality), responsive (reacts appropriately to expected and unexpected changes), and learning (focuses on improvement during and after product development)."[9]

AGILE CHARACTERISTICS

The agility definition highlighted the five fundamental agile characteristics: responsiveness, flexibility, speed, leanness, and learning. These five characteristics can be used to describe and measure the agility of an object or entity.

- *Responsiveness*: is the ability of an object or entity to scan and sense the external and internal opportunities; and form an appropriate response according to the situation at hand.
- *Flexibility*: is the ability of an object or entity to accommodate expected or unexpected changes.
- *Speed*: is the ability of an object or entity to provide a speedy or quick response to expected or unexpected changes.
- *Leanness*: is the ability of an object or entity to provide a speedy and flexible response with optimal or minimal resources without compromising the quality.
- *Learning*: is the ability of an object or entity to learn through continuously managing and applying up-to-date knowledge and experience.[10]

AGILE VALUES

Similarly, the six agile values provide fundamental statements that describe agile preferences:

1. Individual and interactions over processes and tools
2. Working software over comprehensive documentation
3. Customer collaboration over contract negotiation
4. Responding to change over following a plan
5. Keeping the process agile
6. Keeping the process cost-effective

The agile values one to four were provided by the Agile Manifesto (2001). The fifth agile value "keeping the process agile" was provided by Koch in 2005.[11] The sixth value of "keeping the process cost-effective" was provided by Qumer and Henderson-Sellers.[12]

AGILE PRINCIPLES

Agile Software development is based on 12 guiding principles, which are set out in the Agile Manifesto[13]:

1. Our highest priority is to satisfy the customer through early and continuous delivery of valuable software.
2. Welcome changing requirements, even late in development. Agile processes harness change for the customer's competitive advantage.
3. Deliver working software frequently, from a couple of weeks to a couple of months, with a preference to the shorter timescale.
4. Business people and developers must work together daily throughout the project.
5. Build projects around motivated individuals. Give them the environment and support they need, and trust them to get the job done.

6. The most efficient and effective method of conveying information to and within a development team is face-to-face conversation.
7. Working software is the primary measure of progress.
8. Agile processes promote sustainable development. The sponsors, developers, and users should be able to maintain a constant pace indefinitely.
9. Continuous attention to technical excellence and good design enhances agility.
10. Simplicity—the art of maximizing the amount of work not done—is essential.
11. The best architectures, requirements, and designs emerge from self-organizing teams.
12. At regular intervals, the team reflects on how to become more effective, then tunes and adjusts its behavior accordingly.

As the 12 guiding principles make clear, they are software centric, to apply in the BMP context. We will show later how they can be tailored to apply in a different setting with great effect.

AGILE PRACTICES

A number of agile methods exist (e.g., XP, Scrum, and Lean). These methods provide concrete agile practices that adhere to the agile characteristics, values, and principles. The scope of each of the methods is slightly different from the others. For instance, XP focuses on employing technical software development practices such as Refactoring, "Pair Programming", Automated Testing, Continuous Integration and so on. Scrum focuses on project management practices and the use of "Sprints" to deliver functionality. Generally, agile development is supported by a bundle of concrete practices covering areas that may include the full range of product development from requirements, design, modeling, coding, testing, project management, process, quality, and so on. The result is that we learn two things: first, the differences indicate that no standard single agile method is available, which may be applied or adopted off-the-shelf; and second, the best practices from different agile methods can conceivably be combined to create a situation-specific agile method. What is important to note here is that the key to being agile is to focus on harnessing agile characteristics, values, and principles underlying the specific agile practices.

AGILE VERSUS TRADITIONAL WAYS OF WORKING

Agile and traditional waterfall methods are two distinct ways of developing software. The Waterfall model can essentially be described as a linear model of product delivery. Like its name suggests, waterfall employs a sequential set of processes as subsequently indicated in Figure 2. Development flows sequentially from a start point to the conclusion, the delivery of a working product, with several different stages along the way, typically: requirements, high-level design, detailed implementation,

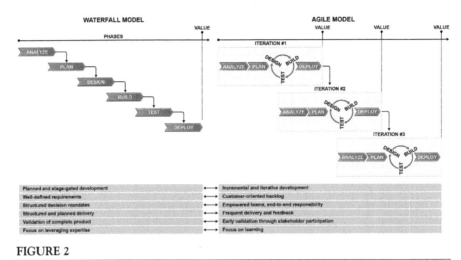

FIGURE 2

Agile versus traditional waterfall.

verification, deployment, and customer validation, often followed with stages to cover the running/maintenance of the product, and to address the need for continuous improvement.

The emphasis of Waterfall is on the project plan and managing all work against the plan. For this reason, a clear plan and a clear vision should exist before beginning any kind of development. Because the Waterfall method requires upfront, extensive planning, it permits the launch of a known feature set, for an understood cost and timeline, which tends to please clients.

Furthermore, Waterfall development processes tend to be more secure because they are so plan oriented. For example, if a designer drops out of the project, it isn't a huge problem, as the Waterfall method requires extensive planning and documentation. A new designer can easily take the old designer's place, seamlessly following the development plan. As described above, Agile offers an incredibly flexible design model, promoting adaptive planning and evolutionary development. Agile might be described as freeform software design. Workers only work on small packages or modules at a time. Customer feedback occurs simultaneously with development, as does software testing and deployment. This has a number of advantages, especially in project environments in which development needs to be able to respond to changes in requirements rapidly and effectively.

By way of comparison, instead of a big-bang waterfall product delivery, Agile focuses on delivering early value or product features in small increments, which is referred to as a minimum viable product or as having minimum marketable features. An agile project is organized into small releases, in which each release has multiple iterations. Within each iteration just enough work is pulled off the stack, planned, analyzed, designed, developed, tested, integrated, and then deployed in the production or a production-like staging environment. During and following the iteration the product is demonstrated to concerned stakeholders for feedback and commitments. Each iteration also involves retrospective activity, which is aimed at identifying and addressing the issues of the agile practices. In each iteration, different developers may work on different modules or requirements (also known as user stories) throughout the development process and then work to integrate all of these modules together into a cohesive piece of working-software release. In summary, this can be seen as a process, which consists of analysis and planning stages, followed by a rapid design, build, and test cycle, all of which then ends with deployment.

Experience with the agile approach has shown that it can be especially beneficial in situations in which it is not possible to define and detail the project requirements, plan, and design upfront. Agile is also an excellent option for experimental circumstances. For example, if you are working with a client whose needs and goals are a bit hazy, it is probably worthwhile to employ the agile method. The client's requirements will likely gradually clarify as the project progresses, and development can easily be adapted to meet these new, evolving requirements. Agile also facilitates interaction and communication—collaboration is more important here than doing design in isolation. Because interaction among different designers and stakeholders is key, it is especially conducive to teamwork-oriented environments.

Figure 2 compares and contrasts key elements of Agile and Waterfall Development. In this figure, we see graphically the life cycle of each development model. Below each type of life cycle are listed the key properties of each method and how they relate to the equivalent properties of the alternative method.

AGILE BPM

Although Agile is not a silver bullet that can be applied to all problems, however, it does provide ways of working that could be suitable to the circumstances in which frequently changing business and customer requirements or other conditions of uncertainty force the organization to pursue quick wins for developing capabilities, services, or systems. As Agile is about making complex things simple or simpler, this section of the chapter will highlight how the agile concepts can be applied to enable BPM in all the various areas and disciplines as defined by Qumer and Henderson-Sellers.[8] We must, however, keep in mind that agility of process is not in and of itself Agile BPM and that to incorporate agility into BPM actually requires a fundamental shift in the strategy, operations, and tactics of the way BPM works and how modeling is carried out in an organization. This section tackles this up-to-date subject in the context of:

1. The benefits and limitations of Agile and how to apply it to BPM
2. An Agile BPM method
3. A firmly defined terminology
4. A concept to develop agile capabilities in the BPM Center of Excellence (CoE).

The Benefits and Limitations of Agile and How to Apply It to BPM

We have seen that Agile offers several benefits (e.g., value to customer, organization, staff, and community) over traditional ways of working. We have seen, for example, that Agile focuses on developing a minimally marketable or viable product or service features, which will provide value to customers and community. In contrast to the traditional waterfall approach, it focuses on delivering value early to customers and community in short increments, which range in duration from anywhere between a few weeks to months. This seems helpful for the organizations and staff seeking to improve time to market and quality while reducing the cost of production and failure. Clearly then, agile ways of working not only help delivering value early, but they also seem appropriate in recognizing the risks and failure early to mitigate their impact.

A part of exploring the potential around Agile BPM also includes understanding the traditional problems and challenges when adapting a new concept. As with so many things, resistance or friction impede adaptation of a new way of thinking and working with agile concepts. For an organization adopting Agile BPM concepts, numerous challenges are possible. However, the most common challenges we have encountered are as follows:

- *Static Friction*: The force that must be overcome before agile concepts can be implemented in a nonagile organization, for example, friction observed before piloting first Agile BPM project.
- *Dynamic Friction*: The force that must be overcome to maintain uniform agile motion and the friction encountered when people don't see immediate results after a new Agile BPM project. It is important for the Agile BPM leader to constantly communicate value of "inspect and adapt." Once the BPM CoE and the organization learn to manage incremental value driven by agile process, dynamic friction starts diminishing by itself.
- *Political Friction*: The force resisting agile progress because of politics that can come from the BPM CoE or the organization itself. A good Agile BPM leader can influence negative politics by persuasive communication in Agile's favor.
- *Knowledge Friction*: The force that must be overcome due to the BPM CoE and the organizational lack of competencies and resources who understand Agile and its precepts, workings, and value. Most organizations use external consultants or hire an Agile BPM specialist to train, coach, and mentor employees so that they gain an agile knowledge base.

Once a solid agile knowledge base is in place in the BPM CoE, this friction will generally start to diminish.

These frictions limit the ability of an organization to maximize the use of Agile BPM in an optimized Way of Working, Modeling, and Governing. Table 1 indicates the typical friction factors across organizational areas.

Friction is not the only challenge organizations will face when moving from traditional BPM to an Agile BPM way of thinking. Other influencing factors cause Agile BPM to fail or to deliver significantly lower value than expected:

- *Innovation is only done from the process perspective*: As it is in the IT world, the current view of Agile is very much defined by the Software/Application

Table 1 *Example of Friction Factors Across Organizational Areas*				
	Static	Political	Dynamic	Knowledge
Organizational	We are unique	Agile BPM versus non agile BPM	Not yet getting value for agile	Waterfall versus agile
Process	Why change?	Change control vs embrace change	Agile process is too fluid	Fear of the unknown, only know BPM water-fall methods
Technical	Where to start?	BPM CoE and pro-cess architecture committee vs community of practice	Not enough resources for process and software auto-mation projects	Resources lack agile compe-tencies.

and underlying technology perspective; this gives rise to a degree of vague-ness of requirements, especially within the business layer. We also see this in the process community, in which they limit business innovation and transformation to what they can see the process can do rather than work-ing in its context. Often this is based on a traditional BPM focus around optimizing the existing processes. However, this view limits Agile BPM concepts from enabling true business agility. The reason is that the current IT Agile methods only have feedback loops between the Plan and Deploy phases for a BPM project, placing an emphasis on the feedback from what is possible in the process and creating a disjointedness loop back to the business: Resulting in Agile BPM teams not having gone through the mul-tiple agile business iterations capturing the value and performance aspects relevant in the Analyze and Plan phase (the Business Layer Context). Therefore, Agile BPM needs a better business requirement loop, which is elaborated on later in this chapter.

- *Multiple changes at once*: Changing both value and performance expecta-tions as well as changing business requires the organization to introduce far too many changes during the iteration's Design, Build, and Test phases. This makes it very difficult for the Agile BPM teams to complete the process analysis, process alignment, process changes, process design, process automa-tion, and so on, in the required 2–4 week sprint cycle. Agile BPM, therefore, needs to build a better requirement and execution approach into the overall approach.
- *Users are not sure of what they can get versus what they want*: Business and process users are not always sure of what they can get from BPM initiatives. As Steve Jobs said, "It's really hard to design products by focus groups. A lot of times people don't know what they want until you show it to them."[14]
- "Having a developer who has a deep understanding of the business is often better than an inexperienced business person with no understanding of how

technology can enable work about "requirements." This also touches upon the challenge we previously discussed in which many process experts limit the business innovation and transformation aspects to what they can see that the process can do. The result is that value derived from the process as well as the execution of the innovation cycle, therefore, for the most part, comes too short and does not deliver the desired result or value.

- *Limited executive sponsorship equals limited agility*: Agility requires sponsorship at the highest level. It requires dedicating top performers and empowering them to challenge the status quo. That is, not just automating the existing siloed approach; executives need to resolve innovation and transformation blockers rapidly and with a focus on the final goal.

- *Agile Focus is operational and not strategic*: Agile teams tend to focus on operational accomplishments and report it to tactical level, however, at the expense of strategic business objectives. In BPM, this is tragic, for missing the big picture can lead to long-term failure at the expense of apparent success in the short term.

- *Agile has too little governance*: Agile teams often lack sufficient checks and balances; if this occurs, they can cause lots of damage in a very short time. Agile BPM must interlink with BPM Governance (see chapter BPM Governance).

- *Giving up on quality*: Because of the high demands or urgency that is placed on process deployment, an Agile BPM team often falls back on the crutch of checking only for process pain points/process defects instead of maintaining a high level of quality of overall BPM changes (see the chapters on BPM Change Management and BPM Governance).

Some of these failure points are indicated in the following Agile figure, which for many organizations represents the current agile method with its failures and problems.

In Figure 3 we see the Agile development method laid out to show the Analyze and Plan stages, followed by the design, build, and test cycle, all of which then ends with the deployment stage with the key criticisms, or weaknesses, mapped to the applicable points in the method.

An Agile BPM Method

To overcome the challenges of the agile method and enable an organization to adapt Agile, BPM must enable strategic alignment and provide the necessary link to performance and value expectations, requirement management, coordination with business impact and changes, better quality, and thereby value creation and realization. For this, we need to augment the traditional agile approach to incorporate a stronger requirement management and an agile feedback loop in the analysis phase. This loop should consider all layers of the enterprise, that is, business, application, and technology, thus allowing the use of these

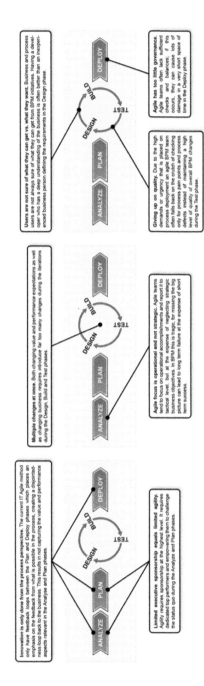

[©LEADing Practice Business Process Reference Content [#LEAD-ES200005BP]

FIGURE 3

Agile weakness point indicators.[15]

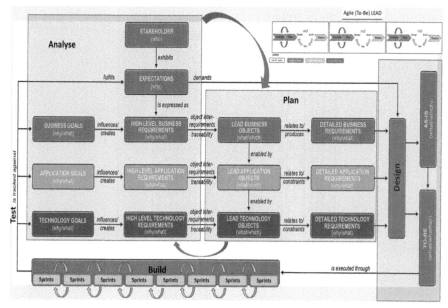

FIGURE 4

Details of agile BPM way of working.[16]

requirements in an Agile Way through the design Build and Test phase and to assess testing against the requirements prior to deployment. This is shown in Figure 4.

Agile Analysis

Agile analysis, in the context of Agile BPM, suggests active collaboration with the stakeholders to identify the requirements with necessary details at the release and iteration levels, instead of trying to get the complete detailed requirements up-front. The key difference (compared to traditional process analysis) is that the Agile BPM focuses on the relevant value and performance drivers and analyses in which and how they can be executed. A process in scope can be identified, modeled, analyzed, and decomposed into subprocesses for the Agile BPM project. Within each subprocess, a set of requirements is documented at high level in terms of process user stories in collaboration with the stakeholder at the beginning of the project. The identified user stories or requirements within each subprocess are estimated and prioritized. The prioritized process requirements are organized into short iterations and releases. A set of high-level process requirements or user stories for a given iteration can be further clarified, detailed, and confirmed (signed off) just before the start of the iteration (Zero Iteration). For instance, user stories planned for any given iteration can be detailed and signed-off beforehand. The detailed signed-off user stories can be made ready (just-in-time documentation) one iteration in advance before the start

Table 2 *Example of an Agile BPM Template Developed in the Analysis and Planning Phase*

Requirement#	Who/Whom Specification For Example, Stakeholder/ Owner	Where Specification For Example, Layer, Objects, Area (Process, Service, Data, Infrastructure, etc.)	What Specification: High-Level Requirements	What Specification: Detailed Requirements
#				
#				
#				
#				
#				
#				

of the process development of those user stories in the next iteration. It is important to note here that high-level user stories should only provide enough details that are necessary for estimation and prioritization, and should not lock in unnecessary low-level details, which may hinder the adaptability of the Agile BPM project.

Agile Planning

Traditional ways of BPM planning focus on the detailed up-front planning. Agile BPM ways of working require planning at project, release, iteration, and day level. Agile BPM focuses on initial high-level project plan that outlines number of project releases, resources, risks, and cost and benefits estimates. Out of the high-level and detailed requirements a project plan is developed to outline when and which requirements can be met throughout as the project progresses in small releases. Table 2 illustrates an example of such a template/artifact, used to relate the captured components relevant in the plan phase aspects that is, Stakeholder/ Process Owner, relevant objects and the high-level (nonfunctional) requirements and detailed (functional) requirements. Such a template typically is in the form of a map, which can start as a simple row, and when information is added produces a catalog of rows. Because a release plan only focuses on the release in hand and the first two or three iterations for that release, such a template has the purpose of building an inventory or index list of the relevant stakeholders, objects, and requirements from the different relevant architectural layers that from the analysis phase can be used and tracked against in the planning phase.

Table 2 is the template of a map that captures requirements in a high-level and detailed form and indicates both who has an interest in the requirement and where within the layers and business objects each requirement resides. This enables the agile practitioner to use the release plan to track the project progress in small iterations. An iteration plan focuses on the iteration that will start next. It provides the detailed information about the time-boxed (2–4 weeks iteration) short-iteration activities and schedule such as additional analysis, the design, the development in the build phase, and the test aspects, and so on, It also includes date and time of iteration, and shows cases and retrospectives. Daily planning in each iteration is achieved via daily stand-up meetings, in which team members discuss what they did yesterday, what will they do today? Are there any impediments? Agile project, release, iteration, and daily planning enable Agile BPM.

Agile Architecture and Design

Agile design for BPM can kick off by reviewing the existing As-Is process model and identified requirements for the target To-Be process model. Instead of a detailed up-front design, a high-level design for the To-Be process can be developed at the start of the project. This high-level design will then emerge with more details in short releases and iterations. Hence, a high-level design can be built on the identified requirements and objects relevant for the target To-Be situation. A high-level design will set the foundation for the Agile BPM project choices and options that enable the detailed design in each iteration (Design Phase-Product Backlog) wanted and specified by the stakeholders within their expectations. It is important to note here that, instead, a target final To-Be process can be achieved via small Transition states. Each project release and iteration should focus on developing a stable Transition state linked to the overall final To-Be state. Once defined, linked to relevant objects and approved To-Be requirements in the execution Build Phase fall under change control. In the Agile BPM way of thinking and working, this means additions to the product backlog will be made if additional requirements are identified in the ongoing Analyze, Plan, and Design Phases. Iteration Build and Testing enable tracking of build completion and quality against the requirements identified in the Analyze phase. This is crucial to ensure that both Backward and Forward Traceability of requirements have been achieved in the preceding phases so that Value generated through the Phases is not lost. This is highlighted in Figure 5 as follows.

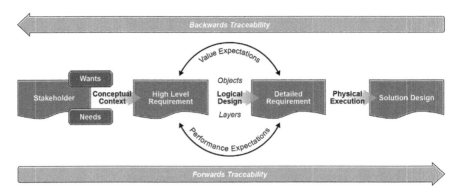

FIGURE 5

Agile BPM backward and forward traceability ensuring value generation.[17]

Agile Build

Traditional ways of working focus on big-bang product or service development in the build phase. Agile ways of working focus on building the product or service minimum marketable or viable features in small iterations based on the just-in-time user stories or requirements. Agile ways of development focus on delivering value early. The focus shifts from documentation to delivering working product or service features right from the beginning. So that Agile BPM initiatives can link strategy, identify value aspects, and focus on the relevant objects, the Agile BPM initiatives in the Build phase use process architecture concepts. There is a misunderstanding that the process architect role and process architecture artifact are not needed in the agile environment. However, various BPM project focused and isolated user stories may overlook the holistic picture of the enterprise architecture and underlying business process and technology assets. To be agile in the build phase, the process user stories need to be connected and classified as described in the Process Architecture chapter.

The impact of the process user stories needs to be considered through the lens of the relevant process architectural categorizations and classifications. Agile process architecture integrated with user stories would not only result in better identification of value, performance, rules, monitoring, organizational change management, risk, and implementation strategy, but it would also provide a shared vision of the enterprise to guide the agile teams working in the distributed Agile BPM development environments. Hence, agile ways of working require process architecture principles. This enables the project architecture, at the beginning of the project, to be linked to the holistic enterprise architecture, and then the details of the architecture will evolve as the BPM project progresses in small iterations. In the specific BPM work, we suggest applying Service-oriented Architecture (SOA) and Process-oriented Architecture (POA) principles. A repeatable process or a part of the process can be developed as a "service". A business process or workflow can be managed through the choreography and orchestration of services. As Qumer and Henderson Sellers[18] point out, the agile service-oriented process is developed in small iterations.

The agile build, test, and deploy phases use the To-Be design identified in the Design phase as the defined Product backlog to work with in the Build phase. The Agile BPM way of thinking and working in these phases uses the standard agile activities:

1. Defining the Product Backlog
2. Sprint Planning Meeting
3. Defining the Sprint Backlog
4. Sprint
5. Interrogating and Testing
6. Demo Release
7. Client Feedback Meeting
8. Retrospective
9. Refactoring
10. System Changes
11. System Testing

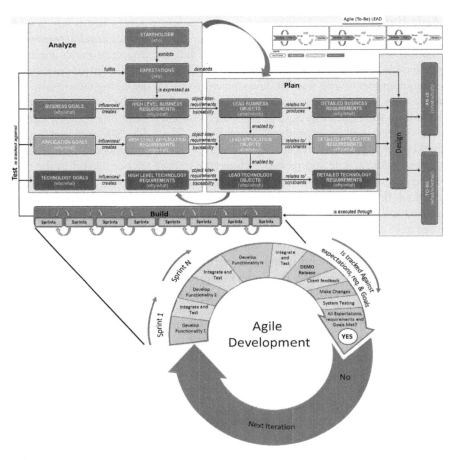

FIGURE 6

The Agile BPM build phase.[19]

12. Decision Point: Are expectations, requirements, and goals of Application and Technology Completed? If YES, then Deploy. If NO, then a new iteration is started.

The build process is presented in context in Figure 6, showing how each set of "build" sprints draws on the design to be executed.

Agile Testing

Although traditional ways of working around testing first do the testing once the whole product or service is developed, agile ways of working focus on testing the product or service minimum marketable or viable features in small iterations while the development is in progress. Agile ways of development focus on automating the testing practices, such as automated unit testing, acceptance testing, integration testing, and so on, Right from the beginning, the focus shifts from testing documentation to actually testing the working product or service features against requirements. This is done not only to ensure that the working product or service meets the customer expectation but also to identify any risks or blockers. In each case, whether within the business, application, or technology layer, the way in which "testing" the requirements is performed is to simulate and compare the As-Is and target behaviors so as to expose possible defects for gaps between that which is desired and what is to be provided. This is achievable as requirements and designs are now addressed through structured models, in which every design object can be traced to its requirement and the various goals it executes. Testing in terms of tracking may occur, not just at the application and technology layers, but within the business layer and within the work system that binds the project choices and options to the specific To-Be solution design that enables the innovation and transformation expressed, for example, demanded by stakeholder expectations. These can also be "tested" against the specific goals that relate to the requirements as well as the full "testing" of solution design into the "work system". This in turn leads to the ability to pragmatically consider design options to fulfill and thereby meet expectations and to verify the quality of the product prior to Deployment.

It is important and now possible to resolve any test-related issues during the relevant iteration. If an issue is not resolved in a given time-boxed iteration, then do not extend the duration of the iteration, rather move the issue to the next iteration, and record and prioritize it on the product or test backlog. A user story related to a product or service feature is considered done when it has passed all the acceptance tests. If a minor issue arises, then it is fine to let the user story pass and fix the issue in the next iteration.

Agile Deployment

The process models, end-to-end flows, and or process changes can be deployed into production either after each iteration or at the end of release. An individual product or service release deployment can be combined with other releases for different products. Organizations may have their own local release cycle. Agile BPM ways of deployment requires tracking the testing and changes. For these reasons, Agile BPM in the deployment phase focuses on collaborative and communication-oriented shared responsibility, accountability, and business value-oriented change and governance. As discussed earlier, as within Agile BPM, the requirements for the product or service features are the responsibility and accountability of the owning stakeholder. Senior management is responsible and accountable for funding, empowering, and supporting the managers. For instance, traditional BPM project governance uses a gated approach to release and monitor the fixed up-front project funding and outcomes. Agile BPM, however, decomposes the project into short releases. Project funding is released based on each successful release of a project. Therefore, agile managers and agile teams are mainly responsible and accountable for the delivery of a valuable quality product or service features to the customer, therefore, in reality, the empowered agile managers, the Agile BPM team, and customer collaborate for the value co-creation. It is important to note that Agile BPM consequently requires empowering the BPM CoE managers and the downstream business managers.

Agile Terminology

Even though agile principles can be applied to Enterprise Architecture, Agile is not an Enterprise Architecture discipline, and hence no direct Objects or Meta Objects apply. However, as shown in the above text, Agile does bring a set of new concepts that are critical to being able to comprehend any discussions on what Agile is, how it works, and how it can be applied within BPM. Having standardized terms provides a structural way of thinking and enables having common terminology in the execution of Agile BPM. It enables the organization of terms around the viewpoints associated with Agile BPM (see chapter What BPM can learn from Enterprise Architecture).

As such, terminology is used with various existing delivery frameworks, methods, and approaches that exist within the BPM CoE and the Project Management Offices (PMO); it is vital when developing such a set of standardized terminology that it be 100% vendor neutral and agnostic from various vendor solutions.

Although the terms are based on a collection of best and leading practices around how to work with Agile BPM within an organization, we do not claim that these terms are all-comprehensive, but rather want to use the terminology that is most common in agile circles and apply to the Agile BPM work (Table 3).

Table 3 *The Most Common Terms that Would Be Used Within Agile BPM*[20]	
Term	Definition
Agile coach	A person responsible for supporting and improving the capability of an organization to deliver in an agile way.
Agile driver and forces (external/internal)	Pressures that arise from outside or inside a system triggering agile approaches.
Backlog	A prioritized list of requirements that are waiting to be worked on.
Bug	An error, flaw, mistake, failure, or fault in the process models, process rules, or process design that produces an incorrect or unexpected result, or causes it to behave in unintended ways.
Burndown chart	A visual representation that shows work remaining over time.
Burnup chart	A visual representation that shows work completed over time.
Business capability	An abstraction that represents the abilities and the quality of being capable, intellectually (logical) and/or physically. Agile enterprise developments must be able to specify the aptitude that may be developed for the enterprise and how it will perform a particular function, process, or service.
Business change	Changes in the way an organization functions brought about through a project or other initiative.
Business resource/actor	A specific person, system or organization internal or external that is part of or affected by the agile development to the enterprise. This can include that the agile development will influence or impact the resource/actor-defined functions and activities.

Table 3 *The Most Common Terms that Would Be Used Within Agile BPM —Cont'd*

Term	Definition
Business service	Agile concepts applied to business concepts will impact the change and development of business services. In terms of the externally visible ("logical") deed, or effort performed to satisfy a need or to fulfil a demand, meaningful to the environment.
Business workflow	A business workflow involved in the agile development, impacting and/or changing the stream, sequence, course, succession, series, progression, as well as order for the movement of information or material from one business function, business service, business activity (worksite) to another.
Continuous integration	When individual process models are combined in, for example, an entire end-to-end process flow and tested as soon as they are produced.
Cross-functional team	A group of people with different skills and expertise working toward a common goal.
Defect trend	A report that shows a rolling average of the number of problems (bugs) the team has opened, resolved, and closed.
Definition of "done"	An increment of a product that is ready for continual use by the end user. Can also be referred to as "done, done."
Deployment	All of the activities that make the process models ready for use and implementation.
Elaborate	When the delivery team adds detail to high-level business requirements.
Function	These are sometimes called epic stories or epics. Functions represent large sets of functionality, for example, Accounts receivable, Accounts payable, month-end close, etc.
Functionality	The behaviors that are specified to achieve.
Information radiator	A large, highly visible display that gives a picture of progress and key issues relating to an area of work.
Iteration	A short time period in which a team is focused on delivering an increment of a product that is useable.
Kanban board	A visual board in which columns represent a state in which a user story can reside, for example, planned, blueprinting, realization, testing, done. Stories are arranged on the Kanban board and moved from one column to another as progress is being made. Many teams build physical Kanban boards by using tape and Post-it notes. Digital Kanban boards are another alternative.
Lean	Techniques to streamline processes and eliminate any activities that do not add value to the user.
Non-functional requirements	Describe how the process models or BPM projects should operate, as opposed to functional requirements that describe how it should behave. Typical examples would be: wished behavior, process security, accessibility, usability, availability, response times, etc.

Continued

Table 3 *The Most Common Terms that Would Be Used Within Agile BPM —Cont'd*

Term	Definition
Owner	The person who is ultimately responsible for prioritization and acceptance of delivered features on a given process or project.
Performance expectations	Although for the most tagged and classified as non-functional requirements, the performance expectations are more as they specify the desire for the manner in which, or the efficiency with which, something reacts or fulfils its intended purpose as anticipated by a specific stakeholder. It will give an input to non-functional requirements, however the performance expectations will also be used in the early validation and thereby be the baseline against performance testing.
Release	Each release is associated with some type of go-live in which a number of processes or BPM projects are moved to roll out/ production. For example, a "big bang" BPM program could have just a single large release. A more phased approach could lead to many releases within a single program.
Release plans	A plan that sets out the order in which user requirements will be released into live service.
Retrospective	A retrospective is a focused session in which your team looks back at how the current agile approach is working and which areas can be improved. Many agile teams conduct retrospectives at set intervals of time (every 8 weeks or at the end of every sprint).
Rework	Components of a project that will need to be revisited to correct bugs or altered to meet new requirements.
Show and tell	When the delivery team demonstrates how the product or service works at the end of each iteration to elicit feedback.
Sprint	A sprint is typically a predetermined period of time (2 weeks, 4 weeks, 6 weeks, etc.) within which a set of identified user stories needs to be complete. Alternatives to sprints are to use a Kanban variation of agile project management methodology.
Stand-up	A short meeting conducted standing up to report progress, share impediments, and make commitments.
Task	We generally try to avoid tracking detailed tasks, but sometimes we need to breakdown a single user story into multiple tasks and assign those to different people. For example, this can be handy for tracking specific process design and development tasks. Each task belongs to one and only one user story. It is the lowest-level entity that we track.
Technical debt	Poor process design in overall process architecture. The consequence of this is that more time is needed later on in the project to resolve process issues
Testing	A set of actions undertaken to assess whether a process or process model behaves as expected.

Table 3 *The Most Common Terms that Would Be Used Within Agile BPM —Cont'd*

Term	Definition
Test coverage	The proportion of a process model that has been assessed.
Time box	A fixed time frame, usually to undertake an intense increment of work
User story	Each user story describes a particular business requirement and is assigned to a single function. In many ways, a user story is the next level down in terms of detail after a function. The standard question approach is followed: "WHO is needed, WHAT we do, WHY we do it". User stories are business-centric, not technology-centric. They do not capture HOW something will be accomplished (that comes later).
Value expectation	Tagging and classifying value expectations as nonfunctional requirements is a part of specifying the anticipated benefits that are of worth, importance, and significance to a specific stakeholder. It will give an input to nonfunctional requirements, however the value expectations will also be used in the customer orientation feedback loop, relating back to the specific stakeholders value expectations.
Value proposition?	A key principle of Agile is its recognition that during a project the customers can change their minds about what they want and need (often -called requirements churn), and that unpredicted challenges cannot be easily addressed in a traditional predictive or planned manner. As such, Agile BPM concepts need to adopt an empirical approach, accepting that the problem cannot be fully understood or defined, focusing instead on maximizing the team's ability to respond to changing value and/or performance expectations and thereby emerging requirements and create specific value proposition to the new need/want.
Velocity	The rate at which a team completes work.

Building Agile Capabilities in the BPM CoE

The establishment of an agile capability in an existing BPM CoE is a challenging task. This is partly because the CoE and teams have a different way of thinking, working, modeling, and implementing. It would, therefore, be appropriate to gradually establish agile capability by introducing agile roles, practices, and tools. One way to do is to use the Agility Adoption and Improvement Model (AAIM). This model (Figure 7) was first developed and published in 2007[21] and then was updated in 2010 as "AAIM Version 2.0".[22] AAIM V2.0 has been developed based on the intensive research in agile adoption at a large scale. The AAIM can be used as a roadmap or guide for agile transformation. Organizations or teams can adopt and improve agile environment to achieve specific agile level(s).

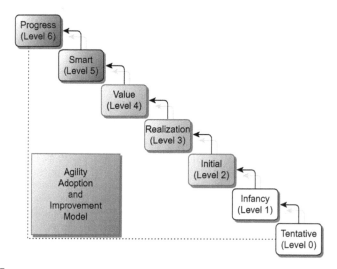

FIGURE 7

The agility adoption and improvement model V2.0.[23]

AGILITY ADOPTION AND IMPROVEMENT MODEL

The AAIM is structured into white, green, and black blocks and six levels (from 0 to level 6—Tentative to Progress). The colors indicate the levels, in which the white blocks are those levels at which initial experience in critical aspects of agility is garnered, whereas the green blocks are the levels at which the agile practices are established and entrenched, and the black blocks show those levels at which agile disciplines become universal. Each agile level has a name and specifies the lean agile principles to follow to achieve the particular level. Continuous improvement is integral to each level. The achieved lean agile level shows the lean agile maturity of an organization or team. The following section discusses the AAIM in the context of Agile BPM capability establishment.

- Tentative (Level 0)
  This level focuses on establishing an experimental environment whereby experience can be gained by BPM teams with some of the agile roles, practices, and tools. Based on this initial experience, BPM teams can communicate the perceived advantages of agile ways of working to the senior management to seek their support to begin with the further systematic establishment of the Agile BPM capability.
- Infancy (Level 1)
  This level focuses on adopting a basic elementary set of agile principles, roles, practices, and tools to support the iterative and incremental test-driven BPM development (evolutionary environment). This level provides the foundation for the further establishment of the Agile BPM capability.

- Initial (Level 2)
  This level focuses on establishing a collaborative BPM environment by adopting agile principles, roles, practices, and tools to support active communication and collaboration among the team members and internal and external shareholders.
- Realization (Level 3)
  This level focuses on establishing a simple result-focused Agile BPM capability by adopting agile principles, roles, practices, and tools to support the production of the executable BPM artifacts with minimal or reduced documentation. This is an advanced agile level, and the teams who are not accustomed to working with less documentation would find it challenging. This level could only be achieved if a well-established communication-oriented culture exists in the organization (e.g., established at level 2).
- Value (Level 4)
  This level focuses on establishing self-organizing BPM teams by adopting agile principles, roles, practices, and tools. Critical here is the fact that self-organization requires working knowledge and experience of Agile.
- Smart (Level 5)
  This level focuses on establishing a knowledge-focused Agile BPM capability by adopting agile principles, roles, practices, and tools to support knowledge management and innovation beyond the scope of an individual Agile BPM project and team.
- Progress (Level 6)
  This level focuses on establishing a continuous improvement by sustaining and continuously improving Agile BPM capability.

Some lessons learned around the Agility Adoption and Improvement journey include the realization that no single agile method or approach is a silver bullet. An organization should not focus too much on mechanically adopting only one agile framework end to end, such as Scrum or XP, but rather should focus on establishing and harvesting an agile mind set, values, principles, thinking, practices, roles, tools, and culture by using some kind of road map or adoption model of progress. The essential lesson is to let agile teams Assess, Tailor, Adopt, and Improve their own agile method suitable to their needs, context, or project, and focus on more "Facilitating and Guiding" teams with appropriate "Reward and Incentive Program" in their agile transformation journey while avoiding the imposition of "Agile" on teams.

CONCLUSION

Traditional BPM ways of working focus on detailed up-front planning, requirements analysis, process analysis, process design, process implementation, and continuous improvement to adjust changes. In other words, traditional takes a waterfall approach to BPM. Here, the assumption is that all the requirements for the process work are fixed, known, or complete. A lot of time and resources are spent up front for achieving this illusion of a fixed or apparently complete list of requirements and plans, without actually delivering a single feature of a working product or service. By the time requirements are completely defined, signed off, and developed, business focus and market competition may have already been changed in response to an always-changing business environment, or changing performance or value expectations. Organizations need to be agile in response to such changing business environments and expectations. We have, therefore, focused in this chapter on the question of why we need to be agile, when, and how Agile BPM could be applied, as well as how to establish an agile capability. Applying the Agile BPM way of thinking and working will ensure that the BPM CoE teams work in a faster way and apply Kaizen principles of continuous improvement directly in their way of working. In that, they learn from what they do and how, Agile adapts and reshapes their manner of delivering the project and involves stakeholders in a new way, for example, as coparticipants in the process.

End Notes

1. Larman Craig., Agile and Iterative Development: A Manager's Guide. Addison-Wesley, (2004) p. 27.
   Ambler Scott., Agile Modeling: Effective Practices for Extreme Programming and the Unified Process. John Wiley & Sons, (12 April 2002) pp. 12.
   Boehm, B. R., Turner. Balancing Agility and Discipline: A Guide for the Perplexed. Boston, MA: Wesley, (2004).
   Sliger, M., Broderick, S., The Software Project Manager's Bridge to Agility. Addison-Wesley, (2008).
   Rakitin, S.R., "Manifesto Elicits Cynicism: Reader's letter to the editor by Steven R. Rakitin", IEEE (2001).
   Geoffrey Wiseman (July 18, 2007). "Do Agile Methods Require Documentation?" InfoQ.
   Abrahamsson, P., Salo, O., Ronkainen, J., & Warsta, J., Agile Software Development Methods: Review and Analysis. VTT Publications, (2002) 478.
   Guide to Agile Practices, the Agile Alliance.
   Aydin, M.N., Harmsen, F., Slooten, K. V., & Stagwee, R. A., An Agile Information Systems Development Method in Use. Turk J Elec Engin, (2004) 12(2), 127–138.
2. Gerald M., Weinberg, As quoted in Larman, Craig; Basili, Victor R. (June 2003). "Iterative and Incremental Development: A Brief History". Computer 36(6): 47–56, doi:10.1109/MC.2003.1204375, ISSN 0018–9162.
3. Edmonds, E.A., "A Process for the Development of Software for Nontechnical Users as an Adaptive System". General Systems, (1974) 19: 215–218.
4. See note 559 above.
5. Larman, C., Agile and Iterative Development: A Manager's Guide. Addison-Wesley, (2004) p. 27. ISBN 978-0-13-111155-4.
6. Agile Manifesto., Manifesto for Agile Software Development, (2001) http://agilemanifesto.org/.
7. Ibid.

8. Qumer, A., & Henderson-Sellers, B., "A framework to support the evaluation, adoption and improvement of agile methods in practice", Journal of Systems and Software, (2008) vol. 81, no. 11, pp. 1899–1919.

9. Ibid.

10. Gill, A.Q., "Towards the Development of an Adaptive Enterprise Service System Model", Americas Conference on Information Systems, Chicago, USA, August 2013 in Americas Conference on Information Systems (AMCIS 2013), Shim, J.P et al., ed., AIS, USA (2013).

11. Koch, A.S., "Agile Software Development: Evaluating the Methods for Your Organization", Artech House, Inc, London (2005), pp. 1–272.

12. Qumer, A., Henderson-Sellers, B. and McBride, T., (2007). Agility Adoption and Improvement Model, EMCIS 2007.

13. Agile Manifesto (2001), Manifesto for Agile Software Development, http://agilemanifesto.org/.

14. Source: Business Week, (May 12 1998).

15. LEADing Practice Business Process Reference Content [#LEAD-ES20005BP].

16. LEADing Practice Agile Reference Content #LEAD-ES30006ES.

17. Ibid.

18. Qumer, A., & Henderson-Sellers, B., "ASOP: an agile service-oriented process", International Conference on Software Methods and Tools, Rome, Italy, November 2007 in New Trends in Software Methodologies, Tools and Techniques. Proceedings of the sixth SoMeT_07, H. Fujita and D. Pisanelli, ed., IOS Press, Amsterdam, The Netherlands, (2007) pp. 83–92.

19. See note 16 above.

20. Taken from the LEADing Practice Agile Reference Content LEAD-ES30006ES.

21. See note 18 above.

22. Qumer, A., A Framework to Assist in the Assessment and Tailoring of Agile Software Development Methods, PhD Thesis, (2010) UTS.

23. Gill, A.Q., Bunker, D., "SaaS Requirements Engineering for Agile Development" in Xiaofeng Wang, N. Ali, I. Ramos, R. Vidgen ed., Agile and Lean Service-Oriented Development: Foundations, Theory, and Practice, IGI, USA, (2013) pp. 64–93.

BPM Change Management

Maria Hove, Marianne Fonseca, Mona von Rosing, Joshua von Scheel,
Dickson Hunja Muhita

INTRODUCTION

In this chapter, we will focus on what Business Process Management (BPM) Change Management is, why it is needed, when it can be applied, and the benefits of applying it. We believe that the principles of BPM Change Management are relevant to any organization, independent of industry, business model, or one's operating model. Change is a challenge faced by all organizations; it not only impacts the strategic aspects, the business models, the employees, and the way an organization utilizes technology. The degree of outside change influences the organization's ability of being able to keep in control the way it works in terms of its activities. When an organization manages the changes befalling the organization, it must also actively manage the change of its business processes. Therefore, in this chapter we will also discuss lessons learned in terms of what works and what does not around BPM Change Management and how the concepts can be developed in the BPM Center of Excellence (CoE), and applied in the BPM Life Cycle method.

LESSONS LEARNED AROUND BPM CHANGE MANAGEMENT

Like many other organizations as well as practitioners working with change management, we make good use of Elisabeth Kübler-Ross's work[1] on stages people go through as they deal with organizational change and transformation. The reason this is important is the phenomenon referred to as "the valley of despair." That, unless tackled rightfully with change management aspects, the organization will suffer, and the benefits wished by the organization will be far less than expected (for further information, read the BPM innovation and transformation chapter). Without a strong change management approach, outcomes can be poor, to say the least (Figure 1).

Many benefits and gains may be obtained by managing change, among them is that it prepares the organization for the "valley of despair" and how the organization can react. There are also Kotter's well-known recommendations for change[2]:

1. Establish a sense of urgency
2. Form a powerful guiding coalition
3. Create a vision

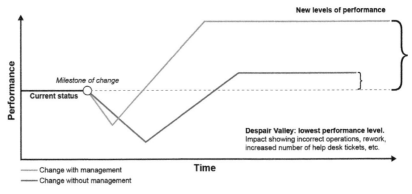

FIGURE 1

The valley of despair based on Elisabeth Kübler-Ross's work around stages of change.[1]

4. Communicate the vision
5. Empower others to act on the vision
6. Plan for and create short-term wins
7. Consolidate improvements and produce more change
8. Institutionalize new approaches

Although this is understood in Organizational Change Management (OCM), this is not really applied the same way to BPM. Although the role of technology, process design, process modeling, and all other factors in the business process management field should not be de-emphasized, this is an intuitively true statement that the major impediment to the successful implementation of a business process change is frequently the poor change management approach adopted.[3]

Therefore, analyzing and understanding the impact of change to the organization must be an integral part of a BPM CoE and the BPM process cycle of continuous improvement. Identifying the process and drawing it in BPM Notations, and then publishing, will not enable change. It can enable standardization, also integration, but not change. As Michael Hammer[4] said in 1993, "Coming up with ideas is the easy part, but getting things done is the tough part. The place where these reforms die is ...down in the trenches. Moreover, who 'owns' the trenches? You and I do, and all the other people working with processes. Change imposed on the 'trench people' will not succeed without being part of the evolution or revolutionary process of change".[5] One needs to consider the change drivers in the various business areas and groups, the organizational competencies impacted, then the flow of the end-to-end business processes—those that span business functions and organizational boundaries. Determine how the change affects discrete business processes as well as how changes in various processes affect related processes and business functions.[6] Some organizations are better than others working with change and adapting it into their BPM work. As Paul Harmon wrote "Process Management and Change Management are tightly coupled".[7]

LESSONS LEARNED OF THE OUTPERFORMERS AND UNDERPERFORMERS

It is generally recommended that an overall change management approach be built, and then link the BPM program of work to the change management tools that the approach has made available.[8] Although these aspects are common knowledge, it is also common knowledge that this is not common practice. In the following we will explore what practices we could learn from leading organizations (outperformers) that know how to go about this, as well as what are bad practices or not the ideal way of working (underperformers in an area).

In the following Table 1 we have listed some differences between the Underperformers' and Outperformers' way of doing BPM Change Management.

Table 1 *List Underperformers' and Outperformers' Ways of Doing BPM Changes*	
Underperformers	**Outperformers**
No formal method or approach for BPM change management. The underlying thought is that BPM models in process notations and process owners publish them to enable change.	Established and documented BPM change management method and approaches.
Capacity (mis)management • Projects often demand huge BPM CoE change capacity and services to deliver. • Change assessment is done by individual project, not integrated to global BPM CoE capacity assessments. • No clear delineation of new and run processes. Roles and responsibilities must be better defined, understood, and tracked for development and change/maintenance.	There is ONE perspective on BPM changes for BPM CoE, including new change and changing to existing, so that only one prioritization process is built into the BPM CoE portfolio management and governance process.
Multiple project owners, change owners. Various process change request documentation. Multiple change management processes and procedures exist today, preventing a proactive/steady state and an integrated, end-to-end change process from requirements to implementation.	Going to integrated, best practices-based BPM CoE change handling, with specific roles and responsibilities, end-to-end processes supported by a single-source of truth.
BPM technology choices is based on: • functional needs • technology requirements • process modeling capabilities Other service organizations involvement not mapped • Current process does not clearly distinguish between BPM CoE services and interlinked business and IT services • Requirement for changes are siloed in various business departments.	BPM technology choices is based on: • business drivers • change enablers Changes scope and governance are defined; entry and exit points are mapped and related coordination, control, and measurements mechanisms are described.

Continued

Table 1 List Underperformers' and Outperformers' Ways of Doing BPM changes—Cont'd	
Enterprise architecture engagement gaps • EA guidelines, parameters, and standards impacting change management are not formalized or integrated into BPM change concepts • Changes identified by the BPM teams are not synchronized with EA teams.	EA change management is formalized, and elements from its various domains affecting BPM change management are integrated throughout the BPM CoE process life cycle.
No standards or interlinks of the various teams and their work around the change concepts, that is, change analysis/strategy, design, creation, deployment, monitoring, and link to continuous improvement.	BPM change management is integrated throughout the process life cycle.

LESSONS LEARNED AROUND BENEFIT AND VALUE REALIZATION

Some of the benefits of doing integrated and standardized BPM Change Management in the BPM CoE among others are:

- Transparency of changes throughout the life cycle—Reducing the number of unauthorized changes, leading to fewer BPM CoE service disruptions, and reduced change-related incidents.
- Enable Organizational Change Management (OCM), minimize the severity of any impact and disruption.
- Delivering change based on change drivers (value and performance drivers) maximizes value and reduces cost of change.
- Not only specifying, but establishing link between performance/value drivers and process changes, and ensuring higher project success rate, reducing failed changes, and, therefore, business disruptions, defects, and rework.
- Implementing changes that meet the clients' agreed value expectation while optimizing costs.
- Reducing the average time to align the process to the right way of working (from misalignment to alignment).
- Contributing to better portfolio, program, and project estimates of the quality, time, and cost of change.
- Contributing that change to meet governance, legal, legislative, contractual, and regulatory requirements by providing auditable evidence of change management activity.
- Ensure that all stakeholders receive appropriate and timely communication about the change so they are aware and ready to adopt and support the change.

LEADING PRACTICE SUGGESTIONS ON WHAT REALLY WORKS WELL

Developing an effective change road map that is integrated into the business process management life cycle and the BPM CoE change and issue management is imperative for change effectiveness, if your initiative is to avoid the "valley of despair". The purpose and objectives of BPM Change Management is to respond to both process change requests as well as the BPM client's changing requirements, while maximizing value and reducing incidents, disruptions, and rework. We feel it is vital to point out that BPM CoE Change Management and BPM Change Management are different. Although both interact, they have different purposes:

- *BPM CoE Change Management*—The resulting concept that combines the vision, strategic considerations, and requirements for Portfolio Change Management within the BPM CoE. This is done through the BPM CoE Change Board and includes alignment of programs and projects ensuring overall value creation for the BPM CoE clients.
- *BPM Change Management*—The set of activities/procedures/processes that, although supporting the BPM CoE, is about the execution of change management. Therefore, it would be the more tactical and operational change management piece of the BPM CoE. The changes are executed through the various tasks and roles in the BPM CoE.

As already pointed out, and although they are different, five common key areas compose BPM CoE Change Management as well as BPM Change Management:

1. Requirements Management
2. Planning with link to process portfolio, program, and project management
3. Value and Performance Management
4. BPM Governance
5. BPM Continuous Improvement feedback loop in terms of degree of change (low, medium, or high)

Out of scope of the above mentioned would be changes with significantly wider impacts than BPM Service Changes or BPM Project Changes. These include:

- Business organizational changes that need to be channeled through the Process Portfolio Management channel
- Structural changes that need to be channeled through the BPM CoE management
- The people-side of change that needs to be channeled through the business change management group

We realize that managing change effectively implies using processes to manage change, whereas it would mean that the BPM CoE would have to take their own medicine, we also realize that this would be a fundamental change for most organizations. It would mean that all BPM changes are recorded and evaluated, and that authorized changes are prioritized in a BPM CoE Change Management procedure. This makes the process life cycle ideal to execute the five key areas around BPM CoE Change Management and enables change in any phase as well as empowering the continuous improvement feedback loop (see Figure 2).

Integrating BPM Change Management into the process life cycle includes both changes to new and existing processes. It increases transparency of changes

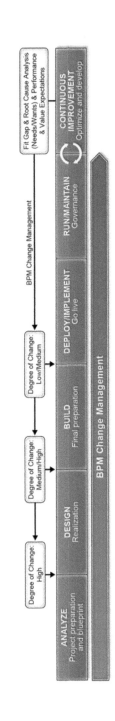

FIGURE 2

The process life cycle with BPM change management.[9]

throughout the life cycle and reduces the number of unauthorized changes, minimizing the severity of any impact and disruption. However, a recent study showed that even though we know we should do something we often do not,[11] even if life depends on it! The results of the study demonstrate that even when doctors tell heart patients they will die if they don't change their habits, only one in seven will be able to follow through successfully. Desire and motivation are not enough: even when it is literally a matter of life or death, the ability to change remains maddeningly elusive. Given that the status quo is so ingrained in our psyches, how can we change ourselves and our organizations? Whereas people and organizations know what they should do, they often do not know how to go about it.

Therefore, we will explore the following in detail:

- The life cycle phase
- The roles involved
- The strategic, tactical, and operational tasks
- The notations that are relevant for the subject (both BPMNotations, x-BPM-Notations, and other business notations)
- Typical enterprise standards involved

We will in Figure 3 illustrate the entire BPM Change Management Life Cycle complete with all the various roles, their tasks, and how the different modeling, engineering, and architecture disciplines interact and are used around each step in the life cycle.

Although the tasks are not that challenging in themselves, the challenge lies in the change control and management of the diverse roles in the various tasks, some that need to interlink and be governed by BPM CoE Portfolio Change Management, and some by BPM Change Management, relating to multiple enterprise standards to enable business and IT change.

BPM Change Management in the Analyze Phase

The first phase of the BPM Life Cycle is the phase in which the organization's processes are analyzed, captured, and defined, based on the business goals and specific process requirements (e.g. business needs and wants), as well as any interlinked business and process demands (Figure 4) Process goals and detailed process requirements are defined, and process choices are clarified through process blueprinting, and the initial process maps are populated with the identified processes. This phase includes Continuous Improvement through Change Management of the BPM Life Cycle, and the degree of changes made during this phase is considered high (Figure 2).

Tasks that have a link to strategic aspects:

1. Log and review change requests.
2. Identify change opportunities.
3. Assess change proposals (depending on scope, it links to appropriate processes)

Tasks that have a link to tactical aspects:

1. Refer to appropriate processes (depending on scope).
2. Raise Requests for Change (RFC) for changes flagged in scope.

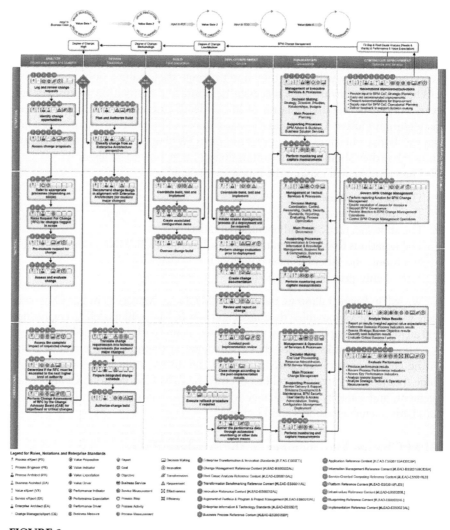

FIGURE 3

The BPM change management life cycle at a glance.[11]

3. Preevaluate request for change.
4. Assess and evaluate change (leads to assessment of the complete impact of requested change).

Tasks that have a link to operational aspects:

1. Assess the complete impact of requested change.
2. Determine if the RFC must be escalated to the next higher level of authority.
3. Perform Change Assessment of RFC by the Change Advisory Board (CAB) for significant or critical changes.

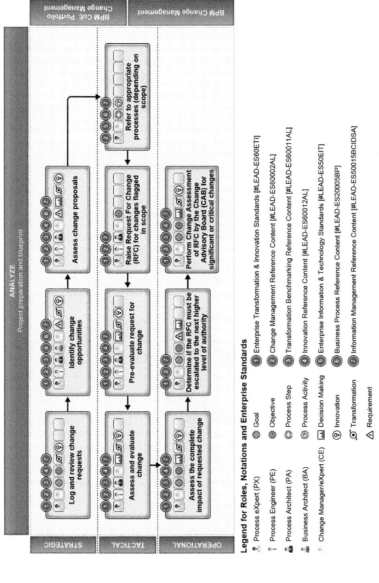

FIGURE 4

The BPM change management life cycle's analysis phase and how tasks, roles, notations, and standards could be applied.[12]

BPM Change Management in the Design Phase

The objective of this process is to take the information gathered in the preceding analyze phase and use it to develop a structured set of activities that *tell the BPM Change Management story for the BPM CoE* (Figure 5).

- Identify and design an enterprise BPM Change Management implantation plan (if required).
- Define and document all work flows or processes required by the stakeholders to perform change management within the BPM CoE; these will be the operations of change management (how to handle a process change, a project change, a service change, an RFC, etc.)
- Develop all supporting policies, guidelines, or best practices required to support the running of change management processes within BPM CoE for our

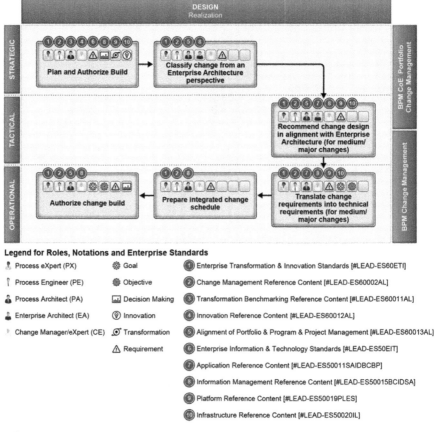

FIGURE 5

The BPM change management life cycle's design phase and how tasks, roles, notations, and standards could be applied.[13]

clients (governance structures, communication mechanisms, change plans, etc.)

Tasks that have a link to strategic aspects:

1. Plan and authorize build.
2. Classify change from an Enterprise Architecture perspective.

Tasks that have a link to tactical aspects:

1. Recommend change design in alignment with Enterprise Architecture (for medium/major changes).

Tasks that have a link to operational aspects:

2. Translate change requirements into technical requirements (for medium/major changes).
3. Prepare integrated change schedule.
4. Authorize change build.

BPM Change Management in the Build Phase

In the build phase (Figure 6) of the BPM Change Management Life Cycle, the tasks focus on carrying out the already-identified design solutions that have been developed during the previous design phase. The new processes and process structures, as well as the redesign of existing processes within the current process portfolio, should be constructed within a coordinated and isolated process testing and simulation environment, and primarily involves participants like process experts, engineers, and architects, as well as change management experts. Configuration foundations are likewise important to adapt to the environment around new processes, in particular, as well as a continuous governance aspect should be implemented to control and oversee the build phase from start to finish, and possibly enforce a construction rollback, if deemed necessary.

Tasks that have a link to tactical aspects:

1. Coordinate build, test, and implement (simulated production environment).
2. Create associated configuration items.
3. Oversee change build.

Tasks that have a link to operational aspects:

1. Execute rollback procedure if required.

BPM Change Management in the Deploy/Implement Phase

In the deployment and implementation phase (Figure 7), all reconfigured, reengineered, as well as new, processes are evaluated for go-live readiness. Change documentation will also need to be created to fully document and define all change aspects that have occurred to the new process portfolio and/or structures. A thorough review analysis will follow up release documentation, and the management will

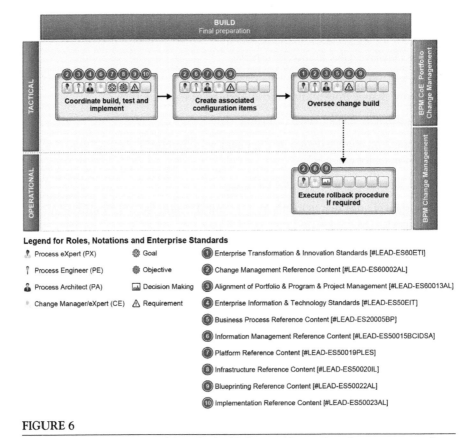

Legend for Roles, Notations and Enterprise Standards

- 🧍 Process eXpert (PX)
- 🧍 Process Engineer (PE)
- 🧍 Process Architect (PA)
- 🧍 Change Manager/eXpert (CE)

- ⚙ Goal
- ⚙ Objective
- 📊 Decision Making
- ⚠ Requirement

1. Enterprise Transformation & Innovation Standards [#LEAD-ES60ETI]
2. Change Management Reference Content [#LEAD-ES60002AL]
3. Alignment of Portfolio & Program & Project Management [#LEAD-ES60013AL]
4. Enterprise Information & Technology Standards [#LEAD-ES50EIT]
5. Business Process Reference Content [#LEAD-ES20005BP]
6. Information Management Reference Content [#LEAD-ES50015BCIDSA]
7. Platform Reference Content [#LEAD-ES50019PLES]
8. Infrastructure Reference Content [#LEAD-ES50020IL]
9. Blueprinting Reference Content [#LEAD-ES50022AL]
10. Implementation Reference Content [#LEAD-ES50023AL]

FIGURE 6

The BPM change management life cycle's build phase and how tasks, roles, notations, and standards could be applied.[14]

then carry out the final decision for go live and process release. Post-implementation review and reporting is also necessary shortly after release to follow up on successes and/or shortcomings of the live process environment.

Tasks that have a link to tactical aspects:

1. Coordinate build, test, and implement (go live).
2. Initiate release management process (if a deployment will be required).
3. Perform change evaluation prior to deployment.
4. Create change documentation.
5. Review and report on change.

Tasks that have a link to operational aspects:

1. Conduct postimplementation review.

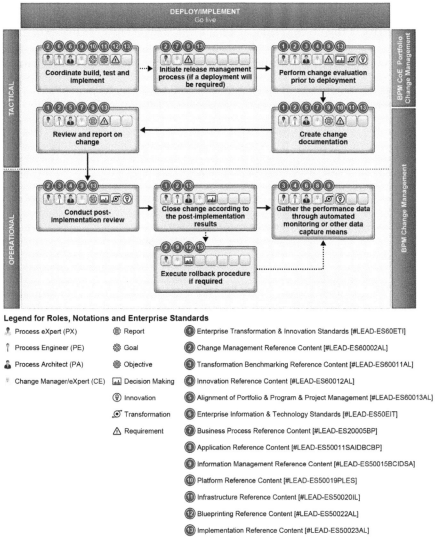

FIGURE 7

The BPM change management life cycle's deploy/implement phase and how tasks, roles, notations, and standards could be applied.[15]

2. Close change according to the postimplementation results (execute rollback procedure if required).
3. Gather the performance data through automated monitoring or other data capture means.

BPM Change Management in the Run/Maintain Phase

The objective of this phase (Figure 8) is to provide a set of processes that, when executed, become the working portfolio change management work flows for the BPM CoE. They are the change management requests that satisfy the client's change

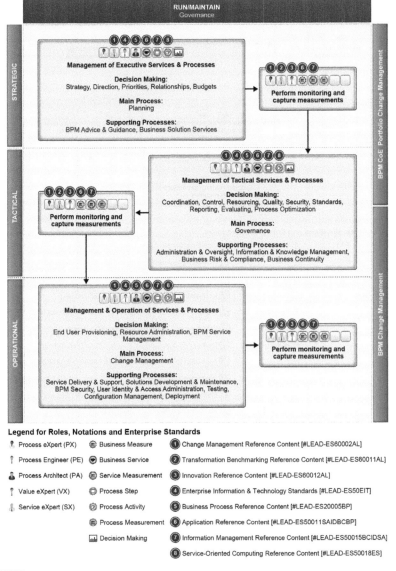

FIGURE 8

The BPM change management life cycle's run/maintain phase and how tasks, roles, notations, and standards could be applied.[1,16]

needs. They should also include step-by-step instructions for performing procedural activities such as impact analysis or user profile assessments when required.

Tasks that have a link to strategic aspects:

1. *Management of Executive Services and Processes*
    a. Decision Making: Strategy, Direction, Priorities, Relationships, Budgets.
    b. Main Process: Planning.
    c. Supporting Processes: BPM Advice and Guidance, Business Solution Services.
2. Perform monitoring and capture measurements

Tasks that have a link to tactical aspects:

1. *Management of Tactical Services and Processes*
    a. Decision Making: Coordination, Control, Resourcing, Quality, Security, Standards, Reporting, Evaluating, and Process Optimization.
    b. Main Process: Governance.
    c. Supporting Processes: Administration and Oversight, Information and Knowledge Management, Business Risk and Compliance, and Business Continuity.
2. Perform monitoring and capture measurements

Tasks that have a link to operational aspects:

1. Management and Operation of Services and Processes
    a. Decision Making: End User Provisioning, Resource Administration, BPM Service Management.
    b. Main Process: Change Management.
    c. Supporting Processes: Service Delivery and Support, Solutions Development and Maintenance, BPM Security, User Identity and Access Administration, Testing, Configuration Management, Deployment.
2. Perform monitoring and capture measurements

BPM Change Management in the Continuous Improvement Phase

The objective of this phase (Figure 9) is to control, monitor, and evaluate the operational change management processes, while addressing escalated issues/concerns and feedback for improvement of the running processes and the BPM portfolio as a whole. They should also include step-by-step instructions for performing any required procedural activities.

Tasks that have a link to strategic aspects:

1. Recommend Improvements/Actions
    a. Provide input to BPM CoE Strategic Planning.
    b. Carry out recommended improvements.
    c. Present recommendations for improvement.
    d. Supply input for BPM CoE Operational Planning.
    e. Deliver feedback to support decision-making.

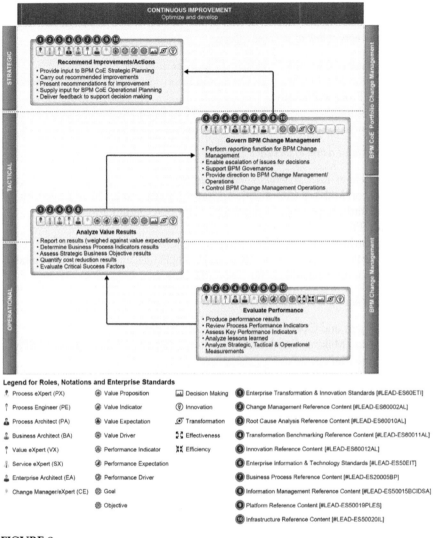

FIGURE 9

The BPM change management life cycle's continuous improvement phase and how tasks, roles, notations, and standards could be applied.[17]

Tasks that have a link to tactical aspects:

1. Govern BPM Change Management
   a. Perform reporting function for BPM Change Management.
   b. Enable escalation of issues for decisions.
   c. Support BPM Governance.

    d. Provide direction to BPM Change Management Operations.
    e. Control BPM Change Management Operations.
2. Analyze Value Results
    a. Report on results (weighed against value expectations).
    b. Determine Business Process Indicators results.
    c. Assess Strategic Business Objective results.
    d. Quantify cost-reduction results.
    e. Evaluate Critical Success Factors.

Tasks that have a link to operational aspects:

1. Evaluate Performance
    a. Produce performance results
    b. Review Process Performance Indicators
    c. Assess Key Performance Indicators
    d. Analyze lessons learned
    e. Analyze Strategic, Tactical, and Operational Measurements
2. Analyze Value Results
    a. Report on results (weighed against value expectations).
    b. Determine Business Process Indicators results.
    c. Assess Strategic Business Objective results.
    d. Quantify cost-reduction results.
    e. Evaluate Critical Success Factors.

The key is to identify, document, and categorize the continuous improvement changes into the degree of change (see Figure 2) and thereby loop it into any of the process life-cycle phases:

- *Degree of Change: Low*
  Changes that can be achieved with low work amount are referred to by different names in the various BPM CoEs. Some of the names are, among others, fast changes, quick changes, or even standard changes. All of them have one thing in common; they have a low degree of change. Low degree changes are, for the most part, preauthorized as they have low risk, are relatively common, and follow a known procedure or work flow.
- *Degree of Change: Medium*
  Changes that can be achieved with medium work amount are for the most part referred to as normal change requests.
- *Degree of Change: High*
  Changes that include a high degree of change can also have different names. Some of the names are, among others, big changes, strategic changes, major incident changes, and emergency changes. All of them do not only have in common that they have a high degree of change, but also that they have a significant relationship to performance and value creation, and therefore must be implemented as soon as possible. This is not always the case, but we see a pattern in the high degree change requests.

Perform Managerial Governance Activities Across all Phases

The objective of this process area is to perform the management and administrative activities to support the running of change management. They should also include step-by-step instructions for performing any required procedural activities.

CONCLUSION

The implementation of a BPM Change Management program demands a whole new way of working in an organization, and implies looking differently at one's organization. Many organizations underestimate this. Old, existing ways of working and managing/directing people must be changed. This fact alone begs for a clear change at the management level, but it also requires change at the lower organization levels. Examples of such changes may include[18]:

- Management and supervision will have to change: management and supervision should be done over the entire process (horizontal point of view) rather than on a hierarchical basis. Attention is to be given to the process instead of on keeping the department up and running.
- The process manager gets a much more prominent role in the organization.
- Cubicle thinking between departments will have to be eliminated.
- Roles and responsibilities will have to be defined better and are likely to change significantly compared to the situation before implementing BPM.
- Another type of management, with a different attitude toward the work floor and the execution in the organization's operations.

This new way of working should be accepted before working in a process-oriented manner can become successful. When organizations decide to implement process improvements and/or BPM, they must not only pay attention to the new possibilities and the factors that stimulate successful implementation, they must also be aware of the restrictions. These restrictions or barriers are often bound to the organization culture, to the comfort one obtains from holding a certain position, and to power and status. Management must deal with these barriers and actively deal with the factors that stimulate implementation as well (Figure 10).

Finally, clear and accurate communication is important for successful change management. This implies a need to build integrity and trust, which will have implications for the specific tactics that will be adopted in implementing the changes required.[19]

Essentially, an organization should focus on these core values:

- Ensure that the need for change is strategically driven
- Outline the BPM strategy together with its program of works
- Develop a change management approach, and devise a tool kit to be used with the implementation of the program of works around three areas of change:
  - Preparing for change

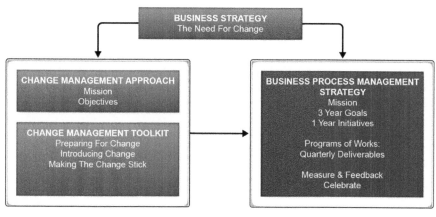

FIGURE 10

The BPM change management approach.[20]

- Introducing change
- Making the change stick

Many tactics can be selected from the tool kit for each area, and the actual tactics adopted will need to match the particular business, but if you have a framework from which to select, the likely success of your BPM Change Management project is increased.

End Notes

1. Kübler-Ross, E, On Death and Dying, Routledge, (1969) ISBN: 0-415-04015-9.
2. Kotter, J.P, "Leading change: why transformation efforts fail," *Harvard Business Review*, (May 1995).
3. Micheal Axelsen, "Business process management and change management analysing the human factor: people, change and governance, Applied Insight Pty Ltd, (2012).
4. Hammer, M., Champy, J., Reengineering the Corporation – A Manifest for Business, Revolution, Harperbusiness, (1994), p.272.
5. Jeston, J., and Nelis, J., Business process management: practical guidelines to successful implementations, Elsevier (2008).
6. Balmes, G., The role of organizational change management in BPM, business process management, organizational performance, BPM institute.org, (2011).
7. Harmon, P., Business Process Advisor, (May 10, 2011).
8. See note 3 above.
9. BPM Change Management Life Cycle Model, LEADing Practice Business Process Reference Content #LEAD-ES20005BP.
10. See note 5 above.
11. See note 9 above.
12. See note 9 above.
13. See note 9 above.

14. See note 9 above.
15. See note 9 above.
16. See note 9 above.
17. See note 9 above.
18. "The importance of change management when implementing BPM", Freek Hermkens.
19. Micheal Axelsen, Business process management and change management.
20. See note 9 above.

Business Process Management Governance

Maria Hove, Gabriella von Rosing, Bob Storms

INTRODUCTION

Companies create value for customers and shareholders (value streams) via the effectiveness and efficiency of activities that flow across organization boundaries—often referred to as the firm's cross-functional business processes. Business process management (BPM) spans both business and technology and provides a layer of visibility and control over the processes. To optimize and sustain business process improvements, it is essential to overlay some form of governance that creates the right structures, metrics, roles, and responsibilities to measure, improve, and manage the performance of a firm's end-to-end business processes.[1] In this chapter we will therefore focus on the concepts of BPM governance from the angles of what it is, why it is needed, where it can be applied, and the benefits of applying it. We believe that the principles of BPM governance are essential to any organization. This chapter is intended for executives, project leaders, and BPM methodology experts, those responsible for governance, and process owners who are responsible for daily operations and are interested in BPM governance.

WHY IS BPM GOVERNANCE IMPORTANT?

Most business processes happen through serendipitous need. Action is needed, someone does something that works, and the organization accepts this as the way things should be done going forward. As such, many organizations do not fully understand how things happen nor have they considered alternative ways to improve their processes, especially in relation to their content and how it moves through the organization. To truly understand organizational processes and the impact they have on content or content with the process, you need to map the process and document the interaction with content.[2] BPM is a management practice that provides for governance of the business process environment toward the goal of improving agility and operational performance. BPM is a structured approach employing methods, policies, metrics, management practices, and software tools to manage and continuously optimize an organization's activities and processes.[3] This means that BPM goes to the root of organizational structures, methods, and operations, and it is important to ensure that the changes it initiates are the right ones.[4]

Besides the ability to govern the processes and provide governance methods, policies, and metrics to ensure BPM governance, BPM governance is required to link the daily process governance to corporate governance, value governance, performance governance, and information technology (IT) governance. As illustrated in Figure 1, BPM governance provides the connection to the other governance disciplines within an organization. It governs performance and conformance at an operational level, and at the strategic level focuses on value identification, planning, and creation. IT related activities of BPM governance focus on cost reduction, whereas corporate aspects of BPM governance focus on activities to ensure revenue generation.

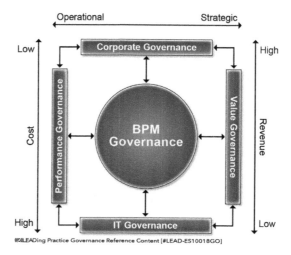

((Ⓒ)LEADing Practice Governance Reference Content [#LEAD-ES10018GO]

FIGURE 1

How business process management (BPM) governance connects to other governance disciplines, and the revenue and cost associated with them.[5]

WHAT IS BPM GOVERNANCE?

A business process is a continuous series of enterprise tasks undertaken for the purpose of creating output. Business processes enable the value chain of the enterprise and focus on the customer when the output is created. The purpose is to make the business process as significant as possible and to link it to multiple functions.[6] All companies have business processes, regardless of size or industry. When maintained and optimized, they will ensure competitiveness and survival in the marketplace.

Business processes have to be managed within an organization to enable and support a long-term business success. This means the continuous reassessment, realignment, and adaptation of business processes that enable strategic objectives to be implemented consistently and translated into everyday operational activity. It also means realignment and continuous adaptation of the related organizational and IT structures to meet the requirements of the market. Based on process analysis, it is possible to make the right decisions, significantly improve product and service quality, boost efficiency, and cut costs.[5]

BPM is a management discipline that provides governance in a business environment, with the goal of improving agility and operational performance.[7] It is a structured approach employing methods, policies, metrics, management practices, and software tools to coordinate and continuously optimize an organization's activities and business processes. Its objective is to control and improve an organization's business through active, coordinated governance of all aspects of the specification, design, implementation, operation, measurement, analysis, and optimization of business processes to effectively and efficiently deliver business objectives.[5,8]

BPM CENTER OF EXCELLENCE AND GOVERNANCE

BPM governance supports the establishment of enterprise-wide processes, rules, methodologies, guidelines, tools, measures, and roles for BPM. For the most part, either BPM governance is found within the BPM center of excellence (CoE) or its concepts are applied within to oversee and manage projects throughout the entire BPM life cycle. Ensuring the operation of one's processes is consistent across the enterprise and reusable and efficient. The development and maintenance of policy, conventions, and standards for an enterprise-wide BPM approach are main tasks of the BPM CoE[5] and are executed through BPM governance (Figure 2).

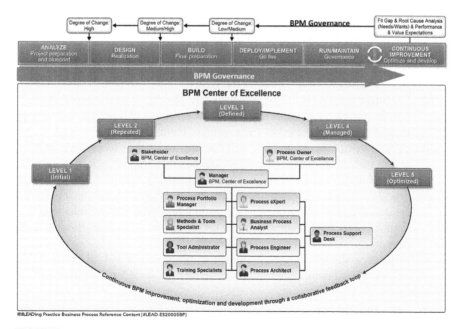

FIGURE 2

Business process management (BPM) governance applied throughout the BPM life cycle and done by the BPM CoE.[9]

Process governance consists of the set of guidelines and resources that an organization uses to facilitate collaboration and communication when it undertakes enterprise process initiatives, such as implementing a new contracts administration process or a new budgeting system. In this context, there are five basic steps for effective process governance[10]:

1. **Establish standards** for implementing new BPM projects. Examples of process standards include:
   a. Implementation methodology: Organizations should subscribe to a specific set of process implementation methodologies
   b. Process modeling notation: When modeling processes, it is important to standardize how different activities and events should be graphically represented
   c. Development platform: Implementing enterprise-wide process initiatives require organizations to standardize on a set of development tools
   d. Integration protocols: Enterprise-wide processes typically require tight integration with back-end data and other enterprise systems. It is important to decide early on which integration standards will be used to connect processes with other internal and external systems
2. **Prioritize BPM projects** so that you work on the most achievable ones first.
   a. Level of complexity: How complex is the proposed process? At the beginning of your process initiative it is important to establish quick wins. If possible, avoid implementing complex processes first
   b. Process reach and impact: How many people will the process impact and how much pain is caused by the current process? Initially, priority should be given to processes that represent the greatest impact to a small group of users
   c. Executive support: Is the process currently a hot topic in the executive boardroom? It is important to decide how priority will be given to processes that are widely supported by the executive team
   d. Subject matter expertise: How well documented is the process on paper and in carbon life forms? Priority should be given to processes that are well documented. You should also consider accessibility to subject matter experts
   e. Process selection guidelines should list and weigh each criterion. This will create some level of transparency regarding how processes are selected for implementation. It is important to gain consensus throughout the organization on the slate of process selection criteria
3. **Clearly define the roles** and responsibilities of everyone involved in the BPM project. At a minimum, responsibilities should be defined for the following roles:
   a. Executive sponsor: As outlined in the previous section, the executive sponsor provides high-level visibility for the process initiative
   b. Process steward: The process steward provides guidance and direction for a particular process. This is typically the business unit manager or director who realizes a direct benefit or pain as a result of the process

   c. Process manager: The process manager is the person charged with leading the implementation of a particular business process. This individual is held accountable for the success or failure of deploying the business process

   d. Functional lead: This individual is responsible for leading process analysis and requirements gathering. Functional leads oversee process discovery sessions with end users and managers, in addition to modeling the process and business rules

   e. Technical lead: The technical lead oversees implementation of technical components of the process. This includes system installation and configuration, application and forms development, and back-end integration

4. Put someone in charge with authority to enforce BPM governance rules

   a. Executive sponsorship is the single most important ingredient required for successful process governance. Without executive sponsorship, most enterprise-wide process initiatives lack a decisive voice capable of resolving process-related conflicts that arise during implementation. Within some organizations, the executive sponsor is a full-time vice president or manager who is accountable to the chief executive officer. However, in most cases the executive sponsor has a part-time role in addition to his or her regular full-time job duties. With either scenario, the executive sponsor must be empowered to enforce agreed-upon governance rules and should have budget authority for process initiatives

5. Establish a BPM CoE to ensure that Steps 1–4 are followed on every initiative. These CoEs serve as internal practices that support deployment of enterprise-wide business processes. BPM CoEs are usually chartered to accomplish the following objectives:

   a. Prioritize and implement processes: The CoE works with the executive sponsor and business managers to identify and prioritize process projects. Process selection guidelines should be developed to help the BPM CoE rank the processes to be implemented. After processes have been prioritized, the CoE can focus on its primary objective: developing and deploying processes

   b. Maintain the process portfolios: This consists of maintaining knowledge and documentation captured for each process. This knowledge is often contained in process requirements documents, training manuals, and project plans. The CoE is tasked with maintaining these artifacts in a physical library or within a virtual knowledge base

   c. Establish process practices: Upon completion of each deployment, the BPM CoE conducts post-project reviews and identifies lessons learned. These reviews are used to establish leading, or at the least, best practices that can be applied to future process implementations

   d. Evaluate process performance: Working with the process steward and executive sponsor, the CoE periodically evaluates the effectiveness of deployed processes. Process effectiveness is evaluated based on key performance metrics established before process deployment

BPM CoEs are growing in popularity as many organizations begin to expand departmental BPM initiatives to encompass the enterprise. CoE are most appropriate for organizations looking to deploy three or more processes that will need to interact with multiple departments. Working closely with the executive sponsor, the BPM CoE should be assigned responsibility for defining and enforcing process governance rules. Once process governance rules have been established, these rules should be institutionalized and automated by the CoE.

HOW DOES BPM GOVERNANCE WORK?

In practice, BPM governance works on two levels: program and project.

At the program level, whereas executive management sets the strategic direction for the BPM initiative, the governance body is responsible for its measurement and enforcement, ensuring alignment using approved frameworks and tools, and managing the road map and selection of projects to meet strategic goals. At the project level, BPM governance directs the project management of solution delivery to work within an engineering and project framework.[4]

BPM governance directs both the conformance and performance aspects in alignment within enterprise governance.

Performance includes:

- Maximizing economies of scale across coexisting processes and value streams
- Efficiency gains (processing time, costs, and throughput capability)
- Customer satisfaction/customer experience
- BPM program/project management (benefits realization and value management)
- Effective and efficient use of resources (e.g., human, financial, assets)

Conformance includes:

- Process compliance (standardization)
- Compliance with enterprise policies and external regulatory standards
- Risk management and control
- Integration of BPM governance across the organization (coexistence with other governances)
- BPM guiding principles and standards
- Alignment of BPM governance with business architecture (e.g., processes mapped to value streams; processes linked to business competencies)

This is accomplished within a continuous improvement life cycle methodology, ensuring BPM governance is relevant, effective, and always in alignment with the strategic objects of the organization.[5] It includes the governance of business process improvement using BPM, as well as governance of the implementation and adoption of BPM in the organization. The life cycle can be described as follows:

Analyze:

- Analyze as-is state of BPM CoE governance (e.g., methodology, organizational structure) and maturity of business processes
- Identify BPM CoE governance objectives and requirements
- Assess alignment of business processes to strategic business objectives and critical success factors of organization
- Identify present pain points, bottlenecks, and weakness clusters
- Analyze the structure and efficiency of current business processes (e.g., process architecture, process flows, times, and costs)
- Assess current state of process accountabilities and compliance with standards

Design:

- Define to-be state of BPM governance CoE (e.g., framework/model, structure)
- Assess BPM CoE resource capacity
- Define process control objectives and practices
- Define targets to support strategic business objectives and critical success factors of organization
- Define enterprise-wide process architecture
- Define BPM standards and policies
- Define measurements and monitoring methods (benefits realization and value management)

Build:

- Develop accountability framework (e.g., Responsible, Accountable, Consulted, Informed (RACI))
- Develop BPM policies and standards (modeling approach and best practices)
- Select process improvement and re-engineering projects (e.g., Six Sigma), grouping projects into BPM programs
- Create to-be state of selected processes (e.g., optimization, agility)
- Allocate BPM CoE governance resources
- Create BPM CoE governance structures

Deploy/implement:

- Implement BPM CoE governance structures
- Direct process improvement projects and programs, including automation opportunities (e.g., using process reference models)
- Implement BPM standards, policies, and procedures
- Deploy BPM CoE change deployment management, including communications and training

Run/maintain:

- Monitor and govern compliance and accountability (audit)
- Monitor effectiveness of BPM CoE governance structures

- Monitor process effectiveness and efficiency (e.g., resource use, costs, processing times) through qualitative and quantitative measures against targets (key performance indicators, Service Level Agreements (SLAs))
- Monitor success of process improvement projects (benefits realization)

Continuous improvement:

- Identify processes with potential for redesign, improvement, and greater productivity
- Identify opportunities to streamline value streams
- Identify/eliminate process redundancy
- Identify opportunities to improve accountability and compliance
- Identify opportunities to improve BPM standards, policies, procedures, and enterprise-wide process architecture
- Identify opportunities to optimize BPM CoE governance structures
- Identify opportunities to optimize resource use
- Modify targets to support changes in strategic business objectives and critical success factors of organization

BPM GOVERNANCE AND INCIDENT MANAGEMENT

In the run and maintain phase of the BPM governance and continuous improvement life cycle (Figure 3), incident management is an important service that supports process governance and control. Incident management should be used for handling

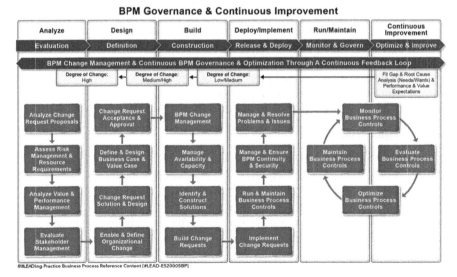

FIGURE 3

The business process management (BPM) governance and continuous improvement model.[11]

all incidents related to both manual/labor-intensive and automated processes. This includes requests for BPM projects (process improvement/redesign), process failures, degradation of services (value streams), and process questions and concerns reported by users or technical staff, or automatically detected and reported by event monitoring tools. In the context of BPM governance the primary goal of the incident management process is to restore normal operations as quickly as possible and minimize the adverse impact on services. BPM governance also uses the information created by incident management to monitor and direct performance and conformance governance aspects. As illustrated in Figure 4, there are there seven main phases of incident management,[12] all of which are interlinked with the BPM CoE, BPM roles, BPM life cycle, process templates, and BPM change management.

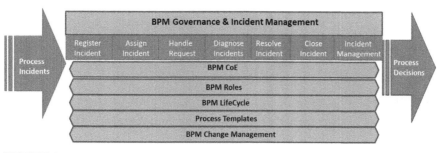

FIGURE 4

Incident management phases are interlinked with various business process management (BPM) concepts.

BPM PORTFOLIO MANAGEMENT AND GOVERNANCE

Process portfolio management has a pivotal role in successful BPM (Figure 5) for a number of reasons. It provides an approach or mind set that is essential in directing limited resources in terms of funds, people, etc., into the processes with the highest demand for an increased process orientation. In the true sense of a balanced portfolio, process portfolio management can be used to diversify the BPM governance activities, leading to parallel projects in different stages of the business process life cycle. In summary, process portfolio management marks the difference between the isolated and uncoordinated improvement and management of a single process and the holistic process-based management of an organization.[13]

In the BPM portfolio management cycle, the following general questions should be asked for every item in your organization's process portfolio[14]:

- Does this process align with the organization's strategic objectives and goals?
- Based on defined key performance indicators and probable risks, does this process initiative meet the requirements for portfolio inclusion?

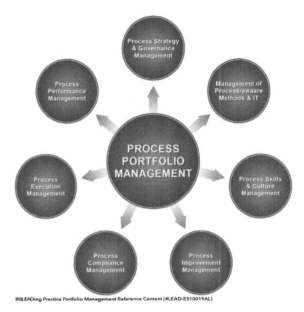

#OILEADing Practice Portfolio Management Reference Content [#LEAD-ES10019AL]

FIGURE 5

Process portfolio management in the context of BPM governance activities.[15]

- Does it still meet the requirements for portfolio inclusion compared with other competing process portfolio items also in consideration?

Many organizations do not have a portfolio management process. To create a process where none exists, the right steps must be taken.

1. Define a process portfolio management structure (organizational chart)
2. Define a process portfolio management plan
3. Define key performance indicators
4. Define process performance indicators

The following are essential steps or activities for process portfolio management, although more process mature organizations may introduce additional steps into the process:

1. Identify process portfolio items
2. Define process portfolio items
3. Evaluate process portfolio items
4. Select your process portfolio
5. Reassess process portfolio
6. Approve process portfolio
7. Transition to process initiative
8. Communicate. Track and report
9. Accommodate and adjust for changes

Although many organizations have significantly matured in their understanding of the opportunities and constraints of BPM, many lack well-defined accountability for their entire portfolio of business processes. In the same way that a manager in charge of strategic marketing is not the product manager, there will be a clear distinction between the role of the centralized process portfolio manager and the duties of decentralized process owners. In terms of BPM governance, a process portfolio manager can be seen as an additional role within the corporate BPM team. The process portfolio manager will be measured by his or her ongoing awareness of the entire range of an organization's business processes and the capability of allocating BPM resources to the most promising processes. The more advanced the organization is in its BPM maturity—i.e., the more it moves from simple overview architectures to a widely populated model repository, even with information about actual process executions—the more critical it will be to shift the initial focus on individual processes to a view that manages the entire landscape of organizational business processes.[16]

LESSONS LEARNED

The organization-wide adoption of BPM typically goes through multiple stages,[17] which can be described as follows:

1. Awareness of the benefits and methodologies of BPM
2. Desire to adopt BPM based on a business-related driver (e.g., mergers, IT system implementations, new business segments, cost reduction activities)
3. Set up, execute, and monitor individual BPM projects
4. Convert from multiple BPM projects to a governing and more centralized BPM program
5. Productize BPM through a BPM CoE

To reach this goal of a holistic BPM approach, the same elements have to be in place that are necessary to run every process efficiently[5]:

- Definition and understanding of the BPM process
- Clear objectives regarding the outcome and benefits of the BPM process
- A BPM organization and a BPM CoE with appropriate knowledge, roles, and responsibilities
- A BPM methodology, BPM standards, and BPM service offerings
- A mature BPM technology and tools that optimally support an efficient BPM approach across the organization.

There are five main responsibilities of a centralized and enterprise-wide BPM CoE[5]:

- BPM leadership
- Regulatory framework
- Project support
- Training and communication
- Process controlling

Rosemann proposed analyzing and managing the BPM services portfolio offered by the BPM CoE based on the two dimensions of demand and capability.[9] Demand reflects the current organizational needs and appetite for a specific BPM service. The capabilities describe the readiness of the BPM CoE to provide a certain service. This dimension reflects the accumulated knowledge, skills, and experience of the BPM CoE, as well as the technological capacities to successfully deliver.[5]

To implement a BPM CoE within an organization to support a BPM governance approach, specific service offerings for stakeholders should be defined, along with internal roles and responsibilities. A service offering is a combination of methodology, tools, and communication activities that together address a strategic BPM target field of the organization. The organization's BPM target fields should be analyzed and prioritized first to identify the necessary BPM service offerings. Every target field (e.g., strategic decision support, Information Technology Infrastructure Library (ITIL) implementation and review, IT system implementation, cost reduction initiatives, or introduction of new products) has to be identified and described.[5]

The greatest value from BPM is found in automating enterprise-wide value streams, and this is where good governance becomes critical. Unfortunately, a number of challenges commonly stand in the way of this kind of cross-functional, enterprise-wide governance, including the following[4]:

- Organizational structures are typically organized by functional silos
- Related to the organizational concern, there is typically a resistance to change and even to cross-functional cooperation
- Formal governance frameworks for this scope are rare
- There is inadequate infrastructure and tools support

It is necessary to understand the scope of BPM governance in relation to other governance concerns and practices to avoid duplication or conflict, but also where appropriate to integrate them for greatest continuity.[4]

BENEFITS AND VALUE OF BPM GOVERNANCE

A Gartner research note stated that 80% of enterprise companies conducting BPM projects will experience a return on investment (ROI) greater than 15%. The survey looked at responses from 20 companies that had completed 154 BPM projects, and 95% of the companies experienced more than a 90% success rate among their BPM projects. All successful projects had an ROI greater than 10%, Gartner found. Seventy-eight percent of the respondents had ROI rates greater than 15%.[18] Organizations with an identified BPM CoE and governance in place can achieve a five times greater ROI over those with no CoE or dedicated process team.[19] Similarly, those with a dedicated business process team in place reported nearly twice the ROI of those without any dedicated team in place.[5,11]

BPM governance is an essential program overlay activity that enforces standards, engineering practices, organization structures, roles, and responsibilities, to measure, manage, and improve the effectiveness of BPM itself. It ensures that your BPM initiative is aligned with your corporate strategies and objectives and that BPM delivers measurable value.[4] BPM governance will help the organization to find and reinforce its control structure and thereby develop its agility and organizational effectiveness.

CONCLUSIONS

In this chapter we have focused on BPM governance and how it is a top priority for executives and BPM CoE. We covered what BPM governance is, why it is important, and how and where it can or should be applied. Furthermore, we detailed typical phases and tasks of BPM governance and illustrated lessons learned in terms of what works well and what does not. We ended with the benefits and value of BPM governance, which is critical for monitoring enterprise-wide and automated value streams.

End Notes

1. BPM Governance, Andrew Spanal, http://www.bpminstitute.org/resources/articles/bpm-governance.

2. *How to Unclog Your Business by Automating Content-Intensive Process* (AIIM Training) http://www.trindocs.com/Portals/3/HowtoUnclogYourBusiness.pdf.

3. Gartner report, *Business Process Management: Preparing for the Process-Managed Organization* (2005).

4. Oracle Practitioner Guide—A Framework for BPM Governance, Release 3.0, E24090-03 (August 2011).

5. LEADing Practice Governance Reference Content #LEAD-ES10018GO.

6. Hammer and Champy, *Reengineering the Corporation: A Manifesto for Business Revolution* (New York: HarperBusiness, 1993).

7. Melenovsky M. J., *Business Process Management as a Discipline*, Gartner Research, ID Number: G00139856 (August 1, 2006).

8. Brabaender E. and Davis R., *ARIS Design Platform—Getting started with BPM* (Springer: London, 2007).

9. LEADing Practice Business Process Reference Content #LEAD-ES20005BP.

10. Clay Richardson, "Process Governance Best Practices: Building a BPM Center of Excellence," (2006).

11. LEADing Practice Governance Reference Content #LEAD-ES10018GO.

12. Lisa Callihan, "Incident Management," from http://www.mais.umich.edu/methodology/service-management/incident-management.html.

13. Michael Rosemann, "Process Portfolio Management" (2006).

14. *Essential Steps to Building a Profitable Portfolio Process*, See more at: http://epmlive.com/portfolio-management/essential-steps-to-building-a-profitable-portfolio-process/#sthash.yxwwdMs3.dpuf.

15. LEADing Practice Portfolio Management Reference Content #LEAD-ES10019AL.

16. See the note 13 above.

17. Rosemann M., *ARIS TV—Episode 6—What are your BPM Services?* (2008) http://www.youtube.com/watch?v=LQ1ZqUq9q-k&feature=channel_page.

18. Dubie D., BPM and ROI (2004) NetworkWorld.com http://www.networkworld.com/weblogs/management/005640.html accessed June 03, 2008.

19. Nathaniel Palmer, "Introduction: Workflow and BPM in 2007: Business Process Standards See a New Global Imperative," *2007 BPM & Workflow Handbook*.

Business Process Portfolio Management

Mark von Rosing, Hendrik Bohn, Gabriel von Scheel, Richard Conzo, Maria Hove

FROM BUSINESS PROCESS MANAGEMENT TO BUSINESS PROCESS PORTFOLIO MANAGEMENT

In today's society, work environment and customers' expectations change on a daily basis. Consequently, it is crucial for the modern enterprise to find a way to adapt itself to new requirements.[1]

After more than 25 years of existence, business process management (BPM) has become the de facto standard in eliminating historically grown and chaotic business procedures by organizing them in a structured, transparent, and standardized way.[2] The growth in acceptance of BPM has been supported by a wide range of tools such as BPM suites, which are entering the plateau of productivity on the Gartner Hype Cycle.[3] This, in turn, will increase the widespread adoption of BPM and lift the BPM maturity in organizations. However, with increasing maturity, organizations face the next challenge.[4] How can they manage the entire set of processes, improve them as a whole, or decide on which processes their limited resources should be deployed?

Organizations apply various process re-engineering, process innovation, optimization, and management techniques to improve their business processes. The impetus for these improvements can range from a specific business problem to a management directive or a need to reduce costs and improve efficiency. Organizations typically undertake periodic process improvements that are focused on specific business processes and may or may not align with the business strategy. Too often, once a project is completed, management attention goes elsewhere and things revert to the way they were. The value realization potential is not used enough, resulting in high cost and low value for the organization. Often the anticipated benefits are not realized or even audited to see whether the goals were reached. Similarly, many pitfalls can appear when process improvement is attempted one process at a time. In these cases, it is difficult to tell which processes contribute the most to achieving the business objectives, which process is the critical process to improve, or which processes are interdependent and therefore influence each other.

To realize all of the benefits of sometimes disparate BPM efforts, there needs to be an ongoing, organization-wide effort to assess and measure the results and continue to use the successful implementations. This organizational wide effort needs to be governed and controlled through a BPM Center of Excellence (CoE) already described elsewhere. Emphasis should be on what needs to be done rather than the location of where it is done, such as a department or area of the company. The processes need to be managed end-to-end to optimize the different silos in an organization where processes normally exist. There is a good chance that in most organizations no one person exists who manages the process end-to-end or even understands the process in that context.

Value chain and value network concepts are approaches to provide a more high-level view on value generation and improvement, linking sequential activities to business strategies and outcomes.[5] However, they often do not allow drilling down or breaking down to specific business processes where the value is created, and thus lack support for process and inter-process relationships.[6] Business process portfolio management (BPPM) is the solution as well as the concept that should be applied, as described in subsequent sections.

COMMON PITFALLS WHEN IMPLEMENTING BPPM

Most organizations, both private and public sector, experience a number of pitfalls when implementing and sustaining successful BPPM, as shown in Figure 1.

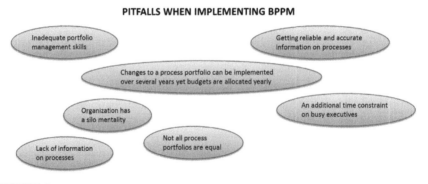

PITFALLS WHEN IMPLEMENTING BPPM

FIGURE 1

Common pitfalls when implementing business process portfolio management (BPPM).

Not All Process Portfolios are Equal

BPPM ought to take place wherever investment decisions are being made; however, the views of the portfolio and the questions that need to be answered will depend on whose perspective affects the decisions. For example, a portfolio of enterprise processes will need much more rigorous evaluation from a number of perspectives than, for example, a portfolio of behind-the-scenes information technology (IT) processes. An enterprise's alignment to corporate strategy may be a score used to determine value at the board level, whereas alignment to Information System (IS)/Information Technology (IT) strategy will be of primary interest to the chief information officer.

Changes to a Process Portfolio Can be Implemented Over Several Years, Yet Budgets are Allocated Yearly

A change initiative to a process portfolio is often a multi-year initiative that is not always aligned to the financial allocation of budget to individual process changes within the portfolio. Furthermore, in most organizations budgets are allocated yearly, which makes the continuum of the portfolio challenging considering that resources might be lowered at key stages based on budget allocation and reallocation. The most challenging periods are normally over the financial year end when existing budgets must be balanced and new budgets have yet to be fully allocated.

Organization Has a Silo Mentality

Silo mentality is an attitude found in some organizations that occurs when several departments or groups do not want to share information or knowledge with other individuals in the same company. A silo mentality reduces efficiency and can be a contributing factor to a failing corporate culture. This occurrence is detrimental in BPPM as processes devalue one another. Inefficiency is exaggerated owing to resources and knowledge being withheld.

Lack of Information on Processes

To prioritize the work successfully on a large portfolio of processes and allocate limited resources adequately, it is important to gather the same information consistently for all involved processes. As mentioned earlier, this information might consist of the risk of failure, client exposure, frequency of use, and cost to run. If desired information is not available for all processes of a portfolio, objective priority calls are difficult to make and remain subjective.

Getting Reliable and Accurate Information on Processes

BPPM also requires a place to store all of the data for processes, preferably a central source that is regarded as being the single source of these data and under change control. Having a single source for reporting also enables the elimination of the double counting that may otherwise arise if each process is permitted to use different sources of data and measures for its reports.

Inadequate Portfolio Management Skills

Managing at the process level is no longer sufficient for organizations. Increasingly, a higher-level perspective is required to ensure that entire ecosystem of processes deliver desired services and products as BPPM allows an organization to take a holistic view of a group (or groups) of its processes to improve return on investment (ROI) and strategic alignment. Process owners or key managers need to be trained to become qualified process portfolio managers. They need to combine strategic alignment and sound financial and risk management to drive large portfolios. The combination of all three elements is often missing and created pain points in all three mentioned areas for executives and organizations looking to improve the ROI successfully in their portfolios. Therefore, irrespective of the benefits theoretically obtainable in one area, a focus in one of these areas will not deliver value without the combination of all three elements of strategic alignment and sound financial and risk management. Furthermore, a focus on the outcome, not the individual performance of processes, is required when dealing with BPPM, a fact with which many previous process owners experience difficulties.

Additional Time Constraint on Busy Executives

Improving the way an enterprise creates and manages value is a change program in itself that will need its own business case. Even with senior sponsorship and a strong appetite for positive change, once executives realize that the effort involved in doing things properly will require time and effort on their part, there is often nervousness, uncertainty, and sometimes push-back. Executives may also struggle with the new data and processes involved and will need guidance, coaching, and support.

The intention is to save these busy executives much more in terms of resources than might otherwise be wasted by enabling them to allocate scarce resources more wisely across the process portfolio, with an acceptable level of risk and more in line with their target investment mix. Gathering lots of data and then putting the data in front of those who make decisions is not necessarily the right answer. Few executives are detail focused and very few would wish to be. They will simply see this data dump as an additional demand on their already overstretched time, or worse, may feel unable to make a decision for fear of making the wrong one. What are called for are the services of impartial experts who do not take the place of the decision makers, but who can offer insight, guidance, and recommendations to decision makers. These services should be offered both proactively and on-demand, so that they can answer questions, including: Are we doing the right things? Are we getting the benefits? The home of such a service might well be called a value management office, process portfolio office, or center of excellence. Whatever the title, its role is essentially that of trusted advisor or secretariat to those who make the investment decisions.

ESTABLISHING BPPM

BPPM borrows its concept from project portfolio management (PPM), which has gone through a similar evolution. The key concepts of PPM can be easily applied: From project to process, from program to cross-functional processes, and from project portfolio to process portfolio.[7] BPPM flips the vertical BPM process horizontally to manage vertical silo organizational processes. The BPPM process will maximize organizational performance as a whole, identify and reduce duplication, and manage process interdependencies.

This section will start with a comparison of PPM, BPPM, and BPM to set the context, which is followed by a discussion of required portfolio information to effectively manage a business process portfolio. To support organizations moving to BPPM, the important steps and considerations in creating a BPPM Office are outlined afterward. The section closes with an overview of the BPPM life cycle.

COMPARISON OF PPM, BPPM, AND BPM

PPM deals with how to undertake the right projects at the right time, whereas process portfolio management addresses the right processes at the right time and process management focuses on performing processes right. Compared with BPM, BPPM focuses on the selection, prioritization, and monitoring of a portfolio of processes to optimize enterprise strategic outcomes, whereas BPM focuses on the individual delivery of a service or product. A comparison is presented in Table 1.

Table 1 *Comparison Between Project Portfolio Management (PPM), Business Process Portfolio Management (BPPM), and Business Process Management (BPM)*

	Project Portfolios (PPM) "Doing the Right Projects"	Process Portfolios (BPPM) "Doing the Right Processes"	Processes (BPM) "Doing the Process Right"
Scope	Project portfolios have horizontal scope that aligns with the strategic framework, objectives, goals, and priorities of the organization.	Process portfolios have horizontal scope that aligns with the strategic framework, objectives, goals, and priorities of the organization.	Processes produce a specific service or product.
Change	Project portfolio managers continuously monitor change in the broader internal and external environments.	Process portfolio managers continuously monitor change in the broader internal and external environments.	Process owners manage change on processes and keep change controlled.
Planning	Project portfolio managers create and maintain processes and communication relative to the aggregate portfolio of projects.	Process portfolio managers create and maintain planning and communication relative to the aggregate portfolio of processes.	Process owners manage detailed plans throughout the process life cycle.
Management	Project portfolio managers manage or coordinate portfolio interdependencies, communications, and benefits in the aggregate portfolio of projects.	Process portfolio managers manage or coordinate portfolio interdependencies, communications, and benefits in the aggregate portfolio of processes.	Process owners manage the performance of a process.
Benefits	Success is measured in terms of the aggregate investment performance, stakeholder satisfaction, and benefit realization of the aggregate portfolio of projects.	Success is measured in terms of the aggregate performance, stakeholder satisfaction, and benefit realization of the aggregate portfolio of processes.	Success is measured by service and product quality, timeliness, budget compliance, and degree of stakeholder satisfaction.
Monitoring	Project portfolio managers monitor strategic changes and aggregate benefits, resources, interdependencies, performance results, and risks of the portfolio of projects.	Process portfolio managers monitor strategic changes and aggregate benefits, resources, interdependencies, performance results, and risks of the portfolio of processes.	Process owners monitor and control the performance of processes to deliver products or services.

As can be seen, the conjunction of PPM and BPPM can be found in change initiatives. Major process improvements are usually run as projects which are planned, executed, and governed through PPM.

CREATING A BPPM COMPETENCY

Once an organization has decided to implement BPPM, the BPPM competency must be planned and its mandate defined; then it can be integrated into the organization. A structured approach to implement BPPM is presented in Figure 2, adapted to BPPM from the portfolio reference content.[8]

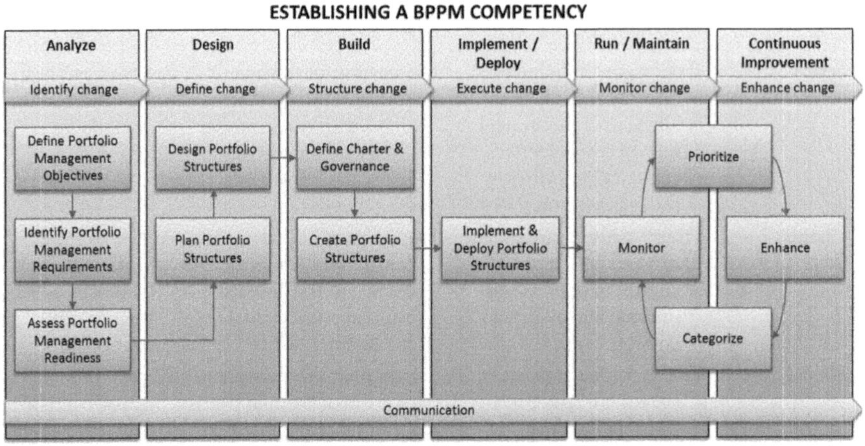

ESTABLISHING A BPPM COMPETENCY

FIGURE 2

Implementing and sustaining a business process portfolio management (BPPM) competency.

The implementation of BPPM is framed by the need for change management, which is highlighted through the ongoing deliverable of communication.

Guiding Principles

The BPPM principles represent the foundations upon which effective portfolio management is built. They provide the organizational environment in which portfolio management practices can operate effectively. These principles apply equally within any portfolio of processes and process improvement projects, whether the individual investment is occurring in the business, application, or technology layers.

Guiding principles are:

- Business process portfolios are aligned to the strategic business objectives as well as the critical success factors of an organization.

- Interdependencies are managed at a business continuum level across portfolios and assessed against business transformation, delivery, and stakeholder commitments.
- Portfolio governance and decision making is clearly defined and integrated across the organization's corporate governance to proactively balance resource capacity against organizational performance.
- Active stakeholder engagement is in place by integrating and coordinating stakeholder requirements within a portfolio where they are recognized as key contributors to the delivery of organizational outcomes.

Analysis Phase

The purpose of this phase is to identify the need for BPPM within an organization. It sets out the basic requirements in terms of what objectives the portfolio management within the organization will fulfill. It details and decomposes the specific requirements needed to meet the expectations and objectives of BPPM and then assesses the portfolio management readiness across the organization.

The section on alignment considerations when implementing BPPM will provide an overview of the different factors to which a BPPM initiative needs to align.

Design Phase

The purpose of this phase is to plan and design the BPPM structures within the organization. The plan and design activities, roles, and deliverables ensure that portfolio management structures are ready for the build phase. Design phase activities should account for variation factor types and feedback communications. Both activities will consider uncertainty events and near real-time performance feedback for process effectiveness. The section on business process hierarchy will introduce a hierarchy concept to provide structure for the business processes in an organization to facilitate prioritization. To compare different process improvement initiatives, certain information is required for the business process portfolio, which is described in the section on BPPM information, measurements, and reporting.

Build Phase

The purpose of this phase is to take the designs created in the preceding phases and build the portfolio management structures and governance within the organization.

Deploy/Implement Phase

The deploy phase executes the change into existence within the organization. It launches BPPM as a framework into the organization whereby process improvement programs and projects fall under the governance of a BPPM office (BP-PMO).

Run/Maintain Phase

The run/maintain phase takes the BPPM life cycle into the business as usual/operational space. BPPM now requires ongoing monitoring, re-prioritization via ranking, and categorization after enhancements have taken place in the continuous improvement phase. The run phase and continuous improvement phase are linked together through the prioritization and categorization activities that lead to the ongoing improvements in monitoring from the continual enhancement of portfolio management.

Continuous Improvement Phase

The continuous improvement phase objective is to look for ongoing enhancements to the BPPM life cycle and method so that these can be used to improve portfolio management over time. The continuous improvement phase and run phase are linked together through the prioritization and categorization activities that lead to prioritized improvements entering the continuous improvement phase; these improvements are then enhanced further where possible before being categorized and applied to the organization's BPPM.

Once an organization has successfully implemented BPPM, the overall BPPM life cycle can be applied in effectively executing, sustaining, and continuously improving their portfolio management. The section on BPPM life cycle deals with the effective daily portfolio management operation.

ALIGNMENT CONSIDERATIONS WHEN IMPLEMENTING BPPM

Alignment to an organization's strategy is the cornerstone of creating a BPPM competency. Clark and Cameron described four alignment factors that need to be taken into consideration when establishing a BPPM competency (as shown in Figure 3): strategic, "processual" (process-centric), social, and technical alignment.[9]

BPPM STRATEGIC ALIGNMENT FACTORS

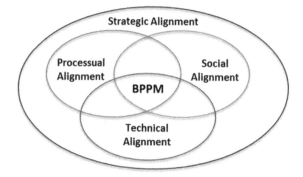

FIGURE 3

Strategic alignment factors when establishing a business process portfolio management (BPPM) competency.

Strategic Alignment

The strategic alignment factors describe when, where, and how BPPM will be applied in the organization and how it will be leveraged for strategic advantage. Vision, scope, and distinctive competencies need to be described here. According to Clark and Cameron, potential outcomes of BPPM might be operational transparency, dynamic executive dashboards tracking process performance, auditing capabilities, ease of business process configuration, and highlighting processes delivering competitive advantage.

Social Alignment

Social alignment factors look at aspects such as the facilitation of collaboration, knowledge sharing, and convergence in perceptions through BPPM as well as the degree of inclusion in decision making. The underlying premise is that process management is highly social and collaborative in many aspects. Clark and Cameron also highlighted that governance is a key social factor.

Processual Alignment

Processual alignment factors deal with methods performed to execute BPPM. According to Clark and Cameron, these include decomposition strategies (top-down, bottom-up, or a hybrid), taxonomies, process classifications, definitions, documentation, and performance metrics, knowledge management, and dealing with process repositories.

Technical Alignment

Technical alignment factors describe the technology used to achieve the desired outcomes of a BPPM strategy incorporating social and processual factors. Technology should be an enabler and not an inhibiter of a successful rollout of BPPM. Clark and Cameron also talked about the facilitation of meeting the top-down approach for BPPM with the bottom-up approach often used in service-oriented architectures deployments that should form part of the BPPM strategy.

BPPM LIFE CYCLE

The BPPM life cycle consists of a series of phases spanning from the opportunity management phase to the realization of an opportunity, right through to its transition into the appropriate operational environment; it concludes with continuous improvement, as shown in Figure 4, which has been adapted from the portfolio reference content.[10] This figure also highlights the value identification, planning, creation, realization, and governance flow across the portfolio management life cycle. It is obvious that the highest value potential can be realized during the earliest phase of the life cycle as well as in the continuous improvement phase.

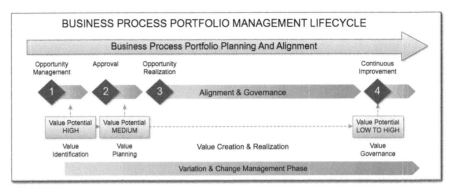

FIGURE 4

Business process portfolio management (BPPM) life cycle.

Each phase in the portfolio management life cycle is described below.

Business Process Portfolio Planning and Alignment Phase

The purpose of this phase is to define the portfolio and ensure the alignment of portfolio planning with organizational strategic goals, priorities, and direction. The portfolio needs to be approved by executive stakeholders.

Business process portfolio planning and alignment phase defining documents include the portfolio road map, portfolio baseline, executive change management strategy, and executive portfolio communication road map.

Opportunity Management Phase

The purpose of this phase is to rank required process improvement projects within the portfolio by assessing the project proposals for portfolio improvements against a defined set of criteria to generate objective ranking (identify, elect, prioritize, and rank) in relation to the organizational strategic outcomes provided by the executive stakeholders.

The opportunity management phase defining document is the project proposal that, at a minimum, describes required process changes by clearly articulating current as-is state, end-state vision, funding, high-level business requirements, benefits, risks, and stakeholders.

The outcome of this phase is to have a prioritized list of project proposals within the portfolio that have preliminary approval in principle with validation that the business unit or organization has the capacity and competency to carry out proposed projects.

Variation/Change Management Phase

Successful portfolio management techniques must consider the effects of variation both internal and external to the business across the life cycle of the portfolio. Programs and projects can start at any time and in most cases do not all start together, so there must be a phase that considers the changes imposed by the new project or new program. This is the variation/change management phase. Internal variations may be defined as missing processes, system requirements, or missing business objectives. External variation may be defined as missing legal/regulatory impacts or missing weather/environmental factors. The portfolio must have the capability to adjust to variations with which it is presented.

The BPPM process could use additional language to support change created by variation. Four variation factor types have been defined that have been found to be most problematic when managing multiple programs within a portfolio. In general, concern must be expressed about exposing what we do not know. The BPPM process should be designed to expose unknown deficiencies, gaps, or duplication as quickly as possible. A feedback loop is required within the process to react to the change and challenge the process to ultimately apply corrective action for each variation factor type. The effect on the portfolio and its related programs is indicated in Figure 5, with portfolio risk increasing as the scope clarity decreases.

Variation Factor Types:

- Variation Type 1: Known project with known "unknowns" (an approved and planned project that knows there are things which it does not know)
  - Documented project with documented requirements or processes to address the known "unknowns"

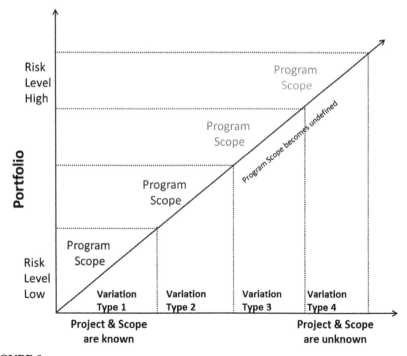

FIGURE 5

Change risk and variation factor type.

- Impacts: Minimal, the team has a known project and is tailoring requirements and processes to the program to address the known "unknowns." Because the project is known the team may have time to apply corrective action
- Variation Type 2: Known project with unknown "unknowns" (an approved and planned project that is unaware that there are things which it does not know)
  - Documented project with no documented requirements or processes to address the unknown "unknowns"
  - Impacts: Minor, the team has a known project and is not tailoring requirements and process to the program to address the unknown "unknowns." Because the project is known the team may have time to apply corrective action
- Variation Type 3: Unknown project with known "unknowns" (an unapproved or unplanned project that knows there are things it does not know)
  - Undocumented project with documented requirements or processes to address the known "unknowns"
  - Impacts: Major; the team has an unknown project that could have a significant impact on the program. However, the team is tailoring requirements and processes to address the known "unknowns." Because the project is unknown and has documented known "unknowns," the team may not have time to apply corrective action.
- Variation Type 4: Unknown project with unknown "unknowns" (an unapproved or unplanned project that is unaware that there are things which it does not know)
  - Undocumented project with no documented requirements or processes to address the unknown "unknowns"
  - Impacts: Critical because the team has an unknown project that could have a significant impact on the program. However, the team is not tailoring requirements and processes to address the unknown "unknowns." Because the project is unknown and has unknown "unknowns," the team will not have time to apply corrective action.

Approval Phase

The purpose of this phase is to formally authorize the business process portfolio improvements. The portfolio improvement projects are presented to executive stakeholders for approval by either the business process portfolio manager or the BP-PMO. The executive stakeholders evaluate the portfolio improvements at an enterprise level and then grant authorization for the improvement projects to proceed based on organizational strategic objectives and corporate capacity.

Once the approval is obtained, the process portfolio is rebalanced. The BP-PMO updates the portfolio delivery strategy within the portfolio road map document to provide an overview of the sub-portfolios, projects, costs, interdependencies, risks, stakeholders, and benefits along with a time frame used within the alignment and governance portfolio phase for effective portfolio monitoring and control.

Opportunity Realization Phase

The purpose of this phase is to provide alignment, oversight, and direction for the effective and timely management of the various process improvement initiatives and projects within the portfolio. The opportunity realization phase focuses executive attention at the portfolio level to primarily address the following considerations:

- Continual evaluation of performance and alignment of portfolio improvement projects against the portfolio road map approval of changes to project and portfolio baselines
- Alignment with other change initiatives (e.g., pure technology improvements with no business process impact) in the organization that might be managed by a separate project management office as well as prioritization across the different portfolios if necessary

This phase also serves to balance and optimize adjoining portfolios with respect to:

- Portfolio improvement project benefits and interdependencies within and between the adjoining portfolios
- Interdependencies between processes that are affected by improvement projects within and between adjoining portfolios
- Limited resource capacity/capability versus substantial demand
- Changes in business strategy/business opportunities
- Managing the portfolio to a predetermined risk profile

Figure 6 shows the relationship between the BPPM life cycle and the project management life cycle for portfolio improvement projects during the opportunity realization phase.[11]

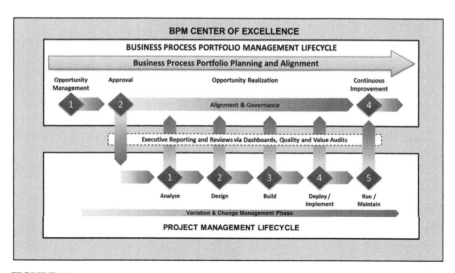

FIGURE 6

Relationship between BPPM life cycle and project management life cycle of process portfolio improvement projects.

Feedback Loop Communication

Successful portfolio management techniques must also consider the effects of communication. A concern in many organizations is about the language used in the documentation that addresses portfolio plans or process requirements approval with senior management. Pushing communication up to senior management and then back down to working management is time-consuming and loaded with risk. How do organizations improve that process so that approval or requirements, especially when impacted by variation and change management, are addressed faster? How do organizations compensate the loop to enable faster response time? Empowerment of middle management ranks that have access to or reside with the BPM CoE to make decisions that do not require executive level approval is an idea or provides a vehicle for frontline communications to flow directly back to senior management. Essentially the organization should create a distributed architecture of empowered middle managers who are part of the BPM CoE and who have the authority to approve tactical and operational changes and program and project management direction and provide a direct line of feedback to the executive team. This builds both the BPPM maturity and strengthens the BPM CoE in its governance.

Executive-level approval and decisions do not always work, for the following reasons:

1. Information is filtered and condensed on executive-level reporting
   a. Executives typically like to see one to three PowerPoint slides
   b. Many times critical information is missing
   c. Complex issue cannot always be quantified in three PowerPoint slides.
2. Executives are primarily concerned with money and budgets
   a. Many executives are too disconnected from the operations/technical issues to make the connection on how this impacts business
   b. Many executives do not have a long-term vision
   c. Many executives are too concerned about short-term gains and putting out immediate daily fires
3. Critical decisions are funneled and bottlenecked for a few select people to review
   a. Vertical communication up to senior management is time-consuming and slow
   b. Often there is no real value added in the process other than rubber stamping the request and moving forward with the project
   c. The decisions is often already been made, so why bother with the exercise?

Feedback Loop

The feedback loop requires the empowerment of a middle manager who has direct dotted line access to senior management. The existing manager, director, executive director, vice president (VP), and senior vice president (SVP) reporting structure stays in place; however, the empowered middle manager provides real team feedback to the VP/SVP team. This new channel will forward unfiltered and near real-time feedback to the senior management team. This new feedback channel will also keep the existing reporting structure and management team in check and ensure that both reports and feedback loops are in phase and in agreement.

An example of this is presented graphically in Figure 7.

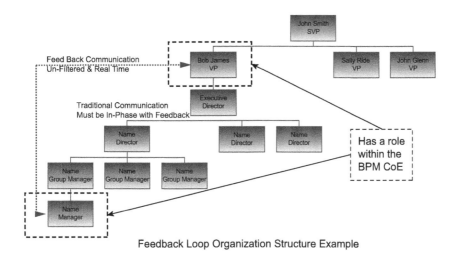

Feedback Loop Organization Structure Example

FIGURE 7

Example of feedback loop.

Continuous Improvement Phase

The purpose of this phase is to evaluate whether the portfolio benefits and contribution to the organization have been effectively realized. This is a consolidation and review of each of the individual projects' outcomes. Furthermore, remaining pain points and new opportunities for portfolio improvements are identified during this phase.

The portfolio continuous improvement phase defining documents are the portfolio benefits assessment and portfolio health assessment.

A portfolio health assessment can be gathered from the health assessment of individual business processes. Process health assessments should focus on costs versus value to the organization.[12]

BUSINESS PROCESS HIERARCHY

One of the tasks performed during the design phase of establishing a BPPM is to create a business process hierarchy, organize existing business processes into the hierarchy, and ideally store the information in a central repository.

Figure 8 presents a way to organize business process into a hierarchy as adapted from the business process reference content.[13] Business process areas and business process groups provide means to categorize existing business process hierarchies including business processes, steps, and activities. Business process areas and business process groups are not business processes.

BUSINESS PROCESS HIERARCHY

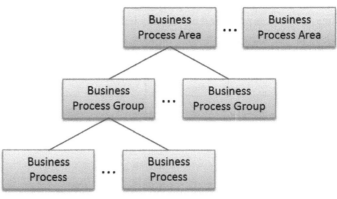

FIGURE 8

Example of a business process hierarchy.

Business Process Area

A business process area consists of business process groups with the same business goal, thus spanning the organization end-to-end or even across to business partners if they are involved in fulfilling that business goal. A business process portfolio should cover at least one business process area. Portfolio prioritization and improvements are also performed at this level.

Business Process Group

A business process group encapsulates logically related first-level business processes that are executed to realize a defined, measurable business outcome for a particular internal or external customer. Process improvements performed concurrently inside a business process group or cutting across different business process groups should be grouped into a program of projects to manage their interdependencies.

Business Process

The business process layer defines the first-level business processes that are organized into a flow to achieve a defined business outcome. Process improvement projects usually operate at this level.

BPPM INFORMATION, MEASUREMENTS, AND REPORTING

Once the requirements for a BPPM and a business process hierarchy are established, it is important to define the information that needs to be tracked for the business process areas, groups, and business processes for measurement and reporting.

BPPM Information for Measurement and Reporting

The required information depends on the strategy behind the establishment of BPPM. The primary objective of BPPM is to increase business value for an organization, whereas contemporary BPM focuses on driving effectiveness and efficiency through optimizing operating models. With that in mind, gathered information around processes must include indicators for business value creation and improvement.

Recommended information to be gathered includes:

- **General information**: Name, goal, and description
- **Value**: Value to the organization as well as value classification (e.g., which processes contribute to competitive advantage)
- **Strategic alignment**: Alignment to strategic goals and objectives, and customer satisfaction
- **Resources and stakeholders**: Stakeholders and resource requirements
- **Interrelationships**: Dependencies and interdependencies
- **Financials**: Costs and financial benefit
- **Risk**: Probability of failure multiplied by impact. Also, customer exposure and customer impact should be tracked, which in relation to frequency provide a holistic overview of risk (Rosemann, 2006)
- **Process metrics**: Volume, cycle time, elapsed time including wait time and nonproductive time, frequency, exceptions, defects, and rework
- **Process classification**: Process types such as core, support, and governing (Bilodeau)
- **Operational and change costs/benefit**: Past process changes including costs and tracked benefits compared with expectations

Figure 9 provides an overview of how important the different types of information are for the different levels of the process hierarchy. For example, gathering strategic and value information is more important at business process area level than at the business process level for portfolio improvements.

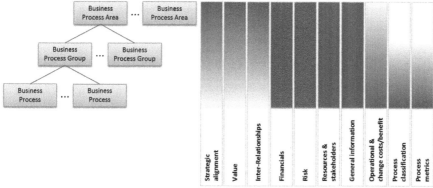

IMPORTANCE OF INFORMATION ACROSS THE PROCESS HIERARCHY

FIGURE 9

Importance of described types of information for different levels of the process hierarchy.

BPPM Measurements and Reporting

There are two levels where measurement and reporting should take place: at the portfolio level and at the process improvement project level.

At the portfolio level, the following measurements and reporting information could be beneficial beside some of the information described above:

- **Total number of processes**: A large process portfolio might be an indicator for increasing duplication of efforts
- **Percentage of processes per process owner**: Indicates accountability spread
- **Cost/benefit of processes**: Fosters decisions around improvement prioritization and driving effectiveness and efficiency
- **Percentage of processes above the desired maturity level and average maturity level**: Indicator of where to deploy resources and investments
- **Number of resources per process**: Indicator for possible composition or decomposition of processes

At the process improvement project level, the usual project measurement and reporting information can be used, such as:[14]

- Alignment to strategic goals
- Cost and return on investment
- Schedule and resourcing
- Scope/productivity
- Project cycle time (time to completion)
- Post project review and customer satisfaction
- Risk management

SUMMARY OF ESTABLISHING BPPM

This section provides an overview of the different considerations when establishing a BPPM in an organization. It discussed the creation of a BPPM competency, alignment issues, the BPPM life cycle, the process hierarchy for portfolio management, and required portfolio information for measurement and reporting. The next sections provides an overview of the lessons learned when implementing BPPM.

LESSONS LEARNED FROM IMPLEMENTING BPPM

This section presents an overview of considerations and lessons learned when implementing BPPM.

RIGHT TIME TO IMPLEMENT BPPM

The right time to implement BPPM and the extent depend on the BPM maturity of an organization. Rosemann distinguished among three phases along the maturity path.[15] The first is the process-unaware organization, in which BPPM can be used to provide an initial process structure with governing strategic (core) and support processes. The process-aware organization already has a good understanding of its important processes, has established sufficient and consistent modeling guidelines, and has an integrated model repository. However, the models are usually underused. In this phase, BPPM can substantially contribute to the organization's next leap in BPM. The focus should be on cross-processes, interdependencies, and prioritization according to the strategy and the risk of the processes. The third is the process-mature organization with an established BPPM that is continuously tracking the process performance, providing appropriate process information at all levels of the organization and established sophisticated audit trails.

The BPM maturity model (Figure 10) indicates the current state of organizations and their awareness of BPM process maturity. Most organizations surveyed exist at Level 2 maturity. An example of a BPM maturity path is also indicated with examples of what BPM deliverables can be expected along the journey. The BPM maturity model further indicates that as maturity is increased there is a proactive rather than reactive approach to processes management, and that industry performance improves for organizations with higher BPM maturity.

EFFECT OF LIMITED OR NO IMPLEMENTED BPPM IN THE LONG RUN

A limited BPPM or no BPPM can have severe effects on the operation and results of an organization, especially in the long term. This risk increases exponentially with the number of processes performed by an organization. Figure 11 shows an overview of direct effects of the lack of BPPM in an organization and their short-term and long-term results.

The sad reality is that many of these causes can be found in most organizations. Internal or external services and products are designed without a need and related processes are established to deliver them. Whereas external services and products fail when the customer does not accept them, unnecessary internal services are less obvious. The common approach to establishing a governance gate to facilitate the use of new internal services often leads to unnecessary or at least inefficient processes, binding resources that are required elsewhere.

CONCLUSIONS

BPPM constitutes the next logical step in implementing successful BPM. It provides an answer to organizations facing challenges with an ever-growing process portfolio with increasing duplication, with deploying their limited resources to the right process improvement initiatives at the right time, and with having an end-to-end view of how their processes create the desired business values. Organizations reaching higher BPM maturity will especially benefit from establishing BPPM.

This work discussed different aspects of implementing BPPM, such as the establishment of the BPPM competency, including areas to which it needs to align, the

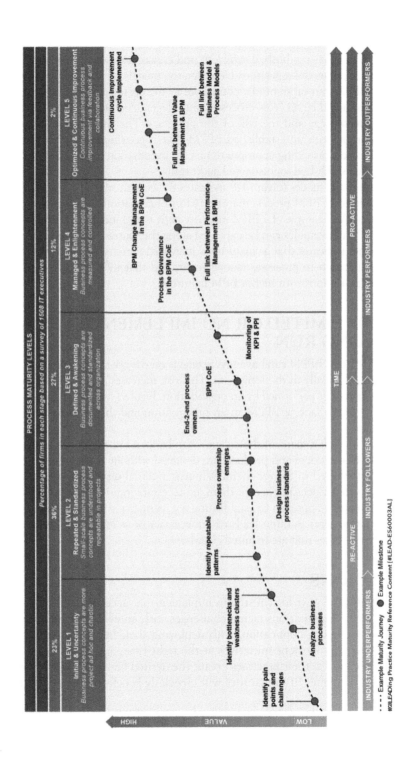

FIGURE 10

Business process management maturity levels.[16]

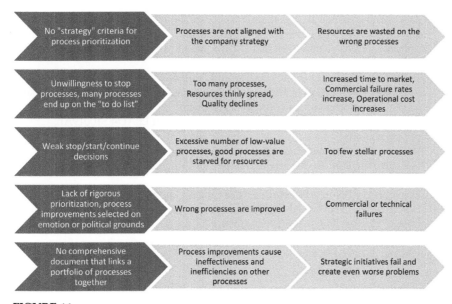

FIGURE 11

Causes of no or limited BPPM with short-term and long-term effects.

running of the BPPM life cycle, the required business process hierarchy, and portfolio information required for measurement and reporting at the portfolio and process improvement level. Furthermore, the timing of BPPM implementations depending on the organizations' BPM maturity was discussed, as well as common pitfalls and lessons learned when implementing BPPM.

Although, portfolio management in other areas such as project and PPM are well established, BPPM is relatively new. It is expected that successful implementations of BPPM in organizations will increase and that BPPM will be joined with PPM in the future.

End Notes

1. Darmani A. and Hanafizadeh P., "Business Process Portfolio Selection in Re-engineering Projects," *Business Process Management Journal* 19, no. 6 (2013): 892–916.
2. Scheer A-W., Feld T., and Caspers R., "BPM: New Architecture Driven by Business Process Planning and Control (BPPC). IM Journal for Information Management and Consulting," *Special Print* (2012): 1–8.
3. Robertson B., *Hype Cycle for Business Process Management*, 2013 (Gartner Inc., 2013).
4. Rosemann M., (2006). "Process Portfolio Management," Retrieved May 20, 2014, from BPTrends: http://www.bptrends.com/publicationfiles/04-06-ART-ProcessPortfolio Management-Rosemann1.pdf.
5. Allee V., *A Value Network Approach for Modeling and Measuring Intangibles*. Presented at Transparent Enterprise (Madrid, Spain, 2002).

6. Clark S. and Cameron B., "Business Process Portfolio Management: A Strategic Alignment Perspective," in *Business Enterprise, Process, and Technology Management: Models and Applications*, ed. V. Shankararaman, J.L. Zhao, and J.K. LeeHershey (Pennsylvania, USA: IGI Global, 2012), 18–31.

7. Bilodeau, N. Déjà Vu! From Project to Process Portfolio Management. Retrieved May 24, 2014, from BPMInstitute.org: http://www.bpminstitute.org/resources/articles/d%C3%A9j%C3%A0-vu-project-process-portfolio-management.

8. Taken from the Portfolio Management Reference Content LEAD-ES10019AL.

9. See note above 6.

10. Taken from the Portfolio Management Reference Content LEAD-ES10019AL.

11. Taken from the Portfolio Management Reference Content LEAD-ES10019AL.

12. See the note 1 above.

13. Taken from the Business Process Reference Content LEAD-ES20005BP.

14. Darmani A. and Hanafizadeh P., "Business process portfolio selection in re-engineering projects," *Business Process Management Journal* 19, no. 6 (2013): 892–916.

15. See note above 4.

16. LEADing Practice Maturity Reference Content #LEAD-ES60003AL.

Real-Time Learning: Business Process Guidance at the Point of Need

Nils Faltin, Mark von Rosing, August-Wilhelm Scheer

INTRODUCTION

Management guru Peter Drucker coined the term "knowledge worker" in his 1969 book, *The Age of Discontinuity*.[1] Although knowledge workers were differentiated from manual workers at that time, Drucker concluded that new industries would primarily employ knowledge workers and that in the information-based economy the role of the knowledge worker would be at the heart of all organizations. When we accelerate and fast-forward to today, the terms "knowledge worker" and "manual worker" are no longer mutually exclusive.[2] People loading product onto rail cars certainly work with their hands, but they may also contribute knowledge to the business. Toffler[3] observed that typical knowledge workers in the age of knowledge economy must have some automated system at their disposal to create, process, and enhance their own knowledge. In some cases, he argued, they would also need to manage the knowledge of their co-workers; so although knowledge workers engage in "peer-to-peer" knowledge sharing across organizational and company boundaries, forming networks of expertise around their activities,[4] they are not currently enabled enough for their activities they execute. It is not only knowledge workers who would benefit from having more and better, readily available information about their work tasks. Employees working in business processes with complex applications need more than training to attain the needed competence level. Experience shows that formal training measures will only build the foundation of what users need to be able to use the new software to its full extent.

Just 48 h after being trained, learners will recall only 30% of the learned knowledge.[5] But could the knowledge workers and learners not just look up the needed knowledge when they need it? Employees usually receive training documents, business process models, and presentation slides, and have information in wikis and blogs at their disposal. However, to look up information the user has to interrupt work and concentrate on looking for a solution to the problem at hand. The same is true for other sources employees consult to fill their knowledge gap, whether it is searching the Internet or online forums or asking colleagues (see Figure 1). Current research provides evidence that knowledge workers spend at least 38% of their time searching for information.[6] Because of all of this, users can be overwhelmed by the

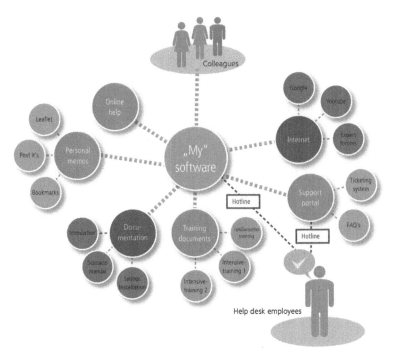

FIGURE 1

Knowledge workers have to find relevant information within a wealth of information sources.

amount of available information and lose much time until they find what is relevant for them. If users resort to trial and error, they may need even more time. As a result, productivity drops, usage errors sneak in, and acceptance of the newly introduced software system is at risk. As a consequence we see a whole new productivity, efficiency, performance management, and even effectiveness challenge for the modern organization. Thus, although there is a high level of standardization and integration enabled by automation, the potential for knowledge workers and other employees to call upon and use the embedded rules, guidelines, and knowledge is limited, hindering the organization's ability to innovate as well as harming its potential for growth.[7]

To give an example of the possible impact on an organization, such problems hit a large German clothing brand in 2006. When they replaced their outdated collection of enterprise resource planning (ERP) systems serving 2400 employees at five company sites with one new system, management expected more flexible, effective, and modern planning of clothing production. Because there are only a few delivery dates per year to dealers, production and logistics have to run reliably. However, the opposite happened. Employees were not able to use the new system correctly and made errors entering data. The wrong type and amount of fabric was delivered to the factories, which led to interruptions in the production of clothes. Insufficient supply to dealers was one reason the company later became insolvent.

All of this shows how important it is not only to train employees before a software rollout, but also to support them directly after going live and beyond. Learning and development (L&D) teams in the human resource departments become increasingly aware of this need and are looking for solutions. A benchmark by Towards Maturity published in 2013 highlighted that L&D teams are looking to technology to help them roll out new systems and processes faster.[8] Although 81% of these teams want technology to help them implement new information technology systems, only 28% of organizations already use such technology. What is troubling is that many organizations' value creation suffers because of lack of collaboration and reuse of existing knowledge[9] by not having the ability to provide the right information when the user needs it.

Because of this complexity and these challenges, today's workers and users want knowledge and skill elements that are concise and fit their need. Most expect the information to be available in a timely manner and easy to access, i.e., the time to consume should be as short as possible, requiring the content to be in small units with specific narrow and relevant topics, i.e., pragmatic and simple usage. These are often referred to as knowledge nuggets.

What seems to be most relevant in terms of these requirements is information that is discrete, concomitant, and directly relevant to the situation. It can be provided by knowledge situated or integrated into the activities, therefore being captured and managed within a process. Because this is a whole new way of continuous improvement of the learning organization, the following sections will explain how such technology support for learning new processes and applications can be made available to process workers.

REAL-TIME LEARNING TO CLOSE THE KNOWLEDGE GAP

Bite-Sized Learning Units

Real-time learning means providing the right information exactly when the user needs it. Information is presented in small, self-contained units to support building up knowledge quickly. This concept is called microlearning and enables learning with small learning units in the work context, adapted to the user. Users can obtain learning content in the midst of the work process, fitting to their context and the problem at hand. Later, if a user is confronted with the same problem again, the content can easily be obtained and consumed again, until it has been learned well.

Microlearning content is designed to enable multiple classes of workers in such a way that it can be easily understood and learned in a short time. Because it helps to solve a current problem, it enables operational excellence, improves efficiency, and helps to keep cost low. Furthermore, it enables self-learning, gives a feeling of success, and strengthens motivation for further work and learning. In a sense, it empowers and therefore is a new perspective on learning processes in mediated environments. Microlearning is especially common in the area of e-learning, where it caters to different learning styles and media preferences. Examples are short text explanations or video sequences, test questions, pictures, screen shots, and Web-based trainings. Also, apps, quizzes, and learning games that are commonly used on mobile devices (such as smartphones and tablets) can be regarded as a kind of microlearning content. As Theo Hug pointed out in *Micro Learning and Narration*,[10] no matter whether learning refers to the process of building up and organizing knowledge, to the change of behavior, attitudes, values, mental abilities, cognitive structures, emotional reactions, action patterns, or societal dimensions, in all cases we have the possibility of considering micro aspects of the various views on more or less persisting changes and sustainable alterations of performance.

ELECTRONIC PERFORMANCE SUPPORT: DELIVERING KNOWLEDGE AT THE POINT OF NEED

An *electronic performance support system* (EPSS) is technology for implementing the idea of real-time learning. It supplies users with small context-related learning units directly at the workplace and increases users' productivity and effectiveness. Usually an EPSS is defined as "a computer-based system that improves worker productivity by providing on the job access to integrated information, advice and learning experiences."[11] It helps reduce work process complexity and processing time, providing exactly the information a user really needs and user decision support for solving specific problems.[12]

BUSINESS PROCESS GUIDANCE

Business process guidance (BPG) takes performance support to the next level. Instead of just supporting users working with a single software application, BPG shows them an overview of all steps (in the business process in which they work) and guides them step by step through the process across several applications. Both software-based and manual work steps can be supported. BPG leaves a degree of freedom to the user regarding how to execute the process. This is in contrast to *workflow management systems* that strictly enforce each step of a process. Another difference is that BPG works well even if the applications cannot be controlled from a central system, whereas workflow management systems need tight technical integration with the applications to be able to start each application and data entry screen automatically.

COMPONENTS OF A BPG SYSTEM

A *BPG system* will be used by content authors and process workers (end users). Each user group needs a different user interface to interact with the system.

Authors create support information for each role and each step in a business process. Support information can be new written text but it also links to existing content such as user manuals, Web-based trainings, user guidelines, business process diagrams, and any other media available on the intranet or Internet. Other important media to support the use of software applications are screen shots and screen recordings. Authors connect support information to user interface elements of the supported application, such as application windows, menus, forms, and data entry fields. This will later allow the BPG system to display the relevant support information automatically when the user reaches a certain process step with the respective application window.

For each business process and role, content authors can create a sequence of user interaction steps. This will enable the BPG system to present the business process as a whole to the user and then guide the user along the process steps.

Process workers use software that detects the application, application window, and process step the user is in. Only information relevant to the current application context and business process step is shown. Such a BPG system is called *context sensitive*. In addition, users can manually search for a process, to be guided along its steps. This will help users to complete the work task. Users can then rate how helpful the content is to their need, ask questions, or suggest improvements to the content. This feedback will be forwarded to the content authors so they can answer questions and improve the support information.

BPG IN PRACTICAL USE

BPG can be applied to all kinds of business processes and application systems. Among the most common areas are support for data entry, multi-application processes, and simplifying communication with the support desk.[13]

SUPPORTING ENTRY OF CORRECT DATA

Large and medium-sized companies rely on ERP systems. They are needed to administer products, customers, orders, employees, and projects and to manage complex production, service delivery processes, and supply chains. Although many data entry forms seem self-explanatory, users can have difficulty figuring out what exactly needs to be entered in a certain input field. Consider the example of adding a new corporate customer into an application: To what industry sector does the organization belong? What is the industry sector code? In what format will the user have to enter a tax number? Do telephone numbers have to be entered with international prefix codes?

A BPG system stores organization specific knowledge and provides it to users while they work with the data entry application. The system detects which processing step the user is in and displays information that is relevant to this context.

SUPPORTING MULTIPLE APPLICATIONS

Process guidance needs to be supported across applications. This allows the business process and its parts to be described in a common platform, structure, and layout, which makes the support media much easier to understand. In any application in which they work, users can get the needed support and thus can work at full efficiency.

As an example, a salesperson creates a quote using several applications. He looks up some customer base data in, for example, the Customer Relationship Management (CRM) system. In Excel he calculates a price offer. He transfers the offer to a Word template, sends the document with Outlook to the customer, and changes the offer status in the CRM system. Classic help systems are installed together with their application and can only support this one application. Therefore, these help systems do not provide real process support. A real BPG system can provide support across applications, available at every work step. It brings business process descriptions for all applications of an organization in a common format to the employees' workplace.

ENHANCING COMMUNICATION WITH THE SUPPORT DESK

When a new application is deployed, users frequently contact the support desk, which can create a high workload on the side of the support desk. User requests can be triggered by software errors, but in most cases they are caused by user errors caused by employees' inexperience with the application or missing training on certain parts of it. Users often find it hard to explain their problem to the support desk with the required level of detail. Many cycles of the support desk asking questions to the user about the problem can occur, which is annoying to both sides and increases the time needed to solve the problem. A BPG system should allow users to send their automatically determined work context (process and process step worked on, application and screen used, and screen shot with data) together with a short problem statement to the support desk. This should be available to users while working with the application: for example, with special keys or buttons added by the BGP system to the user interface. This saves them the effort of switching to an external ticketing system and manually describing the context in detail. In a similar vein, users can comment on the support information provided by the BPG system (with their context being transmitted automatically) to ask for additional information or suggest improvements to the existing information. Both users and the support desk may benefit from such a BPG system, because users find it much easier to ask for support and send improvement requests. On the other hand, the support desk saves many clarification requests and can continuously improve the support information stored in the BPG system based on user suggestions. This, in turn, will give future users the answers they need so they will not need to ask the support desk.

INTRODUCING BPG IN AN ORGANIZATION
Creating a Repository of Microlearning Content

A BPG system offers bespoke microlearning and is therefore not pre-filled for any one application. The learning material must be sourced and entered into the BPG system before it is made available to users. Documentation, handbooks, project groups, specialist departmental knowledge, compliance-relevant information, work instructions, and organization-specific business process know-how from process repositories and databases are all relevant content sources (see Figure 2).

Taking into account the way people learn, decisions must be made on the form of content most applicable to support a specific function or process; these could range from short texts, images and screenshots, videos, and documentation to interactive online learning modules.

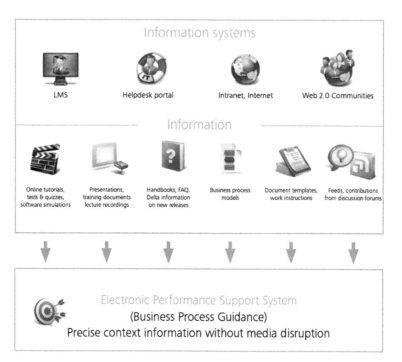

FIGURE 2

Learning content sources for Business Process Guidance.

MAJOR STEPS TO CREATE THE REPOSITORY

Based on these principles, a typical approach to create a relevant, helpful, and up-to-date repository of BPG learning content is to:

1. Define the business process, applications, and functionality to be supported by the BPG system
2. Identify the individual learning groups (according to department, function, etc.)
3. Select and gather learning content (which topics need to be covered and at what level of detail). Focus should be on the most value-adding processes and those where users have most problems in interacting with the applications
4. Upload the content to the BPG system
5. Regularly analyze requests to support desk and improvement suggestions from users and update the learning content accordingly

CONCLUSIONS AND OUTLOOK

As shown, risks of introducing applications to an organization do not stem primarily from the existing or newly introduced technology. They stem from the quality of the software-supported processes and the ability of employees to use the technology correctly.

The same BPG systems support the implementation of new applications and the update of business processes that go with it. They will reduce the effort required for training users up front and the support desk efforts needed in the introduction phase. Users will learn to use new software applications more rapidly and thus become more efficient in their process work. They will also gain a better overview of the overall process and what role different applications have in it. This is an important part in ensuring that business processes are performed as designed.

It is expected that real-time learning through BPG will grow in importance in the future:

- *More changes*: Processes and applications will change even more frequently in the future, triggering a need for training and support among the employees using them
- *More collections of applications*: Instead of one large system installed and configured on premise, we will often see a collection of applications provided as a service out of the cloud. This asks for process guidance that works across applications and that can be configured and equipped with content by the user organization
- *Social networks will be used more at work*: We will also see more knowledge sharing and peer support using social network technologies at the workplace. Social BPG will provide users with access to the social network communication channels and will help to filter and display only messages that are relevant based on the process and application context of the user
- *Users will influence provision of content*: Statistics from software usage and user feedback will become an important source for content authors to provide additional content and improve the existing support content in the BPG system

- *BPG will extend beyond the office*: Mobile devices will bring process guidance to new areas such as repair and maintenance of machines. First prototypes are built in research projects where information and work instructions will be displayed with augmented reality techniques on top of live pictures taken through the built-in camera. Users can call experts who support them directly, seeing the machine in real time through the camera.

BPG already is a good concept to support the introduction of new processes and applications. Its potential will grow in the future as it enables the organization.

End Notes

1. Drucker, Peter F., *The Age of Discontinuity Guidelines to our Changing Society*, 1969.
2. Rosen, E., *Every Worker Is a Knowledge Worker* (Business Week, 2011).
3. Toffler, A., *Powershift: Knowledge, Wealth and Violence at the Edge of the 21st Century*, 1990, ISBN 0-553-29,215-3..
4. Tapscott, Don; Williams, Anthony D., *How Mass Collaboration Changes Everything*, (Penguin, 2006) ISBN 1-59,184-138-0.
5. Güldenberg Stefan, "Wissensmanagement und Wissenscontrolling in lernenden Organisationen," (2003).
6. Mcdermott Michael, "Knowledge Workers: You can gauge their effectiveness," *Leadership Excellence* 22, no.10 (2005), ISSN: 8756–2308.
7. Overton Laura, "5 Practical Ideas for Embedding Learning into the Workflow," Available from towards Maturity Inc., published (July 2013) http://www.towardsmaturity.org/article/2013/07/04/5-practical-ideas-embedding-learning-workflow/.
8. Ibid.
9. Tapscott Don, Williams Anthony D., *How Mass Collaboration Changes Everything* (Penguin, 2006), ISBN 1-59184-138-0.
10. Hug T., *Micro Learning and Narration. Exploring possibilities of utilization of narrations and storytelling for the designing of "micro units" and didactical micro-learning arrangements* (MIT: Cambridge (MA), USA. 2005).
11. Raybould Barry, "An EPSS.Case Study," (1991).
12. Gery Gloria, "*Electronic Performance Support Systems: How and why to Remake the Workplace Through the Strategic Application of Technology*," (1991).
13. Milius Frank and Meiers Christina, "Performance Support für Mitarbeiter, Applikationen und Prozesse—Microlearning als methodischer Ansatz zur mitarbeiterorientierten Softwareschulung," *Information Management und Consulting* 26 (2011): 2.

Business Process Management Alignment

Mona von Rosing, Henrik von Scheel, Justin Tomlinson, Victor Abele,
Kenneth D. Teske, Michael D. Tisdel

INTRODUCTION

Alignment is a concept that dates back to the late 1990s, when it was described by
Paul Strassmann[1]: "Alignment is the capacity to demonstrate a positive relationship
between information technologies and the accepted financial measures of performance." Alignment of business process management (BPM) hence should follow
a similar principle or pattern to be effective. The objective therefore is how this
alignment to and between BPM can create value that is ultimately measurable as a
favorable financial outcome for a commercial enterprise.

Business process management alignment, which is focused on both reusability and
accelerating automation, requires that business managers have an understanding of what
alignment is, how to develop an alignment competency, and what considerations should
be made by organizations to ensure alignment is adequately adopted. This chapter discusses these aspects of alignment and gives credence to the development of aligned BPM.

BACKGROUND TO A NEW WAY OF LOOKING AT ALIGNMENT FOR BPM

The portfolio alignment-unity concept was developed for the United States Department of Defense (DOD), Department of Homeland Security (DHS), Department of
Justice (DOJ), and Department of State (DOS) with the aim of

- Unifying common stakeholders, objectives, and size for common, complex, and
  critical missions and multidimensional warfare such as cyber war, combating
  weapon of mass destruction, combating transnational organized crime, and for
  security corporations.
- Achieving information sharing and unity of effort to meet national security
  objectives for the US DOD, DHS, DOJ, and the DOS.

US Government research involving the DHS, DOS, DOJ, and DOD initiated
an alignment effort to:

1. Identify and specify common and repeatable patterns for business, application,
   and technology areas
2. Support analysis and stability operations planning efforts per JROCM 172-13
3. Change and update joint doctrine

4. Assess for use by the Executive Committee Joint Program Office (JPO) for Assignment of National Security and Emergency Preparedness Communications Functions per Executive Order 13,618
5. Benchmark, research and analyze, and identify alignment and unification patterns
6. Pilot first projects within US Government
7. Join and develop alignment and unity reference content that increases the level of reusability and replication within alignment and unity of stakeholders, portfolios, programs, and enterprise modeling, enterprise engineering, and enterprise architecture concepts
8. Extend with accelerators and templates, such as the:
   a. Alignment and Unity Stakeholder Map
   b. Alignment and Unity Quick Scan
   c. Alignment and Unity Maturity TCO-ROI evaluation
   d. Alignment and Unity Maturity Benchmark
   e. Alignment and Unity Development Path

The alignment-unity framework concept was such a success that DOD Stability Operations recommended the alignment-unity framework concept be used to support analysis and stability operation planning efforts per JROCM 172-13. A Unity of Effort Synchronization Framework Joint Knowledge online course was developed and over 600 DOD and other governmental personnel have taken and completed the course. In addition to this, Joint Doctrine Publication 3.0, 3.22, and others have adopted the alignment-unity framework and are incorporating it into the newest editions.

As of August 2014, the alignment-unity framework concept was being assessed for use by the Executive Committee JPO for Assignment of National Security and Emergency Preparedness Communications Functions. The framework has already been applied by US Special Operations Command to align its information technology portfolio as well as assist the J3-International division in finding commonality while building the Global Special Operations Forces Network (GSN) with its multinational mission partners.

Such a comprehensive alignment management concept uniquely recognizes that any organization, department, or even program, even if it has its own mission, vision, strategies, and critical success factors, is only one element of a larger delivery and service mechanism. In nearly all cases the success of strategy to execution depends on the ability to operate in alignment and therefore unity with the rest of the organizations with a common stake in the issues.

This truly encourages collaboration across areas, groups, portfolios, programs, and projects that will enable value creation and realization. However, realizing higher levels of alignment and unity requires identification of common objectives, initiatives, and standards or requirements.

Most organizations today face significant hurdles to ensure organizational alignment among goals, stakeholder, plans, programs, projects, and portfolios. Identification is the first step toward developing solutions or mitigation strategies. This US DOD Unity of Effort Framework project was developed with several organizational participants to identify important inhibitors to achieving unity of effort. Identifying the negatives is important, however; we learned that identifying the positives such as goals, areas of interest, and categories of effort applied by each of the organizations worked much better for gaining unity.

A lesson learned was that working together with a framework provided many more benefits than detractors on the way to improving unity of effort for complex governmental missions to include operational design, planning, and decision making about scarce resources. The framework also enables orchestrated development of planning to achieve regional and national objectives and is an enabler for building partnership capacity and security sector assistance.

The framework allowed for recommendations based on opportunities for strong organizational partnerships. Another lesson learned while working with stakeholders is that the framework allowed for identification of redundancies or overlaps, gaps in support requirements, seams in the operating environment, and shortfalls in resources.

We also learned that to develop true alignment, it requires representation, participation, and collection of information from stakeholder organizations. To facilitate this, an organization or group must be identified to manage the time and processes to complete a framework. In addition, some events must occur in person to allow time for stakeholders to validate and clarify collected information and participate through staffing activities.

The alignment as indicated in this chapter needs to be specific to business processes and their related objects and enterprise business elements. First, though, we need to define what alignment is in relation to BPM.

ALIGNMENT OF BPM

Most stakeholders across the enterprise landscape have some of the same external and internal forces and drivers influencing them, but different approaches. These stakeholders do not see what is common and hence they do not know how or why to work together. This indicates a lack of alignment maturity and results in enterprise strategy, management, and operations that are disjointed and do not provide the expected return on investment, representing an untapped potential of cost savings and operational excellence for both effectiveness and efficiency only based on the wide range of duplication of goals, competencies, services, process, functions, task, resources, roles, data, etc.

Alignment of BPM provides for the policy or strategy of the organization to drive the alignment of BPM portfolios, programs, and projects that require the relevant stakeholders (business process owners) to develop a common understanding of their business process so that there is a transformation of business process from the "as-is" through to the "to-be." The to-be business processes that have been aligned can then be used in enterprise transformation and innovation to enable improved financial measures of performance. This high level of BPM alignment is described in Figure 1.

ESTABLISHING ALIGNMENT TO BPM

One of the key tasks before even starting to establish alignment to BPM is to confirm that BPM alignment within an organization is even feasible. This requires two questions to be answered in the affirmative:

1. Is there a clear link with the organization's planning and budget commitments?
2. Does the organization have the level of competency required to carry out such a task?

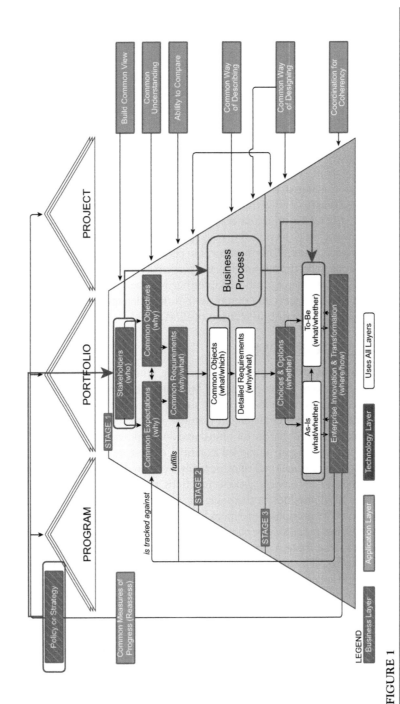

FIGURE 1

Business process management alignment from policy to enterprise innovation and transformation.[2]

If the answer to these two questions is no or if it is uncertain, it is likely that the organization is suffering from one of the following symptoms in the area of BPM:

1. Stove pipes/silos (lack of process information sharing)
2. No visibility of BPM efforts and activities
3. Duplication of efforts and investments across the same set of business processes
4. Lack of planning resources to enable aligned BPM
5. No collective repository of process-centric information
6. Competing priorities among the stakeholders of a specific business process
7. Differing lexicon/taxonomy/language/vocabulary/semantics for BPM
8. Disparate activities across the organization relating to BPM

Overcoming these challenges requires the buy-in and leadership of senior executives. Decision makers and corporate governance requires a higher order of insight to effectively identify gaps and overlaps in its transformation and innovation plans. Furthermore, this is needed to identify opportunities to minimize costs and improve performance of its operational services, as well as to determine a road map for capital investments in corporate infrastructures. Finally, without a methodical way to link strategic business objectives across all layers of a corporate architecture, the organization runs the risk of disjointed execution and a diminished capacity to effectively control and assess the performance of service providers, both internal and external.

In both public and private sector organizations, the consequences translate to higher operating costs, disappointing returns on investment in transformation and innovation, and lost market opportunity.

Throughout business planning and project gating cycles, an organization needs to identify the portfolios, programs, and/or projects that are BPM related and identify aspects that are not aligned to their planning and budget commitments, correct misaligned and redundant efforts, and adjust where possible to an aligned state. Furthermore, the organization needs to identify what competencies are required to achieve the level of BPM alignment, which will bring improved efficiency and effectiveness and advance the organization's financial measures of performance. To methodically assess the potential for business process alignment, it is valuable to take an architectural view of which objects the business processes would relate to and therefore what templates could be used to facilitate improved alignment.

Table 1 describes objects that would be relevant to the overall business processes group object.

As indicated in Figure 1 the alignment starts at the highest level for BPM with the policy and the relevant stakeholders. They then need to ascertain to which business process meta objects can be related and aligned, bringing about synergy to the higher levels.

In Figure 2, alignment of the business process meta objects is highlighted through the relationships that can be made. The way this is achieved is through the development of maps, matrices, and models that cover from forces and drivers all the way to infrastructure high availability. This means that the templates that are relevant

Table 1 *Business Process Group and Its Related Objects Needed for BPM Alignment*

Meta Object	Description
Process area (categorization)	Highest level of an abstract categorization of processes
Process group (categorization)	Categorization and collection of processes into common groups
Business process	Set of structured activities or tasks with logical behavior that produce a specific service or product
Process step	Conceptual set of behaviors bound by the scope of a process, which, each time it is executed, leads to a single change of inputs (form or state) into a single specified output. Each process step is a unit of work normally performed within the constraints of a set of rules by one or more actors in a role who are engaged in changing the state of one or more resources or business objects to create a single desired output
Process activity	Part of the actual physical work system that specifies how to complete the change in the form or state of an input, oversee, or even achieve the completion of an interaction with others actors and which results in the making of a complex decision based on knowledge, judgment, experience, and instinct
Event	State change that recognizes the triggering or termination of processing
Gateway	Determines forking and merging of paths, depending on the conditions expressed
Process flow (including input/output)	Stream, sequence, course, succession, series, or progression, all based on the process input/output states, where each process input/output defines the process flow that together executes a behavior
Process role	Specific set of prescribed set of expected behavior and rights (authority to act) meant to enable its holder to successfully carry out his or her responsibilities in the performance of work. Each role represents a set of allowable actions within the organization in terms of the rights required for the business to operate
Process rule	Statement that defines or constrains some aspect of work and always resolves to either true or false
Process measurement (process performance indicators)	Basis by which the enterprise evaluates or estimates the nature, quality, ability, or extent regarding whether a process or activity is performing as desired
Process owner	Role performed by an actor with the fitting rights, competencies, and capabilities to take decisions to ensure work is performed

LEAD Templates & LEAD Meta Object Relations	FD	VM	Rq	ST	S	V	BSC	Pe	M&R	Comp	Rev	Co	Op	I	Ro	O	OC	Ob	WF	Ru	Ch	Me	P	BPMN	Se	A	AS	ARo	AR	SysM	AI	Asc	C	D	DS	DR	PL	PLS	PLR	PLD	IF	IFS	IFR	IFV	IFH
Business Process																																													
Process Area (categorization)	1.2									2			1										1.2	2																					
Process Group (categorization)	1.2		1.2							2			1										1.2	2																					
Business Process										2													1.2	2.3	2	2																			
Process Step																							1.2	3	2	2																			
Process Activity												2											1.2	3	2	2																			
Events												2											1.2	3	2	2	3																		
Gateways																				2			1.2	3	2	2	3																		
Object (Business & Information & Data)																		1.2					2.3	2.3			3																		
Object Type (main/mgmt./support)													2										1	1																					
Process Flow (incl. Input/output)											3								1.2				3	3	2		3				3	3													
Process Rules												2.3								1.2			2.3	2.3	2				2	2			2												
Process Rules								1.2	1.2														2	2.3																					
Process Measurement (PPI)								1.2	2			1.2			1.2	1.2							1.2	2.3	2																				
Process Owner				2																																									

FIGURE 2

Alignment across business process objects (1, maps, 2, matrices; 3, models).[3]

to alignment within BPM and the strategic, tactical, and operational aspects are covered satisfactorily.

As an example of this alignment, the business processes (meta object) can be related to the requirements map and matrix, to the competency of an organization through a matrix, to cost through a matrix, to business process notations through a matrix and a model, and so on.

Each of the business process meta objects can be aligned in this way to the specific aspects required by an organization to fulfill its portfolio, program, and projects. It furthermore ensures that the business process alignment is applicable across the following layers of business and application.

Why is it important that the business processes be linked to the application layer? This is vital so that the process automation can be executed in line with the to-be business processes designed in the business layer.

BUSINESS SCENARIOS THAT WOULD REQUIRE BUSINESS PROCESS ALIGNMENT

The following section deals with some of the possible business scenarios that would require extensive review of the business processes and a transformation project to bring about alignment.

Stakeholder Alignment

Most stakeholders across the enterprise landscape have some of the same external and internal forces and drivers influencing them, but different approaches. These stakeholders do not see what is common and hence they do not know how to work together.

Alignment Portfolio, Program, and Project Management Challenges

Portfolio, program, and project management (PPPM) has a definite placeholder within the greater enterprise management organizational structure, as depicted in Figure 3. All three of these disciplines have been well documented and researched on their own and in combination. Within the enterprise structure the influence of their alignment is most noticeable and hence most influential. All organizations, whether large or small, across all industry sectors will recognize that they need a combination of portfolio, program, and project management to deliver change initiatives that transform and or innovate their business. For PPPM the alignment context is multidirectional. Alignment needs to flow from both a top-down and bottom-up perspective. Aligning the portfolio at the strategic level through the programs at the tactical level to the projects at the operational level will enable smarter decisions. Alignment of PPPM is also influenced through the stakeholders who influence the enterprise structure at each of the organizational layers and all of the processes involved.

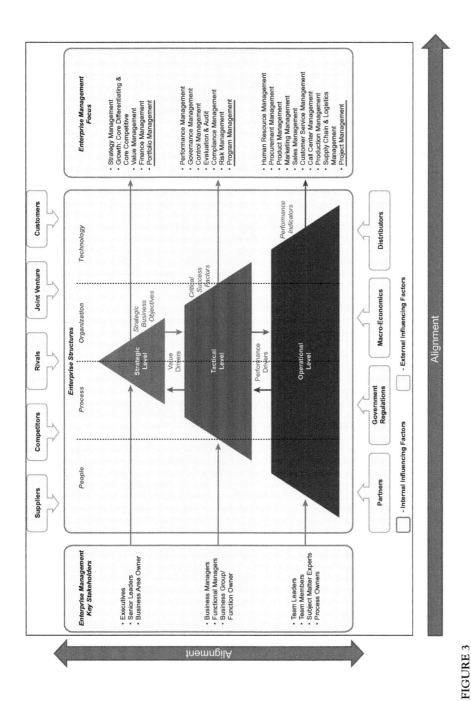

FIGURE 3

Alignment of PPPM across the enterprise structures.[4]

Merger and Acquisition

A typical example of when alignment of BPM would be necessary is when a company goes through a merger or when it acquires a new business entity through an acquisition. The merger or acquisition would require a transformation project that would focus its attention on identifying the common set of stakeholders who have a common set of business processes. The use of Figure 1 and Figure 3 is important to guide the flow from start to finish in terms of a transformation BPM alignment project.

Align BPM with Business Intelligence to Achieve Business Process Excellence

Today, many organizations implement BPM and business intelligence initiatives as separate programs. They are flooded with indicators—mostly process performance indicators and key performance indicators—but performance monitoring is carried out at too local a level in too isolated a way, and with too much focus on lagging indicators. Usually it is hard to see how the various factors measured contribute to different aspects of business value. Combining BPM and business intelligence to achieve closed-loop performance management makes it possible to relate all these indicators to each other. It thus becomes possible to analyze cause-and-effect relationships over different dimensions. As a result, management and staff can make better and more timely decisions and the organization becomes more efficient and effective. This is a crucial step for any enterprise with its sights set on intelligent business operations.

Align BPM with Master Data Management for Master Data Governance, Stewardship, and Enterprise Processes

When organizations align their master data management (MDM) and BPM (BPM) projects, they maximize the value of each solution. Analysts recommend that clients and vendors adopt a strategy that supports this aligned approach. An enterprise can gain differentiating value by aligning its MDM and BPM initiatives. Master data management provides data consistency to improve the integrity of business processes, making those processes smarter, more effective, and productive. Business process management is an agile process platform that can provide consistent visibility, collaboration, and governance. By aligning MDM and BPM initiatives, organizations can optimize their business performance through agile processes that empower decision makers with the trusted information that can provide a single version of truth.

Align BPM with SOA for a Business-Driven, Service-Oriented Enterprise

There is still a gap between business and information technology (IT), because until now the services provided by a Service Oriented Architecture (SOA) could not support the business processes immediately. Thus, combining and aligning SOA and BPM projects results in increased benefits that are achieved more quickly than when either is initiated alone, especially for larger initiatives, achieving a business-driven, service-oriented enterprise and with automated processes across business functions. Processes that need to execute across functions are often hampered by a lack of interoperability of underlying systems. Automate new processes with greater speed and change processes quickly in response to business needs. Avoid costly business errors and focus on improving business processes—not integrating systems. Align IT investments with business needs: With an SOA, it is straightforward to prioritize building services needed for key business processes and to establish service-level key performance indicators. That maximizes not only the alignment with business needs, but also the return on IT investments.

Align BPM with Cloud for Business Process as a Service

Many business processes are good candidates for the cloud service. Alignment of BPM and cloud, called business process as a service, combines business processes and a cloud-based infrastructure enabling core computing resources best directed at the core business to be freed up. With goals of transparency and cost-efficiency in mind, it is logical to outsource many IT functions that are no longer cost-effective or when internal innovation is lacking. Increasing numbers of applications can be provided as a service with the right combination of technology and knowledge, from reporting and trade management to digital rights management and business analytics.

BENEFITS OF BPM ALIGNMENT

The strategic value of BPM alignment and the effect on organizational performance are significant, ranging from better processes produced to lower costs, higher revenues, motivated employees, and happier customers. The benefit checklist for the executive team includes the following:

1. Eliminates unnecessary process steps that are either regional- or system-driven
2. Standardizes and integrates the process across all geographies and business units for better benefit realization
3. Automates after elimination of unnecessary steps and standardizes the process
4. Enables process innovation using historical data from the BPM system once you have automated the process to transform it
5. Creates a repeatable pattern to align stakeholders with various portfolios, projects, and programs
6. Creates a consistent and institutionalized approach to align, plan, and resource programs and projects toward meeting common strategic objectives, expectations, and requirements
7. Improves alignment within planning, investments, and synchronization of effort across multiple portfolios, projects and programs, departments, interagencies, and resources

8. Enables alignment for complex planning efforts
9. Reduces duplication of efforts across business, application, and or technology areas
10. Improves joint delivery and execution
11. Is a proven concept to reduce radical cost
12. Enables better transparency and traceability
13. Does not disturb existing efforts; rather, it provides a means to inform, integrate, synchronize, and control

CONCLUSIONS

In this chapter we have focused on BPM alignment and how it is a top priority for executives. We covered what BPM alignment is, why it is important, and how and where it can or should be applied. Business process management alignment establishes the basis for effective tactical planning and drives continuous improvement and change management. The effectiveness of BPM efforts can be predicted by the maturity of an organization's planning, alignment, and change management. We described this "how and where" to enable replication of the same success across projects, portfolios, and programs. Combined with Business Intelligence (BI), MDM, SOA, and/or the cloud, BPM alignment offers significant potential to drive value and affect organizational performance.

End Notes

1. Paul A. Strassmann (1997), *The Squandered Computer*. Page 27–29 ISBN: 0-9620413-1-9.
2. LEADing Practice Alignment & Unity Reference Content #LEAD-ES60001AL.
3. Business Process Objects Relations from LEAD Template & LEAD Meta Object Relation, LEADing Practice.
4. LEADing Practice Alignment & Unity Reference Content #LEAD-ES60001AL.

Business Process Outsourcing

Mark von Rosing, Gary Doucet, Gert O. Jansson, Gabriel von Scheel, Freek Stoffel, Bas Bach, Henk Kuil, Joshua Waters

INTRODUCTION

The great interest in outsourcing since the start of the 1980s had several causes and was influenced in numerous ways by process work. In this chapter, we will focus on what business process outsourcing is, why it is applied, and which aspects to consider before implementing business process outsourcing strategies in an organization.

Since the industrial revolution, companies have battled with how they can exploit their competitive advantage to increase their markets and their profits. The model for most of the twentieth century was a large integrated company that can own, manage, and directly control its assets. In the 1950s and 1960s, the rallying cry was diversification to broaden corporate bases and take advantage of economies of scale. By diversifying, companies expected to protect profits, even though expansion required multiple layers of management. Subsequently, organizations attempting to compete globally in the 1970s and 1980s were handicapped by a lack of agility that resulted from bloated management structures. To increase their flexibility and creativity, many large companies developed a new strategy of focusing on their core business, which required identifying critical processes and deciding which could be outsourced.[1]

Outsourcing was not formally identified as a business strategy until 1989 (Mullin, 1996). However, most organizations were not totally self-sufficient; they outsourced those functions for which they had no competency internally. Publishers, for example, have often purchased composition, printing, and fulfillment services. The use of external suppliers for these essential, but ancillary, services might be termed the baseline stage in the evolution of outsourcing. Outsourcing support services was the next stage. In the 1990s, as organizations began to focus more on cost-saving measures, they started to outsource functions necessary to run a company, but not related specifically to the core business. Managers contracted with emerging service companies to deliver accounting, human resources, data processing, internal mail distribution, security, plant maintenance and the likes as a matter of good housekeeping. Outsourcing components to affect cost savings in key functions was yet another stage as managers sought to improve their finances.

BUSINESS PROCESS OUTSOURCING: WHAT IS IT?

The short version is that business process outsourcing (BPO) is the contracting of a specific business task, such as payroll, to a third-party service provider. Business process outsourcing is a subset of outsourcing that involves contracting of operations and responsibilities of specific business functions (or processes) to a third-party

657

service provider. Originally, this was associated with manufacturing firms such as Coca Cola that outsourced large segments of their supply chain.[2] Business process outsourcing is not considered only by large multinational organizations, however. Business process outsourcing is not a new field. Rochester, New York-based Paychex, for example, has been outsourcing payroll processing for small businesses since 1971. But the market is heating up these days thanks to companies' keen interest in cost cutting, their desire to improve business methods, and their growing comfort with outsourcing arrangements.[3] Business process outsourcing is something many organizations of any size apply. In this context, BPO is often divided into two categories[4]: (1) back office outsourcing, which includes internal business functions such as billing or purchasing; and (2) front office outsourcing, which includes customer-related services such as marketing or tech support. Business process outsourcing that is contracted outside a company's own country is sometimes called offshore outsourcing. Business process outsourcing that is contracted to a company's neighboring country is sometimes called near-shore outsourcing, and BPO that is contracted with the company's own county is sometimes called onshore outsourcing. Often the business processes are information technology (IT)-based, and are referred to as ITES-BPO, where ITES stands for information technology enabled service. Knowledge process outsourcing and legal process outsourcing are some of the sub-segments of the BPO industry.[5]

BUSINESS PROCESS OUTSOURCING VALUE CASE

The main advantage of BPO is the way in which it helps increase a company's flexibility. In the early 2000s, BPO was all about cost efficiency, which allowed a certain level of flexibility at the time. Owing to technological advances and changes in the industry (specifically, the move to more service-based rather than product-based contracts), companies who choose to outsource their back office increasingly looked for time flexibility and direct quality control.[6] Business process outsourcing enhances the flexibility of an organization in different ways:

- Most services provided by BPO vendors are offered on a fee-for-service basis, using business models such as remote in-sourcing or similar software development and outsourcing models.[7] This can help a company to become more flexible by transforming fixed into variable costs.[8]
- A variable cost structure helps a company respond to changes in the required capacity and does not require a company to invest in assets, thereby making the company more flexible.[9] Outsourcing may provide a firm with increased flexibility in its resource management and may reduce response times to major environmental changes.
- Another way in which BPO contributes to a company's flexibility is that a company is able to focus on its core competencies without being burdened by the demands of bureaucratic restraints.[10]
- Key employees are released from performing non-core or administrative processes and can invest more time and energy in building the firm's core

businesses.[11] The key lies in knowing which of the main value drivers to focus on: customer intimacy, product leadership, or operational excellence. Focusing more on one of these drivers may help a company create a competitive edge.[12]

- Business process outsourcing increases organizational flexibility by increasing the speed of business processes. Supply chain management with the effective use of supply chain partners and BPO increases the speed of several business processes, such as the throughput in the case of a manufacturing company.[13]
- Flexibility is seen as a stage in the organizational life cycle: A company can maintain growth goals while avoiding standard business bottlenecks.[14] Business process outsourcing therefore allows firms to retain their entrepreneurial speed and agility, which they would otherwise sacrifice to become efficient as they expanded. It avoids a premature internal transition from its informal entrepreneurial phase to a more bureaucratic mode of operation.[15]

A company may be able to grow at a faster pace because it will be less constrained by large capital expenditures for people or equipment that may take years to amortize, may become outdated, or may turn out to be a poor match for the company over time. The economic benefits of BPO are clear: the CNET News report[16] states some of these benefits in numbers: Whereas IT outsourcing, such as farming out control of a data center, can cut costs by 10–15%, outsourcing a business process may shave 40–60% off the bottom line, Pool said. "What you're providing on the BPO side is much more valuable to the client."

The business case[17] for traditional finance and administration BPO is well proven; typically the service can be delivered as effectively, i.e., with no worsening in quality of service, and more efficiently in a lower cost location, typically with an improved system of controls. Most of the business case is a combination of efficiency, centralization, standardization, process improvement, and automation coupled with labor arbitrage benefits of low-cost locations. The combination of these levers can often bring benefits of 40–50% on original cost. However, the business case for procurement is about sourcing and compliance savings, i.e., effectiveness savings (doing it better or, in the case of procurement, buying the same or better for less), which can dwarf the efficiency savings (doing it quicker or cheaper). Also, the efficiency savings in procurement are often less (perhaps 20–30%) because the resources will need to be located across regional locations to support language requirements, not just in far eastern low-cost locations; hence, average savings will be less than the 40–50% above (Figure 1).

I therefore believe that the largest portion of the benefit from outsourcing can come from sourcing savings and in particular through better compliance management.

However, it is critical to approach the design of the outsourcing in a way that maximizes the efficiency (process) savings and maximizes the (sourcing) effectiveness savings. You can construct a business case for procurement BPO on efficiency savings, but you will sell it to the business on effectiveness savings.

Building the business case for BPO Procurement

Note: Client with $500 million in indirect source-able spend

FIGURE 1

Example of BPO procurement business case.

THE BPO MARKET

In 2014–2015, the growth of BPO was 4% and surpassed $950 billion; it is expected to average a 5% clip each year through 2018.[18] The global BPO and related IT service market size in 2014 (in billion US dollars) by segment were the following[19] (see Figure 2).

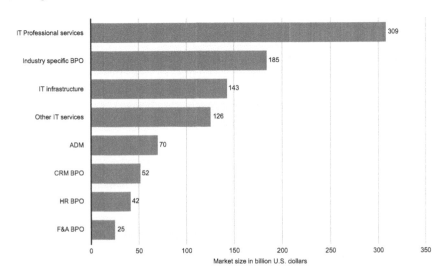

FIGURE 2

The global BPO and the related IT service market size in 2013–2014.

BUSINESS PROCESS OUTSOURCING: POSSIBLE PITFALLS

Although the BPO value case arguments favor the view that BPO increases the flexibility of organizations, management needs to be careful with implementing it because there are issues that work against these advantages. In this section we will try to illustrate them.

These days, outsourcing is often an expression of the facility management way of thinking: that is, how I can minimize my risks and secure the best relevant price/performance, for example, in accounts departments, IT operations, staff restaurants. The challenge for all of these lies in the interfaces. What are the expectations regarding upstream and downstream to have successful outsourcing? This may vary, but it is interesting that 70% of all outsourcings are reported as failures, especially those that are primarily aimed at cutting cost.[20] This is alarming. As Chief Executive Officer Peter Bendor-Samuel of the Everest Group pointed out,[21] part of the reason is that many BPO concepts are large contracts with durations of 3–10 years. Many of these contracts include substantial capital for assets such as people, servers, networks, and capitalized transformational costs. These contracts are notoriously inflexible, driven by a combination of factors including the need to predefine service-level agreements and scope over a long time, pricing that has to anticipate changes in volume and technology, and the substantial capital cost that must be retired over the life of the contract. As you can see from the chart, these contracts delay the profits to the service provider and deliver only modest profitability late in the contract term (Figure 3).

The combination of unrealized earnings and un-depreciated assets has the potential to create substantial stranded costs if the contracts are terminated early or significantly renegotiated mid-term. These stranded costs have been the bane of

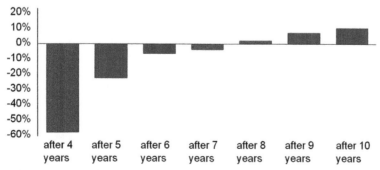

Rate of Return for a typical traditional IT outsourcing contract

Source: Bernstein Research analysis

FIGURE 3

Rate of return within outsourcing.

Source: *Bernstein Research analysis.*

the industry, creating a steady stream of blow-up deals, some of which consistently further suppress earnings in the sector. Sometimes a decision to transfer assets to a service provider was driven by an artificial increase in return on capital that the buyer would show after assets were moved from its books to those of a provider. Nonetheless, even this benefit eventually disappeared owing to changes in assets accounting in an outsourcing transaction.

Among other problems that arise in practice are a failure to meet service levels, unclear contractual issues, changing requirements and unforeseen charges, and a dependence on the BPO, which reduces flexibility. Consequently, these challenges need to be considered before a company decides to engage in business process outsourcing.[22] A further issue is that in many cases there is little that differentiates the BPO providers other than size. They often provide similar services, have similar geographic footprints, leverage similar technology stacks, and have similar quality improvement approaches.[23]

Possible pitfalls and risks are major drawbacks with BPO. Outsourcing an information system, for example, can cause security pitfalls and risks factors from both a communication and privacy perspective. For example, security of North American or European company data is more difficult to maintain when accessed or controlled in the Indian subcontinent. From a knowledge perspective, a changing attitude in employees, underestimation of running costs, and the major risk of losing independence, outsourcing leads to a different relationship between an organization and its contractor.[24] Pitfalls, risks, and threats of outsourcing must therefore be managed to achieve any benefits. To manage outsourcing in a structured way, maximizing positive outcome, minimizing risks, and avoiding threats, a business continuity management model is set up. Business continuity management consists of a set of steps to successfully identify, manage, and control business processes that are or can be outsourced.[25]

BUSINESS PROCESS OUTSOURCING: HOW TO GO ABOUT IT

As mentioned earlier, BPO has to link to the aspects of the core businesses.[26] Therefore, the link between the organization's competencies and process execution provides the means of identifying ways to appropriately define which areas to outsource and thereby increase flexibility and/or innovation to support value creation and revenue growth, or where to improve the effectiveness and efficiency of operations or reduce cost. Without this context there is no means to judge the goodness of a particular process outsourcing strategy. For example, if it is not possible to detect that a process contributes to the unique value creation of the business and helps it differentiate, it is best not to outsource to cut cost; however, if you have business areas and thereby processes that are non-core and do not compete or differentiate in a business context, it should be done in the cheapest way possible.

Figure 4 shows a summary of the concepts for categorizing the six domains of business models, the competencies that enable the business models, and the type of practice standards that correspond to the different competencies.

For non-core competencies, it makes sense to do BPO with standard BPO best practices, in an effort to optimize operations and minimize cost. Similarly, industry

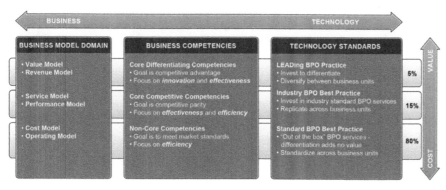

FIGURE 4

When to apply BPO practices and services.[27]

BPO best practice may be adopted for core-competitive competencies because the business only aims to compete effectively with its competitors and maximize its performance. However, to drive growth in revenue and value, new products and services have to be developed to give the business a competitive advantage. By its nature, an advantage requires something that is not offered elsewhere; thus, the business strives toward developing and nurturing core-differentiating competencies. However, applying such differentiating competencies in a standardized BPO offering will at best result in high performance, but not differentiating value.

As shown in Figure 4, true differentiating competencies typically comprise a small portion of the business (only 5%), although it may be a much larger percentage in truly innovative enterprises. Although it could be argued that there are relatively few cases in which a BPO organization could offer unique or even market-leading products and services in a field where you are differentiating, it is crucial for the business to find partners that can support you in your process of innovation and differentiation in the market. Until recently, it had been axiomatic that no organization would outsource core competencies, those functions that give the company a strategic advantage or make it unique. Often, for core-differentiating competencies and all processes involved, some organizations that do not know which competencies are core-differentiating just define it as any function that gets close to customers. In the early 2000s, when BPO matured in the market, this concept of only outsourcing non-core competency areas and the various related processes started to change with the realization that outsourcing some core functions may be good strategy, not anathema, that threatens neither the business model nor the operating model. For example, some organizations outsource customer service, precisely because it is so important.[28]

The key lies in knowing which of the main value drivers and related competencies to focus on, and which produce customer intimacy, product leadership, or operational excellence. Focusing on the drivers that build uniqueness will help a company create a competitive edge (Figure 5).[29]

Before consideration is given to whether to undertake a BPO program, a diagnostic of a company's expenditure must first be undertaken.

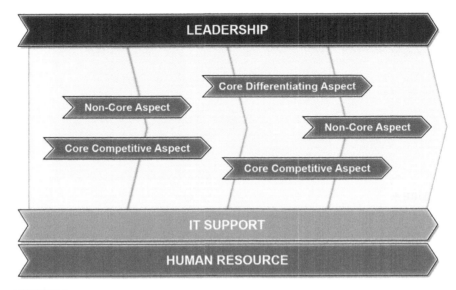

FIGURE 5

Specific processes are within the organization's non-core, core competitive, and core-differentiating aspects across business units.[30]

- Divide the total corporate expenditure into categories that relate to the supplier markets, and then further divide expenditure categories by business units or locations to identify each supplier.
- This initial diagnostic is required to be only around 80% accurate to have relevance and to offer valuable insight.
- If and when BPO teams need to refine spend data for each category, the supplier may be a more accurate source (this is discussed further below).

Diagnostics can provide an expenditure map by category. These expenditure categories should be classified according to competitiveness in the supplier marketplace compared with how important they are to the organization. This results in an expenditure category matrix that will help direct the team toward a potential sourcing strategy for each category.

The Kraljic portfolio purchasing model plots categories as strategic (low supply market competitiveness, high business impact), leverage (high supply market competitiveness, high business impact), bottleneck (low supply market competitiveness, low business impact), and routine (high supply market competitiveness, low business impact) (Figure 6).

Once diagnostics are complete, the business must decide which categories to address immediately and which to delay until internal or external conditions are better. For categories that need immediate attention, the seven-step process begins.

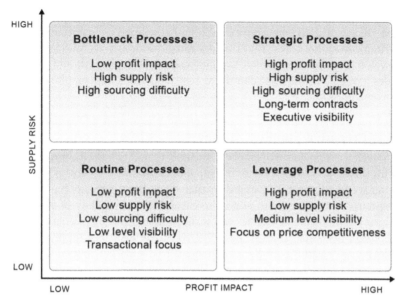

FIGURE 6

Kraljic's purchasing model.

Step 1: Fully Understand the Expenditure Category

This step, along with the next two, is conducted by the business process sourcing team. At this stage, the team needs to ensure it understands everything about the expenditure category itself. For example, if the category is corrugated packaging at a consumer products company, the team will need to understand the definition of the category and usage patterns and why the particular types and grades were specified. Stakeholders at all operating units and physical locations would need to be identified: for example, logistics, which may need to know about shipping specifications, or marketing, which may need to understand certain quality or environmental characteristics, where applicable.

The five key areas of analysis are:

- Total historic expenditure and number of processes
- Expenditure categorised by main, management, and supporting processes
- Expenditure by division, department, or user
- Expenditure by supplier
- Future demand projections or budgets

Step 2: Supplier Market Assessment

Concurrently run supplier market assessment for seeking alternative suppliers to existing incumbents. Understand the key supplier marketplace dynamics and current trends. Prepare should-cost information from the major components of the key products. Take a view on the key suppliers' sub-tier marketplace and analyze for any risks as well as opportunities. Should-cost analysis is not appropriate for every item. In many cases, traditional strategic sourcing techniques work well. However, in cases where strategic sourcing cannot be applied, should-cost analysis provides a valuable tool that can drive cost reductions and supplier continuous improvement efforts.

Step 3: Prepare a Supplier Survey

Next, develop a supplier survey for both incumbent and potential alternative suppliers. This survey will help evaluate the supplier capabilities. At this point, consider verifying spend information using data that incumbent suppliers have from their sales systems. The survey is to assess the capability and capacity of the market to meet your requirements. It enables you to assess at an early stage whether your proposed project is feasible and can be delivered by the identified supply base. It also provides an early warning of your requirements to the market, and enables suppliers to think about how they will respond. The key aim here is to encourage the right suppliers with the right structure to respond to you.

Look to gather knowledge in these key areas:

- Feasibility
- Capability
- Maturity
- Capacity

Step 4: Building the Strategy

This step involves developing the business process sourcing strategy. The combination of the first three steps provides the essential ingredients for the sourcing strategy. However, for each area or category it will depend on:

1. How competitive the supplier marketplace is: Armed with the supplier information, you can build the competitive landscape in the supply marketplace. This can help demonstrate the size of the prize to alternative suppliers and communicates the seriousness of a potential sourcing exercise to incumbent suppliers.
2. How supportive your organization's users are to testing incumbent supplier relationships: A business process sourcing team has two sets of internal stakeholders: people who use the services that are bought and executives who manage overall costs. The people who consume the expenditure category will accept cost reductions as long as the process is started in another department, does not mean a change in suppliers, and does not jeopardize a good relationship with the supply base, generate complaints, or affect issues such as delivery reliability, service, or payments. For executives, cost and service competitiveness is a key objective, but they, too, are users of various corporate services, and so are often caught between the pursuit of cost improvement and a user mentality

of resisting change. To mobilize users' and executives' support for the category strategy, it is vital to communicate all benefits and overcome any potential risks.

3. What alternatives exist to competitive assessment: If the supply base is competitive, you can harness those forces to leverage better pricing or terms owing to increased number of a streamlined product or service specification. Once the result of the competitive sourcing effort is determined, it will be useful to set up a collaborative program that will run until the next competitive sourcing event takes place. If a competitive approach to sourcing is not a viable option, it is worth considering what the alternatives are, such as collaborating with suppliers:
   a. To reduce complexity and in turn increase productivity
   b. To create corroborative process improvements that reduce the cost of doing business
   c. To change the way the relationship is structured. For example, firms may invest in supplier operations to guarantee access to supply, new technology, or process improvements.

These alternatives are pursued typically when a buying company has little leverage over its supply base. They will be relying on good faith that suppliers will share the benefits of a new approach. The sourcing strategy is an accumulation of all the drivers thus far mentioned.

Step 5: RFx Request for ...

Where a competitive approach is used, which is the general case for most expenditure categories, a request for proposal (RFP) or bid will need to be prepared (request for quotation (RFQ), electronic request for quotation (eRFQ), etc.). This will define and make clear the requirements to all prequalified suppliers. It should include product or service specifications, delivery and service requirements, evaluation criteria, pricing structure, and financial terms and conditions. A communication plan should also be implemented at this stage to attract maximum supplier interest. Ensure that every supplier is aware they it is competing on a level playing field.

Once the RFP is sent out to all suppliers, make sure they are given enough time to respond. Follow-up messages should also be sent out to encourage a greater response.

Step 6: Selection

This is about selecting and negotiating with suppliers. The sourcing team should apply its evaluation criteria to the supplier responses. If extra information beyond the RFP response is required, do not be afraid to ask for it. If carried out manually, the negotiation process is conducted first with a larger set of suppliers, then narrowed to a few finalists. If the sourcing team uses an electronic negotiation tool, a greater number of suppliers may be kept in the process for longer, giving more diverse suppliers a better chance at winning the business.

Compare outcomes in terms of total value or implementation cost differences. Departments directly affected can be brought into the final selection process. Senior executives should be briefed on the final selection, to gain their approval and also be given the rationale behind the decision, to prepare them for any calls they receive from disappointed suppliers.

Step 7: Communicate with Your New Suppliers

Once the winning supplier(s) are notified, they should be invited to participate in implementing recommendations. Implementation plans vary depending on the degree of supplier switches. For incumbents, there will be a communication plan that will include any changes in specifications, improvements in delivery, and service or pricing models. These ought to be communicated to users as well. Because the company may have significantly benefited from this entire process, it is important that this be recognized by both company and supplier.

For new suppliers, a communication plan has to be developed that manages the transition from old to new at every point in the process that is touched by the spend category. Department, finance, and customer service are affected by this change, and their risk antennae will be particularly sensitive during this period. It is particularly important to measure closely the new supplier's performance during the first weeks of engagement.

Being able to demonstrate that performance matches, or is superior to, that of the former supplier will be vital during this sensitive time. It is also important to capture the intellectual capital your sourcing team has developed during the seven-step process so it can be used the next time that category is sourced.

CONCLUSIONS

In this section we have gone through what BPO is, and how and why it is applied. We have furthermore detailed where it can or should be applied. We have also elaborated on the current stage in the evolution of outsourcing and the development of strategic partnerships, including the steps and the to-do's such a partnership as well as BPO tendering would include. To gain maximum benefit, a BPO program should go through a formal close-down. There is no point in arguing lost causes once irrevocable decisions have been taken. Staff and companies alike need to accept the new situation and move forward. However, there will be a lot of information generated during the life of the program, and this will have been stored with varying degrees of formality by the team members. This information needs to be formally filed away for future reference.

In this light, there are no simple criteria to conduct an outsourcing versus in-house analysis. The benefits associated with outsourcing are numerous, and one should consider each project on its individual merits. Ongoing operational costs that may be avoided by outsourcing are also a consideration. In a nutshell, outsourcing allows organizations to be more efficient, flexible, and effective, while often reducing costs.

When considering a BPO program, a few main factors influence successful outsourcing. Critical areas for a successful outsourcing program as identified are:

- Understanding company goals and objectives
- A strategic vision and plan
- Identify a business model and operating model in which are core differentiating, core competitive, and non-core competencies
- Map the relevant processes for the chosen business competencies and business functions that are desired to be outsources
- Selecting the right vendor
- Ongoing management of relationships
- Properly structured contract
- Select value and performance measures that are the basis for the service-level agreement
- Open communication with affected individual/groups
- Senior executive support and involvement
- Careful attention to personnel issues
- Short-term financial justification (value case and business case)

Some of the top advantages brought about by outsourcing include the following:

- Staffing flexibility
- Acceleration of projects and quicker time to market
- High-caliber professionals who hit the ground running
- Ability to tap into best practices
- Knowledge transfer to permanent staff
- Cost-effective and predictable expenditures
- Access to the flexibility and creativity of experienced problem solvers
- Resource and core competency focus

End Notes

1. Robert Handfield, *A Brief History of Outsourcing, 2006.*
2. Tas J and Sunder S, 2004, "Financial Services Business Process Outsourcing", *Communications of the ACM* 47, no. 5.
3. C.N.E.T. News, *IT Firms Expand from PCs to Payroll*, ed. Frauenheim.
4. http://searchcio.techtarget.com/definition/business-process-outsourcing.
5. Nellis J. G. and David Parker, "Principles of Business Economics," Financial Times Prentice Hall (2006): 213, ISBN 978-0-273-69306-2.
6. Sagoo A, "How IT is Reinvigorating Business Process Outsourcing" CIO (6 September 2012), Retrieved 25 March 2013.
7. B.P.M. Watch, In-Sourcing Remotely: A Closer Look at an Emerging Outsourcing Trend, http://www.bpmwatch.com/columns/in-sourcing-a-closer-look-at-an-emerging-outsourcing-trend/.
8. Willcocks L. Hindle J. Feeny D and Lacity M, "IT and Business Process Outsourcing: The Knowledge Potential," *Information Systems Management* 21, (2004): 7–15.
9. Gilley K. M and Rasheed A, "Making More by Doing Less: An Analysis of Outsourcing and its Effects on Firm Performance," *Journal of Management* 26, no. 4 (2000): 763–790.

10. Kakabadse A and Kakabadse N, "Trends in Outsourcing: Contrasting USA and Europe," *European Management Journal* 20, no. 2 (2002): 189–198.

11. Weerakkody, Vishanth, Currie L. Wendy and Ekanayake, Y, "Re-engineering business processes through application service providers—challenges, issues and complexities," *Business Process Management Journal* 9, no. 6 (2003): 776–794.

12. Leavy B, "Outsourcing strategies: Opportunities and Risk," *Strategy and Leadership* 32, no. 6 (2004): 20–25.

13. Tas J and Sunder S, "Financial Services Business Process Outsourcing," *Communications of the ACM* 47, no. 5 (2004).

14. Fischer L. M, 2001, From vertical to Virtual; How Nortel's Supplier Alliances Extend the enterprise [online], Strategy+Business.

15. Leavy, 2004, 20–25.

16. See the note 3 above.

17. Capgemini Consulting BPO Research.

18. http://www.horsesforsources.com/hfs-index-q12013_02221#sthash.crBfQZEL.dpuf.

19. http://www.statista.com/statistics/298574/bpo-and-it-services-market-breakdown-worldwide/.

20. Christian Schuh et al.,*The Purchasing Chessboard: 64 Methods to Reduce Cost and Increase Value with Suppliers*, Pages 11–33, (Springer: Berlin Heidelberg, 2009), ISBN 978-3-540-88724-9.

21. Code Red – Stat!, Sherpas in Blue Shirts, Peter Bendor-Samuel, Chief Executive Officer, Everest Group and Ross Tisnovsky, Senior Vice President, Everest Group, (June 2, 2011).

22. Michel V and Fitzgerald G, "The IT outsourcing market place: vendors and their selection," *Journal of Information Technology* 12, (1997): 223–237.

23. Adsit, D, (2009) Will a Toyota Emerge from the Pack of Me-Too BPO's?, In Queue.

24. Bunmi Cynthia Adeleye, Fenio Annansingh and Miguel Baptista Nunes, "Risk management practices in IS outsourcing: an investigation into commercial banks in Nigeria," *International Journal of Information Management* 24 (2004): 167–180.

25. F. Gibb and S. Buchanan, "A framework for business continuity management," *International Journal of Information Management* 26, no.2 (2006): 128–141.

26. See the note 11 above.

27. BPO Practices & Services Model, LEADing Practice Competency Modelling Reference Content (LEAD-ES20013BC).

28. See the note 1 above .

29. See the note 12 above.

30. See the note 27 above.

The Business Process Management Way of Training and Coaching

Mark von Rosing, Henrik von Scheel, August-Wilhelm Scheer

INTRODUCTION

The high demand for skilled and experienced process professionals to both lead and participate in business process management (BPM) initiatives, has created a major skills gap that traditional BPM and BPM notation bodies of knowledge and certifications do not meet. In this part, we elaborate on the way of process training. The way of training focuses on the most effective way to build and mature cross-disciplinary competencies across the breadth of the ways of thinking, working, modeling, implementing, and governance. We advocate an approach that uniquely combines training and coaching with hands-on experience by using all of these disciplines in context with real-life process-oriented projects so as to address the existing knowledge gap.

In this part we explore a standardized and common way to train process professionals with a detailed career path for process experts, process architects, and process engineers. The result is that we turn traditional process education into performance-based project coaching that provides a different set of cost–benefit value ratios, representing the most effective way for organizations to build their process skills.

The Need for a Standardized and Common Way of Process Training

Joshua von Scheel, Mark von Rosing, Marianne Fonseca, Ulrik Foldager

INTRODUCTION

The need for skilled and experienced personnel to lead and participate in business process management (BPM) activities is obvious and in high demand in today's global market. Professional certification can be found in many industries and professions, and BPM is no exception. The market offers a variety of vendor-, technology-, and methodology-driven certifications. Certification in BPM, as described in this chapter, does not refer to certification in well-known methodologies used in BPM such as Six Sigma, Lean, or the IT Infrastructure Library (ITIL), nor in any vendor-specific tool. Instead, we refer to and focus on more generic, broadly scoped training in BPM as a discipline, including a much needed new way of thinking, working, modeling, implementing, and governing process modeling, process architecture, and process engineering principles (see Figure 1). There is rapidly growing interest in this type of certification, and a number of organizations have already established their own distinct approaches to curricula, exams, assessments, and certifications for BPM.

SKILLS REQUIREMENTS

As BPM rapidly matures, the need for a standardized and common way of training for process professionals is also evident. In this chapter, we will outline a fully standardized and common way of training for process professionals, focusing on what skills are required to succeed in BPM today, what career path a process professional should follow to meet the market demand, and in particular what the most effective way is to build on existing process competencies as well as develop new ones.

A recent global business process training and certification research based on a survey of 1765 organizations representing all major countries across both public and private sectors examined which kinds of skills are required to succeed with process modeling, architecture, and engineering in BPM projects. The research identified that:

- 72% of available business process certification programs do not meet the skills required for a process project today
- 93.4% of business process-certified practitioners do not know how to apply the knowledge gained from a classroom setting in a real-life project
- Business process certification programs are not up-to-date. Although businesses matured, applying processes to improve their performance, the certification

673

programs never really followed along. With this significant skills gap, both practitioners and organizations were left on their own to reinvent and piece together the skills required.

- Organizations require cross-disciplinary business process practitioners; this includes skills within process modeling, architecture, and engineering (see Figure 1), although no existing training vendor or organization actually offers cross-disciplinary process certification programs.

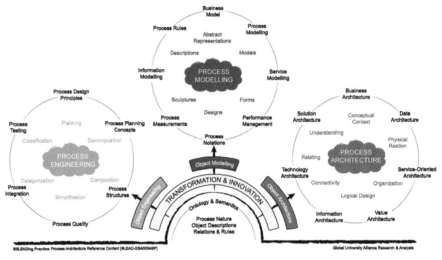

FIGURE 1

Example of cross-disciplinary business process skills: process engineering, process modeling, and process architecture.

Based on the key findings of the research, we can conclude that traditional BPM certification has a high learning versus forgetting curve and it is not up-to-date to meet the skills needed on the market today. There simply is a critical need for cross-disciplinary programs that share common aspects, and existing classroom training programs inhibit and restrain the strong transfer of knowledge from theory to practice in real-life projects.

LEARNING VERSUS FORGETTING CURVE

Academic studies by Profs. P. Quinn[1] and Thailheimer[2] on the most effective way to learn (learning versus forgetting curve) concluded that:

1. Most theoretical content ought to be converted to an e-learning or online setting
2. Traditional classroom training is improved by 58% when it is combined with coaching to convert the new knowledge gain into practical skills acquisition

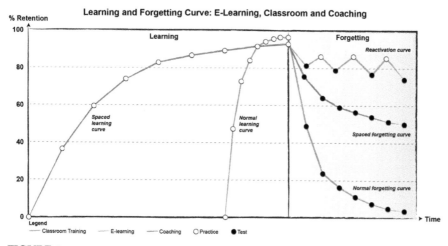

FIGURE 2

Learning versus forgetting curve for e-learning, classroom, and coaching.

3. Combining e-learning with training and coaching improves understanding and decreases the loss of knowledge (forgetting curve) by 79%[3,4] (see Figure 2).

This academic research shows that the most effective way to build process skills is a combination of online training (theoretical), classroom training (theoretical with practical examples), and coaching with hands-on experience using the different disciplines and program content in the context of real-life process-oriented projects. This requires turning traditional education into a performance-based project coaching exercise, instead—something that simultaneously provides a new whole new cost–benefit ratio and, through this new way of training, is achievable for both the individual practitioner and the entire project teams.

STANDARDIZED WAY OF TRAINING FOR PROCESS PROFESSIONALS

To face the skills gap that we encounter today, it is evident that a standardized and common way of training is required to build and develop the skills that process experts, process architects, and process engineers need. In our effort to standardize a common way of training for process professionals, we have:

1. Mapped the skills requirement based on the BPM ontology and the skill sets needed.
2. Structured the entire learning process and educational material into a way of thinking, working, modeling, and governing (see Figure 3).
3. Integrated the most effective way to build skills.
4. Support or exchange physical education with online training.

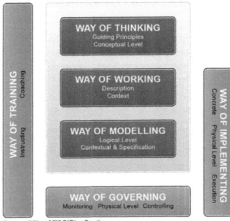

FIGURE 3

Structured way of thinking, working, modeling, implementing, governing, and training with processes.

End Notes

1. Xiao, W.S., Quinn, P.C., Pascalis, O., & Lee, K. "Own- and other-race face scanning in infants: Implications for perceptual narrowing." *Developmental Psychobiology*, (Special Issue on Perceptual Narrowing), 56, (2014): 262–273.
2. Spacing Learning Events Over Time: What the Research Says A Work-Learning Research, Inc. *Publication*. 2006 by Will Thalheimer.
3. Ritter, F.E., & Schooler, L.J. "The learning curve." in *International Encyclopedia of the Social and Behavioral Sciences* (2002), 8602–8605. Amsterdam: Pergamon.
4. Meek, C., Thiesson, Bo, Heckerman, David (Summer 2002). "The Learning-Curve Sampling Method Applied to Model-Based Clustering." *Journal of Machine Learning Research* 2(3): 397.

Process Expert Training

Program duration: Five working days which is supported and/or can be exchanged by online training.

Target audience: This certification program has been designed for professionals with 3 or more years of experience:

- *Specialists*: process experts, business analysts, process specialists, process method specialists (*Business Process Reengineering* (BPR), Six Sigma, *Total Quality Management* (TQM), and/or Lean practitioner) and quality/production/manufacturing specialists
- *Consultants*: process consultants, service consultants, business consultants and transformation consultants
- *Architects*: process architects, enterprise architects, technology architects, solution architects, application architects, business architects, service architects, information/data architects, and value architects
- *Managers*: process managers, service managers, business managers, and project managers
- *Directors*: process owners, business owners, *Line of Business* (LoB) directors, and LoB owners

Program type: The ideal program type would be a classroom (physical location) or online, depending on the size and location of the process team and its willingness to accept online training as a form of skills building.

The process expert certification program has been structured to build on the existing competencies of the practitioner, but most importantly, with a main focus on developing new skills through the use of our unique modeling principles. The aim is also to infuse the practitioner with an entirely new way of thinking, working, and modeling with business processes.

This is done through 5 days of intensive classroom or online training, in-depth tutoring, and coaching coupled with hands-on project experience, in which the practitioner applies the acquired process modeling (Figure 1) techniques and its related disciplines to the practitioner's own company projects.

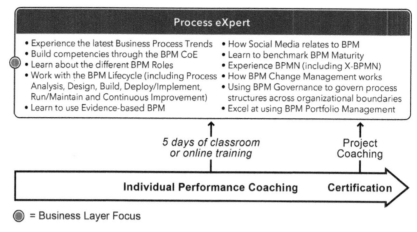

FIGURE 1

Process expert learning model.

CONTENT OF THE PROGRAM

The process expert certification program provides the practitioner with an extensive tool kit and profound knowledge of the Layered Enterprise Architecture Development (LEAD) enterprise standards and industry standards as well as highly detailed and descriptive process reference content that links and connects directly to hot topics such as:

- Business process trends
- How to build business process management (BPM) competencies: the BPM center of excellence
- The various BPM roles
- Working with the BPM life cycle
  1. Process analysis (project preparation and blueprinting)
  2. Process design (project realization)
  3. Process build (final preparations)
  4. Process deployment/implementation (process release and deployment management)
  5. Process run and maintenance (process governance and monitoring)
  6. Continuous process improvement (optimization and improvements)
- Evidence-based BPM
- Social media and BPM
- Business process management maturity
- Business process management notation (BPMN) (including X-BPMN, the extended BPMN discipline)
- Business process management change management
- Business process management governance
- Business process management portfolio management

These topics have already been covered extensively throughout this handbook, and the process expert certification program aims to deliver actual, practical, and hands-on experience by using all of these disciplines in context with real-life process-oriented projects. This ensures the highest level of knowledge transfer and skills building to meet today's organizations cross-disciplinary competency requirements for professionals involved with process-oriented subjects.

PROCESS EXPERT LEARNING MODEL

The process expert learning model (Figure 1) is based on an intensive training module supported by in-depth individual performance coaching on a selected project. The hands-on experience ensures that the BPM and process modeling skills are applied to the following disciplines (Figure 1):

The needed skill for abstraction level for a process expert is:

- *Concrete*: Tangible, existing, and actual
- *Descriptive and specification*: Explanation, depiction/sketch, and portrayal, often using a process map, matrix, and/or model
- *Design*: Plan, intend, and aim

WHAT THE PRACTITIONER GETS

This certification program includes:

- Five working days of classroom and online training
- Training material with practical and usable reference content (i.e., the BPM life cycle, process templates)
- Individual performance coaching during the course
- Three 1.5-hour digital prerecorded sessions
- Process expert certificate

Process Architect Training

Program duration: Ten working days.

Target audience: This certification program has been designed for professionals with 3–10 years of experience:

- *Specialists*: senior process experts, senior business analysts, and Enterprise Architecture (EA) method specialists (The Open Group Architecture Framework (TOGAF), Zachman, and *Ministry of Defence Architecture Framework* (MODAF) practitioners)
- *Consultants*: senior process consultants, senior business consultants, and senior transformation consultants
- *Architects*: process architects, enterprise architects, solution architects, application architects, business architects, service architects, information/data architects, and value architects
- *Managers*: process managers if they have a process ownership

Program type: The ideal program type is to combine classroom training (physical location) with online training, depending on the size and location of the process team. The first week is an optional choice (classroom or online); the second week is always classroom.

The process architect certification program has been structured to build on the existing competencies of the practitioner, but most importantly, with a main focus on developing new skills through the use of our unique architecture principles. The aim is also to infuse the practitioner with an entirely new way of thinking, working, and modeling with business processes.

This is done through 10 days of intensive classroom and/or online training, in-depth tutoring, and coaching coupled with hands-on project experience, in which the practitioner applies the acquired process architecture (Figure 1) techniques and its related disciplines to the practitioner's own company projects.

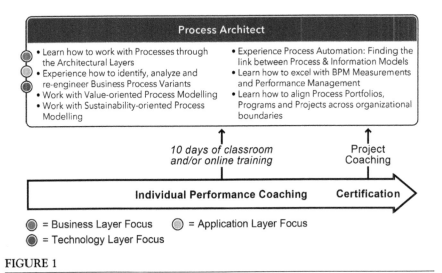

FIGURE 1

Process architect learning model.

CONTENT OF THE PROGRAM

The process architect certification program provides the practitioner with an extensive tool kit and profound knowledge of the Layered Enterprise Architecture Development (LEAD) enterprise standards and industry standards as well as highly detailed and descriptive process and architecture reference content that links and connects directly to hot topics such as:

- How to work with processes in architectural layers
- How to work with and model business process variations
- Value-oriented process modeling
- Sustainability-oriented process modeling
- Process automation: link between process models and information models
- Business process management measurements and performance management
- Business process management alignment

These topics have already been covered extensively throughout this handbook, and the process architect certification program aims to deliver actual, practical, and hands-on experience by using all of these disciplines in the context of real-life process-oriented projects. This ensures the highest level of knowledge transfer and skills building to meet today's organizations cross-disciplinary competency requirements for professionals involved with process-oriented subjects.

PROCESS ARCHITECT LEARNING MODEL

The process architect learning model (Figure 1) is based on an intensive training module supported by in-depth individual performance mentoring on a selected project.

The hands-on learning experience ensures that the business process management (BPM) and process architecture skills are applied in the following disciplines (Figure 1):
The needed skills for abstraction level for a process architect:

- *Conceptual*: Theoretical, abstract, and intangible; the high-level description of the logical
- *Context*: Situation, milieu/environment, and perspective
- *Concrete*: Tangible, existing, and actual
- *Descriptive and specification*: Explanation, depiction/sketch, and portrayal, often using a map, matrix, and/or model
- *Design*: Plan, intend, and aim
- *Execution*: Completing, performing, and realization

WHAT YOU GET

This certification program includes:

- Ten working days of classroom and online training
- Six 1.5-hour digital online sessions
- Individual performance coaching for project and individual development during the course
- Training material with practical and usable reference content (i.e., the BPM life cycle, process templates)
- Process architect certificate

Process Engineer Training

Program Duration: Ten working days.

Target Audience: This certification program has been designed for professionals with 3–10 years of experience:

- *Specialists:* The engineering specialist who needs process knowledge, such as a systems engineer, quality engineer, or software engineer
- *Consultants:* Engineering consultants (depending on whether it is an engineering-centric organization)
- *Architects:* Process architects (depending on whether it is an engineering-centric organization)
- *Managers:* Process managers (depending on whether it is an engineering-centric organization)

Program type: The ideal program type is to combine classroom training (physical location) with online training, depending on the size and location of the process team. The first week is an optional choice (classroom or online); the second week is always classroom.

The process engineer certification program has been structured to build on the existing competencies of the practitioner, but most importantly, with a main focus on developing new skills through the use of our unique engineering principles. Process engineers focus on the design, operation, control, and optimization of business, application, and technology processes. They use specific engineering principles to enable better enterprise-related processes. Process engineering training therefore focuses on the daily job of the process engineer:

- Construct and maintain the endeavor-specific process from the process landscape
- Evaluate process tools for consistency with the organizational process landscape and process life cycle and/or endeavor-specific process
- Ensure that the endeavor-specific process is constructed based on endeavor-specific needs before process tool selection rather than being driven by early selection of a potentially inappropriate process tool
- Provide input to the environments team regarding required process tool support
- Provide local guidance and mentoring in the proper adoption and use of the endeavor process
- Identify and document the enterprise's own leading practices; disseminate and evangelize industry best practices and common best practices
- Work to support strategic process initiatives including recommending improvements to the organizational process framework
- Support multiple endeavors within a local region
- Staff regional process help desks

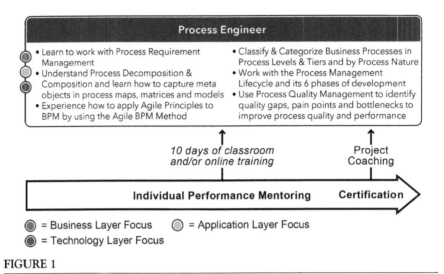

FIGURE 1

Process engineer learning model.

- Present local training on process-related topics
- Research advances in process engineering (e.g., new software development methods)

The aim is also to infuse the practitioner with a supporting process way of thinking, working, and modeling with business processes. This is done through 10 days of intensive classroom and/or online training, in-depth tutoring, and coaching, coupled with hands-on project experience in which the practitioner applies the acquired process engineering (Figure 1) techniques and its related disciplines to the practitioner's own company projects.

CONTENT OF THE PROGRAM

The process engineer certification program provides the practitioner with an extensive tool kit and profound knowledge of the LEAD enterprise standards and industry standards as well as highly detailed and descriptive process and engineering reference content that links and connects directly to topics such as:

- Process analysis techniques
- Process requirement management
- Process design practices and concepts
- Process decomposition and capturing in process templates/models
- Process composition and capturing in process templates/models
- Process categorization and classification
  - Process levels
  - Process tiers
  - Process nature

- Process life cycle management
- Process quality management
- Agile business process management (BPM)

These topics have already been covered extensively throughout this handbook, and the process engineer certification program aims to deliver actual, practical, and hands-on experience by using all of these disciplines in the context of real-life process-oriented projects. This ensures the highest level of knowledge transfer and skills building to meet today's organizations' cross-disciplinary competency requirements for professionals involved with process-oriented subjects.

PROCESS ENGINEER LEARNING MODEL

The process engineer learning model (Figure 1) is based on an intensive training module supported by in-depth individual performance mentoring on a selected project. The hands-on learning experience ensures that the business process management and process engineering skills are applied within the following disciplines (Figure 1):

Needed skills at an abstraction level for a process engineer are:

- *Conceptual*: theoretical, abstract, and intangible—high-level description of the logical
- *Context*: situation, milieu/environment, and perspective
- *Concrete*: tangible, existing, and actual
- *Descriptive and specification*: explanation, depiction/sketch, and portrayal, often using a map, matrix, and/or model
- *Design*: plan, intend, and aim
- *Execution*: completing, performing, and realization

WHAT YOU GET

This certification program includes:

- Ten working days of classroom and online training
- Six 1.5-hour digital online sessions
- Individual performance coaching for project and individual development during the course
- Training material with practical and usable reference content (i.e., the BPM life cycle, process templates)
- Process engineer certificate

CONCLUSIONS

In this chapter we have outlined a standardized and common way of training process professionals with a detailed career path for the process expert, process architect, and process engineer. We have explained which skills are required for the way of thinking, working, modeling, and governing. Our experience has shown that the most effective way to build process skills is a combination of online (theoretical) and classroom training (theoretical with practical examples) and coaching, and by using all of the described disciplines in the context of real-life process-oriented projects, turning traditional education into performance-based project coaching that provides a whole new cost–benefit ratio for the practitioner.

Process Owner Training

Program duration: 0.5 to 2 days.

Target audience: This certification program has been designed for professionals with business experience who want to build process ownership skills:

- **Directors**: Business executives, business owners, Line of Business (LoB) directors, and LoB owners
- **Managers**: Business managers, service managers, operational managers, project managers, and business process managers
- **Specialists**: Business experts, operational process owners, business analysts, process specialists, process method specialists (BPR, Six Sigma, TQM, and/or Lean practitioner), and quality/production/manufacturing specialists

PROGRAM TYPE

The speed of business changes is increasing; because of this, the work of the process owner has become more complex and demanding. In most organizations the process owner is responsible for the governance of processes and their performance as well as continuous improvement. For most organizations this includes defining the process mission, vision, goals, and objectives; relating them to the various business key performance indicators (KPIs) and measures that are a part of multiple reports; and aligning them with the organization's decision making and strategies. Process owners monitor and report process performance against these KPIs and on the health of execution versus established plans. Furthermore, they are involved in synchronizing process improvement plans with other process owners within the value chain and other interconnected processes. Their process aim is to continuously increase the maturity of the processes and sustain each level of maturity.

Because of the nature of the work of process owners, it is not easy to take half a day or 1 or 2 days off work out of an already tight schedule, so training has to be available for whenever it is needed. The ideal program type for process owners and their on-demand model is therefore online training. Depending on the size and location of the process team, however, the program can be taught as classroom training at a physical location. Any process owner training program should be designed to build knowledge for business people who have process ownership and focus on specialized skills in this direction.

The process owner certification program is structured so as to build on the existing competencies of the practitioner, but more important, with a main focus on developing new process-focused skills through the use of our unique strategic, managerial, and operational process principles. The overall goal is to infuse the process owner with an entirely new way of thinking, working, modeling, and governing with business processes.

689

This is done through intensive online training (classrooms are also an option), in-depth tutoring, and coaching coupled with hands-on project experience. The learning route of the process owner program has been designed in three areas:

- Strategic process owner (executive/director focus), which requires 0.5–1 day of training
- Tactical process owner (management focus), which requires 1 day of training
- Operational process owner (execution focus), which requires 2 days of training

The process owner certification program is split into three kinds of training components, but it is possible to train and focus on one, two, or all select areas: for instance, only the strategic or tactical and operational aspects.

CONTENT OF THE PROGRAM

The process owner role is as a specialization of the business owner role, and his or her responsibilities focus almost exclusively on defining and organizational planning of process strategies and goals, governing process execution, and evaluating service delivery through value and performance measurements, as well as setting up and initiating process transformation and innovation through the business process management change management lifecycle.

The process owner certification program provides the practitioner with an extensive tool kit and profound knowledge of the LEAD enterprise standards and industry standards as well as highly detailed and descriptive process reference content. The process owner certification program consists of three areas that focus on different kinds of subject matter content:

- *Strategic process owner*
  - Establishment of process mission and vision
  - Strategy definition and planning (Strategic Business Objectives (SBOs))
  - Process planning aspects
  - Goals and objectives setting (Critical Success Factors (CSFs))
  - Process innovation thinking
  - Value-oriented process thinking
  - Budgeting and forecasting
- *Tactical process owner*
  - Strategic advisory and guidance
  - Performance design and monitoring (Key Performance Indicators (KPIs), PPIs, and Service Performance Indicators (SPIs))
  - Link to business policies and procedures
  - Define process policies and procedures
  - Performance management
  - Link to business innovation and transformation enabling
  - Risk management and communication
  - Continuous improvement

- *Operational process owner*
  - Process governance
  - Operational planning and processing
  - Process maturity and process improvement
  - Operational advisory and guidance
  - Performance measurements and reporting
  - Issue management
  - Communication and collaboration

These topics have already been covered extensively throughout this handbook. The process owner certification program aims to deliver actual, practical, hands-on experience by using all of these disciplines in the context of real-life process-oriented projects. This ensures the highest level of knowledge transfer and skill building to meet today's organizations' cross-disciplinary competency requirements for professionals involved in process-oriented initiatives.

PROCESS OWNER LEARNING MODEL

The process owner learning model is based on an intensive training module supported by in-depth individual performance coaching on a selected project. The hands-on experience ensures that strategic management, tactical administration, and operational execution skills are applied for the following disciplines (Figure 1).

Needed Skill for Abstraction Level for a Process Owner

- **Conceptual**: Theoretical, abstract, and intangible—the high-level description of the logical way of working
- **Context**: Situation, milieu/environment, and perspective regarding the organization's business model

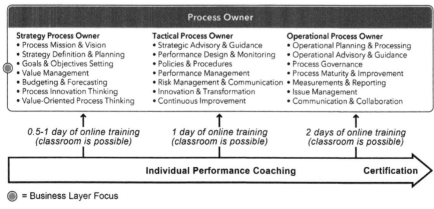

FIGURE 1

Process owner learning model.

- **Concrete**: Tangible, existing, and actual to the organization's operating model
- **Descriptive and specification**: Explanation, depiction/sketch, and portrayal often using a process map, matrix, and/or model
- **Design**: Plan, intention, and aim

WHAT THE PRACTITIONER GETS

This certification program includes:

- 0.5–4 days of on-demand online training (classroom training is also possible)
- Training material with practical and usable reference content (i.e., process workflows, process templates, etc.)
- Individual performance coaching during the course
- Process owner certificate

Conclusion

As it is so often, things have an ending, every story has an ending, and every book has an ending, however, in process modeling the end of something is just the start of something else. In this body of knowledge, we have shared with you concepts, detailed guidelines, methods, and approaches with integrated and standardized templates/artifacts. As a part of your journey we have the following additional recommendations:

For You as an Individual, it is a career opportunity. Our recommendations to succeed in your journey are as follows:

Stay Informed—push the bar and build the expertise required to work with process—do not let the vendors or consultants set the agenda. Follow the websites, webinars, and blogs of thought leaders and pioneers.

Join a Community—get involved in agnostic and vendor-neutral process community and learn from your peers, share insight, best practices, and leading practices.

Get Certified—we see too many process specialists who do not get formal training, missing out on the ability to be able to have any documentation, i.e., certification on their skills. So our clear recommendation, get your vendor neutral certification as a Process eXpert, Process Architect, and/or Process Engineer with focus on cross-disciplines, e.g., Business Process Principles (BPR, Six Sigma, TQM, Lean, etc.), BPMN 2.0, eXtended BPMN (X-BPMN), Process Monitoring, Value-Oriented Process Modeling, Continuous Improvement, and Layered Architecture Modeling (Business, Application, Technology).

For You as a Business, it is a core discipline of any organization to understand the "as is" situation and design the "to be" state in order to model, engineer, and architect how the organization creates and realizes value. With our experience with leading organizations (i.e., outperformers), our recommendations are as follows:

Innovation & Transformation Enablement—Get executive coaching or project coaching on Business Innovation & Transformation Enablement. Due to lack of ability to execute what was defined, 70% of strategies fail to be implemented. The ability to identify what needs to be changed, why it needs to be changed, and how, is a very important aspect for process modeling. Without this link the crossroad to link strategy with operational execution is missing.

Do not Reinvent the Wheel—learn from others and apply business process best practices (reference content) to standardize the noncore competencies of your organization and thereby focus on the Cost and Operating Model.

Thrive on Accelerators—within your own industry, apply industry best practices and accelerators (industry capability models, industry performance indicators, industry measures, and other industry reference content) that will improve competitive parity and standardize core competitive competencies with focus on Performance Model and Service Model.

Become a Leader—learn from leading organizations, the outperformers. Using leading practices will strengthen your competitive advantage, innovation, and efficiency in the core differentiating competencies with a focus on the Revenue Model and the Value Model. Our experience is that only few can do it, linking innovation aspects to BPM, especially since it is done in an executive closed-door session and it takes strategic insight and detailed enterprise modeling, engineering, and architecture knowledge.

We wish you luck in your journey of business process modeling and we realize that your business processes are a big deal, not only because they are in the center of business performance, but also because value creation and realization always is related to business processes. We know it can be a very big opportunity for you and your business.

Finally, if you need any help, we are always up for a challenge.

Prof. Mark von Rosing
Henrik von Scheel

Author Index

A

Aldina, P., 389
Alfred, L., 389

B

Blake, M.B., 389
Boeing, William E., 17
Bose, R.P.J.C., 372–373

C

Champy, J., 580
Chen, N., 372
CoGui, 118–119

D

Deimler, Mike, 360
Deming W. E., 396
Du, J., 372
Dumas, Marlon, 80
Dustdsar, S., 389
Dutton, John M., 318

E

Ejub, K., 389

F

Ferreira D.R., 370–371
Ford, Henry, 7–8

G

Gantt, Henry Laurence, 13
Gartner, 81–82
Gilbreth, Frank B., 2, 14–16
Graham, Benjamin S., 2, 18
Guha, Subashish, 54

H

Hammer, Michael, 50, 580
Harmon, Paul, 81, 580
Harrington, H. James, 316–318
Hays D. W., 396
Henderson-Sellers, B., 559

Hill J.B, 518
Humphrey W. S., 399

J

Juran J. M., 396

K

Khoo S.-C., 372
Koch, A.S., 556
Kotter, J.P, 579
Kübler-Ross, E, 579

L

Lakshmanan, G.T., 372
Lee, K., 674

M

Mito, Setsuo, 27–28
Mogensen, Allan H., 2, 16–17
Mogy. *See* Allan H. Mogensen
Mott, Lucretia, 5

N

Noura, F., 389

O

Ohno, Taiichi, 27–28
Ould, Martyn, 80

P

Pascalis, O., 674

Q

Quan, Z.S., 389
Quinn, P.C., 674
Qumer, A., 559
Quner, A., 556

R

Rebuge A., 370–371
Reeves, Martin, 360

Robertson B., 613
Rozsnyai, S., 372

S

Saleh, I., 389
Scheer, August-Wilhelm, 39–42
Sinur J., 518
Smith, Adam, 4–5
Strassmann, Paul A., 645
Sun Zi. *See* Tzu, Sun
Sun, C., 372

T

Tan, W., 389
Taylor, Frederick Winslow, 5
Thomas, A., 318
Toffler, A., 635
Toyoda, Eiji, 27–28
Tzu, Sun, 2–4

V

van der Aalst, W.M.P., 372–373
Verner, Laury, 516

W

Wang, F., F., 372

X

Xiao, W.S., 674

Y

Yang, Y., 372

Z

Zachman John A S., 42–43
Zakaria, M., 389

Subject Index

Note: Page numbers followed by "f" and "t" indicate figures and tables respectively.

A

Activity, 157
  documentation, 157–158
  identification, 157
  nature, 158
  process activity model, 158f
Ad Hoc process, 451
Advanced case management, 196
Agile, 553–556, 555f
  AAIM, 574–575, 574f
  BPM, 559–573, 570t–573t
    agile analysis, 564–565
    agile architecture and design, 566
    agile building, 567–568, 568f
    agile deployment, 569
    agile planning, 565–566
    agile testing, 568–569
    benefits and limitations, 560–562
    CoE, 573
    friction factors, 561t
  manufacturing, 553
  practices, 557
  principles, 556–557
  project management, 553
  service management, 553
  software development, 553–556
  supply chain, 553
  terminology, 570
  traditional waterfall model *vs.*, 557–559, 558f
  values, 556
  weakness point indicators, 563f
Agility, 555
Agility adoption and improvement model
  (AAIM), 573–575, 574f
Alignment, BPM, 645
American productivity and quality center
  (APQC), 523
American Society of Mechanical Engineers
  (ASME), 12, 18–19, 20f
Anti-pattern information modeling. *See*
  Information and process modeling
Application meta-object group, 111
Application ontologies, 92. *See also* Top-level
  ontologies
Application to Application/Business to Business
  (A2A/B2B), 313, 456

Applied technology in business (ATIB), 43
Approval phase, 624
Architecture of Integrated Information Systems
  (ARIS), 37, 41–42
As-Is analysis, 291
As-Is model, 518–536, 519f
Automated process discovery, 365–367
Automation business process analysis (Automation
  BPA), 205
Axiom, 93
Axiomatization, 93

B

Balanced scorecard cause-and-effect chain,
  543–544, 545f
Boeing B17, 17–18
Break even point (BEP), 536–538
BRMS. *See* Business rule management system
Build phase, 589, 590f
Business activity monitoring (BAM), 215, 516
Business excellence, 69
Business impact analysis (BIA), 314
Business innovation and transformation
  enablement (BITE), 320, 325–327
Business performance indicator (BPI), 521
Business process, 1, 600, 628, 689
  analysis and development, 455
  analyst, 257–258
  area, 136–137
  automation, 517
  chart, 11
  charter, 217–218
  concept drift discovery, 366–367
  engineer, 258
  group, 628
  hierarchy, 627–628
  lifecycle verb taxonomy, 147
  map, 175–177, 176t
  matrix, 177–178, 177t
  model, 178–179, 179f
  nature, 165–169
  outlier identification, 365, 369
  owner, 255–256
  performance analytics, 365
  portfolio manager, 256–257
  professionals, 671

Business process (*Continued*)
  project manager, 257
  scenarios, 161–162
  segmentation, 477–480
  support desk, 259
  process trends, 187, 191, 191f
    early adopter, 193–204
    early adoption, 191–193
    emerging trends, 190–191
    importance, 187–188
    industry adoption, 204–211
    maturity of subject, 188–189
    megatrends, 189–190
    standard adoption, 211–216
Business process analysis (BPA), 204, 513
Business process competency center (BPCC),
    212–213
Business process diagram (BPD), 289, 429
Business process execution language (BPEL), 84,
    289, 429
Business process guidance (BPG), 194–195,
    638–639
  components, 639
  learning content sources for, 641f
  in organization, 641
  in practical use, 639
Business process improvement (BPI), 12, 188,
    316–318
Business process management (BPM), 37,
    79–83, 101, 187, 395, 553. *See also*
    Agile; Evidence-based business process
    management (Evidence-based BPM);
    Maturity models
  agile development, 204
  alignment, 208, 645, 647
    alignment-unity framework, 646
    benefits of, 655–656
    business process group, 650t
    business process objects, 651f
    business scenarios, 652–655
    developing true alignment, 647
    establishment, 647–652
    from policy to enterprise innovation and
      transformation, 648f
    portfolio alignment-unity, 645
    PPPM, 653f
    US Government research,
      645
  application and, 84–85
  BPMS, 84–85
    vendors, 84
  to BPPM, 613–614
  BPPM *vs.* PPM *vs.*, 617–618, 617t

business improvement, 85
case management, 210–211
certification, 199
change management, 208
continuous improvement, 214
cross-disciplinary business process skills,
    674f
and EA, 210
entire organizational units, 85
evidence-based, 197, 209
implementation
  and governance, 551
  of process application not, 86
improving single step of process not, 86
knowledge worker, 196–197
learning *vs.* forgetting curve, 674–675, 675f
maturity levels, 632f
methodology, 199–200
misrepresentations, 84
improving automation of processes, 83
ontology and process templates, 173–175
and operating model, 211–212
optimization and simulation, 202–203
participation in process, 86
by people, 84
performance-based project coaching,
    671
portfolio management governance, 607–609,
    608f
querying process meta-model, 119f
requirements management, 201
roles, 213, 241–246, 253–254, 260
  abilities to act, 250–251
  BPM CoE, 254–260
  context, 248–250
  current methods, 247–248
  involving with role modeling, 252
  motivation for, 241–242
  profile, 251, 252t, 261–262
  relevance context, 242
  standards link, 246–247
as service, 85
skills requirements, 673–674
SNA, 197
social, 198–199
standardized and common way, 671
suggestion for process improvement, 86
sustainability and, 201
tool administrator, 259
way of modeling, 427
way of thinking, 89
way of training, 671, 675
way of working, 185

Business process management as a service model
    (BaaS), 203
Business process management governance, 209,
    599–601, 600f
  benefits and value, 610–611
  BPM portfolio management, 607–609, 608f
  CoE and, 601–604, 601f
  incident management, 606–607, 607f
  lessons learning, 609–610
  working levels, 604–606
Business Process Management Initiative (BPMI),
    430, 448
Business process management life cycle (BPM life
    cycle), 213–214, 265, 266f
  continuous improvement, 316–336
    BITE, 325–327
    improvement area prioritization, 320–324
    industry table index, 319t
    performance and value drivers, 318–320
    performance change management, 324–325
    process update management, 324
  deployment and implementation phase,
      295–296, 299
    add process rewards, 300–301
    harmonize terms, 303
    performance indicators, 302
    process ownership establishment, 303–305
    process performance measurements, 301–302
    rollout phase, 299–300
  final project preparation, 287, 288f
    As-Is analysis, 291
    directly adaptable processes, 295
    harmonize variants, 292–293
    match processes, 294
    process decomposition and composition
      model, 290f
    processes with variants, 294–295
    to-be documentation, 293
    to-be organizational structure, 293
    value-driven process design, 291–292
  process run and maintain phase, 306
    analyze variances, 312–314
    choosing building blocks, 310–311
    impact estimation, 314–316
    potential solution evaluation, 312
    process measurements, monitoring, reporting,
      and audits, 307–309
    scoping of gaps performance, 310
  project preparation and blueprint, 266–268,
      267f
    check for process reference content, 273
    choosing building blocks, 271–273
    critical business factor identification, 270

no process reference content available, 278
process goals description, 270–271
project realization and design phase, 278–280, 279f
  case-based process concept, 283–284
  design solution, 283
  process map, 282–283
  process planning and, 280–282
  process requirement management, 286
  process workflow connection diagram, 281f
  standardization and integration, 285–286
  unadaptable processes, 287
  value-based process concept, 284–285
verb taxonomy model, 269f
Business process management suite (BPMS), 204
Business process modeling, 439, 511. *See also*
    Information modeling; Sustainability
    oriented process modeling
Business Process Modeling Notation (BPMN), 1–2,
    94, 214, 241, 289, 366, 429, 444, 529–531,
    530f. *See also* To-be model
  automatically discovered process model in, 367f
  behavior of diagrams, 444
  case management modeling, 451
  caveats, 447
  choreography, 441, 442f, 445f
  collaboration, 441, 441f, 445f
  conversation diagram, 442, 443f
  data object description, 434t–435t
  diagrams, 439, 444
  event description, 435t–438t
  flow description, 433t
  fulfillment, 448–449
  gateway description, 438t–439t
  graphical notation for business process, 429
  historic development, 430–431
  implementation level modeling, 449, 450f
  marker description, 434t
  private business process, 439–440
  public process, 440–441, 440f
  shapes, 431
  standalone process, 446f
  task description, 432t–433t
  3.0 specification, 452f
  2.0 specification, 429–430, 451
  updating version, 447–448
  usage, 443–444
Business process modeling tool (BPMT), 265
Business process ontology, 101–103, 119–120
  classes and groups, 107f
  decomposed process meta-objects, 102t–103t
  extraction
    application layer meta-object ontology, 115f
    business layer meta-object ontology, 114f

Business process ontology (*Continued*)
    business process composition attribute
        taxonomy, 118f
    business process decomposition attribute
        taxonomy, 118f
    composition relation ontology, 116f
    decomposition relation ontology, 117f
    folksonomy, 101–103
    frame, 114–119
    process composition meta-objects, 104t–106t
    thesaurus, 106–113
Business process outsourcing (BPO), 209, 657–658
    aspects of core businesses, 662
    building strategy, 666–667
    company expenditure diagnostics, 663
    Industrial Revolution, 657
    Kraljic's purchasing model, 665f
    market, 660
    new suppliers communication, 668
    non-core competencies, 662–663
    pitfalls, 661–662
    practices and services, 663f
    procurement business case, 660f
    rate of return, 661f
    RFx request, 667
    selection process, 667–668
    subset of outsourcing, 657–658
    supplier
        market assessment, 665–666
        survey preparation, 666
    understanding expenditure, 665
    value case, 658–659
Business process portfolio management (BPPM), 614
    alignment considerations, 620–621
    alignment factors, 620f
    from BPM to, 613–614
    business process hierarchy, 627–628, 628f
    competency creation, 618–620, 618f
    establishment, 616
    information for measurement and reporting,
        628–630
    life cycle, 620f, 621–627
    pitfalls, 614–616, 614f
    for portfolio management, 630
    PPM *vs.* BPM. *vs.*, 617–618, 617t
    right time to implementation, 630–631
    with short-term and long-term effects, 631, 633f
Business Process Principles (BPR), 693
Business process reengineering (BPR), 38, 50–51,
        188, 265
    cons of, 57
    cycle, 53, 54f

ingredients, 52–53
levels of management, 52, 52f
methods and approaches, 54–55
process redesign steps, 55f
project and success criteria, 55–56
pros of, 56–57
width before depth, 51
Business process variances, 455–457
    allowing process, 459–462
    breakdown of processes, 466f
    business models and life cycle alignment,
        469f
    challenges, 457–459
    complications, 457–459
    defining and justifying, 462
    distinctive process, 465
    LEADing industry, 460f
    lower level variances, 467–468
    management, 468–470
    master-and-variant process, 465–467
    matrix, 464t
    modeling of, 464–468
    process variances cost calculation, 470–471
    solution description, 459
Business rule engine (BRE), 195–196
Business rule management system (BRMS),
        195–196

C
Capability Maturity Model for Software (Software
        CMM), 398–399
Capability maturity model integration model
        (CMMI model), 398–399
Case management modeling, 451
Case-based process concept, 283–284
Center of excellence (CoE), 127–128, 217, 403,
        579, 601, 613–614
    alignment to value, 234–236
    without BPM, 220–222
    BPM maturity holistic view in, 232–233
    cause and effect matrix, 222
    continuous improvement and, 236–237
    faces, 217–220
    governance, 229–232
    lessons learned, 222–237
    manager, 256
    performance management execution, 233–234
    portfolio process management, 227–229
    process life cycle, 227
    roles, 226–227
    stakeholders, 254–255
    work of, 224–226

Career opportunity, 693
Change Advisory Board (CAB), 586
Change management, 579, 597f
    lessons learning, 579–580
        benefit, 582
        outperformers, 581, 581t
        underperformers, 581, 581t
        value realization, 582
    practicing suggestions, 582–583
        in analyze phase, 585–586, 587f
        in build phase, 589, 590f
        in continuous improvement phase, 593–595, 594f
        in deploy/implement phase, 589–591, 591f
        in design phase, 588–589, 588f
        managerial governance activities, 596
        in run/maintain phase, 592–593, 592f
    process life cycle, 584f, 586f
Channel meta-object group, 112
Checking symbol, 19
Chief executive officer (CEO), 494
Chief information officer (CIO), 344–345, 477
Chief operating officer (COO), 344–345
Chief process and information officer (CPIO), 344–345
Chief process officer (CPO), 201, 343, 489
    emerging role, 343–345
    key tasks, 345–346
    positioning of, 346–347, 347f
    process management, 345f
Choreography, 441, 442f, 445f, 456
Class, 92–93
Classification scheme, 92–93
Cloud business rule management services (Cloud BRM services), 195–196
Cloud-enabled business process management (CE-BPM), 203–204
Complex-event processing (CEP), 205–206
Compliance meta-object group, 111
Computer integrated manufacturing (CIM), 40
Conceptual graph (CG), 101, 114
Consortium for Advanced Management–International (CAM-I), 128
Construct deficit, 94
Construct overload, 94
Construct redundancy, 94
Content management interoperability services (CMIS), 353
Context sensitive, 639
Continuous improvement (CI), 316–318, 593–595, 594f
Continuous process improvement (CPI), 316–318

Control Objectives for Information and Related Technology (COBIT), 94–95, 265
Controlled vocabulary, 92
Corporate knowledge, 89, 94
Cost and Operating Model, 693
Cost model, 330–331
Crashing, 22
Critical success factor (CSF), 270, 284, 483–484, 501
Critical way, 22
Cross-disciplinary competencies, 671
Cross-functional business process, 599
Cultural shift, 377
Curricula approach, 673
Customer Relationship Management (CRM), 388–389, 389f, 457, 486, 640
Customer-servicing process, 382, 387

D

Data
    flow, 517
    mart, 538
    meta-object group, 112
    modeling method, 24–25
    warehouse, 538
Data Administration Management Association International (DAMA-I), 43
Data Flow Diagram (DFD), 12, 22–23, 23f
Data-driven process simulation, 370
Dearborn Independent, 8
Decomposed process meta-objects, 102t–103t
Decomposition, 514, 521
Define, measure, analyze, design, and verify (DMADV), 72
Define, measure, analyze, improve, and control (DMAIC), 71
Delay symbol, 19
Delta analysis, 371–372
Department of Defense Architecture Framework (DoDAF), 43
Deploy/implement phase, 589–591, 591f
Descriptive techniques, 365
Design for Six Sigma (DFSS). See Define, measure, analyze, design, and verify (DMADV)
Design phase, 588–589, 588f
Deviance mining, 365, 368–369, 371–373
Digital mind-set, 377–378, 378f
Discriminative sequence mining techniques, 372–373
Distinctive process, 465
Dynamic friction, 560
Dynamic Systems Development Method (DSDM), 554

E

e-learning
  learning *vs.* forgetting curve, 674–675, 675f
Early finish (EF), 22
Early start (ES), 22
80/20 rule, 64–65
Electronic performance support system (EPSS), 638
Emerging trends, 190–191
Enterprise architect, 259
Enterprise architecture (EA), 42–43, 210, 346
  framework for, 43–44, 45f
  perspectives, 44–46
Enterprise content management (ECM), 196
Enterprise portfolio approach, 226
Enterprise Resource Planning (ERP), 218, 350, 457, 486, 636–637
Enterprise-wide metadata repositories, 206–207
Entity relationship modeling (ERM), 511, 534–536, 534f
Environmental sustainability, 497
Event-driven process, goal-driven process to, 353–354
Event-driven process chains (EPC), 39, 427, 481, 511, 531–534, 533f
Evidence-based business process management (Evidence-based BPM), 363–364
  automated process discovery, 366–367
  case studies, 370–371
  descriptive techniques, 365
  deviance mining, 368–369, 371–373
  model enhancement, 367–368
  predictive process monitoring, 373
  predictive techniques, 369–370
  process mining, 364–365
  process outlier and variant identification, 369
  process performance analytics, 366
Evolutionary Project Management (EVO), 553–554
Excel, Word, PowerPoint (EVP), 205
Executable process, 440
Executive Council for Information Management and Technology (ECIMT), 43
Extended business process modeling notation (X-BPMN), 95, 511, 693
eXtensible Markup Language (XML), 351–352, 430
Extensible Stylesheet Language Transformations (XSLT), 431

F

Fast tracking, 22
Federal Enterprise Architecture Framework (FEAF), 43

Feedback loop, 626–627
  communication, 626, 627f
Financial business model, 380–381
Float. *See* Slack
Flow meta-object group, 110
Folksonomies, 92–93
Foundational ontologies. *See* Top-level ontologies
Functional Flow Block Diagrams (FFBD), 20–21, 20f

G

Gantt chart, 13–14, 14f
Global market, 673
Global Special Operations Forces Network (GSN), 646
Global University Alliance, 475
Goal-driven process, event-driven process to, 353–354
Governance disciplines, 599–600
Government Accountability Office (GAO), 43. *See also* Joint Program Office (JPO)

H

Hammer, Michael, 50
Happy paths, 363
Hasso-Plattner-Institut (HPI), 42
Heterogeneous groups, 102–103
Human resources, 382

I

IDEF. *See* Integrated definition
IDEF0 method, 23
IDEF1 method, 24
IDEF1X method, 24–25
IDEF3 method, 25
IDEF4 method, 25
IDEF5 method, 25
IDS scheer, 39
  ARIS, 40f–41f, 41–42
  important aspects, 42
  linking process and information concepts, 40–41
Implementation level modeling, 449, 450f
Incident management, 606–607, 607f
Industrial Revolution, 657
Inference rules, 92–93
Information and process modeling, 200
Information engineering (IE), 511, 538–543
Information modeling, 511
  As-Is model, 518–536, 519f
  BPMN collaboration, 544, 546–547
  business process modeling, 544

enterprise tiers, 522f
intended audience, 511–512
mapping
   information models, 527f
   meta objects, 525f
method, 24
problems and challenges, 517–518
process attributes, 516–517
process life cycle, 512–516, 512f
SAP document flow, 531f
to-be model, 518–528, 519f, 536–544
Information System (IS), 614
Information technology (IT), 37, 124–125,
   218–219, 506, 614, 654–655, 657–658
Information Technology Infrastructure Library
   (ITIL), 94–95, 246, 265, 673
Infrastructure meta-object group, 113
Initial public offering (IPO), 359
Instances, 92–93
Institute of Electrical and Electronics Engineers
   (IEEE), 247
Integrated definition (IDEF), 12, 23
   data modeling method, 24–25
   information modeling method, 24
   object-oriented design method, 25
   ontology description capture method, 25
   process description capture method, 25
Intelligent Business process management (iBPM), 198
Intelligent Business Process Management System
   (iBPMS), 349
   from automation to orchestration, 351–352
   big data, 356–359
   evolution, 350–351
   phase three, 354–356
   realizing adaptability, 353–354
   SOA strategies, 352–353
   social media value, 359–360
Internal business process. *See* Private business process
International Organization for Standardization
   (ISO), 57

J

Jidoka, 28
Joint program office (JPO), 646
Just-in-time (JIT), 28–30, 63

K

Key performance indicator (KPI), 336, 477,
   503–504, 528, 689
Knowledge
   friction, 560
   worker, 635, 636f

Knowledge Based Systems, Inc. (KBSI), 12
Knowledge interchange format (KIF), 95

L

Lag time, 22
Latest finishing point (LF point), 22
Latest starting point (LS point), 22
Layered Enterprise Architecture Development
   (LEAD), 94–95
Lead time, 22
Lean, 46
   consumption, 47–48
Learning and development (L&D), 637
Lightweight agile software development methods,
   553–554
Logical clustering, 123–125

M

Marketing, 382
Massachusetts Institute of Technology (MIT),
   38
Master data management (MDM), 654
Master-and-variant process, 465–467
Master's degree in engineering (ME), 13
Material usage variance, 470
Maturity
   benchmark, 421–424
   levels, 403–405, 421–424
   BPM, 403, 407f
      maturity development path, 423f
      maturity self-assessment, 408t–420t
   grids and models, 401f
   historic development, 396–399
   from maturity level assessment to maturity
      benchmark, 421–424
   missing parts, 401–403
   models, 395, 398f
   ROI, 406f
   stages of, 399–401
ME. *See* Master's degree in engineering
Media meta-object group, 112
Megatrends, 189–190
Meta information objects, 524–528
Meta-objects, 101–102, 111
Metadata, 206–207
Methods and tools specialist, 259
Microlearning, repository of, 637–638, 641
Model enhancement, 365, 367–368
Model extension, 367–368
Model repair, 367
Model-driven design, 515
Move-based overhead efficiency variance, 470

N

Near-shore outsourcing, 657–658
Network-based business process, 389
Non-executable process, 440
Nongovernmental organization (NGO), 494

O

Object management group (OMG), 194, 246, 429
Object-oriented design method, 25
Objects, 101–102
  groups, 101–102
  meta-models, 101–102
  meta-object group, 109
Office of Secretary of Defense (OSD), 399
Oil and Gas Petroleum Engineering business
      model, 462, 463f
Online process performance analytics, 366
Ontology, 91–92
  classification based on context dependency, 92
  description capture method, 25
  maturity and maturing process, 92–93
  state of art, 93–95
Ontology web language (OWL), 95
Open Group, 246
Operating model, 333–335
Operation symbol, 19
Operational process owner, 691
Opportunity management phase, 622
Opportunity realization phase, 624–625
Orchestration, 351–352
  automation to, 351–352
Organizational Change Management (OCM), 580,
      582
Organizational development (OD), 318–319
Outsourcing, 657
Owner meta-object group, 109

P

Paperwork, 18
Pareto
  diagrams, 64–65
  principle, 64–65
Peer-to-Peer (P2P), 380
Performance model, 336
Plan, Do, Check, Act Cycle (PDCA Cycle), 38,
      66–69
Platform as a service (PaaS), 195–196
Platform meta-object group, 113
Political friction, 560
Portfolio, program, and project management
      (PPPM), 652
Portfolio alignment-unity, 645
Predictive deviance monitoring, 369

Predictive process monitoring, 373
Predictive techniques, 365, 369–370
Price of Nonconformance (PONC), 27
Private business process, 439–440
Procedure, 159–160
  documentation, 160
  identification, 160
Process. See Business process
Process architect certification program, 681–683
Process architect learning model, 682–683, 682f
Process architect training, 258–259
  process architect certification program, 681–683
  process architect learning model, 682–683,
      682f
  program duration, 681
Process classification framework (PCF), 132
Process composition meta-objects, 104t–106t
Process concept evolution 1. 0, 1–8, 3f, 143–144
  defense Navy process map, 145f
  documentation, 144–147
  identification, 144
  nature of, 147
  process map, 146f
  tier, 165
  type, 162–164
  variance modeling, 197–198
  variances cost calculation, 470–471
  variant identification, 365, 369
  workers, 639
Process concept evolution 2.0, 11
  ASME, 18–19, 20f
  Boeing B17, 17–18
  DFD, 22–23
  Gantt chart, 13–14
  Gilbreth, Frank B., 14–16
  Graham, Benjamin S., 18
  IDEF, 23
  IDEF0 method, 23
  IDEF1 method, 24
  IDEF1X method, 24–25
  IDEF3 method, 25
  IDEF4 method, 25
  IDEF5 method, 25
  Mogensen, Allan H., 16–17
  PERT, 20–22
  TPS, 27–34
  zero defects, 25–27
Process concept evolution 3.0, 37
  BPR, 50–57
  IDS scheer, 39–42
  John A. Zachman SR., 42–46
  lean and lean consumption, 46–49
  six sigma, 70–73
  TQM, 58–63

Process description capture method, 25
Process deviation analysis, 372
Process engineer training
  certification program, 687
  process engineer certification program, 686
  process engineer learning model, 686f, 687
  program duration, 685
  program type, 685
Process expert, 257
  process expert certification program, 677–679
  process expert learning model, 678f, 679
  program duration, 677
Process group, 139
  and business service, 140
  defense Navy process map, 142f
  documentation, 142
  identification, 140–141
  nature of, 143
Process mining, 364–365
  in healthcare, 370
  service refund process, 371
Process owner certification program, 690
Process owner training
  content of program, 690–691
  process owner learning model, 691–692
  program type, 689–690
Process performance indicator (PPI), 108, 447,
    483–484, 503–504, 516
Process reengineering life cycle (PRLC), 54
Process step, 147, 157
  documentation, 150–155
  with exceptions, 156f
  identification, 147–150
  model, 151f, 153f
  process verb taxonomy, 148f
Process tagging
  activity, 157–158
  classification and categorization, 125–128, 127f
  data classification and categorization, 124f
  defense Navy process area example, 137f
  enterprise/business high-level relations, 138f
  layered architecture categories and relations,
    126f
  logical clustering, 123–125
  miscategorization and misclassification, 169
  nature of process decomposition, 130–133
  nested dolls and processes, 131f
  procedure, 159–160
  value-added chain diagram, 138f
  work, 133–136, 134f
Process templates, 175, 181, 182f, 207
  benefits of, 181–183
  BPM ontology and, 173–175
  process map, 175–177, 176t

  process matrix, 177–178
  process model, 178–179
Process-oriented architecture principles (POA
    principles), 567
Processual alignment factors, 621
Proctor and Gamble (P&G), 357
Professional certification, 673
Program Evaluation Review Technique (PERT),
    21–22. See also Structured Analysis and
    Design Technique (SADT)
  diagram, 22f
  FFBD, 20–21
  methodology, 12
Project management offices (PMO), 570
Project portfolio management (PPM), 616
  BPPM and BPM vs., 617–618, 617t
Prospect qualification process, 386
Public process, 440–441, 440f. See also Private
    business process.

Q

Quality function deployment (QFD), 38
Quality management maturity grid (QMMG), 396,
    397t

R

Real business value, 175
Real-time learning
  BPG, 638–639
    components, 639
    in organization, 641
    in practical use, 639
  communication with support desk establishment,
    640–641
  EPSS, 638
  knowledge gap, 637–638
  knowledge worker, 635, 636f
  L&D team, 637
  multiple applications, 640
  repository creation, 642
  supporting entry of data, 639–640
Real-time process performance analytics. See
    Online process performance analytics
Representational state transfer (REST), 352
Requests for change (RFC), 585
Research and development, 383
Resource description framework (RDF), 95
Resource-based overhead efficiency variance, 470
Return on Investment (ROI), 218, 405, 610, 615–616
Revenue model, 329–330, 694
Role-oriented process modeling, 196
Root cause analysis, 38
Run/maintain phase, 592–593, 592f

S

SADT. *See* Structured Analysis and Design
Technique
Sales and distribution (SD), 531–532
Scientific management, 6–7
Security risk management (SRM), 457
Semantic mapping, 94
Senior vice president (SVP), 626–627
Service
  meta-object group, 113
  model, 331–333
  refund process, 371
Service-oriented architecture (SOA), 207, 185,
    351–352, 486
  BPM realignment, 351–352
  principles, 567
  strategies, 352–353
Simple Object Access Protocol (SOAP), 351–352
Six sigma, 70
  DMADV, 72, 72f
  DMAIC, 71, 71f
  purpose of, 70–71
Skills gap, 671
Slack, 22
Smith, Adam, 4–5
Social alignment factors, 621
Social media, 377
  alternative channels for sales, 387
  BPM for customer servicing, 387–388
  changing business, 380f
  CRM, 388–389, 389f
  customer notifications, 387
  customer profile data, 386–387
  digital mind-set, 377–378, 378f
  enabling customer-centricity, 383–384
  iBPMS, 359–360
  interaction circles, 381f
  interaction response and combination, 392f
  process flow, 390–392, 391f
  prospect qualification process, 386
  reshaping business, 379–383
  right offering/solution selection, 387
  social-oriented process modeling, 384–385
  target marketing campaigns with, 385
Social network analysis (SNA), 197
Socially oriented process modeling, 377,
    384–385
Software development method, 555
Software Engineering Institute (SEI), 398–399
Software process maturity framework, 399
Spanning system, 349
Stakeholder alignment, 652

Standalone process, 446f
Standard cost adjustment variance, 471
Standardized training, 675
Star scheme, 538
Static friction, 560
Statistical process control (SPC), 38, 66
Storage symbol, 19
Strategic alignment factors, 621
Strategic business objective (SBO), 284, 483–484,
    502, 521
Strategic definitions, 89
Strategic process owner, 690
"Stop-watch" approach, 15–16
Structured Analysis and Design Technique
    (SADT), 23
Supply chain management (SCM), 457, 486
Supply chain operations reference model (SCOR),
    523
Sustainability, 493
  revenue model, 504–505
  value model, 502–504
Sustainability oriented process modeling
  BPM, 501f, 508–509
  business model for sustainability, 498f
  circumstances, 494–495
  complexity, 494–495
  complications, 493–494
  conditions, 494–495
  example of, 505f
  questions, 493–496
  situation, 493–494
  solution, 496
  sustainability, 493
  way of governing, 508
  way of implementing, 507–508
  way of modeling, 505–507
  way of thinking, 496–497
  way of working, 497–505
Symbols, 94
Systems applications product (SAP),
    456

T

Tactical process owner, 690
Taguchi techniques, 64
Targeting value, 476–477
Taylorism, 5–7
Technical alignment factors, 621
The Open Group Architecture Framework
    (TOGAF), 94–95
Theory of Constraints (TOC), 318
Thesaurus, 92–93

To-be model, 518–528, 519f, 536–544
  e-business scenario map, 543f
  for SAP business object, 539f
  SAP HANA data model analytical view, 540f
Token, 444
Top-level ontologies, 92
Total quality management (TQM), 38, 58–59, 396
  business excellence and EFQM, 69
  cause and effect analysis diagrams, 66
  house of quality, 62f, 63–64
  implementation, 59, 60f
  key elements for change, 59–61
  Pareto diagrams, 64–65
  PDCA Cycle, 66–69
  process diagrams, 65–66
  SPC, 66
  Taguchi techniques, 64
  use of, 61–63
Toyota Production System (TPS), 13, 27–28, 29f,
    37–38
  Jidoka, 28
  JIT, 28–30
  principles of, 30–34
Training specialist, 259–260
Transport symbol, 19

U
Underlying thoughts, 89
Unified Modeling Language (UML), 289, 484–486,
    511, 538
United States Department of Defense (DOD), 645
United States Department of Homeland Security
    (DHS), 645
United States Department of Justice (DOJ), 645
United States Department of State (DOS), 645
United States General Accounting Principles
    (USGAP), 529
Unity development path, 646
Unity maturity benchmark, 646
Unity maturity TCO-ROI evaluation, 646
Unity quick scan, 646
Unity stakeholder map, 646
Universal Description, Discovery, and Integration
    (UDDI), 351–352
User Interface (UI), 313, 456
User stories, 558–559

V
"Valley of despair", 579, 580f
Value
  case, 658–659
  chain, 614

model, 327–329, 694
network, 614
realization, 582
restrictions, 93
value-based process concept, 284–285
value-driven process design, 291–292
Value Chain Diagram (VCD), 287
Value Delivery Modeling Language (VDML), 481
Value-oriented process modeling, 194, 475, 482f,
    483–484, 503–504. See also Business
    process
  business process segmentation, 477–480
  next generation process automation, 487f
  process assessment matrix, 479f
  for process teams, 475
  targeting value, 476–477
  traditional software architecture, 488f
  value oriented process governance, 489, 490f
  value-driver tree, 478f
  value-oriented
    design, 481–483
    implementation, 489
Variance, 457–458
Variation/change management phase, 622–624,
    623f
Vice president (VP), 626–627

W
Waterfall model, 557–558
"Way of governing", 551
"Way of implementing", 551
"Way of modeling", 427
Web Services Business Process Execution Language
    (WSBPEL), 430
Web Services Description Language (WSDL),
    351–352
Work, 133–136, 134f
  spaces connection, 160–161
  system, 158–159
    determination, 159
    documentation, 159
Work Simplification, 17
Workflow management system (WFMS), 265

X
XML Metadata Interchange (XMI), 431
XML Schema Definition (XSD), 431

Z
Zero defects, 25–27
  theory, 12